Consumer market research handbook

CONSUMER MARKET RESEARCH HANDBOOK

Editor in chief: ROBERT M WORCESTER

London · New York · St Louis · San Francisco · Düsseldorf ·
Johannesburg · Kuala Lumpur · Mexico · Montreal · New Delhi ·
Panama · Paris · Rio de Janeiro · Singapore · Sydney · Toronto

Published by

McGRAW-HILL Book Company (UK) Limited
MAIDENHEAD · BERKSHIRE · ENGLAND

---

07 094234 X

Reproduced and printed by photolithography and bound in
Great Britain at The Pitman Press, Bath

Preface

For some years practitioners and users of market research in Great Britain have deplored the lack of a comprehensive summary of consumer research techniques and applications. There are many books available which treat this or that aspect of the subject, but evidently none that are widely considered to be comprehensive.

Thus, when approached by the publishers to take on the task of such a work, I found widespread appreciation of the need for the book among potential contributors, and an almost universal willingness, on the part of the acknowledged experts in their fields who were asked to contribute their experience and thought, to set aside time and commercial pressures in order to share their expertise with others. We saw the potential audience for the book in three distinct groups: the general marketing student, as a reference, and as a text for advanced course; for practitioners, including those working in research and advertising agencies and on the staffs of manufacturing and service companies; and, finally, those executives in agencies and companies who are charged with responsibility for the use and application of research findings.

At the outset, it was clear that the book would necessarily be a large one indeed if it was to have any claim whatsoever to being reasonably comprehensive. For this reason, I first turned to the task of gathering a team of advisory editors together whose functions included both the assumption of responsibility for an individual section of the book and also service as a board of editors. These section editors' unstinting efforts over the many months that have elapsed since our first meeting are the foundation on which the book is built. If this book accrues any credit whatsoever, the credit must be given to Liz Nelson, Paul Harris, John Downham and Bert de Vos who served in this role. I also need add that, especially in the initial developmental phase of the book, sound and willing advice was provided by Frank Teer.

While the focus of the book is British, an effort has been made to include references to work being done in America, Europe and elsewhere. Another decision made early on was that the contributors were to be drawn entirely from the ranks of practising consumer market researchers rather than from academics. No offence to our brethren in the universities is intended and, indeed, all of us draw frequently on the work of such contributors to the field as W. Belson (references to his work and the work of others are included where appropriate at the conclusion of each chapter). It was felt, however, that the annealing process of commercial experience would lend strength to the fundamental purpose, which is to provide guidance to the efforts of those studying, doing and using commercial consumer market research. In a way, our theme became one of, 'But will it help him to understand the problem tomorrow morning at 9.30?' Obviously, even a work of this size cannot be comprehensive. It is intended to be reasonably instructive in each of the subjects covered, and also to give guidance as to where to extend the search if more information is needed.

The organization of the volume became almost chronological in the process of conducting a study. We felt the overall content could be broken into what have, by sheer magnitude of the contributions, become two parts; the first devoted to the techniques of consumer market research and the second to the use of research. Further, each part, we felt, lent itself to further subdivision, the 'techniques' half being split into two sections: 'Collecting the Data' and 'Analysing the Data'. The second half was divided into 'Consumer Research Applications' and 'Media Research'. This, then, is the concept behind the organization of the book. The internal rationale behind the inclusions and exclusions within each section is covered in the introduction to each section.

Thanks are due to each contributor and section editor, to McGraw-Hill for the idea in the first place and patience in the end, and I am indebted to the Literary Executor of the late Sir Ronald A. Fisher, FRS, to Dr Frank Yates, FRS, and to Oliver & Boyd, Edinburgh, for permission to reprint tables from their book *Statistical Tables* for biological, agricultural and medical research. Also, thanks to Yvonne Levy who prepared the index, to my wife, Joann Worcester, who did the prodigious job of reading the proofs and, finally, to Joseph C. Bevis, retired Chairman of the Board of Opinion Research Corporation of Princeton, New Jersey, whose lifelong career and maintenance of high standards in research sets a target for us all.

Robert M. Worcester
London, 1971

Contents

Preface: Robert M. Worcester, Editor in Chief

PART ONE: TECHNIQUES OF
             CONSUMER MARKET RESEARCH

Section 1: Collecting the Data   3

Introduction: Elizabeth H. Nelson, Section Editor   4
Chapter 1:   Qualitative Research and Motivation Research,
              Peter Sampson   7
Chapter 2:   Experimental Designs and Models, James Rothman   28
Chapter 3:   Sampling, Martin Collins   52
Chapter 4:   Questionnaire Design, Jean Morton-Williams   69
Chapter 5:   Interviewing and Field Control, John F. Drakeford   103
Chapter 6:   Trade Research, Gerry Arnott   120
Chapter 7:   Panel Research, John Parfitt   143
Chapter 8:   Omnibus Surveys, J.P.H. Kendall   178
Chapter 9:   Mail Surveys, Brain Allt   194
Chapter 10:   Other Techniques, Leonard England   220

Section 2: Analysing the Data   235

Introduction: Paul T. Harris, Section Editor   236
Chapter 11:   Coding, Editing and Processing, Geoffrey R.
              Roughton   239
Chapter 12:   Statistics and Significance Testing, Paul T. Harris   265
Chapter 13:   Multivariate Analysis of Market Research Data,
              C. Holmes   312

PART TWO: USE OF CONSUMER MARKET RESEARCH

Section 3: Consumer Research Applications   339

Introduction: John Downham, Section Editor   340
Chapter 14:   Segmenting and Constructing Markets, Tony Lunn   345

Chapter 15:   Research for New Product Development, Colin
              Greenhalgh   378
Chapter 16:   Advertising Research, Mark Lovell   410
Chapter 17:   Packaging and Symbolic Communication, William
              Schlackman and John Dillon   448
Chapter 18:   Research on 'Below the Line' Expenditure, Martin
              Simmons   471
Chapter 19:   Market Testing and Experimentation, John Davis   485
Chapter 20:   Corporate Image Research, Robert Worcester   505
Chapter 21:   Market Research in the Financial Field, Michael
              Burrows   519
Chapter 22:   International Market Research, Lucy Law Webster   533

Section 4: Media Research   545

Introduction: Bert de Vos, Section Editor   546
Chapter 23:   Print Media Research Objectives and Applications,
              Michael Brown   548
Chapter 24:   Television Media Research, W. A. Twyman   577
Chapter 25:   Radio and Cinema Research, Frank Teer   627
Chapter 26:   Outdoor Advertising Research, Brain Copland   640

Biographies of the contributors   661

Index   673

Part I. Techniques of market research

Section 1. Collecting the data

Introduction

This section concentrates on marketing research *techniques*. While the section is aimed principally at practitioners and students of market research, it may also prove useful to the market research user as a guide to the methods by which the answers he seeks are obtained.

The section is written around the time sequence involved in carrying out a market research project. Thus, it starts with defining the problem and gaining the necessary background information before going on to techniques employed to solve marketing problems.

An attempt has been made to cover all of the major research techniques now employed perhaps at the sacrifice of depth analysis of the use and limitations of each technique examined. Each contributor has attempted to show the purpose of the technique covered in the chapter, its advantages and disadvantages, how it actually operates and, in some cases, practical implications such as costing.

Market research techniques are changing rapidly. As an example of this growth, there is an emphasis in this section on two major areas which would not have appeared five years ago—multivariate analysis using computers and extensive use of applied behavioural sciences.

Some readers may be concerned that this section does not have a chapter on desk research and the preliminary investigation of secondary source material. Unfortunately, there has not been room to include such a chapter. The editorial board is, however, very grateful to Mrs Patricia Millard for her advice on this important aspect of market research. The reader is urged to recognize the real need for collecting as much necessary background information as practicable. Past experience suggests that too many market researchers go straight to collecting primary data rather than first assessing whether or not they can solve the problem by the use of published information. As Mrs Millard has pointed out:

> Essentially desk research provides the means for the rapid assembly of relevant published material which will be of help when assessing the scope and nature of further research. At best, desk research can provide a basic picture of a market or market sector; it can pinpoint

available material, comment on the thoroughness and accuracy of the published information and provide a useful list of references and sources. Desk research can also highlight areas where further research is needed and thus save the market research practitioner a considerable amount of time in the initial stages of a survey. Taken a step further, the desk researcher can make use of such tools on his desk as the telephone and calculating machine, the latter for amplification and expansion of statistics, the former for a modest amount of telephone interviewing to establish attitudes and the like.

Basic statistics about the population of the country and other basic data are published annually in the yearbook of the Market Research Society. Basic population data has not been reproduced in this book since it is inevitably quickly out of date. Readers are urged, however, to consider the MRS yearbook as a first source of important data.

Before leaving the subject of desk research it is worth noting that it can produce information speedily and accurately on a variety of subjects e.g., product information, business opportunities and background marketing information.

Definition of Problems and Client Involvement

Marketing research is characterized by its use of orderly scientific procedure. A discussion of techniques, therefore, must begin with the first step of that procedure, i.e., define the problem. There is a saying that, 'when your marketing problems are known, they are half solved'. The role of the researcher in helping to define problems is crucial. When the researcher is properly involved, he will be able to suggest not only which technique is most applicable but what data needs to be gathered. He can separate out the essential data from 'interesting information'. He can also say when market research cannot assist in the solution of the problem. Proper involvement by the researcher can overcome the common pitfall of expecting too much from research.

Marketing research data can be helpful in predicting the future, but as yet not with any degree of accuracy. Marketing research cannot yet make decisions. The marketing man must still operate in the area of uncertainty. Thus, looking ahead, market researchers will become more involved in making decisions; they will become more involved in clients' problems both before research is carried out and afterwards. There will be more of a continuous relationship between researchers and marketing men. The more that the continuous relationship concept develops, the more researchers will be asked to solve problems which are not of the bushfire type. Much problem solving will then be not of the 'outright difficulty' type. Research should be involved in the recognition of hitherto unnoticed opportunities and, often, research can provide the most profitable type of problem solving, i.e., finding gaps for new products and finding the right approach for the most profitable target group of consumers.

The Layout of the Section

To return to the design of this section, chapter 1 is concerned with defining the parameters of the problem which rely largely upon qualitative and psychological techniques. Having defined the parameters of the problem from the research point of view, chapter 2 goes on to experimental design and models. Models are included in this section. They are only briefly discussed, since this subject cannot be thoroughly treated except by expanding into another book. Chapter 3 provides a 'short course' on sampling, chapter 4 covers survey questionnaire design using personal interviews. It seemed necessary to cover interviewing and field control in chapter 5 before discussing other widely-used techniques, audits (chapter 6), consumer panels (chapter 7) and omnibus surveys (chapter 8). The point of view that retailer research is closer in its techniques to consumer rather than industrial research has been taken. Thus, trade research as well as retail audits is covered in chapter 6.

The present near total dependence on the personal interview will be likely to diminish in the future. There will probably be a greater inclination to have a short personal interview and to use a postal, telephone, or self-completion follow-up. Thus, the last two chapters in this section deal with mail surveys and other techniques such as telephone surveys and observation.

Certainly, large users of research do not rely upon one technique alone. They use a combination of panels and audits, panels and surveys, audits and surveys. If any general point can be made about choice of techniques, it is that if the client does not know much about his market or indeed much about a particular problem, he is best advised to use desk research and qualitative research and to proceed from that stage learning more and more about his market as he proceeds.

Elizabeth H. Nelson

1. Qualitative research and motivation research

Peter Sampson

What is Qualitative Research and How Does It Differ from Quantitative Research?

Qualitative research is usually exploratory or diagnostic in its nature. It involves small numbers of people who are not usually sampled on any probabilistic basis. They may, however, be selected to represent different categories of people from a given section of the community. In qualitative research no attempt is made to draw hard and fast conclusions. It is impressionistic rather than definitive. With quantitative research, on the other hand, we are concerned with large numbers of people who are usually members of some carefully drawn sample that is representative in some way of a much larger section of people. The data obtained is quantified on some basis or other to indicate the numbers and proportions of sample members who fall into different response categories. A degree of statistical significance is usually attributed to quantitative data and within the confines of a known margin of error, its conclusions are generalized to the universe of which the sample purports to be representative.

Motivational Research

Motivation or motivational research is not synonymous with qualitative research. Very often, motives are sought and explored by qualitative techniques, but these techniques are used for a wide range of purposes other than being concerned with motives.

The concept 'motive' is a complex one in the field of psychology. Motivation explains *why* specific behaviour takes place. Gellerman[1] has commented that, 'The first and most important thing to be said about motives is that everybody has a lot of them, and that nobody has quite the same mixture

7

as anybody else'. This comment merely points to the fact that every individual is unique, which is of little consolation to the market researcher who is concerned with identifying groups, segments, target audiences, etc., on the basis of some common characteristics. Notwithstanding, sufficient people seem to have enough in common for us to recognize fairly homogeneous groups on the basis of certain parameters that include motives, thus making the identification of these valuable.

Early psychological theories of motivation took an 'animalistic' viewpoint, with the emphasis upon biological or physiological needs such as hunger, thirst, and sex. Motivation towards the satisfaction of these needs or drive states may be regarded as being universal, automatic, and self-regulatory. However, they provide little explanation of social or consumer behaviour. Social or 'secondary' drives may be regarded as explaining a good deal of the variation in human behaviour. They are enduring characteristics of the individual, but vary in strength from time to time, depending upon the extent of arousal or satiation. There is general agreement amongst social psychologists that there are six major social drives or motives. These are the:

(a) affiliation motive (the desire to be associated with or to be in the presence of other people);
(b) acquisition motive (the desire to possess or hoard material things);
(c) prestige motive (the desire to be highly regarded by other people);
(d) power motive (the desire to control or influence other persons);
(e) altruism motive (the desire to help others);
(f) curiosity motive (the desire to explore and investigate one's surroundings).

It has been said that motives tell us why people behave as they do, but there is rarely a simple, single explanation for human behaviour. This is especially the case with the type of consumer behaviour studied by market researchers. Here, we are more likely to be concerned with discovering the reasons why people behave as they do in terms of a number of variables, some of which go to make up this complex psychological construct, 'motive'. For example, we can employ characteristics such as demographic variables (sex, age, socio-economic class, etc.,) and behavioural variables (e.g., heavy, medium, light consumption) and, in addition, those which are closer to motivation like attitudinal, personality and life-style variables.

In the market research context, motivations are important, but only in conjunction with other information. Lunn[2] distinguishes two categories of attitudinal-type variables:

(a) relatively specific requirements which reflect the importance given by the consumer to product attributes;
(b) more general *motives* and attitudes that are, nevertheless, close to product context, e.g., traditionalism, economy-mindedness, experimentalism, and health-consciousness. They may be regarded as 'broad

consumer values' that influence and *motivate* consumers. Insofar as 'motivations', such as those described above by Lunn, are more likely to be actually identified by multivariate analysis methods based upon large-scale quantitative studies, the role of qualitative research to elicit motives may be regarded as a diminishing one.

The Uses and Limitations of Qualitative Research

Some research problems require a more flexible approach than can be provided by the standardized interviewing techniques offered by a structured questionnaire. Under these circumstances, qualitative research may be employed. The writer[3] has listed ten common examples of the use made of qualitative research techniques:

(a) to obtain some background information where absolutely nothing is known about the problem area or product field in question;
(b) in concept identification and exploration;
(c) to identify relevant or 'salient' behaviour patterns, beliefs, opinions, attitudes, motivations, etc.;
(d) to establish priorities amongst categories of behaviour and psychological variables like beliefs, opinions, and attitudes;
(e) generally defining problem areas more fully and formulating hypotheses for further investigation and/or quantification;
(f) during a preliminary screening process in order to reduce a large number of possible contenders to a smaller number of probable ones;
(g) to obtain a large amount of data about beliefs, attitudes, etc., as data input for multivariate analysis studies;
(h) conducting post-research investigations or 'post mortems' to amplify or explain certain points emerging from some major study, without having to repeat on a large scale;
(i) in piloting questionnaires to test comprehension, word forms, the 'memory factor', etc.;
(j) where we cannot discover in a simple, straightforward way like direct questioning, why people behave as they do because the field of enquiry is personal or embarrassing in some way. In these circumstances some 'oblique' approach is called for in which projective questioning techniques may be used in a qualitative research setting.

The Techniques of Qualitative Research

In qualitative research we are primarily concerned with two main interview types, the:

(a) individual 'depth', or intensive, interview;
(b) group interview or group discussion.

9

The individual 'depth' or intensive interview

Many practitioners[4] argue that the term 'depth' interview is a misnomer in that it is too often used generically to describe a wide range of different types of interviews. A suggested classification of interview types that covers a range of possibilities is put forward, covering such diverse descriptions as clinical, free, focused, non-directive, extended, unstructured, semi-structured, intensive.

Collectively, these interviews represent an interview type which may be described as *less-structured–more-intensive* than a standardized question-naire-administered interview. The classification delineates three broad types. The:

(a) true depth or clinical interview that corresponds to the psychothera-peutic interview and requires far longer than a single session, and is, strictly speaking, outside the scope of conventional market research;

(b) non-directive interview where, although the interviewer retains the initiative regarding the course of the interview, the respondent is given maximum freedom to respond in the manner he wishes, within reasonable bounds of relevancy;

(c) semi-structured, or focused interview, where the interviewer is required to cover a specific list of points and, although the respondent is allowed to respond freely, a much tighter control is exercised by the interviewer in order to maximize the collection of relevant data. Specific areas may be focused upon. The interviewer (or researcher) has determined *a priori* the sort of questions to which he is seeking answers and is merely seeking the appropriate responses from the respondent.

The group interview or group discussion

In the case of the group discussion we are concerned with a number of respondents or group 'participants' brought together under the direction of a 'group leader'. There is no 'correct size' for any group. The number of participants may vary according to the type of participant, the subject matter for discussion and the group leader's preference. For example, with highly articulate and fluent professional people, the ideal size is perhaps five or six participants. With members of the public, seven or eight would be preferred. Under certain circumstances, like conducting a group discussion amongst elderly people or groups of inarticulate people, and dealing with a subject not likely to be of great interest to them, the number may be in-creased from nine to twelve. It is important to remember though, that the value of any particular group discussion is quite independent of its size. Another question that is often asked is whether participants should be seated around a table with the leader at the head, or on chairs in a circle. In the author's experience it makes no difference at all. Given the accommodation available people should be seated as comfortably as possible in full view of each other and the leader. If they are required to write anything down or fill in questionnaires, a table is necessary.

Whereas, in the case of the individual intensive interview, the flow of response is from the respondent to the interviewer, in the case of the group interview the leader should play a relatively more passive role since we are primarily concerned with group *interaction*. Each participant is encouraged to express his or her views, and is likewise exposed to the views of fellow members of the group. The leader says as little as possible and merely guides the course of discussion by, first, ensuring that participants are in fact discussing issues which are relevant to the problem or subject matter in question, or at least, do not stray too far from this. (Often a move off at a tangent can be profitable but if in the judgement of the moderator this is not proving so, the group is refocused towards the issue under investigation.) Second, ensuring that each person participates fairly equally, which means encouraging less forthcoming members of the group, suppressing the loquacious, and seeing to it that no leadership force emerges from the group and takes over effective control. Goldman[5] has described five characteristics of the group discussion:

(a) the interaction amongst group members stimulates new ideas regarding the topic under discussion that may never be mentioned in individual interviewing;
(b) group reactions provide the opportunity to observe directly, the group process;
(c) the group provides some idea of the dynamics of attitudes and opinions;
(d) discussion often provokes considerably greater spontaneity and candour than can be expected in an individual interview;
(e) the group setting is emotionally provocative in a way that an individual interview cannot be.

Brainstorming and Synectics

In attempting to increase the involvement of individuals in the group situation, increase the amount of group interaction, reduce the inhibition of group members and encourage creative thinking, the writer[6] describes some experimentation carried out with brainstorming and synectics techniques in the area of new product development.

In the brainstorming group a heterogeneous collection of participants is selected (compared to the usually fairly homogeneous group of participants in the conventional group discussion). Typically, if the problem was one concerned with an infant food product, instead of merely talking to mothers of infants, the brainstorming group would encompass men, women, young, old, married and unmarried, and those with and without children. Rather than just sit down at a table or in a circle around the moderator, they may get up and walk about, break up into smaller groups, enact various role situations, etc. Whereas the average length of a group discussion is $1\frac{1}{2}$–$1\frac{3}{4}$ hours, the brainstorming group would be likely to continue for much longer, perhaps 3 or 4 hours. The conventional group discussion would normally be a one-off affair but the brainstorming group may meet on several occasions or regularly over a period.

Synectics is a fairly recent method of directing creative potential towards the solution of problems (Gordon[7]). Synectics means, literally, the joining together of different and apparently irrelevant elements. In the group interview sense this means participants. These must be drawn from a wide spectrum of educational academic, social, and work backgrounds. They must, however, have one thing is common, the ability to think creatively. The synectics process harnesses this diverse source of creativity, directing it towards the group goal which may be the solution of a problem or generation of ideas.

Participants may be screened for high 'creativity' or 'divergent thinking' (Getzels and Jackson[8], Hudson[9]) or 'lateral thinking' (de Bono[10]) in a number of ways.

The synectics process involves a number of mechanisms, including the requirement that participants employ four different types of analogy thought processes. For a detailed discussion of what is involved in synectics the reader is referred to Gordon[7].

The synectics groups that the writer[6] describes are a very considerable modification of the Gordon approach. They involved five participants, carefully screened, and two moderators. The groups were undertaken on an *ad hoc* basis whereas the approach really required a continuous and regular operating group run over a lengthy period of time. The author concluded that in the context of generating new product ideas the synectics approach might be of value.

The Repertory or 'Kelly' Grid Technique. Criticism of traditional exploratory research techniques from the standpoint of their subjectivity and the occasional failure to obtain responses in the 'true language of the consumer' led to the development of the repertory grid interview in the context of market research practice. The repertory grid technique was felt to be a much better way of locating attitude scale items or 'constructs', from which semantic differential scales for multivariate analysis procedures could be devised.

A detailed discussion of personal construct theory is outside the scope of this book. The interested reader is referred to Kelly[11], Bannister[12,13], Frost and Braine[14], and Bannister and Mair[15].

In market research practice, for most exercises, the repertory grid interview varies little from the original Kelly approach in its basic form. The respondent is presented with a list of stimuli numbering from a half dozen or so to a maximum of around thirty. Somewhere in the region of sixteen to twenty is about optimum. A wide variety of different types of stimuli may be used. For example:

(a) products, e.g., tea, coffee, milk, drinking chocolate, etc.;
(b) brands, e.g., Lyons, Typhoo, Brooke Bond, Tetley's, etc.;
(c) concept statements, e.g., 'slow-roasted coffee granules', etc.

12

Stimuli may be presented in the form of word labels, written statements, drawings, photographs, actual packs or products, advertisements, etc.

After removing any stimuli from the list that the respondent has not heard of, or on some other grounds that require exclusion, three stimuli are presented to the respondent, who is asked to state one way in which two of them are alike and yet different from the third. The basis for similarity (the emergent pole) and the difference (the implicit pole) are recorded. The remaining stimuli are then sorted, equally between the two poles. Then another three stimuli are presented and the respondent asked to state *another* way in which two of them are alike and different from the third. The interviewer continues to present the respondent with different triads until the respondent can no longer think of any reason why two items are different from the third. When this occurs, the respondent's repertoire of constructs is said to be exhausted and the interview completed. The triads are selected according to some random procedure which ensures that identical triads are never repeated.

With the repertory grid the interview situation resembles more a test than an interview. Considerable skill is required to administer such a test. A good interviewer or 'tester' is not necessarily a good 'depth interviewer' or vice versa. The information sought and collected is extremely specific. Although repertory grids may be administered in conjunction with an individual intensive interview, if the grid is executed properly, it should be exhaustive and, at the end of it, both the respondent and the interviewer will have had enough. The case for combining repertory grid interviews and individual intensive interviews is a weak one, if either is to be done properly, but there may be special circumstances where this is justified. For example, we may have a problem that can be explored initially, albeit in a somewhat speculative way, by conducting a short (perhaps highly focused) intensive interview followed by a repertory grid test using no more than half a dozen stimulus items.

A major drawback of the repertory grid interview is the tendency for some responses to be utterly valueless in terms of the type of information that is being sought. Two types of such responses are found. First, there are those which are too descriptive or irrelevant, and secondly, those which are too evaluative. Examples of the first type are:

(a) 'Those two come in bottles; that one comes in a cardboard packet';
(b) 'Those two are made by Cadbury's; that one is made by Nestle'.

Typical of the second type are:

(a) 'I like those two; I don't like that one'.

Given a response like, 'My children like those two; they don't like that one', the researcher is able to transpose this into something that could form a scale, such as, 'Is liked by children'—'is not liked by children'.

This particular example shows up another problem that is faced in utilizing grid responses. According to Kelly, 'is liked by children—is not liked by children' is not a proper construct, whereas 'Is liked by children—is liked by adults' is a construct.

Similarly, responses like, 'Fizzy—not fizzy' and 'Fizzy—still' may often be obtained. A good deal of editing, rephrasing, etc., is usually required. This is bound to reduce the overall objectivity of the exercise in that an element of subjective interpretation is called for. (A categorization for the different types of responses provided by repertory grids is described by the writer elsewhere[16].)

The following diagram shows a typical completed grid sheet.

NOP Market Research Limited, Repertory Grid Sheet — EMERGENT POLE (√)	TEA	OVALTINE	COCA-COLA	COFFEE	LUCOZADE	WATER	DRINKING CHOCOLATE	MILK	RIBENA/BLACKCURRANT	SOUP	ORANGE SQUASH	MILK SHAKE	IMPLICIT POLE (×)
Harmful to teeth	(×)	√	(√)	×	(√)	×	√	×	√	×	√	×	Not harmful to teeth
Add sugar	√	(√)	×	(√)	×	(×)	√	×	×	×	√	√	Do not add sugar
Comes in bottles	×	×	(√)	√	(√)	×	(×)	√	√	×	√	×	Comes in other containers
Not stimulant	×	√	×	(×)	√	(√)	√	(√)	√	√	√	√	Stimulant
Opaque	√	√	×	×	×	(×)	√	(√)	×	(√)	×	√	Clear
Nutritive value	×	√	×	×	√	×	(√)	√	(√)	√	(×)	×	No nutritive value
Can drink through straw	×	×	√	√	√	×	×	(√)	×	(×)	√	(√)	Cannot drink through a straw
Not addictive	×	√	(×)	×	√	(√)	√	(√)	√	√	√	√	Addictive
High calorie content	(×)	(√)	×	×	√	×	(√)	√	√	×	×	√	Low calorie content
Derived from plants	(√)	×	×	(√)	×	×	√	×	√	√	√	(×)	From other source
Dairy product	×	(√)	×	√	×	×	(√)	√	√	(×)	×	√	Not dairy product
Fizzy	×	×	√	×	(√)	√	×	√	(×)	×	(√)	√	Still
Cannot buy frozen	Could not divide equally					×	(√)			(√)	(×)		Can buy frozen
Thirst quenching	√	(×)	√	×	×	(√)	×	×	√	×	√	(√)	Not thirst quenching

A single repertory grid sheet such as this will, on its own, tell the researcher very little. A series of these (any number from say, 12–40 or 50 is usual, depending on time/cost factors and the problem in hand) is content analysed by sorting, classifying, and listing the items. The collection of items obtained from the set of repertory grids would be used to form scales for subsequent attitude research. In this particular example respondents would be asked to rate various drinks or beverages on a series of scales. Because of the specificity of the repertory grid interview, its main value lies in seeking 'constructs' or the dimensions by which people perceive objects or other stimuli. These interviews may provide a great deal of valuable input data for multivariate analysis, but in themselves, they will tell us little about how, what, when, where, and why specific behaviour takes place.

Sorting all the elements in the set of stimuli, other than the actual triad presented, into two *equal* piles between the emergent and implicit poles is an interesting notion. If the respondent is allowed to nominate as many or as few elements as he wishes for each pole, the distribution becomes lopsided. This results in problems of statistical analysis. By distributing the stimuli equally, these statistical problems are overcome. However, one may well ask whether or not it is wise to have subjects distort their judgements in order to achieve statistical convenience. Frost and Braine[14] claim that respondents normally provide between ten to thirty responses, while the average number is around eighteen. The writer[3,17] regards this average of eighteen as being much higher than his own experience has indicated. He has demonstrated[17] that the number of constructs generated appears to be independent of sex, age, and socio-economic class, and is a function of high divergent thinking[8,9]. The following table summarizes the results of the experimental work reported. Significance testing, correlating the divergency scores with numbers of constructs generated, and analysis of variance all indicated that, for the population tested, the performance on the repertory grid was independent of sex, age, and social class but dependent upon divergency.

	BASE (N)	DIVERGENCY SCORE	GROSS NO. OF ITEMS GENERATED
		Mean	Mean
MEN	20	23.8	13.4
WOMEN	20	20.8	13.6
OVER 35 YEARS	20	22.8	13.5
UNDER 35 YEARS	20	21.7	13.4
ABC$_1$ (Upper and Middle)	24	22.9	15.4
C$_2$DE (Lower)	16	21.3	11.3
HIGH DIVERGENT	20	32.5	17.7
LOW DIVERGENT	20	12.0	9.3

Descriptions of the use of the repertory grid in market research exist. Frost[18] has described an interesting use of the repertory grid technique in respect of television programmes. Clemens and Thornton[19] describe the role of the repertory grid as the first stage of a 'gap analysis' approach to locate new product ideas. Sampson[3] describes how repertory grids were used to obtain pack image dimensions for male toiletries.

These examples of the use of repertory grids and, indeed, their commonest use, employ the rotated triads approach. This need not be so. A simple variation is to have one fixed element in a succession of different triads, e.g., abc, abd, abe, acd, ace, ade. Equally, although Kelly suggested that the minimum context within which a construct can be formulated comprised three elements, the grid approach can be used with just two stimuli being presented. Yet a further variation is to 'fix' one pole, and ask the respondent to supply the other, rather than supply both poles.

Very simply, completed grids may be regarded as data sheets that provide lists of actual or potential semantic differential scale items. It has been suggested that immediately after obtaining constructs, the interviewer may transform these into five, six, or seven-point scales and undertake a further scaling exercise with the same respondent. The writer[3] has argued that considerable editing and tidying up of verbalized constructs is necessary in order to produce meaningful scale items.

Frost and Braine[14] describe various statistical treatments that can be carried out on repertory grids, and make some suggestion as to how the data may be checked for reliability and validity.

Problems Encountered During the Interview Situation and How They May Be Overcome

The writer[3] has described the various problems that may be encountered during the interview situation which serve to distort the accuracy of responses. These barriers to communication are:

(a) psychological barriers, i.e., the memory factor, emotional factors, and unconscious or repressed material;
(b) language barriers;
(c) social barriers.

Different Types of Interview Situations

The use of projective techniques

Within the context of the individual intensive interview or conventional group discussion, use is very often made of a wide range of projective techniques.

Oppenheim[20] suggests that suitably designed projective techniques can penetrate some of the following barriers:

(a) barrier of awareness—when people are unaware of their own attitudes and motives;
(b) barrier of irrationality—to overcome the rationalizations that people make when they talk about themselves;
(c) barriers of inadmissibility and self-incrimination—when people are disinclined to admit things in a conventional interview situation;

16

(d) barrier of politeness—when respondents are disinclined to be critical because they are, by nature, polite and tend to behave so towards the interviewer.

By projective technique is meant the utilization of vague, ambiguous, unstructured stimulus objects or situations in order to elicit the individual's characteristic modes of perceiving his world or of behaving in it (Chaplin[21]). The underlying theory of projective questioning is that in certain circumstances it is impossible to obtain accurate information about what a person thinks and feels by asking him to explain *his* thoughts and feelings, but this information can be obtained by allowing a respondent to project these on to some other person or object. Some examples are given below.

(a) *Sentence Completion Tests*

The respondents are asked to complete statements like, 'Women who give their families tinned vegetables are . . . . ' 'People who don't have bank accounts are . . . . ' 'Women who use Lux Toilet Soap . . . .';

(b) *Word Association Tests*

Here the respondent may be presented with a list of stimulus words and, for each one, asked to say what he thinks about when he sees the word;

(c) *Fantasy Situations*

Here, respondents may be asked to imagine that they are motor cars, lawn mowers, or boxes of chocolates and describe their feelings;

(d) *Cartoon Completion*

Here, the respondent is shown a cartoon similar to a comic strip with 'balloons' indicating speech. Usually, two people are shown in conversation but only one balloon contains speech. The respondent's job is to fill the other balloon with his idea of what the other person is saying.

(e) *Draw a Picture*

A respondent may be asked to draw or sketch a picture. Often reported studies describe how people with bank accounts, when asked to draw the interior of a bank, draw what appears to be a friendly place, whilst people without bank accounts tend to draw rather awesome and grim interiors.

(f) *Picture Interpretation*

This technique is based upon the Thematic Apperception Test (TAT) which, along with the Rorschach Ink Blot Test, must rank as the most widely known and probably widest used projective test in clinical work. Here the respondent is shown a picture—either a line drawing, illustration, or photograph—which is rather ambiguous and asked to say what is going on or tell a story about what is illustrated.

In projective questioning, the individual's responses are not taken at face value, i.e., with the meaning that the respondent would expect them to have, but are interpreted in terms of some pre-established psychological framework. It is here that projective tests have come in for major criticism. A considerable degree of subjectivity is exercised in the interpretation of responses to projective tests, and very often 'experts' may be in disagreement amongst themselves. For an extremely detailed review of projective techniques, the reader is referred to Murstein[22].

Abelson's 'Role Rehearsal' Technique

An interesting exploratory research technique is that described by Abelson[23] which was developed at Opinion Research Corporation, Princeton, New Jersey. In practice, role rehearsal consists of asking respondents, in a group discussion situation, to alter their behaviour pattern in some extreme way by offering some incentive for them to do so. Abelson describes a study where he asked housewives to serve chicken three times a week for a year to their family in return for $15.00 a week, and an agreement not to tell them that this arrangement had been made. According to Abelson, the approach yielded useful information on the reactions of the individuals to this offer, in terms of perceived obstacles and problems they would face, which gave some insight into their attitudes. Studies undertaken by NOP Market Research Limited, using this approach to see just how loyal consumers were to their regular brands, have brought to light some interesting information. The offer can be progressively increased in the attempt to break down strong brand loyalty. Failure to achieve this transfer at a given size of offer, and the reasons why a person will not switch brands, illustrated why brand loyalty was so strong. Furthermore, the group situation provided some interesting interaction between the 'disloyals' who caved in at the offer of a small incentive and the 'loyals' who either held out for a larger incentive or remained loyal at 'any price'.

Immediately after this section of the interview has taken place (and it is recommended that it is towards the end of a group session) respondents are told that the offer was really fictional. Participants appear to enter into the spirit of the exercise and do not mind being misled.

The Selection and Training of Interviewers

Many of the basic requirements for individual intensive interviewing are the same as for interviewing with a standardized, structured questionnaire (see chapter 6). However, over and above these basic skills, additional skills are required because non-standardized interviewing is a more complex task and the quality of information is to a much greater extent dependent upon the skill of the interviewer. Precisely what these are is difficult to determine and there is a distinct lack of any detailed research on this question.

There is general agreement that 'depth' interviewers must be very carefully selected and thoroughly trained (Berent[24]). However, on the questions of on what basis selection should be made and the type of person that makes a good interviewer, there is less agreement. Berent argues for selecting qualitative interviewers from amongst the 'normal quantitative field force'. He lists the necessary qualities as:

(a) the ability to relax in the interviewing situation;
(b) a friendly manner;
(c) the ability to instil confidence;
(d) to like people and be interested in them;
(e) to be broadminded.

He considers that people with strong ideas about politics, religion, or morals and people with a conventional and narrow outlook are likely to be unsuitable. Whereas the first set of qualities are obviously desirable, narrowness and rigidity a likely disadvantage, it is difficult to imagine why the possession of strong views should be a drawback, providing the interviewer has sense enough to keep his or her views from entering into the exchange. It should be quite possible for a rabid racialist to interview about race relations or even to interview a coloured person. Providing that such an interviewer was capable of controlling or ignoring his own feelings, beliefs, opinions, attitudes, etc., the interview could be quite satisfactory.

From the standpoint of selecting 'depth' interviewers, Berent argues in favour of having intelligent people without academic qualifications rather than psychologists. Many practitioners have expressed a preference for graduates, especially in one of the social sciences and, particularly, psychologists. This preference one way or the other must be regarded as very much a personal one. There is no conclusive evidence to suggest that graduates are better than non-graduates and graduates in one discipline better than any other.

As far as training is concerned, some basic instruction in interviewing methods like achieving rapport, questioning approaches, prompting and probing, is absolutely vital. The trainee interviewer should be made to listen to tape recordings of an experienced interviewer's work and to undertake a number of trial interviews on different subjects, with different respondents. These should be tape-recorded and subject to criticism by the training officer in the presence of the trainee. Even amongst interviewers who exhibit a flair for this sort of work, the commonest mistakes are invariably to ask leading questions and the failure to probe. This can be corrected if they are pointed out. Trainee interviewers should be allowed to listen to the recordings of other trainees and, through constructive criticism, improve their own performance and that of their fellow trainees. Even with experienced interviewers it is a good idea to constantly comment on their work and to run refresher courses in order to develop their skills and improve their performance still further.

With group discussions, many of these considerations in respect of selection and training apply. Certainly, there is far more to conducting a group interview than merely sitting round a table with a group of people and getting them to talk. Failure to achieve interaction will result in a series of dialogues between participants and the group leader. With inexperienced group leaders this often tends to happen.

Assessing Performance

Apart from fairly obvious errors, like asking leading or loaded questions and the failure to probe when this was clearly called for, a skilled qualitative researcher can, by listening to the tape recording of an interview, usually make a fair assessment of the interviewer's performance from the general run of the interview and the nature of the data (notes and/or edited transcripts perhaps) provided by the interviewer. Obviously, not all interviews will be good ones. Even the most skilled interviewer can have an 'off-day' or, more commonly, a poor respondent. If a respondent is very poor at communicating and verbalizing, there is a strong case for terminating the interview and finding another respondent.

The Use of Tape Recorders

There is some measure of disagreement about the advisability of using tape recorders for individual depth interviews; there is no disagreement about using tape recorders for groups, where they are considered essential. Berent[24] claims that the advantages (a complete record of the interview obtained without effort by the interviewer who is thus able to concentrate on the actual interview without worrying about recording information) are outweighed by the disadvantages. He describes these as:

(a) the likelihood of the respondent becoming inhibited and selfconscious;
(b) tape recorders attract the interest of other members of the family;
(c) the likelihood of interruptions through tape recorder failure or having to change a tape;
(d) transcription is arduous and costly.

Wilson[25] states that a tape recorder at an interview creates anxiety and inhibits the discussion.

The writer[26] has opposed these viewpoints and argued that the advantages of using a tape recorder outweigh the disadvantages. A friendly relaxed approach and manner and the clear guarantee of anonymity by the interviewer can very quickly allay any suspicion and anxiety about the tape recorder on the part of the respondent. True, there are some individuals who flatly refuse to have an interview recorded but in the author's experience, they represent less than one per cent of people approached. Moreover, it is likely that some of these people would refuse to be interviewed without a tape recorder. That tape recorders attract other members of the family does not appear to be a major disadvantage. Interviewers should be instructed to always conduct the interview with the chosen respondent *alone* and preferably in a quiet part of the house. Unfortunately, the home environment of some people does not allow this. In some instances there is only one available room in the house which may have to be shared with children and other adults. The interviewer is instructed to be as polite as possible in restraining other members of the family from joining in. Another problem in crowded homes is the television set, which the interviewer would politely ask to be turned off. If the circumstances under which the interview has to be conducted are too unfavourable, an appointment to carry this out at another time may be made or another respondent found. However, if the respondent happens to be one of an extremely small minority located only after a long and intensive search, and the only time and place the interview can be obtained is a room full of children, adults, dogs, cats, and a television set, there may still be a strong case for going ahead.

In the case of individual intensive interviews, making the interviewers produce a 2000–3000 word edited transcript, including the most interesting verbatim comments, rather than produce a complete verbatim transcript, is often a satisfactory compromise.

In a study to determine the effect of accuracy of response in survey interviews by using tape recorders, Belson[27] concluded that,

> ... the use of the machine was rarely a source of overt objection. Despite possible expectations to the contrary, this is the common experience of others reporting on the use of tape recorders in interviews. ... for the sample as a whole, the tape recording of the interview did not appear to reduce the accuracy of respondent estimates.

Video-Tape Recording

For group discussions and individual interviews in the past few years, increasing use has been made of video-tape recorders to provide a visual as well as sound recording. A special filming studio is required as are skilled technicians to film, record, and set lighting. Participants must be told that they are being filmed and, providing that the camera is sited in some unobtrusive place (like a hole in a wall, and operated from the adjoining room) they do not manifestly appear to be adversely affected. The precise effect that filming has could, however, be the subject for some empirical research.

Video-taped groups have been found to be especially useful with children (playing with toys, eating sweets, etc.) and adults who are required to use their hands or undertake some other activity like eating, drinking, smoking, opening packs, etc. Filming merely to record facial expressions to supplement voice intonation and verbal responses is, in itself, likely to be of little value in cost-benefit terms.

Analysis and Interpretation

The results of an interview or group discussion may be regarded as the results of communication between the interviewer and the respondent and in the case of the group discussion, between respondents themselves. Communication may be analysed by a technique known as 'content analysis'. Berelson[28] defines content analysis as 'a research technique for the objective, systematic, and quantitative description of the manifest content of communication'. Berelson describes seventeen types of uses of content analysis that in some way or another call for the quantification of content elements like words, themes, characters, items, and space-and-time measures. (It is outside the scope of this chapter to discuss approaches to content analysis in detail. The interested reader is referred to Berelson[28], and Holsti, Loomba, and North[29].)

The content analysis forms of Berelson and others have been primarily concerned with the analysis of written documents and items of communication, like newspapers. Some attempt at quantification lay behind the analysis. With the analysis of qualitative research interviews, the objective of content analysis is to abstract the relevant and important data without quantifying. Precisely how this should be done and the criteria that should be used is an area that has been entirely neglected by market researchers. The analysis and interpretation of qualitative data is very much an individual skill possessed more by some researchers than others.

The Psychological Interpretation of Qualitative Data

At the simplest level, analysis of overt content, 'content analysis', represents the most objective treatment. If one is looking for clues as to what behaviour is relevant to a particular problem or product field purely in a descriptive sense or what 'attitude dimensions' appear salient, this will suffice. It is when the researcher is asked to explain *why*?, why people behave as they do, why people hold the attitude they do and so on, that the question of interpretation becomes a contentious one. The non-psychologist has his own private viewpoint, experience, perception, insight, call it what you will. The psychologist has all of these things and, in addition, a familiarity with a body of theory derived from many and conflicting schools of thought. Rarely do we have, amongst contemporary market research psychologists, an exclusive commitment to a school of thought like Freud, Adler, Jung, Rank, etc. There may, however, be a tendency to incline slightly towards a particular viewpoint. Very often a 'psychologist's interpretation' may be full of conclusions like 'a *hoarding or collecting instinct* is, therefore, necessary in order to save the coupons from the cigarettes smoked'. Or, 'they were also more *guilt-ridden*, than smokers of X'. The reader or user must be very careful to look for, discuss and be satisfied by, sufficient evidence to support conclusions like these which, on the face of it, always appear speculative.

It has been argued that the psychologist or more appropriately, perhaps, the social scientist, can find good utilization for his skills in data collection. His discipline can also be of value in data interpretation. What is of greater value than these learned skills is a sense of pragmatism when it comes to interpreting data, in terms of appreciating what it is going to be used for, either to provide hypotheses for future testing, data for some subsequent research input (i.e., scale items) or the basis upon which some decision will be made.

The choice conflict—which technique?

Amongst the two major techniques, individual intensive interviews and group discussions and, then, the repertory grid approach as an alternative, there may often be a choice conflict over which to use for a given problem. While certain points may be made that can guide technique selection, the deciding factor is sometimes a personal preference, but most often a question of logistics.

As a general rule, individual intensive interviews provide more 'depth', i.e., compared to a group discussion where 'breadth' is provided. This is not implying 'depth' from the standpoint of probing the unconscious mind. It is obvious that a one-to-one interview lasting between one and two hours will generate more information appertaining to the individual than in the case where seven or eight people are interviewed collectively for the same time. If it is necessary to obtain information *in considerable detail* about people's past and current behaviour, their beliefs, opinions, and attitudes, then an individual intensive interview may be preferred. If certain broad indications are sought, a group discussion may be more appropriate. In some instances, this could mean undertaking some group discussions initially to obtain a broad understanding of the problem area and *then* undertaking individual intensive interviews to either obtain more detail, information in greater depth or to focus on specific issues.

Historically, it has often been argued that in specific instances, where the nature of the subject matter precludes the likelihood of a group of people discussing it, individual interviews would be called for. In practice, we find that there are very few subject areas where group discussion participation is found embarrassing and it is possible to conduct groups on such hitherto taboo subjects as contraception, sanitary protection and so on. The problem here is not that people refuse to discuss personal matters in the presence of others but that the amount of inhibition which does exist tends to produce a rather superficial discussion. Thus, although we are able to talk to groups of people about sanitary protection, it is likely that we could obtain much more information from an individual interview situation. The whole area of financial research presents a similar problem. Whereas people are prepared to discuss their finances in the presence of others, they are much more forthcoming when interviewed alone. The rule must be, therefore, that if detailed information on personal matters is required, individual depth interviews are to be preferred to group discussions.

The repertory grid technique has been claimed to be the most appropriate one[19,18,14] where the problem is merely to obtain image and attitude dimensions for subsequent scaling exercises. The writer[3] has shown how, for a given problem, group discussions and repertory grids proved equally satisfactory, with neither being exhaustive in generating pack image dimensions. Current thinking suggests that, where possible, both groups and/or individual interviews should be used in conjunction with repertory grids to ensure that the total dimensionality of the product or problem field is located[16].

Very little experimental work has been done to compare the actual data obtained from repertory grids with that obtained from group and individual intensive interviews on a 'qualitative' basis. For example, the author has some experimental evidence to suggest that the items derived from repertory grids are mainly denotative (or descriptive) while response items derived from group discussions and individual interviews are mainly connotative (or evaluative). However, the evidence does not yet justify any firm conclusions being drawn[16].

In deciding how many of what type of interview to be carried out, time and cost considerations are likely to be the determining factors. For example, in the case of group discussions there are sometimes good reasons for not mixing social classes, particularly DE and ABC_1, in which case class composition of groups may be on some basis like:

$$AB$$
$$C_1$$
$$C_2$$
$$DE;$$

or
$$ABC_1$$
$$C_2DE;$$

or
$$AB$$
$$C_1C_2$$
$$DE.$$

However, there is little evidence to support the viewpoint that men and women should not be mixed for most general discussions or that a spread of ages (excepting extremes) is disadvantageous.

If some regional split is sought (although it is unreasonable to expect the group discussion technique to do more than provide the hypothesis that 'there may be regional differences') it is unlikely that the number of groups to be carried out will allow for all possibilities. For example, a two-class, two-age split in two areas would require *eight* groups. In many instances

24

this would be undertaken but, in others, some compromise would be effected like:

$$\text{south } ABC_1 \ldots \text{under 35 years;}$$
$$\text{south } C_2DE \ldots \text{over 35 years;}$$
$$\text{north } ABC_1 \ldots \text{over 35 years;}$$
$$\text{north } C_2DE \ldots \text{under 35 years.}$$

A group discussion can cost anything between £80 to £150 depending upon:

(a) who is being recruited, i.e., housewives are easy to find and recruit but women over 65 years with a full set of teeth are not;

(b) whether verbatim transcripts are required and whether a detailed report is to be provided;

(c) the amount of travelling time, expenses, and overnight accommodation involved;

(d) who actually conducts the group session. There are many psychologists acting as consultants scattered throughout Britain, acting as 'sub-contractors' who can conduct groups for a relatively low cost. In the author's experience some of these people are very competent but others are not;

(e) whether participants are to be paid. It now appears fairly standard to pay respondents even for nothing else than to provide them with an incentive for turning up. Payment varies from 50p for housewives coming to a morning or afternoon session, to £1.00 for, say, an evening session and as much as £2.00 for some considerable inconvenience.

Drakeford[30] has questioned whether payment or, indeed, the whole manner of recruiting, tends to attract certain types of respondent. This may be so but in the context of a qualitative research exercise where no generalizations should be made for the total population, it is unlikely to be a major drawback to this sort of research. What is undesirable, though, is the 'professional' group discussion participant whose regular attendance can lead to her providing what information she thinks the moderator wants to hear.

Similarly, with individual intensive interviews costing between £10.00–£20.00, and repertory grid interviews costing between £5.00–£15.00, time and cost considerations will be important in determining numbers.

The writer has never found a case for conducting dozens of individual depth interviews since, after a certain point, they become extremely repetitive. Depending upon how categories are broken down, 5–6, 10–12, 20–24 seem adequate for most purposes. For example, if the subject was credit cards, something like:

$$\text{men card owners} \quad = 10$$
$$\text{women card owners} = 10$$
$$\text{men non-owners} \quad = 10$$
$$\text{women non-owners} = 10$$

would probably be adequate. If time and money were vital considerations, a total of 24 (6 in each group) may suffice. Certainly, one should not need 20–25 in each category.

With repertory grids, it has been shown by the writer[17] that high divergers produce, on average, twice as many constructs as low divergers, which could suggest that it is more worthwhile to undertake fewer repertory grid interviews than one would normally expect exclusively amongst respondents who are high divergers.

A Final Note*

The whole area of qualitative research is one which has received an increasing emphasis in recent years. This has occurred without a parallel increase in attention to methodology. It is an area which appears to be familiar to almost everybody but really known and understood by a much smaller number of market researchers. To the many, it is a field of market research which lacks subtlety and requires little skill. To the expert it is the complete reverse.

References

1. GELLERMAN, S. W. *Motivation and Productivity*, American Management Association, 1963.
2. LUNN, J. A. *Recent Developments in Market Segmentation*, ESOMAR Congress, 1969.
3. SAMPSON, P. *An Examination of Exploratory Research Techniques*, ESOMAR Congress, 1969.
4. SAMPSON, P. Commonsense in Qualitative Research, *Commentary*, 9, 1, 1967.
5. GOLDMAN, A. E. The Group Depth Interview, *Journal of Marketing*, 26, 1962.
6. SAMPSON, P. Can Consumers Create New Products?, *Journal of the Market Research Society*, 12, 1, 1970.
7. GORDON, W. J. J. *Synectics: the Development of Creative Capacity*, Harper and Row, New York, 1961.
8. GETZELS, J. W. and JACKSON, P. W. *Creativity and Intelligence*, Wiley, New York, 1962.
9. HUDSON, L. *Contrary Imaginations*, Methuen, London, 1966.
10. DE BONO, E. *The Five-day Course in Thinking*, Basic Books, New York, 1967.
11. KELLY, G. A. *Psychology of Personal Constructs, Vols I and II*, Norton, New York, 1955.
12. BANNISTER, D. Personal Construct Theory: a Summary and Experimental Paradigm, *Acta Psychologica*, 20, 2, 1962.
13. BANNISTER, D. A New Theory of Personality. In B. M. Foss (Ed.), *New Horizons in Psychology*, Penguin Books, London, 1966.
14. FROST, W. A. K. and BRAINE, R. L. The Application of the Repertory Grid Technique to Problems in Market Research, *Commentary*, 9, 3, 1967.
15. BANNISTER, D. and MAIR, J. M. M. *The Evaluation of Personal Constructs*, Academic Press, London, 1968.
16. SAMPSON, P. Using the Repertory Grid Test, *Journal of Marketing Research*, (In press).
17. SAMPSON, P. *The repertory Grid and its Application in Market Research*, American Marketing Association Conference on Attitude and Motivation Research, Mexico City, 1970.
18. FROST, W. A. K. The Development of a Technique for Television Programme Assessment, *Journal of the Market Research Society*, 11, 1, 1969.
19. CLEMENS, N. J. S. and THORNTON, C. Evaluating non-existing Products, *Admap*, 4, 5, 1968.

---

* For an interesting review of the history of motivation research, see Collins and Montgomery[31].

20. OPPENHEIM, A. M. *Questionnaire Design and Attitude Measurement*, Heinemann, London, 1966.
21. CHAPLIN, J. P. *Dictionary of Psychology*, Dell, New York, 1968.
22. MURSTEIN, B. I. (Ed.). *Handbook of Projective Techniques*, Basic Books, New York, 1965.
23. ABELSON, H. I. A Role Rehearsal Technique for Exploratory Research, *Public Opinion Quarterly*, **30**, 1966.
24. BERENT, P. H. The Depth Interview, *Journal of Advertising Research*, **6**, 2, 1966.
25. WILSON, A. Industrial Marketing Research in Britain, *Journal of Marketing Research*, **6**, 1, 1969.
26. SAMPSON, P. *A New Look at Qualitative Research*, Market Research Society Seminar on Psychological Methods in Market Research, 1967.
27. BELSON, W. Tape Recording: its Effect on Accuracy of Response in Survey Interviews, *Journal of Marketing Research*, **4**, 1967.
28. BERELSON, B. Content Analysis. In G. Lindzey (Ed.), *Handbook of Social Psychology*, Addison-Wesley, Cambridge Mass., 1954.
29. HOLSTI, O. R., LOOMBA, J. K., and NORTH, R. C. Content Analysis. In G. Lindzey and E. Aronson (Eds.), *The Handbook of Social Psychology*, Addison-Wesley, Cambridge, Mass., 1967.
30. DRAKEFORD, J. *Critical Appraisal of Pilot Techniques used Prior to Attitude Quantification*, ESOMAR seminar on attitude and motivation research, Elsinore, 1970.
31. COLLINS, L. and MONTGOMERY, C. The Origins of Motivational Research, *British Journal of Marketing*, Summer, 1969.

2. Experimental designs and models

James Rothman

This chapter is divided into two distinct parts: experimental design and models. The researcher must consider the question of experimental design and models before proceeding to the choice of sampling techniques, sample size or questionnaire design, hence the placing of these two subjects early on in this section.

Experimental Designs

The role of experiments in marketing

An experiment can be defined as an attempt to measure the effect of a given stimulus or to compare the effects of different stimuli. There is a sense in which, on this definition, all market research can be considered to be an experiment; since any question is a stimulus. If we believed that the questions we ask are completely understood and answered absolutely correctly by every respondent, then the sense in which market research was an experiment would be trivial. However, we know from the research carried out by Belson[1] and others that, in many cases, respondents do not understand questions or do not answer them correctly. In other words, we should try to make as few assumptions about our questions, and the answers we are likely to get from them, as possible. This means that even when preparing basic questionnaires we should bear in mind the principles of experimental design.

To take an obvious example, if we wanted to test two advertisements to find out which of them was the more persuasive, we could, if we believed that respondents always answered questions correctly, just show the two advertisements to each respondent and ask them which of the two they thought would be more likely to make them buy the product. However, life is not as easy as that and we have to find a suitable experimental procedure for testing the two advertisements, such as splitting our sample in two, exposing one advertisement to each half of the sample and then, possibly, measuring their buying behaviour after the exposure.

One point which it is convenient to make here is that in most market research we are more concerned with comparing the effects of different stimuli, rather than with making an absolute measurement of the effect of a single stimulus, and this is probably particularly true of those areas where experimental design can be used. Thus, for example, we are more likely to be asked to say which premium offer would have the better effect on sales rather than to attempt to estimate the absolute sales increase that will be achieved by a given premium offer. Consequently, much of this chapter will be concerned with experimental designs for the purposes of making comparisons.

Definition of experimental design

If a given stimulus were always followed to exactly the same extent by exactly the same effect, and the effect of the stimulus could be measured with perfect accuracy, then experimental designs would probably not be needed. However, in most of our work, the measurements we make of the effects of stimuli are affected by many other factors. In a product test, for example, we will not find that everybody prefers one product by exactly the same amount to the other product; instead, we will find that some people like one product and some like the other and, moreover, that other factors such as the order in which the products are tried will affect our results. An experimental design, then, is a method of planning experiments in such a way that as far as possible the results are neither affected as little as possible by either random errors nor confused by other factors and, moreover, so that the sampling error can be measured.

Techniques for achieving good experimental designs

There are four basic ways of achieving the objectives of a good experimental design. First, we can remove or minimize these sources of error, e.g., we can reduce the effect of between-interviewer variation by ensuring that all our interviewers have been carefully trained. Again, if we are doing some type of split-sample operation we can remove the effects of between-polling district variation by ensuring that the sample is split exactly in half in each polling district. Second, if we cannot remove these random fluctuations, then we can attempt to control them, in other words, attempt to allocate them equally between the samples receiving the different stimuli. This is not always as easy as it sounds, particularly when there are many different sources of fluctuations and the number of experimental units we have is limited. One of the things which we will be talking about are the types of experimental design which are useful in these circumstances. Third, besides controlling the effects of some types of fluctuation we can measure their effect and make due allowance for them, e.g., if we want to compare the effectiveness of two different forms of packaging for a product by using two samples of stores and putting the product on sale in each of the stores in one of the forms of packaging, then we have two alternative possibilities for splitting the sample and analysing the result. Firstly, we can try to match the stores by ensuring that for every store in one sample there is a store in the other sample which is identical to it in terms of turnover, type of location, etc. However, although we might be able to match our stores in terms of type of location, it is very probable that we could not match them exactly in terms of their turnover. In these circumstances, it may well be a better procedure to measure the effect of turnover on sales of the product before comparing the effects of the two different packages. Finally, if all else fails, the least we can do is to ensure the effects of these fluctuations are randomized. In other words, even if in our store test the store managers all refused to declare their turnovers, we can still assign the stores to the samples in a random fashion rather than, for example, allowing each store manager to put on sale the package he likes best. These, then, are the four procedures which we have at our command for reducing the effect of fluctuations on our measurements: we can attempt to remove or reduce these effects; attempt to control them; attempt to measure their effect separately and make allowance for them or, at the very least, ensure that there are no systematic errors and that the effects are randomized.

Conditions for good experimental designs

However, besides this there are four other requirements which we must bear in mind when we design our experiment. First, we should design our experiment in such a way that it will have adequate precision, i.e., we must employ enough experimental units on each treatment. This is the familiar problem of ensuring that our sample size is adequate so that we do not conclude that there is no significant difference between the effects of the stimuli when, in fact, the difference between them is sufficiently large to be of commercial importance. Second, the results should be applicable over a wide range, e.g., if we are comparing the effectiveness of two advertising campaigns, each of which contains a number of advertisements, then it is obviously not adequate merely to compare one advertisement from one campaign with a single advertisement from the other campaign. These two advertisements might be freaks and, whereas campaign A might in general be better than campaign B, one advertisement from campaign B might still be better than another given advertisement from campaign A. Third, as stated earlier, we must in any experiment be able at the end of all this to calculate the error in our measurements and to assess the significance of the comparisons which we make. Finally, the conditions in which the experiment is conducted must be such that the results are capable of real life application. All experiments are artificial to some extent so whether or not a particular experiment is too artificial needs to be either a matter of judgement or the subject of an empirical comparison with another experiment which, although more realistic, would be too costly for regular use.

30

Types of experimental design

Split Runs.   The simplest form of experimental design is the split run. This is the arrangement in which, say, half the sample is administered one stimulus and half the other.

In market research, split runs, in spite of their simplicity, can be extremely useful, e.g., one form of assessing the likely demand for products at different prices is to ask respondents to indicate their likelihood of buying the product if it were on sale at a given price. The price quoted can be varied between respondents and the information derived used to plot a demand curve. Again, split sample techniques can be used to test the effects of alternative question wordings and, hence, to set upper and lower bounds for the prevalence of a given opinion or attitude.

Split runs should only be used in cases such as the above where, for one reason or another, it is not advisable to administer both stimuli to the same respondent since otherwise this would be the more sensitive design.

In designing split runs, two alternatives are possible, either each interviewer can be instructed to administer all the stimuli rotating them across respondents with different starting points for different interviewers, or the different stimuli can be issued to the different interviewers for administration.

From a theoretical standpoint the former method is always preferable since it eliminates between-interviewer variance; and also if, as is usual, different interviewers operate in different sampling areas, it eliminates between-area variance. From a practical point of view, on the other hand, the former method puts a heavier strain on the interviewer and, if the sample is to be split into more than three segments, it may be necessary to employ the second method.

'Before and After' Test.   The second elementary experimental design frequently used in market research is the 'before and after' test in which a measurement is made and a stimulus is administered, either by artificial means, such as posting an advertisement to respondents, or by real life means, such as a test advertising campaign after which a measurement survey is conducted.

Two forms of 'before and after' surveys are possible: that in which the second measurement survey is conducted on the same respondent as the first, and that in which it is conducted on a different sample of respondents.

Here again, the first method is theoretically preferable. However, unless the interval between the two surveys is long, there is the danger that the initial survey may itself act as a stimulus, e.g., respondents asked a brand awareness question may become conditioned and take a greater interest in brand advertising for that product group after the interview than they did before. For these reasons most 'before and after' surveys are conducted on different samples of respondents.

In this instance, as for split sample tests, there are two alternatives, the second survey can be conducted in the same sample points as the first or a fresh sample of points can be drawn. From a sampling point of view the first method is preferable. However, if the initial survey is itself likely to create so much interest that the respondents talk to their neighbours about it and so condition them it may be necessary to use the second one. A further refinement of the 'before and after' survey is to carry out an additional control survey, i.e., a 'before and after' survey taking place at the same time as the test survey but in which the respondents have not received the stimulus material during the interim period. The advantage of doing this is that a correction can be made for other changes that may have been taking place during the intervening period apart from the administration of the test stimulus e.g., there may have been competitive advertising during the interim period or, in some circumstances, changes in the weather may have affected the results of the survey. Here again, the question arises as to whether the control survey should be carried out in the same area as the test survey.

The answer this time normally depends on the way in which the stimulus has been administered. In general, the principle is to have the control sample as close to the test sample as can be achieved whilst avoiding the danger of 'carry over' effects. However, if the stimulus has been administered in a real-life situation, the control area will have to be different, say a different television area or a different newspaper circulation area to that used for the test survey.

If the control area is widely separated from the test area, the researcher must then consider carefully if it may not indeed be so widely separated that it will be unlikely to have received the same external stimuli as the test area. If this is the case, then the use of the control area will only confuse rather than assist the interpretation of the results of the experiment. Ideally, this type of problem can be overcome by the use of several test and control areas. In the UK this is possible, but expensive, for local press advertising but virtually impossible for national press or television.

From these two relatively simple experimental designs, we now proceed to the more complex designs which are occasionally used in market research.

Latin Square Designs. This design normally arises when the effects of a number of alternative stimuli need to be compared, and the units over which they are to be administered are known to differ along two different dimensions. One may wish, for example, to carry out a store test on an item with a very high rate of sale, in four stores for one week only. The sampling unit in this case is a week in a store. If we label the four different test stimuli A, B, C, and D, it will be seen that if an arrangement as shown in Fig. 2.1 is employed, each test stimulus has been employed once in each week, and once in each store. Arrangements such as this, where the design can be represented by a square with the same letter appearing just once in each row and each column of the square, are known as 'Latin squares'.

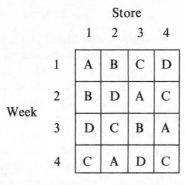

Store

	1	2	3	4
1	A	B	C	D
2	B	D	A	C
3	D	C	B	A
4	C	A	D	C

Week

Fig. 2.1

More advanced versions of the same type of design known as 'Graeco Latin squares' can be used to control the sample across three or more dimensions.

The arrangement shown in Fig. 2.2, which might be used to test a product sold at four different prices W, X, Y, Z, in four different stores, in four different weeks from four different types of display stands A, B, C, D, is an example of the 'Graeco-Latin square'.

Store

	1	2	3	4
1	WA	XB	YC	ZD
2	YB	ZA	WD	XC
3	ZC	YD	XA	WB
4	XD	WC	ZB	YA

Week

Fig. 2.2

As will be noted, designs of this type can be used either to control the tests across a number of different dimensions or to enable the researcher to test two or more variables such as prices, display stands or pack designs at the same time. At first glance, it may seem that testing two different variables in the same test should halve the effectiveness of the sample and consequently no advantage would be gained. In fact, whilst the accuracy of a test of several variables using the same experimental units is slightly less effective than a test across just one variable, the loss of efficiency is relatively small and more information is gained.

Factorial designs

A related type of situation which is also found in market research is that in which a product or an advertisement can be considered as being made up of a number of different factors; e.g., a food product may be considered as containing two or more flavouring ingredients in differing proportions, together with different levels of a texturizing process. Again, in an advertisement, alternative visuals may be under test together, perhaps with the inclusion or absence of some specific product claim or free offer and the use or non-use of the company logotype as well as the brand name. In these circumstances, we may wish to measure the influence of each of these factors separately—in technical language, their main effects. In addition, we may also wish to see if the presence or absence of one variable influences the effect of another, known in technical language as an 'interaction' effect.

Interaction effects can, of course, arise at several levels; e.g., in the food product sample quoted above, if both flavouring ingredients were present together, the product might receive a high appreciation score, but if either were present separately, the product might receive a lower than expected appreciation score and could even do worse than if neither were present at all. Effects of this nature are known as 'first order interactions', a 'second order interaction' being the differential effects produced by combinations of three variables taken together, and so on.

If every combination of factors is tested, we have a so-called 'complete' factorial design which enables us to measure all main effects and all interactions. If we have a large number of different factors to test, the number of combinations required can become large, especially if we need to test these at more than two basic levels, such as present and absent or high concentration and low concentration; e.g., a test of the effects of three different flavouring ingredients at three different concentration levels would require the preparation of twenty-seven different test products.

Whilst sample sizes used in most market research studies are sufficiently large to accommodate this sort of number of test items, the cost of their production can be high. In these circumstances, an incomplete experimental design can be employed. For example, with a design such as that shown in Fig. 2.3 it will be seen that using only nine different test products we have enough information to enable us to measure main effects and first order interactions for three different ingredients A, B, and C each used at three concentration levels 1, 2, and 3.

$$A_1B_1C_1 \quad A_2B_1C_2 \quad A_3B_1C_3$$
$$A_1B_2C_2 \quad A_2B_2C_3 \quad A_3B_2C_1$$
$$A_1B_3C_3 \quad A_2B_3C_1 \quad A_3B_3C_2$$

Fig. 2.3

In many tests it is reasonable to assume that higher order interactions will be small compared with the main effects and the first order interactions, and

34

the cost savings achievable by the use of incomplete factorial designs more than offset the slight risk of making this assumption. Several works in this area such as Cox[2] contain examples of such incomplete experimental designs for various combinations of factors and levels.

Paired comparisons

An experimental design frequently found in market research is the paired comparison design in which respondents compare two different products or other stimuli. Use of these designs will also be discussed in chapter 16. A point which is worth making here, however, is that in a situation in which three or more products are to be assessed by means of a test of this nature, two alternatives are available:

(a) one product can be selected as a standard and each of the others can be tested against this;
(b) each product can be tested against every other one.

It will be seen that in general, the second method known as the 'round robin' method involves a larger number of tests than the first. For this reason, some researchers have been tempted to use the first method. Nonetheless, it can be shown that the 'round robin' method is more efficient and can, in some circumstances, even yield information which is lost completely when the first method is used. Say, for example, we have three products to be tested, A, B, and C and the research budget permits the use of a total sample of 300 respondents. The first approach then would be to test A against C and B against C using a sample of 150 respondents for each test. On this basis, our information about the performance of A and B would be derived from 150 respondents. On the other hand, we could use the 'round robin' technique of testing A against B, B against C, and A against C, using three samples each consisting of 100 respondents. In this case, information on the performance of each of the three test samples is based on 200 respondents so that the variance is reduced by a quarter. In addition, when this is done, it may be found that product A performs better than one would expect when tested against B, but worse than one would expect when tested against C. This might arise if the different pairings encourage respondents to make comparisons along different dimensions; e.g., if A and B are similar in colour but different in flavour then when B is tested against A, respondents tend to express their flavour preference, rather than their colour preference and vice versa when B is tested against C. In these circumstances, the so-called effect of non-additivity described above can be observed. Whilst the interpretation of these non-additivity effects is often difficult, the presence of this type of effect may not be noticed and valuable information lost if the system of testing against a standard is employed.

A full description of the method for analysing 'round robin' tests, including testing for departures from the assumption of additivity will be summarized in chapter 13 in this handbook.

Carry-over effects

These occur when the use of one stimulus effects the results obtained with another; e.g., if in a store test, one particular stimulus administered in one week gives a high rate of sale, then this may pre-empt potential purchases that might have been made in a later week so that the effect observed for the stimulus administered in the store in the following week will be artificially depressed.

If a Latin square design is used the size of these carry-over effects can be measured if the test is continued for an additional week, without changing the stimuli between the stores. If there were no carry-over effects the sales observed in the last week should be the same as those observed in the previous week. The difference between the sales in the two periods shown represents a measure of the carry-over effects delivered by each stimulus which can be then used to correct observations made in the previous weeks[3].

Difference tests

In product tests especially, the researcher may find himself attempting to test for preference between products before it has been established whether or not the ordinary user is capable of detecting any difference between the test products. In some cases we may even be more concerned to know whether people notice a difference between the products than to know which they prefer; e.g., in existing products, the possibility of substituting a cheaper ingredient for a more expensive one can arise. However, if buyers notice the difference, the product may lose some of its franchise even if the majority of users preferred the product with the cheaper ingredient. Designs to test whether people are capable of noticing the difference between test products, are known as 'difference tests'. The most common form of these is the so called 'triadic difference test' in which respondents are given three samples to try and informed that two of these are the same and one is different, and then asked to guess or state which one is the odd one out. If each of the three test products is selected by a third of the sample, the conclusion can be reached that there is no real difference between the two versions of the product. If, on the other hand, the odd one out is selected by significantly more than a third of the respondents, the opposite conclusion can be drawn. It should be noted that this type of test, since it is based on a variance of one third times two thirds, i.e., two ninths is slightly more sensitive than a conventional product test where, if there is no preference between the two products, the variance would be one quarter.

One point to be noted in the use of this type of test is that it is important that respondents are informed that one of the three products in the triad is different from the other two. A frequent temptation is merely to ask respondents if they can notice any difference between the three and to say which one is the odd one out. This, however, means that respondents who notice a slight difference but are reluctant to commit themselves, and therefore claim that they can detect no difference, are eliminated so that the test results are distorted.

The sensitivity of difference tests can be increased by giving respondents more samples to assess; e.g., respondents may be given five samples to try and asked to sort the products into one group of three and another group of two. Analysis methods for this type of test which gives credit to respondents not only for getting a completely correct result but also a partial result such as A, B in one group and A, B, B in the other are given by Greenhalgh[4]. Another type of difference test is to ask respondents to test a number of test samples and say for each one whether or not it is the same as a standard which they are given to try.

The advantage of these more elaborate techniques is that not only do they enable a greater test precision to be obtained from a given sample size but they also enable respondents to be identified as good or poor discriminators. On the other hand, in the conventional triadic difference test, since even a non-discriminator stands a one in three chance of getting the right answer it is normally not possible to identify discriminators in a situation in which, say, 30% of the population can discriminate and the remainder not.

Analysis of experiments and choice of sample size

Apart from the case of the simple split run with a two-way split where a conventional student 't' test can be employed, the standard method of analysing the results of experiments in which experimental designs have been employed is the analysis of variance or, where the test result is known to be correlated with some characteristic of the sample unit which it is not possible to stratify out completely in the experimental design, the analysis of covariance. This last method can be reduced to an analysis of variance of deviations about a regression line.

Details of these analysis techniques are given in chapter 13. One point, however, that should be made here is that it is often mistakenly believed that the size of samples to be used in an experiment is the minimum size of sample that can be accommodated within the experimental design. Thus, if the experimental design indicated is a four by four Latin square, then the experiment could be conducted on a basis of sixteen sample units. This, however, is merely the minimum size of sample that can be used. The size of the sample that is necessary must still be calculated on the same basis as for any other survey (see chapter 3). Whilst experimental designs can be more efficient than conventional sampling procedures because of the way in which they stratify out the between and within unit variance, the improvement in efficiency is usually not large and it is still necessary to estimate the within unit sampling variance and, hence, derive the size of sample that is required for any given degree of accuracy. This size of sample is then achieved by means of duplicating the experimental design, i.e., by repeating the experimental design for the required number of times.

Generally speaking, it is more efficient if the replications differ from each other, e.g., if it is calculated that 32 sample units are required and the sample design is to be two four by four Latin squares then the Latin squares employed should be different from each other.

Examples of the use of experimental designs

(a) *Voting Experiment*

In August, 1964 when the two main political polls showed different parties in the lead, Sales Research Services Ltd carried out an experiment to test the hypothesis that political polls had a bandwaggon effect encouraging voters to vote for the party which they believed stood the greatest chance of winning. A continuous survey sample was split into three equal sub-samples and each of these sub-samples was asked a standard voting intention question together with another question designed to estimate turnout. The introduction to the questions, however, differed between the sub-samples, one being told that the latest survey showed that the Conservative party was most likely to win, the second that the Labour party was most likely to win and the third being given no information on recent survey results.

The results of the experiment showed no significant difference between the sub-samples on voting intention. On turn-out however, the experiment showed that supporters of a particular political party showed greatest determination to vote when told that the opposing party was in the lead and least determination to vote when told that their own party was in the lead. The differences were very small; nonetheless, this example is of interest since it illustrates how a simple experiment can often throw more light on a controversy than can the most powerful argument.

(b) *Store Front Tests*

The next experiment illustrates the way in which a suitable experimental design for the stimulus material under study can be used to test a general concept, i.e., to ensure that the results of the experiment are applicable over a wide range. The purpose was to determine whether the style and quality of shop-front design influenced attitudes towards stores such as grocers and drapers. Each member of a panel of designers was asked independently to assign pictures of shop-fronts to one of three categories, good modern, bad modern and old-fashioned design. A check was made to ensure that designers agreed on their assignment of photographs and a few pictures where there was substantial disagreement on their category were rejected. From the remaining pictures, three examples of each design style were selected. A Latin square design was then used to assign the pictures into groups of three in such a way that each group contained one example of each design style and that each picture appeared once with each of the pictures in either of the other two categories.

An omnibus survey sample was then split into nine equivalent sub-samples, each sub-sample being shown one of the groups of three pictures and asked to select the shop-front they thought best on a number of different aspects. Scores for the different shop fronts were then summed over the categories in which they appeared to yield ratings for each of the nine pictures and these ratings, in turn, were summed to yield average ratings for the design styles.

The results showed that, whilst clear differences emerged for the different design styles, it was possible for particular examples of a design style to yield inaccurate results; e.g., on drapery stores the overall preference scores were as follows:

good modern   . . . 48%;
bad modern   . . . 23%;
old fashioned . . . 29%

The average scores for three individual photographs, however, were:

good modern (photograph A)   . . . 38%;
bad modern (photograph C)   . . . 27%;
old-fashioned (photograph B) . . . 43%.

If these three shops only had been tested, because the good modern design was a relatively inferior member of the good modern design category whilst the old-fashioned shop was a superior member of its category, we would have reached the wrong conclusion.

An Exhibition Test. It was required to obtain data at low cost on the effects of different types of stimuli which can, for the purposes of this example, be considered as different prices, on the rate of sale of a product. Advantage was taken of an exhibition at which the product was placed on sale. The exhibition lasted for four weeks and the Mondays, Tuesdays, Wednesdays, and Thursdays of each week were selected as test days on which sales of the product were measured. A Latin square design was used to allocate the prices to days of the week in such a way that each price was administered once on each day of the week and once in each of the four weeks that the exhibition lasted. A count was also maintained of the number of people visiting the stand on each day of the week.

From analyses of the results it was possible to produce what amounted to a demand curve for the product and also, as a by-product, to investigate the effect of day of week and week of exhibition on the sale of the product.

Store Tests. Similar techniques to the above are used to assess the effects of varying stimuli on the rate of sale of the product. The use of stores rather than an exhibition enables greater flexibility and more realism to be achieved albeit at a higher research cost. Normally speaking, a period of a week or a month rather than a day is used as the test period so as to accumulate an adequate number of sales under each stimulus without the necessity of introducing too many changes into the stores. Store Tests are discussed in greater detail in chapter 6.

Dummy Stores and Laboratory Experiments. Another area in which test designs are frequently used is in test centre experiments in which respondents are asked to visit a centre for the purposes of research; e.g., in these centres 'find time' tests can be administered to compare the time it takes to find a brand in alternative pack designs on self-service style shelving. In these experiments the position of the test product on the shelves can be varied in accordance with the experimental design to ensure that the results are not biased by this factor.

Factorially Designed Product Tests. An important area for the use of experimental design is in the field of product tests. Products can be made up on the basis of a factorial design, whether complete or incomplete, with the proportions of key ingredients being varied or alternative processing systems being altered. These products can then be tested against each other using a 'round robin' design and from the results a score for each product calculated. These scores are then subjected to an analysis of variance so that the effect of each factor is tested to see whether it has a significant influence on product preference and the presence or absence of interactions are also explored. Tests of this nature are valuable not only in that they enable an optimum formulation of a product to be reached but because they can throw light on respondents verbal statements as to their reasons for preference in a product test.

Postal Surveys and Mail Order Advertising. Here too, experimental designs are valuable. A factorial design can be used in the pilot of a postal survey to test the effect on response rates of such factors as the wording of a covering letter, questionnaire layout, inclusion or absence of a question on a sensitive subject, etc. Further details on mail surveys are given in chapter 9. A similar approach can be used in testing advertising designed to achieve a direct mail type of response.

Models

Definition of the term model

A model is a set of assumptions about the factors which are relevant to a given situation and the relationships which exist between them. The term model is normally taken to mean a formal developed model in which the assumptions are stated explicitly and relevant conclusions have been drawn by formally deductive (usually mathematical) methods. Hopefully, the model has been also tested in various ways by adducing evidence in favour of the initial assumptions or by testing conclusions drawn from the model. (An assumption can be derived from observed relationships. The more evidence one has the more confident one is of one's assumption.)

The role of models in research and marketing

The first way in which models are used in market research is that virtually every method of analysing research results involves a set of assumptions about the data which as we have seen is equivalent to the use of, at the least, an implicit model. Usually for example, when a scale question is employed an average score implies the assumption that the scale is of equal interval, i.e., the difference between the fourth and fifth position on the scale is assumed to be equivalent to the difference between, say, the first and second position. Methods are, of course, available for checking the equal interval assumption (see chapter 5) and experience has shown that even if a scale is not exactly of equal interval, the departures from this property are not normally sufficient to effect the conclusions one draws from the results. Nevertheless, it is important to realize that this assumption is being made.

Another example of the way in which we assume a model when analysing research results (including, of course, those from experimental designs) is the assumption of the order of interaction present in the data. As we have seen, incomplete factorial designs are frequently employed on the assumption that interactions above a certain order are unlikely to be important. Again, we normally assume that the data inter-relates in a certain way e.g., we might assume that, within a certain range, liking of a soft drink can be calculated by some equation of the type: 'appreciation score equals constant times quantity of flavour component one plus constant times quantity of flavour component two plus a small interaction effect'. We do not countenance the concept that the appreciation score might be a function of these quantities multiplied together rather than added together, i.e., we assume an additive rather than a multiplicative model. By and large, most of these assumptions are justified by the fact that, within the sort of range of variables normally found in the market research situation, it can be shown that models are reasonably robust to departures from these assumptions.

Principles of behavioural models used in market research

Behavioural models in market research perform three main functions:

(a) the construction of such a model prior to the carrying out of a survey can assist in ensuring that all the relevant data is collected and, in addition, can prevent the construction of over-long questionnaires asking 'interesting' but irrelevant questions;
(b) they can simplify the analysis of the survey results by enabling the answers to several questions to be combined in a meaningful fashion and ensuring that only relevant analyses are conducted on them;
(c) they reduce the gap between the market research report and the marketing decision it is intended to assist.

One point which should be noted about models in market research is that, whereas the conventional operational research model normally has to use data which is already available and consequently is restricted by the form in which the data is produced, the market researcher building his own model can choose the method of collection and analysis of the data to suit the requirements of the model exactly and, consequently, is not restricted in this fashion. Normally, for example, an operational researcher using data on the prevalence of a certain characteristic analysed by age and class would not be able to incorporate in his model the possibility that there is an interaction effect between age and class so that the characteristic is prevalent amongst say, young working class individuals and older middle class individuals. The researcher, on the other hand, is free to decide whether he wishes to have his analyses conducted in terms of class within age or on these characteristics taken separately. This leads to the first of our distinctions between different types of models used in market research, i.e., the distinction between global and individual models.

Global or individual models

A global model is one which takes data in its conventional form for a population or a sample and attempts to relate it to other characteristics under study. An individual or simulation model on the other hand, takes each individual or unit in a sample in turn and relates the characteristics of that individual to the factor under study; it then combines the results for the individuals in the sample to produce a final result; e.g., in assessing a media schedule, a global model might simply work with conventional readership and duplication data, whereas an individual or simulation model would take each individual in the sample, calculate his expected number of exposures from the campaign, relate this to a response function and thus calculate the average response for the total sample.

The individual simulation technique is a practicable proposition if a computer is available, and it has the advantage of allowing all the complexities in the data to be taken into account. On the other hand, the global model is simpler to operate; it can be more readily understood and, providing it is a correct representation of the situation, is likely to yield more accurate results than would a simulation technique. The best method is probably to work from an individual model and to attempt to build up from this an appropriate global model; e.g., the original inspiration for Ehrenberg's[5] NBD theory of consumer purchasing behaviour was that a negative binomial distribution of consumer purchases within a period would result if the assumption was made that each individual's purchases within a finite period would follow a Poisson distribution, whilst the long term frequency of individuals' purchasing behaviour followed a gamma distribution.

Formal and informal models

It should be noted that not all behavioural models used in market research follow or are expressed in exact mathematical terms; e.g., various models of the advertising process such as the DAGMAR model[6] have been hypothesized. Whilst purists may wish to argue whether models of this type are, in fact, worthy of the name, such a discussion is outside the scope of this chapter. It should, however, be noted that a model is only useful in so far as it is expressed sufficiently precisely either for the model itself to be validated or for one or more of the conclusions that can be drawn from it to be verified.

Occasions or people

Many behavioural models used in market research work on the principle that people can be divided into types, e.g., buyers or non-buyers of brand A. An examination of the buying behaviour for most products, however, would appear to indicate that truly brand loyal buying behaviour is relatively uncommon; consequently, models which assign probabilities of buying brand A on a given occasion to individuals and, hence, work in terms of expected numbers of buying occasions rather than in terms of people, must be considered to be more realistic. Again, in interpreting test results, the conventional model is that they indicate, say, that 60% prefer brand A to brand B; unless further evidence is available a more precise model could well be that brand A is preferred to brand B on 60% of the occasions on which it is tested. This is related to the next distinction between model traits and types.

Traits or types

It is often convenient to divide people up into different type groups, e.g., housewives who enjoy cooking and housewives who cook as a duty, people willing to try new things, people not willing to try new things, and so on. However, if these characteristics are studied in detail, it is often more likely that they will be found to be traits which people may have to a greater or lesser extent rather than type groups into which people may or may or not fall. The difference is shown in Fig. 2.4.

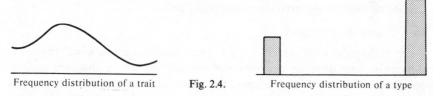

Frequency distribution of a trait   Fig. 2.4.   Frequency distribution of a type

Segmentation and taxonomic models normally work on the type rather than the trait principle. In many instances, the type assumption is a convenient approximation and may well not distort the research results. However, if the type assumption is being made, it is important to verify either that it is valid or that the interpretation of the results is unlikely to be affected greatly if the trait principle is, in fact, more appropriate.

Static or dynamic models

Most models used in market research work on the principle of finding an explanation for behaviour in terms of attitudes or other characteristics and then assume that if an individual's characteristics or attitudes can be changed, his behaviour will alter in the direction predicted by the model. Models of this nature can be described as static since they assume that the system is not altered by its dynamic characteristics. There is, in fact, very little evidence in favour of this assumption and, indeed, the work of, for example, Hovland[7] tends to support the view that attitudes may continue to change long after the stimulus causing that change has been removed. It would seem reasonable, then, to suppose that the same process of change might apply to behaviour.

The discussion now current as to whether or not changes in attitudes preceed or follow changes in behaviour is, of course, related to the same question. Whilst researchers may be forced to continue to use static models and to make the static assumption until workable procedures for developing and operating a dynamic model have been discovered, it is still necessary that the nature of the static assumption should be clearly recognized.

Points in space

(a) Congruity or Dominance

Coombs[8] has pointed out that data used in the social sciences can be considered as being represented by a series of points in space. It is convenient to consider models used in market research in these terms. Thus, for example, many models work on the congruity principle, i.e., that individuals will tend to purchase products which come close to their requirements. Other models, however, work on the dominance principle, i.e., that individuals will tend to purchase the product which in their space can be represented by a point farthest along one or more evaluative axes. A congruity model can be used as an approximation to an evaluative one by placing the requirement points at the extremes of the dimensions but normally an evaluative model cannot be used to approximate a congruity one.

(b) Measures of Distance

Once the space with which we are concerned occupies more than one dimension, we have to consider the method by which distance will be measured, either for the purpose of determining relative congruity or dominance. The obvious form of measure to employ is the so-called Euclidean measure, that is to say the distance as the 'crow flies' between the two points. Those who recall Pythagoras' theorem will appreciate that this measure of distance, depending as it does on the sum of the squares of distances along each dimension, is essentially a quadratic function. Many marketing models, however, employ linear functions. The effect of using a linear instead of a quadratic function is equivalent to the use of what is called a 'city block' measure of distance, i.e., the distance between two points where one has to travel between them along a grid of roads running at right-angles to each other. There is no evidence to suggest whether subjective distances are most appropriately measured by 'city block' or Euclidean measures.

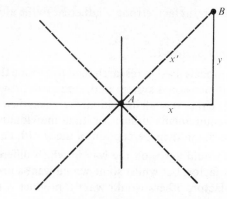

Fig. 2.5

It should, however, be noted that, whereas the Euclidean measure of distance is robust to rotations of the dimensions which constitute the space, the 'city block' measure is not. This will be seen more clearly if we consider Fig. 2.5. In this diagram, it will be seen that the Euclidean distance between the two points A and B will be the same regardless of whether the orientation of the axis is chosen to be the solid lines or the dotted lines. If a 'city block' measure of distance is employed, however, the distance between the two points in the one case will be $x + y$, whereas in the other case, it will be $\sqrt{x^2 + y^2}$ which will be seen to be smaller.

(c) *Orthogonal or Oblique Axes*

If data is to be represented by a system of points in space, it is necessary to consider whether the axes used to represent these points should be orthogonal or oblique. Using a static model it is possible to determine whether two measures are orthogonal or oblique to each other by considering whether or not they are correlated across respondents. However, the fact that two dimensions are correlated in the static case does not necessarily mean that they would also be correlated in the conduct of a dynamic model; again they might be orthogonal for one population and oblique for another. There is, therefore, some justification for systems of market segmentation or other types of models which use correlated measures, such as scores on different scales, as if they were, in fact, orthogonal to each other. Moreover, if a 'city block' system of measurement is employed, there is no reason for supposing that the 'streets of the city' must run at right angles to each other. So long as they run parallel to the axes of the system, whether or not the axes were orthogonal in this model would be irrelevant. For small correlations between measures in the static case, the question of whether the distance measure employed should or should not correct for the obliqueness of the axes, is relatively unimportant. If, however, the measures do show correlations with each other which are greater than, say, 0.3 it is important either to consider carefully whether or not a correction should be applied or to verify that the model is, in fact, strongly adherent to the alternative assumption.

(d) *The Dimensional System Itself*

Most behavioural models used in research tend to assume that all individuals employ the same dimensional system and, frequently, it will be found that they further assume either that all individuals agree on their perception of the world but their requirements differ; or that individuals have the same requirements but differ in their perception of the world, i.e.

(a) all individuals would agree on the way in which different products rate on a particular factor, but whilst some would want a product with a high score on that factor, others would want a product with a moderate or even a low score; or

(b) all individuals are agreed that a certain factor has an evaluative content so that a high score on it is always considered to be a good thing, but that individuals differ as to which products possess this quality to the greatest extent and, thus, differ in the items they purchase.

In most instances, however, the true situation is probably that individuals differ both in their requirements and in their perceptions and models which allow both these assumptions are preferable to the more restricted type which enables only one or the other assumption to be made. Again, it is normally recognized that the weights applied to different dimensions can vary; thus, in calculating a distance measure, dimension A might be given twice the weight to that applied to dimension B. In some models the assumption is made that these weights are the same for all individuals whilst other models enable the weights to be varied between individuals so that for some, dimension A might be more important than dimension B, whereas for others the opposite would be true.

Further to these complications, however, there is also the possibility that the dimensionality of the space itself may differ between individuals. This may simply be a matter of the rotation of the dimensions differing between them. If so, correct results can still be achieved if a Euclidean space is assumed. On the other hand, it is also possible that, whereas factors A, B, and C are salient for one individual, for another three totally different factors, say D, E, and F might be salient. In theory, the question of saliency can be overcome if the importance weights can be varied between individuals. This may, however, mean that the number of dimensions that may need to be studied can become unduly large either for the analysis itself or for measurement purposes.

Interactive or non-interactive models

In addition to the above, a further complication is that most behavioural models will assume that there is no interaction between the scores on different dimensions. Some models of individual behaviour, however, work on a hierarchical basis such as that shown in Fig. 2.6. It will be seen that this type

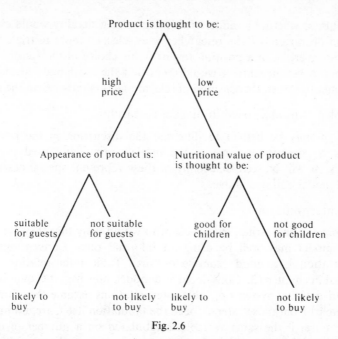

Product is thought to be:

high price

low price

Appearance of product is:

Nutritional value of product is thought to be:

suitable for guests

not suitable for guests

good for children

not good for children

likely to buy

not likely to buy

likely to buy

not likely to buy

Fig. 2.6

of model is equivalent to assuming a high degree of interaction between the dimensions.

In theory, this can be overcome by treating the interaction components as additional dimensions. In practice, however, the number of dimensions that are created becomes too great for the model to be usefully manipulated. At this point, then, it may be convenient to depart from considering data as a representation of points in space and employ other approaches. In this case, though, we need to consider whether or not the system of hierarchical needs has the same arrangement for different individuals.

General model

To sum up, the most general behavioural model would need to incorporate the following:

(a) a congruity principle instead of or as well as an evaluative one;
(b) the possibility for individuals to differ both in their perceptions and requirements;
(c) the incorporation of a dynamic element for the time that has elapsed since the change of attitude took place;
(d) the possibility for individuals to differ in the importance weight which they assign to different dimensions and even to differ in the dimensions which they select as salient;
(e) the incorporation of interaction terms whose weights differ between individuals;
(f) the interpretation of the results for each individual in a probabilistic rather than a deterministic fashion.

It is doubtful whether a model of this degree of generality would ever be a practical proposition. The researcher who selects a more restricted model must, however, be in a position to justify his choice of the factors that he considers to be relevant. It would seem that the availability of the model determines too often the selection of relevant factors rather than the reverse.

Examples of models used in market research

Finally, it may be helpful to illustrate the discussion in the preceeding sections by describing some of the models principally used in market research. It will be seen that many of these represent special cases of the general model outlined above.

Table interpretation

As we have stated earlier, even those who would deny that they are using a formal model may well be using an informal one. Conventional table interpretation is a good example of this. Table interpretation itself is discussed in chapter 12. Considered as a model, however, it should be noted that conventional systems of table interpretations assume that interaction effects apart from those catered for in the tabulation itself, are unimportant. Furthermore, if the same variable is tabulated on a number of different factors, straightforward table interpretation tends to ignore the effects produced by correlations between these factors. Thus, a report may state that young housewives tend to buy brand A more than older ones and those with young children tend to buy brand A more than women with older children or adult families. The analysis, however, does not consider whether both of these factors influence separately the purchase of brand A or whether housewives with young children tend to have the characteristic merely because they are also younger.

Models of attitude change

Models of attitude-change clearly have considerable relevance to advertisement planning and testing and they are frequently referred to when interpreting research results both in test situations and before and after surveys. They have, however, tended not to be used directly in market research. The reason for the lack of direct use of models of attitude change is probably two fold:

(a) the client, quite correctly, is interested in influencing behaviour and not attitudes and, consequently, models which relate attitudes or attitude change to behaviour are likely to be considered more useful;

(b) most models of attitude change normally have a qualitative rather than a quantitative format and, consequently, are not suitable for direct use.

A typical example of a model of attitude change is the Rosenberg and Abelson[9] balance model. This assumes that, if an object is associated in a positive fashion with a second object towards which the respondent already has an attitude, the attitude he will adopt towards the first object will be similar to that which the individual holds towards the second one. Conversely, if the two objects are negatively associated then the attitudes between the two objects will diverge.

The St James' model[10]

This is a model which has been widely adopted in UK market research. The model can be categorized as a 'city block' distance type of model since it states, in effect, that individuals will buy the brand of a product which comes closest to their requirements using a 'city block' distance measure. The procedure for employing the model is as follows. Respondents rate brands using say, a battery of semantic differential scales, they also rate on the same battery of scales the characteristics they would wish an ideal brand to possess. The scale scores then are factor-analysed to yield a smaller set of orthogonal or, more usually, oblique factors. For each respondent the absolute distance between his rating of each brand and of his ideal is calculated and a regression is then conducted using these distances as independent variables and the likelihood of buying the brands as the dependent ones. This likelihood is estimated either from claimed purchase data or from respondents preference ratings. This regression is then used to derive the importance weights to be associated with the different dimensions for all respondents. Whilst the obvious measure of these importance weights might seem to be the regression coefficients themselves, the classical version of the model employs, in their place, the squared correlation coefficients between the dependent and independent variables. The results from the model are normally expressed in terms of the average distance scores for each brand from the ideal along each dimension together with the derived importance weight for that dimension and these two measures can be summarized by multiplying them together.

The Fishbein model[11]

This differs from most research models in that it concentrates on the act of purchasing the brand rather than on the brand itself and allows for the incorporation not only of beliefs about the brand but also of normative beliefs, i.e., beliefs about how the respondent himself feels he ought to behave or about how he feels others, whose opinions he considers important, would expect him to behave. Each respondent scores first his opinion of the importance of different belief statements to the decision under consideration and then of the extent to which he believes the brand under study possesses them. These two scores are multiplied together for each respondent and then summed, again for each respondent, across belief statements. A check is then made to verify that the sum of these products is correlated with the respondent's overall attitude towards the act of purchasing the product measured on a separate set of scales. A similar procedure is adopted with respect to the normative beliefs.

Finally, the relative weight to be assigned to attitudes to the purchasing act and to the normative beliefs is obtained by means of a regression between these two functions with behavioural intention as a dependent variable. It should be noted that this is the first occasion on which a regression is used in the model. The correlations between the attitudes towards the act and the beliefs/importance products is a direct and not a multiple correlation derived from a regression equation.

The model, then, does incorporate an internal check on its own validity which avoids the danger that, with a large number of variables, high multiple correlations can be produced merely by capitalizing on random effects.

The NBD/LSD model of consumer purchasing behaviour

This model, which was originally developed by Ehrenberg[12] states that the number of purchasing occasions for an individual within a certain period follows a particular statistical distribution known as the negative binomial distribution. Moreover, where the penetration of the product or brand is relatively low, the distribution of purchasing occasions for buyers of the product follows an even simpler distribution known as the 'logarithmic series distribution'.

From these laws it is possible to derive a number of interesting conclusions about, for example, the number of individuals who, having purchased in one period, will cease to purchase in a following one, or the relative number of buyers to be expected in two periods of differing lengths. The occurrence of these distributions has been observed in a wide range of product fields and in overseas countries as well as in the UK and consequently it can, perhaps, claim to be the best founded of all market research models.

Television viewership

Another model derived by Ehrenberg and Goodhardt[13] is that for the duplication encountered between viewers of two television programmes. This states that the number of individuals seeing both programmes is (subject to small discrepancies, and with the exception of programmes closely following each other or occurring at the same time on the same day of the week) proportional to the product of their ratings. Moreover, the constant of proportionality is dependent only upon the days of week and the channels over which the programmes are broadcast. This model is a valuable aid to television media scheduling since it enables duplication factors to be calculated readily.

References

1. BELSON, W. A. *Studies in Readership*. Published on behalf of the Institute of Practitioners in Advertising by Business Publications Ltd, 1962.
2. Cox, D. R. *The Planning of Experiments*, Wiley, New York, 1958.
3. HOOFNAGLE, W. S. Experimental Designs in Measuring the Effectiveness of Promotion, *Journal of Marketing Research*, May, 1965.

4. GREENHALGH, C. Some Techniques and Interesting Results in Discrimination Testing, *Journal of the Market Research Society*, Jan., 1967.
5. EHRENBERG, A. S. C. The Pattern of Consumer Purchases, *Applied Statistics*, 8, 1959, 26–41.
6. COLLEY, R. H. *Defining Advertising Goals for Measured Advertising Results*. Association of National Advertisers Inc., New York, 1961.
7. *Thomson Medals and Awards for Media Research*, Silver Medal papers, 1966.
8. COOMBS, C. H. *A Theory of Data*, John Wiley and Sons, New York, 1964.
9. ROSENBERG, M. J. and ABELSON, R. P. *An Analysis of Cognitive Balancing* from *Attitude Organisation and Change*. Hovland, C. I. and Rosenberg, M. J. (Eds.) New Haven, Yale University Press, 1960.
10. HENDRICKSON, A. E. *Choice Behaviour and Advertising*, ADMAP World Advertising Workshop, Southampton, Oct., 1967.
11. COWLING, A. B. and NELSON, E. H. *Predicting the Effects of Change*, Brighton Market Research Society Conference Paper, 1969.
12. EHRENBERG, A. S. C. The Practical Meaning and Usefulness of the NBD/LSD Theory of Repeat Buying, *Applied Statistics*, 17, 17–32, 1968.
13. EHRENBERG, A. S. C. and GOODHARDT, G. J. Practical Applications of the Duplication of Viewing Law, *Journal of the Market Research Society*, Jan., 1969.

3. Sampling

Martin Collins

The Theory of Sampling

Sampling is an essential ingredient of market research and can be justified on a number of grounds. In terms of practicality, it would simply not be feasible to establish the habits, views or requirements of every member of the population each time market research was called upon. Again, quite clearly, the cost of such a mammoth exercise would be prohibitive. Less obviously, sampling allows us to concentrate our attention upon a relatively small number of people and, hence, to devote more energy to ensuring that the information collected from them is accurate.

We do not even need to excuse sampling in these terms; it should not be regarded simply as a more or less unsatisfactory substitute for total coverage. Over the years, both the theory and the practice of sampling have developed to the extent that we are in possession of a reliable means of learning about the whole from a study of only a part. Properly conducted, sampling will produce results which are, for all practical purposes, as good as those which would emerge from a fully exhaustive study.

The use of sampling processes does, nevertheless, bring problems with it. Most of these lie in details of a particular use; they are not inherent in the overall process. This is an area where quantity can certainly not replace quality; the biggest is not necessarily the best. Before looking at some aspects of sample design, however, we must consider the pattern of theory underlying our use of sampling. This theory is basically concerned with chance and its inevitable effects upon data drawn from a sample. Without some appreciation of these effects, sample results become dangerously prone to misinterpretation.

Sampling error

If we measure some property, say height, for every member of a population, we produce answers which are indisputable facts (given, of course, that our measuring instrument is accurate). A measurement based upon a sample, in contrast, can provide only an *estimate;* an estimate which may be more or less close to the true population value being studied. It is an unfortunate fact that the estimate is unlikely to be exactly correct.

Suppose we have a 'population' of nine men:

Alf, aged 26;	Dave, 29;	George, 25;
Bert, 21;	Ernie, 22;	Harry, 20;
Charlie, 21;	Fred, 24;	Ian, 28.

By studying the whole of this population we can state the fact that their average age is 24. We might, however, wish to estimate this average using a sample of only three of the nine men. Putting all the names in a hat and withdrawing three of them, we produce, perhaps, a sample consisting of Alf, Fred and Harry. This sample will give us an estimate of the average age of our population of just over 23—not far from the truth. This is, however, only one of the samples which we might have drawn from the hat. We might have chosen Alf, Dave and George to arrive at an estimate of rather under 27, or Ernie, George and Harry with an estimate of just over 22 and so on. In all, there are 84 different samples of three men which we could happen to draw; samples which would yield us estimates of the average age of our population ranging from under 21 to almost 28. Of all these possible samples, only six would actually yield a correct answer.

Clearly, then, sampling involves a risk; we stand a 6-in-84 (or 1-in-14) chance of getting the answer exactly right whilst, at the other extreme, the possibility exists that we might be almost four years astray. When we produce some measurement on the basis of a sample, therefore, we must qualify it; how accurate is it likely to be; what is the risk of its being wrong by more than some stated amount?

The science of sampling theory is concerned with this problem, the element of chance and probability, and is based upon two main properties. First, if we took all the possible samples of three men from our population of nine and averaged out the 84 different estimates of age, this average would be exactly equal to the correct population value (a fact which can be verified by the more disbelieving reader). Second, the scatter of the various sample estimates about this overall average (and, hence, about the correct answer) will tend to follow a known pattern, called the *normal distribution*. This pattern can be seen in Fig. 3.1, where the 84 different sample estimates from

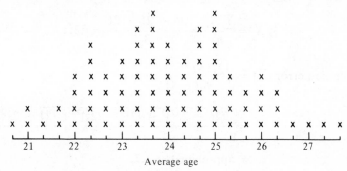

Average age   Fig. 3.1.

our example are plotted, each X representing one sample estimate. Thus, one sample yields an answer of $20\frac{2}{3}$, two yield estimates of 21 and so on. Even with the very small numbers involved in this example, we see the clustering of the estimates around the true value and the emergence of the bell-shape of the normal distribution.

The standard error

With reasonably-sized samples, then, we know how the various possible answers will be scattered, in terms of their mid-point and the shape of their distribution about this mid-point. We must now investigate the likely extent of this scatter; when we select just one of the many possible samples, how wrong might we be?

The precise extent of the scatter of the different sample estimates could only be measured by actually drawing all the possible samples and studying the answers they yield, hardly a practical or worthwhile proposition! We can, however, obtain a good estimate from the results of a single sample, an estimate which we call the *standard error*.

The standard error of a sample estimate is a measure of the extent to which chance may influence its accuracy. It is calculated as follows:

where X_1 is our measurement for the first person in the sample, X_2 the measurement for the second person and so on, X_i being the measurement for the ith person; where $\overline{X}$(x-bar) is the average of these measurements (i.e., our sample estimate) and where n is the sample size:

$$\text{standard error of } \overline{X} = \sqrt{\frac{\sum (X_i - \overline{X})^2}{n(n-1)}} .$$

Note that

$$\sum (X_i - \overline{X})^2 = (X_1 - \overline{X})^2 + (X_2 - \overline{X})^2 + \cdots$$
$$+ (X_i - \overline{X})^2 + \cdots (X_n - \overline{X})^2.$$

As an example, we can apply the formula to a sample of Alf, Bert and Charlie from our population of nine men. In this case, n is equal to 3, X_1 is 26, X_2 is 21 and X_3 is 21.

$$\overline{X} = \frac{\sum X_i}{n} = \frac{26 + 21 + 21}{3} = 22\frac{2}{3};$$

$$\text{standard error } (\overline{X}) = \sqrt{\frac{\sum (X_i - \overline{X})^2}{n(n-1)}}$$

$$= \sqrt{\frac{(26 - 22\frac{2}{3})^2 + (21 - 22\frac{2}{3})^2 + (21 - 22\frac{2}{3})^2}{3 \times 2}}$$

$$= \text{approximately } 1.7.$$

If our sample estimate takes the form of a percentage, say p, the formula is much simpler:

$$\text{standard error } (p) = \sqrt{\frac{p(100 - p)}{n}} \quad \text{or} \quad \sqrt{\frac{p \cdot q}{n}} \quad \text{where} \quad q = 100 - p.$$

We might estimate, for example, from a sample of 100 adults that 50 per cent of all adults are men. The standard error of this estimate is:

$$\text{standard error } (p) = \sqrt{\frac{p \cdot q}{n}} = \sqrt{\frac{50 \cdot 50}{100}} = \sqrt{25} = 5.$$

Confidence limits

We use our calculation of the standard error to construct statements which must qualify our sample estimate in terms of its probable accuracy. Such statements are couched in terms of *confidence limits* and take the general form:

Our sample estimate is p. We are X per cent confident that the true population value lies between $p - a$ and $p + a$.

Various levels of confidence (i.e., X) may be adopted, we might talk about the 90 per cent confidence limits, a range of values within which we are 90 per cent confident the true population value lies (i.e., there is only a 10 per cent risk that it lies outside these limits). Alternatively, we might refer to the 95 per cent confidence limits, the range of values within which we are 95 per cent confident the true population value lies. The more confident we wish to be, however, the wider the range of values we quote must be.

Confidence limits are calculated by multiplying the standard error by some value and adding the result to the sample estimate to obtain the upper limit, subtracting the result from the sample estimate to obtain the lower limit. The multiplier to be used depends upon the level of confidence required:

Level of confidence required	Multiplier of standard error
50%	$\frac{2}{3}$
68%	1
87%	$1\frac{1}{2}$
90%	$1\frac{2}{3}$
95%	2
99%	$2\frac{1}{2}$
99.7%	3

If we require the 95 per cent confidence limits of an estimate, therefore, we define these as being our sample estimate plus or minus *twice* its standard error.

Influences on the size of the standard error

There are two main factors which influence the size of the standard error of a sample estimate. The first is the amount of variation, or scatter, exhibited by the population being measured. The more variation there is the greater the standard error of a sample estimate will be. The second is the size of the sample. A larger sample will produce a more precise estimate, i.e., an estimate with a smaller standard error. The two are not in direct proportion, however; to halve the standard error we must *quadruple* the sample size, since the error varies inversely with the square root of the sample size.

It is important to note that, for most practical purposes, the size of the population being studied can be ignored. Only when the sample represents 10 per cent or more of the total population need we apply a correction factor. This factor, the *finite population correction*, has the effect of reducing the standard error:

where n is the sample size and N is the population size,

$$\text{true standard error} = \sqrt{1 - \frac{n}{N}} \text{ times the basic standard error.}$$

Bias

It was stated earlier that the average of all the possible sample estimates will be exactly equal to the true population value. In fact, this will only be true provided the sampling method used does not involve *bias*.

The standard error measures only random discrepancies, the inaccuracies which might arise purely from the element of chance involved in any sampling operation. Bias is a second type of error, one which cannot be measured by the standard error. Its existence implies that, if we were to measure every possible sample selected by our biased method, the average of their estimates would *not* be equal to the true population value. As a result, the existence of a bias in a sampling procedure will invalidate the exercise.

Bias arises, basically, from the use of a sampling method which does not allow every member of a population an equal chance of contributing to the sample estimate. To avoid bias, every individual must have a known chance of being selected. If, for some practical reason, this chance is not equal for every member of the population, the final sample estimate must be adjusted by applying differential weights to each informant's response, such that:

Where P_i is the ith person's probability of being chosen, n is the sample size and N the population size, the weight to be applied to the ith person,

$$W_i = \frac{n}{NP_i}.$$

Sampling in Practice

The theory of sampling discussed above underlies the practical processes of sampling in market research. It is, however, tempered by considerations of cost and practicability. Thus, the design of a sampling method cannot be concerned only with maximizing accuracy in the simple statistical terms we have discussed. The problem can be expressed as a need to maximize statistical accuracy for a given expenditure, within certain constraints of practicability and data quality. This requirement leads to modifications of the simplest form of random sampling (e.g., a lottery) and, even in some instances, a complete departure from the principles of random sampling. These modifications and departures demand adjustments to the calculations set out above.

Clustering

Clustering is one of the major modifications normally made to the simple random process. It is the process whereby interviews are not spread throughout the population but are concentrated into groups, e.g., into a restricted number of constituencies or in certain administrative districts. This procedure is, of course, absolutely essential to the practicability of survey conduct. It is an example of the consideration of cost-effectiveness: the additional expense which would be involved in conducting a survey without clustering would be so great as to outweigh the advantages which would be gained in terms of accuracy.

Clustering will certainly reduce the accuracy of sample estimates. The extent of this reduction will depend upon the number and size of the clusters used and the homogeneity of members of each cluster (generally related to the area covered by a cluster). It would be foolish to attempt to formulate hard and fast rules since these could not give adequate consideration to such practical considerations as the desirable interviewer workload. Certainly, however, it is generally inadvisable to cluster interviews into areas smaller than polling districts. If areas as small as this are used, the number of interviews in each cluster should probably not exceed fifteen to twenty. If larger areas are used, the number of interviews might be increased to, say, twenty-five or thirty.

Weighting

Samples are sometimes drawn in such a way that differential weights need to be applied in order to yield unbiased estimates, e.g., in order to increase the number of interviews in some specialist group without, at the same time, increasing the number of interviews with other groups of the population which are already adequately represented.

Except in special cases, too complex to be dealt with in this chapter, the effect of any such weighting will be to reduce the accuracy of the resultant estimates. Certainly, there should be good reasons before weighting is adopted for any sample design and excessively large weighting factors should be avoided. (Opinions differ as to a proper definition of excessively large in this context but a weighting factor of five or six would probably be regarded as a desirable limit.)

Stratification

One complexity normally found in survey design, stratification, is not a harmful one. This is a process used to ensure that different strata of the population (e.g., regions, age groups) are represented in a sample in the correct proportions. This is achieved either at the selection stage, by selecting a separate sample in each stratum or, less satisfactorily, at the analysis stage, by a process known as post-survey stratification, where differential weighting is used to ensure appropriate representation in the sample.

Stratification will normally have the effect of reducing the standard error of a sample estimate. The extent of this contribution will depend upon the relevance of the stratification factor or factors involved. Thus, a stratification by region will only help when the property or characteristic being measured varies much more between the different regions than it does within any given region.

The design factor

The overall effects of any complexities in a sampling design are summarized by the *design factor*, which is used to multiply the simple standard error calculation. Thus, if our basic calculation yields a standard error of four per cent and our sampling method has a design factor of two, the true standard error is $(4 \times 2 =) 8$ per cent.

The design factor, despite its potential significance, tends to be ignored, largely because its calculation is complex. Even the National Readership Survey, however, has been estimated as having a design factor in the order of 1.4, and this is recognized as being a particularly good sample design. Many random samples have design factors of two or even more. The calculation of the design factor for every survey can certainly not be recommended as a practical proposition. Safer than totally discounting it, however, is making some arbitrary allowance by always multiplying the basic standard error calculation by a factor of, say, 1.5.

The precise sampling method used will certainly have a profound effect upon the accuracy of our sample estimates and, hence, upon the conclusions we can draw from them, e.g., a sample of 1000, yielding an estimate of 5 per cent for some proportion, has a simple standard error of about 1.6 per cent. In a well-designed sample, with a design factor of about 1.5, the real standard error would actually be about $2\frac{1}{2}$ per cent, whilst, with a less efficient sampling method with a design factor of about 2, the real error would be over 3 per cent.

The importance of the design factor can, perhaps, best be appreciated in financial terms. Suppose we ask two research agencies to quote for conducting a survey amongst a random sample of 2000 informants. One agency might quote us £7000, the other £5000; costs per interview of £3.50 and £2.50. The more expensive quotation might, however, include provision for a technically better sampling method. Supposing the two have design factors of 1.4 and 1.8 respectively, we should go through the following calculations to show that the more expensive quotation in fact provides better value:

	Agency A	Agency B
(a) quote	£7000	£5000
(b) sample size	2000	2000
(c) design factor	1.4	1.8
(d) effective sample size		
$= b \div c^2$	1020	617
(e) cost per effective interview		
$= a \div d$	£6.86	£8.10

Bias in sampling

The design factor provides a useful summary of the effects of details of sample design. Like the standard error itself, however, it relates only to random or chance fluctuations and errors and we must still consider elements of practical sampling which might produce errors of another type, namely, biases.

One important potential source of bias in a sample is the *sampling frame*, the list from which the sample is selected. This list may be incomplete or inaccurate, with the result that some members of the population do not have their due chance of being selected for the sample.

To avoid bias from this source, one must clearly take all possible steps to ensure that the sampling frame is completely accurate. More important, it must be recognized that such complete accuracy is unlikely and a sampling method must take account of any residual errors in the frame used. This is a point which will be discussed further when we turn to the use of the electoral registers in sampling, certainly the most widely used sampling frame in UK survey research.

A second major source of bias is *non-response*. In no survey is an interview successfully achieved with every person selected for the sample. Indeed, we count ourselves as having been successful if we manage to interview 80 per cent of the selected individuals, even after making allowances for 'dead-wood'—selections no longer available for inclusion for one reason or another. In the remaining 20 per cent or more of selections we will meet with refusal to co-operate or simply failure to contact the person involved.

Clearly, non-response must be kept to a minimum, involving us in the use of well-trained interviewers and of methods which maximize the likelihood of contact being made with selected informants. Whatever our efforts, however, some non-response will remain. Bias will then be introduced if those people who do not respond differ from the respondents in respect of the characteristics being measured.

By definition, bias is not measurable, although various methods are used to assess the probability of its existance. None of these can lead to anything more than a fairly subjective assessment, however, and it is such a sub-jective opinion which must always temper the scientifically drawn conclusions of a sample survey.

Quota sampling

Thus far we have discussed only various forms of random (or 'probability' or 'pre-selected') sampling. One can probably say, however, that the majority of commercial survey research in the UK is not done through such methods. A random sampling procedure will result in an interviewer being issued with a list of names and addresses of pre-selected informants. Contact-ing and interviewing these people is never easy and is an expensive process. In many market research projects this expense is felt to be simply not justified.

The most common form of non-random sampling is the *quota sample*. In this form of sampling, the interviewer receives, instead of a list of names and addresses, a quota to fill. This will instruct her to conduct a set number of interviews with people in various categories, e.g., six interviews with women, aged under 35, in the AB social grades. Generally, it is much easier for the interviewer to achieve this target than to interview an equivalent number of pre-selected informants. The main advantage of quota sampling lies, then, in cost-saving. Not only will the interviewer's work rate be much higher (perhaps even doubling that achieved with random sampling) but also one is saved the not inconsiderable expense of actually drawing a sample, e.g., from the electoral registers.

A concomitant advantage lies in the speed which is possible with the use of quota sampling. First, time can be saved at the stage of setting-up a survey because no names and addresses have to be selected. Second, time can be saved in the field; an average assignment for an interviewer working to a quota is probably three days, whilst effective random sampling usually demands a minimum assignment of five days.

These advantages must be weighed against the undeniable disadvantages. In theory, the main disadvantage is that the idea of sampling errors cannot be applied to this type of sample because it does not satisfy the conditions which define an unbiased random sample. In practice, however, sample estimates are useless without some statement of their accuracy and we tend to apply the same theory. Various attempts to qualify this approach by the application of arbitrary design factors have been suggested, although there is no con-clusive evidence to show that quota sampling necessarily produces estimates which are less precise than those produced by random sampling.

A far greater danger is that bias may be introduced. Within the framework laid down by the survey designer in terms of quota controls, the interviewer has a good deal of freedom in choosing her informants. As a result, certain sections of the population are likely to be over-represented in the sample: those who are easy to contact and interview, people who are at home a lot, who are readily accessible at work and, especially, those whose jobs demand an accessible presence with a good deal of waiting time (firemen, inspectors at bus garages, police station sergeants, etc.) and those who most obviously fit the required quota—the stereotype AB; those aged from 20 to 25 to fit a quota cell of 16 to 34; and those whose appearance is more acceptable to the interviewer.

This danger cannot be removed, although it can be minimized by the thorough indoctrination of interviewers as to the requirements of survey research and by the application of controls. Such controls might include restrictions on clustering of informants, quota limitations on non-working women, on people working in non-manufacturing industries, etc.

In judging quota sampling, it must be remembered that the criticisms levelled at the approach are, in practice, also true of most random samples. With an achievement or response rate of only 75–80 per cent or less, the average random sample is certainly exposed to many of the biases attached to the quota sample. Again, the people successfully interviewed are likely to be those who are most accessible. This factor is of importance when the survey subject is related to accessibility, e.g., leisure pursuits, drinking, etc. In such instances, it may well be that the biases incorporated in a well-designed quota sample which allows interviewing at work will be less severe than those arising in a random sample which depends upon availability at home.

There are other forms of non-random sampling, which generally share the advantages and disadvantages of quota sampling, e.g., random-route sampling is frequently used. In this approach, an interviewer is instructed to follow a predetermined route, calling on households at a set interval. At its worst, this method is open to even greater errors than a quota sample; at its best it becomes virtually as expensive as a random sample. Alternatively, streets or blocks are selected at random and the interviewer is then instructed to fill a quota, usually defined in terms of sex and age, within the selected area. One should not be led by the rather confusing name given to this form of sampling, *quasi-random sampling* into thinking of it as a randomized method. It is open to all the biases arising from inaccessibility and may well be less satisfactory than the *at work-interview* quota sample.

Sample Size

Just as the statistical theory underlying sampling allows us to compute the accuracy of an estimate made on the basis of a sample of a given size, so the operation can be reversed in order to calculate the sample size which would be required in order to yield a set level of accuracy. The formula to be used in this case is:

$$\text{sample size } (n) = \frac{k^2 DF^2 p(100 - p)}{L^2}.$$

So, in order to calculate our required sample size, therefore, we must pre-set

61

the following four terms:

k: k is used here to denote the multiple associated with the standard error in defining confidence limits. Its value will depend upon the level of confidence (or, conversely, the level of risk) acceptable in the qualifying statement. Thus, if the user of the research demands 95 per cent confidence in its results within certain limits, the value of k to be used is 2.

L: L represents the other term in the qualifying statement, the limit (above or below the estimate) within which the required level of confidence holds. Taking k and L together, if we demand a result the accuracy of which we are 95 per cent confident to within plus or minus 4 per cent, we insert values of 2 for k and 4 for L.

DF: DF is the design factor of our sample design. If this is not known, we take an arbitrary value of about 1.4 (such that $DF^2 = 2$).

p: p is the answer we expect to obtain. Clearly, we are unlikely to be able to state this precisely but a reasonable estimate may be possible on the basis of earlier research or knowledge of correlated measures. If no estimate of p can be made, it should be set at the level at which it will have the maximum effect on sample size: 50 per cent.

As an example, we might be asked to provide an estimate of the proportion of the population who wear spectacles. We are asked to provide an estimate which is accurate to within two per cent with only a five per cent risk of greater inaccuracy. Our calculation is then:

$$n = \frac{2^2 \times 1.4^2 \times 50(50)}{2^2}$$
$$= \frac{4 \times 2 \times 2500}{4}$$
$$= 5000$$

All too often, the result of such a calculation is a sample size which would go beyond the budget for the research. At this point, it is up to the research user to amend his demands either by accepting a greater risk of error outside the given limits (e.g., by taking the 90 per cent confidence limits) or by widening the actual limits.

The effect of such revision will be quite marked. If the demands in the foregoing example were revised so that a range of accuracy of plus or minus five per cent and a risk of greater error of ten per cent were acceptable, the sample size required would be reduced from 5000 to rather over 500:

$$n = \frac{1.64^2 \times 1.4^2 \times 50(50)}{5^2}$$
$$= \frac{2.7 \times 2 \times 2500}{25}$$
$$= 540$$

There are, however, other ways of reducing the total sample size required and, hence, cutting the cost of the research. Three approaches are outlined below.

Sequential sampling

The basis of this method is the gradual building up of a sample by a series or sequence of subsidiary sampling operations until the point is reached where a sufficiently conclusive answer can be drawn from the research. The approach is most often used where the result needed from research is an answer to the question of whether a characteristic is held in a population at a level above or below some threshold or critical level. We might, for example, be conducting research to define the circulation area of a regional newspaper. Our approach is to divide up the likely area into zones and to include a zone in the defined area if household coverage by our paper is at least 10 per cent. As a first step, we might conduct, say, 400 interviews in each zone. In one zone this might yield an estimate of 20 per cent coverage. With our sample size, this estimate has a standard error of 3 per cent (assuming a design factor of 1.5) and we can be very confident that the true coverage in this zone is above the threshold level. In another, more marginal, zone we might obtain an estimate of 14 per cent coverage. This estimate would have a standard error of around $2\frac{1}{2}$ per cent and, hence, 95 per cent confidence limits of about 9 to 19 per cent. On this basis, we could not reach a firm decision as to whether the zone should or should not be included in our definition of the circulation area.

Applying our formula for the calculation of required sample sizes would show us that we would require a sample of about 700 households to give us enough precision to make a firm decision about the meaning of an estimate of 14 per cent. On this basis, we conduct a second phase of interviewing in this zone in order to increase our sample base. For safety, we might add a further 400 interviews, bringing our combined sample for the zone up to 800. If our estimate is still 14 per cent, the larger sample will now permit us to say with more than 95 per cent confidence that coverage in this zone is, in fact, above the threshold limit. Clearly, the advantage of this approach lies in the economy which is possible when a relatively small sample yields a sufficiently accurate result. Larger samples are only used when they are found to be essential.

Disproportionate sampling

In most surveys our interest is not restricted to opinions or behaviour reported by the total sample. We also need to know about certain subsections of the population, e.g., in assessing reaction to a new version of a product, the manufacturer will wish to know how users of the brand, as a special category, react. If these users make up only a relatively small proportion of the total population, we will need a large total sample in order to obtain sufficient accuracy within the group of users of the brand.

Economies can be achieved in such a situation by the use of disproportionate sampling. Very simply, we would interview more users in our sample than would be warranted if we followed the population proportions. Thus, if a brand was bought by about 25 per cent of the population, we might interview all the users we came across but only one in three of the non-users (apart, of course, from asking the questions needed to establish non-use). In this way, our total sample would be equally divided between users and non-users. If this approach is adopted, it is important to remember that the results for the total sample will be meaningless until the correct proportions are restored to the sample by differential weighting of the groups affected.

Multi-phase sampling

Few surveys set out to measure only one characteristic. When a number of different properties are to be estimated, it may well be that we can attach varying demands of accuracy to them. Thus, we might conduct a study to measure both purchasing behaviour and attitudes in a product field. The accuracy demanded of the purchasing data might be such that 1000 interviews would be required, whilst 500 would suffice for some rather less stringent demands placed upon the attitudinal data. In order to economize both in the field and in data processing, we can apply the purchasing questions to a sample of 1000 informants but only apply the longer questionnaire including attitudinal measures to alternate informants.

Some Mechanics of Sampling

This chapter has so far only outlined some of the many ways in which sample designs may vary. Because of the number of options available (many of which are a matter of personal preference rather than scientific judgment) it is not possible to give an authoritative 'blow-by-blow' description of exactly how a sample should be drawn. The methods which follow are selected only as examples of the mechanics of drawing samples in order to illustrate some of the basic principles.

A sample of adults (aged 15 and over)

Let us suppose that our brief is to select a sample of 1000 adults aged 15 and over, clustered into 50 polling districts. Our method is as follows:

Step 1. A sampling frame of administrative areas (i.e., boroughs, urban districts and rural districts) is drawn up. This is a full listing of the areas, grouped (or stratified) under headings and subheadings (e.g., area type within region). Against each area we give its population and then, through the list, we add a cumulative population figure:

Conurbation	POPULATION	CUMULATIVE
Area I	6345	6345
Area II	2070	8415
Area III	4813	13 228
Area IV	7962	21 190
Area V	8054	29 244

Other urban

etc.,
etc.

(An admirable frame of this type is available in published form.[1])

Step 2. We can now move on to the selection of our fifty interviewing areas by a process known as sampling with *probability proportional to size*. This process can best be explained by reference to a simpler example.

Suppose we have four towns, A, B, C, and D, from which we wish to select two as interviewing areas. Our sampling frame is:

	POPULATION	CUMULATIVE
town A	4500	4500
town B	7000	11 500
town C	6000	17 500
town D	2500	20 000

First, we divide the total population of the four towns by the number of interviewing areas required: 20 000/2 = 10 000. The result is known as our *sampling interval*. Using a table of random numbers we select a random number between 1 and our interval, i.e., between 1 and 10 000—let us say 7325. This number determines our first interviewing area, in which the 7325th person in our list lives—town B. (Town A houses the 1st to the 4500th persons, town B the 4501st to 11 500th, and so on.) Next, we add our sampling interval to the random number. The result, 17 325 then determines our second area, town C, which houses the 17 325th person in the list.

In our main example, then, we would divide the total population of our universe by fifty, the number of areas required, in order to obtain a sampling interval. We would select a random number between 1 and this interval to define the first area to be used. We would then add the interval to determine our second area, add it again to determine the third and so on, until we have our fifty areas.

Step 3. At this point, we have selected fifty administrative areas and must now move on to the selection of polling districts, again with probability proportional to size. Within each selected administrative area, we list out the polling districts, in descending order of size:

	POPULATION	CUMULATIVE
town B, polling district I	2500	2500
II	2000	4500
III	1500	6000
IV	1000	7000

We now refer back to the number which led us to select the area for the sample. In our simple example, this was 7325 in the case of town B. This we described as a pointer to the 7325th person in our full list. This person is the $7325 - 4500 = 2825$th person in town B. In the same sense as before, this person is housed in the second polling district of town B.

The effect of sampling with probability proportional to size is to give a large area a greater chance of selection than a small one. As a result, we can interview an equal number of informants in each of our selected areas, regardless of the relative sizes of the areas, and still meet the need to give an equal chance of selection to every member of the population.

Step 4. We now turn to the selection of individual informants for our sample, using the electoral register. We do this by a process known as *serial sampling*. We divide the total number of electors registered in our selected polling district by the number of interviews required in that area (plus some allowance for non-response). In our example, we require 20 interviews in each polling district. Making an allowance for non-response, we will give the interviewer 25 names within her area, so we divide the population of the district by 25 to yield a sampling interval. As before, we turn to a table of random numbers for a number between 1 and this interval. This number selects our first informant; if the random number is N, we take the Nth person listed in the register for the district. Adding our interval, say, K gives our second selection—the $N + K$th person in the list. We continue in this way, adding our interval repeatedly until we have our full list of 25 names and addresses. (The process is rendered fairly easy by the fact that every person in the electoral register bears a serial number.)

Step 5. We are now left with only one problem, i.e., that the electoral register is not a full or completely accurate sampling frame. It will not list the youngest adults, those too young to vote, nor will it list some other special categories of residents not qualified to vote. The register is six months out of date by the time it is published and is eighteen months out of date before it is replaced. During this interval, some of those listed in it will have died or left the country; far more will simply have moved their residence since it was compiled.

If our final sample is to provide unbiased estimates we must take account of non-electors amongst our defined universe of people aged 15 and over and of the mobile members of the population. This is done as follows. The interviewer is given the list of selected names and addresses. She calls at an address and interviews the named person if he is still resident there. If he is not, even if he has only moved to the next street, she does not attempt to contact him. Whether the named person still lives at the address or not, the interviewer prepares a list of all the adults who are resident in his household (or in the space formerly occupied by his household). She compares this list with the list given in the electoral register for the address. If she finds a resident adult who is not entered in the register, she seeks an interview with him (even if she has already taken one interview at the address with the originally selected person). If she finds more than one such non-registered person, she selects one of them at random for interview. This can be done either by the use of a selection chart or by the use of the 'birthday rule', selecting for interview the person whose birthday is the next to come round.

Step 6. This process of covering non-electors disrupts the equal probabilities in our sample. In order to restore these, we must apply differential weighting at the analysis stage, multiplying the responses of each non-elector interviewed by the function:

$$\frac{\text{number of non-electors found in household}}{\text{number of electors registered for household}}$$

This is just one way in which a sample of individuals can be selected and it is by no means universally adopted. It is, however, probably the most commonly encountered approach and is similar to that used in the National Readership Survey[2]. (The Technical Appendix to the report on this survey is worth reading for further enlightenment.) Of course, not all surveys use samples of individuals; many are concerned with households. These surveys involve us in an extra problem in the selection of names and addresses from the electoral register.

We proceed as above for steps 1, 2, and 3, resulting in our selection of interviewing areas. Step 4 is, however, quite different. We obtain an interval by dividing the total electorate of the area by a number three times the number of households to be interviewed, so, if we require interviews with 15 households in the area, we divide by $3 \times 15 = 45$. Then, as before, we take a random number and proceed to select our list of 45 individuals from the electoral register. We then check each person on our list and, if they are the first person listed at their address, we take that address for our sample; if not, we reject it. In this way, we ensure that each address in the electoral register has only one chance of being selected for our sample. In this instance, we ignore the problem of non-electors since it will be far less serious. (There are few households made up entirely of people not eligible to vote.) The problem of mobility does not arise because we are selecting addresses and we interview whoever lives there.

A new problem does, however, arise, in that some addresses will be shared by more than one household. The normal procedure in such a case is to list all the households found at the address. If only one is found, that household is interviewed. If two are found, both are interviewed and the next address on the list is deleted in compensation. If three households are in residence, all three are interviewed and two addresses are deleted in compensation. If there are more than three households at the address, three of them are randomly selected for interview and two addresses are deleted from the list.

Further Reading

It has only been possible here to give a broad outline of a quite complex subject. Statistical theory in relation to sampling and practical aspects of sample design have been dealt with in a multiplicity of books, articles, and papers. Most of these the reader would be well-advised to avoid.

One book that must, however, be compulsory reading, and not just for its coverage of sampling, is by Moser[3] and for comprehensive coverage of the subject it is hard to fault Kish[4].

References

1. *Population Statistics*, IPA and Research Services Ltd.
2. *National Readership Survey*, JICNARS and Research Services, Ltd.
3. MOSER, C. A. *Survey Methods in Social Investigation*, Heinemann, Ltd.
4. KISH, L. *Survey Sampling*, John Wiley and Sons Inc.

4. Questionnaire design

Jean Morton-Williams

Every stage of a market research survey is of vital importance if valid conclusions are to be drawn from it. But the design of the questionnaire is certainly one of the most critical phases. If the required information is not covered or if the questions are posed in such a way that they make nonsense to the informant, no amount of clever interviewing or ingenious analysis can produce useful results.

This chapter is mainly concerned with the design of structured questionnaires for use in face to face interviews. It does not deal with the development of guides for depth interviewing nor with the problems of questionnaires for special populations, such as retailers or professional investors, since these are covered in other chapters.

The aims of this chapter are modest; it attempts to lay down a few tentative general principles, indicate some of the hazards met in collecting information of various kinds and to describe some of the main techniques used at present, especially in the area of attitude measurement. But in the last analysis, questionnaire design cannot be learnt from books; it is a skill that has to be acquired through experience. The best method of learning the skill is to write a questionnaire, to go out and interview people with it and then to analyse it oneself.

Unfortunately, it is usually only at the trainee stage of a researcher's career that there is the opportunity to do this. Researchers are usually too busy and under too much pressure to delegate to be able to find the time to go out into the field; the result is that they tend to become remote from the realities of the interviewing situation. A considerable amount of useful 'feedback' from the field can be obtained, however, if full use is made of that invaluable ambassador between researcher and informant, the experienced interviewer. 'Debriefing' conferences after pilot studies can provide the opportunity for the researcher to learn how informants reacted to the questionnaire, which questions caused difficulties and whether all sectors of the population to be covered by the survey could understand and answer validly. It is unfortunately true that a questionnaire must be designed to be comprehensible to the least able informants.

Planning the Questionnaire

The precise ground to be covered by a questionnaire arises from the brief. The first step is to decide what *specific* information is required in order to solve the marketing problems and to answer the questions raised in the brief.

There are often limitations of money and time which dictate the length of the questionnaire, quite apart from considerations of the amount of time that members of the public might be prepared to spend in being interviewed! Of all the information that *could* be useful, it is necessary to have some means of assessing what should be given priority. The brief obviously provides the main criteria for assessing what is most important but exploratory research can also contribute; the insight it provides into the market leads to the development of hypotheses about motivations which the survey may be required to validate. Information to test the hypotheses must be gathered in the questionnaire, e.g., depth research suggested that women who used a lot of a certain brand of disinfectant were particularly conscientious housewives who had babies or very young children. To test this hypothesis it was necessary to include a measure of the extent to which they were conscientious housewives and also to make sure that full details of household composition were collected.

Before starting to formulate actual questions, it is advisable to list in detail *all* the information that the questionnaire will be designed to obtain; this gives a broad indication of its length and enables a review to be made at an early stage of the degree of detail that can be covered. It is also a valuable aid to organization of the various sections and of the order in which questions will be asked. If the subject is complex and different groups within the sample need to be asked different questions, it is helpful to use a flow chart as set out in Fig. 4.1 to plan the questionnaire and to ensure that all the ground is covered with the optimum efficiency.

In planning the content, the requirements of the analysis stage must be borne in mind. If the views of the brand-loyal are to be compared with the views of those who constantly change brands, questions must be included to identify the brand-loyal and the changeable. If hypotheses are to be tested about the motivations that lead housewives to be heavy users of disinfectant, then some measure of amounts of disinfectant used must be included.

Some General Principles

A questionnaire is a tool for the collection of data from informants. If it is to be an efficient tool, its role in all aspects of the interview situation must be considered in:

(a) maintaining the informant's co-operation and involvement;
(b) communication to the informant;

70

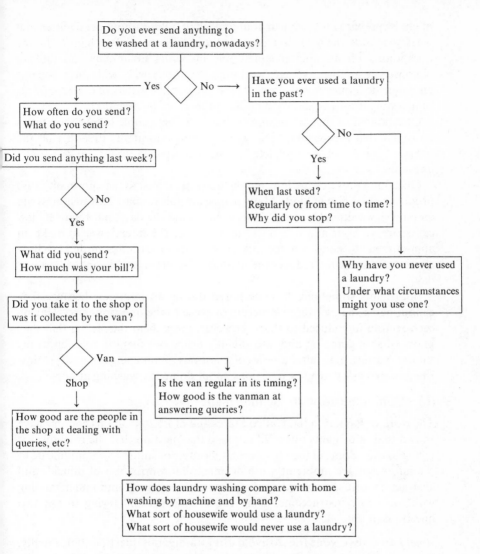

Fig. 4.1 Example of a flow chart plan for a questionnaire.

(c) the informant's working-out of his response;
(d) the interviewer's task in asking the right questions and recording the answers.

(a)   Maintaining the informant's co-operation

Maintaining *rapport* during the interview is obviously an important part of interviewing skill but the questionnaire can help or hinder the interviewer's task. The longer it is the more is demanded of the informant in terms of time and attention. No absolute rules can be laid down about length; a housewife might be prepared to spend an hour and a half talking about her children and what she feeds them on but be bored and exhausted after half an hour's questioning on an uninteresting topic involving unfamiliar and difficult concepts; e.g., the average working class housewife will soon become antagonistic if questioned closely about the relative merits of different forms of investment for people paying different levels of income tax.

Questionnaires that are boring or that try to get people to give their views on topics that are beyond their scope lead to informants breaking off the interview before it is completed. An uncompleted interview is usually unusable.

Questionnaires that are long but on topics of interest to the informant cause problems of a different kind. Many people are able to spare half an hour when an interviewer knocks on the door, even during the day; but relatively few can spare an hour and it is often necessary for the interviewer to make an appointment to carry out the interview. This necessitates more travelling around and radically reduces the number of interviews she can achieve in a day.

Informants sometimes become bored during an interview because they cannot perceive any overall structure or sense to the questionnaire. Having each section introduced to them, however, gives them the feeling that they know what is going on and also usefully orientates them in relation to the subject matter; e.g., (after a series of questions about using a laundry) 'Now I'm going to ask you a few questions about doing the washing at home . . .'.

(b) Communication to the informant

The work of Payne[1] in the United States and of Belson[2] in this country have shown that informants often fail to grasp the question that the researcher is trying to ask. Some of the most common causes of failure to communicate to the informant are ambiguity, use of unfamiliar words, use of difficult and abstract concepts, overloading the informant's memory and understanding with too many instructions, using vague concepts and trying to ask two questions in one.

Ambiguity. Everyone tries to avoid using ambiguous questions but, equally, everyone finds from time to time that a question is interpreted differently by different informants. Only careful piloting can guard against this.

Use of Unfamiliar Words. A study by Belson and the author when in the BBC's Audience Research Department[3] indicated that many words which appear to be in quite common use are in fact not properly understood, e.g., words such as 'incentive', 'proximity' and 'discrepancy' are known by only about half the population whereas words such as 'paradox' and 'chronological' are known by only about a fifth. Although the context in which a word is used can sometimes help people to understand the word, often the effect is reversed and the unfamiliar word prevents comprehension of the whole sentence.

Use of Difficult and Abstract Concepts. Research in the field of education has shown that both intelligence and educational level are related to the degree to which people are able to think in terms of abstract concepts. Most researchers and their clients are both highly intelligent and highly educated and the use of abstract concepts is second nature to them. They often find it difficult to grasp that the mode of thinking of a large proportion of the population differs quite markedly from theirs.

In a recent pilot survey, informants were asked to say what region of the country they felt they belonged to; they were then shown a map with a region marked on it and asked whether they agreed with this definition of their region. It was apparent that those who had not travelled about the country much, whose friends and relatives came from a small nearby area and who had not had an extensive education in geography and the reading of maps had no concept of a region as such; they were able to think only in terms of their neighbourhood or town. Their answers to the series of opinion questions which followed on how things were run in their region could have referred only to the more limited area where they lived. For the main survey it was essential to identify those who could not grasp the key concept of region or quite invalid conclusions might have been drawn.

Those not used to abstract concepts tend to turn them into concrete concepts. An interviewer asked, 'How would you feel if your neighbour didn't use disinfectant?' 'Oh, I'm sure she does!'' replied the informant, 'she's ever such a clean woman!'

Overloading the Informant's Memory with Too Many Instructions. When an interviewer reads out a question, the informant has to remember what has been said long enough to work out the answer. People's short-term memory for aural material varies considerably and some people find it quite difficult to hold even two ideas in their head at the same time.

Every time an informant is asked to rate a brand on an attribute he has to hold two ideas in his head, the name of the brand and the scale dimension that he is to apply to it; it is common practice to help him by presenting one or other on a card. But many questions are loaded down with explanatory and conditional phrases that confuse rather than clarify; e.g., 'Do you read regularly any daily newspapers; that is, at least three out of every four issues? By 'read' I mean read or look at?'

Using Vague Concepts. Vague questions tend to produce confusion in the informant or else equally vague answers. The question 'Do you think your house is the right sort of house for your family?' was interpreted by some as meaning 'Do you like your house?' whereas others counter-questioned 'What do you mean? "Right" in what sense?'

Trying to Ask Two Questions in One. It is often tempting to try to save time in an interview by letting one question be subsumed within another and hoping that the informant will say if the question is inapplicable to him; e.g., 'How many hours did you spend at work last week?', instead of; 'Did you do any paid work at all last week?' 'How many hours did you work?', which makes quite clear that we are asking about any form of paid employment and not simply the regular job or unpaid work.

(c) Working out the response

Sometimes the mental tasks which the informant has to perform in answering the questions put to him are quite arduous. Some of the difficulties that informants experience are related to the problems of communicating that have already been discussed, e.g., if he is asked to hold a number of defining concepts in his head while trying to work out his answer, not only does he find it difficult to grasp the question but he may forget some of the concepts and make a mistake, a mistake which may not be apparent from his answer.

Manipulating Abstract Concepts. The difficulty that many people have in using abstract concepts can also cause problems and lead to errors in working out the answer. 'How would you rate the performance of your car overall?' asks the interviewer. 'Well, the acceleration is very good but it doesn't pull well on the hills' replies the informant. 'How would you rate the performance *overall?*' prompts the conscientious interviewer. But the informant may not know how to add together 'very good' for acceleration and 'rather poor' on hills to form an overall rating.

Asking the informant to say 'on average' how many times he buys sweets in a week demands that he has a clear idea of the variability of his behaviour from week to week and then applies an arithmetical concept to the data. Most informants would fail on both counts. In order not to reveal their ignorance and because they want to oblige the interviewer, many would say what they 'usually' do or what they did last week, which might or might not approximate to the concept the researcher had in mind in asking the question. Requesting the informant to work out proportions is likely to cause similar difficulties unless kept very simple, e.g., 'Less than half, about half, more than half'.

Memory. Informants are sometimes asked to perform prodigious feats of memory. They are asked to remember where, when and how they purchased something, how much they paid for it and where they saw it advertised. They are asked to remember what magazines they have read during the past month, when, exactly, they last decorated a room of their house, what brand of paint they used, and so on.

Trying to remember something that has been more or less forgotten or has merged into a number of other similar acts, demands considerable mental effort and concentration. Informants are not always willing or able to make this effort.

What little research has been done on this subject (Belson[4]) suggests that memory is fairly accurate where behaviour is regular, e.g., where magazines are bought on subscription but much less accurate for the occasional departure from regularity, e.g., the informant might not remember that he did

74

not get around to looking at the most recent copy of his magazine or for the informant whose behaviour follows no regular pattern, e.g., takes no magazines on subscription but sees some each week at the hairdresser.

Pilot questioning as to how certain the informant feels that he has remembered accurately is no proof that he has in fact done so but suggests that the relatively rare and important event is more precisely remembered than the trivial, often repeated event. The purchase of a car may be remembered in some detail for years whereas the purchase of a packet of cigarettes may be forgotten twenty-four hours later.

Steps can be taken to optimize memory accuracy by getting the informant to recreate in his mind the total context in which the event occurred and by asking only those for whom the event occurred very recently to try to remember the details of it. But, however skilful the questioning, it will still remain likely that many informants will not give accurate information. Pilot checks can at least establish whether the informant *thinks* he remembers what he actually did. Beyond this, retrospective question and answer techniques cannot go; diary, home audits or observation techniques have to be used instead.

Indicating the Answers Required. An important part of helping the informant both to understand the question and to arrive at his answer is to make sure that he knows what type of answer is required. There are basically two types of question, 'open-ended', to which the informant replies in his own words, and 'pre-coded' where he chooses his answer from those provided. It should be clear to him which type of answer he is meant to be giving. If the question is 'pre-coded', all the alternatives should be presented to him either verbally by the interviewer or on a card. Bias can result if only the positive or only the negative answers are presented.

A practice that should be avoided in most circumstances is that of asking a question in 'open-ended' form and then requiring the interviewer to code the answers into a set of pre-codes given in the questionnaire. This procedure works very well for simple factual data, e.g., 'How long have you lived in this house?'; but for more complex questions, and in particular for attitude questions, it should be the informant's task to decide which of a set of pre-codes best represents his views. The interviewer is unlikely to be able to assess the informants' reply fully or to code it accurately while in the midst of coping with the interview.

The Use of Cards. Cards can be a valuable aid to the informant in helping him to work out his answer. They can be used to help him grasp and remember the concepts in the question and can indicate to him the response categories from which he is to choose his answer. Sometimes, the card bears a list of items, such as brand names, and the informant is asked to pick items from the list in answer to the question put by the interviewer; e.g., 'Which of these brands have you ever used?' or 'Which of these brands are particularly good for colds?'.

Alternatively, the card presents a series of response categories and the informant picks the one which expresses his opinion of a proposition put to him by the interviewer; e.g., 'I am going to read out some statements that people have made about doing the washing. Please tell me how much you agree or disagree with each one; pick your answer from this card'.

If items are to be put in order of preference, each item should be put on a separate card, otherwise it is difficult for the informant to remember which items he has already selected. Separate cards are also useful if a second question is to be asked about some items; e.g., 'Please sort these cards into two piles, those brands you think you might use and those you would avoid' and 'Now from those you might use, select the three you would be most likely to use'.

'Open Ended' questions tax the skill of the interviewer even more than other types. She has to record the informant's answer verbatim and simultaneously consider whether the answer makes sense in terms of the question that has been asked and whether it is likely to be fully intelligible to someone in the office who was not present at the interview. She also has to ensure that the informant has said all he has to say on the subject.

The answers to open questions must be recorded verbatim, otherwise 'interpretation' on the part of the interviewer is likely to distort the informant's views.

If the informant gives an answer which does not make sense in terms of the question that was asked, the interviewer should *repeat the question as it is written on the questionnaire;* she should not re-word or explain it since this would mean that each informant was not being asked the same question. At most, she should change the emphasis in order to stress that part of the question which the informant seemed to misunderstand.

If an answer is vague or lacking in specific detail, the interviewer should 'probe', i.e., ask questions to obtain further information. It is in this area of interviewing skill that thorough training is most necessary since it is essential that probes should be of a very general kind; e.g., 'In what way . . . ?' 'Can you explain about the . . . a little more fully?'. Even if the informant has already talked in the course of the interview about the subject of the question, the interviewer should not assume she knows the answer and that it is safe to ask a leading question, e.g., if the informant says, 'I wasn't satisfied with the way the machine washed my husband's shirts'; the probe should be, 'Can you explain that a little more?' or 'In what way were you not satisfied?'; not, 'Is that because it didn't get the collars and cuffs clean as you mentioned earlier?'.

When the informant has fully elucidated the first answer given, the interviewer should not assume that that is all he has to say on the subject but ask, 'Anything else?' or, 'Any other reasons?' before moving on to the next question.

If the researcher wishes to obtain reasonably full answers to open-ended questions, plenty of space must be left on the questionnaire. The interviewer will not believe that verbatim answers with careful probing are really required if there is room on the questionnaire for only about ten words.

The importance of the interviewer's role in putting over open-ended questions and probing to elucidate the answers means that the usefulness of open-ended questions in self-completion questionnaires e.g., in postal surveys is very limited. They can be used in telephone interviews but there are difficulties of hearing accurately and of maintaining *rapport* with the informant while probing and writing down the answer. It would, therefore, be unwise to use a questionnaire that consisted almost entirely of open-ended questions for a telephone survey.

(d)   The interviewer's task

The task that the interviewer has to perform can be made easy or difficult by the way the questionnaire is laid out. A badly laid out questionnaire leads to mistakes on the part of the interviewer in asking the right questions, putting the questions correctly to the informant and in recording the answers.

There is a fairly widespread belief that informants are put off by the sight of a questionnaire several pages long; efforts are made to make the questionnaire look as short as possible by using small print and cramping the questions together. But it is doubtful whether a five page questionnaire looks less intimidating to the informant than one of ten pages and the interviewer's task is made much more difficult for no good reason. Many interviewers are in their forties and fifties and find it difficult to read very small print; lack of space between pre-coded answers (especially vertically) leads to errors in recording answers; and lack of space in which to write down the answers to open-ended questions means that the interviewer is forced to paraphrase instead of recording verbatim.

How the question is to be asked should be indicated in the way it is laid out, including the point at which cards should be introduced. The questions should be in lower case and the instructions to the interviewer in capital letters; e.g.,

> SHOW CARD   On this card are the names of some brands
> of toothpaste. Which ones would you say are particularly
> good at making your teeth white?
> PROBE: Any others?
> REPEAT FOR EACH ITEM IN TURN.

The instructions to the interviewer to omit certain questions on the basis of the informant's responses to other questions are usually called 'skip instructions'. A good method, and one that minimizes error, is to indicate which question should be asked next against each set of response categories. It is then a simple matter to indicate that different response categories lead on to different questions (see Table 4.1). This method obviates the necessity for lengthy verbal instructions ('IF YES ASK Q.2., IF NO GO TO Q.30'), or arrows which tend to be confusing and difficult for the typist to draw accurately.

Table 4.1   *Example of questionnaire layout with skip instructions*

Question	Answer	Code	Skip
1. Have you ever had any of your washing done at a laundry?	Yes	1	2
	No	2	30
2. Do you ever use a laundry nowadays or have you given up using a laundry?	Use nowadays	3	3
	Have given up	4	25
3. Do you use a laundry every week, every two weeks or just from time to time?	Every week	1	4
	Every two weeks	2	
	From time to time	3	10

(The skip instructions indicate that those who have never used a laundry go to question 30, past users go to question 25 and irregular users go to question 10.)

The Use of Piloting

There are two main types of piloting, methodological pilots which are specifically designed to provide data for the development of measuring tools such as attitude scales, and questionnaire pilots designed to ensure the efficiency of the questions. Methodological piloting is discussed in the section on measuring attitude and beliefs. This section deals only with questionnaire piloting.

Piloting plays a vital part in questionnaire development but it too often consists of only getting some interviewers to conduct a few interviews 'to see if the questionnaire works'. Simply using a questionnaire will reveal the most obvious ambiguities and incomprehensions because the informant will ask questions or give answers which clearly indicate incomprehension, but questionnaires can apparently work quite well in that informants give what appear to be reasonable answers while, in fact, there are wide variations in interpretation or even complete misunderstandings hidden below the surface.

Interviewers should be specially trained in the requirements of piloting. It is useful, however, to use some relatively inexperienced interviewers on pilots, as well as highly skilled and experienced ones, because they throw more light on the sorts of problems which the less experienced interviewer is likely to come across in the field.

Pilot questionnaires should be laid out with plenty of space so that interviewers have room to record any spontaneous comments or explanations that informants give while working out their answers. Interviewers should be instructed to write in any alterations made to the wording of the question or additional explanations that they gave in order to help the informant understand. (This often reveals that the purpose and meaning of the question was not clear to the interviewer.) The interviewer should also follow-up some of the questions by asking, 'Can you tell me what you understand by this question (or statement)?' and, 'Can you tell me what you had in mind when you answered . . . ?'. This probing reveals the hidden ambiguities and misunderstandings. Questions involving memory can be followed up by, 'How clearly can you remember this particular purchase? What fixed it in your mind?'

To go back over the whole questionnaire in this manner can be very time-consuming; it is sometimes carried out as a separate operation, a different interviewer calling back on the informant later on in the day. Often, however, just key questions are picked out for this treatment and they are followed up during the course of the interview or, if this disrupts the flow too much, at the end. The interviewer might say, 'We are trying out this questionnaire and want to make sure that the questions make sense, so can I go back quickly over some of the answers you gave?'. This positions the process as a trial of the questionnaire and not an examination of the informant's ability to understand. The amount of time taken can be reduced by dividing the questions to be examined in detail among the interviewers so that each deals with only three or four.

Apart from studying the pilot questionnaires, it is useful to have reports from the interviewers working on the pilot in which they summarize their findings under a number of headings provided by the researcher. These might be:

'selling' the survey and persuading the informant to take part;
the opening questions;
the length of interview;
the flow of the interview;
any particularly difficult questions;
any problems of interviewers' instructions;
any layout problems.

Questions for Behavioural Information

Information on consumer behaviour is usually required in order to give a picture of where and when the product is being bought, how it is used and into what context of more general behaviour its usage fits. It is also needed in order to provide a basis for discovering what sort of people use the product in terms of characteristics and attitudes. For this latter purpose, it is usually necessary to identify particular 'behaviour groups' for use in tabulation such as present and past users, heavy and light users, and so on. These groups must be precisely defined and questions asked to identify them.

The main difficulties in designing questions to collect behavioural information concern the problem of getting informants to remember accurately and trying to get them to distinguish between what they 'usually' do and what, precisely, they did last time. There can also sometimes be difficulties in getting informants to generalize about their behaviour. Techniques other than question-and-answer surveys have to be used when accuracy is essential. The information collected from surveys can be only an approximation. The researcher's job is not only to make the approximation as close as possible but also to have some idea from piloting as to what kind of errors are likely to occur.

Some of the most common types of behavioural questions and their problems can be discussed separately.

(a) Product group definition

Before asking people whether they have ever used a product, make sure they know what is included, e.g., in asking housewives whether they have ever used a laundry, it may be necessary to ensure that they understand that this does not include launderettes or dry cleaning. In asking people whether they have ever taken a tonic, indicate whether tonic wines, doctors' prescribed tonics or vitamin pills etc., are included or not. Make sure that they understand that by 'ever use' you mean tried once and gave up as well as used regularly.

(b) Frequency questions

When an informant is asked to say 'how often' he does something or 'how many times' he does it within a particular time period, he is usually being asked to generalize about his behaviour since there is almost certain to be some irregularity. The tendency is for him to give his *ideal* behaviour, from which he may frequently deviate, e.g., a person may think that the proper number of baths he ought to take in a week is four, though more often than not he may only get around to taking two, but may quite honestly believe that he usually takes four baths a week. Furthermore, he may be reluctant to admit that he only took two last week. To obtain accurate information it is not sufficient to follow up the 'how often?' question with a casual, 'How many did you happen to have last week?'. It is necessary, first, to make him feel that he is not the only person who misses baths with some reassuring preamble; e.g., 'Quite a lot of people find it difficult to take as many baths as they wish because of shortage of time or because they're tired, or for other reasons; do you ever find you miss baths for this sort of reason?'. This can then be followed up with questions about the number of baths taken last week, preferably by getting him to recreate the week in his mind rather than by just asking him to give the number of baths taken; e.g., 'Now would you think back over last week, and tell me on which days you happened to take a bath?'.

Questions which proceed from what the informant 'usually' does to what he 'happened to do last week' assist accuracy because the informant is less tempted to falsify his account of what he did last week on the grounds that it is atypical. It must be remembered, however, that what the informant claims he 'usually' does is likely to represent his ideal rather than his average behaviour.

'How often' questions are sometimes applied to completely irregular behaviour and this can cause considerable difficulty to the informant; e.g., the true answer to, 'How often do you take indigestion remedies?', may be 'Everytime I suffer from indigestion'; but the pre-coded answer categories are given in terms of number of times a week or month. The form of question tends to assume that all sufferers are chronic sufferers whereas many have indigestion only from time to time or have periods when they suffer quite frequently followed by periods free of the complaint. On top of the variability of suffering from indigestion, consumers may vary in the extent to which they take remedies when they have an attack. A series of questions is necessary to give a true picture of the market rather than a single 'how often' question.

(c) 'Where?' questions

Questions which ask where a product was purchased or where advertising for the product was seen are particularly subject to memory failure unless the event was a particularly important one for the informant or clearly linked to a date. Because it is difficult to remember precisely, the informant tends to say what he thinks was most likely to be the case. He has the idea that toiletries are *normally* bought at chemists and therefore gives this as his answer, with the result that the proportion of sales through groceries is very much underestimated from interview surveys. Similarly, because he sees more advertising on television than anywhere else, he considers that this is probably where he saw the advertisement he is being asked about. The only remedy is to try to get informants to recreate in their minds the actual occasion of purchase or the actual moment of seeing the advertisement, and not to press for an answer if he feels uncertain as to whether he has remembered correctly.

(d) 'When?' questions

Time tends to contract in memory with the result that people tend to remember events as having happened more recently than they really did. Difficulties of remembering again lead informants to substitute what they think *usually* do for what they actually did. In answer to questions such as, 'When did you last buy a bottle of disinfectant?' informants are likely to claim that they bought one within the last seven days because they feel that it ought to be part of their once a week grocery purchasing and they know that they bought some not very long ago. Yet estimates of the total disinfectant market based on those claiming to buy within the past seven days are usually of the order of four times the most conservative estimate of the market from other sources.

(e) 'How much?' questions

Informants can usually remember how much of a product they bought or used on a recent occasion as long as the units are clear cut, but they frequently cannot remember how much they paid for it (especially if the item was part of a larger bill) and are usually unaware of bottle or can sizes, especially when a number of size variations are available.

(f) Brand names

In some product fields where brand attachment is not strong, informants sometimes cannot remember accurately which brand they last purchased or have in the house at present. Brands of stockings or tights are rapidly forgotten and a pantry check might reveal confusion between 'Sunfresh' and 'Suncrush' and between 'Daz' and 'Omo'.

Measuring Attitudes and Beliefs

The measurement of attitudes is a vast subject that can only be touched on in this chapter. For a more comprehensive review of measuring techniques and also for papers on the main theories of attitude, the reader is referred to Fishbein[5].

It is useful to distinguish between the more general 'life-style' attitudes, such as attitudes towards the job of being a housewife or towards saving, and the more specific attitudes to brands or products. The term 'image' is reserved for these more specific brand evaluations.

The relationship between attitudes and beliefs

Attitudes can be defined as emotionally toned evaluations about events, objects or activities. They are *evaluations* because they assess things as good or bad, desirable or undesirable. They are *emotionally toned* in that the events, objects or activities with which the attitudes are connected arouse pleasure, joy, pain, anger, fear, anxiety, etc.; e.g., people who hold the attitude that saving money is a very good thing are likely to feel happy when they have a lot of money deposited in a Building Society and very anxious when they have no money saved.

The direction that the evaluation of the object or event takes, however, and the type of emotion felt is likely to be affected by a person's *beliefs* about the object, event or activity. If he believes that having money saved gives security, he is likely to feel anxious if he has no savings. If, on the other hand, he believes that one can only save by stinting one's family, he may feel guilty of meanness if any money accumulates in the bank. This last example demonstrates that beliefs also can carry evaluations.

Fishbein[6] has pointed out that it is important in attitude research to distinguish between evaluations of the subject that is being investigated, beliefs about it and evaluations of these beliefs. All three may be included implicitly within one measuring technique. Sometimes, this results in a valid measure of attitude because everyone agrees with the evaluation placed on the belief. The statement, 'Coloured people are less intelligent than white people,' for example, is a statement of belief. Everyone may agree, however, that intelligence is a desirable and admirable attribute; therefore anyone who agrees with the statement is giving a low evaluation to being coloured. The belief statement, 'Coloured people are more athletic than white people', may not carry the same evaluation for everyone and those who agree with it are not necessarily giving a high evaluation to coloured people. The evaluation attached to the belief would, in this case, have to be measured separately in order to know whether it was contributing positively, negatively or neutrally to the overall evaluation of the subject being studied.

Saliency of attitude

One of the problems of investigating attitudes with structured questionnaires is that it is difficult to avoid putting words into people's mouths. It is impossible to ask someone whether he agrees or disagrees with a proposition without putting the subject of the proposition into his mind. He may agree strongly with the proposition, yet he may never have given the matter any thought before. The term 'saliency' is used to describe the extent to which a particular attitude is actively in people's minds before the interviewer asks specific questions about it.

The saliency of an attitude is usually measured by a series of open-ended questions which progressively 'home in' on the target attitude. In a study of attitudes to the noise of aircraft around Heathrow[7], for instance, informants were asked a series of questions designed to discover whether aircraft noise was sufficiently annoying for it consciously to affect their pleasure in living in their home; e.g., 'What do you dislike about living around here?'; 'If you could change just one thing about living round here, what would it be?'; 'Have you ever thought of moving away from here? Why?' and, 'What are main kinds of noise you hear round here?' No mention of aircraft or aircraft noise was made in the interview until all these questions had been asked. The answers to these questions indicated the extent to which people were consciously aware of aircraft noise as a source of disturbance.

Dimensionality of attitudes

Open-ended questions can indicate whether a particular subject is uppermost in people's minds and what the main opinions are that people hold about the subject, but they can, at best, be only crude indications of how people feel. In particular, open questions cannot assess how *strongly* people feel about a subject.

The main purpose of measuring attitudes in market research is usually in order to be able to make *comparisons* between the attitudes of different groups of consumers, e.g., users and non-users of the product or brand. In order to make valid comparisons between groups, it is essential to be able to measure the position of *all* the people in the groups on the attitude, to measure whether they are favourable or unfavourable in their attitude and how strongly they feel about it. This implies that attitudes are *dimensions* along which people can be positioned. This concept of the dimensionality of attitudes underlies all the main techniques of attitude measurement.

Attitudes and opinions that are simple, clear-cut and readily accessible to conscious introspection can be measured by single questions, e.g., people's optimism about their future financial prospects was measured by a simple self-rating scale, 'Over the next five years or so, do you expect your financial situation to:

improve a lot;
improve a little;
stay about the same;
get a bit worse;
get a lot worse?

The more complex and fundamental attitudes which underlie specific opinions cannot be so easily measured, however. It is unlikely, for instance, that people would give a valid answer if asked to rate themselves on the extent to which they were conscientious housewives or concerned with maintaining their financial independence. This is partly because people are not usually aware of their broader and more fundamental attitudes and therefore cannot introspect accurately about them, and partly because these broad attitudes are *generalizations* about the people and, as already discussed, people find it very difficult to generalize.

The broad underlying dimensions of attitude are usually measured by batteries of questions which measure different aspects of the attitude and are then combined in some way to give an overall measure of the underlying attitude. The main methods of forming attitude batteries are discussed later in this chapter, but first it is necessary to consider the basic ingredients of attitude measurement, the questioning methods used in the interview situation.

Questioning techniques

The most common basic tool of attitude measurement is the *rating scale*, by which the informant is asked to indicate his position on a dimension of opinion. Other techniques involve the ascription of adjectives to concepts, or vice versa, or a choice between alternative attitudinal positions. Rating scales can be verbal, numerical or diagrammatic.

Verbal Rating Scales may take the form of the 'financial optimism' scale given above in which a single clear-cut concept is rated on a specific scale which embodies an attitude to the concept or a belief about it. Alternatively, a more complex concept may be presented which embodies the attitude or belief. The informant is then asked to say whether he agrees or disagrees and how strongly (or whether he believes it to be true or untrue). Several concepts may be presented one after the other and the informant may be asked to use the same response framework for replying to each; e.g., 'Tell me how much you agree or disagree with each of these statements:

(a) everyone should disinfect their drains everyday;
(b) only those in old houses need use disinfectant;
(c) those who use a lot of disinfectant must be dirty people'.

A 'no opinion' or 'don't know' category should be provided for the interviewer to use if the informant is unable to give an answer though it need not necessarily be offered to the informant.

Belson[8] has investigated the effects of the order in which the categories are presented in verbal rating scales on the distribution of answers along the scale. He found that the positive answers were more frequently endorsed when they were presented at the top of the scale than when the scale was reversed and the positive answer appeared at the bottom. Putting the negative response categories at the top of the scale tended to give a better distribution of answers across the categories. There are, therefore, advantages in presenting the negative categories first, provided that it does not lead to confusion for the informant.

There is no case for varying the order of presentation of rating scales from one interview to another, since this could lead to a situation where apparent differences in attitude between sub-groups of the sample were due to there being more people in one group than in the other having the scales presented in a particular way.

Numerical Rating Scales take several forms. Informants may be asked to give scores out of ten or out of five (on an analogy with school marks). They might be asked, for instance, to score a cake mix that they have just tested on a number of attributes such as ease of making, lightness, tastiness and so on. Alternatively, they might be asked to give scores to different brands relating to their suitability for some purpose.

In using scoring systems the evaluation to be placed on the top score must be indisputable. (A product could not be scored for 'sweetness' for instance, because informants cannot be certain whether the top point of the scale meant 'too sweet' or 'just right'.) Shorter scales are usually preferable to longer scales since it has been found that people tend to use only part of longer scales. Scores out of ten tend to carry particular connotations from school marks in that a score of five is often regarded as a low score rather than as the mid-point; the informant may in effect use only the top half of the scale. The top and bottom point of a numerical scale should be defined verbally in order to avoid variability of interpretation between informants.

Diagrammatic Rating Scales are as varied as the imaginations of the research people who invent them. They may be representational or abstract. The example in Fig. 4.2 below is a simple way of measuring pure evaluation independently of descriptive content by a representational scale; 'Which of these faces best expresses how you felt about the sweetness of the product?'. In this example, the most favourable response means 'just right' whilst the

Fig. 4.2

least favourable response might mean, 'too sweet' or 'not sweet enough'. It would clearly be necessary to ask those who gave a poor rating what was wrong with the sweetness of the product.

Diagrammatic scales can present the dimension as a set of abstract categories:

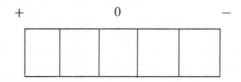

or as a continuum:

The informant is simply asked to indicate his position on the scale. Numerical values can easily be assigned to informants' positions on the scales which are presented with abstract categories but continuous scales present more of a problem. It is usually necessary to impose categories on the continuum for scoring purposes.

The argument in favour of continuous diagrammatic scales is that they do not impose a set of categories of a pre-defined size and number on the informant. On the other hand, all diagrammatic scales tend to involve the informant in abstract thinking and to present ideas in a way that is less familiar than either verbal or numerical scales.

Semantic Differential Scales are very popular in measuring brand, product or company images. These combine elements of both verbal and diagrammatic scales.

The technique was developed by Osgood[9] to investigate the meaning which concepts had for people. He presented a concept e.g., 'the American nation' or 'coloured people' and asked informants to rate them on seven-point scales, the end points of which were defined by pairs of adjectives:

good | | | | | | | | bad

strong | | | | | | | | weak

Market researchers have adapted the technique by using a brand, product, or company name as the concept and often using quite complex descriptive and evaluative phrases to define the ends of the scale. The advantage of the technique is that several brands can be quite rapidly rated on several different scales (say four brands on fifteen scales or six brands on ten scales) and comparisons made between them. Often, the informant is shown how the scales are to be used and then asked to fill them in himself. Numerical values can be assigned to the scale positions and comparisons made between the various brands (or between users and non-users of a brand) in terms of mean scores.

The pairs of adjectives or phrases used to define the ends of the scale should, of course, be very carefully selected to be meaningful in the market being investigated. The Kelly Repertory Grid technique, described by Sampson in chapter 1 on Qualitative and Motivational Research is often used to throw up meaningful attributes and to define the scale ends.

Some people prefer to use only 'monopolar' scales such as 'sweet—not sweet' while others may use 'bipolar' scales, such as 'sweet—sour' where appropriate. The mid-point of the scale has different meanings for these two types of scale. On monopolar scales, the mid-point is simply a step on the scale from 'not sweet' to 'sweet' whereas on a bipolar scale the mid-point is a neutral point meaning 'neither sweet nor sour'. It can also be used to represent a 'no opinion' point on bipolar scales while a separate 'no opinion' category is necessary for monopolar scales.

Some researchers prefer to use five point rather than seven point semantic scales on the grounds that five points are easier for the interviewer to explain and for the informant to grasp. Inspection of informants' answer patterns on seven point scales certainly seems to suggest that many fail to use all the positions but confine their answers to the extreme position and one other on each side of the mid-point. The meaning of the scale positions on five point scales can easily be described by turning it into a verbal rating scale.

Interviewers need to be carefully instructed on how to explain semantic differential scales to informants and a few trial examples should always be provided for demonstration purposes and to make sure that the informant has understood.

Ascription of Adjectives to brands is another questioning technique for measuring brand images. The informant is handed a list of brands and asked to say which of them fit a particular adjective well; e.g., 'Which of the brands on this list are particularly sweet?' or 'And which are not at all sweet?'.

By presenting both ends of an attribute, as in the above example, a simplified brand rating can be achieved; i.e., a brand is rated either as 'particularly sweet' or 'not at all sweet' or, by implication, as neither one nor the other.

Two measures for each brand on each attribute can be derived from this: 'image strength', which is the proportion of the sample mentioning the brand as being either sweet or not sweet and 'image direction', which is the proportion of those mentioning it as sweet or not sweet who assign it to each side of the dichotomy.

Joyce[10] has indicated that this simple technique is quicker and easier to administer in the field than semantic scales, that it provides sharper discrimination between brands and that it is more sensitive in pinpointing changes in brand images over time. It is not suitable, however, for making comparisons between brands which differ markedly in share of the market and familiarity, since the unfamiliar brands tend to be swamped by the familiar brands and, thus, are not mentioned.

Presenting Alternative Attitude Positions is a useful technique for avoiding the superficial socially acceptable response. Most people would agree for instance, with the proposition that they ought to save when the country is in financial difficulties yet many people do not do so because they feel that inflation makes saving pointless. If two propositions are presented as equally sensible alternatives, the tendency to agree glibly is reduced and the informant is forced to think out his position; e.g., 'Which of these two statements do you agree with most?'

(SHOW CARD AND READ)

'People should save money when the country is in financial difficulties', or, 'It's better to spend your money when the country is in financial difficulties because prices keep going up'?

Similarly, most people would like to consider themselves to be safe and careful drivers and also to be skilful and confident drivers, but the relative degree of importance which an individual motorist attaches to these adjectives could indicate important differences in driving attitudes and values. Motorists were, therefore, asked to choose between a number of opposing adjectives, as follows.

As a motorist, would you rather be described as:
    considerate or quick-witted;
    confident or safe;
    careful or skilful?
Which of these descriptions would you object to more:
    timid or foolhardy;
    aggressive or hesitant;
    impatient or slow?

One of each pair of words described a more introverted type of motorist while the other described a more extrovert type. Each word was paired with another which, in the opinion of a panel of judges was equally favourable or unfavourable.

The use of projective techniques in attitude measurement

Most projective techniques are not suitable for use in attitude measurement in structured questionnaires. The majority require open-ended answers, which cannot be used as efficient means of measurement, and they often require a high degree of subjective interpretation. (See chapter 1 for a full picture of the use of projective techniques in qualitative research.)

Indirect questioning techniques can, of course, be used in structured questionnaires, such as asking the informant to say what sort of person would or would not use a particular product or brand. Most of the different measurement techniques described above could be applied within this framework; semantic differential scales, for instance,

| used by hard-working housewives | | | | | | | used by lazy housewives |

Such questions as, 'If your car were to become a person, what sort of person would it be?', can also be structured in the same way.

Sentence completion can be used in a structured form in which the informant is asked to select one of several alternative ways of finishing a sentence; but this moves away from the truly projective nature of the technique and it becomes simply another method of presenting a scale or a series of propositions.

Attitude batteries

The development of attitude batteries which combine the answers to several questions to measure a general underlying attitude usually requires special preparatory work. In order to ensure that the items that go into the battery all contribute efficiently to the measurement of the attitude it is usually necessary to try out a large number of items in a methodological pilot study of 100 to 200 informants and then to apply various criteria for selecting those items which are the most appropriate. This procedure is commonly called 'attitude scaling'.

There are four main types of attitude scaling technique:

(a) the Thurstone method of 'equal-appearing intervals';
(b) the Likert method of summated ratings;
(c) Guttman cumulative scales;
(d) scales based on factor analysis.

The last is the most commonly used in market research nowadays.

Each will be described briefly in turn but the reader is referred to the relevant literature for a more complete exposition.

Thurstone scaling[11] involves devising (or collecting from free interviewing) a large number of opinion statements on the attitude subject. Preferably about 100 statements are collected. The attitude dimension to be measured is broadly, but clearly, defined. A panel of people (at least 100) is then asked to rate the opinion statements according to how favourable or unfavourable each one is in terms of the attitude to be measured. The procedure is to ask the panel to divide the statements into eleven piles ranging from 'very unfavourable' at one end, through a neutral mid-point to 'very favourable' at the other end. This panel is referred to as the 'panel of judges' since their function is to evaluate the statements in terms of their favourability for the defined attitude subject and not to say whether they themselves agree or disagree with the statements.

The next step is to select those items from each of the eleven scale positions about which there is most agreement from the judges. (Fishbein has pointed out that this procedure eliminates all statements in which there is little agreement on the evaluation attached to the *belief* component of the statement.) Each item is given a weight according to its median scale position. It is called the method of 'equal appearing intervals' because the eleven groups into which the judges divide the statements are meant to be equally spaced along the favourable/unfavourable continuum. The scale, now reduced to a minimum of eleven items but preferably about twenty is then ready for use. Informants are asked to read through the statements and simply to endorse all those with which they agree. They are given a score on the attitude dimension by averaging the scale weights of all the items they have endorsed. This method of scaling is very laborious and its validity depends on the judges being drawn from the same population as that on which it is intended to use the scale. The average member of the public is likely to have some difficulty in acting as a judge without his agreement or disagreement with the statement influencing or confusing his judgement.

Likert scaling[12] also starts with a large number of opinion statements but, instead of using a panel of judges, a sample of informants is asked to rate each statement on a verbal scale from 'agree strongly' through a 'no opinion' mid-point to 'disagree strongly'. The answer categories are given weights from 1 to 5 or 5 to 1 depending on whether the statement is positive or negative in relation to the underlying attitude. Each informant is then given a score by summing the weights attached to each of his answers. Items are then selected for inclusion in the final scale by applying a criterion of internal consistency. Criterion groups consisting of the upper and lower 10 per cent, or some other percentage, of the informants in terms of their total scores are compared to see whether the individual items differentiate between the two groups. The means for each item for each of the two groups are computed and the items which show the biggest difference between the means are retained.

Guttman Cumulative Scales[13] utilize the heirarchical property of questions that lie at different points along the same attitude dimension. A simple example illustrates the principle: if we ask people to say (a) whether they are over 20 years of age, (b) over 40 years of age, or (c) over 60 years of age, their answers will form a 'scalogram' pattern in that all those over 40 would also endorse that they are over 20, and those who are over 60 would endorse that they are over both the lesser ages:

	(a)	(b)	(c)
over 60's	×	×	×
over 40's	×	×	
over 20's	×		

If the answers are hierarchic, a person's answer pattern can be deduced from his overall score.

To discover whether the scalogram pattern exists, the items are placed in order of the number of people endorsing each along one dimension of a sheet of paper and the individuals are placed in order of number of items endorsed along the other dimension and their answer patterns entered in the matrix.

In practice, if attitude items are used rather than physical measurements, there is a considerable amount of 'error' in the pattern of answers, i.e., departure from the ideal pattern illustrated above. The 'scalogram analysis' is usually performed using a special scalogram board which allows individual items or people to be shifted about slightly in order to optimize the scalogram pattern. The closeness with which a series of questions approaches perfect scalability is measured by the coefficient of reproducibility which is assessed by the following formula:

$$\frac{\text{number of errors}}{\text{number of questions} \times \text{number of respondents}}$$

A value of about 0.90 for the coefficient of reproducibility is usually taken as the lower acceptable limit for inferring scalability.

Guttman scales have the property of being strictly 'unidimensional', i.e., of measuring one, and one only, underlying dimension of attitude. In practice, it is extremely difficult to develop a satisfactory Guttman scale to measure attitudes unless the attitude to be measured has a logical hierarchical foundation such as attitudes to aircraft noise. In the study of the effects of aircraft noise round Heathrow already quoted[7], a Guttman scale of annoyance was used. This took the form of a series of questions about the effects of aircraft noise, e.g., 'Does the noise of aircraft ever wake you up? Interfere with conversation? Make your television flicker?' etc., followed by, 'When this happens, how annoyed does it make you feel?' It can be argued that the louder the aircraft passing overhead, the wider the range of disturbances caused and the more annoyed people are likely to be; the scale is thus in a sense based on the hierarchic nature of noise measurements.

Scales Based on Factor Analysis contain elements of both Thurstone and Likert scales but statistical measures of the extent to which the scales contribute to the measurement of an underlying general attitude are used rather than subjective judgement.

Factor analysis is a statistical method widely used in psychological research, not only in the development of attitude scales; its application in the field of market research has grown rapidly with the availability of well-tried program for the technique for large computers which has brought the cost down within the reach of most attitude survey budgets.

There are different types of factor analysis of which the one most appropriate to attitude scaling problems is that known as 'principal component analysis'. (Experts might argue that this is not really a form of factor analysis at all but a separate technique. Colloquial usage has led, however, to principal component analysis being called 'factor analysis'; it is notable that the computer print out from Cybernetics Research Consultants Ltd., one of the leading exponents of principal component analysis, labels the emerging components 'factors'.) The basic function of principal component analysis is quite easy to grasp without there being any necessity to understand the mathematics underlying it. Its use, therefore, need not be confined to statisticians. Along with factor analysis it can be applied when there are a lot of different measurements for the same sample of people. In attitude research it can, for instance, be applied to semantic differential scales, to ratings applied to opinion statements or any other measurements provided the total sample is rated on each item.

The first step is to calculate the correlation between each and every other item. The matrix of correlations provides the input for the principal component analysis. (A program for calculating the intercorrelations is usually an integral part of any factor analysis program.)

Principal component analysis sorts all the measurements into a number of groups or 'factors' on the basis of the extent to which they are measuring common ground. This is assessed by examining within the computer each individual's pattern of answers for all the items and identifying the items which tend to have common patterns. The assumption is made that items which are shown to belong to the same factor are measuring something in common, e.g., an underlying attitude dimension. Examination of the content of the items usually indicates fairly clearly what the underlying dimension is.

In addition to grouping attitude items into factors and indicating any which do not fit the factors, a 'factor loading' is given to each item. This is a figure from -1.0 to $+1.0$ which indicates the extent to which each item is associated with the dimension underlying the factor. The factor loading is therefore an indication of the efficiency with which each item measures the underlying factor. Another measure given by most programmes of factor analysis indicates how much of the total variance of all the items is accounted for by each of the factors.

Principal component analysis can be used in two ways in attitude research; to help identify the relevant attitude dimensions and to examine the efficiency of specific items in measuring the attitude dimensions.

In a study of attitudes to savings, a number of hypotheses about the attitudes that led people to save were developed on the basis of a qualitative study. A list of about 25 statements of opinion were derived from the depth interviews and administered to a sample of 130 members of the public as a methodological pilot. The results were subjected to principal component analysis. A 'four-factor' solution grouped the statements broadly as had been expected from the qualitative study but indicated which statements were the most efficient at measuring each factor. The four factors are listed below together with names which were given them after examining the content of the main items to identify the common element underlying them.

FACTOR I   Temperamental difficulty in saving

Loading

−0.75   I have never been able to save.
−0.74   Unless you have some specific reason to save, it's better to spend and enjoy it.
−0.69   I believe in enjoying my money now and letting the future take care of itself.
−0.63   I don't feel it's necessary to save just now.
−0.55   I can't help spending all I earn.

FACTOR II   Sense of solidity

Loading

−0.81   If you've got a bit of money saved you are not so likely to be pushed around.
−0.72   Your opinions carry more weight if you've got money saved.
−0.68   You don't feel successful until you've got money saved.
−0.54   I'd like to feel I was worth something.

FACTOR III   Concern with independence

Loading

−0.85   I hate to feel I might have to ask someone for financial help.
−0.80   I hate to feel that a minor emergency could cause me financial embarrassment.
−0.54   Money not needed should be saved rather than spent on luxuries.
−0.43   It would worry me if I had no savings at all.

FACTOR IV   Feeling of financial security

Loading

−0.65   I feel it's unlikely I shall have any financial emergencies in the near future.

0.54   I always feel there might be a financial emergency at any time.

−0.45   I can't help spending all I earn.

Items can be selected from each factor to use in the main survey to measure the attitudes which have been identified. The number of items selected depends on the degree of reliability desired (the more items, the more reliable the measure) and the amount of space available in the questionnaire. Each informant can be given a score for each attitude by using the Likert method of weighting each response category and summing the weights. A further refinement is to weight each item by its factor loading so that the more important items in measuring the attitude play a bigger part in the overall score.

A slightly different use of factor analysis is in developing a single attitude scale, when the aim is to select those items which measure the single attitude dimension most efficiently. By obtaining a one-factor solution, it is possible to discover whether there is, in fact, a single unified attitude dimension underlying the statements and to identify the items which measure it best.

Principal component analysis is often applied to measures of brand image using semantic differential scales. It is used in a methodological pilot to identify the main image dimensions and to provide a logical criterion by which the number of scales to be included in the main survey can be reduced.

The value of factor analysis in attitude scaling is that no previous assumptions are made about the precise nature of the attitude to be measured or the type of consistency between the items of the scale that is desirable. The Thurstone, Likert, and Guttmann methods all assume that a particular type of consistency (that between individual items and overall score) is the most important one and tend to oversimplify the definition of the attitude. The attitudes we are normally interested in are complex and we require to understand the nature of their complexity rather than to force them into a simple 'pro' and 'anti' continuum.

The 'unidimensionality' of Guttman scaling is an attractive concept to many people but, except in rare cases, it is extremely difficult if not impossible to develop a Guttman scale that both scales well according to his criterion and ends up containing items that have a high degree of face validity.

Classification of Informants

It is usual practice to collect personal details about the informant and his household at the end of the interview, such as age, occupation, socio-economic class, household composition, etc. The purpose of this information is to provide:

(a) control over the sample;
(b) a check on the sample;
(c) profile descriptions of sub-groups of the sample;
(d) breakdown groups for analysis.

(a) Control over the sample

Many market research surveys are based on quota sampling in which the interviewer is asked to find so many men and so many women, so many in each age group, so many in each socio-economic group, and so on. To check that the sample has been correctly constituted, it is necessary to record on the questionnaire the details of the variables used in controlling the selection of informants. Region, town size and urban/rural classification is usually controlled by the allocation of interviewing areas and is not left to the discretion of the interviewer; these data are often identified on the questionnaire by a quota number. The interviewer, however, has to select informants from within her area to fit the quota she has been given using, perhaps, three or four variables, some of which may be 'interlocking', e.g., her age and social class quota may be specified separately for men and women, thus making them interlock with sex.

(b) A check on the sample

It is practical to use only a small number of variables in selecting a quota sample. The variables chosen are obviously those which are considered to be most relevant to the particular survey; there may, however, be others which have some relevance but which could not be used as controls without making sample selection extremely difficult and expensive; for example, housewives might be selected using age, socio-economic class and working status as controls; in such a case, it would be likely that a cross-section of mothers with children in different age groups would also be obtained because this is related to age and working status. The socio-economic class control should also ensure a correct proportion with the use of a car, but both these variables could usefully be checked against published statistics based on large random samples to ensure that no bias has crept in.

When random sampling methods are used, it is also useful to check the distributions of the classification variables against those collected from other large-scale random sample surveys or against census data in order to ensure that sampling error, refusals, or problems in contacting people have not resulted in bias.

(c) Profile description of sub-groups of the sample

Much of the value of survey research comes from making comparisons between sub-groups of the sample who show different purchasing, usage or attitude patterns. An important use of classification data is to provide profile descriptions of these different sub-groups in the market.

(d) Breakdown groups for use in analysis

In examining survey results, it is also often relevant to compare the purchasing, usage, and attitude patterns of different segments of the population; analysis may therefore be carried out using classification variables to define breakdown groups. This underlines again the point made earlier that it is essential to consider the requirements of analysis in some detail when the questionnaire is being designed.

Classification variables for inclusion

The classification variables that should be included in the questionnaire will depend on the particular requirements of the survey for controlling and checking the sample and for providing profile descriptions and breakdown groups. A classification manual produced by Social and Community Planning Research[14] lists the following variables for each of which there is an established system of classification and published population statistics.

Area variables:

geographical region;
type of area;
density of population;
socio-economic index;
person per room index.

Accommodation variables:

type of accommodation;
type of tenure;
length of residence;
age of building;
number of rooms;
accommodation amenities;
garage facilities.

Household variables:

household size;
household structure, (alternatives A and B);
gross household income;
socio-economic group of head of household, (as shown in The Classification of Occupation);
socio-economic grade of household, (used in National Readership Surveys);
types of vehicle owned;
household vehicle ownership;
household possessions.

Name			**(10)–(12)**
Address	Quota District Number		
	Quota District Name		

		Age:		**(13)**
			16–24	1
Position in family:	**(19)**		25–34	2
head of household	1		35–44	3
housewife	2		45–64	4
other adult	3		65+	5
Occupation of head of household		Class:	A	6
			B	7
			C1	8
			C2	9
	(20)		D	0
Informant: not working	1		E	X
┌──────working	2			
↓		Sex:		**(14)**
Is there a pension scheme with	Yes	3	male	1
your job?	No	4	female	2
IF YES: are deductions made	Yes	5	Status: married	3
from your pay for it or not?	No	6	┌───── single/widowed/divorced	4
			↓	
			Are you engaged or planning Yes	5
Do you have an income of your	Yes	7	to get married? No	6
own?	No	8		**(15)**
┌────			IF MARRIED 0–2 years	1
↓ (Skip to age)			How long have you 3–5 years	2
			been married? 6–10 years	3
IF YES: Which of these income			Longer	4

			Total	Earns
groups do you come in?			**(16)**	**(17)**
(CARD 9) (Gross income)	**(21)**	(a) *Total in household:* One	1	1
Yearly (*Weekly*)		Two	2	2
—£500 (Under £10) 1		(b) *How many of them* Three	3	3
£500—£749 (£10—£14.95) 2		*are wage earners?* Four	4	4
£750—£999 (£15—£19.95) 3		Five	5	5
£1000—£1249 (£20—£24.95) 4		Six +	6	6
£1250—£1749 (£25—£34.95) 5				
£1750—£2249 (£35—£44.95) 6		Is your home: (READ OUT)		**(18)**
£2250—£2749 (£45—£54.95) 7		rented furnished		1
£2750 + (£55 +) 8		rented unfurnished		2
	(22)	being bought on mortgage		3
Do you pay tax at the standard		fully paid for and owned		4
rate of 0.41p on any of your Yes 1		or rent free with the job?		5
income? No 2				
Don't know 3		Interviewers name:		
		Date of interview: / /		
Do you pay surtax? Yes 1				
No 2		Length of interview: mins.		
Don't know 3				

97

Individual variables:
age of individual
sex of individual .
status in the household
relationship to head of household
marital status
activity status, e.g., working full/part-time, retired, studying, etc.;
socio-economic group;
personal income (gross or net);
terminal education age;
educational qualifications;
type of school attended;
driving characteristics.

There may be others, not included in this list, which are important in a particular case. The National Readership Survey[16] provides information on a number of variables of interest to specific markets, e.g., pet ownership, possession of gardens, etc.

There are several arguments in favour of using standard methods of classification wherever possible; apart from enabling proper sample control and checking to be maintained, it ensures at least some comparability between surveys taken at different times and on different subjects. The National Readership Survey[16] is the most widely-used source of information for setting quota controls in the market research field and, because it is the main source of media information, is also a standard to which other survey data is often compared; for this reason the conventions set up by it for defining classification variables are generally established in market research.

As the typical 'classification page' of a questionnaire (p. 97) indicates, the questions which the interviewer should ask in order to collect the classification information are not always specified. This is a practice which can be carried too far since it relies overmuch on the assumption that all interviewers have received the same type and amount of training. It also depends heavily on interviewers remembering definitions accurately while trying to conduct the interview. Collection of enough detail on occupation of the head of the household to classify his socio-economic group accurately is probably the item that suffers most from this practice.

Appendix: Excerpt from National Savings Survey Questionnaire

No.	Question	Answer	Code	Skip to
	SHOW CARD 5		(69)	
36.	Can you tell me, very roughly, how much	£50 or less	1	
	money you have saved or invested	£51–£200	2	
	altogether in these forms of saving?	£201–£500	3	37
		£501–£1000	4	
		£1001–£3000	5	
		More	6	
		Don't know	7	

No.	Question	Answer	Code	Skip to
7.	In which form of saving do you have *most* money?		(70)	
		Only one form held	1	
		Premium Bonds	2	
		National Savings Certificates	3	
		Building Society	4	
		P.O.S.B. Ordinary Account	5	
		P.O.S.B. Investment Account	6	
		Bank Deposit Account	7	
		National Development Bonds	8	38
		Defence Bonds	9	
		Unit Trusts	0	
		Stocks and Shares	X	
		Trustee S.B. Ordinary Account	V	
			(71)	
		Trustee S.B. Special Investment A/c	1	
		Local Authorities	2	
		Other	3	
8.	SHOW CARD 6 What is this saving for? For any of these purposes (CARD) or for other purposes?		(72)	
		For emergencies	1	
		For meeting large household bills	2	
		For holidays, Christmas, etc.	3	39
		For security in later life	4	
		To provide an income	5	
		Other _____	6	
9.	Why did you choose that particular form of saving? PROBE		(73)	
				40
			(74)	
	IF ONLY ONE FORM OF SAVING, GO TO Q. 41. IF MORE THAN ONE, ASK FOR EACH REMAINING IN ORDER OF SIZE: ASK SEPARATELY FOR ALL OTHER TYPES OF SAVING HELD	(WRITE IN TYPE) Type of saving...	(10)	
40. a	SHOW CARD 6 What are the savings in ....for?		(11)	
		For emergencies	1	
		For meeting large household bills	2	
		For holidays, Christmas, etc.	3	
		For security in later life	4	
		To provide an income	5	
		Others	6	
b	SHOW CARD 5 What are the savings ....for?	(WRITE IN TYPE) Type of saving...	(12)	
			(13)	
		For emergencies	1	
		For meeting large household bills	2	
		For holidays, Christmas, etc.	3	
		For security in later life	4	
		To provide an income	5	
		Others	6	

No.	Question	Answer	Code	Skip to
c	SHOW CARD 5 What are the savings in .... for?	Type of saving .... (WRITE IN TYPE)	(14)	

	(15)
For emergencies	1
For meeting large household bills	2
For holidays, Christmas, etc.	3
For security in later life	4
To provide an income	5
Others	6

SHOW CARD 7

41. a | Are there any types of saving on this list which you held in the past but no longer hold?

b | IF YES: ASK FOR EACH HELD
How long ago did you cash the last of them:
  Within the last 2 years
  3–5 years ago
  6–10 years ago
  or longer

(CR = Can't remember)

	Held (16)	0–2 (17)	3–5 (18)	6–10 (19)	11+ (20)	CR (21)
None	1	1	1	1	1	1
Premium Bonds	2	2	2	2	2	2
Nat. Sav. Certs.	3	3	3	3	3	3
Building Society	4	4	4	4	4	4
P.O.S.B. (O)	5	5	5	5	5	5
P.O.S.B. (I)	6	6	6	6	6	6
Bank Deposit A/c	7	7	7	7	7	7
Nat. Devel. Bonds	8	8	8	8	8	8
Defence Bonds	9	9	9	9	9	9
Unit Trusts	0	0	0	0	0	0
Stocks and Shares	X	X	X	X	X	X
Trustee (O)	V	V	V	V	V	V
	(22)	(23)	(24)	(25)	(26)	(27)
Trustee (I)	1	1	1	1	1	1
Local Authority	2	2	2	2	2	2
Other	3	3	3	3	3	3

Skip to: **42**

No.	Question	Answer	Code	Skip to
42.	Do you yourself pay any life insurance premiums?	Yes	(28) 1	43
		No	2	45
43.	Can you tell me about how much you pay per month in premiums?	£1 or less £2 to £5 £6 to £10 £11 to £20 More Don't know	3 4 5 6 7 8	44
44.	In general, do you think of your life insurance as a method of saving or just as insurance?	A method of saving Just insurance Don't know	9 0 X	45
45.	Do you have a current bank account at present?	Yes No	(29) 1 2	46

SHOW CARD 8

46. a | Which of these is *most* important to you in choosing a form of saving or investment?

b | Which others would you also consider to be *very* important?

		(a) Most	(b) Very
		(30)	
A chance for the capital to grow		1	7
Complete security of the capital		2	8
A high interest rate		3	9
Tax concessions on the interest		4	0
Quick and easy to get your money out		5	X
(Don't know)		6	V

Skip to: **47**

No.	Question	Answer	Code	Skip to
47.	Do you think of yourself as being	READ: Well off Fairly well off	(31) 1 2	

No.	Question	Answer	Code	Skip to
		Neither well off nor hard up	3	48
		A little bit hard up	4	
		Very hard up	5	
		(Don't know)	6	
48.	Over the next couple of years, do you think your income/your family income will:	READ: Increase a lot	7	
		Increase a little	8	
		Decrease	9	49
		or Stay about the same	0	
		(Don't know)	X	
49.	Do you feel that your future financially is:		(32)	
		READ: Completely secure	1	
		Very secure	2	
		Fairly secure	3	50
		Rather insecure	4	
		(Don't know)	5	

No.	Question	Code	Skip to
50.	I am going to read a pair of statements. Will you tell me which you feel is closest to your opinion:	(33)	
a	When the country is in difficulties:		
	People should save all they can	1	
	OR People would be wiser to spend before inflation makes prices rise	2	
	(Don't know)	3	
	CONTINUE WITH REMAINING PAIRS		
b	When the country is in difficulties:		
	People should buy government sponsored savings	4	
	OR You should still buy the type of saving which suits you best	5	
	(Don't know)	6	
c	I prefer not to buy Government savings when the wrong Party is in power	7	
	OR The Party in power does not affect my choice of savings at all	8	51
	(Don't know)	9	
d	I never consider how the money I save is being used	0	
	OR I would only choose savings methods which I felt would make good use of my money	X	
	(Don't know)	V	
e		(34)	
	Your savings are put to best use by the Government	1	
	OR Your savings are put to best use by private enterprise	2	
	(Don't know)	3	
51. a	It is best to spread your savings	4	
	OR It's best to put all your savings in one good form	5	(b)
	(Don't know)	6	52
b	Can you tell me why you think that it's best to ....?	(35)	
			52
		(36)	

101

References

1. PAYNE, S. L. *The Art of Asking Questions*, Princeton University Press, Princeton, New Jersey. 1951.
2. BELSON, W. A. *Respondent Understanding of Survey Questions*, Polls, Survey Research Centre Reprint Series 40, **3,** No. 4, 1968.
3. BELSON, W. A. *The Impact of Television*, London, Crosby Lockwood, 1967.
4. BELSON, W. A. *Studies in Readership*, London, Business Publications, on the behalf of the IPA, 1962.
5. FISHBEIN, M. (Ed.). *Readings in Attitude Theory and Measurement*, John Wiley and Sons, Inc. 1967.
6. FISHBEIN, M. *Readings in Attitude Theory and Measurement, A Consideration of Beliefs and Their Role in Attitude Measurement*, John Wiley and Sons, Inc. 1967.
7. MCKENNELL, A. C. *Aircraft Noise Annoyance Around London (Heathrow) Airport*, Social Survey Report 337, Central Office of Information.
8. BELSON, W. A. *A Study of the Effects of Reversing the Order of Presentation of Verbal Rating Scales*, Survey Research Centre Report, 1965.
9. OSGOOD, C. E., SUCI, G. J., and TANNENBAUM, P. H. *The Measurement of Meaning*, Urbana, University of Illinois Press, 1957.
10. JOYCE, T. *Techniques of Brand Image Measurement*, paper read at Market Research Society Annual Conference, 1963.
11. THURSTONE, L. L. Attitudes can be measured, *American Journal of Sociology*, **33,** 529–554, 1928. (Reprinted in 'Readings in Attitude Theory and Measurement', Ed.: Fishbein, John Wiley and Sons, Inc. 1967.)
12. LIKERT, R. The Method of Constructing an Attitude Scale, *Readings in Attitude Theory and Measurement* (Ed. Fishbein), John Wiley and Sons, Inc. 1967.
13. STOUFFER, A. A., GUTTMANN, L., SUCHMAN, E. A., LAZARSFELD, P. F., STAR, and CLAUSEN, Studies in Social Psychology in World War II, *Measurement and Prediction*, Vol. 4, Princeton University Press, 1950.
14. HOINVILLE, G. and JOWELL, R. *Classification Manual for Household Interview Surveys in Great Britain*. Produced by Social and Community Planning Research, 1969.
15. *The Classification of Occupation*, HMSO, 1966.
16. *National Readership Survey*, JICNAS.

5. Interviewing and field control

John F. Drakeford

The Role of the Interview in Survey Research

Most survey research requires the collection of information, or observations, from representative samples of particular populations. These samples can comprise individual members of the public where information, when aggregated, aims to reflect the behaviour or opinions of the total population and/or sub-samples of it. Alternatively, these samples can comprise individuals within specialist groups such as manufacturers, retailers, businessmen, where information may be needed either about the behaviour and opinions of these respondents as individuals or about the establishments, e.g., companies, shops etc., that they represent.

Irrespective of the *type* of information to be collected, virtually all of this work, if postal surveys are excluded, demands *personal* contact of some kind between an interviewer and a respondent. The fundamental importance of this requirement cannot be overstated; as far as the sponsor of a particular survey is concerned, this *personal* contact between an interviewer and a respondent is nearly always the only direct link he has with the user or potential user of his products or services. In certain circumstances, particularly in small (usually industrial) markets or where the identity of customers or potential customers is known, it may be possible for a manufacturer to establish this direct and personal contact himself or through his representatives; indeed, it is not uncommon for salesmen to be used to report back to management with information collected by them from customers or potential customers. There are a number of serious dangers in this approach, principally that representatives or salesmen are almost certainly not able to collect relevant information, nor trained to collect it in a systematic and controlled way. They may often have a particular axe to grind; the special relationship between salesmen and customers or potential customers is almost certain to introduce bias in responses. Where a research sponsor seeks information from a 'mass market' it is, of course, impossible for him to have direct contact in this way. Nevertheless, the dangers of ever using 'committed' or involved people as interviewers, without adequate training and control in the special kind of personal content required in survey research, cannot be overemphasized.

It must be stressed that, during this chapter, we are concerned with the role of professionally trained research interviewers who alone should be responsible for this vital phase in any project.

Putting the Interview in Context

The need for information in survey research to be collected most often by *personal* contact of this kind must, nevertheless, be seen against the background of how particular surveys are structured and planned. The complex nature of survey research nowadays, and the need to employ specialists at various phases in a project, means that the questionnaire, recording form, diary, or inventory designed for use by the interviewer cannot be designed solely with him or her or, indeed, the respondent in mind. Of particular importance here is the need to appreciate that the:

(a) survey sponsor will have his own special requirements in terms of the information or observations he needs to collect;
(b) researcher in control of the project, who is translating these requirements into practical survey methodology, will have open to him a wide range of techniques and procedures;
(c) questionnaire, recording form, diary, or inventory incorporating these must be usable by the interviewer in a face to face situation, and comprehensible to the respondent;
(d) completed documents must be capable of subsequent handling, both manually (in check editing and coding) and mechanically (in transfer to punched cards and computer tape) as rapidly as possible with the minimum of error;
(e) resultant findings must be capable of interpretation in depth by the researcher, and of *real use* ultimately to the survey sponsor.

Any project, therefore, will pass through a number of phases, and no one phase can be allowed to dominate; even the 'best' questionnaire must be something of a compromise, in needing to take account of these various requirements.

In the recent past, a great deal of attention has been paid to new techniques and procedures in questionnaire design, and to ways of assembling and analysing the data collected in the most meaningful (albeit often highly complex) way, with all the refinements in, for instance, multivariate analysis, that the widespread and still growing use of computers can bring. Less attention than it deserves has perhaps been paid to the vital interviewing phase in survey research, and the clear need to impose on this standards of the highest quality.

The need for training and control

If the need for professionally trained interviewers in survey research is accepted, it follows that detailed attention has to be paid to the ways in which these interviewers are selected, trained, and subsequently controlled in their day to day work. This is necessary especially because:

(a) the range of problems that survey research is now called upon to solve is now extensive and varied;

(b) to the researcher planning a project, an evergrowing corpus of survey techniques, interviewing methods, and analysis procedures is available. These can often be used in various combinations with equal effectiveness to solve a particular problem; in other words, the ways in which different research organizations will use the techniques available in attempting to solve similar or even identical problems will vary; indeed, it is unreasonable to suggest that there is always a single, standard method of approach;

(c) the characteristics of respondents from whom information is to be collected, or about whom observations are to be made, will vary widely within a particular survey, and even more between surveys;

(d) whatever standards are imposed on interviewers by adequate selection, training, and quality-control, interviewers will themselves vary in being members of field forces with different structures, in their own personal characteristics and backgrounds, in the depth and variation of initial training and subsequent retraining, in the types of survey in which they may specialize, and in the frequency with which they are engaged. It is worth noting here that some interviewers will be full-time members of small, tightly controlled, field forces operated by individual manufacturers, media owners, and so on, although these are comparatively rare and tend to be confined to large organizations who are heavily engaged on survey research on a continuing basis; some interviewers will work for field forces controlled by independent research organizations offering a comprehensive service, where they are more likely to be exposed fairly often to the other phases of survey research; other interviewers will operate in specialist field forces offering an interviewing service alone, where they will have perhaps less opportunity to see how their particular contribution fits into the total picture. Many interviewers, furthermore, who are in most cases likely to be working on a part-time basis, will be engaged by a number of *different* field forces over time; indeed, this 'overlapping' is widespread among those interviewers who may welcome substantial amounts of part-time work on a regular basis.

These variations in types of research, characteristics of respondents, and structure and methods of field forces, can only emphasize further need for a high degree of overall efficiency in day to day fieldwork and, wherever possible, the aim of standardizing and further improving basic procedures.

Types of Interviewer and Interviewing

The wide ranging nature of survey research includes many projects where it is inappropriate to use part-time interviewers in a field force, however well-trained and controlled they may be in 'conventional' face to face interviewing.

Such projects will need information collected by:

(a) structured or unstructured interviews, especially in industrial and commercial companies, with top-level management or employees who need to be approached because of the specialist (often highly technical) nature of the information they can provide. In industrial research surveys for instance, it is often necessary. to employ specially selected and trained interviewers of a rather higher calibre than those used on day to day research surveys of a fairly standardized and conventional kind. These interviewers may also need to have some technical knowledge of the particular survey topics being investigated;

(b) group interviewing, or single interviews of an extended and unstructured kind, most often described as 'group discussions' or 'depth' interviews. Work of this type is usually of an exploratory nature where attitudes and beliefs are examined and collated, but in an unquantified way, in order to elicit hypotheses for further study, or to ensure that the full range of attitudes and beliefs held are extracted early enough to ensure inclusion in a subsequent quantified stage of research. Here, ideally, psychologists or sociologists specially trained in this type of work should be used, particularly where the topics to be explored are of a particularly personal, delicate, or intimate nature. It is, of course, not uncommon for researchers without special psychological or sociological training to be used in work of this kind and, indeed, this has some value if the main purpose is to inform the researcher planning and controlling the survey about the way in which people behave and think about the particular topic. There are, however, great dangers in relegating this type of interviewing to inexperienced researchers, who will fail to appreciate often enough the subtleties of approach required and the all-important and difficult task of extracting the appropriate data, and putting the right emphasis on it in subsequent stages of the research.

The task of a conventional field force

Having said this, it is nevertheless clear that the great majority of survey research projects are likely to use interviewers who belong to field forces of the kinds described earlier. Before dealing with how these field forces operate, it is worthwhile reviewing the range of tasks which such interviewers can be called upon to carry out. Major areas of activity here will include:

(a) the selection and recruitment of individual members of the public to attend subsequent research sessions, e.g., group discussions, hall tests, advertising testing, etc.;

(b) the selection and recruitment of individuals to be members of a panel required to report, over a lengthy period, on purchasing behaviour, etc.;

(c) shop audits and domestic pantry checks, where interviewers are required to inspect and check ranges of products held and to calculate from invoices or other records sales volume, purchasing rates, etc.;

(d) courtesy calls, made from time to time on individuals reporting as panel members, to check on performance, answer queries, and possibly to re-activate disinterested panel members;

(e) exploratory interviewing, often of a fairly unstructured nature, sometimes at the pilot stage of a project, where experiments are being conducted on the design and content of a questionnaire or recording form, whose final version will subsequently be used in a major survey;

(f) conventional face to face interviews where behavioural, or attitude and opinion information, is being collected;

(g) invitations to members of the public to participate in product testing, where existing or new products are to be placed in homes for subsequent use over a controlled period;

(h) telephone interviewing, either to collect information on the spot using a structured or unstructured questionnaire or to arrange an appointment for a subsequent face to face interview;

(i) industrial or commercial interviewing;

(j) observing, counting, and classifying individuals, and/or vehicles, in traffic studies, parking studies, shop research, etc.

The varying nature of the types of tasks interviewers are called upon to perform further emphasizes the need to maximize the efficiency of field force operations and impose stringent interviewer control.

Field Management Organization

Head office organization

Such control, and the day to day administration of a field force engaged on this varied work, requires a carefully structured central organization from which field work can be planned, and to which individual interviewers and supervisors must report. The complexity of this central organization will, of course, vary with the size of the field force and the nature of its work.

In a small field force, perhaps operated by a manufacturer solely for his own research purposes, full-time salaried or part-time interviewers may work only in a particular town or region of the country. Such a force will require only a small head office team to control adequately the comparatively few interviewers involved; indeed, these interviewers will be seen personally by head office staff fairly frequently. In larger, mostly nationally spread, field forces of the type operated by many independent research organizations, teams of several hundred interviewers will be employed, often regularly for several days of the week on repeat surveys, panels, omnibus surveys and so on, but nevertheless usually on a part-time rather than a full-time basis. Field organization here must be on a much larger scale, and there will often be separate field managers at head office looking after separate teams of interviewers, some of whom will operate 'across the board' on a wide variety of projects, and some of whom will be confined to continuous audit and panel work for which they will be specially trained.

The work of head office field staff in the larger organizations is likely to be sectionalized, different staff members having different responsibilities. These separate sections of responsibility will include:

(a) the selection, training, and re-training of interviewers;
(b) costing surveys, negotiating the rates of pay with interviewers, and ensuring prompt payment on delivery of completed work of an acceptable standard;
(c) booking interviewers for survey work or arranging for them to be booked through supervisors, and despatching work material;
(d) day to day supervision and control of interviewers in the field;
(e) the receipt and checking of completed work;
(f) following up substandard work, arranging for re-interviewing or substitute interviewing, checking on suspect interviewers etc.;
(g) administrative matters concerned with quality control, training sessions, briefing conferences, etc.;
(h) the continual updating of the interviewer manual on basic procedures.

Supervisors

The volume and complexity of this work in large field forces will also almost certainly necessitate a supervisory level, interposed between head office staff and individual interviewers. Supervisors of this type will have had considerable depth of interviewing experience previously, and will probably be employed now in their supervisory role on a full-time salaried basis. They will be in frequent contact with head office staff and responsible, usually on a regional basis, for controlling a team of interviewers in their areas. This control will include the allocation of work to individuals in an area, attending briefing conferences, dealing with queries arising from interviewers about research projects or from head office about interviewers, maintaining day to day supervision in the field and assisting in interviewer training. In a large field force, a supervisor has a very real part to play in maintaining interviewer efficiency and morale, and it must be emphasized that supervisors' allegiance must be firmly to the head office and not to individual interviewers for whom they are responsible.

Maintaining sufficiently frequent personal contact with interviewers working relatively infrequently, or with those in remote areas, can be a real problem. Maintaining interviewer efficiency and morale is considerably helped by the existence of a supervisory force, and of course also by the attendance of interviewers at briefing conferences and training sessions. Nevertheless, there is no substitute for head office contact with individual interviewers as often as is practicable. Personal briefings held at head office or regionally on major 'ad hoc' surveys or at suitable intervals on audit and panel work, with attendance by head office field force and research executives handling projects, have a most important role to play here.

The Selection and Training of Interviewers

Selection

National and local press advertising, spontaneous application, 'word of mouth' recommendation are the main ways in which prospective interviewers can be contacted initially. If selection is to be effective, at least one personal interview with each candidate, certainly at the supervisory level and more preferably at head office level, will be required. The qualities and basic characteristics that go to make up a successful interviewer, notwithstanding the necessary training to follow initial selection, are such that it is extremely dangerous to engage new interviewers (even if they claim extensive past experience) by correspondence, without this important face to face contact.

The first exploratory interview will need to establish such factors as the prospective interviewer's sex, age, previous business experience, previous research experience, availability (daytime, evenings, and weekends), car-ownership and general mobility in her area, educational level, social class, personality, speech, accent, and so on. Clearly some of these factors can *only* be established at a personal interview, which gives the head office staff or supervisor the opportunity also to explore the applicant's attitudes in general to market research. This first interview will lead to a decision about whether or not the applicant is suitable for training. While attention will, no doubt, be paid to the applicant's previous research experience, individual field forces within research organizations have different requirements and (sad to say) different standards and there is no doubt that some fresh training will be needed.

Formal training

Irrespective of past experience and apparent future potential, formal 'in office' training is advisable as a first stage. Whether this is undertaken at supervisory level in the regions or at head office will depend on the size and structure of the field force, and the number of candidates coming forward at a particular time. The duration of such a formal training session will vary from one field force to another, but there will be general agreement that such training shall occupy not less than two, and preferably up to five, days.

The formal training course, after a suitable introduction to the nature and purpose of survey research and the way in which the interview is integrated with the other phases of the project, will include:

(a) instruction on basic sampling procedures to be followed, use of maps to determine boundaries and grid references, sampling at preselected addresses, the concept and implementation of random walk sampling, and quota sampling method;
(b) questionnaire design, with particular emphasis on how to ask questions, strict adherence to the written content, prompting and probing, questionnaire routing and skips and recording demographic and other classification data;
(c) methods of introduction to a potential respondent, how to deal with queries about survey sponsorship, keeping respondents to the point, clarifying vague replies, dealing with unsuitable respondents, possible refusals, and with queries as to why the respondent was chosen for interview;
(d) methods of quality control used by the field force (supervisor checks, postal checks, office check editing etc.), and steps that are taken on queried or suspect work;
(e) administrative details about procedures for interviewer booking, briefing methods, allocation of work, receiving return of completed work, methods of payment and the relationship and method of contact between the interviewer, her supervisor, and head office staff.

As part of this formal training, interviewers should be encouraged to conduct 'in office' interviews with dummy questionnaires; demonstration interviews will be given by head office staff and supervisors and, ideally, some system of rating interviewer performance even at this early stage should be devised. It is helpful to tape-record demonstration and test interviews and to play these back during the training sessions. If training is on a large enough scale, initial criticism of performance here should be actively encouraged. It is well worth while at the close of such formal training sessions to administer short written tests to interviewers, which will further assist in decisions about potential for further training.

Training in the field

Formal first stage training of the kind described above will eliminate applicants who for one reason or another are below standard or, less dramatically, felt to be suitable only for certain types of survey work.

There is, however, no substitute for training in the field and prospective interviewers passing successfully through formal training need to move on rapidly to this phase before final decisions are taken about their acceptability for future work.

Most often, training in the field will be conducted by a supervisor (who will of course have been similarly trained in the past) in which she herself will demonstrate various interviewing techniques in the field with the trainee observing; this will be followed by test interviews by the trainee in the presence of the supervisor and, finally, if at all possible, the assessment by the supervisor of a batch of interviews completed by the trainee on her own. This assessment can be achieved by a detailed examination of completed questionnaires, a full discussion with the applicant of any problems she encountered, or by supervisor call-backs on the respondents interviewed during this test phase. The stark reality of this training in the field will almost certainly show which trainees may have mastered the theory adequately enough but are unlikely in practice to be of a sufficiently high standard.

Formal and field training of the kind described above should be regarded as the least that should be done to ensure competent performance once successful candidates have been enlisted for future work. Obviously, during the first few weeks in the field a new interviewer will have to be supervised and controlled very closely, to ensure that standards are being maintained.

Both the formal and field training described are essential for new interviewers; they are also advisable as a method of retraining and bringing up to date older-established members of a field force.

The interviewing manual

To complement this training, all interviewers need to be supplied with a manual which sets out in detail general procedural rules and methods to be followed on the various types of project that the interviewer is likely to encounter. Basically, these rules will comprise those dealt with fully at the initial training session but, of course, they will need to be amended frequently and brought up to date by head office staff as new procedures and new techniques are developed.

Any interviewers engaged on repeat surveys or on audit and panel work will need to be supplied with detailed instructions about checking methods to be used, products, prices and pack sizes to be checked, and so on. Every interviewer must be encouraged to master the contents of the manual and to use it for day to day reference in the field, prior to attempting to contact their supervisor or head office to resolve day to day queries.

In addition to the manual she carries an interviewer is, of course, likely to be supplied with further instructions in writing specific to each project on which she is working.

Briefing Interviewers

As we have said, contact between interviewers and head office staff or supervisors needs to be maintained as frequently as possible. Formal training or retraining sessions held periodically, however, will tend to deal mostly with basic issues of a general nature. On each specific survey special briefing procedures need to be adopted to deal with problems and procedures peculiar to that survey. This briefing can take one of a number of forms depending on the complexity of the project, the extent to which it introduces new requirements, the number of interviewers required to work on the project, and the time available for prefield-work instruction.

Briefings on panel and audits work

Where interviewers are in contact regularly with panel members, reporting weekly, monthly, or perhaps quarterly in individual shops or homes, basic interviewing and checking procedures are unlikely to vary substantially from period to period. Keeping the instruction manual on a project of this kind up to date should allow these procedures to be followed satisfactorily each time a contact is made. This does not mean, of course, that an interviewer may not receive additional instructions for each new visit or that the normal quality control checks in the field will not be imposed.

There will be a need to call all interviewers working on such projects for refresher briefings together from time to time, in order to discuss problems which arise, the implementation of new checking techniques, and so on. In continuous audit or panel work it is essential for slackness and boredom, because the interviewer feels the project is of a routine repetitive nature, to be avoided. Here, either random or specially-timed supervisor checks on interviewers will prove invaluable in ensuring the maintenance of accuracy.

Survey briefings

Where special 'ad hoc' surveys are concerned, briefing practices will vary more widely. On major surveys, particularly those involving fresh interviewers or new survey techniques, it is certainly worthwhile briefing personally all interviewers, either at head office or regionally, with research staff and head office field staff and area supervisors in attendance. Such briefings, however, are often costly and, sometimes, the time required for them prior to commencement of field work may not be available.

Personal briefings

Where they take place, these personal briefings will comprise:

(a) a detailed description by the appropriate member of head office staff of the background to, and the nature and purpose of, the survey;
(b) instructions about how respondents are to be selected for interview, with particular emphasis on any changes in standard procedures for pre-selected address sampling, random routes, or quota controls;
(c) an exposition of the questionnaire to be used, to ensure that interviewers fully understand the nature of the questions, how they are to be asked, question routing, skips, etc.;
(d) general discussion with interviewers of any problem arising;

(e) test interviews, either between pairs of interviewers chosen at random on the spot or by interviewers with a member of head office staff;

(f) further discussion of any additional problems arising;

(g) the allocation of work material and discussion of any administrative problems relating to field work dates and deadlines, methods of payment, and so on.

Ideally, personal briefing of this kind should be attended by head office representatives; where this is impracticable, similar personal briefings can be run at the supervisor level on a regional basis. Ideally, personal briefings can only really be considered unnecessary where *all* interviewers concerned have worked fairly recently on an identical or very similar project.

Postal and telephone briefings

These are necessary substitutes for personal briefings in many cases, and in certain circumstances can be regarded as adequate, provided interviewers so briefed are encouraged to raise any queries immediately with their supervisors or with head office, so that these can be dealt with before field work commences. In all cases like this it is essential that the interviewer thoroughly reads and completely understands the written instructions that will have been supplied with her work material. It is worthwhile also building-in the additional safeguard of inspecting the first batch of each interviewer's work to decide whether any interviewers should be debarred from continuing.

Pilot briefing

A special comment about briefings on pilot research is worthwhile, because here both the requirements and the procedures tend to be different. At the planning stage on major projects, it is a widespread practice for a research organization to test and develop a number of versions of a questionnaire in draft, prior to agreeing the version to be used in the main survey.

Pilot interviewing may be needed at various stages, with a highly-structured and almost final draft which has been worked on for some time by head office staff who may also have tested early versions by pilot interviews in the field or with a much more flexible document which now needs further refinement with the guidance of interviewers who have used it in the field. On normal survey work, the very fact that interviewers are required to adopt a consistent approach and not to deviate from written instructions and the printed questionnaire, makes some interviewers unsuitable for use in exploratory pilot work. What is required here is a much more flexible approach, where interviewers are actively encouraged to use their initiative, and to report back to head office staff about the best way in which questions can be phrased or ordered in a questionnaire and whether there are any significant errors or omissions. It follows that supervisors themselves or interviewers of the highest calibre are likely to be best-suited for this pilot work. After briefing and the pilot field work, debriefing sessions, where each interviewer is invited to contribute to further improvements in questionnaire design prior to the main survey, can be invaluable.

Quality Control

A rigorous and planned approach to selecting and training interviewers, and the implementation wherever possible of briefing sessions prior to field work, will do much to ensure that high standards in the field are maintained. However, there are great differences between theory and practice in interviewing, not least because of the very real stresses that are imposed on interviewers in the course of their day to day work. No matter how carefully a project is planned, the nature of the project itself, the characteristics of the respondents and differences *between* interviewers or, indeed, variation in performance of a single interviewer from day to day, can and often do give rise to problems in interviewing that could not have been foreseen. It is necessary, therefore, to impose additional checks on a day to day basis against these eventualities, with the aim of maintaining overall performance in the field at the highest possible level.

Control by supervisors

The ratio of supervisors to interviewers will, of course, vary from one field force to another, and, indeed, with variations in project nature and interviewers there can be no 'correct' level of supervision. The ratio obviously must be such that no single interviewer goes too long without contact with, and checks by, her supervisor on projects, quite apart from additional contact through briefings and training sessions. A considerable amount of time here will be devoted by supervisors to the control of new interviewers or interviewers whose performance for some reason is suspect.

Day to day control imposed by supervisors will usually take the form either of accompanying interviewers on an assignment, or of conducting spot checks on respondents and re-interviewing them as soon as possible after their first interview or else of scrutiny of completed work before it is passed back to head office for subsequent processing. Accompanying interviewers in their work has some advantages, particularly in terms of ensuring that no deviations are occurring in the basic methods laid down, and is useful on the one hand for keeping interviewer morale high, and on the other for making it clear that field force management are concerned on a continuing basis with maintaining the standards of performance of individual interviewers. However, the advantages of this type of control are limited; any interviewer can have an 'off-day', or be at a stage in a project where unusual difficulties appear to be arising, atypical of a more normal situation. A more useful form of control is spot checks at random on interviewers' 're-calls' on respondents, to establish first whether the interview took place, and second, how it was conducted in broad terms, how long it took, and so on. Such spot checks will need to be conducted rapidly after the first interview, otherwise a respondent may reflect changes in behaviour or opinion of a real nature which give the false impression that a first interview was inaccurate in some way.

There is some merit in having completed work routed through supervisors before transmission to head office. This will ensure that genuine problems can be dealt with quickly and suitable corrective action taken. Checking of this kind may not be practicable for all interviewers all the time, but is useful even if based on some system of rotation. In practical terms, how much of this scrutiny can be achieved at the regional level will depend on how many interviewers a supervisor has under her control and variations over time in workload.

Postal checks

It is a widespread practice to send prepaid postcards or letters to respondents to enquire whether an interview was carried out and the opportunity is often taken to ask additional check questions. Such a postal check, however, can only be a partial check, and extreme care has to be taken in the selection of any check questions to be asked, otherwise differences in response will be apparent which are quite unrelated to interviewer performance. In theory, it is possible to conduct 100 per cent postal check on all work of all interviewers all the time but this is extremely costly, cumbersome, and probably unnecessary, because the very nature of postal checks means that replies from respondents themselves will never be at the 100 per cent level. A more common approach is to:

(a) select batches of interviewers in rotation over time, and submit all their work on one survey to postal checks at the 100 per cent level;
(b) check a randomly selected proportion of all interviewers' work on *all* surveys, but at a much lower level, say 10 to 20 per cent.

Both of these approaches have advantages and disadvantages; actual practice will depend on the nature of the surveys being conducted by a particular field force, the number of interviewers involved, and background knowledge at head office of individual interviewer performance over time.

Check editing

Even if some scrutiny of completed work is undertaken at the supervisor level, it will be essential to impose further check editing procedures on work that has reached head office for subsequent processing. This check editing can again be operated in various ways, either by sampling proportions of interviewers or of their work; it will concern itself principally with sources of error such as:

(a) failure to adhere to sampling instructions—the failure to select appropriate individuals at preselected addresses or failure to complete set quotas of work;

(b) the omission of vital demographic data such as age, occupation, income level, socio-economic class, family size, etc.;
(c) the omission of specific questions, or failure to follow correctly routing instructions through a questionnaire;
(d) a tendency, most often apparent on open-ended responses, to generate inadequate or vague replies.

Apart from the additional measure of control this check editing imposes on a day to day basis, it is of considerable importance as a basis for head office to build up a backlog of performance data about each interviewer. This data will come from a number of sources, and needs to be compiled into readily available records which show, for each interviewer, such aspects of performance as:

(a) levels of response rate by respondents to postal checks carried out;
(b) any evidence from these of possible falsification of interviews (e.g., interviewing someone other than the alleged respondent recorded) or of 'making-up' replies for interviews which never took place;
(c) the number of errors found in recording classification data;
(d) the levels at which omissions or misrouting occur;
(e) rates per day achieved in initial contacts and in successfully completed interviews.

Ideally, a data bank of information of this kind should be compiled to enable performance of individual interviewers to be compared with average performance. The aspects of performance listed above can be built into this system, as also can analyses on particular projects of the kinds of responses different interviewers are obtaining to questions. Obviously if suspicion is aroused at any stage about an interviewer's performance, through supervisor checks, postal checks, check editing, or cumulative evidence from the data bank, immediate follow-up action will need to be taken.

The aim of all quality control of this kind must be to minimize errors and maintain individual interviewer standards at the highest possible level. Deliberate cheating, despite all the precautions taken is, of course, extremely difficult to detect. In general, the evidence is that such cheating is at a low level, not least because of this very rigorous approach to quality control that most research organizations adopt. In order to be effective of course, it is absolutely *vital* that *all* interviewers are fully aware that these various checks are made, and they should be equally aware of the penalties which can follow from substandard performance; in particular, knowledge that black lists of interviewers exist and that confidential information about individual performance is exchanged among research organizations.

A Check List For Buyers

Some readers, as members of independent research organizations or specialist field companies, will be actively engaged with the problems of interviewing and field control on a day to day basis, especially if their responsibilities include operating and controlling a field force. Most of these readers will already be well aware of the problems in interviewing that can arise, and will be implementing the quality control procedures described here. Other readers however, as sponsors of survey research, will be buying expertise from independent research organizations or specialist field forces. They will, no doubt, be equally concerned about the problem in research of maintaining high interviewing standards, and will wish to satisfy themselves that the organizations from whom they buy research are, in fact, adopting acceptable control procedures where appropriate. Perhaps a useful way to summarise what has been said is to present, particularly for the benefit of these readers, a check-list of points which need to be borne in mind when checking upon the credentials of a particular research organization. Such a check list would certainly include the following.

Research planning and design:
(a) is the right degree of emphasis placed upon the interviewing phase of a project, compared with the other phases through which the project has to go?;
(b) how are questionnaires, recording forms, diaries, or inventories laid out, and by whom are they designed?;
(c) has the designer any interviewing experience, and has he at any stage piloted the questionnaire?;
(d) are instructions to interviewers comprehensive?;
(e) are the sampling procedures to be used in the project feasible in the field?;
(f) how are interviewers instructed on these sampling procedures, and under what circumstances, if any, are they allowed to deviate from instructions?;
(g) what checks are imposed to ensure that a sampling plan is followed?

Field control:
(a) how is field management at head office organized in general and in relation to the implementation of a particular project?;
(b) how much contact is there between head office staff and the supervisors and interviewers?;
(c) what documentation exists as a control on contact rates, interviewing rates etc?;
(d) how is day to day supervision in the field organized and how are queries that arise in the field dealt with?;
(e) what is the ratio between supervisors and interviewers and what responsibilities have the supervisors for maintaining adequate interviewer standards?;
(f) what procedures are followed in briefing interviewers, either personally, by post or by telephone?;
(g) how well are these procedures supported by written material of a general kind (e.g., the interviewer manual) or of a kind specific to the survey (e.g., instructions, call-sheets, etc.)?

The interviewers:
(a) what is the composition of the field force and how has it been built up?;
(b) how are interviewers initially selected?;
(c) how are they trained, either at formal training sessions or in the field?;
(d) how frequently are interviewers seen by head office staff and supervisors?;
(e) are they aware of the nature and depth of the quality control procedures conducted?;
(f) what are their terms of employment and how are they paid?

Quality control:
(a) what checks are imposed on interviewers while work is in the field and how are problems and queries resolved?;
(b) how often and at what level are supervisor spot checks, postal checks, revisits to respondents conducted as further control measures?;
(c) what are the check-editing procedures once work has been returned to head office and how are queries and suspect interviewing dealt with?;
(d) has the organization been able to build up a data bank on individual interviewer performance; if so, what does this data bank comprise?

While the vital importance of controls on interviewing will be recognized, the way these are imposed will vary from one organization to another. Clearly, no perfect system of control can exist, in a situation where survey research deals with such a wide variety of projects and where the composition and structure of field forces necessarily differs. The aim, however, must be to achieve the best possible combination of controls, consistent with the nature of the field force, the money available, and the time span (often relatively short) over which particular projects are conducted.

Suggested Further Reading

1. ATKINSON, J. *A Handbook for Interviewers*, The Government Social Survey, 1968.
2. BELSON, W. A. *Studies in Readership*, Business Publications Ltd, 1962.
3. BELSON, W. A. *Tape-recording: its Effect on Accuracy of Response in Survey Interviews*, The Survey Research Unit, The London School of Economics, 1963.
4. BELSON, W. A. *Respondent Understanding of Questions in the Survey Interview*, The Survey Research Unit, The London School of Economics, 1968.
5. BERENT, P. H. *Interview Recruitment and Training*, ESOMAR Congress, Evian, 1962.
6. BRANDSMA, P. The Role and Influence of the Interviewer, *European Marketing Research Review*, **4**, 1, 1969.
7. DRAKEFORD, J. F. *A Critical Appraisal of Pilot Techniques in Qualitative Research*, ESOMAR Seminar on Attitude and Motivation Research, 1970.
8. FERBER, R. and WALES, H. G. Detection and Correction of Interviewer Bias, *Public Opinion Quarterly*, **XVI**, 1, 1952.
9. HAUCK, M. and STEINKAMP, S. Survey Reliability and Interviewer Competence, *Studies in Consumer Savings No. 4*, Bureau of Economic and Business Research, University of Illinois, Urbana, 1964.
10. HAUCK, M. Interviewer Compensation on Consumer Surveys, *Journal of the Market Research Society*, 14, 1964.
11. HYMAN, H. *et al. Interviewing in Social Research*, Chicago, 1954.

12. MACFARLANE SMITH, J. Selection and Training of Interviewers, *Journal of the Market Research Society*, **12**, 2, April 1970.
13. MARKET RESEARCH SOCIETY, First Report, Working Party on Interviewing Methods.
14. MAYER, C. S. Evaluating the Quality of Marketing Research Contractors, *Journal of Marketing Research*, May 1967.
15. TWIGG, J. *What is Interviewer Bias?* ESOMAR Congress, 1969.

6. Trade research

Gerry Arnott

Trade research is a collective term for a series of specially developed techniques serving the needs and objectives of marketing management at the various stages of the distribution network. Just as the elementary methods of consumer research have been adapted and improved to gear them more specifically to particular problems, so the basic techniques of research among the distributive trades have been refined from the original to meet current demands. This chapter deals with the basic techniques and illustrates a few of the applications and developments that have occurred. It makes no attempt to be comprehensive.

Of all the expenditure on trade research, by far the most is spent on retail and wholesale audits, the remainder is probably divided evenly between distribution checks and 'ad hoc' studies. Almost inevitably, therefore, the emphasis in this chapter will be upon trade audits. For those who are particularly interested in the latter, the reader is referred to Melhuish[1], Nowik[2], and Yates[3].

Trade Audits

With few notable exceptions, most manufacturers requiring national retail audit data subscribe to the services offered by those research agencies that specialize in these studies. A few manufacturers, however, continue to conduct their own, largely for reasons of frequency of reporting, speed of preparation, the need for product panels rather than shop indices and the volume of information required. In test markets, i.e., audits in test towns or TV regions, perhaps a few more manufacturers venture to carry out the audit measurements independently, even though there are adequate facilities available from the specialist agencies who almost invariably have active (sometimes dormant) panels of shops in their territories. It is with this concentration of syndicated audit facilities among a few specialist research agencies in mind, and the continuing existence of some manufacturers

120

independently conducting their own, that the following pages attempt to serve the interest and needs of readers.

The use of retail audits to management

Information from retail audits is vital to marketing management in the areas of both strategic and tactical decision making.

Information leading to strategic decision making can frequently be obtained by simple observation of long-term trends indicated by this source. These trends enable management to predict with some accuracy the size of the market in which the company is operating currently and in the future. It can tell management how the company is performing relative to its competitors in terms of market share and, within the overall picture of market share, it can pick out dramatic movements by individual brands, brands of a certain type, formulation, or price range, perhaps indicate a need for the company to review its product mix, its pricing policy, where it should concentrate its promotional expenditure, etc.

Provided the company possesses the other information necessary to assess which brands are likely to be profitable and which relatively unprofitable in the long term, retail audit can contribute to a large extent in successful long term profit planning. To put it another way, retail audit data can provide a framework of basic knowledge of market movements to which may be linked a myriad of other marketing factors—such as raw material prices and availability, machinery and labour requirements, competitive strengths and weaknesses—and, equally important, movements in consumer behaviour and retail attitudes to equip a company with signposts to find the direction in which profitability is most likely to lie in the long term.

The use of audit data in a tactical role is also essential, although this use tends to be evaluative of what has happened in the past as much as predictive as to what is to happen in the future, e.g., management will look back on recent promotional campaigns to assess their effectiveness and, by building up a picture composed of evaluations of several such recent performances, be better able to select those courses of short term activity which are effective. Likewise, this study of past action can help management avoid the more obvious pitfalls, e.g., the repetition of clearly disastrous sales promotions. Perhaps the major short term value is the ability to read quickly and to act upon competitive successes and failures.

In summary, audit data, imperfect though it may be in part, is one of the best aids at the disposal of marketing management for keeping informed about the market place in a quantitative, relatively unbiased way, month by month and year by year.

Collecting the information

The technique of auditing is simple and straightforward. The auditors visit the sample shops at predetermined intervals and at each visit they count the stock and record deliveries to the shop since their last visit. Sales during

Shop name
address

1. BRAND:	NAME SIZE VARIATION		A Lge		A Hdy		B Lge		B Lge 2p off	
2.	Sales last audit		224		82		43		12	
3.	Brand code	6 - 11	010.121		010.141		010.221		010.324	
4.	Price information	12 - 14	7p		4p		10½p		10½p	
5. Delivery details since last audit	Whole-sale	15 - 19								
	Cash and carry	20 - 24								
	Direct and head office	25 - 29	96 96 +8 +8	288	36	36			48 48 48	144
6.	Opening stock	30 - 34	71		73		89		132	
7.	Opening stock plus deliveries	(5 + 6)	359		109		89		276	

8. Stock this audit and use of display material			Forward	Reserve	D	Forward	Reserve	D	Forward	Reserve	D	Forward	Reserve	D
	a. Counter													
	b. Shelf		9			7			12			27		
	c. Window													
	d. Floor													
	e. S/S Stand													
	f. Dumper													
	g. Storeroom			144						40			30	

9.	Total stock a. - g. incl.	35 - 45	9	144		7			12	40		27	30	
10.	Closing stock	46 - 50	153			7			52			57		
11.	Sales this audit (7 minus 10)	51 - 55	☆ 206			☆ 102			☆ 37			☆ 219		
12.	Special information													
13.	Comments													

Fig. 6.1. An example of an audit form.

the interval between visits is simply calculated thus:

PAST STOCKS + DELIVERIES − PRESENT STOCKS = SALES

It should not be inferred from this bald statement that auditing is easy; considerable discipline and an organized approach are essential to obtain accurate estimates. Auditors must be trained to examine each stock location searching for the brands that make up the product class. As these are observed and counted they must be recorded separately against the location in which they are found so that stock in dump bins, shelves, or self service stands, i.e., in the selling area, can be distinguished from that held in the stockroom, the yard, or elsewhere, i.e., out of the selling area. The same care and attention is necessary in annotating delivery information. Each invoice, delivery note, or daybook entry must be scrutinized to be certain that all relevant delivery information is collected. Each delivery must be recorded against the source of purchase to distinguish between the conventional wholesaler, cash and carry, head office, or direct from the manufacturer. The whole operation must be systematic, deliberate, and rigorous for errors in stock counts, or missed invoices will give false sales readings, possibly leading to a misinterpretation of the expanded results. Additional

122

data is also collected by the auditors, selling price, promotional packs, special offers and any other information that could be of value. Thus, for each sample shop, a pattern of trading in the period is prepared; when added to the data collected from other sample shops a comprehensive picture of the market as a whole is constructed.

An example of an audit form is given in Fig. 6.1.

Preparing the data

Each entry and calculation made by the auditors in the shops must be subject to rigorous examination at the processing centre, each notation of stocks and deliveries, addition and calculation of sales for each brand size and type, must be physically checked. The most recent sales must be compared with the previous sales history of that brand and size in that shop and, only if it is 'reasonable' or anomalies explained by known activity such as promotions or price changes, should it be used in the preparation of the report. The auditor's notes are of great importance here to help account for changes or unusual levels of sales, deliveries or stocks following marketing activity. The emphasis at the processing centre, as in the field work, must be upon accuracy and thorough checking.

Once this scrutiny is completed, totals are made up of the stocks, the deliveries, and the sales for all the shops for each of the 'itemized' brands and sizes separately (collectively for that group of less important brands that are to be shown in the report as 'all others'). For small audits, such as those in test towns, the bulk of the processing is then complete except for the totalling of the shops found to be either in stock or to have made sales during the period of the various brands. These small audits are the exception, however. Most audit data needs to be grossed or expanded to universe levels. The process of totalling is common to both small and large 'national' audits, except that in the latter case the shops are first sorted into cells (shop type within area) and then totalled. For each cell the value of the universe is known and the expansion is simply:

$$\frac{\text{UNIVERSE}}{\text{SAMPLE}} \times \text{SALES (OR STOCK OR DELIVERIES)}$$

By adding the expanded cell data, area totals and shop type totals are obtained and thus, a representation of the national market is constructed.

The bulk of national audits today, of course, are processed by computer and the methods vary in detail from the one described. But whatever facility is used it is essential that the most stringent checks are applied at every stage.

The data provided

Though each of the service companies, and those manufacturers who conduct their own audits, have developed their own distinctive style of table presentation, the same basic data is common to them all. A description of these essential tables is followed by a brief outline of some of the additional analyses that are possible.

Consumer sales are sales made over the counter to customers during the audit period and shown both on a sterling or cash paid basis and as volume when the expression is package or weight. These tables normally also feature the share of the market accounted for by each itemized brand.

Retailer deliveries or purchases from wholesalers and manufacturers made by the shop during the audit period and normally expressed as volume on a package or weight basis.

Retail stock, the stock of the product encountered at the last shop check, expressed in packages or weight.

Stock cover, a tabulation of the length of time stocks will last, based upon current rates of sale. With seasonal products, this table is more meaningfully presented in terms of anticipated future sales which is not difficult to calculate once sufficient back data is available.

Average stocks and average sales per shop handling, literally averaging the total stock and sale by the number of shops in current distribution in order to present the true-life situation of the stockist.

Average prices paid by consumers, as the heading implies, a simple average of all the items and brands based upon prices encountered at closing stock.

Distribution, which takes two forms, the first, 'numerical', is based upon the proportion of shops handling the product at some time during the audit period (maximum), and subsequently the proportion actually in stock (effective) at the end of the period, the difference between the two figures being the shops 'out of stock'. The same basic information, but calculated upon the proportions of total annual grocery turnover represented by the shops handling it and 'in stock' at the end of the period, is termed 'sterling distribution'.

Showings, or information about the display material encountered in the shops at the last check. This is usually divided into groups, e.g., advertising material, which would include showcards or mobiles, self-selection, incorporating dispensers, outers from which customers make their own selection and dump bins and, lastly, stock presentations, pyramids, or features.

These basic tables represent the bulk of the tables provided as standard in most audit reports both from research agencies and by those manufacturers conducting their own audit. Each of these is analysed or broken down by region, either television area, the Registrar General's standard regions, or into individual or combinations of the manufacturer's sales divisions.

Further analysis by shop type or form of organization, multiple, co-operative and independent, the latter divided by size, or membership of voluntary group, is also normal. By this means, a total and composite picture of the retail trade is obtained.

There are several other useful tabulations which can be prepared from the basic data, some examples of these follow.

Forward and reserve stock, which is a simple division of the stock levels already annotated but divided between that which is in the forward selling area, the shop itself and, thus, available to the consumer, and that which is in the stock or storeroom.

Source of delivery, a broad division of the volume of retail deliveries from the three main sources, wholesaler, manufacturer, and the multiple head office.

Frequency distribution of shops selling at individual prices, literally an annotation of the proportions of stockists selling each brand size at given prices and most useful when contrasted with frequency distribution of prices paid.

Frequency distribution of prices paid, when the volume sold at each price can be compared with the proportion of stockists selling at these prices so that the extent and impact of price cuts, promotions, and dealing can be better assessed.

Frequency distribution of stock which shows the proportion of stockists holding either given levels of stock, or expressed as stockists holding levels equal to given weeks' sales (stock cover). From this, an analysis can be made of marginal stockists.

Marginal stockists which identifies the areas and shop types holding minimal stock levels, either in absolute or relative stock cover terms.

Marginal purchases analysis, another frequency distribution analysis of the amounts delivered to retailers during the audit period.

Analyses of combinations of brands stocked puts into real terms the extent to which individual brands are competing together in stores.

Cumulative distribution, a useful measure to check on the developments in distribution of new brands and the extent to which new stockists are being attracted and old stockists failing to re-order. It is particularly appropriate in test market evaluations.

There are many other forms of special analyses, each designed to answer a specific problem. No useful purpose will be served in making an exhaustive list in this chapter, a little thought and some ingenuity is all that is required to conceive yet another presentation, more meaningful or pertinent to the matter in hand. For those who buy a syndicated service, the client executive allocated to the account, is the most useful source for discussion, consultation, and general advice in the matter of special analyses. He can warn of the problems and difficulties and he understands the extent to which the audit information can be reliably adapted.

Omitted from the list of basic and supplementary tables is 'back data'. For manufacturers entering a new product field much useful background can be obtained from past history; all retail audit companies will sell back data at a discount, obviously at a greater discount if a forward contract is entered into. Special analyses of back data, however, are not generally available and the cost of re-analysis is normally prohibitive.

The sample

The types of sample used in retail audits fall into two distinct types, those that mirror a particular trade or type of shop, e.g., grocers, chemists, or hardware, and the, at present, relatively specialized which attempt to reflect the characteristic distribution of a product class, e.g., confectionery, or tobacco. In the latter, a combination of store types is used in the panel of shops, grocers, confectionery/tobacco/newsagents, cinemas, public houses, canteens in factories and offices, restaurants, garages, etc., all linked in such proportions that the data represents the totality of outlets selling the product.

When investigating the sample of outlets covered by A. C. Nielsen, Retail Audits, Stats MR, and any other audit firm it is advisable to check the representativeness of the sample. It has been impossible for audit firms to gain the co-operation of *all* large multiple grocery groups, large chemists such as Boots and important food outlets such as Marks & Spencer. Obviously, the lack of representativeness can affect estimates of turnover by units and volume. Therefore, when assessing the validity of the estimates, the user is well advised to look for minimum/maximum estimates with some indication of 'best guess'.

More and more interest is being shown by manufacturers in a 'product class' index. A manufacturer of aerosol air fresheners, for example, can buy an audit sample which reflects the distribution of the product, adequate numbers of grocers, chemists, and hardware stores all linked by the research agency, audited at the same time and processed and presented to the client as fully representative of the product class distribution and, thus, a market totality.

While this development of product sample as opposed to shop type sample continues, there are several basic rules followed by all the agencies and those few manufacturers who conduct their own audits, in constructing their samples. Figure 6.2 describes more than adequately the problem that faces the sample designer. From it can be seen the problem posed by attempting to reflect just one type of shop. Later, the application of this same principle is used with modifications when a product class sample is drawn but the same basic principles must be enforced.

The fundamental rule is to sample the volume of sales, rather than the number of stores. The principle used is simple and effective and the method titled 'disproportionate' sampling. While Fig. 6.2 simplifies the problem and ignores the modifications normally made to account for variations in size and organization within the type of shop, it describes adequately the basic rules followed by most designers of audit samples. This is to audit most where most of the sales lie.

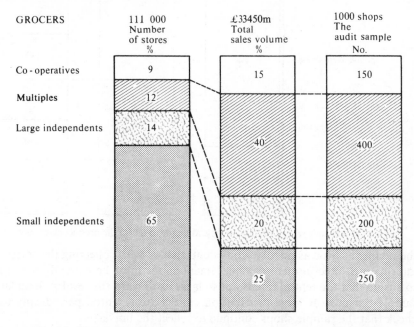

Fig. 6.2. The relationship of sales volume, number of stores and audit sample.

Taking the concept a stage further, where the sample attempts to reflect the whole spectrum of sales of the product class, a sample could be constructed in the following manner (see Fig. 6.3). Here, the considerations of adequate sample cell size and the need to expand the data to national estimates force the designer to reflect the total sales volume of the product only in each shop type, and within each to contain sufficient of the various organizations to give approximately equal cell bases in order to provide the most reliable estimates, consistent with the economies of a modest sample.

Whatever type of sample is favoured (product class or shop type index) it is clearly important that the sample itself should be, as far as possible, stable; inevitably with rebuilding, reorganization, sickness, and expiry of leases, there will be sample losses from time to time and these are unavoidable, but positive steps must be taken to keep refusals to co-operate further to a minimum. Some companies operating audits make a point of providing panel retailers with information, all make payment for the facility, make appointments for the following visit, are courteous and take care to trouble

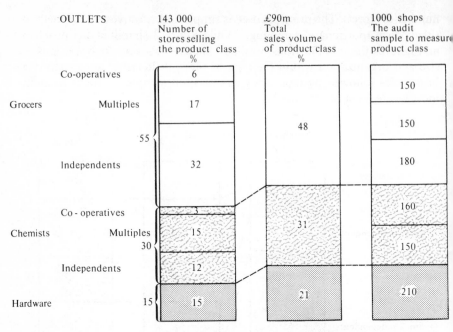

OUTLETS			143 000 Number of stores selling the product class %	£90m Total sales volume of product class %	1000 shops The audit sample to measure product class
	Co-operatives		6		150
Grocers	Multiples		17	48	150
		55			
	Independents		32		180
	Co-operatives		3		160
Chemists	Multiples	30	15	31	150
	Independents		12		
Hardware		15	15	21	210

Fig. 6.3. An example where the audit sample attempts to reflect the product class sales.

the retailer as little as possible consistent, that is, with collecting the correct information. Recruitment of replacement shops must be carefully policed to ensure that the refusal rate is not so large as to warp the results. Regular sample censuses or large distribution checks are essential periodically to check that the sample shops continue to reflect the universe.

All companies who operate audits guarantee that the identity of organizations and the individual shops who co-operate with them will be preserved and under no circumstances revealed to anyone. This is an assurance which all research agencies involved in this type of work respect most thoroughly.

Frequency of reporting

Most of the national syndicated audit services are geared to preparing reports every two months; for nearly all the major manufacturers this frequency is adequate since the basic object is to study trend data. There are, however, several product classes for which more frequent reports are desirable, particularly seasonal ones where a 'burst' pattern of reports is more appropriate. Examples of these would include soups in winter, salad cream and mayonnaise in summer, paints and decorating materials in spring and autumn, and so on. Of course, the level of stock held in the retail trade at the end of the season is the most important item of data to manufacturers. Increased frequency of reporting is more expensive, however, and unless the time required by the agency to prepare the reports is considerably shortened, a more frequent service is difficult to use fully and properly.

In test market audits where the sample of shops is comparatively small and the processing simple, audits are generally available at four-weekly intervals. Indeed, this is usually demanded since the object of test audits is often to measure short term activity or to obtain quick assessments of competitive tactics. An audit can be prepared to report even more frequently but this is inevitably by special arrangement, and one example occurred some years ago when a national audit of approximately two hundred grocers was set up to audit daily, though reports were prepared only each week. The project ran successfully but once the pattern of sales by day of week was established and the seasonal differences observed, the auditing frequency dropped to weekly for reasons of cost. In national audits a bimonthly report is normal, more frequent reports can be arranged, at a price.

Client service

One of the attractions of buying from a syndicated service is that most companies that provide audits to manufacturers and distributors feature as part of their service, the availability of a client service executive. It is his duty to maintain regular and frequent contact with clients in order to ensure that the data obtained from the audit is related to current problems and is presented in the most easily understood way.

In contrast, the client service executive can never know more about the client's business than the client himself. Although he can only advise the client he can compare current market situations with what has occurred in others, since one of the duties of a client service executive is that he serves a number of non-competitive accounts and that he has a wide experience of the problems that face manufacturers, gained from practical experience. The experienced client service executive is not concerned with theories but with the practical, profitable, successful selling of his client's product. His purpose in life can be summarized as the responsibility to provide his client with the precise marketing intelligence necessary to aid the taking of sound marketing decisions. The value of his service, however, is directly correlated to the degree to which he enjoys his client's confidence and all who consider subscribing to a retail audit service need to be satisfied that the client service executive allocated to their account is a man with whom they feel they can discuss fully the problems of the company, in order to profit from that man's experience.

Validation

This is a necessary exercise to gauge the extent to which ex-factory shipment is being recorded by the audit. It forms the basis of the level of confidence that can be put upon the results, it indicates the adjustment necessary to account for differences and, of prime importance, the interpretation and use that can be made of the information about the market as a whole and competition, both strategically and tactically.

129

Table 6.1

| PRODUCT | Change in Stocks | | | | Over-counter sales (5) | Total (4) + (5) (6) | Factory despatches (7) | per cent (6) to (7) (8) | 1967/68 per cent | 1966/67 per cent | 1965/66 per cent | 1964/65 per cent |
	Retail (1)	W/S (2)	H.O. (3)	Total (4)								
Brand A	+28.4	+21.4	+0.3	+50.1	1693.4	1743.5	1752.0	100	100	98	96	101
Brand B	+1.6	−6.2	−2.2	−6.8	891.7	884.9	998.6	89	89	88	91	77
Brand C	−0.1	−7.6	+4.7	−3.0	1398.9	1395.9	1341.5	104	100	97	98	100
Brand D	−10.8	−10.2	−4.5	−25.5	354.0	328.5	333.7	98	99	129	—	—
TOTAL ALL BRANDS	+19.1	−2.6	−1.7	+14.8	4338.0	4352.8	4425.8	98	98	96	96	99

The calculation should be made at least half-yearly, more frequently for seasonal products, but always using moving annual totals of consumer sales and factory shipments in order to smooth the figures and avoid freak results caused by the inevitable varying time lapse between shipment and delivery to the store. Basically the formula is:

$$\frac{\text{CHANGES IN STOCKS} + \text{CONSUMER SALES}}{\text{FACTORY SHIPMENT}}$$

In Table 6.1 it can be seen that in the ideal situation, using audit information from a sample designed to reflect the full spectrum of outlets (a product class audit rather than a type of shop index, e.g., grocers) the changes in stock at retail, wholesale, and multiple head office levels are all taken into account. Individual companies will need to make other adjustments. If the audit information available relates to only one type of shop, say, grocers, and significant company sales are made through other outlet types, some allowance for the unaudited sales volume must be made. Other adjustments, not featured in Table 6.1 should be made for sales through particular important retailers known not to co-operate with the audit.

As a general rule the higher the distribution and the greater the sales volume, the better the validation is likely to be.

Costs

It is most important to realize that the nature of an audit is its measurement of changes in the market over time, and that its value, therefore, is long term. Though it can, no doubt, help to resolve immediate problems, its real worth is the facility it gives management to observe, understand, and profit from changes both in the market as a whole and the individual parts of the market, pointing out areas of opportunity and weakness. It is essentially a continuous research vehicle and becomes integrated in company marketing thought. Once available as an aid to planning and market assessment, it is insidious in that it becomes difficult to conceive of ever having been without it.

The cost of an audit, whether as part of a syndicated service, a specially set up 'exclusive' panel or a test market, naturally reflects the complexity and amount of work involved. The number of shops, the frequency of visits, literally the volume of individual brands to be itemized and their incidence or distribution, the size of the market under study, the degree of breakdown required, the extra analyses, the interpretative function provided as part of the service and the length of contract, are all components of the cost. Some economies can be made by asking competing agencies for quotations and making use of the slightly different specifications, the different sample sizes providing the greatest opportunity for economy.

Case histories

Such is the confidential nature of the relationship between the research agency providing retail audit facilities and their clients (and the jealously guarded examples held by the manufacturers who conduct their own audits) that the illustrations of the practical use of audit information is limited to the few that follow. Nonetheless, they serve adequately to show the practical use of the data.

Case history 1. Quite apart from the special analyses of audit information carried out by the service company for a particular manufacturer, there are obvious gains in information and a fresh understanding of changing market characteristics to be made by reassembly of the standard data. In the

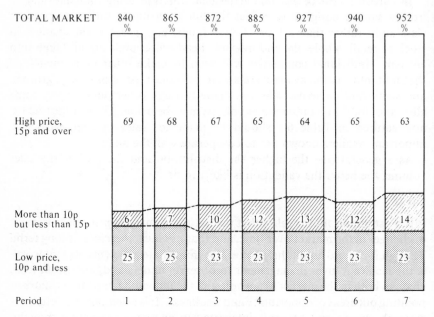

Fig. 6.4. Case History 1.

following example the grouping of individual brands with an empirical but meaningful (to the manufacturer) reassembly of the data revealed to him the growth in a particular sector of the trade. A number of individual minor brands had been seen to be enlarging but the full significance of this growth was only demonstrated when the data was re-presented (see Fig. 6.4). Re-analysis of audit information by pack size, price, product type, company, or other meaningful grouping should be carried out as a matter of course, in order to get the most from the data and to determine the early indications of change.

Case history 2. Confident of success following pre-tests of his commercial, the manufacturer required reassurance so tested the sales effectiveness of the advertising for his new product by buying time in all television areas except the Midlands. Linked with the television campaign was a heavy sales drive to obtain distribution. The data in Table 6.2 shows that, although

132

Table 6.2   Case history 2

	London	South	West	Lancs	Yorks	Tyne	Scotland	Midlands
Brand A								
Sales share								
Pd 1	23	25	10	8	16	23	27	25
Pd 2	27	23	20	14	24	14	23	14
Pd 3	54	53	62	69	48	44	42	23
Sterling distribution								
Pd 1	81	82	60	79	61	53	55	56
Pd 2	85	86	61	80	69	58	70	53
Pd 3	92	94	84	90	75	79	82	69

(Courtesy A. C. Nielsen)

there were apparent increases in distribution for the brand in the Midlands, the consumer reaction was much less marked than in the areas where television had been used.

Case history 3. This example features the use of audit data to assist management in forward planning. The figures shown in Table 6.3 are indices on a bimonthly moving annual total basis, in sterling turnover, for the total market.

In making the first forward projection, management took simply the average of the growth for the first seven periods, 10.6 per cent. At that time, distribution was already high at 85 per cent numerical, 94 per cent by value and it was assumed that advertising expenditure, as a percentage of sales, would remain constant at 22 per cent as it had been in the two earlier years. With the benefit of hindsight, the final projected figure of 447 was remarkably close to the actual market size reached of 451, although there were signs in the periods immediately following the projection that the market had begun to slow down indicating that the projection would overstate. Management thus elected to make a second projection once again based on the average growth, this time for the preceding twelve months, which was 9.6 per cent. There had been a marked increase in advertising expenditure, however, which, as a proportion of sales, now stood at 33 per cent. Further, distribution had improved and for the last four periods of the projection stood at 88 per cent numerical and 97 per cent sterling (by value). Both these factors contributed towards the substantial difference between the two estimates and also from the actual market levels achieved.

Table 6.3   Case history 3

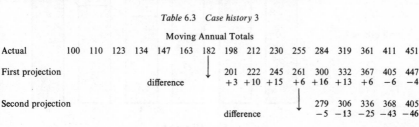

(Courtesy A. C. Nielsen)

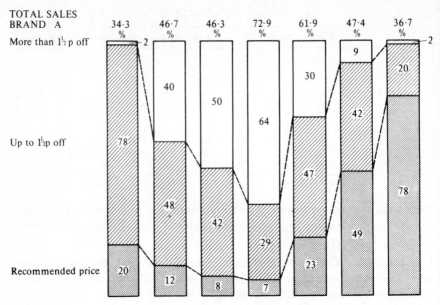

Fig. 6.5 Case History 4.

Case history 4. Sales of a recent nationally launched brand were seen to develop at a very fast rate (see Fig. 6.5). It was known from salesmen's reports that the brand was being dealt in heavily with selected retailers and was also being supported by a national 'money-off' offer. The intention was

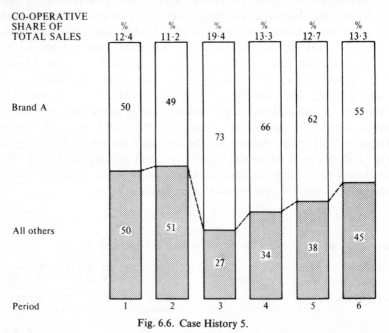

Fig. 6.6. Case History 5.

clearly to encourage trial. Analysis by price noted by the auditor at closing stock, enabled sales to be analysed in detail which revealed the very extensive below-the-line activity and entirely explained the rise in sales. Though backing at these levels could clearly not be maintained, the brand leader countered by more modest retail dealing and consumer offers, reducing the impact of the new brand and, as support was withdrawn, the brand reverted to its pre-promoted level.

Case history 5. This example also features a relatively short term promotion. In one of the earlier Co-operative National promotions, one brand in each of six separate product classes was featured. In this single example the substantial gain in the Co-operative share of the total product class sales was the highest ever observed. For the featured brand A, the gain in share is quite remarkable (see Fig. 6.6).

For general interest it is perhaps worth adding that the manufacturers of brand A repeated the promotion with the Co-operatives some eighteen months later. Although they achieved similar gains in sales volume they did not enjoy the same long term effects. One reason why the momentum slowed was that the success of the first promotion had prompted the Co-operatives to feature the display and prominence of their own brands more strongly in the stores (see Fig. 6.7).

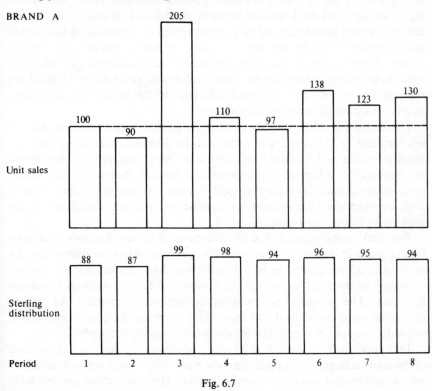

Fig. 6.7

135

The second chart shows how the manufacturer continued to derive benefits from the promotion months later, enjoying substantial increases in sales across the year and higher distribution many months after the promotion.

It is no exaggeration to state that any of the many market research agencies listed in the MRS handbook will set up and conduct an audit for a client. Obviously, many will capably carry out test audits but only a few have the experience to operate a full national audit efficiently. Some of the leading companies currently engaged in the area of national audits are:

Marplan Ltd.	A. C. Nielsen Co. Ltd.	Research Services Ltd.
Retail Audits Ltd.	Sales Research Services Ltd.	Stats (M.R.) Ltd.

Invoice Analyses

As the name suggests, these are analyses of the delivery notes and invoices of goods bought by the retailers or wholesalers. No attempt is made to count stock, unlike the full retail audit and, consequently, tabulations are limited. This is adequate, however, for some product classes, the notable example being the full range of ethical pharmaceuticals. To all intents and purposes the retail stock level of the bulk of ethicals is constant, the retailer either ordering specifically for each prescription or replenishing his limited stock promptly. Obviously, the vast range of items prohibits any but the largest chemist carrying adequate stocks and one consequence of this is the remarkable wholesale service provided to chemists, twice daily. In this trade then, stocks are constant and thus deliveries to the retailer are equivalent to over-the-counter sales to the customer.

The technique offers several advantages in that retailer co-operation is not strained, it is cheaper since the auditor does not need to spend time stock counting and it should be faster since fewer analyses or tabulations are necessary. Where it is reasonable to assume that stocks are either constant or immaterial since their sale is imminent because of their nature, such as when shelf life is short, an invoice analysis is a useful and cheap alternative to the retail audit.

The next logical stage in the development of invoice analysis is already taking place in America. The research agency involved in pioneering the method is taking advantage of the (relatively) high degree of stock control exercised by distributors, to sell the concept of invoice analysis to manufacturers. The service is not confined to samples of retailers but reflects the whole structure of the distributive chain—wholesalers, head offices, and individual shops. It is fast, less expensive, and highly successful.

This application in the UK is likely to be slower, the less 'organized' end of the trade is larger and it could be some time before the process of rationalization makes this technique more obvious. However, there are products that could already be adequately measured by invoice analysis such as cigarettes, perishables such as sausages, whole cheeses, fresh and chilled meat, bacon, fish, fresh fruit, and vegetables, and other merchandise which should only be handled by shop staff. Currently the sales or deliveries of most of these products are not recorded or available to management even though organizations for their promotion and marketing exist. It can only be a matter of time before this development is generally available here.

Distribution Checks

The battle for distribution and shelf space is continuous. While manufacturers seek to maintain or increase availability to retain a competitive edge and to obtain representative facings, the retailer strives to rationalize the range of brands held and to reduce stock levels to a minimum.

Accurate information about distribution is therefore vital, particularly during times of competitive activity. As already stated, information about distribution is available from retail audit but not every manufacturer buys audit information for all his products and even those who subscribe to a retail audit sometimes do so on a limited scale, such that many products (principally minor competitors) are shown grouped. There is also a clear limit to the breakdowns possible because of the relatively small samples used; audit data on distribution is simply not sufficiently detailed for the diagnostic information required by manufacturers with distribution problems. To remedy deficiencies or assess competitive pressure it is necessary to examine shops of a particular type in a particular area, e.g., multiple grocers in the Midlands, co-operatives in Scotland. Only with this information can manufacturers pinpoint weaknesses and strengths and direct the sales force or distributor to specific defined targets.

Clearly then, large numbers of outlets must be sampled, the number dependent on the breakdowns required, around 3000, for example, to measure distribution among four types of grocer in the eight major television regions and the remainder of the country. Using such a sample size to its maximum efficiency by 'equal cell sampling' would yield for each area sample a total of 336 shops each containing 84 shops of each of the four types—co-operatives, multiples, symbol independents, and other independents—the imbalance of the sample being restored at the expansion stage to provide correctly weighted national and area totals and within these, the shop-type totals.

The basic data obtained from a distribution check shows simply the proportion of shops of a particular type in a particular area found to be in stock at the time of the fieldwork. This is the equivalent of numerical distribution obtained from a retail audit. Putting a value to the distribution, in other words to attempt to show the volume of sales represented by the shops stocking, is more difficult since retailers are most unlikely to give reliable information about their turnover. Some approximation can be made, however, by basing the calculation upon the numbers of staff employed. Thus, distribution achieved in a shop staffed by ten persons is worth ten times the distribution value of a shop staffed by one person. Other devices include square footage of the shop, rateable value, number of check-outs or cash registers, all reflecting, to a greater or lesser extent, the volume of business carried out. In addition to these two basic tabulations a number of additional analyses are also possible. If, in addition to the simple annotation of shops stocking, a listing is made of the prices at which the various brands are being sold, three useful further tables can be constructed, i.e., the:

(a) range of prices at which individual brands are being sold;
(b) proportion of stockists selling at each point in the range;
(c) 'average' price and the degree of dispersion about the mean (the standard deviation).

By some further work by the interviewer in the store, other helpful analyses can be prepared:

(d) counts of 'facings' on self-service shelves to obtain the share held by each brand stocked;
(e) the incidence of displays, special features, dump bins;
(f) special packs, 'flash' packs, old and new labels;
(g) by questioning, to establish the source of supply, i.e., the use of cash and carry wholesalers by symbols and other independents.

Most distribution checks can be carried out by observation, certainly in the case of self-service and supermarket grocers the products are on the shelves, if in stock. This was confirmed by a recent survey designed to measure the incidence of stock in the reserve area (storerooms, stockrooms, and yards) not being on sale in the forward selling area. Checks were carried out at two hourly intervals over five days among a sample of 300 stores on a high volume range of products. Only late on Saturday afternoons and the early opening hours on Monday mornings was it found that any significant proportions (between four and ten per cent) of brand stockists were out of stock in the forward selling area. By midday on Monday, only two per cent of the stores had failed to relocate the brands. The advantage of observation rather than questioning is the facility to carry out checks among particular multiple groups whose managers would perhaps refuse information were they to be questioned.

Several research agencies offer syndicated distribution checks. These are carried out periodically three or four times a year; most feature calls on a continuous sample, a form of panel operation. Syndication enables the cost to an individual client to be kept to the minimum but requires complying with predetermined field dates and sample demographics. Information is processed relatively quickly, the full report is normally despatched within three weeks, preceded by advance information on key items available a few days earlier by telephone.

A summary of several circumstances that have precipitated a number of recent distribution checks follows, rather than illustrations or case histories. Basically the efficiency of distribution policies, strategies, and tactics need to be reliably measured by distribution checks. Many manufacturers experiment with varying cover and call rates, merchants are concentrated in some areas and thinned out in others, free mail-outs for immediate initial distribution are increasingly used as are commando sales forces. The effect on distribution of bonusing and dealing needs to be offset against the cost and the sales achieved. Reciprocal trading agreements are developing in outlets controlled by competing manufacturers, each naturally anxious to establish independently the levels achieved. The development of line extensions and varieties (the umbrella brands) is another frequent reason for distribution checks. Salesmen's reports of competitive price activity need to be assessed for extent and depth. Reported growths in distribution from retail audit reports are sometimes checked out by larger sample distribution surveys. One syndicated service carries out a number of these studies in named outlets to verify developments and to obtain measures of facings.

Ad Hoc Trade Surveys

Surprisingly few surveys are carried out among the retail trade but as competition between manufacturers intensifies and as the trade structure changes in the process of rationalization to form voluntary groups, combines and larger organizations, manufacturers have become increasingly aware of the need for more information about the wholesaler and retailer, their needs, opinions, attitudes, and behaviour.

Perhaps content with salesmen's reports in the past, manufacturers are now turning to market research for a deeper, more accurate assembly of relevant facts. There are pitfalls, however, and a short résumé could well help to avoid the more obvious. Most important, is to understand and use the language and idiom of the sector of the retail trade under study. Expressions which are familiar to managers of multiples are not necessarily as well known to the independent. Grocery terms are not those in common use among the hardware trade.

Restricted to the grocery trade only, the examples seen at top of page 140 have been found to be confusing even within that trade and serve to illustrate the very real need for preparation and care in this area.

The refusal rate, i.e., the number of calls made on retailers that are unsuccessful or in which interviews are only partially completed, is frequently higher than those encountered on consumer surveys. Sometimes this stems from a failure to understand his working week. A recent survey by Gordon Simmons Research, the 'grocery trade index' estimated the distribution

allocation	in-store-promotion	return
backing card	lines	run
broken bulk	long run	shelf talker
bonus	marketed	shrink wrap
cover	merchandise	spectacular
direct	movement	splits
expanded	offer	stack
fixture	operator	stand
flash pack	pack	stand strips
floor display	period	stock loading
group	promotion	units
indirect	quote	volume.

of grocery sales through the week (see Table 6.4). This points to the pressure on the retailer towards the end of the week and clearly indicates that interviewers should avoid the busy shopping days and never attempt to make an interview with the retailer when the store is full of shoppers. However, it would be erroneous to believe that interviews can be made with ease in the early days of the week. It is then that the retailer is re-ordering, restocking, receiving, and dealing with representatives and carrying out his administrative duties. Patently the retailer is a busy man and his time is limited. It follows, therefore, that a short interview will have a lower rate of failure to complete. Edit from the questionnaire any peripheral questions and obtain as much information as possible by observation rather than questioning. The brands stocked, the number of fixtures, floor displays, product locations, and space, the use of particular forms of promotion material can all be observed or noted and need not require questions to be put to the retailer. Use as little of the retailer's time as possible. Remember he is a busy professional.

Courtesy should be the rule. The interviewer should be prepared to make a second call if another time is more suitable for the manager or his staff. Instructions to the interviewer should never be vague; 'interview that person best able to answer the questions', is a lazy approach. A few interviews at the pilot stage will establish the identity of the correct respondent and, naturally, courtesy demands that the manager be approached first for permission.

Table 6.4

Total sales	100 %
Monday	7
Tuesday	13
Wednesday	10
Thursday	18
Friday	29
Saturday	23

Distribution of Grocer Sales   January–March 1970
through the week

Research at the point of sale often involves questioning shoppers as they make their purchases, go through the check-outs, or emerge from the store. Sometimes research designs require that the interviewer observes the buyer in the 'choice' situation, carefully stationing herself so that she can watch undetected. In all of these it is clearly vital that the co-operation of the retailer is obtained. Sometimes head office permission is also necessary and a wise precaution, if interviewers are to stand just outside the shop for any length of time, is to inform the local police station so that interruption from the law, provoked by earnest citizens, is minimized. Do not question multiple or co-operative retail management about buying procedures, purchasing behaviour, or attitudes concerning the buying function. Decisions or action is rarely taken at the retail manager's level in this area. More pertinent, relevant, and accurate information can be obtained from the appropriate buyers at the multiple or co-operative head offices.

Defining the outlet is a problem to be faced early in the course of a trade survey. Errors can easily occur (e.g., the distinction between a department store and a furniture store, wholesalers that are both cash and carry and conventional). These definitions must be agreed before fieldwork starts and this is particularly important if it is intended to gross up the results to national levels. This is difficult enough with the current paucity of relevant census data, particularly with the present constantly changing characteristics of the retail and wholesale trades. It leads, naturally, to difficulties in sample design though steps are being taken by the Board of Trade, largely at the instigation of the Market Research Society, to meet the needs of marketing and research. An ideal frame would be type of trade × form of organization × turnover size within region, to adequately describe the skewed distribution of some shop types (48 per cent of all the grocers with a turnover of less than £20 000 per annum, the small independents, are located in the Midlands, Lancashire, and Yorkshire television regions). Fortunately, the television contractors and the BBTA realize this and, commendably, have attempted to compensate for the deficiency by conducting their own censuses and by re-analysing and updating Board of Trade estimates. Other useful sources for sampling are the many trade registers such as Benn's Hardware Directory, the Chemist's Register, the Self-Service and Supermarket Directory and, curiously, but not ominously, fairly exhaustive listings can be obtained through the Inland Revenue and local authority rating lists.

In any research plan it is a useful caution to verify the flow of product from the factory to the retailer; what proportion is delivered direct to multiples and co-operative head offices, individual stores, wholesalers, both those involved with voluntary (symbol) group trading and the remainder? How many of the questions posed by the research objective can be answered at the retail level? Would it be wise, perhaps only as a precaution, to include an element of head offices or wholesalers in the sample?

Elsewhere in this volume the advice and recommendations applying to 'ad hoc' research among consumers should be employed even more rigorously

141

in surveys of the retail trade. Understanding the problem clearly, care in constructing the questionnaire, pilot interviews to check interpretation and flow, relevance of questions, ability of the respondent to answer the questions, adequacy of the sample, must all be thoroughly checked-out before the main fieldwork starts.

References

1. MELHUISH, R. M. The use and operation of the Nielson Indices, *Journal of the European Society for Opinion and Market Research*, **1**, 64–71, 1954.
2. NOWIK, H. *The use of Retailer Panel for Test Marketing*, ESOMAR Conference, 1963.
3. YATES, W. A. *Shop Audits in Marketing Evaluation, Now and in the Future*, Market Research Society Conference, 1967.

7. Panel research

John Parfitt

This chapter is concerned with panels. Like so many common English words placed in a market research context, its special research meaning is entirely familiar to the practitioners and confusing to the layman. Its nearest common meaning is a list of names (doctors, jurors, etc.), but in its research meaning this list of names has to be performing certain functions for certain desired objectives before it takes the form of a panel.

There are a wide variety of panel techniques available in Great Britain and some are permanent and some short term. Their functions and characteristics are described later in this chapter. All these panels have two common distinguishing characteristics with regard to the type of data they are designed to obtain and the method of obtaining it:

(a) panels are based on a representative sample of individuals or households from the universe being studied (e.g., all private households, all households with ITV sets, all cigarette smokers, etc.). Each individual or household panel member records (or permits the recording of) their complete activity in some factual aspect of consumer behaviour, such as their purchases in a defined range of consumer products or their television viewing;

(b) this measurement is ideally a continuous process over time, by virtue of retaining the same sample of respondents over the full period of measurement and obtaining from them a continuous and complete record of the required data. The collection of these data has, therefore, to be at regular and frequent intervals.

There are two basic objectives of panels, whatever specific data they are designed to collect. These are to:

(a) collect detailed and accurate information of the anatomy of consumer behaviour and the characteristics of the consumers; in other words, to obtain such precise information about the behaviour of each consumer or group of consumers that the differences in behaviour can be clearly

143

recognized and the relevant characteristics recorded. This refers, of course, to basically factual data about behaviour and not attitudinal data and in this respect panels offer the possibility of much greater accuracy and detail than is normally possible from single-call interviewing techniques;

(b) obtain information on the dynamics of consumer behaviour over time. The continuous study of the behaviour of individual consumers over time, made possible by the panel techniques, enables measurements to be made of the consistencies and inconsistencies of consumer behaviour, exact measurements of the frequency and volume of purchases/viewing/reading (whatever is being measured) and the response to given stimuli—advertising, brand launches, programme changes, or whatever.

Why Use Panels?

It requires little knowledge of research to see that these can be difficult objectives to obtain in full. The problem of respondent co-operation alone is a formidable one. Panels require a lot of 'know-how' to be run efficiently and, above all, they are expensive to operate. It is relevant to ask, therefore, why bother to set up panels anyway, what use do they have and in what sense do they have advantages over research techniques that may be cheaper and easier to operate? After all, sample size for sample size it will be far cheaper to call on a sample of respondents only once and interview them on, say, their purchasing behaviour for the last three months than to set up a panel which records these data for three months, so what advantages do panels offer for the extra money and time?

The answer to this question is in two parts:

(a) panels have marked advantages in the amount and accuracy of the data that can be obtained from one source, compared with the normal alternative of single call interview techniques (see 'Technical considerations in panels');

(b) the depth of analysis of the dynamics of consumer behaviour possible from the continuous nature of panel measurements offers unique opportunities to understand the ways in which the consumer behaves under given stimuli (see 'Analysis of panel data').

The Marketing Need For Panel Data

The wide range of panel and repetitive survey services currently available in Great Britain has grown not out of the steady widening of technical research knowledge as to how to operate them, since this was known substantially long before the majority of the services began (even if it has been polished en route), but out of the marketing need and, therefore, demand for the data they provide. The first of these services to be launched in Great Britain was the household consumer panel technique (the Attwood panel started in 1948). In fifteen years from 1955 and, particularly, in the six years from 1964 to 1970, many other panel services have been set up to meet specific marketing requirements for data. What were the marketing requirements which caused the development of the consumer panels?

A recent leaflet published by Arthur D. Little Inc. makes the challenging statement: 'Marketing managers are being inundated with data but starved of information'. The distinction drawn by the writer is between data (facts about the world) and information (answers to specific questions). In measuring consumer purchasing and attitudes, one is gathering 'data' (as defined) but one is also gathering it selectively with a view to transmuting it into 'information' (as defined). There are certain recurrent questions in marketing which the manufacturer's research department knows to be of perennial interest and, therefore, facilities have been created to provide the 'data' which will yield the necessary 'information'. The questions are of the type:

> how many people buy my product?;
> how much do they buy?;
> who are my competitors?;
> how strong are they?;
> are we/they gaining or losing?;
> what sort of people buy our/their products?;
> is any brand responsive to promotion?;
> has it regional/shop-type strengths and weaknesses? etc.

Marketing people are very interested in the detailed anatomy of the market and also in its dynamic characteristics. Monitoring services of various sorts have grown up to satisfy this need and among these the consumer panel technique.

The type of service which has evolved reflects the nature of the need. A mail order house, for instance, obtains a great deal of information from its own internally collected statistics. The exact response to any advertisement may be determined right down to the last unit sold and the name and address of each customer. A seller of expensive consumer durables such as Rolls Royce may go even further and seek to maintain a 'cradle to grave' record of each vehicle that leaves the factory. A soap powder manufacturer, on the other hand, may sell 5 million units per week of a big brand, and without some fairly elaborate system of data collection, he will have little idea of the final destination of these packets after his own transport and distribution organization has offloaded them at the delivery point. Similarly, apart from a few rather barren industry statistics, supplied by his trade association, he will have little knowledge of what his competitors are doing. It is with the information needs of manufacturers at this 'low cost/repeat purchase' end of the spectrum rather than at the 'high cost/consumer durable' end that consumer panels are mainly concerned.

The manufacturer who is interested in the market standing of low-cost repeat purchase items is faced with two main choices of data source. He may choose a method which takes a measurement at some point in the chain of wholesale and retail distribution. Commercial services are available which measure such things as warehouse withdrawal (mainly in the US), retail sales, retail distribution (retail audits and distribution checks). Such techniques are described elsewhere in this volume. His alternative is to pick a method which goes directly to the final link in the chain, the consumer, and again there are many commercial services which take measurements at this point. They fall into two broad categories—interview survey techniques, and continuous consumer panels. Some of the relative merits of interview surveys and panels with regard to the accuracy and detail of the data that can be obtained from respondents are discussed in a later section. For the time being it is sufficient to mention that it is the continuity of the data supplied by consumer panels which gives them particular value in providing marketing information.

People's actions are often a better guide to their character than their expressed opinions. Consumer panels are concerned mainly with consumer *behaviour*, i.e., actions not opinions. Again, a motion picture conveys more information than a snapshot. A snapshot of a hundred housewives might reveal that thirty of them were wearing hats. A second picture of another hundred might turn up the same proportion of hat-wearers. What does one conclude?, that 30 per cent of housewives wear hats? A continuous film record of the behaviour of one of these groups might show that all its members wear hats, but that they do so only 30 per cent of the time. Such a finding would be entirely consistent with the snapshot evidence, but might well lead to different conclusions, particularly if one happened to be a hatter. Consumer panels are *continuous:* they aim to cover *all* the purchases of each panel member over time in the field under study.

Thus, the consumer panel technique operates by confining itself to the collection of basically factual data about consumer purchasing behaviour, containing the minimum of respondent bias or conditioning resulting from seeking opinions or searching the respondents' memories about purchasing behaviour, and transmuting it by analysis into marketing 'information' for the study, not only of the detailed anatomy of the market under study but also of the dynamics of consumer behaviour over time.

The Types of Panel Services Available

Continuous consumer purchasing panels

The majority of permanent panel services are purchasing panels, based either on samples of households or individuals. The principals of these operating in Great Britain in 1971 were:

Panel service	Date of formation	Reporting sample size	Data collection method	Type of data collected	Standard reporting periods
Attwood Consumer Panel	1948	4800 households	Postal diary	Details of purchases of household consumer goods	4-weekly and/or quarterly
AGB Television Consumer Audit	1964	5600 households	Home audit	Details of purchases of household consumer goods	4-weekly
RBL FBI Personal Panel	1970	11 400 individuals	Diary and interviewers	Details of purchases of personal consumer goods	4 weekly and/or multiples thereof
Attwood AMSAC Personal Panel	1970	projected 16 000 individuals by Sept., 1971	Postal diary	Details of purchases of personal consumer goods	
KBMS Baby Panel	1967	1000 mothers with babies	Diary and interviewers	Purchases of of consumer goods for use by babies	4 weekly and/or quarterly
RBL Motorists Panel	1964	4000 individual motorists	Postal diary	Purchases of Petrol, oil and car accessories	4 weekly

There are two basic alternatives for collecting data in consumer purchasing panels. These are the home audit and the diary method.

The Home Audit. A panel is recruited and agrees to one main condition, i.e., that once a week (or at some other agreed interval) the panel member will admit an auditor into her home and will permit her to check household stocks of any product field in which she may be interested. Secondary conditions are that the panel member will save up used cartons, wrappers, etc., in a special receptacle provided by the auditor and that she will also answer a short questionnaire when the auditor calls (since some required information about the purchase will not be obtainable from the package alone). The auditor then checks all household stocks and *marks* the packets that have not been marked in previous weeks. She then checks the receptacle for used packs, ignores anything that has been marked at a previous call, and adds to the total any used pack which has not been marked. Thus, the purchases for the week are counted as all packets found in stock, in use or in the empty packet receptacle that had not been marked at previous calls.

The Diary Method. A panel member is recruited and undertakes to record in a preprinted diary all purchases, made either by herself or by other members of the family, in certain nominated product fields. Every week (or at some agreed interval) she returns the diary to the research company. She may or may not be provided with a receptacle for used packets (as an aid to memory). If she normally receives and returns diaries by post, she will be visited periodically by a representative of the research company so that the contact is kept 'alive' and is not allowed to grow stale, and to provide an 'educational' function where necessary. Some diary panels rely on interviewer collection of the diaries anyway—this is more expensive but it does combine some advantages of both systems.

All operators of consumer purchasing panels use one or other of these methods of data collection but predominently it is the diary method that is used. A great deal has been said about the advantages of the one method or the other in the collection of panel data and remarkably little has been written for publication. The home audit method appeals to the imagination more as an objective method putting less burden on the panel members than the diary method, which may be subject to problems of understanding, memory, and fatigue. In practice, the differences between the two methods appear to be much less marked than they appear to be in theory, i.e., judging from parallel data from the Attwood panel (postal diary) and the TCA panel (home audit). Nevertheless, there are differences and the principal advantages and disadvantages of the two data collection methods appear to be as follows:

(a) postal diary collection methods are cheaper to operate than home audits and, as the method is not dependent on regular personal calls, the sample does not need to be so closely clustered as for home audits. A part of these two advantages disappears when interviewers are used for diary collection;

(b) the initial panel recruitment rate is probably higher for the home audit method than for the diary method. In both cases recruitment is by personal interview. How important this factor is is a moot point bearing in mind that in the USA national diary panels are usually recruited by mail and produce a 10 to 15 per cent recruitment rate, compared with say, 50 per cent for diary panels in Great Britain and higher for home audit panels; and yet the American panels are reported to produce very reliable purchasing data;

(c) the continuity of panel membership is probably higher for the home audit method than for the postal diary method. A 'drop out' rate of 25 to 30 per cent/annum can be expected from a postal diary panel and 10 per cent has been quoted for home audit panels, although this latter figure sounds low allowing for the normal rates of death and home-removal in this country. The use of interviewers to collect diaries almost certainly reduces the 'drop out' rate below the level quoted above for diary panels, since it is known that regular calling has a beneficial effect on continuity of panel membership;

(d) home audits are entirely dependent on getting regular access to the home for the collection of data, which postal diary panels are not. On the other hand the non-receipt of a diary for a particular week calls for very quick action from the research company to collect the diary if the record is not to be lost;

(e) the two methods have different advantages and disadvantages in the collection of certain types of data. Thus, home audits record very accurately any promotions, special offers, etc., marked on the pack. Pick-up of other promotions is adequate but probably no better than diary records. Foodstuffs which are bought loose and consumed quickly are hard to check in home audits, and wrappers which may start to smell after a brief storage may be missing from the audit bin and missed from the audit. These present no particular problem in a diary record. Diaries are probably better than audits at picking up the purchases of 'other family members', e.g., the teenage daughter's personal bottle of shampoo or father's extra tube of toothpaste packed in the overnight bag may well be missed even in a conscientious audit;

(f) the diary method can cover a wider range of goods and services than the home audit method as such, since it is not dependent on physical evidence of purchases for its data collection. Thus, it can collect data on products with important unbranded sectors, like eggs, sausages, and cheese or products difficult to audit in the home, like paint or garden products or services like hairdressing, cinema visits, or dry cleaning. Naturally, these data can be collected on home audits also but only by the introduction of diaries or by interviewer-administered questionnaires.

Although both audit and diary panels have their imperfections, both methods have over long periods (twenty years for diaries and six years for audits at time of writing in 1970) been shown in Great Britain to provide accurate market share and trend data over a wide range of product fields. The technical weaknesses do not manifest themselves to any very great extent if the aim is simply to produce aggregate market share data by weekly or quarterly periods; and this was the type of service which the panel companies were originally set up to supply. Indeed, the bulk of their income is still derived from the sale of such standard reports.

Of the continuous consumer purchasing panels operating in Great Britain in 1971 one, the TCA panel, relies on the home audit method and the remainder on the diary method, with or without interviewer collection of diaries. Two are household panels (the Attwood Consumer Panel and the AGB home audit panel) set up for the collection of purchasing data on products which are basically for household use. In these panels it is the housewife who is recruited for co-operation in the collection of the data, both because she is usually the most readily available of the household members and also because she will normally be the main agent of purchase for products of this kind. The Attwood consumer panel has for some years relied on supplementary data from diaries issued to other household members for recording purchases of a more personal kind, e.g., shampoos, toilet soaps, records, etc. This has been done on the grounds that these are purchases which the housewife might not otherwise be aware of and therefore would not record in her household diary, and as such, points the way to the most recent development in continuous panel services—personal panels.

Two personal panels have been set up on a national basis in 1970—the RBL FBI panel and the Attwood AMSAC panel. The method of operation of these is basically similar to that of household diary panels except that the data is collected from individuals rather than households and the range of products on which data can be collected goes far beyond what is considered to be feasible from a household panel, e.g., it includes cigarettes, confectionery, etc., which are essentially personal purchases for personal consumption often beyond the home. The principal problem in collection of these types of data is to ensure that the panel members record their purchases as soon after making them as possible, since the frequency of purchase is often far higher than for products normally recorded in household panels; and the evidence of purchase, i.e., packaging, often disappears quickly after purchase as does the memory of the purchase. Experimental work has suggested that a more portable form of diary than is necessary for a household panel is a valuable aid to complete and accurate recording of personal purchases of this kind.

The other two continuous consumer purchasing panels mentioned in the summary—the KBMS Baby Panel and the RBL Motorist Panel—are essentially aimed at special interest groups (mothers with babies, and motorists) but otherwise work on normal diary panel lines. The motorist panel comes closer to a personal panel than the others and relies on a pocket-size diary which can be kept in the car to ensure that petrol and oil purchases are recorded as soon after they are made as possible. The baby panel has particularly acute recruitment problems, compared with the normal run of panels, since only mothers with young babies are of interest and they need to be recruited as soon after the birth of the child as possible. And once the baby is over two years of age panel membership is no longer required.

Short-term consumer purchasing panels

Unlike the continuous panels, the short-term consumer purchasing panels do not usually operate on a syndicated service basis. They are designed for a specific purpose, usually only for one client, and their duration is determined by the measurements necessary to answer the marketing problems for which they were set up. A minimum of twelve weeks and a maximum of a year are the usual limits of these short term panels. The objectives of these are numerous but the most important of them are:

(a) to measure test marketing activity, particularly in terms of product penetration and repeat purchasing, in test towns or in small areas where the continuous panel services do not yield samples of a sufficient size;

(b) to test out alternative marketing choices, e.g., alternative promotional activities, in controlled conditions in order to determine which is likely

150

to be the most efficient in general use, or to discover whether existing policies could be modified without detriment to the product's sales. To do this, different matched panels are subjected to the different marketing pressures under observation and the purchasing behaviour of the samples are compared, usually in penetration and repeat purchasing terms. There are sometimes as many as half a dozen matched panels under observation at the same time, although the number is usually only two or three. They may all be located in the same district or town, or sometimes they are located in different areas depending on how closely the stimuli being applied can be confined to the households under observation. Thus, a test of different advertising campaigns usually has to take place in several areas, as the advertising cannot be confined to small districts; whereas a comparison of different promotional activities can often be carried out within the same district or town;

(c) a third use of short term consumer panels is where information is required from the panel households or where they are subjected to special marketing pressures which would be considered conditioning and detrimental to the future buying behaviour of permanent panel members. Thus, purchasing behaviour collected from the panel may need to be related to information on their attitudes to the product or awareness of its advertising, etc. This is perfectly feasible with a short term panel. Indeed the application of awareness and attitude questions at the end of the panel's life is a standard feature of the technique, whereas such information obtained from a permanent panel might be considered harmful to the representativeness of the panel's future buying behaviour.

The data collection methods employed in short term panels are much the same as those described earlier for the continuous panel services. The principal difference is that the recruitment rate for short-term panels is usually higher than for permanent panels since more respondents are prepared to participate in panels when they know exactly how long it is for.

Television-viewing panels

The television-viewing panel technique was developed by Nielsen in the USA and, at the time of the start of commercial television in Great Britain by TAM. The service in this country is now operated by AGB on behalf of JICTAR.

The panel is recruited from households with television sets and the primary measurement is achieved by means of a meter attached to the set which records on a tape the time when the set is turned on or off and the station it is tuned to. This information alone gives no indication of the actual audience and this is usually obtained by means of a viewing diary in which the viewing times of the individual household members (and guests) are recorded. From these data are estimated the total household viewing audiences to each channel in each ITV area and also the household composition of these

151

audiences. The methods have remained virtually unaltered in the fifteen years since commercial television began in Great Britain. One important exception in data collection is that meter tapes are now returned by post, instead of being collected every Monday by an employee of the research company.

By consumer purchasing panel standards panel sizes in each area are comparatively small, as is shown below, and this can be attributed to the comparative simplicity and stability of television viewing behaviour compared with the complexities of consumer purchasing behaviour.

JICTAR panel sample sizes in each ITV area.
Television meter households in each area:

London	350	Central Scotland	200	Ulster	100
Midlands	300	North East England	200	Border	100
Lancashire	300	Wales and the West	200	South West England	100
Yorkshire	300	East of England	200	North East Scotland	100
		Southern	200		

Total in Great Britain 2650 households

The recruitment rate for television viewing panels and the continuity of panel membership is traditionally higher than for consumer purchasing panels (particularly of the diary panels). This can be attributed to the smaller burden on the respondents, the relatively greater attractiveness of television panel membership and to the higher rewards offered. This subject of television viewing panels is covered in greater depth in chapter 24.

Consumer product consumption panels

In the same way that consumer purchasing behaviour is complex and liable to exaggeration and over-simplification in single-call interview situations so, too, is consumer consumption behaviour of the products they buy or make. The pattern of product consumption, the uses to which products are put, the occasions of consumption, who consumes them, in what quantities and with what other products, etc., can be measured most accurately over time by means of a panel. These are normally very short term panels set up long enough to allow for running-in and the normal cycle of consumption behaviour, for which an average period may be eight weeks duration, dependent on the average frequency of consumption and purchase of the product under observation.

Like short term purchasing panels, the panels to measure product consumption are usually set up for one specific purpose and for one client. The purpose normally requires some disguise as far as the respondent is concerned to avoid over-reporting of consumption behaviour, and this is usually achieved by measuring a wider range of product consumption than is required for the study. The scope of product consumption panels is wide. In the experience of the author examples of them give some illustrations of

152

the size, subject, and duration of panels of this kind. Panels set up to measure the preparation and consumption in the home of soups and canned puddings, had a sample of 1000 housewives and lasted for 8 weeks. During this time, housewives recorded the occasions of serving the products, details of other foods eaten with them, who ate them, full details of the product served, etc. An edible fats consumption panel consisted of 1000 housewives and lasted for 3 weeks (some in winter, spring, and summer) and obtained full details and the quantities of the purpose for which butter, margarine, etc., was used. A clothes washing habits panel of 300 housewives ran for 6 weeks and obtained full details of the washes carried out, the main clothes categories washed and of the washing products used.

It is normal at the finish of the panel operation to interview the respondent in order to obtain attitude and awareness data and to relate this to consumption habits.

Shopping panels

This research technique is really a variant of the consumer purchasing panel. It has been developed in the USA and is relatively widely used there. The only example currently available in Great Britain is RBL's mini-test-market service. The panel consists of a demographically controlled sample of housewives in one town (RBL have a 500 housewife panel in Southampton, for instance) who have expressed their willingness to purchase products from a travelling shop. The travelling shop is, in fact, run by the research company and calls on each housewife once a week. Each housewife is regularly supplied with a brochure containing illustrations of all the products and brands she can purchase and an order form (which, in effect, is the equivalent of a panel diary). The operation carries the usual range of brands in each product field it covers, and these are at carefully controlled but competitive prices. In addition, however, it introduces new brands or varieties which are not available on the general market and using the brochure as an advertising medium and applying normal promotion schemes where necessary it promotes these products to the panel. The result is that it usually achieves an abnormally high penetration for the new brand, compared with what would probably happen in a real test market situation. It provides, however, a realistic impression of the likely repeat purchasing rate the brand would achieve in the market. It is on this latter measurement that the panel largely depends for its assessment of whether the brand would be successful or not if it were launched. It is, therefore, not a substitute for a consumer purchasing panel in a test marketing situation, but rather it permits an earlier measurement to be made of a brand's likelihood of success prior to test marketing.

Product testing panels

Product testing panels are more in use in the USA, e.g., NFO and HTI panels than in this country. Their title is slightly inaccurate since they are usually used for collecting data quite as much as for testing products. They lack many of the common characteristics of the panels so far described since there is seldom any continuity in the data collection or product testing functions; their continuity is solely in the fact that a particular sample of respondents of known characteristics is retained for a semi-continuous miscellany of research enquiries. They are at their optimum use when the cost of interviewer field work for national enquiries is at its maximum in relation to postal costs (as in the USA or France) and for this reason have made rather less headway in this country where travelling distances and field work costs are comparatively low. Their principal use in this country has been by manufacturers running their own panels, and this has been primarily to retain the maximum control and secrecy in their product development.

Technical Considerations in Panels

Sample selection

As panels are intended to operate for a considerable length of time, if not indefinitely, considerable care is applied in sample selection at recruitment. The Attwood consumer panel, for example, is based on 250 local government sample district clusters of 16 households in each. These were selected in a four stage stratified random sample, the last stage of which was the selection of addresses at a fixed interval from the electoral registers of wards selected at the third stage. The resulting sample was proportionately correct by four town size groups within 15 control areas in the country and demographically balanced within each of the 15 areas.

It is not sufficient, however, just to exercise this care at the initial recruitment stage. Similar controls have to be applied in two other panel sampling procedures. The first of these relates to panel maintenance, i.e., the replacement of households which are removed or remove themselves from the panel. This is a continuous process and each removed household has to be replaced by another with similar demographic and area characteristics. To provide these 'quotas' a large number of households selected by the methods described above have to be surveyed and held in readiness for the occasion when they need to be used as panel replacements.

The second sampling procedure relates to actual reporting periods. Any panel has a reserve over and above its basic reporting number to allow for slow or non-return of purchasing records in any one period. This reserve (usually about 10 per cent) has to be large enough so that in any period a fully balanced area and demographic sample of reporting households can be drawn within a minimum waiting period, otherwise panel reporting would be delayed whilst the returns from demographically deficient groups were awaited.

154

The validity of panel data

The fact that panel recruitment rates may vary from as little as 10 to 15 per cent of initial contacts in postal recruitment in the USA, to around 50 per cent for diary panels in Great Britain and higher for home audit panels has already been discussed. Thus, there are a lot of people who refuse to join panels, and this sometimes raises doubts about the representativeness of those who do. A source of evidence which suggests that panels are representative comes from some experimental work to create psychological or attitude grouping scales with which to classify panel housewives. An initial set of attitude scales designed ultimately to be related to consumer purchasing behaviour on the panel were applied initially to a random sample of 3600 non-panel housewives. The results obtained from the random sample and later from the panel housewives show a close similarity in attitude groupings, as may be seen in Table 7.1.

The extremes of each scale are composed largely of different housewives. It is not unreasonable to assume that if the consumer panel sample was fundamentally unrepresentative of the domestic household population then significant differences would appear in these attitude scales and, in its turn, in purchasing behaviour.

In theory, the simplest way to test the validity of purchasing data obtained from panels is to compare it with data obtained from other sources. In practice this is difficult, partly because very little other reliable information is available and, where it is available, it is often hard to make direct comparisons with panel results. This is because household consumer panels measure only purchases taken into the home and, in some fields, this excludes important areas of consumption beyond the home. Where such information does exist, and it is usually in the form of total production figures for the retail market, then the panel results (grossed-up) normally range from about two-thirds to 100 per cent of these tonnages, depending on how much purchasing occurs beyond the home. In the case of flour, for instance, where there is little non-domestic consumption of retail packs the panel pick-up is virtually 100 per cent. In the case of toilet soaps, where there is much more consumption of the retail pack beyond home, then the panel pick-up is about 90 per cent, and so on. In general, with one or two notable exceptions, consumer panels reflect total domestic purchasing of products with accuracy, where valid comparisons can be made.

The question of whether panel housewives get conditioned in their purchasing behaviour by long membership of the panel is one on which some direct evidence can be produced. Two separate studies are shown which, while not being fully conclusive, do at least provide no evidence of this type of conditioning. The first example is taken from the STAFCO consumer panel in France and it compares two demographically matched samples of panel households, the first long-serving panel members (five years or more) and the second more recently recruited members. Two potential types of

Table 7.1 A comparison of attitude groupings in a random sample of the total housewife population and among Attwood Consumer Panel members

Attitude scale:	Rigidity in housework		Traditionalism in housework		Economy consciousness		Conservatism in shopping	
	Random sample 100%	Consumer panel 100%	Random sample 100%	Consumer panel 100%	Random sample 100%	Consumer panel 100%	Random sample 100%	Consumer panel 100%
Total housewives								
No. of housewives falling into each group on the scale								
1. Very rigid/ traditional/ economy conscious/ conservative	9%	7%	13%	12%	10%	10%	10%	10%
2.	13%	12%	21%	24%	38%	35%	13%	13%
3.	22%	24%	29%	29%	24%	31%	44%	48%
4.	35%	35%	25%	24%	16%	16%		
5. Flexible/modern minded/not economy conscious/not conservative	21%	22%	11%	11%	11%	8%	33%	29%

Source: Attwood Consumer Panel, Great Britain.

156

conditioning are studied; the first that panel membership tends to induce greater brand loyalty, and the second that it tends to produce greater price consciousness and, therefore, more attention is paid to obtaining price advantages (see Tables 7.2 and 7.3).

Table 7.2   Average number of brands purchased—by length of panel membership

	(Brands purchased in a 12 week period)			
	Dentifrice	Margarine	Toilet Soap	Washing Powder
Long service panel members (recruited 1955–1960)	1.23	1.29	1.45	1.98
Shorter service members (recruited 1961–1964)	1.22	1.31	1.42	1.98

Table 7.3   Average price paid per 100 grms—by length of panel membership

	Average price paid in a 12 week period (francs per 100 grms)			
	Dentifrice	Margarine	Toilet Soap	Washing Powder
Long service panel members (recruited 1955–1960)	2.05	N.A.	0.77	N.A.
Shorter service members (recruited 1961–1964)	2.09	N.A.	0.77	N.A.

Source: STAFCO Consumer Panel 12 weeks ending
27 December, 1964.

This study at least shows that there is no progressive conditioning of panel housewives. The behaviour of the longer serving panel members is virtually identical with that of shorter service members. A similar study carried out in the Attwood panel in Germany showed similar results. It does not, however, preclude the possibility that all the conditioning occurs in the first few months of panel membership and thereafter ceases. The second analysis is taken from the Attwood Consumer Panel in Great Britain at the time when the basic sample size was increased from 2000 households to 4000. The purchasing levels in 25 product fields were compared between the old 2000 panel (containing a high proportion of long service members) and the newly recruited 2000 panel (who by definition were all short-service members) to see whether any variations which occurred were beyond those which would be attributed to chance after allowing for the variations in the range of chance differences which would occur for fields of different size and frequency of purchase. In fact, 13 of the fields showed some upward movement in total purchases and 12 showed some downward movement but in only two cases were these movements statistically significant. These results suggest that even during the first year of panel membership there are no basic differences in product purchasing levels from those obtaining after longer service.

Table 7.4   Normalized deviates of percentage differences between purchasing levels of old and new panels

Normalized deviate	over -2	-2 to -1	-1 to 0	0 to 1	1 to 2	over 2	Total fields
Actual	0	3	9	7	4	2	25
expected	0.6	3.4	8.5	8.5	3.4	0.6	25

If conditioning does not seem to occur to any great extent in practice—and in general terms the evidence suggests that a continuous consumer panel is a representative measuring instrument—there still remains the fact that consumer panels do tend to have minority areas of unrepresentativeness. There are at least three known minorities of the domestic population that consumer panels tend to under-represent. These are the two extremes of the population, the very prosperous and the very poor (particularly the very poor and old). The third group are the fluctuating and transitory households composed mainly of young single men (or women) living particularly in the centres of the larger cities. It is likely that these groups tend to be under-represented to some extent in most market research samples.

Continuity of reporting

As one of the principal advantages of panels is the continuity of the data, clearly continuity of reporting by panel members is of paramount importance. This is particularly true of the more sophisticated analyses of panel data, which rely heavily on complete continuity of reporting by the panel members included.

Continuity is directly influenced by three factors: the rewards offered for panel membership, the degree of interest the panel members have in participation, and the ease with which they can supply the data required. Probably all panel operations offer some reward for the services of the members; these range from direct money payments, through stamp schemes in exchange for gifts, to free television set maintenance in the case of television-viewing panel members who own their own sets. Clearly, there are limits set by the commercial viability of the panel operation itself to the size of the payments to its members. Suffice it to say that the payments themselves can hardly be regarded as the 'rate for the job' and therefore continuity is very much dependent on the interest of the panel member.

The degree of interest the panel members have is a very important factor. There is little doubt that frequent visits by friendly auditors/interviewers has an important effect, as does the exchange of chatty notes between a *nom de plume* at head office and the panel members (the Americans are so much better at this than researchers in Great Britain). A cordial relationship between the panel member and the panel company is at least as important as the payments.

The interest of the panel members is very much influenced by the ease with which they can supply the data required of them. Confusion about what they are supposed to do, even on small points, is a great destroyer of interest. People essentially like to co-operate and do not like to be made to feel inadequate to what has been set them, by a failure to understand what they are supposed to do. Clarity, particularly in diary layout, is vital. One special feature of this factor is the problem that respondents usually do not understand that to report a non-purchase is as important as reporting a purchase, i.e., a genuinely empty audit-bin is as important as a full one. There is a danger, particularly in the early stages of panel membership, that respondents will create purchases or find packages rather than report nothing. Thus, in short-term panels in particular it is necessary to cover a wide enough range of products for most of the sample to have purchased at least one thing once a week; for the rest it is a matter of respondent education that a non-purchase is as interesting as a purchase.

The Volume and Accuracy of Panel Data, Compared with Interview Surveys

Panels are used to measure aspects of consumer behaviour which are complex and variable, e.g., purchasing or viewing behaviour over time and where a relatively high degree of accuracy in the measurement is required. This second point is important because, for instance in the measurement of purchasing behaviour, for many purposes the high degree of accuracy and detail offered by a panel may not be necessary to obtain the information required for a particular marketing decision. In such cases, and there are many, using a panel might prove to be an expensive luxury and a cheaper simple interview survey would suffice adequately.

How complex and subtle purchasing behaviour can be is often not fully appreciated. This is illustrated in Figs. 7.1 and 7.2. In Fig. 7.1 the purchases of 350 households in seven product fields (of high purchase frequency) over two consecutive eight-week periods is studied by individual households, showing the amount of variation in total purchases between the first and second periods. The average change for the total sample over these two periods was negligible—from 21.3 to 21.5 packages per household, or an increase of less than one per cent. However, in 49 per cent of the households studied purchases changed by more than 20 per cent thus illustrating that even in the most apparently stable market situations there is considerable and diverse movement below the surface.

Figure 7.2 illustrates the purchases of a brand of washing powder over the period of a year and the proportion of these purchases that were made with promotions. The complexity of this situation speaks for itself, and it is only part of the picture since the problem of purchases of competitive brands is ignored in this illustration.

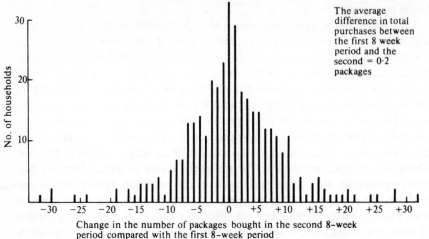

The average difference in total purchases between the first 8 week period and the second = 0·2 packages

No. of households

Change in the number of packages bought in the second 8-week period compared with the first 8-week period

Fig. 7.1. Individual household variations in purchasing levels in the total of seven product fields between one 8-week period and the next. Source: Attwood Consumer Panel.

It is generally accepted among researchers that if you interview a respondent asking him (or, more likely, her) to recall purchasing behaviour in a consumer product field, there is a strong likelihood that the frequency and quantity of purchases will tend to be exaggerated and the complexity of purchasing behaviour over-simplified. This hypothesis was tested in an experimental research study in which 1000 consumer panel housewives were interviewed about their purchasing behaviour in 12 product fields and the

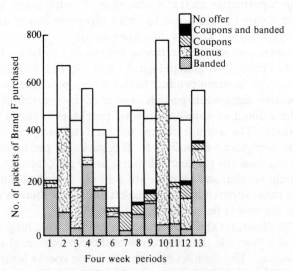

No offer
Coupons and banded
Coupons
Bonus
Banded

No. of packets of Brand F purchased

Four week periods

Fig. 7.2. Proportion of purchases of a washing powder brand made on promotions. Source: Attwood Consumer Panel.

data obtained were compared with the data recorded by the same housewives in the panel to which they belonged. The results obtained from this study[1] suggested the following conclusions:

(a) that respondents when interviewed are prone to exaggerate their purchasing behaviour;

(b) this exaggeration is very closely related to the respondent's average frequency of purchase of the product. Thus, the more frequently a respondent actually purchases a product the more accurate he/she is likely to be in recalling that frequency and, conversely, the less frequently a product is purchased the more likely that the purchasing behaviour will be exaggerated;

(c) in its turn this conclusion has two effects. The first is that products with a high average frequency of purchase tend to be exaggerated least in interview surveys. Table 7.5 summarizes these findings from the experimental study. The second effect is that within any product field the gap between the volume of purchases of high- and low-frequency buyers is artificially narrowed in an interview situation because the latter tend to exaggerate their purchases more than the former;

(d) there is dramatic over-simplification of brand switching behaviour over time in an interview situation. Broadly, respondents tend to equate their most recent brand buying behaviour to their 'normal' behaviour over time, whether this is accurate or not.

Table 7.5   *The relationship between average frequency of purchase and interview exaggeration of total purchase volume*

| Product field | Average frequency of purchase | | Interview exaggeration factor—volume of purchases (panel diary returns = 100) | | | |
| | Average interval between purchases— weeks | Rank order | Panel housewives when interviewed | | Matched non-panel housewives* | |
			Exaggeration factor	Rank order	Exaggeration factor	Rank order
Tea	1 week or less	(1)	116	(1)	136	(2)
Margarine	1.1	(2)	128	(3)	123	(1)
Washing powders	3.0	(3)	124	(2)	143	(4)
Washing-up liquids	3.5	(4)	178	(5)	210	(5)
Baked beans	4.5	(5)	152	(4)	140	(3)
Toilet soap	4.9	(6)	208	(9)	261	(8)
Canned soups (summer)	5.3	(7)	200	(8)	298	(10)
Instant coffee	6.2	(8)	179	(6)	245	(7)
Jam	9.4	(9)	194	(7)	235	(6)
Dentifrice	9.7	(10)	217	(10)	282	(9)
Floor and furniture polish	15.9	(11)	292	(11)	396	(11)

* A Matched Sample of 1000 housewives who were not members of the Attwood panel were also interviewed, using the same questionnaire as for the panel housewives. In general they exaggerated their purchasing behaviour more than panel housewives and this is attributed to the fact that the latter had a better idea of their purchasing behaviour from their habit of recording it in the panel diaries. The rank order of exaggeration is, however, similar.

Broadbent and Mooney in their follow-on to this study[2] point out that for certain purposes (in this case selection of print media against light, medium, and heavy buyers of products) the exaggeration obtained at single-call interviews does not distort the rank order of purchase volume too seriously and does not, therefore, invalidate the results obtained. This may be so, but as this is a relatively insensitive use of purchasing data it does not alter the fact that a high degree of exaggeration and distortion of purchasing behaviour is present in purchasing data obtained from single-call interviews; and for many of the studies of purchasing behaviour required from panel data such distortion would seriously affect the accuracy of the results obtained.

As well as the accuracy possible in panel techniques in obtaining the sheer volume of purchasing, or consumption habits, or television viewing data or whatever over time, there is also an advantage in comparison with interview surveys in the volume of ancillary data that can be obtained. This advantage is, as yet, relatively unexploited. Because a panel sample is by definition available over a long period these ancillary data can be collected, and perfected, at intervals and not cause respondent fatigue which might result from their collection at one point in time as would be necessary in single-call interview surveys. These ancillary data fall into two distinct categories:

(a) consumer classification data for the better identification of types of consumer behaviour. Into this category fall all the normal demographic characteristics of the consumer which would be collected as a matter of course in the recruitment of a panel. In addition there is a vast range of classification characteristics which might prove relevant to the purposes of the panel, the ownership of goods and services, leisure time activities, shopping habits, consumption habits, income and occupational categories, etc. It has also proved possible to obtain psychological or attitude classifications of panel members. The advantage of the panel technique is that classification data can be collected and tried by analysis for its relevance and usefulness in isolating consumer behaviour characteristics and, if found wanting, can be rejected or modified. It is a continuous process;

(b) ancillary data which is known, or suspected, to have an influence on consumer behaviour and therefore can be collected alongside the main data of the panel and applied to get a better understanding of the processes of consumer activity. Into this category comes the collection of readership and television-viewing data for application to consumer purchase panels, and holiday and other travel activities in relation to motorist panels.

As far as the collection of ancillary data from the single source of the panel is concerned, there is still a considerable potential to be tapped. This should be one of the major areas of development of panel techniques.

The Analysis of Panel Data

Panels, whether they are short-term or continuous, provide an almost indigestible mass of data which has to be translated into a limited amount of information which can be absorbed and acted upon. This is, of course, true of almost all research work but it is a particularly acute problem for panels simply because of the sheer volume of data flowing in as a continuous process. The efficient use of panels, therefore, lies in the standard and relevance of the analyses obtained from the data.

The analyses derived from the data of consumer purchasing panels can be conveniently divided into three groups:

(a) standard trend analyses produced at regular intervals, usually four weekly, which show the progress of the market and of its principal brands;
(b) 'simple' special analyses designed to show the anatomy of the characteristics of purchasing behaviour and of the consumers. These are not usually produced on a continuous basis but rather as and when required, usually when some significant change is thought to have occurred in the market which requires further study;
(c) 'complex' special analyses designed to examine the fundamental patterns of consumer behaviour, particularly in relation to specific bursts of major marketing activity.

The remainder of this section illustrates examples of analyses in the three groups.

Standard trend analyses

These differ in detail from one purchasing panel operation to another but are similar in purpose and provide the content of the basic reports. The normal reporting period is four weeks, long enough to provide enough data of significance to analyse and short enough to show trends while there is still time to take action. In special and urgent cases data may be produced on a weekly basis, but this is rare.

The analysis tables in the four weekly report shows the number of buyers in the total product field in the period and the buyers of each of the brands and subsections (if any) of the field. A similar table shows the total quantities purchased (again by brands) expressed in whatever quantity measure is most appropriate to the field—expenditure, weight, packets, standard units, etc. The current four-weekly period is usually shown alongside similar data from previous periods, going back for perhaps as long as a year, and this provides a ready reading of trends. Other data may also be shown in the report where this is relevant to the interpretation of the trends, such as the proportion of purchases made in different types of consumer promotions, etc.

The trend analyses of purchasing panel data are the essential preliminaries to all other panel analysis work. They provide the broad picture of the market but they are not the *raison d'être* of panels since similar information could be obtained from other research techniques, e.g., shop audits, regular 'ad hoc' surveys and they make no use of the real advantage of panels, their continuity of reporting.

'Simple' special analyses

The term 'simple' is derived not from the ease with which the analysis is provided (it may in fact be relatively difficult to provide) but from the nature of the information it supplies. The examples given here are not meant to provide a comprehensive list of the analyses that are possible but are meant to be illustrative of the range of analyses.

The first example, in Fig. 7.3, relates consumer demographic characteristics to purchasing behaviour. In this particular example it relates the weight of total self-raising flour purchases in 13 weeks to the age of housewife purchasers for the total market and one particular brand. The brand in question shows a higher average age of purchaser than the total market. This is a particularly simple example of the great range of consumer classification analyses possible from panel data. A second example is shown in Fig. 7.4, which relates the quantity of purchases of baby products in a 12 week period to whether the baby is the first, second, third, etc., in that family. Clearly, experience in bringing-up babies influences purchasing behaviour.

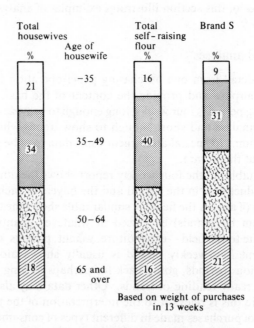

Fig. 7.3. Self-raising flour purchases, by age of housewife.

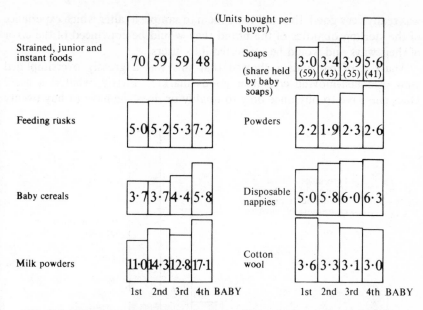

Fig. 7.4. The volume of purchases of a range of baby products related to whether the baby is the first child or not. Source: KBMS Baby Panel.

Panels habitually collect a lot of associated data about the item purchased—for example, the price paid, the day of the purchase, and the type of shop from which it was made and whether any promotions were involved. These data provide useful information.

In Fig. 7.5 a series of analyses have been summarized to show the trend in importance of the different types of outlets in the growth of a fast-moving food product. It shows clearly that the rate of growth of purchases of the product differs markedly from one type of outlet to another and gives a clear warning light to any brand which is not keeping pace in the outlets expanding at the fastest rate. It does, incidentally, give strength to the point made in the chapter on trade research of the importance of measuring a product in more than one type of outlet.

Another example, shown in Fig. 7.6, relates purchases of a food brand to the average price paid by the consumer and shows a clear elasticity of demand related to price. The brand was a premium priced product and it should be emphasized that the same degree of price elasticity might not be present for a lower priced brand in the same market or for any brands at all in some other product field.

'Simple' analyses begin to lose some of their simplicity once they get into the realm of defining 'users' and 'non-users' of a product. There was a time when many marketing men would divide their world quite simply into these two categories. The brand had a franchise, which could be termed 'users' and beyond them were a lot of people who could be termed 'non-users'. Marketing skill consisted of persuading the 'non-users' that your brand

165

was really very good, then inducing them to sample it, after which experience of the sterling qualities of the brand they would be convinced of the error of their ways and would be converted into 'users'.

Analysis of panel data showed that this was a grossly oversimplified view of a fast-moving consumer goods market. Firstly, what is a user? Does she have to buy once only to qualify or does she have to buy twenty

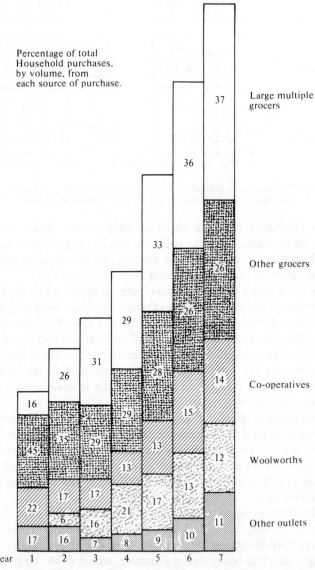

Fig. 7.5. Consumer purchases by type of outlet in a rapidly expanding food field. Source: Attwood Consumer Panel.

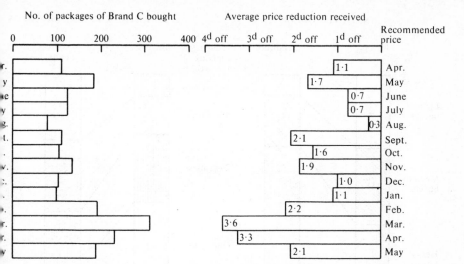

No. of packages of Brand C bought   Average price reduction received

	Average price reduction received	Recommended price
	1·1	Apr.
	1·7	May
	0·7	June
	0·7	July
	0·3	Aug.
	2·1	Sept.
	1·6	Oct.
	1·9	Nov.
	1·0	Dec.
	1·1	Jan.
	2·2	Feb.
	3·6	Mar.
	3·3	Apr.
	2·1	May

g. 7.6. The relationship of the volume of purchases of food Brand C to the average price paid by the consumer. Source: Attwood Consumer Panel.

times? Does she have to take all her purchases in the product field in your brand or only part of them—if part, then what proportion would you settle for? Secondly, how much substance is there in the belief that persuasion will induce trial, which will in turn induce loyalty to the brand? Experience shows that the trial/conversion process can happen when a significant innovation hits the market place, but that more often than not there is a constant battle for position going on between closely matched brands, with smallish strongholds being held on a long-term basis and much of the territory in a more or less fluid state, being held sometimes by one brand and at other times by another, and with no brand making permanent gain.

The following analysis examples illustrate some of the purchasing behaviour characteristics described above.

Figure 7.7 shows the frequency of purchase of buyers of instant coffee and the buyers of a brand of self-raising flour. In both cases it is a relatively small minority of buyers who account for a majority of total purchases of the product.

Figure 7.8 shows a measure of continuity of purchasing, i.e., a form of loyalty measurement, for a leading brand of toothpaste in which it will be seen that nearly half the quantity of the brand purchased in a six month period was accounted for by less than 20 per cent of the buyers who were 'loyal' to the brand, and that 46 per cent of the buyers were moving in or out of the market for the brand and accounted for only a small proportion of the total purchases.

The user/non-user concept of a market is replaced, therefore, in analysis terms by the two concepts of 'market penetration', i.e., those who buy the brand at least once in a given time period, and 'brand loyalty'. Brand

167

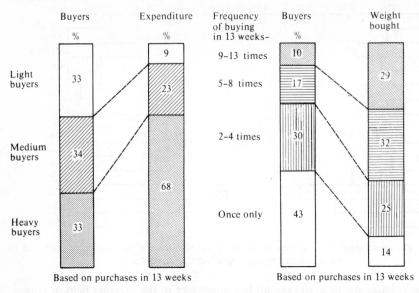

Fig. 7.7. Analyses of frequency of purchase—examples from instant coffee and self-raising flour Brand S. Source: Attwood Consumer Panel.

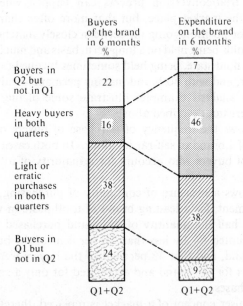

Fig. 7.8. Continuity of purchasing over a 6-month period—example of a brand leader in the toothpaste market. Source: Attwood Consumer Panel.

loyalty is subject to a number of interpretations depending upon the analyses used. The analysis of continuity of purchasing in Fig. 7.8 is a relatively crude definition, and the type of analysis which examines total purchases in a product field for each individual panel member in a given period of time and then expresses purchases of a given brand as a proportion of the total comes closer to an exact definition. This has its problems, however, since very light buyers tend to show brand loyalty merely because they have less opportunity to switch brands, and in this type of analysis need to be isolated from the heavier buyers.

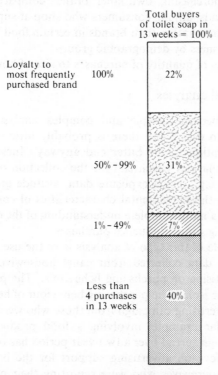

Fig. 7.9. The extent to which buyers of toilet soap are completely loyal to one brand in a 13-week period.
Source: Attwood Consumer Panel.

Figure 7.9, which shows the extent to which buyers of toilet soap are loyal to one brand, illustrates both the relatively limited extent of 100 per cent loyalty to a brand in a highly competitive market and, what we have already seen, that a high proportion of the buyers in any field accounts for only a small part of total purchases.

There are many other forms of special analyses, each designed to answer specific problems and the illustrations here are meant only to indicate a little of the possibilities of 'simple' analyses from panel data. Nothing has been said at all of many of the analysis types regularly produced from panel

169

data of which the following is a list of examples:

(a) purchases by size of pack;
(b) quantity of the product bought on each purchase occasion;
(c) day of the week on which purchases are made;
(d) extent to which different individual consumers purchase products with the same 'family' brand name, e.g., Lux, Ajax, Heinz, etc.;
(e) the limits of duplication between brands by which consumers confine their purchases to a limited group of the total brands available;
(f) the extent of purchasing 'own label' brands compared with nationally advertised brands, among consumers who shop at supermarkets;
(g) loyalty to flavours rather than brands in certain food fields;
(h) price consciousness by demographic groups;
(i) the relationship of quantity of purchases to size of household.

'Complex' special analyses

The dividing line between 'simple' and 'complex' analyses of panel data is not an easy one to define and there is probably little to be gained from pursuing the definition to the bitter end anyway. Included in the latter category are the analyses which call for the collection of special ancillary data from panels, e.g., media exposure data, attitude grouping data, etc., or which examine the fundamental characteristics of consumer behaviour for the purpose of a more complete understanding of the complex processes by which marketing stimuli influence purchases.

The first example of this type of analysis is of the use of readership and television viewing data collected from panel housewives to measure the influence of advertising on purchasing behaviour. The principle employed in this analysis is to isolate the purchasing behaviour of housewives exposed to a particular advertising campaign from those who were not.

In this particular example, involving a food product brand, a press advertising campaign spread over a two-year period has been superimposed on the normal television advertising support for the brand. A common sample of panel housewives who were reporting their purchases over the full two years has been selected and these have been classified according to their likely exposure to the advertising (based on their readership of the publications used in the campaign) into heavy, medium, light, and non-reader categories.

The purchases of the brand (in volume and market share) were measured in the quarter year prior to the start of the press campaign and in the same period in the two succeeding years, as shown in Table 7.6.

After the first year of the advertising campaign the volume of purchases and share indices have a consistent relationship with the amount of exposure to the press advertising—those not exposed showing a decline in purchases, those most exposed showing the greatest increase in purchases. By the end of the second year there had been an absolute decline in purchases of the

Table 7.6   The sales effect of a press campaign for brand X, by readership categories

	Total housewives		Heavy readers		Medium readers		Light readers		Non-readers	
	Volume of purchases	Brand share index	Volume	Brand share	Volume	Brand share	Volume	Brand share	Volume	Brand share
Q4 1964*	100	100	100	100	100	100	100	100	100	100
Q4 1965	106	105	115	116	112	109	104	106	96	95
Q4 1966	91	97	107	112	102	111	75	84	90	91

* Before press campaign began.

Source: Attwood Consumer Panel, Great Britain.

brand for reasons beyond the control of this particular press campaign. The only groups whose purchases have not fallen below the 1964 level are the heavy and medium reader groups. It would seem that in the second year light readership was not sufficient to counteract the tendency for purchases of the brand to decline.

There is a further analysis which has been extracted for this study and this relates to the relative effectiveness of the press advertising on housewives who have (or have not) been exposed heavily to the television advertising for the same brand. The television advertising is a relatively common element running through the whole period of the study, including the period before the press campaign began (Q.4, 1964). Table 7.7 illustrates this analysis. The readership groups have been split into two (rather than four) in the interests of sample size.

Almost all the increase in purchases among the heavy and medium reading groups is confined to those who had *not* already been exposed heavily to the television advertising. The implication of this is that the television advertising had already raised the level of purchasing of its heavy viewers as far as it was likely to go before the press campaign began. Certainly, the general level of purchases of the heavy and medium ITV viewers was some 10 per cent higher than that for the light and non-ITV viewers before the press campaign began.

The second analysis example is drawn from relating an attitudinal classification of panel housewives to their purchasing behaviour. The principle adopted in this approach is that housewives with identical demographic

Table 7.7   The trend of purchases of brand X by the volume of exposure to the TV and press advertising

Readership:	Heavy and medium readers				Light and non-readers			
Television:	Heavy and medium viewers		Light and non-viewers		Heavy and medium viewers		Light and non-viewers	
	Volume	Share	Volume	Share	Volume	Share	Volume	Share
Q4 1964*	100	100	100	100	100	100	100	100
Q4 1965	105	105	123	119	97	99	105	103
Q4 1966	96	104	113	119	83	91	80	83

* Before the press campaign began.

Source: Attwood Consumer Panel, Great Britain.

characteristics show considerable differences in purchasing behaviour and it is possible and, indeed, likely that these relate to differences in fundamental attitudes to activities like shopping, housework, cooking, trying new products, etc., which in their turn reflect in their purchasing behaviour. If this hypothesis is correct, and the attitudes which relate to the differences in the purchasing behaviour can be measured, this will have an important bearing not only in understanding the marketing approach to be made to purchasers of a particular product but also in identifying where potential purchasers are most likely to be found. Table 7.8 shows an analysis based on experimental work on the Attwood Consumer Panel where two types of floor and furniture polish (wax and aerosol) show similar demographic profiles among purchasers but strongly contrasting attitude profiles. This type of analysis is represented in the continuous consumer panel services at the present time only by experimental work; it is not offered as a regular service but it is an important indicator of the direction in which these services can develop in the future. There are, of course, limits to the extent to which attitude data can be collected in the permanent panels without conditioning future purchasing behaviour; but general attitude data not related directly to questions on brand or product purchasing are certainly well within these limits. Such limitations do not apply to short-term panels, where the attitude questioning is confined to interviewing immediately after the end of the panel operation, and this service is regularly applied in short-term panels to provide an additional dimension in the interpretation of the purchasing data.

Table 7.8   Social class and attitude to housework profiles of purchasers of two types of polish

	Social class				Attitude to housework scale				
	AB	C	D1	D2E	1 Very traditional	2	3	4	5 Modern- minded
Proportion of housewives buying:			100 =	Average	level of buying of the polish types				
Wax polish	134	111	94	93	110	110	105	84	68
Aerosol polish	170	110	98	85	45	91	100	109	146

Source: Attwood Consumer Panel, Great Britain.

The remaining examples of 'complex' analysis of panel data are derived from the study of the underlying patterns of consumer purchasing behaviour using a model which predicts future market share by measuring the likely penetration and the likely repeat purchasing rate for the brand under study. The analysis was originally devised to predict the share of newly launched brands but has since been developed to study the longer term effects of promotions, or advertising campaigns, or other marketing activity for established brands.

The launch of 'Signal' toothpaste is shown in the next example. Figure 7.10 shows the penetration and repeat purchasing rate achieved by the

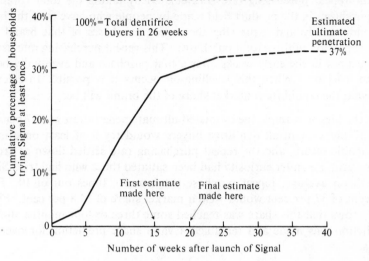

CUMULATIVE PENETRATION OF SIGNAL

Cumulative percentage of households trying Signal at least once

100%=Total dentifrice buyers in 26 weeks

Estimated ultimate penetration 37%

First estimate made here

Final estimate made here

Number of weeks after launch of Signal

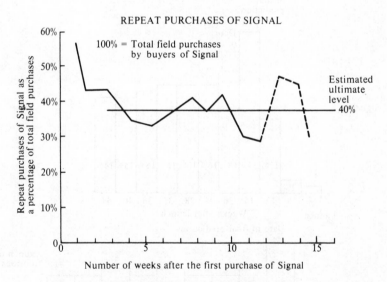

REPEAT PURCHASES OF SIGNAL

Repeat purchases of Signal as a percentage of total field purchases

100% = Total field purchases by buyers of Signal

Estimated ultimate level 40%

Number of weeks after the first purchase of Signal

Fig. 7.10. The cumulative penetration and repeat-purchasing rate for Signal in the period immediately after its launch.

brand in the weeks following the launch of the brand. They show two characteristics which are common to virtually all analyses of this kind:

(a) after a time the cumulative penetration of the brand, i.e., the number of people buying the brand for the first time, shows a declining rate of increase. Once the shape of the curve is determined and a declining rate of increase is observed, it is possible to make a reasonable estimate of the ultimate likely penetration;

173

(b) the repeat purchasing rate is calculated by taking the total volume of purchases in the product field made by people who have tried the brand under study and expressing the repeat purchases of that brand as a proportion of these total purchases. This repeat purchasing rate usually declines in the early weeks after a first purchase and eventually begins to level off. When this levelling-off occurs it is possible to calculate what the equilibrium market share of the brand will be.

In the Signal example the estimated ultimate penetration was 37 per cent, i.e., 37 per cent of all dentifrice buyers would try it at least once in the reasonable future, and the repeat purchasing rate settled down at around 40 per cent, i.e., after curiosity had been satiated those who had tried Signal would, on average, repeat purchase the brand 4 times out of 10. Forty per cent of 37 per cent would yield a market share of 14.8 per cent. Figure 7.11 shows that this share was reached some three or four months after the prediction was made and remained a valid share prediction for over two years.

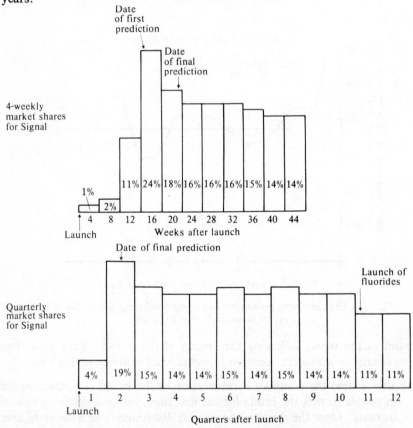

Fig. 7.11. The extent of validity of the brand share prediction made for Signal.
Source: Attwood Consumer Panel.

174

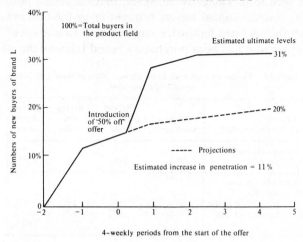

CUMULATIVE PENETRATION OF BRAND L

100% = Total buyers in the product field

Estimated ultimate levels

31%

Introduction of '50% off' offer

20%

----- Projections

Estimated increase in penetration = 11%

4-weekly periods from the start of the offer

Fig. 7.12. The effect of a 50% price cut on the cumulative penetration of detergent Brand L. Source: Attwood Consumer Panel.

There are a number of refinements and qualifications to this analysis which were not included in this early example and there is not space in this chapter to deal with them. Readers who wish to pursue them should read the published work on this subject[3].

The product of the penetration × repeat purchase analysis has proved to give a forward estimate of market share which has been found to be very reliable in frequently-purchased product categories. The accumulation of many examples of the analysis has also contributed to a greater understanding of the way consumer purchasing responds to marketing stimuli. In particular, one 'rule' that has emerged has important implications. This 'rule' is that on average the later a buyer enters the market for a brand for the first time the lower her repeat purchasing rate will be and the smaller the contribution to the future brand share. Thus, it can be concluded that any attempt to improve the penetration of a brand, e.g., with a particularly attractive promotion, will not yield a repeat purchasing rate for buyers brought in by the promotion higher than the rate of the marginal buyers existing before the promotion began; and in all probability it will be lower.

An example to illustrate this concept is taken from an established detergent brand, brand L. In the normal way the brand would penetrate about 20 per cent of the buyers in the market in, say, a six month period and achieve an average repeat purchasing rate of 25 per cent (which would be normal in a highly competitive relatively disloyal market with five or six major brands to choose from) thus indicating that its market share is around five per cent. In this example a 50 per cent price-cut promotion was introduced and Fig. 7.12 illustrates the effect of this on the cumulative penetration of the brand, with an increase from 20 to 31 per cent.

175

It will be seen from Table 7.9, however, that the repeat purchasing rate of the 11 per cent additional buyers brought in by the offer was only four per cent after the offer had finished, compared with an average of 25 per cent for those buyers who had been purchasing brand L before the offer began.

Table 7.9   The contribution made to the ultimate share of brand L by buyers introduced by the offer

BRAND L (50% price cut offer)	Ultimate penetration	×	Repeat purchasing rate	×	Buying rate index	=	Ultimate brand share
Before introduction of the offer	20%	×	25%	×	1.03	=	5.15%
After introduction of the offer buyers before offer buyers after offer	20% 11%	× ×	25% 4%	× ×	1.03 1.01	= =	5.15% 0.45% 5.60%

Thus, the offer produced a 55 per cent increase in penetration (which would have produced a large temporary increase in brand share at the time of the offer) and only an 8.5 per cent increase in brand share after the offer. This is not to say that that was an unsatisfactory result for the offer but purely that the long-term effects, measured in terms of repeat purchasing, are very much more subdued than the immediate increase in penetration would suggest. There is also reason to believe that the immediate penetration effects of marketing activity are not necessarily a very good guide to the strength of the longer-term effects; a promotion, for instance, that yields a relatively high immediate increase in penetration does not necessarily make the biggest contribution to the longer term strengthening of that brand's market share.

The Continuous Study of the Underlying Patterns of Consumer Purchasing Behaviour

Somewhere locked in the panel data accumulated over the years lie the answers to a range of marketing questions. Some important work has been carried out to extract the essence of these data and find marketing 'laws', e.g., Ehrenberg[4] but for the most part the more sophisticated analysis of panel data has been carried out primarily to pursue specific and 'limited' objectives, such as to predict the future share of a new brand or to measure the sales effect of a particular advertising campaign. The analyses have been relatively expensive to carry out and, therefore, no attempt has been made to introduce them as a matter of course at each point of major change in advertising, promotion, etc. A data bank of case histories in a particular market would reveal far more of the fundamental factors influencing purchasing behaviour in that market than the occasional isolated analysis, however sophisticated. The increasing use of panel raw data for computer analysis by client companies must eventually lead to this situation and, assuming that the appropriate ancillary data mentioned in this chapter is also by then regularly available, panels will at long last be used to their full advantage. Panel analysis will then fully serve its dual purpose, to provide:

(a) immediate data on the development of trends and consumer characteristics in the market—the traditional rôle of panels;
(b) the more fundamental data on how consumers react to given marketing activity to determine how they are likely to react to future marketing activity.

References

1. PARFITT, J. H. A Comparison of Purchase Recall with Diary Panel Records, *Journal of Advertising Research*, **7**, 3, Sept., 1967.
   Also *How Accurately can Product Purchasing Behaviour be Measured by Recall at a Single Interview?*, Paper 26, ESOMAR, Vienna Congress, August, 1967.
2. BROADBENT, S. and MOONEY, P. *Can Informant Claims on Product Purchase made at an Interview be used for Media Planning?* Paper 14, ESOMAR, Opatija Congress, Sept., 1968.
3. COLLINS, B. J. K. and PARFITT, J. H. The use of Consumer Panels for Brand-Share Prediction, *Journal of Marketing Research*, **V**, May 1968.
   McGLOUGHLIN, I. and PARFITT, J. H. *The use of Consumer Panels in the evaluation of promotional and advertising expenditure*, Paper 28, ESOMAR, Opatija Congress, Sept., 1968.
4. EHRENBERG, A. S. C. *Pack-Size Rates of Purchasing*, Paper 33, ESOMAR, Opatija Congress, Sept., 1968.
   EHRENBERG, A. S. C. The Practical Meaning and Usefulness of the NBD/LSD Theory of Repeat-Buying, *Applied Statistics*, **17**, 1968.
   EHRENBERG, A. S. C. The Discovery and Use of Laws of Marketing, *Journal of Marketing*, **32**, 1968.

8. Omnibus surveys

J. P. H. Kendall

The fieldwork costs for most market research surveys are very high. In some surveys, they can reach 80 per cent of the total expenditure. A more detailed examination will reveal that these costs are incurred almost entirely in making contact with the respondent, whereas the length of the eventual interview will only marginally influence expenditure. In other words, a survey amongst 2000 women, asking one question only, will cost almost as much as a survey of similar design and sample size, asking 30 questions. This situation arises because the majority of interviewer time is taken up in travelling to the place of interview and attempting to make contact with the respondent, and only a relatively small percentage with the actual questioning. It is primarily the relatively high costs of making contact and the insensitivity of costs to the length of the questionnaire, which have given rise to what are called omnibus or syndicated surveys.

An omnibus survey is similar to an 'ad hoc' survey with the exception that the questionnaire, instead of being devoted entirely to one research project, is made up of a number of sub-questionnaires, each one being a survey in its own right. These sub-questionnaires, with a few reservations indicated below, can be on entirely different subjects and deal with different aspects of those subjects. By this device it is possible to share the costs of interviewer time between several different surveys and thereby very substantially reduce the expenditure on each project. Although cost is the main reason for the development and use of this kind of survey, there are other reasons for using them which are indicated later in this chapter. Furthermore, omnibus surveys are defined here in a fairly narrow sense and there are associated areas which are considered briefly in the section below called 'Other Forms of Syndicated Research'.

As is frequently the case with cost saving ideas, particular care must be taken to ensure that these are genuine savings and that in the end an even greater expenditure has not been involved. Whilst there are many market research problems which can be solved using these approaches, there are also problems where the omnibus survey would not be appropriate, even though at first sight it may appear to offer a cheaper alternative. The major part of this chapter is concerned with indicating the advantages and disadvantages of this type of survey, and to assist the reader in deciding whether the omnibus survey is appropriate for his particular problem.

Basic Methods of Operation

In theory it would be possible for any researcher to set up an omnibus survey. All that is required would be to find a number of other researchers concurrently planning a survey with similar sample designs and to create one master questionnaire from the individual questionnaires. In practice, the problems of obtaining agreement on all aspects of the survey design and the financial commitment involved are such that few individual researchers would attempt this. The field is left to market research companies who, by weighing up the likely demands and offering space on a master questionnaire, carry out the planning, fieldwork and analysis of these omnibus surveys themselves. These research companies usually undertake their omnibus surveys at frequent intervals on a standard sample size and design. The researcher can, therefore, select from a range of such services the sample design and timing that he believes to be most appropriate. The services offered by research companies vary widely, in terms of the frequency with which they carry out these surveys, the sample size, the type of sample interviewed and the methods of working. (A list of actual examples can be found at the end of this chapter.)

Most research companies place certain restrictions, particularly on the type and number of questions which can be asked on their omnibus surveys. The restrictions vary from company to company and it would be necessary in practice to check with each research company. Such areas which should be considered are:

(a) the number of questions permitted;
(b) use of prompt cards and other additional materials;
(c) number of code positions permitted;
(d) confidentiality of results;
(e) position in the master questionnaire;
(f) classification details that can be collected;
(g) range of cross analysis available.

The above method of operation, whereby a research company offers service to the clients and takes the risk of not filling the questionnaire, is by far the most common method of operating omnibus surveys. One other approach is the research company undertaking a survey on a particular project but willing to allow one or two additional clients to add questions to the end of their questionnaire. This is most common where the major research project is a continuous one and, therefore, the company is able to offer the service at regular intervals. This can be considered similar to the normal omnibus surveys with one of the clients having a substantial part of the questionnaire.

Aspects of Design

Questionnaire

Questionnaire design has been fully examined in chapter 4 and it is assumed that the reader is aware of the major problems. There are some aspects peculiar to omnibus surveys which are considered here in more detail.

The first point to remember when designing questions for an omnibus survey is that the questions will be appearing with many others, often in completely different fields. Unless the questions happen to be first in the master questionnaire, for example, the final question from the previous research will occur immediately before the researcher's questions. It is, therefore, advisable to begin the questions for any particular subject with an opening indicating to the respondent that the following questions will be in a new field. The following sequence of questions could occur if attention is not paid to this particular point.

Q   Which of the following brands of toothpaste have you heard of? (Show list.)

Q   And which brand of toothpaste did you last purchase?

Q   And could you tell me the names of all the brands of toothpaste that you have in the house at present?

Q   Have you flown in an aircraft in the last twelve months? If 'No', go to Question 12. If 'Yes' ask:

Q   On the last occasion that you flew in an aircraft, from where and to where did you fly?

The above questions may have appeared perfectly reasonable to the client interested in toothpaste usage and the client interested in obtaining travel information, but to the respondent, the switch without warning from one subject to another, is liable to create considerable confusion, and will undoubtedly effect the accuracy of his response. The use of an opening paragraph, 'I would now like to change the subject and talk about something completely different . . .' can help this difficulty, but the reader should always remain aware of this problem.

Even where there is an adequate introduction to any changes of subject in the questionnaire, it is clearly desirable to keep these changes to a minimum. This is largely the task of the research company offering the syndicated service to arrange this, so that clients may find their questions refused for a particular period or placed in such a position in the questionnaire so as to avoid clashing with another client. Although this is usually carried out responsibly by the research company, it is advisable for the client to try to check which product field is being used immediately before and immediately after their particular questions. This is sometimes difficult as, for reasons of confidentiality, the research company may not be willing to disclose details of other clients.

Invariably, the more complicated the question technique, the less likely it is that an omnibus survey will be adequate. It is difficult to be exact as the complexity of other questions in the questionnaire is relevant. An interviewer should be able to handle one or two difficult questions but there is clearly a limit, particularly if each client uses different types of questions. There is also a limit to the amount of additional material an interviewer can carry around with her in the form of prompt cards, samples and so on. It is, therefore, particularly desirable to use the simplest possible questions when using omnibus surveys, even if this involves increasing the total number of questions.

Coding

Coding problems are similar to those used for ordinary 'ad hoc' surveys. It should be remembered that most research companies will charge for the number of positions used on the coding of their questionnaires. The costs involved are usually relatively small and it would be an unwise researcher who limited the amount of coding he required merely on the grounds of cost. Unlike an 'ad hoc' survey where the client can leave the coding entirely to the research company, in an omnibus survey the client should be prepared to define the exact coding positions he requires at the same time as indicating the questionnaire requirements. He should also make his requirements on whether, for open-ended questions, the questionnaire should be pre-coded or whether coding should be carried out after the interview.

Analysis

In theory, it is possible to undertake any form of analysis on an omnibus survey which would be feasible on an ordinary 'ad hoc' survey. In practice, the researcher is advised to use the standard analysis package offered by the company if he is to keep within reasonable costs. Most research companies operating omnibus surveys will offer, at very low cost, an analysis giving most standard breakdowns; most will charge a substantial additional fee for any analysis required which is not of a standard pattern. Furthermore, the requirements for additional analysis tend to effect the timing of results as well as the overall costs. If additional analysis is required, it is recommended that this be kept separate from the main body of the report and issued at a separate time, otherwise the client will find that his major results are delayed awaiting more detailed analysis.

Sampling

The primary problem facing the user of omnibus surveys in the area of sampling is that to all intents and purposes the sample is decided and fixed by the research company offering the service and the client cannot make modifications. This raises problems both in the areas of the design of the sample and in the selection of respondents. As far as the design is concerned, in the author's experience, the sampling design of omnibus surveys tends to be less rigorous than some used in 'ad hoc' surveys. This does not imply inaccuracies as there are many different approaches possible in sampling presenting equally satisfactory alternatives. However, any particular problem may demand certain requirements from the sample or, at least, indicate a priority in forming the sample frame. The number of call-backs made on a random sample, for example, can vary from none to as many as five, depending on the requirements of the sampling design. Clearly, a survey which is concerned with a problem relating to the absence from the home of the individual to be interviewed (such as a survey into the habits of the working woman) will have a high priority for as many call-backs as possible. However, a survey into the brand image of different dog foods might not place multiple recalls with as high a priority.

It is always possible for the researcher to look at the various alternative omnibus surveys and select one that comes nearest to his requirements, and in most countries there are a range of surveys offered. Unfortunately, by their very nature these surveys tend to be designed on the basis of the average requirement. There is a tendency not to satisfy any individual requirements particularly if they are slightly out of the ordinary. It cannot be too strongly emphasized that the researcher should be prepared to investigate fully the exact sample specifications of the various omnibus surveys and not assume that, since there are many other reputable companies using the survey, it necessarily fills his own particular requirements.

As an omnibus survey is likely to be repeated at frequent intervals with the same sample design, it is possible for a research company to examine the design and to rectify inaccuracies or, at least, give an indication of the errors involved. This is usually not possible on an 'ad hoc' survey, partly by virtue of the fact that only one survey will take place, also because the total costs of any particular additional analysis must be borne on that one survey, whereas for an omnibus survey the costs can be spread over several surveys.

Interviewers

Since the research company is operating the omnibus survey on a continuous basis, it should be particularly easy for the company to recruit and train competent interviewers. Yet, probably because one of the prime reasons for using omnibus surveys is the cost element, interviewers used for them do not always measure up to those used in 'ad hoc' surveys. The researcher should question the research company in depth on the interviewers they use and their method of operating. There is an undesirable tendency for interviewers, for example, not to receive a personal briefing on the omnibus survey. To some extent this can be justified as the interviewers will have become fully acquainted with the omnibus survey problems and therefore a personal briefing is not so essential. In the author's opinion, there will still be problems on most questionnaires which warrant a briefing directly between the executive organizing the survey and the interviewers.

Costs

It will have been apparent from the beginning of this chapter that the primary reason for using an omnibus survey is to save money. Figure 8.1 below indicates for a typical survey of varying questionnaire length the appropriate expenditure for that survey if it was carried out on an 'ad hoc' basis or on an omnibus survey basis. It will be noticed that there will be a point when the questionnaire becomes so long that, even from a cost point of view, it is cheaper to do the survey on an 'ad hoc' basis.

Cost of omnibus versus 'ad hoc' surveys

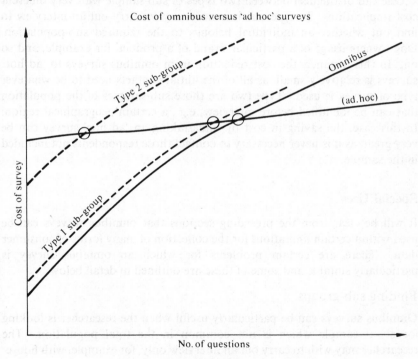

Fig. 8.1. Cost of omnibus versus 'ad hoc' surveys.

Although costing systems vary from company to company, most companies operate on the following principles:

(a) a basic joining charge, usually about £50 to £100;
(b) a cost per question, sometimes with a discount for a number of questions;
(c) a cost for each position of coding—usually not very large in relation to (a) and (b);
(d) additional costs for extra analysis, extra reports, open-ended questions, and so on.

183

Care should be taken by the researchers to ensure they have included costs which may not at first appear relevant. It is essential, for example, to define the universe to be sampled before approaching the various companies. In an 'ad hoc' survey it is often possible to restrict the survey entirely to the required population, at least after the initial contact. In an omnibus survey, it is usually necessary to pay for the total sample covered and, if the required sample is a small percentage of the total, then the costs will rise proportionally for the omnibus survey as is indicated by the dotted lines on the graph above. It will be noted that the researcher should not reject omnibus surveys purely on the grounds that the interviewing will take place on a wider sample than is required for his particular research. It may still be cheaper to use the omnibus survey rather than the 'ad hoc' approach.

One can distinguish between two types of sub-sample with very different cost implications. In type one it is necessary to carry out an interview to find out whether an individual belongs to the required sub-population. Dog-owners usage of a particular brand of a product, for example, and so on. In this instance, the cost reduction from omnibus surveys to 'ad hoc' surveys is relatively small, as all of the initial contacts need to be whatever type of survey is used. Type two are those sub-samples of the population that can be identified before interview, e.g., a certain geographical region. In this case, the saving in cost by undertaking an 'ad hoc' survey can be very great, as it is never necessary to contact those respondents not included in the sample.

Special Uses

It will be clear from the preceding sections that omnibus surveys can be used within certain limitations for the collection of many forms of consumer data. There are certain problems for which an omnibus survey is particularly suitable and some of these are outlined in detail below.

Finding sub-groups

Omnibus surveys can be particularly useful when the researcher is looking for a sub-sample which is not common in the total population. The researcher may wish to carry out an interview only, for example, with house-wives who own a particular type of washing machine. Clearly, in these instances it is extremely expensive to find the sub-groups by means of an 'ad hoc' survey as the total number of contacts will have to be very large indeed. It is possible to ask questions concerning the attributes (which in the above sample would be the type of washing machine owned) on an omnibus survey where the sample is large. In this way, the costs of finding a sub-group may be very significantly reduced. Having obtained a sub-sample of the required type, it is possible to carry out the interview with this sample on the omnibus survey itself or, because of the restrictions already outlined in relation to omnibus surveys, it may be necessary to carry out a second interview. The costs of the second interview will be substantially reduced in that the interviewer will have a list of respondents known to belong to that particular sub-group. The cost savings of this mode of operation are not always as large as might at first sight appear, for two reasons; first, the members of the sub-group will be geographically widespread in accordance with the original omnibus survey sample and so a considerable amount of travel will be necessary at the second interview; second, not every member interviewed on the first occasion will be available because of absence or refusal at the second interview. If the respondent can be given a questionnaire to return by post at the first interview, so that no second interview is needed, these reservations do not apply and a substantial cost saving may be made.

Sequential or cumulative sampling

Since most omnibus surveys are carried out on a continuous basis, it is possible to build up a very large sample by adding the same questions to a series of consecutive omnibus surveys. This is of value when building up a sub-group of the population (as above) in order to obtain a sufficiently large sample for accurate measurement.

A second use of omnibus surveys in this area is one which, at least in theory, could save substantial expenditure. Most surveys are carried out to estimate the proportion of the population or a sub-group of the population which have a particular attribute or make a particular comment. This estimate is subject to sampling error which depends on the sample size and the actual population proportion being estimated. This latter statistic is usually unknown. By using an omnibus survey series it is possible to cumulate samples until a sufficiently large sample is obtained to give the required degree of accuracy. As soon as this degree of accuracy has been achieved no further purchases of omnibus survey space are made. The risk of having a sample that is too small and with an insufficient degree of accuracy, or a sample which is unnecessarily large incurring a considerable excess cost, is avoided. This approach appears to be rarely used in practice. Probably this is partly because most surveys include a range of estimates each requiring different sample sizes and partly because the time of the survey would be seriously delayed by waiting for repeat results in order to make the accumulation. Finally, another reason may be the unfortunate, but general, lack of interest in the degree of accuracy of the results obtained.

Experimental designs

In chapter 2 the many aspects of experimental design are outlined in detail. It is worth noting that a number of these designs are easily incorporated into the omnibus survey and some market research companies offer such designs as part of their standard omnibus survey. The simple experiment, for example, of a split-run between two samples to test, say, an alternative form of question can be easily incorporated into an omnibus survey. The advantage in using omnibus surveys for this type of experiment lies primarily in the availability of the design. Again, many researchers use them as a form of pilot survey for their main research project.

Unfortunately, the facilities for such experiments are limited by the omnibus operators themselves and the researcher will find considerable degrees of difference between the various omnibus research companies in the extent to which they can carry out the more complicated forms of experimental design. Where an omnibus survey does include these facilities, the actual design should be checked to ensure that it is adequate, for example, when a research company offers a split-run facility, the researcher should examine carefully the method used by the research company for obtaining the two matched samples as it may be found that their method does not adequately match the sample in terms of the variable to be measured. An example of this occurs when the sample is split by sampling points so that there is a tendency for different interviewers to be involved in the two matched samples, as opposed to the alternative method where each interviewer alternates between the two variations. Clearly, any problem concerned with measuring the effect of interviewer bias between two questions will not be so adequately measured by the former of these two approaches.

Time series

Many problems require a variable to be measured over a period of time; for example, a researcher may be interested in the purchasing trend for a particular product; or, he may wish to measure average purchases over a period of time where he suspects the purchase rate varies from one time period to another. In both examples, it is then necessary to undertake a continuous series of surveys. The omnibus survey may well be the cheapest and easiest form of research for both. The advantages of cost and organization are more in favour of the omnibus survey although there are the same restrictions as usual on the number and type of questions.

It is important to distinguish two types of fieldwork timing offered by market research companies. Some companies carry out literally continuous interviewing every day, every week, and every month. Other surveys are repeated at given intervals but the interviewing is not evenly spread out over that interval; for example, the interviewing for a monthly omnibus survey may be carried out in the first week of each month. When using omnibus surveys to obtain time series, it is clearly necessary to obtain these details on the timing of fieldwork.

Advantages and Disadvantages

Already a number of advantages and disadvantages have been indicated to the reader. In this section there is a summary of the major advantages and disadvantages of omnibus surveys.

Summary of advantages

The primary advantage to the researcher in the use of an omnibus survey is that within the limitations of the number and complexity of questions, there will be a substantial saving in cost compared with carrying out the survey on an 'ad hoc' basis. Another important advantage is that the use of omnibus surveys can often be carried out more quickly. First of all, the work of preparation before undertaking the fieldwork can be considerably reduced since the sampling and fieldwork will have already been organized, unlike an 'ad hoc' survey where it is often necessary to begin with a newly designed sample and to make special arrangements for fieldwork. Second, because the survey is usually spread over a number of clients, it is possible to use more interviewers, so reducing the fieldwork time. This is particularly true when a very large sample is required as, in 'ad hoc' surveys, interviewing may have to be spread over a long period of time in order to avoid over-loading the fieldwork staff. Third, analysis of results is usually quicker after the survey has finished because a greater degree of automation in the production of results is possible. The saving in time here is probably not very substantial, particularly if the alternative 'ad hoc' research company is selected for their ability to produce fast results. Finally, a certain degree of 'bottle-necking' occurs in availability of interviewers for 'ad hoc' projects with the result that a researcher may have to wait until there is vacant fieldwork time. With omnibus surveys it is usually possible to commission an immediate survey.

The design of an omnibus survey should be reliable as it will have been used by a substantial number of different companies. Thus, the various aspects of design of the surveys will have been examined critically by a wide number of people. This is particularly useful for the researcher who does does not have time to go into the facilities and reliability of a particular research company in detail. This may occur in international research where research is conducted at some distance from the country concerned. In theory, this should be a substantial advantage for the researcher as it is rarely possible for him to examine in great detail the sample design of a particular research company for an 'ad hoc' project. However, the author should add in caution that, in his experience, whereas the variation in quality between different omnibus surveys is less than the variation obtained in undertaking an 'ad hoc' project, it is not true to say that the omnibus research designs are in general any better. Indeed, there is some evidence that the design of these surveys is less efficient than for some 'ad hoc' projects. Omnibus surveys do, to some extent serve to ensure the researcher that he does not undertake a survey using a particularly inferior design although it does not act, as might be hoped, as a guarantee that the research design is more than adequate.

Because the research company is carrying out a continuous series of these omnibus surveys, it is possible for the company to invest a substantial amount in their design, particularly in the area of sample design. Furthermore, it is possible for the research company to indicate the effect of errors contained within their particular sample design because they will have already carried out a series of tests. Thus, for example, it will probably be possible for an omnibus research company to indicate the clustering of the sample design. This advantage of carrying out the research on a continuous basis should enable them to improve not only aspects of sampling but also such problems as the production of reports, analysis of results, training of interviewers and so on.

Another advantage of omnibus surveys occurs when a researcher is interested in carrying out multi-national research. Partly because the survey operator is able to invest in the design of his surveys it is simpler to operate a similar service in a number of different countries. It is, therefore, possible to use the omnibus survey approach in different countries, virtually simultaneously, and to obtain results which would be more nearly comparable than if an 'ad hoc' survey was undertaken in each individual country.

Summary of disadvantages

The most obvious limitation of the omnibus survey is the number of questions which can be asked on it. First, in order to achieve a cost saving, the number of questions must be restricted or it will be as cheap to undertake a full scale 'ad hoc' survey. Second, because the omnibus survey operator is unlikely to allow any one client to dominate a particular questionnaire, there may well be a limitation on the number of questions permitted by one client. Finally, of course, there is a limit to the total length of a questionnaire used by an omnibus operator and this in itself may limit the individual users. A second disadvantage closely associated with this is the inability of the omnibus survey to handle complex questions. Some researchers claim that any question can be asked in a simple form. However, most would agree that there are a number of problems which are best solved with a more complex type of question. In addition, the more complex questions may entail supplementary equipment such as prompt cards and this in itself is usually restricted on an omnibus survey.

Any survey that involves carrying around any substantial quantity of material, such as products for placement or advertisements for testing, may well put a burden on the interviewers which they would be unable to handle. This bars a number of types of research project from using the omnibus survey approach.

Any survey requiring an unusual or specific sample design is not suitable for an omnibus survey as no operator can adapt the sample design for any individual user. Similarly, if a particular target is required the omnibus survey may not be the best way of achieving it. However, in both these cases it is possible that a sub-group of the total omnibus survey will give the required results and it may be cheaper to use an omnibus survey and to discard unnecessary information.

188

Any other peculiarity in the total survey design that is essential to a particular project may, of course, prohibit its use on an omnibus survey; for example, a survey requiring a series of interviews with the same respondent will be unlikely to be suitable. Requirements for specific fieldwork dates are another example, although some companies will permit questions for part of the fieldwork period.

Although in theory it should be possible to receive as detailed a report and as comprehensive an analysis from an omnibus as from an individual 'ad hoc' survey, in general, if such a facility is required it is probably more advisable to use an 'ad hoc' survey. The operators of an omnibus survey do not usually wish to give an extensive analysis service other than the normal forms of analysis which are required for most surveys and they do not usually wish to give a detailed marketing report. Furthermore, the type of executives who operate such surveys are not necessarily the researchers who would be required for a more detailed and extensive analysis of the problem.

Problems to watch

In addition to the disadvantages outlined above, there are a few other problems in the use of omnibus surveys of which the user of this type of research should be aware. One of these is the omnibus survey operator who is offering a service which is not fully operational. Some research companies, in order to set up an omnibus survey on a working basis without initially investing funds in that service, form their first few omnibus surveys by attempting to persuade clients to join before they have finally made it a viable proposition. In some instances this may be the only practical way of getting a survey operational, e.g., an unusual minority group survey. Unfortunately, some research companies do not make it clear whether the omnibus surveys offered are going concerns or of the nature mentioned above. It is, therefore, possible for a researcher to place questions on an omnibus survey which, for various different reasons, never actually takes place. Although the researcher is unlikely to involve himself in any expenditure, it is more than probable that he will have difficulty in maintaining his timetable. The researcher should always enquire from the research company the status of the omnibus survey and, if possible, obtain some guarantee that the survey will take place even if sufficient clients are not forthcoming.

The next problem concerns the sampling frame used by the research company. Particular care should be taken by the researcher to ensure that the sample is as required and no researcher should ever assume that any particular omnibus survey will match his own particular requirements. For some reason, researchers appear to accept research company statements about the design of omnibus surveys far more readily than if they were carrying out an 'ad hoc' survey themselves. This may be because they would be

189

unable to change the system even if they found it was unsatisfactory; although, of course, they are always at liberty to move to another omnibus operating company. However, even if the researcher continues to use that omnibus survey it may be possible to make an allowance for differences between what is required and what is actually happening. The researcher, for example, might require adults over the age of 21 whereas the omnibus survey might contain all adults over the age of 15. In this instance, it would be extremely simple for the researcher to deal with the difference but only if he realized that such a difference existed.

Another problem requiring care has already been outlined in some detail previously, i.e., the positioning of the questions within the omnibus questionnaire. The researcher should always discuss with the omnibus company ways of overcoming the difficulties of positioning effects of these questions and should ensure that his questions do not suffer from the fact that they are on an omnibus survey. Far too often the research company is left to choose the layout of the questionnaire itself and the result is that in many instances questions are placed in inappropriate places.

One final problem worth mentioning is that, in the experience of the author, a number of omnibus surveys are operated on a less efficient basis than the average 'ad hoc' survey, although this is difficult to establish in practice. Exactly why this should be so is difficult to determine, as one would expect that the investment possible on an omnibus survey would enable the many aspects of design, such as sampling, to be more critically examined than in most 'ad hoc' surveys. The probable reason for this is that omnibus surveys are still regarded by a number of researchers as a form of cheap research. For some reason they are willing to accept a lower standard of results from such research than from an 'ad hoc' survey which would involve a greater expenditure. The majority of research companies operating omnibus surveys will tend to disagree for obvious reasons, although they would probably agree that in 'ad hoc' research there is a far greater breadth in the quality of the surveys between the best and the worst than on omnibus research surveys. The research company will correctly point out that it can only operate an omnibus survey on the basis of obtaining a wide range of clients and, therefore, the quality of these surveys is a reflection of the average quality of the requests from their various clients. So long as the researcher recognizes the situation he will have little difficulty in carrying out these surveys. If he is not wary he may well be disappointed in the results.

Other Forms of Syndicated Research

It has been the main purpose of this chapter to consider the omnibus survey where the questionnaire is a combination of smaller questionnaires designed by a variety of different clients and with the total research project being administered and controlled by a research company which sells space on

190

this master questionnaire to the different clients. Two variations should be mentioned. First of all, there are a number of research companies which operate omnibus surveys strictly limited to one particular type of research but still allowing for a variety of clients and a variety of different question-naires on the same master questionnaire. An example of this is the Advertis-ing Planning Index (API) operated by the British Market Research Bureau. On this survey it is possible for clients to obtain information on brand awareness, attitudes and so on. Each client has questions on the master questionnaire but the questions are of a standard form and designed by the research company so that the whole questionnaire follows a consistent pattern. In some instances it is possible to add a few additional questions on these questionnaires in exactly the same way as for an ordinary omnibus survey. Since this is designed for a specific purpose the number of additional questions is limited. The second type of syndicated research occurs when a research company carries out a survey and sells the results, either in part or in its entirety, to a number of different clients. An example of this is the consumer panel. This type of syndicated research is covered elsewhere in this book and except in certain specialized areas it is not common practice for a research company to carry out its own research project and then sell the results to a number of different clients.

Examples of Existing Services

It is difficult to present a practical list of omnibus surveys currently in existence. Companies operating such services are continually changing and as many as four or five companies come into existence each year and an equal number drop out. Furthermore, companies change, from time to time, aspects of the design of these surveys such as the sample design or the coverage. Despite these difficulties, it is felt useful to give some indication of the companies operating this type of service.

Table 8.1 below indicates the current situation with regard to service being offered by companies in the UK. Every attempt has been made to make this as comprehensive a list as possible, at the time of going to press, but it is strongly recommended that the reader checks the individual facts with the research companies for himself. With regard to costs, the expendi-ture clearly depends on the type of questions demanded by the researcher. In order to get some meaningful comparison on costs, a standard question-naire was designed which involves the following (based on total adult population as far as the survey would permit):

(a) three pre-coded questions using one column of punch card;
(b) two open-ended questions using two columns of punch card;
(c) standard analysis and report.

Table 8.1 overleaf omits those panels aimed at particular sub-groups. Table 8.2 lists some examples of these more specialized groups.

Table 8.1   Examples of UK omnibus surveys

Name of company	Sample size	Coverage	Type of sample	Cost standard unit	Frequency
British Market Research Bureau	4000	Adults, 16+, national (except North Scotland)	Random walk	£280	Fortnightly
Ellis Marketing Research	1000	Adults, 21+, national	Quota	£460	Monthly
Gordon Simmons Research	1000	Housewives, national	Quota	£320	Monthly
Gallup Poll	1000	Adults, 16+, national	Quota	£275	Weekly
KBMS	2100	Adults & children, 8+, national	Quota	£380	Monthly
Louis Harris (Research)	2500	Adults, 16+, national	Random	£520	Monthly
Market Information Services	1000	Housewives 16–64	Quota	£275	Monthly
Mass-Observation	2000	Adults 16–64 national	Quota	£880	Monthly
Market Search Unit	1000	Housewives, 16+, national	Quota	£330	Monthly
NOP Market Research	2200	Adults, 16+, national	Random	£500	Fortnightly
Opinion Research Centre	2500	Adults, 16+, national	Random	£590	Monthly
Speedsearch	1100	Adults, 15+, national	Random	£370	Weekly
Sales Research Services	500	Adults, 16+, national	Quota	£135	Weekly

Table 8.2   Examples of minority group omnibus surveys

Name of company	Special group	Sample size	Frequency
Group Marketing and Research	Southern Television area	1000	Monthly
Marketing Economics Ltd	Teenagers	1000	Quarterly
Marplan	London Television area	500	Weekly
Midland Market Research	Motorists	5000	Quarterly
Public Attitude Surveys	Children	1000	Monthly

Table 8.3   Examples of omnibus surveys in different countries

Country	Research company	Sample size	Type of sample	Total £ =
Australia	Roy Morgan Research Centre	1000	Random	£480
Austria	Dr Fessel Institut	2000	Random	£340
Canada	Canadian Facts Co. Ltd	3150	Random	£1900
Denmark	Gallup Markedsanalyse A/S	2000	Random	£370
Finland	Suomen Gallup	1000	Random	£320
France	SOFRES	2000	Quota	£890
Germany	GfK	2000	Quota	£820
Greece	Institute for Research in Communication	1400	Quota	£230
Holland	Nederlandse Stichting Voor Statistick	1800	Random	£860
Italy	Demoskopea	2000	Quota	£940
New Zealand	Research Marketing Services Ltd	1150	Quota	£1050
Norway	Norsk Gallup Institut A/S	1600	Random	£250
Spain	ECO	3000	Random	£340
Sweden	SIFO	1200	Random	£930
Switzerland	AES	4000	Quota	£1030
USA	Gallup	3000	Random	£1940

It has already been mentioned earlier in this chapter that a valuable use of an omnibus survey is in the commissioning of international market research. It would clearly be impossible to give as comprehensive a list for the whole world as had been attempted for the UK above; but in order to give an indication of the scope and possibilities of such surveys, an example is given in Table 8.3 of one omnibus survey operator, in several countries, with a similar cost estimate to that given for the UK companies above. It should be emphasized that this does not in any way indicate approval for these particular research companies, nor does it imply that there are not other equally, if not more, appropriate omnibus research companies in each country.

Reference

1. JENKINS, J. and KENDALL J. *Formulating Quantified Objectives and Evaluating Progress without Profit or Sales*, ESOMAR Conference, 1969.

9. Mail surveys

Brian Allt

Operational Definition

Because the classification is physical rather than related to essence, the phrase 'mail surveys' cannot be said to connote a type of survey substantially different from all other types of survey.

In this chapter the phrase is used to describe surveys where the respondent is responsible for completing and returning the questionnaire (or other representation of opinion or behaviour) to the organization carrying out the survey. In most cases the discussion also applies to those surveys where the questionnaire or response document is *also* mailed *to* the potential informant. Most applies even if the document is conveyed to the informant by other means.

Approach

Since mail surveys are not seen as a discrete entity, but simply as one variant of survey method, it is essential that they are approached in this light. This chapter is designed to draw attention to the problems which arise, to the decisions which are necessary, and to the possible pitfalls when this particular method is used, rather than to be an economy-research-pack. Mail surveys are easy traps for the unwary, and the attempt to rely on them without thorough knowledge or experience of other methods can be disastrous, since the feedback element may be minimal. Hence, this chapter is designed to indicate the considerations governing the choice of the mail method, and the problems and stages which have to be thought through if a mail survey is to be effective. The discussion is rarely in terms of detailed rules to be rigidly followed. There will always be exceptions to any generalized dicta on survey method, and the researcher will have to find out which of these emerge in his particular market. Further reading (a list is provided at the end of this chapter) may provide conflicting views on detailed points, and the researcher will have to decide how much the studies, upon which those views are based, have in common with his own potential studies.

194

Summary of Advantages and Disadvantages

Below are outlined the major advantages and disadvantages of using a mail survey. These will be discussed in detail later in the chapter.

Advantages:

(a) immunity from variable interviewer-effect;
(b) survey as a whole is more *reliable*, i.e., identically repeatable, than a personal interview study;
(c) informant can work at his own pace;
(d) even ignoring cost, it is sometimes the only possible way of contacting the relevant population;
(e) many of the contexts in which mail research is particularly appropriate also provide a basis for economies through differential rates of sampling of particular sub-groups;
(f) the relative level of response to different parts of the questionnaire can provide a valuable indicator of informant interest and, hence, relevance;
(g) points (a) and (b) can make it a particularly suitable tool for multi-national studies.

Disadvantages:

(a) data-gathering stage usually takes longer than personal interview;
(b) the researcher cannot control the attention given to the questionnaire or know when differences of interpretation are taking place, unless piloting on comprehension has been undertaken;
(c) response material in free-response questions may be excessive or inadequate—it cannot be controlled as in a personal interview;
(d) informants may be more unrepresentative of the population studied than in a personal interview study. Though the *nature* of the unrepresentativeness is rarely automatically studied as an integral part of personal interview surveys it is quite possible to do so, and is easier in many mail studies. With either mail or personal interview studies there may be cases where nothing can be done to elicit response from important categories of the population;
(e) the informant may read and/or answer the questions in any order. Thus, one cannot assume that answers to any question are independent of the effects of reading and/or answering later questions;
(f) tests of 'awareness' must be interpreted with great caution.

When to Consider Mail Surveys

It is assumed that these questions have already been asked: 'What can we do with any information?'; 'What information do we need?'; 'How precise does the information need to be?'; 'How much are we prepared to spend?'. If they have not been asked, and mail surveys are being considered, then the context for correct decisions *at all stages* will almost certainly be wrong, as is the case with all survey research where these questions have not been asked and answered.

The above cautions relate to points which are made as positive assertions in the rest of this book. The reason for stressing these cautions is based on observation. In all forms of survey research, once the gathering of data has been initiated, there are social and psychological pressures (quite apart from contractual obligations) which drive the initiator to complete the task, to 'see what we can get out of it', 'to suck it and see'. Probably through limited human or financial resources, people without experience in survey research are much more prone to attempt postal research than personal interview research, and many of the 'horrible warnings' in this chapter are based on knowledge of such cases. Nevertheless, even experienced market research workers sometimes appear disorientated when committed to a mail survey, and throw their accustomed criteria and caution to the winds.

The apparently lower cost of data gathering and, hence, the lower cost of *initiating* a mail survey, and the relatively simpler organizational task make this type of study particularly seductive, once any original resistance has been overcome. Large quantities of data fall as manna from heaven, and are much too good to waste!

It is hard for even a crudely conducted personal interview study to represent only five per cent of the universe it is meant to cover. It is possible for a mail survey response to represent as little as this or as much as 80 or 90 per cent.

When to Employ Mail Surveys

In this section, a distinction must be drawn between *essentially* mail studies, and *optionally* mail studies. *Essentially* mail studies are those where the special nature of the problem strongly indicates that postal methods are the only relevant approach through the nature of the interview situation, as in product tests for products sold by mailing-shot, etc., or where the only possible method of contact is postal, lack of primary access to lists of special populations, etc. *Optionally* mail studies are those where the study could feasibly be conducted by personal interview, but considerations of cost or logistics make a personal interview study less attractive or virtually impossible.

In the first category the considerations which apply at this stage are the same as those which apply for any survey.

Optionally mail surveys

The most likely reason why mail is considered as a substitute for personal interview, or even apparently 'the only possibility', will be cost. In a number of instances the difference in the cost of data *gathering* will be so enormous as to need relatively little cost-comparison beyond this stage. However, it is a useful exercise to attempt this in all cases where mail surveys are being considered. This is because cases often can occur where the cost-saving is apparent rather than real, and the time-scale disadvantageous.

Assume that the concern is only with the number of interviews, *ignoring response rate*. For many universes, given numbers of completed questionnaires can cost a quarter or more of the cost of personal interviews. An apparent large saving can pale into insignificance when the total job is costed in detail. If data-gathering is, for example, a quarter of the *total* cost of a personal interview survey,* and n personal interviews cost four times as much as n postal interviews, then the personal interview study will be only $12\frac{1}{2}$ per cent dearer than the postal. The point is laboured, because too often a decision is made on the basis of savings at the first stage.

Deciding between personal interviews and mail surveys in practice

Making the comparison involves a combination of hard figures and subjective judgments. The attempt should be made to quantify the latter. Planning and design time, outward postal costs *or* personal interview costs, coding, data processing, and reporting can all be accurately forecast in terms of the organization's costing experience. The 'soft' part of the assessment relates to response rate, possible limitations of range or detail of data which it is felt can be gathered by post, and urgency.

The most important of these is obviously the response rate. The researcher is faced with assessing the relative merits of 70, 60, 40 per cent, etc., response and, quite clearly, no objectively valid yardstick can be applied without infinite experience of the relative danger or damage to the client of marketing decisions based upon descending levels of response. Even if a disproportionately increasing 'disadvantage cost' is not actually included in the comparative estimates, the concept should always be borne in mind (perhaps a more vivid self-question should be, 'Suppose all the non-respondents use the competitor's brand?'). If ample time is available, much of the guesswork can be removed by one or more small pilot runs. This also gives a better idea of the total outward and inward postal costs necessary.

The difference in time between initiation and completion of a postal survey, and that of a personal interview survey (or vice versa), can also be thought of as a 'disadvantage cost', again subjectively assessed. Thus, the various possibilities are costed. If there is no time for pilot runs, several different mail survey estimates should be made to allow for different response rates. (These should obviously also take account of the different number of outward mailings to achieve a given sample, costs of reminders, incentives, personal interview validation, etc.). These should be compared with the quota-sample personal interview, and probability sample personal interview, where these are feasible.

The precision of the comparison estimates will often not need to be great, but some attempt at relevant comparison is essential.

---

* Commissioners of research should usually include own 'interpretation' costs.

Summary

Compare costs of survey as follows:

To yield *n* completed interviews	Probability personal interview £	Quota personal interview £	Postal: response rate A £	Postal: response rate B £	Postal: response rate C £
Planning and design time	X	X	X	X	X
Questionnaire printing/paper, etc.	X	X	X	X	X
Personal interviews and quality control	X	X	—	—	—
Outward costs (addressing, recording, postage, and despatch)	—	—	X	X	X
Inward postal costs (stamps or reply-paid)	—	—	X	X	X
Incentives	—	—	X	X	X
Reminder (addressing, recording, postage, and despatch)	—	—	X	X	X
Personal-interview validation	—	—	?	?	?
Response rate disadvantage cost	X	X	X	X	X
Editing and coding	X	X	X	X	X
Data processing	X	X	X	X	X
Reporting	?	?	?	?	?
Time disadvantage cost	?	?	?	?	?
Total					

X = Essential cost entries   ? = Recommended possible cost entries

The Universe and the Sample—Mechanics

General

In practice, the particular researcher's starting point may be a universe or population, or some sample of a universe.

In extreme cases, the total list of all members of the relevant universe will be smaller than a normal sample survey—only 100 or 200. In such cases, the representativeness of a given size of sample (as distinct from the proportion of the universe which the sample forms) must be particularly borne in mind (see chapter 3).

At the other extreme, it may be that the population to be sampled is virtually total, e.g., all men and women over 21, via the electoral register, in which case normal probability sampling methods operate. Most cases will fall between these two extremes. For any *given* list the normal principles of sampling operate, i.e., every *n*th name (or number, if the actual names are not in the possession of the researcher). The sampling frame should obviously be as relevant to the marketing problem as possible.

Establishing a frame where none exists—chance distribution and the two-stage study

In certain cases no frame of identifiable people exists. In these cases there are two alternatives. One is to distribute questionnaires in the package, or along with the service, to a proportion of 'buyers' or 'users'. In these

198

circumstances it is very difficult to tell what causes a low response. *Alternatively* one may adopt some strategem to get consumers to provide their name and address. The long term aim is, of course, to obtain a higher initial response and thus provide a basis for follow-up of non-responders to the survey proper. Some manufacturers have such an operation as a constant feature for other reasons, e.g., guarantee cards. In other cases, a one-off insertion of some attractive offer (payment simply in return for completion of a simple question on a card) may provide an economically worthwhile frame. Of course, this is effectively a preliminary mail survey in its own right. Its merits depend once again upon the response rate, and, if this method is attempted, it is *essential* to control rigidly the number of insertions. It is most satisfactory when a known number are supplied, *and received* by the consumer, within a short controlled time period.

A study of the purchasers of a single issue of a minority periodical would be a good example, providing that replies after an appropriate interval are rejected as likely to come from pass-on readers.

In these cases, both chance distribution of the actual questionnaire *and* the two-stage operation, care must be taken over the numbers, and hence the costs incurred. The usual method for either is the reply-paid folded sheet or card. Enthusiasm over a response higher than expected may be quickly tempered as the postage costs mount up. Again, a pilot exercise may save red faces.

Structuring the sample

It is at this stage that certain economies, not normally possible in personal interview studies, can begin to operate, and be the foundation of effective response maximization. In many cases one will be working with samples from earlier personal interview surveys. In other cases, lists may be separated into highly relevant segments. In the former case one may be able to classify names as heavy, medium, and light buyers; by class or age group and so on. In the latter, one may have long-term members, short-term members, enquirers who didn't join up and so on.

If separate lists are available (or can be rearranged) for the relevant sections of the market, each can be sampled separately. If a mail order supplier of luxury foods, for example, wished to sound out reactions to a new range among his existing market, it would probably prove wiser to conduct a survey among his own lists than undertake a study of a sample of the total population. He might have 25 000 names and addresses on his list. If he has found it otherwise cost-effective to log purchases over time against each name on his list, he may well be able to analyse his addresses to show that he has among his customers 1000 making six or more purchases in the last year, 4000 who have made two to five purchases in the last year, 20 000 who have made only one purchase in the last year. If he mailed a questionnaire to all 25 000 he would be faced with very high postage costs. If he simply decided to mail 1000 picked at random, even if all replied, he would end up with 40 who had made six purchases or more, 160 who had made two to five purchases, 800 who had made only one purchase. Were he to do this, it would imply either ignorance of the principles of sampling and research, and/or a lack of concern with possible market strategies. Those who have such mail markets as relevant sampling frames, often ignore their potential in this way and draw a sample from the list as a whole. In this example it would obviously be wiser, in almost all situations, to mail questionnaires to equal *numbers* of each group. (Such an opportunity would be regarded as a godsend by those conducting personal interview research on most consumer goods.) In this way one has the opportunity to assess both the different sections, with a reasonably-sized sample in each case, and also assess the list as a whole, via appropriate weighting to the universe profile.

A similar approach would apply to use of a previous personal interview sample. The net result may, indeed, provide a much more representative sample (say, of users) if based on a probability sample, than a personal interview quota study employing 'usership' as a crude quota control.

As mentioned, a further advantage lies in response maximization. Response rate can vary appreciably among different subsections. Separation of the mailings to each group, and the separate recording of their response, will tell the researcher whether any subsection's response is substantially lower than others, and whether extra reminders are merited to attempt the raising of the response level. Alternatively, should time not permit, he will be forewarned of the relative weakness of the section(s) when reporting.

The Mailing Out of Questionnaires

Very little need be said here, though the scale of the operation may be considerable. (Detailed differences in the mailing method which might affect response rate are discussed below.)

The operations are simple clerical tasks but must be carried out systematically.

Names and addresses should be recorded as envelopes are typed (or carbon-labels used) since they are essential for checking-in, and for reminders. Whether or not the respondent is asked to sign his name (and possibly confirm his address), a serial number will, in most cases, be given to each mailed questionnaire, and listed against each recorded addressee. In *some* studies, particularly industrial, this *may* militate against good response but, in most cases, numbering the questionnaires does not materially affect response rate, and facilitates checking-in, particularly with large samples. It also saves making an alphabetical list. If, as is usual, it is essential to obtain replies from a specific person rather than some other member of the household, do everything to make this clear. The envelope should obviously be personally addressed and, if costs allow, the letter and questionnaire bear the same name/address. Anonymity of respondent is often overrated as an incentive and, in most cases, it is perfectly acceptable to ask informants to sign their name and address.

What the Potential Informant Receives

Aims of the mailing as a whole

Obviously, the addressee may receive a number of items. Examples of covering letter, reminders and mail questionnaire are found in the appendices, but before discussing the separate parts of the mailing, e.g., whether the envelope should be stamped or not, whether the covering letter should be signed or not, the researcher should project himself into the role of the informant, and thus think about what the addressee gets.

The mailing must be considered as a whole. It is easy to say, 'If the addressee is put off by the envelope he won't open it, so this is all-important', and to proceed to the covering letter, etc., sequentially. This is only relevant if one has foreknowledge of the fact that substantial numbers leave letters (or letters of a particular appearance) unopened, or that people peruse the mixed contents of envelopes sequentially.

The effects of different approaches to the design and content of survey mailings is often discussed in such a way as to suggest that 'stamp-response', 'signed-/or unsigned-response', green paper- or pink paper-response etc., represent fundamental human drives. Sight appears to be lost of the fact that the mail survey is addressed to human beings who have the same, or wider, range of potential responses as the people one knows or among whom one conducts personal interviews.

Published research upon particular methods or detail of method can be useful, but unless it is appraised in the proper context it can be misleading, since there is usually no real basis for assessing the similarity of the reported studies to the immediate problem. Further, there is a natural tendency for experimental variation to be concentrated on those factors which can relatively easily be systematically varied, and/or are unlikely to drastically upset the survey. It may be that some of the attempts to increase response stem from a feeling that the mail interview is an antipathetic task. This leads to the key consideration which should underlie the *whole* mailing. *It should aim to elicit maximum involvement on the part of the informant.* To do this the mailing must:

(a) arouse his curiosity;
(b) make its importance clear;
(c) make its relevance *to him* clear;
(d) be easy to understand;
(e) be interesting;
(f) be easy to complete;
(g) be easy to return.

The word 'easy' needs amplification. Obviously, it must not make educational or cultural demands greater than the sample is likely to possess. On the other hand, it should not be at the level of a child's first reading book. As with any interview, it should be easy in the sense that it does not leave the informant unclear as to what he is being asked to do, nor put him in a 'puzzle-solving' situation so that he responds 'don't know' or effectively refuses the interview, to escape from the conflict produced.

The parts of the mailing

The contents of the mailing are considered in terms of its essential characteristics and objectives.

A common form of a mail survey is an envelope containing an explanatory letter and a questionnaire. The instructions for specific questions are often alongside those questions. The *general* instructions may be in the letter or at the beginning and end of the questionnaire. *There is no automatic necessity for this to be the format.* Informant's address, survey purpose, general instructions, questions, could all be in one unit, even a single sheet of paper to be reverse-folded to show the organization's address for mailing back. The possibilities are myriad, and the combination used should depend upon what effect and results are sought, rather than what has been done before. The following sections mean to highlight the questions the researcher should ask *himself* and no step by step guide is attempted. This applies also to the actual layout of the recording document. It is only too easy to replicate something which may be ideal for a trained interviewer, coder, or puncher, but be unattractive and unintelligible to its recipient.

The Basic Properties of the Postal Interview

The contraints and freedoms in a postal interview differ from those in personal interview situations:

(a) mail survey questionnaires are self-completion questionnaires;
(b) hence, the informant can grasp the whole gist of the questionnaire, with potentially positive or negative effects upon co-operation;
(c) he may answer questions in any order;
(d) interpretation of the survey-purpose *and of the questionnaire* will be an *informant*-variable—each may interpret in his own way. Hence, variation in interpretation by particular informants, or uniform 'misinterpretation' by the total sample, or by sub-groups, is usually not discernible from the returned documents, and unless gross or illogical, cannot be corrected or allowed for;
(e) at the same time, it is thus a *standard stimulus*, in a way never attainable in a personal interview survey. Considering samples as a whole, it is thus in scientific terms a more 'reliable' stimulus than a personal interview.

Piloting

Whereas the negative effects mentioned above cannot be assessed from the returned documents, valuable warnings and indications can be obtained from feasibility-piloting. This must be under the same conditions as the eventual survey, the test informants opening an envelope and working through. A subsequent *individual* 'de-briefing' with the filled-in questionnaire as a guide, to establish what the informant understood, even among only a handful of informants, will usually throw up most of the potential problems and ambiguities. Coupled with final general questions on 'anything else you feel we should have asked you', on interest, relevance, etc., this will provide a good basis for question finalization.

The Recording Document

Limits on topics covered by questions

In the view of the writer there is no type of question which should automatically be rejected in the context of postal surveys, providing it does not infringe the rules of comprehension and ease of completion. A few of the questions can be boring, irrelevant, unimportant, even slightly annoying, providing that the overall reaction to the questionnaire is likely to satisfy the criteria mentioned above. It would seem sensible to say, 'It would help us to gain a better understanding of your views and circumstances if you would tell us whether you are married/widowed/divorced/or single', rather than baldly list such questions. Similarly, the need for questions which are less interesting or apparently relevant can often be briefly explained in the body of the question or questionnaire. Questions which are tests of awareness or immediate knowledge cannot be assumed to achieve their object, and may not reflect what would come out of a personal interview. It may be more effective to adopt an approach which better invites the informant to play the game and understand what you are after; for example, instead of saying, 'Write down all the names of brands of margarine you can think of', it may be better to say, 'Write down in this box the brands of margarine that come into your head immediately, and in this box all the others you can think of'. If a partially incomplete questionnaire will be useful, make this clear. If there is reason to expect resistance to particular questions, particularly in industrial research, explain that non-response to them does not invalidate. Similarly, if index values are better than refusal of actual values, give informants the chance of answering in either way.

Sequence

One has to be prepared for informants reading and answering questions in any order (as well as filling in the answers before reading the covering letter or general instructions). It follows that the sequences should, other things being equal, be such as to arouse and maintain interest through each page of the questionnaire.

Interesting *questions* may be much more likely to produce a filled-in questionnaire than any amount of explanation or introduction. Avoid filling the first page with the dullest questions. Order constraints stemming from personal interview design sequence or convenience should be discarded and/or thought through afresh.

Length of questionnaire and amount of space

Beware of cramping the questionnaire to make it appear shorter—the effect is often the reverse. Ample spacing automatically introduces more rest-pauses. One can make no categorical statements as to upper time limits or length limits. There is no reason why a questionnaire expected to take an hour or more should automatically be rejected, again provided that it satisfies the conditions above.

Layout of individual questions

This, again, cannot be rigidly specified or restricted. Open-ended questions with plenty of recording space can often produce more information, or more carefully considered indications of attitude, than are produced by a personal interview. On the other hand, there is no point in incurring coding costs on fixed-choice questions, when pre-coding (small numbers in the answer boxes to be ticked), or other punching guides can be used. However, many punching operators can work efficiently from a coded master and do not need printed codes on the questionnaire. Nevertheless, allow some white space around all questions (margins, etc.). The questionnaire designer is unlikely to think of all the possible responses to a fixed-choice question unless it is *very* simple. Whereas an interviewer, hopefully, will know to which specified answer category a reply best approximates, the informant will often not recognize that his all-important individual opinion so fits and may be put off. Some space around fixed-choice questions, or a dotted line, allows him to express his views. This may well emphasize the researcher's concern with the informant's own views and may make the difference between a usable and unusable questionnaire or between replying and not replying.

Attractiveness

The questionnaire should not be actually unpleasant to look at. However, the possible effects of 'glamourizing' the documents must be carefully considered.

Clearly, if the study is a dummy run to test purchase effects of a mail order mailing, e.g., a new catalogue, it should be in a form close to that of the envisaged final version. In *other* mail studies we are concerned with response maximization in a different sense.

204

Once again, providing the contents satisfy the conditions above and are clear, legible, and incorporate obvious routing instructions, further beautifying, such as colour-printing, expensive paper, etc., may be even negative in effect. A highly 'attractive' one may carry overtones which appeal to some and are 'off-putting' to others. Mail questionnaires and covering documents are sometimes produced which look like mailed promotional material. They may be perceived, and treated, as other than intended. Further, something which appears to be published 'at large', may foster less desire to complete than something which gives a more personal impression and potential involvement.

Representativeness of Sampling Frame

Listed below are a number of possible types of sampling frame. Obviously, a similar possible range exists for industrial studies.

1. *New contacts with total population:*
named individuals, *not previously* contacted, selected from the electoral register (anything from a true random sample to multi-stage samples).

2. *Existing selective lists:*
(a) lists of people which include *all* of the population the study aims to cover. Customer lists, enquiry lists, e.g., mail order buyers for a study of reactions to current services provided by the company;
(b) lists of people selected in a way not, or less, relevant to the survey purpose, e.g., the same mail order buyers as in (a), used for a *general* study of holiday habits or for a *different* mail order product range;
(c) other lists—directories, salesmen's contacts, enquiry lists; customer lists, circular distributor's lists, mailing lists, etc.

3. *Informants from previous personal interview surveys:*
(a) all, or selected, respondents via previous probability samples;
(b) all, or selected, respondents obtained via previous quota samples, random route, etc.

The above list serves to point out that the first approach to sampling must be to assess the relevance of potential sampling frames to the study. Only in example 1 and 2(a), is the sampling frame by definition correspondent with the population which should ideally be studied. In 2(a) it is automatic, in 1 effectively automatic since one would only use it if wanting, or forced to use, a general sample of the population.

Ideally, the list or frame used should not only consist entirely of the type of person we wish to contact, but also represent *all* of the types of person which exist. The electoral register (if new) effectively contains all the people of the type we require if we are studying electors at large. A company list of enquirers or customers contains equally all the people if the study is meant to be *exclusively* one of customers or enquirers. The same list will be a much less known quantity if we really want to carry out a study of *all* purchasers of the goods, whether or not they buy also or only from other companies.

Survey objectives are often effectively muddled by careless and rushed thinking at this stage. The feeling, 'They are going to be the same sort of people', i.e., as the universe which should really be sampled, is one which must be guarded against.

It is thus essential with practically all sample sources to assess the representativeness of the frame. If we start with a list of respondents from a previous personal interview survey, we must consider firstly the response rate to *that* survey, e.g., if we interview by post informants from a personal interview probability sample which had a 70 per cent response rate, and obtain a 70 per cent mail response, we end up with only a 49 per cent response from the *original* sampling frame. This may or may not be adequate for the survey purpose. (Of course, in certain circumstances it may be worth mailing to all the persons not contacted at the personal interview.) The above holds for appraisal at any stage, i.e., initial mailing, first reminder, second reminder, etc.

In many cases, the only conceivable source is a clearly inadequate list. In many cases it will be impossible to assess quantitatively its inadequacy. Theoretically, any personal interview quota sample cannot be *independently* assessed for representativeness, and on any probability sample it is always possible that, in relation to the topic investigated, the 10, 15, and 20 per cent non-responders behave in bizarrely different ways. The acceptance of the data is based on other knowledge, reasonably justified belief or hope about the relative homogeneity of the population, and so on. By spelling out the limitations beforehand, a proper decision can be taken as to whether the frame is any use at all, and if so, what problems can justifiably be tackled.

Response Maximization

Monitoring

The first requisite is information to judge how and when to act. If the mailing is all made at once, the number of replies will be logged and graphed by reply date. If the despatch was made over a period, ensure that the questionnaires have a despatch date code so that they can be counted separately. Always code the questionnaires in terms of despatch-return interval as this may be wanted for tabulating differences between early and late responders. Keep the graph up to date at the end of each day. Except in most unusual cases, the first mailing will not produce the maximum response and reminder(s) will be necessary. Guard against impatience, it can waste money. Carefully keep any mailings returned as 'gone away', 'address not known', etc. Compare them with the list to eliminate confusion from clerical errors. The number of true erroneous addresses will serve as one indication of the adequacy of the sampling frame. If lists have to be bought at substantial cost, it is worth asking the vendor for his assessment of the likely level, and consider whether a clause in the sale contract should take account of possible erroneous claims.

Reminders

As soon as the curve has flattened, mail out reminders, again marking the names and addresses of those to whom reminders have been sent. The writer usually prefers to include a further copy of the questionnaire, again with appropriate informant number and code to distinguish it from original questionnaires.

A dilemma now faces one: should the nature of the reminder request be the same as the original, or different. Logically, it should be different, the first one apparently did not have the right effect. However, theoretically, a different letter could restructure the stimulus complex and produce different responses to some or all of the questionnaire. Unless one is in a position to systematically experiment, the wisest course is probably to get over the points that:

(a) you are not only interested in people who are very actively interested in the topic;
(b) you are not only interested in people who like to fill in questionnaires;
(c) you really need their reply;

and then repeat the gist of the original letter.

In practice, it is usually worth sending out at least two reminders (see Appendices 2 and 3) but again no automatic rule applies. Remember that some people make a practice of leaving things for a time before doing them. The diagram in Fig. 9.1 below gives some idea of a typical response pattern before and after reminders. Be wary of impatience in another sense, deciding to mail an additional *sample* because the absolute number of early responses suggests that the final *numbers* will be too small for analysis. Assuming that one is *not* patient, and does mail out to an additional sample while still reminding the original sample, do not be tempted to throw in the single-shot second sample replies with the total responses to the first; at least, not without checks on the similarity of early and late repliers.

Eye-catching coloured labels with cryptic messages such as, 'Please deal with this now' are sometimes used on reminder letters, or on the original letters, but beware of making these look too much like 'selling' literature. As mentioned earlier, considerable economies can be effected if one can split the mailed-out sample in terms of previously known data. Thus, in the example cited it is almost inevitable that different rates of response would be achieved from heavy, medium, and light buyers. Only one reminder might be needed to achieve satisfactory response from heavy buyers, perhaps several for medium and light buyers. Any other relevant breakdown may be used, demographic or topic-related.

If one has a low response, and any reason to believe that little further response is likely, a sub-sample can be reminded to assess the merits of fullscale reminding.

Other factors affecting response, and special techniques

The first requisite is involvement, and the second is reminder letters. Over and above these, there are particular techniques and factors which may also make appreciable differences.

The first type involves rewards and incentives. One is a straight payment to each informant on receipt of the questionnaire. For normal consumer work small sums are appropriate, a few shillings. For studies which impose a large workload upon informants, particularly industrial studies, a fee of a more substantial size can be appropriate. One must be prepared to pay for lengthy work, unless one wants a small response based on executives with little to do. Try a pilot, with and without payment, if in doubt.

A quite different type of reward is the competition at the end of the questionnaire, and this is now very popular. Depending upon the overall cost of the study and size of prize, it can be quite cheap, and usually results in higher response levels than if no incentive is used. These competitions must not, in legal terms, be lotteries. The type of competition appearing in consumer goods advertising can serve as examples, e.g., rankings of listed attributes of a perfect holiday, with a short description of where it would be, and why. If this is used, beware of the nature of the competition having any effect upon the replies to the main enquiry; choose a different field. The type of informants should be borne in mind in selecting the form of incentive or prize.

Deadlines are of some help, and are not necessarily incompatible with competitions, nor with reminders. Simply explaining in the reminder letter that you have decided to extend the period does not appear to produce any negative reaction upon the reminded informants, and produces further response, even if stated that the competition entry chance has now passed. If the competition incentive is still retained it should, of course, be a new competition for further prizes. Figure 9.1 shows responses to an initial mailing with competition, reminder with competition, and second reminder with direct payment incentive. (Prizes were £25 in premium bonds.)

Some studies have suggested that sponsorship of the survey may have an effect upon response rate. Clearly, people who are under an obligation to the organization carrying out the survey or are members of it, may be more inclined to respond. Again, if there is doubt and also a choice, a trial run will be useful to indicate whether vast differences occur. Differences of a few per cent between initial runs should not be taken too seriously, since reminders may redress the balance or tip it the other way. Where knowledge of the organization's name may condition or distort response, the name of a less specific subsidiary may be used. Alternatively, this problem may dictate use of an independent agency.

It is virtually essential to provide a return envelope, preferably addressed, and either stamped or printed with a business reply system. On the whole the stamped envelope appears to produce slightly higher response rates, but beware of the cost implications. If pilot tests or prior knowledge imply a low response rate considerable stamp costs may be wasted. If the response rate is high, higher costs may be incurred because the reply-paid system in the UK is more costly per missive than a stamp. Given the appropriate values, costs per reply can be graphed and the crossover point used as a guide. If business reply is to be used and a licence from the Post Office does not already exist, allow time for design approval procedures and licencing.

An endless list of factors possibly affecting response could be made, together with subjective speculations and/or experimental evidence to support or refute any given hypothesis. Few have been tested in a sufficient variety of contexts for generalizable conclusions to be drawn. A balance has to be struck between desperate concern over every word, comma, and physical aspect of the mailing, and the blithe unconcern which results in a 'military order of the day' or an impression that one doesn't really care whether replies are received or not.

The golden rules are: imagine that you are the recipient of the mailing; try it out, even if somewhat artificially, upon some objective informants of

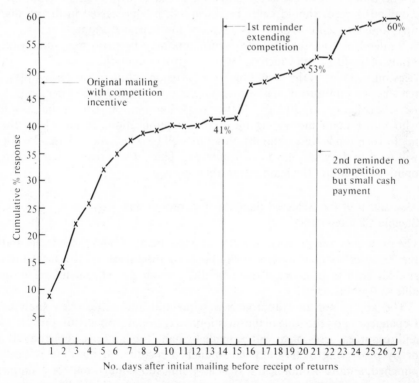

Fig. 9.1. Response in mail survey with competition incentive and small cash payment.

appropriate characteristics; conduct a trial run if you can. Remember, in the last case, that you can always contact some of the non-respondents to a pilot, personally, by telephone, or by letter, to find out why they didn't reply.

Response accuracy

The final response rate to a mail survey is unlikely to be over 90 per cent, and can be anything below that. How true a representation of the universe or sample required has been achieved, and how accurate are the data recorded by informants?

Response by wrong person

In some surveys it may not matter whether the respondent is some other member of the household, but in most cases it does. Every effort should be made to impress upon the informant that you need *his* reply, and to get him to sign his full name. One may consider inserting the question, 'Was this questionnaire filled in by the person to whom it was addressed, or someone else?' or, 'Do the opinions and facts you have given represent your own ideas?'. This is raised purely hypothetically.

The usual simple test is to compare signatures with original addressee. Conflicting cases should never be discarded, but processed in the normal way, and assessed separately, as discussed in the next section.

Remember, too, that 'wrong' informants may be performing a service. Many of the lists from which one works do not contain the name of the most relevant member of the household; e.g., if recontacting by post a sample of readers of a publication, mail-order purchasers, etc., the named person may be of secondary importance. If they pass the questionnaire to the person who is the main motivating buyer of the publication, or for whom the mail-order goods were obtained, this may well be of much more use. People will tend to do what they *think* you want. Thus, if you really require their opinions when not the main buyer, then say so.

Assessment of the Achieved Sample—Respondent and Sample Characteristics

The principles and practices underlying assessment of both the sample, and the answers to questions, are similar, and discussion of the mechanics enables both to be covered more briefly, though the judgements relate to different problems.

The key to the best approach is sequential and categorized analysis. Dependent upon the scale of the questionnaire, size of sample, time pressures, and resources, assessment will be made by hand tabulation as replies arrive, or by processing of the fully card-punched records. If the data is card-punched, a more economical way of assessing sub-samples may be a simple 'hole-count' tabulation performed separately for each sub-section.

210

One wishes to be able to compare some or all of the following, and obviously it will be necessary to have appropriately coded all replies:

(a) *already known characteristics* of informants, by speed of response and in total; thus early, late, and latest responders, by overall interval *or* in terms of which of the sequence of mailings and reminders they replied to; hence, by elimination, the known characteristics of the non-responders. This will provide one basis for assessment of the merits of yet further reminders, and for possible weighting to correct imbalances (dependent upon (b));

(b) *survey findings*—all or selected, by speed of response, and in total. These will be the answers to questions the survey was designed to find out and may be demographic, facts, opinions, etc. Again, they serve to indicate how much one's sample is modified by later or more recalcitrant repliers, and give some indications of potential error from absent replies, and basis for confidence. Remember, however, that extrapolated conclusions about the ultimate non-responders are a matter of systematic enlightened guesswork. Again, further reminders may appear merited.

The assessment of the achieved sample as a whole, and the subdivisions thereof, is crucially important to the interpretation of the findings.

Personal or telephone interview follow-up is probably more talked about than performed, but is the ultimate check on differences between responders and non-responders, other than those already known. It is not necessarily as costly as might appear. Ideally, every *n*th name from the non-response list should be contacted, but rather than do nothing it is better to contact *all* the non-responders in one or two towns. In designing the initial sample, if selected from a very large list, it may be worth deliberately over-sampling in one or two towns simply with non-response assessment in mind.

Obviously, if follow-up interviews on non-responders are carried out, there must be sufficient numbers for meaningful analysis.

The follow-up can lead to two different types of conclusion. One is in terms of whether the responders are, or are not, an adequate representation of the desired universe. The other can be that the initial universe was not adequately defined, i.e., the non-responders are people who are not relevant to the survey problem, and should not have been contacted in the first place.

Assessment of the accuracy and validity of the replies

Some clues may emerge from the *analyses* discussed above, but many aspects demand either faith or selective personal follow-up.

It is essential when making such assessment to be certain of the potential stability of the facts or opinions in question, *and* the potential stability under different interview conditions and design. Thus, the same question, in a different *setting*, will frequently produce an element of discrepancy which is a survey variable, albeit apparently random in operation. This applies to some 'simple factual' questions as much as to opinion and attitude questions (some would say opinions are likely to be more stable).

It is important to have both the potential stability of the 'facts' or opinions and the nature of the survey problem in mind, in any check procedure. One can then decide more clearly whether the *appropriate* criterion of accuracy is gross or net error, and how important is informant reliability or consistency, as against sample reliability or consistency. Thus, from what may be known already about an irregularly read newspaper one might accept high gross, and low net error, as satisfactorily accurate. Here, one would be demanding high reliability of overall sample response, but not of individual response.

The source of assessment data is usually by personal interview. *Some* assessment may be made via the actual mail questionnaire, if crucial invariant characteristics are available in the pre-existent data about the informant, and these characteristics are covered again in the mail survey. *Cross* tabulation of the earlier data by the new data, for the same informants, will assess both the gross and net error in respect of these characteristics. Again, if data assessment is carried out by personal interview, previous structuring of the sample may make this more economical.

Suitability for Different Types of Problem

General guides

In general, a mail survey will have a higher chance of success (high response rate) *where some relationship exists*. The 'existing relationship' may be a previous interview, membership, previous purchase or use of goods or services, etc. It probably stems from a variety of factors—interest in the topic, a thin strand of human involvement, and/or ability to respond relevantly. The ideal mail survey would be of a widely scattered minority persecuted for their extreme beliefs, being questioned on self-protection by their acknowledged leader.

Technically, the results of a mail survey will often be much better than that of a personal interview where:

(a) considered thought, 'work', consultation, etc., is necessary for a useful reply;
(b) the respondents are effectively unreachable by normal interview methods. The 'out seven days a week', the geographically isolated, etc. Postal interviews could possibly sometimes be used to fill response gaps on personal interview samples, perhaps on a redrafted crucial section of the original interview;
(c) as mentioned earlier, interviewer variability is eliminated, and any topic where this is likely to be a particularly damaging factor may be better covered by mail.

Some counter-indications may be:

(a) where language and literacy problems cannot be coped with other than by the potentially adjustable and explanatory mode of the personal interview. (Be sure that such a conclusion does not stem from limitations of the questionnaire *design*);
(b) where spontaneous unaided knowledge or awareness is being measured. This also extends to areas where it is crucial to measure fleeting or 'trivial' behaviour and experience, and not only substantial experience. An unaided informant may concentrate upon the things he does frequently, with strong awareness, with depth of emotion etc., and interpret a deliberately superficial question according to *his* level of interest. Instead of giving the papers 'ever seen', for example, he may give the papers he sees regularly. This problem exists with personal interviews, but under good interview conditions can be dealt with;
(c) for simple logistic reasons 'stop-press' studies are not feasible by post. The sort of study where results are needed one or two weeks from initiation does not lend itself to a mail survey. If this is simply a product of having a rapid service available and postal methods are otherwise suitable, then it is worth attacking the organizational operations to obtain earlier problem formulation. What can be very dangerous is giving early outline results based on first returns. In a personal interview study the danger usually stems from the number of observations. In a postal study early replies must be expected to be atypical.

Specific problems

The above types of case excepted, practically any problem may be considered for mail study.

Factual and opinion studies, panels, product tests, public topics, intimate topics, interesting studies, and, on the *face* of it, boring studies all seem possible providing the relevant technical and logistic constraints and indications are acceptable.

Perhaps the most striking example of an apparently low-appeal questionnaire seemingly finding wide informant acceptance is the British Market Research Bureau's 'Target Group Index' study (October 1968—March 1969). Here a random route sample is asked to accept a questionnaire at the end of a personal interview and mail it in when completed. Competition incentives are used, though experimental work suggested that they made only a moderate difference. The percentage of informants accepting was 88 per cent and the percentage returning usable questionnaires, after two reminders, was 58 per cent of the original contacts, i.e., 66 per cent of those accepting. (These figures are not offered as indices of sample quality since the basic interview, sample design and response rate are not here being discussed.) The relevant points are that the questionnaire deals with broad buying or usage, and brand information for 350 products and services, questions on readership frequency for 100 or more publications, and considerable questions upon television viewing. The questionnaire runs to about 75 pages. While the response rate (66 per cent) is not among the highest, it certainly suggests that one never knows what is possible until it is tried.

A quite different type of study was the recent JICNARS 'Calibration of Reading Intensity'. Here, informants were re-contacted by post to calibrate generalized claims, made in a previous personal interview, about amounts of publications read or looked at. They had to mark *each page*, of up to three publications, if they had seen it. A high proportion (77 per cent) did so (again the competition incentive was used). Personal interview validation at pilot stage showed low net error (this was the relevant criterion).

While there will undoubtedly be many areas which, for the reasons discussed, will never be particularly suitable for mail work, the true boundaries have yet to be mapped. Ideally a mail sub-sample should be incorporated into all studies to test its comparability and possible inferiority, or superiority, so that these boundaries can be established and understood.

Appendix 1

Letters.

(a) First covering letter:

Dear

We are carrying out a survey among members of the Venturer Book Club to find out their views on the Club and book reading in general.

You have been chosen to take part in this survey, and the information you give us will be used to help the Venturer Book Club select even more interesting books for its new range.

The questions are quite easy and we reckon it should take you about ten minutes to work through the whole form.

We have combined this survey with a simple competition. The first prize will be at least £50; the more people that send in a reply to the questionnaire the more we will add to the prize money, so you could win much more than this! To qualify for the competition we need to have your completed form within the next two weeks. Full details of the competition are printed on the enclosed entry form.

If you cannot answer all the questions, please do not let that put you off, any information you can give will help us. If you don't read many books nowadays, we are still interested in your replies, so please answer all the questions as best you can. It is *your* opinions we are interested in, so if you have any criticisms to make, don't hesitate to say so.

We explain exactly what we would like you to do on the front page of

214

the questionnaire. We are sure you will enjoy filling it in and your replies will be extremely valuable to us.

Thank you so much.

Yours sincerely,

Tom Archer

Appendix 2

(b) First reminder:

Dear

VENTURER BOOK CLUB SURVEY

To date we have not received the questionnaire we sent you two weeks ago. Only a small cross-section of people were selected to take part in the survey and it is very important to us that we get completed forms from all of them. You may be the kind of person who doesn't like filling in forms or perhaps you just haven't had time to get around to completing the questionnaire. This makes it doubly important for us to know your opinions or else we will only be getting information from the kind of people who have the time and the patience to respond to our request, and their opinions could be very different from yours.

In case you have mislaid the first questionnaire, we are sending you another. Please help us by filling it in and sending it to us as soon as possible.

We have decided to extend the competition so if you return your completed entry form to us within the next two weeks, you will still be able to qualify for the competition which could win you a prize of £50. Should you have lost your original competition entry form, a further one is attached to the enclosed questionnaire.

Let me stress again that if you cannot answer all the questions exactly please do not let that put you off. It is *your* opinions we are interested in, so if you have any criticisms to make, don't hesitate to say so. Answer each question to the best of your ability. If you don't read many books nowadays still answer the questions. We are interested in your replies no matter how many or how few books you read. Details of how to fill in the questionnaire are shown on the first page.

It is only by your filling in the questionnaire that we will be able to know your views. The questions are quite simple, and we reckon it should take you about ten minutes to work through the whole form.

Thank you for your co-operation,

Yours sincerely,

Tom Archer

PS: If, in the meantime, you have already sent in the first questionnaire, don't bother to send in this one as well.

Appendix 3

(c) Second reminder:

Dear

VENTURER BOOK CLUB SURVEY

We really want to know your opinions so we are having one last try even though you haven't returned the previous questionnaires we sent you. This is because it's almost more important to get the opinions of people who don't like filling in questionnaires.

In case you have mislaid the previous questionnaires, we are sending you another. Please help us by filling in all the questions you can answer and sending it to us as soon as possible.

We look forward to hearing from you.

Yours sincerely,

Tom Archer

Appendix 4

Extracts from an actual questionnaire (proper nouns altered)

(a) Front page of questionnaire:

On the following pages you will find the questions we would like you to answer. In most cases, they can be answered by placing ticks in the appropriate boxes. A few questions, however, require replies in your own words. It is always your own opinions we are after, so answer the questions exactly as you feel. There are no right or wrong answers.

The enclosed ball pen is for you to use when completing the form. Please keep it for your own use after sending back to us the completed questionnaire in the addressed envelope provided (no postage is necessary).

Remember that to qualify for the competition, we need to have your completed form within the next two weeks. The competition entry is on the back page.

WE HAVE ADDRESSED THIS QUESTIONNAIRE TO YOU AS THE PERSON WHO TOOK OUT MEMBERSHIP OF THE VENTURER BOOK CLUB. HOWEVER, IF THE MEMBERSHIP WAS FOR SOMEONE ELSE IN YOUR HOUSEHOLD, PLEASE PASS IT ON TO THAT PERSON.

Appendix 5

(b) Some specimen questions:

(1) How many books, *any* books, not necessarily Venturer Book Club books, would you say you have read since last Christmas? By books we mean full-length books, including paperbacks. We do *not* mean magazines. (WRITE IN ALONGSIDE) ————→

Office only

And, out of this number about how many would you say:

were books you, yourself, bought from a shop ————→

were books you got from a book club (*any* book club) ————→

were books you got out of the library ————→

were books you borrowed from friends or were given as gifts ——→

Office only

(2) About how many books, would you say, you have at home altogether? ————→
And, out of this number, about how many would you say are Venturer Book Club books? ————→

Office only

(3) Where do you keep *most* of your books?
I keep *most* of my books in/on...
in the:...room..
....

Office only

(4) This is a list of statements about books in general (not just Book Club books). We would like to know how *you* feel about them. Please read each statement and indicate for each the extent to which you agree or disagree with it. All you have to do is to put ticks in the boxes which best describe your feelings. (Please tick only one box for each statement.)

	I strongly agree	I agree to some extent	I have no real feelings either way	I disagree to some extent	I strongly disagree	Office only
A home isn't a home without books						
I haven't enough time to read books nowadays						
Etc.						

(15) We would like you to tell us how you feel the Venturer Book Club lives up to your expectations. Please tick the box alongside the statement which best describes your feelings.

	Tick appropriate box	Office
It lives up to my expectations entirely		
It lives up to most of my expectations		
It lives up to very few of my expectations		
It does not live up to my expectations at all		

If the Club does not live up to your expectations, could you please tell us why in the space provided below.

....	Office
....	
....	

(13) We should also like to know what things you particularly like about the Book Club and what things you particularly dislike. Would you write in details of these things in the appropriate space below.

Things particularly *liked*		Things particularly *disliked*	
....		....	
....		....	
....		....	
....		....	
....		....	
....		....	
Office only		Office only	

References

1. BAUR, E. J. Response Bias in a Mail Survey, *Public Opinion Quarterly*, 1947–8.
2. COX, W. E., Jnr. Response Patterns to Mail Surveys, *Journal of Marketing Research*, **3**, 4, 1966.
3. ERDOS, P. L. Successful Mail Surveys, High Returns and How to Get Them, *Printers Ink*, March, 1957.
4. ERDOS, P. L. *Professional Mail Survey*, McGraw-Hill Publishing Co. Ltd, 1970.
5. FORD, N. M. Questionnaire Appearance and Response Rates in Mail Surveys, *Journal of Advertising Research*, **8**, 3, 1968.
6. FORD, N. M. Consistency of Responses in a Mail Survey, *Journal of Advertising Research*, **9**, 4, 1969.
7. FORD, N. M. The Advance Letter in Mail Surveys, *Journal of Market Research*, **4**, 2, 1967.
8. FRANCEL, E. G. Mail Administered Questionnaires: Success Story, *Journal of Marketing Research*, **3**, 3, 1966.
9. HEADS, J. and THRIFT, H. J. Notes on a Study in Postal Response Rates, *Journal of the Market Research Society*, **8**, 3, 1968.
10. HOCHSTIM, J. R. and ATHANASOPOULAS, D. A. Personal Follow-up in a Mail Survey: its Contribution and its Cost, *Public Opinion Quarterly*, Spring, 1970.
11. *Postal Questionnaires*, Industrial Market Research Association, October, 1968.
12. ISAACSON, H. L., KOENIGSBERG, A., and SMITH, H. Mail Survey Research in Britain: an Experiment in Incentitives, *Journal of the Market Research Society*, **9**, 4, 1967.

218

13. KARLSSON, H. K. E. *Postal Contact: Methodical or Practical Dilemma*, ESOMAR Congress Papers, September, 1968.
14. KEANE, J. G. Low Cost, High Return Mail Surveys, *Journal of Marketing*, 3, 1963.
15. LAWSON, F. Varying Group Responses to Postal Questionnaires, *Public Opinion Quarterly*, 13, 1949.
16. LeROUX, A. A. A Method of Detecting Errors of Classification by Respondents to Postal Enquiries, *Applied Statistics*, 17, 1, 1968.
17. MADDAN, M. Maximising Mail Responses, *ESOMAR Journal*, 1, 1954.
18. MANFIELD, M. N. A Pattern of Response to Mail Surveys, *Public Opinion Quarterly*, 12, 1948.
19. MYERS, J. H. and HAUG, A. F. How a Preliminary Letter Affects Mail Survey Returns and Costs, *Journal of Advertising Research*, 9, 3, 1969.
20. NUCKOLS, R. C. Personal Interview Versus Mail Panel Survey, *Journal of Marketing Research*, 1, 1, 1964.
21. O'DELL, W. F. Personal Interview or Mail Panels, *Journal of Marketing*, 26, 1962.
22. OGNIBENE, P. Traits Affecting Questionnaire Responses, *Journal of Advertising Research*, 10, 3, 1970.
23. PAYNE, S. L. Combination of Survey Methods, *Journal of Marketing Research*, May, 1964.
24. REUSS, C. F. Differences between persons responding and not responding to a mailed questionnaire, *American Sociological Review*, 8, 1943.
25. SCOTT, C. Research on Mail Surveys, *Royal Statistical Society Journal*, 124, Pt. 2, 1961.
26. SIMON, R. Responses to Personal and Form Letters in Mail Surveys, *Journal of Advertising Research*, March, 1967.
27. STAFFORD, J. E. Influence of Preliminary Contact on Mail Returns, *Journal of Marketing Research*, 3, 4, 1966.
28. SWAIN, G. R. Techniques of Field Research Postal Questionnaires, *IMRA Journal*, Feb., 1968.
29. VINCENT, C. E. Socio-Economic Status and Familiar Variables in Mail Questionnaire Responses, *American Journal of Sociology*, May, 1964.
30. WATSAR, J. J. Improving the Response Rates in Mail Research, *Journal of Advertising Research*, 2, 1965.
31. WAISANEN, F. B. A Note on the Response to a Mailed Questionnaire, *Public Opinion Quarterly*, 18, 2, 1954.
32. WOTRUBA, T. R. Monetary Inducements and Mail Questionnaire Research, *Journal of Marketing Research*, 3, 4, 1966.

10. Other techniques

Leonard England

Of the chapters in this section of the book, the majority are basically concerned with forms of market research which imply personal confrontation of interviewer and respondent. It is probably impossible ever to estimate the proportion of all market research carried out in this way, either by volume or by number of contacts, but an estimate of 75 to 85 per cent, judged either by cost or by volume, seems reasonable enough. What is more, changing and developing techniques are unlikely to alter this proportion to any dramatic extent in the years to come.

Most of the research which does not involve the direct interview is, in fact, related to measurement of television viewing by means of meters (chapter 25) the auditing of shops by means of various forms of counts (chapter 7) or mail surveys as described in the previous chapter. Over a very wide range of problems, however, there are occasions when standard forms of interviewing become inappropriate. This chapter is concerned with such occasions.

In general terms, three such situations call for use of techniques other than the standard interview. The *first* of these operates when those to be interviewed are likely to be acutely difficult to contact, probably because each person of relevance to the survey is a long way away from all others, possibly because a large number of interviews are required almost simultaneously. In these instances use is likely to be made of the:

(a) postal survey;
(b) telephone survey.

The postal survey is considered in chapter 9. Our concern here is therefore with the telephone survey alone.

The *second* situation occurs when surveys involve the co-operation of respondents over a long period of time or when the interviewer is unable to be present for the whole of the interview time. The need here is for the self-completion questionnaire.

The *third* area—and this is by far the most important—operates when it is thought likely that standard techniques will fail to uncover the basic reasons involved in decision-making. In many cases (see chapter 2) careful preliminary work will mean that the questionnaire developed will allow useful and relevant answers to emerge rather than those which are superficial and 'expected'. There are, however, other occasions when perhaps respondents themselves have no idea of what they do, let alone why they do it; or where they are unable to report accurately how they order a beer, how long it takes them to cross a road or why they buy brand X rather than brand Y and so on. For these occasions the following techniques might need to be considered:

(a) the use of ironmongery;
(b) counts;
(c) observation;
(d) anthropological participation.

The seven techniques (i.e., all except mail surveys) are each the subject of their own section in this chapter, while Table 10.1 summarizes very briefly the most likely uses for each method together with their advantages and disadvantages. In a final section some general comments are made on the value of, and the problems involved in, using techniques other than the direct interviewer respondent confrontation.

Table 10.1

Method	*Some uses*	*Some advantages*	*Some disadvantages*
Telephone	(a) When simultaneous interviews needed	Cost, Speed	Lack of *rapport*, Interviews must be fairly short
	(b) When individual calls are very far apart		
Self completion	(a) When interview should be completed if interviewer cannot be present	Cost, Accuracy of reporting close to action reported	As with mail surveys (e.g., misunderstanding bias; only short questionnaire possible)
Psycho galvanometer	When respondent unlikely to be aware of own responses	Prestige and similar answers need not be considered	Unreal surroundings, Little data about why, Cost of large samples
Tachistoscope etc.,	To test detailed physical behaviour, particularly of eye reaction	Ability to measure action in a detail not available by other methods	Unreal surroundings, Little data about why, Cost of large samples
Count	When requirement involves total numbers of people involved in certain actions	Cost, Speed, Large samples	Little data about why, No analysis possible by profile of individual
Observation	When the concern is more with *how* people act than *why*	Direct observation of what people do rather than what they *say* they do	Cost, Sample structure
Participant observation	When only information at a very detailed level is of value	Depth of response	Very high cost and very long time taken, Problems of representative sample

Telephone Surveys

No researcher training can be complete without the classic story of one of the earliest of all surveys, carried out to predict the results of the American presidential elections. The survey was conducted by telephone, only the sponsors being unaware that those with telephones were richer and more likely to vote Republican. The result was wildly wrong; yet personal interviews carried out at the same time by another organization showed how clearly opinion polls could predict voting patterns.

By now, most people in the US may have telephones, but the proportion in this country is still no higher than 27 per cent, thus clearly precluding their use for any form of survey involving a cross-section of the whole population or for groups other than those for which there is reason to suppose that telephone ownership is almost universal. If this were the only problem, it is true that almost all interviews with executives or professional people *could* be carried out by telephone; it could be used with groups for whom a telephone is essential, e.g., builders, individual car hire operators, and so on.

There are, however, further problems with telephone interviews. Whether more useful results are produced as a result or not, it is a fact of modern research that there is a consistently greater use of aids—pictures of mastheads of papers, illustrations of advertisements, lists of scales or words to choose from and so on. No technique involving aids can be used on the telephone, and to send the aids through the post in advance, as is sometimes suggested, inevitably raises an unknown degree of bias because of the advance knowledge provided in the respondent.

More important than either of these limitations is the difficulty of establishing *rapport* through a telephone. Those likely to be available for telephone interviews are also those most likely to need to be reassured as to the credentials of the interviewer, the purpose of the survey and so on; the interviews which finally emerge may be of the highest quality but only if the respondents are first satisfied on points such as these. It is true here that a letter can provide advance warning and explanation and a prearranged time for the call can be made, but this provides far less *rapport* than that of a responsible interviewer fully briefed to explain the purpose of the survey and the importance of the respondent's personal contribution.

When all this is said it remains true that the telephone interview plays a major part—and probably one of increasing importance—in the researcher's armoury. We are not concerned with industrial research in this book, but in the consumer field there are many surveys which involve interviews with those almost certain to be on the telephone but equally likely to be hard to contact personally—owners of expensive cars, of deep freezers, readers of business papers, users of credit cards and so on. Lists selected from client's records would probably provide the framework of the survey, but even with a car and by making prior appointments an interviewer would usually be hard put to it to do more than two such interviews an evening. If a great deal of data is required, then the costs involved in personal contact are worthwhile. What happens, however, if one's only concern is a comparatively simple piece of information? Do they belong to one particular professional group? Can they remember the context of a commercial recently shown on television? Have they had particular forms of trouble with their car? And indeed the cost differential becomes even more dramatic when a before-and-after interview may be involved in order to assess changing views as a result of an advertisement and two such calls are necessary.

There are refinements and rather more special uses of this approach. While in general simultaneous recall techniques never seem to have found much favour, the telephone is ideally suited (again if the nature of the sample to be interviewed justifies it) for calls immediately after a television programme or related to an evening newspaper advertisement where it is essential to check recall within a given period after exposure, and where a large number of calls must be done in a short time. Probably even more important, as with many other techniques discussed in this chapter, is the use of the telephone interview *in conjunction with* the personal interview. It might, for example, be sensible to ask a few extra questions *after* a launch to those selected from a pre-launch survey as the most likely users. These additional questions can be asked by telephone to all recorded originally as having the use of a telephone; other interviews would have to be carried out personally.

It is the writer's contention that telephone surveys by their nature can never be as efficient as the personal interview; even with coincidental recall the theoretically correct solution must be to use a very large number of interviewers for a very short time. In practical terms the cost differential is sometimes so great and the efficiency loss so small that telephone interviewing may well become a perfectly reasonable solution. On certain types of interviewing with small minority sample, for example, personal interviews might well cost £10.00 to £15.00 each while telephone calls could cost only £1.50 to £2.00. If 200 or 300 such interviews are required, then the use of the telephone becomes almost inevitable.

Self Completion Questionnaires

Chapter 9 has been devoted to mail questionnaires. These by their nature are self-completion questionnaires. Reference should perhaps be made here, however, to other forms and particularly to the fact that self-completion questionnaires can be of considerable value *in conjunction with* standard interviewer studies as part of what is, in effect, one questionnaire. In these circumstances they are not usually sent by post but left by the interviewer.

This is particularly the case in product tests. In some cases, the test can be made on the spot, in others it does not matter a great deal if comments are not collected until the interviewer returns to obtain views on the product. There is an intermediate group of cases, however, when the *immediate* reaction of the housewife, and perhaps also of her family, is of considerable importance. As examples of this we may cite:

(a) a cough mixture left with people to take when they get a cough. Although those taking part were asked to contact the market research company as soon as the cough developed to arrange a personal interview, some report on the immediate interchange of cough and remedy seemed essential and this was done by means of a form left with the respondent;
(b) a new product which involved unfamiliar cooking patterns. When the housewife was in the process of making it, it was essential that she should also make a note of snags which she encountered, the immediate results and the immediate comments of the family;
(c) a paired comparison test of two cigarettes. To do the test while the interviewer waited would make it most unreal. To leave it to the respondent in his own time was far more realistic provided that he was sure to record what his feelings were at the time rather than recalling them at a later stage.

An alternative approach involves the self-completion questionnaire as a form of *aide memoire*. Development of new products may be assisted by knowledge of how current products are used in a detail for which memory may be dangerous except over very short periods. A new form of instant coffee, for example, may depend for its success on how many cups are made at any one time, or a new baby food on whether the mother usually prepares food for the baby at the same time as food for adult members of the household. Recording of this kind is, of course, close to the diary panels considered in chapter 8, but there is no need for a panel to be involved, the respondent being asked to co-operate only in a single study.

This type of approach is also of value on occasions where respondents would be *able* to tell the interviewer their answers but might be somewhat embarrassed to do so. Probably, this is less important today than it was even ten years ago, e.g., on a recent survey a few sudden questions on brands of contraceptives used appeared to cause very little problem even though both interviewers and respondents were specifically told to omit these if they wished. On the other hand, answers thought to be *socially unacceptable*, e.g., strong approval of South African apartheid policies, could well be expressed by some people more forcibly on a piece of paper than to a total stranger.

Self-completion interviews of the kinds so far considered assume completion in the home. A separate use of the same technique is involved when self-completion means mass-completion. The most obvious instance of this is that of theatre tests when a representative sample is invited to see a series of films interspersed by commercials. At various stages in the performance the audience is invited to answer questions usually about the products concerned in the advertisements. Which would they buy? What do they see as particular advantages and disadvantages of each?

224

Questionnaires are distributed for self-completion primarily because of the expense and time involved in the simultaneous personal interviewing of all people in a theatre, but in consequence the approach suffers from most of the same limitations as any other form of self-completion and mail questionnaire. It does, however, have one major advantage over other forms. In the course of an evening respondents may well fill in half a dozen *separate* simple questionnaires. However, they have filled in the first ones unaware of what is to follow. This removes the bias which sometimes can exist in any form of self-completion survey caused by respondents knowing in advance what further questions he is likely to be asked.

Ironmongery

In the techniques so far considered, the main variations from the standard interview approach are in the *method* of collection of data rather than in what is collected. Whether the interview is asked personally, or left for the respondent to fill in, or asked over the telephone, the question-and-answer approach applies, and the information collected is recorded and coded in a generally standard form. For the further techniques discussed in this chapter, this no longer applies; the interviewer is no longer a recorder of what is said, the respondent is no longer necessarily expected to provide in words or writing what she is doing and saying and thinking. Actions are now speaking rather than words. Hardware and counts and observation imply the use of an interviewer to report what is happening; they watch, they do not ask.

In operations of this kind, much help can be given by the use of mechanical equipment; indeed, in some instances such equipment can, in fact, provide data which could not be obtained in any other way. Almost without exception, however, apart from the use of television meters* such 'hardware' has been found to have only limited uses in market research, and a description of how some current machinery works may in itself indicate the reason for the limitations.

We must include in this category the *camera*. On occasions this may be used only to provide still photographs, e.g., for use in a survey covering a representative sample of kitchens to discover the extent to which there was room in them, (if necessary after rearrangement) to add extra durable goods. It is more likely, however, to be a moving record. A recently reported case using this technique was carried out by the London Transport Executive[1]. The object of the study was to assess the proportion of the

---

* Although audience measurement devices are of the same kind as those considered in this section, they are the subject of separate discussion in chapter 25. It is perhaps relevant to point out, however, one basic argument against such machines is very similar to that considered here; the fact that the television is on is recorded by the meter, but this on its own tells us nothing about who is in the room and whether, in fact they are watching.

population given the opportunity to view posters on bus sides. On special buses following randomly selected standard routes, cameras were placed above the advertisement used as a test. By replaying the film thus made available it was possible to analyse in part the nature of the potential audience (defined as those passing the bus and at least part facing) and from this to make deductions as to the total audience.

Such a survey naturally cannot be concerned in any way with whether respondents did see the advertisement concerned, only with whether they had the *opportunity*. Much of the equipment devised is more specifically concerned with what the eye does, in fact, see and what it passes to the brain. For a year or so in the early 1960's work with special equipment was carried out on subliminal advertising and the effect of messages displayed too fast for the eye apparently to see but yet probably absorbed by the brain; and at a later stage there was a belief that data as to the state of mind of a purchaser in a supermarket could be disclosed by recording the 'blink rate.' A concealed special camera recorded the speed at which the shopper blinked; the slower the blink rate the more 'hypnotised' she was said to be by choice, the more open to suggestion. A separate technique widely discussed a few years ago involved pupil dilation, the average percentage change in this being assumed to measure the degree of interest in the advertisement or display being studied[2]. On another study—this time not involving a camera—fingerprints were recorded to test page traffic on a magazine. All these 'machines' are now generally discredited.

The *psychogalvanometer* remains with us and has been used far more[3]. The respondent watches television or reads copy 'wired' by means of small suction cap electrodes fitted to the back of his hand and connected to a machine recording sweat variations. Precise nervous reactions are thus recorded to what he is seeing. As with many other techniques considered in this chapter the main objection is the question of what any reaction means. In certain cases, it must be admitted, tape recording provides *in parallel* what the respondent is saying as his reactions are being recorded on the psycho-galvanometer, but this again does not necessarily mean that the respondent will behave in a predictable way in a subsequent behavioural situation.

The *tachistoscope*[3] is far more widely accepted although it is probably far less used than five or ten years ago. This machine tests to calibrations of $\frac{1}{100}$th of a second the reaction of a respondent to what he sees through a shutter: it may be a test of the comparative legibility of pack or label design or the extent to which one pack stands out against all its competitors, or the *part* of the advertisement which is most likely to be seen first. A simple tachistoscope measures a single stimulus at a time, but further developments with stereoscope or binocular models allow the exposure of two stimuli simultaneously with independent and variable light densities and at the same time allow tests to be made on eye dominance. Other things being equal, it is assumed that the name or the display which is recognized in the fastest time is the most likely to be successful. However, of course, other things rarely are equal, and there is a good deal of evidence that the most effective advertisement is the one which is less likely to be seen immediately, but is studied in detail when it is. Used side-by-side with other techniques, however, the tachistoscope can be of considerable use.

All these techniques are, in fact, best used in conjunction with direct interviewing. A rather newer form of eye camera can *only* be used in such conjunction, by a procedure known as DEMOS[4]. This springs from the need to be able to relate what is remembered in advertisements to what has definitely been seen. Is complete lack of recall of an advertisement due to the fact that the respondent has not, in fact, seen it all, her eye having completely overlooked the page, or has she seen it and found it so totally uninteresting that she has no recollection of having seen it? By means of an ingenious lay-out of mirrors and camera the respondent is watched unobserved as she turns the pages of a magazine, and a record is made of the time she has taken page by page, and area by area. A later questionnaire considers her recall of advertisements and relates this to what she has seen and how long she has spent reading it. This is a case where mechanical aids are used to assist the interviewing technique rather than to replace it. There are other forms of hardware with much the same purpose, and in the foreseeable future, portable video machines or cassettes may be attached to television sets to allow this kind of advertising testing to be carried out in the more realistic surroundings of the respondent's own home. There are already, however, other useful aids of this kind; to take one example, the purchase of any major item—a car, a house—involves the consideration of a number of factors, on which the buyer must place varying stress to keep within his budget. He is unlikely, for example, to be able to afford a house which meets all his requirements, or even most of them. What 'premium' does he place on the number of rooms, or nearness to the shops, or proximity of other houses? In market research terms it is usual that one ranks such attributes in order of importance but can rarely force the respondent into a position where he can put a cash value on what he has chosen.

Gerald Hoinville[5] has developed an appliance which in some ways resembles the children's general knowledge game where plugs connected to the right answer to a question bring on a light. In the market research instance, within a box are illustrated a series of different attributes which people might bear in mind when buying, say, a house; against each there is a price. The respondent is given pegs to represent money which he can use as he likes to 'buy' advantages. What he has bought lights up, the other attributes remain dark. What is important about this technique is that it reveals to the respondent that his willingness to 'buy', for example, garage space and a corner site, may mean that he has no money left to ensure nearness to a bus route or the fact that he is not overlooked. The technique at the moment is a crude one, but is useful as an illustration of a way in which, in the future, hardware may develop as an aid to interviewing rather than as a replacement.

Counts

Between the use of mechanical equipment and of observation lies the simple count. 'Simple' is, perhaps, a misnomer if the count technique is seen (as is technically possible) to embrace almost all forms of audience meter recording and retail audits. Occasions exist, however, when a count carried out by interviewers can provide more useful data than an actual interview.

At the beginning of the Second World War civilians were supposed to carry their gas-masks wherever they went[6]. These were, however, cumbersome articles and most people chose to forget them. On certain occasions, it was noticed that the proportions carrying them seemed to rise sharply, and a study of the news on the progress of the war revealed what appeared to be a consistent relationship between the proportions carrying gas-masks and the state of general morale. Counts were consistently carried out to assess morale until such time as the fear of gas attack so abated that few people carried masks on any occasions at all. This technique could not be validated, since direct questioning (at a time when it might have been thought unpatriotic to be depressed) revealed that the stated comments of the general public showed a far closer relationship to the official attitude of 'do or die'. In more recent applications, however, the same technique has been used in a number of projects to provide data difficult to collect in other ways; to take one example, operational research has apparently established that pedestrian subways will not generally be used when the time taken to travel through the subway is markedly longer than that taken above ground. It is highly doubtful, however, if people consciously realize this fact, and certainly they would not have been able to answer with any precision before a particular subway was built. Simple timing of road-crossing under laboratory conditions were meaningless when little was known about traffic flows or the difference in speed of crossing at different times of day.

An unpublished survey of this kind was conducted with the traffic entering and leaving one of London's main railway stations. Brief interviews first established the proportions likely to be crossing given roads where subways were planned, and preliminary counts checked the numbers crossing such roads at various times of the day. Then, using a random selection technique and stopwatch, interviewers timed pedestrians from the moment they *reached* the curb they planned to step off, to the moment they were able to *step on to* the opposite one. Average times were calculated and it became apparent that subways costing many thousands of pounds would be unlikely to be used at least for some years to come; for the most part, people did not have to wait long enough to make them likely to go down one flight of steps and up the other.

Counts can also establish data which would again not be forthcoming from direct questioning because of difficulties of obtaining either correct samples or answers unaffected by memory or feat or consequences of reply. The 'dustbin audit' of AGB described in chapter 8 is one such example.

In similar vein, however, it is possible to estimate the extent of all-day parking in meter areas by checking registration numbers of cars either remaining on one meter (with the meter being fed) or moving very short distances. It is a simple matter on the computer if regular counts are held through the day to record the time at which a car enters the area and the time at which it leaves it, and by so doing to calculate the extent to which meters are used by all-day parkers. Direct questioning presents alternative problems.

Counts suffer from the same problems as many other techniques described in this chapter: they record but they do not explain. There are many cases, however, where accurate reporting is all that is, in fact, required, and where direct interviewing will not provide such clear data.

Observation

The research use of investigator observation was made widely known in this country as a result of work before the war by Mass Observation: basically its founders, Tom Harrisson and Charles Madge[6], argued that there were very many areas of knowledge in which people would not answer correctly, either because they did not know the correct reply or because they would be unwilling to tell from embarrassment or from various reasons of prestige.

In the thirty or so years since the founding of Mass Observation, many arguments have weakened the original thesis. Their early work was epitomized by vivid descriptions of public events such as wrestling matches and election meetings or of private and family matters, but these are now covered more simply, if not more efficiently, by the use of documentary film particularly in television. Techniques of asking questions have improved and extended, and in parallel with this the principle of the question-and-answer survey has become more widely accepted; respondents are thus less reticent in revealing intimate information or that which is difficult to collect, and motivation research has helped to define in what areas questions are appropriate. Nevertheless, the need for observation remains. Observation has been described[7] as a primary tool of social enquiry which becomes a scientific technique when it:

(a) serves a formulated research purpose;
(b) is planned systematically;
(c) is recorded systematically and related to general propositions;
(d) is subject to checks and controls on validity and reliability.

In the intense forms of the technique, which are mainly anthropologically inspired, there are a separate set of problems discussed later. Simpler techniques, however, are now gaining wide favour again. Many recent developments, for example, involve a skilled investigator watching some simple household process to find areas for new product development. At what stage, for example, in her cleaning routine, does the housewife find something difficult to clean but where a new gadget might help[8]? Are there new products which the housewife could use as instant or convenience foods which would help here with her regular routines? This can be expanded more widely in many areas. No housewife could probably tell exactly how much salt or cornflour she uses in simple recipes and she would be unlikely even to admit that she often guessed; certainly for whatever reasons estimates from direct questionnaires are almost always very inflated. Observation, however, particularly when its main purpose is masked, can provide better data on how the housewife acts.

Few beer drinkers would know in exactly what terms they asked for their beer—they would *think* or *report* that they said, 'Half of light ale, please', when what they probably said was, 'The same again, Fred'. Nor would they always know the extent to which what they had ordered was, in fact, supplied. Do they get the same in all pubs, for example, when they ask for a 'pint of the best', or 'a half of keg'? To brewers, this is vital in terms of advertising copy and in the extent to which criticisms of their product perhaps spring from the wrong product being provided by the barman.

Observation techniques are also of use in studying more detailed behaviourist patterns. A recent unpublished study, for example, related the actual driving of motorists to their driving personalities assessed by a series of psychological questions. The driving assessment involved three observers taking drivers on a standard test route, one in the front giving instructions as to where the driver was to go, two in the back recording handling of gears and clutch, use of side mirrors, number of times the car concerned was overtaken or overtook, and so on. The driver knew that he was being studied but the system was so simple and the observers so well concealed that it seemed almost certain that after the first few minutes driving behaviour became normal.

There remain two basic problems about all observation work. The first is that the cost involved, not only in observation but in writing up and training, usually implies limited regional areas, or small sample bases, and the critic can in consequence always fault it on the grounds that what has been found out would not apply elsewhere. Most of the early work done by Mass Observation, for example, concentrated on studying one Lancashire town in great detail, and even though a few further towns were studied with less concentration there is little evidence available to indicate that what emerged from one town was true even for another ten miles away, let alone for another part of the country.

It is also true (although not for participant observation) that studies can only report on what happens and draw conclusions from this, excluding the 'why's' of what is done. Sometimes these speak for themselves, like the elaborate treating rituals found in many pubs whereby all those involved in groups find themselves at the end of the evening having paid out the same sums; but others are open to a series of different interpretations. Work was carried out, for example, on the selection of books from public libraries. People were observed at a distance; details including the extent to which they read titles, looked at books, the parts of the books which they looked at and so on were noted. What did it mean if a person picked up a book, looked at the cover, read the last page and put it down again? That he had read it already? That it had an unhappy ending? That there were too many long words or too many pages? All these interpretations were possible, none could be accepted as definitive; and probably the reader, even if he had been asked, would not have been able to unscramble his motives.

One must also stress that these forms of observation require training, and that few interviewers, however skilled at questionnaire techniques, are able to carry out this sort of work. It is necessary to spot and record the relevant detail and to report it in quite objective terms. An interviewer may well be used to writing down precisely what has been said; it is quite a different thing to decide herself what should be recorded about actions rather than words.

Participation

In the observation techniques so far described the interviewer has served in the function of an impartial observer—almost an automaton—and an essential of the observer's function has sometimes been that those observed do not know that they are being observed. We have seen that one of the serious limitations of such techniques lies in the fact that little or no information is obtained for the *reasons* behind the actions observed.

It does not follow however, that the observer *has* to be anonymous. There is a sense in which any group discussion involves an observer playing a role in the exploration of the subject of the study and certainly in synectic groups this aspect becomes increasingly important (see chapter 1). Even if we exclude this field, however, this section must include reference to what may be called participant observation. This technique owes much to the early work of the anthropologists and ethnologists and, again, was introduced into the market research field by Tom Harrisson (who would probably not draw the division made here between participant and non-participant observation[9]). It is now widely accepted by journalists and users of the documentary (witness the recent television film on the Royal Family where journalists and cameramen accompanied the Queen through private and public engagements over a long period) but its research uses are even more strictly limited than those of simpler forms of observation, almost entirely because of the length of time involved in laying the groundwork.

Many sociological studies make great use of the continuous observation of a single family to reveal, for example, kinship patterns or socialization of children, but it is not often that market research needs to explore issues at such depth. An observer using this approach must first find a family he thinks will be likely to illustrate the problems with which he is concerned: he has then to persuade them to accept him into the family circle for all events, weddings, funerals, quarrels, and so on, and he must then continuously ask his questions slowly and carefully so as not to destroy any mutual trust or create suspicion. And when results are written up he is open to constant criticism, which is extremely difficult to answer, that had he taken a family in a different road, let alone a different town, the conclusions which he had drawn would not have been the same. He must prove too, that his presence has not affected the situation.

There is little doubt of the value of these techniques at the academic level and it is probable that the method has considerable uses in market research not so far really exploited; for example, for studies of shops, and their customers, or reactions to given events taking place over a short period. It seems unlikely, however, that it will ever be of very general importance in the market research armoury.

The above, of course, assumes that the researcher must be 'injected' into a group and must make himself accepted by it; but what if a series of observers all report on their own family circle, in which they are already accepted? This, again, was a technique developed by Mass Observation in the years before the Second World War, and used fairly widely until the end of that war. Some hundreds of people reported monthly on what they themselves were doing, and how those with whom they were directly concerned were reacting to events.

Changes in social climate and in sociology itself tended to make this work increasingly less useful and it is doubtful if there could be a revival in this approach except in specialized areas, such as the recording of dreams or fears. Reports were inevitably subjective, to a degree which made it difficult to know what weight to put on individual comments, however graphically expressed; but perhaps more important was the fact that in the mid-thirties there were many working class people, anxious to express themselves in this way but unable to get a job which allowed them to do so; today the increasing influence of higher education has meant that panels of observers of the kind considered here become more and more composed of teachers and civil servants, precisely those groups most likely to be willing to answer postal and other forms of questionnaire when the need arises.

Some General Comments

In many sections of this chapter reference has been made to the fact that the techniques described are open to serious criticism on the grounds that they do not necessarily describe a representative sample. How does one know that the person who answers on a telephone has the same views as the person without a telephone? How does one know that the people who have been counted are representative of the population concerned?

Almost always, the answer is that one does *not* know, and to find out at a level to satisfy the statisticians would be impossibly expensive. Many of the hardware techniques described are, of course, carried out in laboratories and respondents can be selected to reflect a representative cross-section; but here the costs per interview can be high (as they are in most forms of observation) and, while statistical tests can often be done to prove significance, there is very widespread doubt as to the validity of samples of fifty or sixty. With counts, on the other hand, many thousands may be involved: but from what universe have they been taken?

It is probable that the researcher will always have to live with this problem and the only practical solution is the compromise of the largest and 'best' sample which is feasible within the prescribed budget. Certainly, if the techniques employed seem to be producing results not obtainable by other methods but which appear to be of real use, then the argument for using them in whatever detail possible seems a strong one.

A second point is, perhaps, more fundamental although not often discussed. A convention of market research (although it is obviously open to much argument, especially from the psychologists) is that the nature of the direct interview is such that it provides information only at *one* level of consciousness or communication and that this is a useful level. There are many others which could be used from the subconscious world of dreams to the purely formal one of polite and meaningless conversation. In another dimension, the interview usually (though by no means always) involves an immediate answer to an immediate question while, to take an extreme, the anthropological approach to a subject may be discussed intensively over weeks. A 'deeper' answer is not necessarily a 'better' one or, in more practical terms, one of which greater use can be made, but it is not measuring the same thing.

Similarly, while a good deal of evidence is to hand that interviewer personality makes less difference to the nature of answers provided than was at one time assumed, the degree and nature of the *rapport* must in some way show through the answers to any study. This *rapport* must be different if, on the one hand, the 'interviewer' is a person who lives as part of the family circle for months, on the other he is seen as the hand on the switch of the psychogalvanometer. Again, recommended action must, to some extent, be on pragmatical grounds.

For all their weaknesses and unsolved difficulties of comparison, do the special techniques considered here add something not otherwise provided? If they do, then there is a reason for using them. If they do not, there is none.

References

1. DAY, P. S. and DUNN, J. Estimating the Audience for Advertising on the Outside of Buses, *Applied Statistics* **18**, 3, 1961.
2. KONIG, G. and LOVELL, M. *The Measurement of Pupil Dilation as a Research Tool*, ESOMAR Conference Paper, 1965.
3. CAFFYN, J. A. and BROWN, N. A. The Application of Psychological Ironmongery to Commercial Problems, *Commentary*, Jan., 1965.
4. FLETCHER, R. *Reading Behaviour Reconsidered*, ESOMAR Conference Paper, 1969.
5. HOINVILLE, G. Paper given at Market Research Society Seminar Research for Social Policy, Feb., 1970.

6. Madge, C. and Huxley, J. *Mass Observation* 1937 (see also Harrisson, T., *Pub and the People*, Gollancz, 1943; *War Begins at Home*, Chatto and Windus, 1940).
7. Selltiz, J. Deutsch and Cook, *Research Methods in Social Relations*, Methuen, 1960.
8. Patrick, M. How to do the Washing Up in 41 Easy Stages, *Campaign* **20**, 4, 70.
9. Malinowski, R. *A Nation-Wide Intelligence Service*, First Year's Work, Lindsay Drummond, 1938.

234

Section 2.   **Analysing the data**

Introduction

The stage has now been reached when the data has been collected by using the techniques described in section 1. What the user requires now is that the data are analysed quickly and efficiently so that the maximum amount of usable information is obtained. He also wishes to know how accurate the results are and whether the results are 'real' or can just be explained as the fluctuations of random sampling. In addition, the user needs to be told of the complex interrelationships of various parts of the data. Only when he has been given all these things is he able to use the research results with confidence, and be sure that they can profitably assist in the marketing decisions. Of course, any analysis of the data is only as good as the data that has been collected. No amount of 'playing with numbers' can get over such problems as questions asked in a biased way, questions missing from the questionnaire and incorrect measuring techniques.

In the last decade tremendous advances have been seen in the analysis of of market research surveys. Most of this has been due to the advent of the computer, which has brought speed and flexibility to the handling of data. This advance, though bringing obvious advantages, is not without its drawbacks. Previously the researcher had, because of time and cost considerations, to limit the number of tables produced from any survey, and thus it forced him to think objectively about the analysis. It was necessary to consider only the most important hypotheses about the data, and this had the effect of disciplining the researcher in his approach to survey analysis. Now, as the on-cost of producing a large amount of survey tabulations or extra analyses is small, there is a tendency to analyse 'everything by everything' and just 'see what comes up'. In some cases, where a new topic is being investigated, for example, this may pay dividends; but as has been pointed out[1] this testing of a large number of hypotheses simultaneously has to be handled carefully to avoid incorrect conclusions being drawn from the data. With this reservation, however, it must be stated that the increasing technological nature of survey analysis methods has mainly had a good influence on the analysis and interpretation of market surveys. Nowhere is this more true than in the use of advanced statistical techniques to discover important and complicated relationships in the data that has been collected (see chapter 13).

The inclusion or exclusion of certain topics in the three chapters that follow was a matter for lengthy discussion. Some of the notable omissions are briefly discussed below when reviewing each chapter. References are given where possible so that readers whose interest is in these topics may investigate them further.

Chapter 11 describes what happens to a batch of questionnaires that have been sent in by the fieldworkers. It tells how the questionnaires are checked, and how the data are transferred to a medium, such as punched cards or paper tape, which is used as input to an electronic computer. The methods of analysis given are mainly in terms of a general 'one off' quantitative survey. The temptation was resisted to include the special problems and methods of specific types of surveys such as qualitative surveys or panels and audits. Details of the analysis of data from such sources are given in the chapters devoted to them or in the references given in those chapters. The field of market research survey analysis is a continually changing one. Apart from the introduction of electronic computers themselves, there have been a number of peripheral advances in such things as the automatic conversion of questionnaires into punched cards or magnetic tape. This has been done by introducing machines which can sense pencil marks in certain places on the questionnaire, or can recognize characters such as letters or numbers which have been recorded in boxes on the questionnaire. At present very few surveys are actually using such processing methods, as the machines like to have pre-printed fixed format questionnaires. In the case of single 'ad hoc' surveys, where the layout of the questionnaire is unique, this would mean designing a special version of the questionnaire each time and 'programming' the sensing device to deal with it. Where such techniques are most useful is for analysing the panel or shop audit survey, where the data collection form remains standard over a long time. However, such data handling techniques are continually being developed and during the next few years we can expect technological advances in this field which will overcome the questionnaire format problem and lead to automated data handling for most surveys.

The next chapter is concerned with elementary statistics obtained from survey tabulations and the testing of statistical hypotheses using a group of testing procedures which come under the general heading of significance tests. These are used to explain whether observed differences in the data are due to the errors of sampling. It is well known, however, that the total error in any survey result comes from non-sampling errors, e.g., non-response and measurement errors, as well as sampling errors. Market researchers have paid too little attention in the past to estimating these non-sampling errors. Attempts have been made to quantify such errors[2] and to build them into a framework for estimating total survey error[3], but not much of this work has passed into current practice. The results of surveys are sometimes used as input to market forecasting exercises, especially when a survey has been repeated over a number of years. There is a body of statistical techniques subsumed under the heading of time series analysis, which can assist the researcher whose statistical analysis of surveys includes future projections of market size, etc. Details are not included in this section's chapters as this would have taken too much space, and it was thought that such techniques were more often used by the statistical specialists in marketing departments than by the average market researcher. For those who wish to read about such techniques three references[4,5,6] are given at the end of this introduction.

Chapter 13 deals with the more advanced statistical techniques used to analyse market research data. The techniques go under the general heading of multivariate analysis. In most cases no single thing determines what makes consumers buy the products they buy or makes them behave in a certain way. The influences on consumers are many and varied, including such things as past behaviour and attitudes to the product. It is not surprising, therefore, that multivariate statistical methods, i.e., those which examine a large number of survey characteristics simultaneously, are widely used by survey analysts. The methods used are mathematically complicated but the description of them in this chapter only involves simple algebra.

Paul Harris

References

1. SELVIN, H. C. and STUART, A. Data Dredging Procedures in Survey Analysis, *The American Statistician*, pp. 20–23, June, 1966.
2. COCHRAN, W. G. *Sampling Techniques, Sources of Errors in Surveys*, John Wiley and Sons, Inc., Second Edition, 1963.
3. BROWN, R. V. Evaluation of Total Survey Error, *The Statistician*, **17**, 4, pp. 335–356, 1967.
4. GREGG, J. V. *et al. ICI Monograph No. 1—Mathematical Trend Curves: An Aid to Forecasting*, Oliver and Boyd Ltd, 1964.
5. COUTIE, G. A. *et al. ICI Monograph No. 2—Short Term Forecasting*, Oliver and Boyd Ltd, 1964.
6. KENDALL, M. G. and STUART, A. *The Advanced Theory of Statistics*, **3**, Chapters 45–50, Charles Griffin and Co. Ltd, 1966.

11. Coding, editing, and processing of market research data

G. W. Roughton

In earlier chapters techniques have been described for obtaining market research data. These techniques mostly provide raw data. Before the data can be used in most types of surveys it must be converted from its raw state into finished tabulations. These show the practitioner what the findings of the survey are, and will allow statistical and other appropriate tests to be applied. This usually involves coding, editing and processing. Editing is carried out to correct or remove obvious logical or factual errors in the raw data; coding, to classify informant responses in terms of a predetermined coding frame, and processing, to produce summaries of the results as well as cross tabulations to show the presence or absence of relevant relationships in the data. It may be useful to begin by considering the more common forms of data.

Forms of Data

By far the most common document in market research is the interviewer-administered questionnaire. These consist of lists of pre-coded and open-ended questions. In pre-coded questions, interviewers mark or 'code' the appropriate pre-printed answer to show into which of the categories (pre-codes) printed on the questionnaire the informant's reply falls. To a question such as, 'Have you purchased a washing-machine in the past twelve months?', an obvious set of pre-coded answers would be 'Yes', 'No' and for the sake of completeness, 'Don't know'. It is important to include categories such as 'don't know' so as to leave as little doubt as possible in the interviewer's mind as to the category into which the particular answer should be placed. Badly designed pre-codes will mean that the interviewer has some difficulty in fitting answers into the pre-coded list. As a result, errors may be introduced by inadvertently forcing answers into pre-codes to which they do not belong. In open-ended questions, informants' replies are written out by the interviewer. There may be some probing with answers of several sentences. In other cases, where a question is purely a factual one, an open-ended answer may consist of only one or two words; for example, a question about consumption could elicit a number as an answer.

Generally, it is unwise to use pre-codes where the interviewer, unless specially trained, requires to exercise any degree of judgement in determining into which category the answers should fall. On the other hand, pre-coding greatly reduces processing time and the cost of coding. It also tells the interviewer the kind and detail of answers you are expecting. Questionnaires involving a mixture of open-ended and pre-coded questions with space for the answers to be either coded or written in by the interviewers, are by far the most common form of questionnaire administered in market research. Some brief notes are given below on other types of document. In certain kinds of study, e.g., postal surveys, a self-completion questionnaire is used. They are largely pre-coded and extremely simple. Although they are different in certain respects from interviewer questionnaires, the steps through which they subsequently pass are exactly the same.

Instead of, or in conjunction with, carrying out interviews using a questionnaire, interviewers may record the activities or behaviour of informants on specially designed transfer or other forms of document involving such things as mark sense cards and optical reading. Mark sense cards are a special form of punch card (punch cards are fully described later in this chapter) measuring about $3\frac{1}{4}$ in. $\times$ $7\frac{3}{8}$ in. on which a number of small rectangular boxes are printed. Each box may be marked with a line using a special graphite pencil. These marks can then be interpreted by appropriate card reading devices. Optical reading enables marks placed in special boxes on ordinary paper to be similarly interpreted. The speed, reliability, and flexibility of optical reading is, however, very much more highly developed than mark sensing.

There are other more advanced methods of data recording which are appropriate for large scale or repetitive types of project where there is ample time available to design the entire data recording procedure. One of the better known examples is the use of special meters to record household television viewing.

Editing

The first stage through which the data must pass is editing. It is a truism to say that not every interviewer will ask and correctly record answers to every question that should have been asked of every informant. Nor indeed, will every informant necessarily be so obliging as to answer every appropriate question. The result is that survey data is normally less than perfect. Although one could reject data which contained any errors at all, this would

240

mean that a considerable amount of useful information was being thrown away simply because of possibly one or two trivial errors at some stage in its collection. The purpose of editing is to reduce or remove the effect of these minor errors. Some common causes of errors are as follows.

Poorly Designed Questionnaires and/or Instructions. These invoke the GIGO principle familiar to all in the computer world (Garbage in = Garbage out). There is usually little if anything, that can be done at the editing or coding stage to retrieve fundamental survey design errors. There is little remedy for missing questions, or incorrect instructions. The best thing to do is to try to make as much use as possible of the data which has been correctly obtained (see chapter 4).

Poor Quality Interviewing. Poor quality interviewing, and the consequent poor quality answering are probably the principal causes of errors that can be corrected at the editing stage. It is often possible for an experienced editor to patch up the questionnaire which has been badly completed by an interviewer who may have been working on a doorstep in bad weather. Despite this, the GIGO principle applies to poor quality interviewing. Although editing can ameliorate the effect, it cannot remove it. The justification for editing in these circumstances is that it is wasteful to reject a questionnaire which has been reasonably well administered, but on which one particular question may not have been correctly asked. The more common types of data errors arising from poor quality interviewing are discussed below. Procedures for dealing with these are, to some extent, a matter of judgement. Policies vary from one organization to another. Some of the more common practices now in existence are noted.

(a) *Missing Data*

For a variety of reasons, it frequently occurs that an interviewer omits to ask a question which she should have asked. In these circumstances, one would begin by attempting to infer the answer from other data on the questionnaire. There are certain circumstances in which this is possible, but there are, of course, dangers if this is taken too far. Alternatively, one may raise a specific 'not answered' category or perhaps base answers to the question at the tabulation stage, only on those informants who actually answered the question rather than on those who should have answered it. In either of these cases the questionnaire is accepted in its present form, and passes through the editing stage. However, it may be of vital importance that an answer to the question concerned is obtained. In these circumstances the questionnaire has to be returned to the interviewer with a request for them to obtain the missing information from the informant. Timing and other administrative considerations may cause difficulties in this latter approach. Interviewers are not particularly co-operative in returning to ask informants one of two additional questions, particularly if the interview was a long one. Often, it is not possible to obtain the information in any case.

(b) *Incorrect Logic*

This occurs when a question or group of questions are answered which should not have been answered or are not answered when they should have been. This latter case obviously comes under the heading of missing data. In the former case, a decision has to be made whether to use the information which should have been collected, in other words, should the logic of the questionnaire be amended to fit the response pattern which appears to exist on the questionnaire. This enables one to accept the redundant data as a sort of bonus. The alternative is to delete the redundant answers, maintaining the original logic of the questionnaire. It is difficult to give a general ruling on which procedure to adopt as it would depend upon the objects of the survey, the size of the sub-bases required for meaningful analyses, and what sort of logical errors are occurring. Generally, however, greater homogeneity in the data will result if the original logic in the questionnaire is adhered to, and the 'bonus' data is rejected.

(c) *Informant Misunderstanding*

It is sometimes clear to an experienced editor that an informant has misunderstood the question. This will usually result from bad questionnaire design. Sometimes it is possible for the editor to infer the answer from the data that is given but, if not, it may be possible to distinguish between those informants who have understood the question correctly and those who have not. If an appropriate code or codes are raised to indicate this, then answers to the partially misunderstood question can be based only upon those informants who have understood it correctly. The resultant data is generally more useful than combining answers of those who have understood with answers of those who have misunderstood.

(d) *Inconsistent or Erroneous Answers*

It frequently occurs that informants will change their mind during the progress of an interview. As a result, it becomes clear that answers given towards the end of the interview are inconsistent with those given at the beginning. It is a matter of judgement as to what should be done in these circumstances. Informants do change their mind, particularly as a result of intensive questionning, which can condition them on a subject, if not actually educate them. One opinion is that to edit out these sort of inconsistencies is to force an unreal pattern of consistency upon the answers. In other cases obviously erroneous factual answers may arise. The editor must determine whether these are due to incorrect recording by the interviewer or arise from the answers to the questions themselves. In the latter case, the fact that the informant has given an erroneous answer may itself be an important item of data. In certain other cases, however, the recording of obviously erroneous data does cause trouble; e.g., in computations of consumption it is important that pack sizes, prices, etc., are correctly recorded. Not to do so would mean that market size estimates, the calculation of which are fraught with difficulties even with proper data, are likely to be badly effected.

(e) *Frivolous Data*

Occasionally it is obvious to an editor that an informant has been insincere in the conduct of the interview. Questionnaires of this kind should not really be submitted by interviewers. These questionnaires, should, without question, be withdrawn. Questionnaires in which the informant has obviously lost interest and has given up half-way should similarly be withdrawn.

Editing may be carried out as a separate operation or in conjunction with coding. It may be carried out manually, mechanically or electronically. It is extremely rare for data to be useable without some form of editing. The aim of editing is to do whatever is legitimately possible in dealing with errors of the type listed above. In dealing with these errors, most of them can be dealt with by modifying the input i.e., the raw data. In certain cases, however, when basing tabulations on those who have answered rather than those who should have answered a question, for example, it is possible for the editing to be carried out, in effect, at the output or table stage. Editing the input data is obviously more thorough, and will ensure that the results of the survey are more consistent. However, editing of the output data is very much quicker and less costly. It is normal, therefore, to make decisions early on in the editing process as to what type of errors are to be dealt with by modifying the input and what kind are to be dealt with at the output stage. At the moment, we are concerned only with editing the raw data at the input stage. The principle reasons for editing should now be clear but it may be useful to review them briefly.

Editing can in many circumstances improve the data itself. Second, the effect of unedited data upon the inexperienced can be disturbing. Many laymen studying survey data have doubts about the legitimacy of taking samples of a population rather than carrying out a census. They are not aware of the various stages to which the data has gone and they may, indeed, find the results highly distasteful. It is not uncommon, therefore, for considerable importance to be attached in these circumstances to minor obvious faults in the data. It is important, in order to establish the proper level of confidence in the data itself, that it should appear to be accurate.

Trivial errors, e.g., resulting in percentages adding to less than 100, e.g., 96, 97, etc., will rarely effect any conclusion likely to be drawn from the data. However, if trivial errors are obvious in the final tabulations which, in the view of the reader could be put right with only five minutes effort, then it obviously conveys a slipshod and unsatisfactory impression.

On the other hand, 100 per cent consistency gives a delusion of accuracy that is not real and is fairly time consuming to achieve. It is important that users of data should be aware that it has limitations, but at the same time, have complete confidence in what they see before them. Editing has to draw a happy medium between pressing a completely unreal rigidity upon data and at the same time preventing the more obvious idiocies appearing in the final output.

Editing can be carried out manually, in which case an 'editor' goes through each data document amending it in accordance with the set of editing instructions. It can be carried out mechanically on a machine such as a counter sorter or electronically using an appropriate computer program.

Manual Editing. In manual editing each survey document is thoroughly examined by an editor who is fully conversant with the conditions which the document should meet. The editor must have a complete written set of instructions, setting out each condition the document is to satisfy, and what they are to do in the event of the condition not being satisfied. As little as possible must be left to the judgement of the individual editor. Different individuals will edit differently, and this will introduce differences into the data which arise from differences between editors rather than in the data itself. Comprehensive written instructions will avoid this. Editing will involve raising or deleting codes on the original survey document. It is essential that this should be carried out in a distinctive colour, e.g., green, which the interviewers had been specifically told not to use. It is then clear afterwards on any particular document, exactly what editing has been done. In this way it is also possible for a supervisor to examine the work done by any particular editor.

Editing instructions should take the editor systematically through the questionnaire or other document showing for each question in the order on the questionnaire what should have happened. The editing instructions will, therefore, follow the logic of the questionnaire. It is customary to lay them out in a stylized format and for these to include coding instructions for the open-ended question as and when they come up. (Coding is discussed separately later on in this chapter but is, in fact, almost invariably carried out simultaneously with editing.) Written instructions are also important to users of the data, so they know what editing has been done. The precise form in which editing instructions are written vary from one organization to the other. However, an example of some typical editing instructions are given below in Table 11.1.

Manually editing, say 1000 questionnaires, each one of which comprised a 20 minute interview might typically require 80–100 manhours to complete by an *experienced* editor. It is perhaps important to say that editing is something that requires experience to be done effectively and accurately. Although it is simple in concept, it can prove tedious and demanding to inexperienced people. The use of unskilled students or other office staff for this function, can sometimes result in a greater number of errors being introduced into the data than had been removed.

Manual editing must be used where any element of judgement has to be exercised by the editor; in other words, where it is not possible by means of a

244

Table 11.1 *Some typical editing instructions*

Question	Editing/coding instructions	Code category	Code	Col
	Classification. *Occupational grouping.* Check group ringed against Occupation of Head of Household *Age.* One pre-code to be ringed between V–2 in C.10 *Children.* Code V or X to be ringed in C.11 *Product tried first.* Code V or X to be ringed in C.12 *Area.* One pre-code to be ringed in C.13			
1	At least one pre-code to be ringed in C.14.			
2 (a)	Code V or X to be ringed in C.18 *All coded X in* C.18. Code V or X to be ringed in C.19			
3	Check that following sections are asked of correct members of the household by checking with Q.1 as to the composition of the household. At least one pre-code to be ringed in relevant columns. If N/A leave blank Columns 21, 23, 25, and 27 will not be used.	Milk.. 8 All other foods.......................... 9		20 and 22 and 24 and 26

simple set of logical rules to say what should happen in a given set of circumstances. This will occur whenever an editing instruction lays down that the editor should try to infer the answer to the question from elsewhere in the questionnaire without specifying where. Manual editing has the advantage that it can be started during the course of the fieldwork, often in sufficient time for interviewers to be informed of the more obvious errors which are occurring. The editor can exercise judgement as to whether or not to accept a questionnaire in total, and is in a better position than any mechanical or electronic method to assess the overall plausibility of a survey document. It is easier for them to write appropriate reports to interviewers on the quality of the work that has been done.

The principle drawbacks with manual editing are that it is usually more costly than other methods and, though it is rarely critical in the timing of a survey, it requires more manhours. Editors, being human, also make errors, and it sometimes happens that errors are still found in data which has been 100 per cent manually edited.

Mechanical Editing. Mechanical editing is possible where data has been transferred to punched cards. It is carried out on the cards rather than on the original document, using punch card unit record equipment, principally the counter sorter. This is a device which enables one to sort cards into groups, dependent upon whether or not holes appear on particular parts of the card (a fuller explanation of punch cards is given later in this chapter). It is therefore possible to check whether informants with a hole on one part of the card,

245

also have a hole, or holes, on some other parts of the card. This enables thorough and exhaustive logical checks to be carried out. Clearly, little judgement can be exercised in respect of individual informants. What the procedure does is to isolate those informants, i.e., cards, which contain a particular error and additional codes may then be raised on the cards concerned. This type of editing is extremely quick and effective for logic checking. It is therefore inexpensive and there is little or no room for error (assuming the machine is working correctly, which is not always the case). Instructions are necessary only in the form of punch card logic.

Computer Editing. Computer editing is similar to mechanical editing. The principle difference, however, is that whereas only one editing instruction can be executed at one time on the counter/sorter, several hundred can be executed at one time on the computer. Computer editing is very much faster, more accurate, and far more complex logical instructions can be specified. A certain amount of skill is normally required in setting up jobs running on the computer, and this is best handled by an appropriate bureau. A number of the computer programs for cross-tabulation have a certain number of built-in editing features. Nowadays, this is the principle form of editing carried out.

In an editing operation, a rigorous attitude must be taken to the question of replacing missing data. Legitimate inference is generally acceptable but, at a certain point, inspired guesswork can begin to add information to the data not inherent in its original collection. At a certain point, this would clearly become unethical.

The effect of guessing answers and thereby inserting missing data, is to introduce a random element into the results. It is as though there had been a reduction in the effective sample size on which the survey was based. Clearly, to amend two or three questionnaires out of 1000 on each question is not likely to cause any differences to the results of the survey, but may tidy up one or two irritating inconsistencies. However, since tabulations are often based upon sub-samples, a correction rate of one per cent in a total sample can easily transfer itself into a correction rate of 20 per cent on a sub-base, and clearly a figure of the latter magnitude would be totally unacceptable.

An important element of editing is to provide a method of checking on the quality of the interviewing. In many organizations, editors will compile reports on interviewers' work which can be forwarded to fieldstaff who can take appropriate remedial action. Computerized methods enable analyses by interviewer to be carried out automatically. The advantages of this latter form of quality control are obvious but are beyond the scope of organizations without the appropriate data processing facilities. Editors can often provide useful information on the quality of questionnaire design and layout and if their advice, though from a lowly source, is heeded some useful minor improvements to questionnaires may result.

Coding

In open-ended questions, it is common to obtain a wide variety of answers. It is usually necessary to group these answers together in some way. This is the first function of coding. The second function is to assign numeric or other codes to each category of answers so as to allow subsequent mechanical or electronic processing of the results. Grouping of answers is required because few practitioners can cope with responses to a question where there are dozens of different answers. The proportion of informants giving each answer is often extremely small and many of the answers are either very similar or convey exactly the same sense. Grouping enables the practitioner to see the wood for the trees.

In order to carry out coding, it is necessary to prepare clear printed instructions on both the groupings of answers and on the codes which are to be subsequently assigned to each group. A coder (who may also be the editor) then compares the actual answers on each questionnaire with the various categories given on the coding frame. The coder then decides into which category or categories the informant's answer falls and then assigns the appropriate code or codes. The codes assigned are usually written on the questionnaire and, as with editing, a distinctive colour should be used for this purpose. Part of a typical coding frame might look as shown in Table 11.2.

Before coding can begin it is necessary to prepare a coding frame. This

Table 11.2   Some typical coding instructions for open-ended responses to what informants disliked about a food product

4(b) and 5(b)	Code for R.42 in Cols. 21 and 22 Code for M.51 in Cols. 25 and 26	Not enough taste/flavour..........	V	
		Powdery taste/uncooked taste....	X	
		Disliked oatmeal taste/like porridge................................	0	
		Too dry............................	1	21
		Too mushy/soggy.....................	2	
		Dislike appearance/looked horrible............................	3	and
		Disliked fruit/raisins hard..........	4	25
		Too bitty/lumpy........................	5	
		Too much fruit/raisins...............	6	
		Not enough fruit/raisins.............	7	
		Not a good texture/coarse/ not smooth............................	8	
		Takes too long to eat.................	9	
		Disliked the nuts........................	V	
		Disliked flakes of oatmeal..........	X	
		Stuck in teeth............................	0	22
		Too heavy/stodgy.....................	1	
		Too sweet................................	2	and
			3	
			4	26
			5	
			6	
		Just disliked it (unspec.).............	7	
		Other dislikes..........................	8	
		DK/NA/nothing disliked...........	9	

involves taking a sub-sample of the data and producing an exhaustive listing of all the answers obtained from each question which requires coding. At this stage no attempt is made to group the answers although it will rapidly become clear that there is a considerable overlap both in words and sense, between some of the separate answers which are listed. Each time an answer is found on a questionnaire the entry on the listing sheet is marked. This will give a very rough count of the number of times each particular answer has occurred.

The disparate answers are then inspected and appropriately grouped together. There are certain problems in preparing coding frames which are discussed below.

In producing the preliminary exhaustive listing referred to above, a proper sample of the data should be taken. This should consist of at least 100 questionnaires. If the first 100 questionnaires that are received are taken, it will quite often happen that this is in no way representative of the total number. It may overrepresent the work of certain interviewers, certain areas or certain time periods. Although timing considerations often press for coding to be carried out simultaneously with the latter stages of fieldwork, a poorly-designed coding frame would frequently result. What then happens is that answers are found in subsequent questionnaires for which no code has been generated at the time that the coding frame was devised. Although coding frames should always provide for the addition of codes when necessary, it will quite frequently happen that coders will put answers for which there is no code into an 'others' category. It will usually be found, therefore, that coding frames based upon a poor sample of total data will have a higher proportion of answers coded as 'others'.

The actual formation of codes can derive from the data itself and are therefore oriented round the replies which informants give; alternatively they may be oriented round the objectives of the survey. A question on informants' comprehension of an advertisement, for example, can be coded on the replies they gave or in terms of whether, from their reply, they appeared to understand a specified message in the advertisement.

In certain cases, a combination of the two is required. In these circumstances two separate sets of codes may be used for the question(s) concerned with double coding in each case. Whatever form of coding is adopted, however, it is important that the coding frame should be considered in the light of survey objectives, and in the light of whether or not an analysis of the answers to the question in terms of the codes proposed will provide useful and actionable data. Failure to do this will often result in a feeling of 'so what' when the results are examined.

The designer of a coding frame must find a compromise between having a sufficiently large number of codes to provide sensitive discrimination between different answers, and too few codes, which result in coders tending to lump answers together in the same categories, even though there may be important, though subtle, differences between them. The best way to avoid this is

248

for the practitioner to examine the preliminary listing in terms of survey objectives, and the proposed coding frame. At the same time the proposed codes should be examined to ensure that they are not ambiguous as this also reduces the efficiency of the coding.

Like editing, coding may in concept seem a comparatively simple operation. However, unless it is carefully organized and appropriately skilled staff used, the quality of the results can be extremely poor. It is not particularly easy to find staff with the intellectual ability to carry out interpretive work of this kind who are also willing to accept its tedious nature. In actually organizing coding, it is important that careful control is kept of the code sheets, so that in the event of additional codes being added after coding has started, this is transcribed on to all of the coding sheets in use. It is not an uncommon practice for the supervisor responsible to keep all coding sheets and to hand these out on a daily basis to the coders concerned. In addition, the supervisor must ensure that coding is carried out consistently; that each coder will code a particular response in the same way(s). This requires thorough checking of each coder's work at the beginning of the coding operation. Consistency grows over time within a particular team of coders.

Another method of ensuring consistency is for a particular question or set of questions to be entirely coded by one coder, another question or set of questions by a different coder and so on. Though greater consistency is achieved, more time is involved in the total coding operation. In some cases, a mixture of both methods is used. This is applicable where the majority of questions are straightforward but where there are perhaps one or two questions requiring a very high degree of consistency or special technical knowledge. In these cases, the latter questions may be reserved for one specially appointed coder.

Analysis

Once data has been edited and coded it is ready for analysis. The object of analysis is to summarize individual items of data, questionnaires or whatever, so that the practitioner can readily know how many informants in the sample gave each of the possible replies to each question. This summary data is usually presented in the form of tables which may show the results not only for the sample as a whole, but also for sub-groups of it, e.g., for males and females separately, young people/old people, etc. This kind of cross-tabulation is extremely important in discovering relevant relationships within the data, and is nowadays carried out more and more extensively. An example of a typical table is given in Fig. 11.1.

Analysis may be carried out by hand, by mechanical methods, or by computer. Although, nowadays, computers are the principal method of analysis, the three methods are described in some detail below. Hand and mechanical methods do have applications, particularly for the smaller, more simple surveys, though for certain kinds of operations, and especially where

TABLE	DISTRIBUTION OF PRODUCT X AND PRODUCT Y
ANALYSED BY	FORM OF ORGANISATION · SELF SERVICE · ESTIMATED SALES PER WEEK
BASE	ALL GROCERS INTERVIEWED IN GREAT BRITAIN

TABLE NO 2
QUESTION

COLUMN PERCENTAGES

RESPONSES	Total	FORM OF ORGANISATION				SELF SERVICE			ESTIMATED SALES PER WEEK				Not Given
		Co-operative	Multiple	Volunt Chain	Independent	+2000 Sq. ft.	-2000 Sq. ft.	Count. Serve	-£100	-£200	-£500	+£500	
	2724	409	611	632	1072	436	700	1588	223	531	811	1068	91
	* * *	* * *	* * *	* * *	* * *	* * *	* * *	* * *	* * *	* * *	* * *	* * *	* * *
PRODUCT X IS	14.	9	23	18	12	24	16	12	4	7	16	24	14
TOS	3.	3	3	3	2	3	5	2	1	2	4	3	4
PRODUCT Y IS	29.	38	33	34	24	43	35	25	15	23	30	40	20
TOS	5.	5	4	5	6	4	4	5	5	6	6	4	1

PROJECT NO 2839

REF 1/61/70   1485

Fig. 11.1. Example of a table showing distribution of products X and Y in grocers.

multivariate methods (see chapter 13) are being used, computers are the only method of analysis.

Hand Analysis

Hand analysis involves the preparation of outline tables or hand summary sheets. One or more of these sheets is prepared for each question. The replies to questions are written down the left-hand side of the sheet with appropriate columns, across the sheet for any cross-tabulation that may be required. This latter point is explained more fully later on.

Analysis is carried out one question at a time. Using the appropriate hand summary sheet, every questionnaire is examined and an entry made on the appropriate line of the hand summary sheet corresponding to the answer(s) given to that question. It is customary in many organizations for the marking of the summary sheet to take the form of five bar gate scores—four upright marks; with the fifth marked across, e.g., ⼞⼞, ||, etc. Each complete 'gate' represents five responses. This simplifies subsequent counting-up. Where more than one answer is possible to a question the sum of scores against each response will add to more than the total number of questionnaires involved. In order to ensure that this is not due to errors in summarizing, it is normal to provide at the bottom of the sheet concerned appropriate 'overlap' categories. Thus, when the two entries to the sheet are made for one question, an additional entry is also made to a category called 'Overlap 1'. Where three entries are made, the additional category would be made to a category called 'Overlap 2', etc. In this way, a record is kept of the extent of multi-coding of replies. On completion of the summarizing the replies and overlap scores are added up. The overlap scores are further weighted by 1, 2, 3, etc., according to the number of overlaps they represent to give the number of replies which were second (or more) replies. This figure is subtracted from the total replies. The result should be equal to the number of questionnaires which have been summarized. This kind of checking is essential in hand analysis. It is extremely easy for errors to creep in, particularly when this kind of work is done quickly or by inexperienced staff.

In hand summarizing, questionnaires are first bundled into groups or batches. Each bundle is counted and the total number of questionnaires written on each bundle. Each person summarizing then deals with one particular question, i.e., summary sheet, going through one bundle at a time. On completion of each bundle the cumulative scores including overlaps can be counted and checked. Not only does this emphasize the need for accuracy all the time, but if the recording of replies for each bundle is kept separate on the summary sheet, then it is an extremely easy matter to put any errors right by only going through the bundle in error. Not to follow this kind of procedure means that if checking is left to the end, and errors are found, it is necessary to resummarize every bundle for the question(s) in error.

When it is desired to carry out cross-tabulations in which replies to one question are analysed either by classification information or replies to other questions, it is essential to sort the questionnaires into bundles correspond-ing to the breakdowns involved. This must be done one break within the other. This ensures that the figures within each breakdown add back to the same total figure as well as keeping the actual summarizing to a minimum. As an example, let us suppose it was desired to analyse some data by two area codes, three age groups and two social classes, the questionnaires would be sorted into twelve bundles of the following composition:

Bundle	Area code	Age group	Social class
1	1	16 to 34	ABC1
2	1		C2DE
3	1	35 to 54	ABC1
4	1		C2DE
5	1	55+	ABC1
6	1		C2DE
7	2	16 to 34	ABC1
etc.			

Results for each bundle would be summarized within separate columns on the summary sheets. The replies would then be added up within each column. From these subtotals the breakdown total is obtained. Thus results for areas 1 and 2 are obtained by adding the subtotals for columns 1 to 6, and 7 to 12 respectively on the summary sheets for the 16—34 age groups by adding columns 1, 2, 7, and 8 etc. This method obviously ensures that inconsistencies across breakdowns are removed. Where this method cannot be followed, hand analysis should only be used for surveys with compara-tively small samples (under 200).

It is clear from the foregoing that hand analysis has certain limitations; for example, it frequently happens that on examining data, the practitioner requires different or additional tabulations. In hand analysis this involves repeating the above operations, perhaps with the questionnaires bundled in a different way or ways. Rigorous control is essential if errors are to be avoided. The process lacks flexibility and requires tight quality controls. However, it does have some advantages. It can be extremely quick in producing rough results to say, a few key questions, e.g., which product was preferred in a product test. Summarizing may be carried out simultaneously with booking-in of questionnaires from the field. Because of higher fixed costs associated with other forms of analysis, including the possible need for special equipment, or the need to deal with outside suppliers, hand analysis can be extremely economic to practitioners carrying out only occasional surveys on limited samples.

Most survey organizations, however, use hand analysis mainly for advance results, analysing pilot surveys and handling certain kinds of complex data, e.g., depth interviews, calling for special interpretative techniques. It is not recommended procedure for the ordinary type of survey.

Card punching, tape, document reading

Both mechanical and electronic methods of analysis involve converting the original data into some other medium. This conversion itself is usually carried out by machines, which may be manually operated. Whatever the medium into which the data is transferred, its resultant format is entirely rigid. This must be taken into account in the design of the original questionnaire or other survey document. Failing this, it may be necessary for the data to be manually transferred to a special transfer sheet from which the subsequent transformation takes place.

The principle medium at present is punch cards. The most commonly used card measures approximately $7\frac{3}{8}$ in. $\times$ $3\frac{1}{4}$ in. and is notionally divided into 80 columns. On each column a rectangular hole or set of holes may be punched in any of twelve positions. Cards may be singly punched, in which case there will be a maximum of one hole per column, or multi-punched where there may be any number of holes punched in up to all 12 positions. The latter case is rare, and should be avoided as some card reading devices (principally, the mechanical ones) cannot read columns with more than a specified number of positions punched. The bottom ten positions on any column are referred to by the numbers 0 to 9 respectively. The top two positions are referred to variously as V and X, A and B, Y and X and 12 and 11, etc. Nomenclature varies from one organization to another. Columns are referred to by the numbers 1 to 80. An example of a punch card is given below in Fig. 11.2. Any position on a card can, therefore, be defined by its column number and hole code, e.g., column 13, code 1, or 13/(1), column 61, code 2 or 61/(2) etc. Thus, analysis can be specified in a form such as: give a count of the number of times each code position on, say column 48, contains a hole (a hole corresponds to a particular answer either already printed on the questionnaire, or subsequently assigned when the coding frame is prepared). Such counts may be based on all the cards for the survey or only on a sub-group, e.g., those with, say 2 punched on column 14. This enables extremely complex logical filtering to be carried out. The assignment of columns and codes on a questionnaire is an integral part of its design. Figure 11.2 shows how this was done for a code sheet. When codes are printed directly on the questionnaire, the punch operators punch the cards from the questionnaire itself.

Instead of card, paper tape is occasionally used. Paper tape is normally about $\frac{3}{4}$ in. in width, and punching devices allow for a varying number of holes (eight is common) to be punched across the width of the tape. Whereas a punched card contains a fixed number (80) of columns regardless of the number of columns required per questionnaire (many questionnaires require more than one card to accommodate all the data obtained), paper tape can provide as many 'columns' as are required per item. One record

Fig. 11.2. An 80 column punch card.

is punched consecutively after another on the same tape, one reel of tape being capable of accommodating a large number of records. Although tape can show cost savings and avoidance of the matching problems sometimes associated with multi-card data, it can only be processed by computer. Preliminary processing by mechanical methods is not possible. It is also relatively less common than card; in consequence, skills in structuring questionnaires for tape may be less common, and equipment suitable for processing tape less universally available. Furthermore, the fact that one card column can accommodate twelve codes means that the answers to many questions can be very conveniently punched on one column. A reduction to eight codes reduces the number of questions which can be so accommodated. The use of one column for a complete set of answers to a question greatly simplifies checking and analysis specifications.

An alternative method is to punch directly onto magnetic tape. This method of data preparation is increasing in other fields. It does, however, further restrict both the organizations which can punch the data in the first place and those who can subsequently process it. Because of the density with which the data is packed on the tape, one reel of tape (usually 2400 feet) can accommodate a very large amount of data. The precise amount depends upon the format of the data and certain technical considerations but could be the equivalent of 60 to 70 000 eighty-column punch cards. Generally, however, the same points apply as to paper tape.

All of the above methods involve the data being read by an operator who then punches keys on special machines which make the appropriate holes or entries on whatever medium is being used. Experienced operators can expect to achieve punching speeds of 6 to 7000 key depressions per hour on market research questionnaires, although for short periods or on simple work e.g., transfer sheets, speeds may be very much higher. Alternatively, for badly structured questionnaires or where the punch operator is asked to check the data as it is punched, the rate may fall, sometimes considerably. After data is punched, it is customary as a quality-control measure for all or part of it to be repunched on verifying machines. In the case of cards the original cards are fed into the machines and the punching operation repeated. However, instead of actually punching the card, the image of the column punched on the verifying machine is compared with what is already on that card 'column'. If the two are the same, the card moves to the next 'column'. If they are different, a red light (the method varies from machine to machine) appears and the operator can then check that column to identify the error. The principles are the same for paper and magnetic tape, although the actual procedures are slightly different. A typical survey involving, say, 1000 punch cards may involve some 100 000 key depressions requiring perhaps 20 to 30 hours for punching and verification.

Document reading devices are beginning to provide an alternative method of translation for certain kinds of questionnaire. Instead of the document being read by human operators they are read by a machine which generates, usually, a magnetic tape of the data read. These may be used directly as input to a computer or converted back mechanically into punch cards or paper tape. Document reading cuts out the need for verification, and enables data to be transcribed very much more quickly. However, considerable care must be taken in the design and printing of the document to be read. Interviewers must take greater care in marking questionnaires. In certain, but not all, cases an error in marking means filling in a fresh questionnaire. The quality of printing required, particularly in the registration of the answer spaces with respect to the top and side of the paper, is beyond the scope of most organizations with only the normal stencil or small offset printing facilities. This method will provide a substantial increase in speed at the processing stage but takes slightly longer to set up at the design stage. Recent technical development in readers is rapidly making them suitable for a wide variety of 'ad hoc' surveys. It is probable that this form of transfer will become much more important in the future.

Given, then, that the data has been transferred to a suitable medium, analysis may now be carried out mechanically or by computer. Mechanical methods replaced hand summarizing in the early 'fifties' and were the predominant analysis method for well over ten years. Mechanical methods are still used for many kinds of smaller surveys.

Mechanical analysis

The principal machines used in mechanical analysis are counter/sorters, tabulators and statistical analysis machines. These machines are (or were) made by IBM, ICL, and other suppliers of punched card equipment.

The best known mechanical device is the counter/sorter. This is a machine which consists of a hopper into which punched cards can be placed, and thirteen output pockets into which the cards fall after passing through the machine. As the cards go through the machine they pass under a bar with 80 serations on it on which a small brush is mounted. The mounting of the brush is usually spring-loaded. The brush may be moved along the bar by the operator and placed on any one of the 80 positions on the bar which correspond to the 80 column position on the card. As the cards pass under the brush they pass over a metal roller with the brush exerting a slight downward pressure on the card against the roller. Whenever a hole is encountered on the card, electrical contact is made between the brush and the metal roller under the card. In this way, the code positions on a particular column are sensed by the machine. The resultant electrical impulse may be used to drive counters, one for each code position, which are incremented by one each time a hole is encountered in a particular code position. The electrical impulse may alternatively, or additionally, be used to 'open' one of the output pockets corresponding to the position punched. In this way, both a counting and a sorting facility are provided.

There are thirteen output pockets to provide for all twelve code positions and the case where nothing is punched on the column, usually referred to as

256

the 'reject' pocket. Where a card is multi-punched it will normally fall into the pocket corresponding to the code position nearest the bottom edge of the card. If, for example, a card contained a hole in both the 'three' and 'eight' positions, the cards would fall into the output pocket for the 'eight' code. The operator may close any or all of the twelve pockets corresponding to the twelve code positions. This provides the extremely important facility of allowing sorting to take place on selected codes only on a particular column.

For each column on which data is required, the cards are passed through the machine with the brush set to the appropriate column. Figures are copied manually onto sheets, the counters set to zero, and the operation repeated. This may be done on the whole pack or sub-groups as desired. The best known machines are the 082, 083, and 084 made by IBM. These operate at varying speeds from 650 to 2000 cards a minute. A basic point to remember about a counter/sorter is that it can only process one column at a time. In certain cases, tabulators have been used where it is desired to use numbers punched across a field of columns. A tabulator is able to read sets of columns and carry out simple manipulative operations on the numbers in the different fields. Results are printed onto continuous paper. Instructions are communicated to the machine through wired panels. Usually, a particular panel is permanently wired-up for a particular operation. Tabulators were principally designed for accounting applications, and their use in market research was therefore restricted to specialized fields such as retail audit and other types of panel processing.

The best-known statistical analysis machine was the IBM 101. (There were others which were specially made.) The IBM 101 was able to 'sense' all 80 columns simultaneously. By appropriate wiring of the control panel up to five columns could be read at any one time. At the end of passing the data pack through the machine the results for the five columns concerned were printed out automatically by the machine. The much greater flexibility in logical capability, and the printing feature meant that the machine's output was very much greater than the counter/sorter's. Errors arising from inconsistent manual transcription by the operators on counter/sorters were avoided. Although the form of output was fairly rigid, with ingenious wiring it could be made sufficiently similar to the tables required to make translations to their final form—a manual task—fairly simple.

When mechanical methods became widely available they had numerous important advantages on hand methods. However, with the advent of computers, many of their advantages are no longer relevant. The IBM 101 is no longer manufactured and there are fewer and fewer of these machines around. The same is largely true of tabulators.

The counter/sorter is still found in many organizations. It is extremely useful for checking odd items of data, editing and a variety of other miscellaneous functions. When processing on the counter sorter, however, weighting can only be carried out by either removing some data from over-represented cells or duplicating a sample of the cards in under-represented cells. The cards must be passed through the machine several times, and the resultant figures may require considerable additional manipulation before they can be used by the practitioner. For these and other reasons more and more analysis is done on computers which is discussed below.

Computers

Computers have not only revolutionized the way in which analysis is done but have had an equally major effect on the form and value of analysis. Whereas mechanical and hand methods meant that data was virtually confined to producing raw numbers and simple percentages, computers enable a variety of other kinds of statistics to be produced. Statistical tests of various kinds can be carried out on an exhaustive scale. They allow rigorous checking and manipulation of the data. At the same time, they have reduced the absolute cost of analysing data. Weighting of data to remove biases due to over- or under-representation of the sample can be carried out more accurately. There are numerous other advantages which is why upwards of 95 per cent of survey analysis is now computer-based.

A computer consists of at least the following devices: facilities for reading punch cards, paper or magnetic tape, a central processing unit (CPU) and an output device such as a line printer on which results will be given. A common additional feature is for the computer to have one or more magnetic disks or tapes which are attached to the CPU and may be used for the storage of programs, data and results. The actual devices vary from one installation to another. Larger installations usually have a greater number of peripheral units as well as bigger and more powerful CPU's.

In brief, for a computer to analyse some data the following is necessary. The data must exist in a form that can be read into the computer. A set of specifications must be prepared which will tell the computer what to do and one or more computer programs must be available which are capable of accepting the specification cards, interpreting them, accepting and processing the data cards, and outputting the desired results. Usually, several programs are required which are linked together to form a comprehensive analysis system, referred to in jargon terms as a 'software package'.

The principle limitation in the use of computers lies in the 'software packages' available. However, with the simplification of programs brought about by the increasing sophistication of high-level programming languages, and the substantial improvements in hardware performance inherent in third generation machines, early difficulties have largely been overcome. Computers can carry out virtually any analysis which the practitioner can conceive.

The actual writing of an appropriate software package is not something with which the survey practitioner need be concerned. This can only be done by a team of computer programmers. Such teams are normally found in computer bureaux or software organizations. Once the package has been written it remains fixed for some time. The user does not need to concern

258

himself with the actual mechanics of the programs but rather with how to use them. To use most packages involves writing specifications on special forms. These are punched on cards which then tell the package concerned what to do.

It is important to distinguish between the writing of a program or package and the writing of a set of specifications to be read by a program or package in processing a particular survey. The latter operation, 'spec writing', is something with which the practitioner may well be concerned.

Most organizations offering analysis facilities are able to offer 'spec writing' as part of their service. It is possible for practitioners to do this themselves with savings in time and cost. The ease or difficulty in using any particular software package depends very much on the way in which the 'specs' have to be written.

The 'specs' will cover such things as labels for tables, rows, and columns, the filter base for each table, the punch card definition in logical form of the rows and columns of each table, the form of output, any editing or re-arrangement of the data, etc. Most packages have a wide variety of options which provide considerable flexibility to the user. There are considerable variations in the variety and ease of using software packages for cross-tabulations.

Although a practitioner can, of course, contract processing to whichever computer organization submits the lowest quotation for carrying out the work involved, it pays to have some knowledge of the characteristics of the software packages being used. There are a number of reasons for this. First, some packages are particularly appropriate for some forms of analysis whereas others are not. Computer organizations sometimes quote for jobs for which their software is either completely inappropriate or can only be made appropriate with a greater or lesser amount of reprogramming. Although the job may be done at the original budget, (there are many cases where this has involved the computer organization in substantial losses) the execution is likely to be more difficult, and involve the practitioner in substantial additional time in dealing with queries and problems. A knowledge of the characteristics of different packages enables the practitioner to avoid the inappropriate ones. Second, where a practitioner is able to match the way he specifies his analysis to the input requirements of a particular package, there will be a considerable saving in time and costs. Most of the cost savings will come from the improvement in communication. This awareness of the range and capability of particular packages enables the practitioner to exploit their potential much more fully.

Although the nature of the specification cards varies from one package to another, the amount of skill involved in completing them also varies. Some packages will accept specification cards, the format of which is very similar to the way in which the practitioner actually thinks of his analysis requirements. Other packages involve cards containing instructions in, perhaps, a special language. It will often be found that the latter type of package will have more powerful capabilities; on the other hand, the former type is easier to use.

A somewhat obvious point is that any software package is of necessity a compromise between a number of desirable objects, which may to some be incompatible. Efficiency in execution, for example, may be sacrificed to some extent for ease of specification. The software package that is best for everything is more or less an impossible dream. It is very much a case of horses for courses. Simple software packages are right for simple surveys. Small computers are cheaper for small surveys and so on.

Clearly, some judicious shopping will enable the practitioner to gauge for himself which packages to use for the different kinds of project he may be carrying-out.

Some of the factors which a user might consider in deciding whether a particular package was suitable for a particular job are the following:

(a) how easy is it to specify the analysis requirements to the specification writer(s)?;
(b) are table, column, and row labels adequate without further annotation?;
(c) does the package have sufficient editing and recoding features to ensure that 'clean' data is produced?;
(d) can multi-card surveys present problems?;
(e) is the layout of the tables sufficiently clear that secondary transcription by typing, etc., is unnecessary?;
(f) are the output options sufficiently flexible to produce data in the form appropriate to the practitioner's need?;
(g) can tables be formed with sufficient flexibility to allow virtually any code or set of codes on any card to appear in a single table?;
(h) can weighting be carried out easily without, for example, having to punch factors for each informant?;
(i) is the package able to cope with the size of the job without numerous re-runs or very long runs?;
(j) do your requirements mean changes to the package, or can they be handled easily within the existing control card procedure?

These are some of the main questions upon which the practitioner himself should be satisfied. There are others, of course, particularly when the processing is atypical in any way.

It is beyond the scope of this chapter to make more than a passing reference to specific software packages. Some of these are discussed below. For fuller information it is really necessary to study the user manuals produced by the proprietors of the packages concerned. This is also necessary because the packages themselves undergo continuous development and up-grading. In selecting companies with software packages, one may consider either an appropriate market research company or a computer bureau.

A number of market research agencies in Great Britain have their own computers, and most of them carry out a considerable amount of work for

260

other agencies or practitioners who require cross-tabulation. Names of such companies may be obtained by reference to AMSO, The Association of Market Survey Organizations. The principle computer bureaux or specialist organizations carrying out market research processing in Great Britain at the moment include Computer Projects, IBM, ICL, Pritchard Brown and Taylor, Scicon, Surveytab, and Whittle Data Services.

Some of the better-known packages are very briefly commented upon below. Fuller details can be obtained from the relevant manuals. In each case, some guidance is given as to where the package may be used. It is probable that around two thirds of the survey processing in Great Britain uses one or other of these packages.

AGSP (*Atlas General Survey Program*). The first really powerful general survey package. It is extremely flexible but specifications have to be written in a special processing language. The Atlas computer for which it was written is a rare machine now being phased out; (ICL Baric only).

DONOVAN. This package was designed for the IBM 1130 computer which is certainly the most widely-used small computer in market research. The package has been developed over several versions with progressive improvements in ease of setting-up; (available on most 1130's).

QUICKTAB. Also designed for the 1130. Its principal advantage is the extreme ease in setting-up, and its efficiency in execution. These more than compensate for a number of limitations which the ingenious 'spec' writer can get round by appropriate preparation of the data packs beforehand; (available on some 1130's).

SABLE. This package is designed for the ICL 1900 series and is the result of several years development. It has many highly-developed features with powerful editing and recoding abilities. The control cards generate a machine language code which makes the program very fast; (Pritchard Brown and Taylor only).

SAMPLE and STONEWALL. Sample is designed for the CDC 3200 machine. The control cards set up a series of machine language instructions. This makes the package both fast and powerful. Specification writing, however, requires a good deal of skill. Stonewall will produce simple matrices using a control card set-up which can easily be written by the user. It is suitable for the simpler single card surveys; (Computer Projects only).

SPL and SPS. SPL is a formal specification language which is very comprehensive but involves a user in special training. SPS on the other hand is a quick, easy to use system, well within the grasp of most survey practitioners. Both packages are designed for the XDS Sigma 5 machine; (Surveytab only).

TABLEAU. This package presently operates on the Univac 1108 computer. 'Spec' writing requires medium skill, and is usually carried out by the bureau. Its capability is similar to the more advanced Donovan packages. There are a variety of statistical test options; (Scicon only).

Computer input requirements

A good deal of discussion has taken place earlier on input data. There are certain aspects of this which need to be borne in mind in relation to computers. First, computers are more sensitive to faults in data and are, at the same time, more accurate in tabulating what is, in fact, there. Thus, the GIGO principle applies. Data cards with errors must be 'cleaned' or the tables will also contain errors. This is particularly important when it is desired to present computer output directly to the final user. The cleaning-up operation is likely to involve, among other things, the removal of redundant, erroneous or rogue codes, logic checking with resultant amendments to the data and general sense checking. To ensure 'perfect' output these operations themselves must be carried out by computer. Manual or mechanical editing is seldom good enough. Although this takes extra time at the preparation stage, it is well worthwhile in terms of the time saved at the output stage.

Some packages contain comprehensive editing features. However, it is quite frequent for this to be carried out at a prior stage by special programs. The data is then checked on the computer to ensure that it is 100 per cent correct before the tabulation runs are carried out.

In multi-card surveys it is usually necessary to check that the correct number of cards are present for each informant. Most packages which accept multi-card data will reject invalid or mismatched sets. This can result in a substantial loss of data. Many bureaux have special programs for checking matching and identifying which serial numbers or cards are invalid. Corrections of this kind are usually done manually, and sometimes involve referring back to original questionnaires. The pack may then be checked again on the computer.

In some bureaux, data is stored for as long as it may be required either on disk or tape. However, in some cases it is stored on card only. In these latter cases great care must be taken to avoid degradation of the data pack through wrecking, mishandling or other causes. The consequences of this are that tables run on separate occasions may well contain differences when they should, in fact, be the same.

Computer weighting

It is frequently necessary to weight data to correct for differences in the composition of the sample achieved, and known characteristics of the universe from which it was drawn. If, for example, one found that one's sample contained too many men, most cross-tabulation packages can correct this by assigning separate fractional weights to male and female informants such that the sample which is used for the analysis has the correct composition. It is not easy to do efficiently when using hand or mechanical methods. Usually, it is necessary to specify the desired composition of the sample in terms of the appropriate characteristics. Common ones include age, class, sex, area, etc. A preliminary run is then carried out to determine the actual composition, and from this appropriate factors may be computed. Packages differ in the ways in which weighting is handled. In some cases, it is possible to enter the weights directly, in other cases it is necessary to punch them on to the data cards.

Checking computer output

Occasionally, very occasionally, computers themselves make mistakes. When they do so, more often than not the result is obvious and spectacular. However, most errors in computer output arise either because the input data contains errors (referred to above) or because errors have been made in the specifications of the table concerned. It is very rare, especially on a survey of any size, for there to be no errors at all on any of the output. For this reason some kinds of checking should be carried out. How this is done will vary from one organization to another. The procedure outlined below is less than perfect, but rigorous checking procedures are no longer worth the delay they will cause in terms of the increased accuracy which may result. Here are some simple steps:

(a) if any weighting was carried out, calculate what the weighted sample size should have been manually. If the computer gives you another result, there may be something wrong with the weighting. If so, all the tables may be wrong;

(b) similarly, if the unweighted sample size is markedly different to what you expected, a serious fault may have occurred;

(c) the base figures should then be checked for each of the different base filters for each analysis breakdown. These should add back, where appropriate, to the total sample. It is probable that if they are correct for the one table with a particular base and breakdown, that they will be correct for all other similar tables;

(d) tables now need to be examined individually for the presence of correct labelling;

(e) the total column should be examined for sense and its addition to 100 per cent (may be slightly different due to rounding off), although this latter check may be done by the computer in some cases;

(f) the number of rejects should be examined. Rejects are informants who qualified for inclusion in the table but for whom no information was found in the data to the question being tabulated. If this number is high it is indicative of an error.

It will be noticed that checking of the data within the table has not been suggested. If the margins, i.e., the base figures and the total column are checked and correct, then the data within the table will also normally be correct. The elimination of this part of the checking greatly reduces the time involved.

Conclusion

Editing, coding, and data processing are obviously an important part of producing any market research survey. They are largely clerical operations which to a greater or lesser extent make use of modern data processing techniques. The general principles are much the same as those applying to other forms of paper processing. The disciplines necessary in an automated accounting system have much in common with those necessary in market research. Although there is considerable literature on market research or statistical techniques, and also on data processing in general, there is comparatively little literature available on this latter area applicable to market research. It is an area which tends to be taken for granted. In the absence of further reading, attention to detail and common-sense will enable the conscientous practitioner to handle the editing, coding and processing of most kinds of survey.

12. Statistics and significance testing

Paul Harris

Statistics may be defined as 'the collection, analysis and interpretation of numerical data'. As market research is concerned mostly with counting and measuring it, it is not surprising that the theory of statistics can play an important part in assisting researchers to collect valid samples of data, and in helping them to draw correct conclusions from that data. The 'collection' aspect of statistics had already been covered in chapters 3 and 4 on experimental sampling and design. In this chapter, the emphasis will be on the 'analysis and interpretation' aspects of statistics dealing mainly with simple descriptive measures calculated from survey data and the testing of hypotheses about that data. The more advanced statistical techniques used for interpreting market research data will be covered in chapter 13. The techniques and significance tests described below are those which have been found most useful in interpreting survey tabulations. This is not an exhaustive list, by any means, and the reader who wishes to know more about statistical analysis in market research may consult the texts given in the references at the end of the chapter.

Types of Market Research Data

Classified data

This is defined as data which has been collected using only different classifications or categories as the measuring scale. Much of the demographic data collected on market research questionnaires, for example, is of this type, consisting of groups of respondents who fall into one of a number of classifications. Two obvious examples are sex and marital status, where the categories would be:

Sex	Marital status
Male	Single
Female	Married
	Widowed
	Divorced

The numerical data is simply obtained by counting the frequency of occurrence of respondents in each classification. The various classifications used form a type of measurement scale known as a *nominal* scale. The basic property of this weakest form of measurement scale is that items or people that fall into one classification are different in some way from those falling in the other classifications. When the frequency counts for each classification are each divided by a base figure, such as the total number of respondents in the survey, and are multiplied by 100, a percentage is obtained for each classification. A frequency count and a percentage for a number of classifications is one of the most commonly occurring formats of market survey tabulations. The statistical treatment of these counts and percentages will form a large part of this chapter.

Ranked data

Data is often collected by classifications which are not only different, but where some classifications are 'higher' or 'lower' than other classifications in some sense. A common example in market research is where purchasers of various amounts of a product are classified as:

(a) heavy buyers (e.g., over ten packets);
(b) medium buyers (e.g., five to nine packets);
(c) light buyers (e.g., one to four packets).

Another example is where respondents are asked about their attitudes towards a product on semantic scales such as:

(a) very sweet;
(b) sweet;
(c) neither sweet nor bitter;
(d) bitter;
(e) very bitter.

A third example is when respondents are asked to rank a number of products in order of preference, giving classifications of 1st, 2nd, 3rd . . . etc. When the number of products is two this is the often-used 'paired-comparison design'. In all these examples the classifications on the scales have a natural ordering, which distinguishes them from the previously defined classified data. Numerical data is obtained from the count of respondents for each

266

classification and its associated percentage. The natural order of classifications for ranked data gives the researcher more scope in analysing data of this type, which is often referred to as *ordinal* scale data.

Measured data

Under this heading is included all data where the scale of measurement consists not of labelled classifications, but real numerical values. Obvious examples are height (in metres), age (in years), and number of packets of 'brand B' bought last week. Measured data includes the two types of measurement which are known as *interval* scales and *ratio* scales. In the former, the distance between two positions on the numerical scale is known and is interpretable numerically, and in the latter the ratio of two positions on the scale is independent of the unit of measurement. The ratio scale has the further property that its zero point is known and meaningful. An example of interval measurement is temperature which can be measured on Fahrenheit or centigrade scales. Height is a good example of the use of ratio measurement, where the ratio of two heights is the same, irrespective of whether they are measured in feet and inches or in metres.

A further distinction between types of measured data is that of *discrete* (*or discontinuous*) data and *continuous* data. Discrete data occurs when the measurement scale consists of a number of distinct numerical values such as 'the number of times a certain advertisement has been seen in the last month'. The values on the scale must be 0, 1, 2, 3, . . . etc., with intermediate values such as 1.5 being impossible. No such restriction is applicable to continuous data where the measurements may be taken to any number of decimal places, depending only on the accuracy of the measuring instruments being used. In practice, continuous data such as height is usually collected to distinct values such as two decimal places of metres.

Under the heading of measured data is included data obtained from semantic rating scales, to which simple discrete numerical scores have been attached. An example of two such scoring systems commonly used is given below:

	Score	Score
A preferred to B very much	5	+2
A preferred to B a little	4	+1
No preference	3	0
B preferred to A a little	2	−1
B preferred to A very much	1	−2

This practice of taking an ordinal or ranked measuring scale and giving the various classifications a numerical score is widespread in market research. By doing so the researcher is assuming that underlying the semantic scale is a continuous numerical scale which it is not possible to measure accurately,

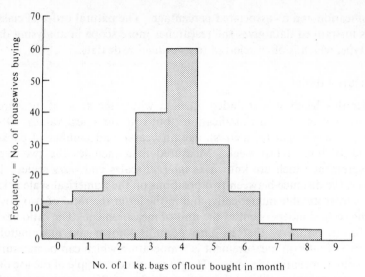

No. of 1 kg. bags of flour bought in month

Fig. 12.1. Histogram of frequency distribution of flour purchases.

and that the numerical values given correspond approximately to positions on that scale. If such assumptions can be validly made, then a lot more can be done with the data statistically.

Simple Descriptive Statistics

In this section a number of summarizing features of measured data will be given.

Frequency distributions

If data has been collected on the number of 1 kg bags of flour bought by 200 housewives each month, it would be confusing to list all 200 values obtained. It is much better to display the data in the form of a *frequency distribution* as below:

Number of 1 kg bags bought	Frequency of occurrence = no. of housewives buying
0	12
1	15
2	20
3	40
4	60
5	30
6	15
7	5
8	3
	200

268

In this form, the data can be more easily understood and interpreted, especially as this frequency distribution (or 'distribution' as it is often simply called) may be represented pictorially as in Fig. 12.1. This graphical representation of a frequency distribution is known as a *histogram*. In the above example the data is given for a discrete distribution, but these two ways of displaying data are equally useful for continuous data. All one has to do is group the continuous data values into convenient groupings or class intervals and count the number of observations in each class. A number of classes between 8 and 15 is usually adequate. If data on height was collected in metres, part of the frequency distribution might be as follows:

Height (m)	*Frequency = no. of people*
1.51–1.55	20
1.56–1.60	27
1.61–1.65	34
1.66–1.70	46
.	.
.	.
.	.
.	.

Continuous data that has been grouped into class intervals may also be represented by a *frequency curve*, which is obtained by drawing a smooth curve through the mid-points of the top of each bar on the histogram. An example of a frequency curve derived from a histogram is shown below in Fig. 12.2.

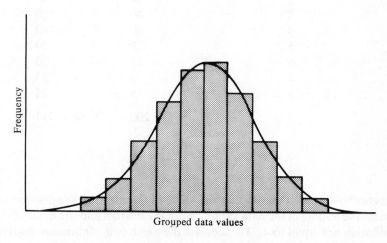

Fig. 12.2. Frequency curve.

The mean, variance, standard deviation and standard error of a distribution

Although the frequency distribution and histogram describe a set of data in simple terms, an even more valuable condensation of the data may be obtained by calculating a single value which summarizes the distribution. Such a value is the *arithmetic mean* or just simply the *mean* of the distribution. It is often referred to as the *average*, but this is not strictly correct as the mean is only one of a number of averages that may be calculated from a distribution. Other averages are the *mode* defined as the data value with the highest frequency, and the *median* defined as the middle value when all the data values are arranged in order of magnitude. To show how to calculate the mean of a distribution the previous data on bags of flour will be used. It is customary to denote the data values by 'x' and the frequency of occurrence of those values by 'f'. The mean, which is usually denoted by $\bar{x}(x - \text{bar})$, is calculated by using the formula,

$$\bar{x} = \frac{\sum fx}{\sum f} \qquad \text{where } \sum = \text{the sum of.}$$

Putting the formula into words we have—multiply each data value (x) by its associated frequency (f), add up these multiplications and divide their total by sum of the frequencies. This has been done below for the data on flour.

Number of 1 kg bags bought	Frequency	
x	*f*	*fx*
0	12	0
1	15	15
2	20	40
3	40	120
4	60	240
5	30	150
6	15	90
7	5	35
8	3	24
	$\sum f = 200$	$\sum fx = 714$

$$\bar{x} = \frac{\sum fx}{\sum f} = \frac{714}{200} = 3.57.$$

Reference to Fig. 12.1 shows that the value of the mean of the distribution lies near the middle of the data values. Both the median and the mode of this distribution are equal to 4. To calculate the mean of a continuous distribution it is necessary to take the mid-points of the class intervals as the data values (x). In the height example given above the values would be:

Height (m)	Mid-point	Frequency
	x	f
1.51–1.55	1.53	20
1.56–1.60	1.58	27
1.61–1.65	1.63	34
1.66–1.70	1.68	46
.	.	.
.	.	.
.	.	.
.	.	.
.	.	.

Not only is it useful to have a summarizing value such as a mean for a distribution but it is also of interest to have another value which indicates how much the individual data values are spread around the mean. Such a value is given by a quantity called the *variance* of the distribution or by the square root of the variance, known as the *standard deviation*. In terms of the data values (x), the frequencies (f) and the mean ($\bar{x}$) they are defined as:

$$\text{Variance} = s^2 = \frac{\sum f(x - \bar{x})^2}{\sum f - 1};$$

$$\text{Standard deviation} = s = \sqrt{\frac{\sum f(x - \bar{x})^2}{\sum f - 1}}.$$

The calculation of these two quantities, using the data on bags of flour, is demonstrated below.

Number of 1 kg bags bought	Frequency	$x - \bar{x}$	$(x - \bar{x})^2$	$f(x - \bar{x})^2$
x	f			
0	12	−3.57	12.74	152.88
1	15	−2.57	6.60	99.00
2	20	−1.57	2.46	49.20
3	40	−0.57	0.32	12.80
4	60	0.43	0.18	10.80
5	30	1.43	2.04	61.20
6	15	2.43	5.90	88.50
7	5	3.43	11.76	58.80
8	3	4.43	19.62	58.86
	$\sum f = 200$		$\sum f(x - \bar{x})^2 =$	592.04

271

$$\text{Variance} = s^2 = \frac{\sum f(x - \bar{x})^2}{\sum f - 1} = \frac{592.04}{199} = 2.98;$$

$$\text{Standard deviation} = s = \sqrt{\frac{\sum f(x - \bar{x})^2}{\sum f - 1}} = \sqrt{2.98} = 1.73.$$

It is quite usual to replace $\sum f$ by the symbol n, i.e., $n = \sum f$. Figure 12.3 below shows two hypothetical distributions, each with the same mean of $\bar{x} = 5$ units. For distribution A, which has data values ranging from 3 to 7 units, the variance and standard deviation would both be smaller than that for distribution B, where the data values range more widely from zero to ten (see Fig. 12.3).

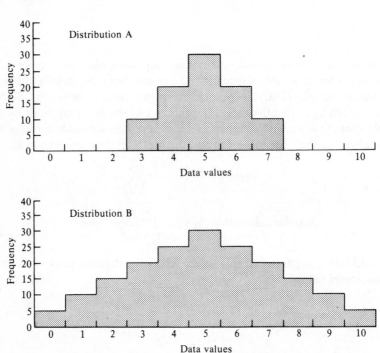

Fig. 12.3. Frequency distributions of hypothetical data.

There is a further important statistic that can be calculated from a distribution, namely the *standard error of the mean*. To explain this term it is necessary to refer back to the theory of random sampling given in chapter 3. Suppose it is known that in a certain town the true average number of persons per household (based on *all* households) is $\bar{X} = 3.12$ with a standard deviation of $S = 1.00$. The values are denoted by capital X and S as they are population values and not sample values. If a random sample of 250 households is selected from the town it would be possible to calculate the mean number of persons per household for this sample. Let the mean of this sample be denoted by $\bar{x}_1$. Putting this value to one side, a second random sample of 250 households is selected and the mean ($\bar{x}_2$) is calculated. Similarly, a third sample of 250 is selected, giving $\bar{x}_3$, and so on, until 100 samples have been collected. The resulting 100 values of $\bar{x}$ may then be grouped into a frequency distribution. In general the 100 values of $\bar{x}$ will all be fairly close to the population mean, $\bar{X} = 3.12$. In fact, their distribution should have a mean, i.e., the mean of all the 100 means, which is indistinguishable or nearly indistinguishable from the value 3.12. Certainly, if all possible samples of 250 households were selected from the town, then the mean of the frequency distribution of all possible sample means, would be exactly 3.12 (see page 53 of chapter 3). The distribution of sample means will have a bell-shape distribution, which is known as the *normal distribution*. The standard deviation of the distribution of 100 means may be calculated and it is usually called the *standard error of the mean*. Fortunately, it is not necessary to draw a large number of samples to estimate the standard error, as its value may be calculated from the single sample that is normally selected. If a sample of n members is selected and the standard deviation (s) calculated for some data values (x) then the standard error of the mean ($\bar{x}$) is given by:

$$\text{Standard error } (\bar{x}) = \frac{s}{\sqrt{n}}.$$

If the data collected consists of percentages (p) then the statistics defined above take a simple form:

Values for percentages data

mean	$\bar{x}$	p
variance	s^2	pq, where $q = 100 - p$
standard deviation	s	$\sqrt{pq}$
standard error	$\dfrac{s}{\sqrt{n}}$	$\sqrt{\dfrac{pq}{n}}$

Principles of Significance Testing

The market researcher, when interpreting the results of a market survey, has a large number of tables of frequencies and percentages to examine. These results, being based on a sample, will be subject to sampling errors. When the researcher selects two figures for comparison he has to assure himself that any difference between the two figures cannot be explained solely by sampling error. Only then may he validly draw attention to the difference in figures. The *significance test* is a device which enables the researcher to reach a decision objectively in such matters. In this section, the general principles of significance testing will be described. In later sections significance tests for use with various types of market research data will be given.

The null hypothesis and the alternative hypothesis

A significance test is used to decide whether to accept or reject hypotheses concerning the sample data that has been collected. The first step in a significance test is to set up a special hypothesis known as a *null hypothesis* (usually denoted by H_0). It is so called because it is quite often expressed in null or negative terms. A typical one in market research, not in negative terms would be 'The percentage of men in the population who smoke is $P = 50$ per cent'. Next, the researcher must define an *alternative hypothesis* (H_1) which may be accepted if the null hypothesis is rejected. The corresponding alternative hypothesis to the null hypothesis stated above might be, 'Percentage P is not equal to 50 per cent'. A significance test based on this alternative hypothesis would be of the type known as a *two-tailed test*, as it states that P may be either higher or lower than 50 per cent. Two examples of alternative hypotheses each of which lead to a separate *one-tailed test* are given below:

(a) P is greater than 50 per cent;
(b) P is less than 50 per cent.

Both of these predict a difference in *one* direction only.

Testing the null hypothesis

The steps employed in conducting a significance test are best explained in the context of an example. In this section the hypothesis concerning the percentage of men who smoke will be tested using the two-tailed alternative hypothesis. To test the validity of the null hypothesis a random sample of n men, e.g., $n = 250$, is selected from the population of all men, and from the data values the statistic to be tested (p_1) is calculated, p_1 being the proportion of men who smoke. This is the result from just one sample. It would be possible in theory, as described in the previous section on the standard error of the mean, to draw all possible samples of size $n = 250$ from the population to produce a large number of estimates $p_1, p_2, p_3, \ldots$ etc. If these estimates were formed into a frequency distribution it would be a normal distribution. If the null hypothesis is true, this distribution, which is called the *sampling distribution of the test statistic*, will have a mean of $P = 50$ per cent and a standard error of:

$$\sqrt{\frac{PQ}{n}} = \sqrt{\frac{50(100 - 50)}{250}} = \sqrt{10} = 3.16 \text{ per cent.}$$

Figure 12.4 shows this particular distribution, from which it can be seen that if the null hypothesis is true, then a sample value of p_1 lower than 40 per cent or higher than 60 per cent is very unlikely. Of course, it is possible that a sample of $n = 250$ will give $p_1 = 40$ per cent even when the null hypothesis of $P = 50$ per cent is true; but this would probably not occur. What the researcher has to decide now is where to place cut-off points on this distribution beyond which he is not prepared to accept that the null hypothesis is true but that an alternative hypothesis is true. These cutoff points are normally referred to as critical values in the statistical literature. To assist in this decision a valuable property of the normal distribution may be used. In any normal distribution the area of the distribution outside the limits, arithmetic mean $\pm z$ standard deviations (where z is any number), can be calculated.

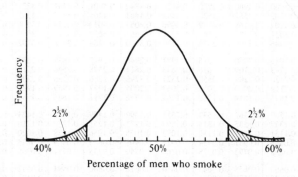

Fig. 12.4. Sampling distribution of a test statistic.

Three examples are given below:

(a) only 5 per cent of the area is outside the limits, mean ± 1.96 standard deviations;
(b) only one per cent of the area is outside the limits, mean ± 2.58 standard deviations;
(c) only 0.1 per cent of the area is outside the limits, mean ± 3.29 standard deviations.

Tables of the areas of the normal distribution have been calculated and one version is given in Table 12.1. It gives the area of the distribution beyond certain multiples of the standard deviation for one tail of the distribution only. The value corresponding to $z = 1.96$, for example, is 0.025 on one tail and, therefore, as stated above, 0.05 or 5 per cent of the area of the curve is outside 1.96 standard deviations.

Figure 12.4 shows the critical values for the men smokers example, giving the limits outside which five per cent of the area of the distribution lies (two and a half per cent on each tail). As this is a distribution of a mean, the standard error of the mean must be used in place of the standard deviation

275

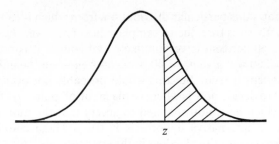

Table 12.1   *Table of probabilities associated with values as extreme as observed values of z in the normal distribution*

The body of the table gives one-tailed probabilities under H_0 of z. The left-hand marginal column gives various values of z to one decimal place. The top row gives various values to the second decimal place. Thus, for example, the one-tailed p of $z \geq 0.11$ or $z \leq -0.11$ is $p = 0.4562$.

z	0.00	0.01	0.02	0.03	0.04	0.05	0.06	0.07	0.08	0.09
0.0	0.5000	0.4960	0.4920	0.4880	0.4840	0.4801	0.4761	0.4721	0.4681	0.4641
0.1	0.4602	0.4562	0.4522	0.4483	0.4443	0.4404	0.4364	0.4325	0.4286	0.4247
0.2	0.4207	0.4168	0.4129	0.4090	0.4052	0.4013	0.3974	0.3936	0.3897	0.3859
0.3	0.3821	0.3783	0.3745	0.3707	0.3669	0.3632	0.3594	0.3557	0.3520	0.3483
0.4	0.3446	0.3409	0.3372	0.3336	0.3300	0.3264	0.3228	0.3192	0.3156	0.3121
0.5	0.3085	0.3050	0.3015	0.2981	0.2946	0.2912	0.2877	0.2843	0.2810	0.2776
0.6	0.2743	0.2709	0.2676	0.2643	0.2611	0.2578	0.2546	0.2514	0.2483	0.2451
0.7	0.2420	0.2389	0.2358	0.2327	0.2296	0.2266	0.2236	0.2206	0.2177	0.2148
0.8	0.2119	0.2090	0.2061	0.2033	0.2005	0.1977	0.1949	0.1922	0.1894	0.1867
0.9	0.1841	0.1814	0.1788	0.1762	0.1736	0.1711	0.1685	0.1660	0.1635	0.1611
1.0	0.1587	0.1562	0.1539	0.1515	0.1492	0.1469	0.1446	0.1423	0.1401	0.1379
1.1	0.1357	0.1335	0.1314	0.1292	0.1271	0.1251	0.1230	0.1210	0.1190	0.1170
1.2	0.1151	0.1131	0.1112	0.1093	0.1075	0.1056	0.1038	0.1020	0.1003	0.0985
1.3	0.0968	0.0951	0.0934	0.0918	0.0901	0.0885	0.0869	0.0853	0.0838	0.0823
1.4	0.0808	0.0793	0.0778	0.0764	0.0749	0.0735	0.0721	0.0708	0.0694	0.0681
1.5	0.0668	0.0655	0.0643	0.0630	0.0618	0.0606	0.0594	0.0582	0.0571	0.0559
1.6	0.0548	0.0537	0.0526	0.0516	0.0505	0.0495	0.0485	0.0475	0.0465	0.0455
1.7	0.0446	0.0436	0.0427	0.0418	0.0409	0.0401	0.0392	0.0384	0.0375	0.0367
1.8	0.0359	0.0351	0.0344	0.0336	0.0329	0.0322	0.0314	0.0307	0.0301	0.0294
1.9	0.0287	0.0281	0.0274	0.0268	0.0262	0.0256	0.0250	0.0244	0.0239	0.0233
2.0	0.0228	0.0222	0.0217	0.0212	0.0207	0.0202	0.0197	0.0192	0.0188	0.0183
2.1	0.0179	0.0174	0.0170	0.0166	0.0162	0.0158	0.0154	0.0150	0.0146	0.0143
2.2	0.0139	0.0136	0.0132	0.0129	0.0125	0.0122	0.0119	0.0116	0.0113	0.0110
2.3	0.0107	0.0104	0.0102	0.0099	0.0096	0.0094	0.0091	0.0089	0.0087	0.0084
2.4	0.0082	0.0080	0.0078	0.0075	0.0073	0.0071	0.0069	0.0068	0.0066	0.0064
2.5	0.0062	0.0060	0.0059	0.0057	0.0055	0.0054	0.0052	0.0051	0.0049	0.0048
2.6	0.0047	0.0045	0.0044	0.0043	0.0041	0.0040	0.0039	0.0038	0.0037	0.0036
2.7	0.0035	0.0034	0.0033	0.0032	0.0031	0.0030	0.0029	0.0028	0.0027	0.0026
2.8	0.0026	0.0025	0.0024	0.0023	0.0023	0.0022	0.0021	0.0021	0.0020	0.0019
2.9	0.0019	0.0018	0.0018	0.0017	0.0016	0.0016	0.0015	0.0015	0.0014	0.0014
3.0	0.0013	0.0013	0.0013	0.0012	0.0012	0.0011	0.0011	0.0011	0.0010	0.0010
3.1	0.0010	0.0009	0.0009	0.0009	0.0008	0.0008	0.0008	0.0008	0.0007	0.0007
3.2	0.0007									
3.3	0.0005									
3.4	0.0003									
3.5	0.00023									
3.6	0.00016									
3.7	0.00011									
3.8	0.00007									
3.9	0.00005									
4.0	0.00003									

The above table is reproduced from *Non-Parametric Statistics for The Behavioural Sciences* by Sidney Siegel by permission of the McGraw-Hill Publishing Co. Ltd, the publishers.
Note: The blanks in the lower part of the table indicate that the values do not differ appreciably from those in the column headed '0.00'.

276

to calculate the critical values. These are given by:

$$\text{mean} \pm 1.96 \text{ standard errors} = P \text{ per cent} + 1.96 \sqrt{\frac{PQ}{n}}$$

$$= 50 \text{ per cent} \pm 1.96 \,(3.16)$$
$$= 50 \text{ per cent} \pm 6.20 \text{ per cent}$$
$$= 43.80 \text{ per cent and } 56.20 \text{ per cent.}$$

If all possible samples of size $n = 250$, therefore, were drawn from the population and the null hypothesis were true, five per cent of these samples would give a value less than 43.80 per cent or greater than 56.20 per cent. If the calculated value of p_1 from the one sample actually selected is outside these two limits, then the null hypothesis is rejected and the alternative hypothesis is accepted. Alternatively, if p_1 is within the limits, then the null hypothesis is accepted. When such a decision is made in practice there is a chance that an error will be made. There is a five per cent chance that the null hypothesis may be rejected when, in fact, it is true because the sample just happened to be one of the five per cent of all possible samples that will always fall outside the specified limits. This chosen value of five per cent is known as the *significance level* of the test and is often stated in the form $\alpha = 0.05$. In other words, it is often stated as a probability of 5 in 100, i.e., a 1 in 20 chance, that an error will be made. The significance level is often referred to as the *type I error*. Of course, there is nothing to stop the researcher using the ten per cent or one per cent, or any other significance level; it depends on the error he is prepared to accept when making the decision. If the calculated value of the test statistic p_1 obtained from the sample is found to be outside the calculated limits it is said to be *significant* at the chosen level of significance. If it was found from the sample, for example, that 42 per cent of men smoke, this result would be significant as the difference 50 to 42 per cent is greater than 1.96 standard errors, and the null hypothesis that the population percentage is 50 per cent would be rejected.

It is important to note that, although $P = 50$ per cent has been rejected, nothing has been said in this significance test as to the true value of P, except that it is different from 50 per cent. In this case the best estimate of P is given by the sample estimate $p_1 = 42$ per cent. This estimate will be subject to sampling error and it is not possible to state categorically that $P = 42$ per cent. All that can be done is to give limits known as *confidence limits* within which the true value of P will lie. These limits are based on the areas of the normal distribution and are given by:

$$p_1\% \pm Z \sqrt{\frac{p_1\%(100 - p_1)\%}{n}}.$$

When $Z = 1.96$ standard errors, then 95 per cent of the area of the normal distribution is covered by these limits which would then be known as 95 per cent confidence limits. In the present example for sample size $n = 250$ and

$p_1 = 42$ per cent, the 95 per cent limits are given by:

$$42\% \pm 1.96 \sqrt{\frac{42 \times 58}{250}}$$

$$42\% \pm 6.12\%$$

$$35.88\% \text{ to } 48.12\%.$$

Appendix A gives 95 per cent confidence limits for various sample sizes and a selection of observed percentages. It may be used to give approximate answers to confidence limit problems.

The type I error (or significance level) is not the only error that can be made when doing a significance test. Whereas the type I error is the error of saying a result is significant when it is not, the *type II error* is the error of saying a result is not significant when it is. To explain this new concept the previous null hypothesis H_0 will be tested against the one-tailed alternative hypothesis (H_1) that 'P is greater than 50 per cent'. The assumption will now be made that, unknown to the researcher, in fact the alternative hypothesis is true and that $P = 54$ per cent in the population of all men. Just as it is possible to have the sampling distribution for the null hypothesis, so it is also possible to construct a theoretical sampling distribution for when the alternative hypothesis is true. This distribution will also be a normal distribution based on the principle of selecting all possible samples from a population where $P = 54$ per cent and its standard error will be given by:

$$\sqrt{\frac{54\%(100 - 54)\%}{250}} = \sqrt{9.94} = 3.15 \text{ per cent.}$$

The sample size is assumed to be $n = 250$ as before and a five per cent significance level will be used. Figure 12.5 shows the sampling distribution of samples of $n = 250$ when the null hypothesis (H_0) is true and beneath it is the sampling distribution for samples $n = 250$ when the alternative hypothesis (H_1) is true, and in particular when $P = 54$ per cent. As the alternative hypothesis only specifies values of P greater than 50 per cent, only the right-hand tail of the null hypothesis sampling distribution is used in the significance test. Table 12.1 of the area of the normal distribution can be used to find the cut-off point, beyond which five per cent of this distribution will lie. This value is given by:

$$\text{mean} + 1.645 \text{ standard errors} = 50\% + 1.645 (3.16\%)$$
$$= 50\% + 5.20\%$$
$$= 55.2 \text{ per cent.}$$

If, in the one sample actually selected, it is found that the proportion of men who smoke is $p_1 = 55.2$ per cent or greater, then the null hypothesis that $P = 50$ per cent in the population is rejected. If p_1 is any value less than 55.2 per cent then there is no reason to doubt the null hypothesis, as 95 per

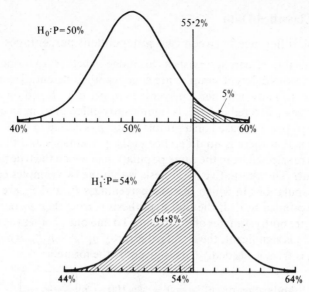

Fig. 12.5. Sampling distributions of the null and alternative
hypotheses.

cent of all possible samples will give a result less than 55.2 per cent when the null hypothesis is true. However, if the latter decision is made in the present example where, unknown to the researcher, P is actually equal to 54 per cent, there is a 64.8 per cent chance that the decision will be wrong. This can be seen by referring to the bottom distribution of $P = 54$ per cent in Fig. 12.5. The area of the distribution to the left of the significance criterion (55.2 per cent) may be calculated using Table 12.1 of the normal distribution. It is the area shown shaded thus ▨ and is found to be 64.8 per cent. This chance of error is known as the type II error. It is quite often denoted by β and is sometimes expressed, like the significance level, as a probability. The present example would give $\beta = 0.648$.

If the chances of reaching a correct decision in a significance test are to be high, then both the significance level and the type II error ought to be kept to a minimum. This can be done by increasing the sample size, as this reduces the standard error and the spread of the sampling distributions of the null and alternative hypotheses. To make $\alpha = \beta = 0.05$ in the present example, when testing H_0 against the specific alternative hypothesis that $P = 54$ per cent, would require a sample size of approximately $n = 1680$.

Some Useful Significance Tests in Market Research

This section will be concerned with giving examples of a number of the most frequently used significance tests in market research. Some tests are more suitable for use on certain types of data than others. For this reason the tests most suited to the three types of data previously defined will be given under those three headings below.

Tests on Classified Data

Testing the difference between two independent percentages

Very often, the researcher wishes to judge whether two independent percentages from different samples are significantly different. He may wish, for example, to know whether a percentage p_1 per cent, based on a random sample of size n_1 selected in 1970, is significantly different from an equivalent percentage p_2 per cent based on a sample of size n_2 selected in 1968. The null hypothesis is that there is no difference in the percentages and that the two samples were selected from the same population in which the true percentage is P per cent. The alternative hypothesis is that the two samples come from different populations in which the two percentages P_1 and P_2 are different, giving a two-tailed test. If the null hypothesis is true, then p_1 per cent and p_2 per cent are both estimates of P per cent. To find out whether the difference $p_1\% - p_2\%$ is significant, the standard error of $p_1\% - p_2\%$, when the null hypothesis is true, is needed. This is given by the formula:

$$\text{Standard error } (p_1 - p_2) = \sqrt{p(100 - p)\left[\frac{1}{n_1} + \frac{1}{n_2}\right]}$$

where

$$p = \frac{n_1 p_1 + n_2 p_2}{n_1 + n_2}$$

is the best estimate of the unknown population percentage P per cent. Tables giving the value of this standard error for various values of n_1, n_2, and p are available[1]. If the difference $p_1 - p_2$ is greater than 1.96 times its standard error then this observed difference can be declared significant at the five per cent level. Appendix B may be used to give approximate answers to this problem. It shows for various values of n_1, n_2, and p the differences needed between p_1 and p_2 to be significant at the five per cent level.

Example. In 1968 a random sample of $n_1 = 400$ men showed that $p_1 = 42.5$ per cent of them regularly read a certain newspaper. Two years later, in a random sample of $n_2 = 200$ men it was found that $p_2 = 35.0$ per cent of them read that newspaper. Is the difference significant or can it be explained as the random fluctuations of sampling? The first step in this test is to calculate:

$$p = \frac{(400 \times 42.5) + (200 \times 35.0)}{400 + 200} = 40.0 \text{ per cent.}$$

The standard error of $(p_1 - p_2)$ is then:

$$\text{Standard error } (p_1 - p_2) = \sqrt{40 \times 60[\tfrac{1}{400} + \tfrac{1}{200}]} = 4.24 \text{ per cent.}$$

Dividing $p_1 - p_2$ by its standard error gives:

$$\frac{p_1 - p_2}{\text{standard error } (p_1 - p_2)} = \frac{42.5\% - 35.0\%}{4.24\%} = \frac{7.5\%}{4.24\%} = 1.77$$

The observed difference is less than 1.96 times its standard error and, therefore, it is not an unusual value to obtain from the sampling distribution when the null hypothesis is true. Accordingly, the conclusion is reached that this data does not give any reason to reject the null hypothesis that there has been no change in the percentage of men reading the newspaper.

Testing the difference between two correlated percentages

(a) *Mutually Exclusive Classifications*

Questions to which the respondent may give only *one* of a number of answers occur frequently on market research questionnaires. The analysis of such questions results in a series of percentages adding up to 100 per cent based on a sample of size n. The testing of the difference between two such percentages is complicated by the fact that if one of the percentages goes up, then one or more of the other percentages must go down, as they all must add to 100 per cent. The test differs from the previous one on independent percentages by having a different formula for the standard error:

$$\text{Standard error } (p_1 - p_2) = \sqrt{\frac{1}{n}(p_1 q_1 + p_2 q_2 + 2p_1 p_2)}$$

where

$$q_1 = 100 - p_1$$
$$q_2 = 100 - p_2.$$

Example. From a random sample of $n = 400$ housewives the following results were obtained in answer to the question, 'Which brand of coffee do you buy most often?':

brand A	$p_1 = 40$ per cent;
brand B	$p_2 = 30$ per cent;
brand C	$p_3 = 12$ per cent;
brand D	$p_4 = 11$ per cent;
no regular brand	$p_5 = \underline{7}$ per cent;
	$\underline{100}$ per cent.

The null hypothesis to be tested is that there is no difference between brand A and brand B and that the observed difference in percentages can be explained as sampling variations. The alternative hypothesis is that there is a difference in the percentage share held by these two brands. The standard error of the difference is given by:

$$\text{Standard error } (p_1 - p_2) = \sqrt{\tfrac{1}{400}[(40 \times 60) + (30 \times 70) + 2(40 \times 30)]}$$
$$= 4.15 \text{ per cent.}$$

The observed difference $p_1 - p_2 = 10$ per cent is 2.41 times this standard error and is significant at the five per cent level. The data, therefore, suggests that there is a real difference between these two brands.

(b) *Overlapping Classifications*

With some market research questions the respondent may give more than one answer. The results of analysing such a question will be in the form of a number of percentages adding up to more than 100 per cent, being based on the sample size n. As an example consider the question, 'Which brands of soap did you buy in the last seven days?' The housewives asked this question could possibly have bought more than one brand. To test the difference between two brand percentages a different standard error formula is needed to account for the overlap between brands.

$$\text{Standard error } (p_1 - p_2) = \sqrt{\frac{1}{n} [p_1 q_1 + p_2 q_2 + 2(p_1 p_2 - p_{12})]}$$

where p_{12} = the overlap proportion, i.e., the proportion buying both brands.

For arithmetical reasons it is best to convert all the percentages in the above standard error formula to proportions when doing the calculations and multiply the answer at the end by 100 to give the standard error as a percentage.

Example.   The following data was obtained from a sample of $n = 2000$ men who were asked which brands of petrol they had used in the previous three months:

brand 1	$p_1 = 25$ per cent;
brand 2	$p_2 = 20$ per cent;
brand 3	$p_3 = 18$ per cent;
brand 4	$p_4 = 18$ per cent;
brand 5	$p_5 = 11$ per cent;
brand 6	$p_6 = 13$ per cent;
brand 7	$p_7 = \underline{12}$ per cent;
	$\underline{117}$ per cent.

The difference between brands 1 and 2 is to be tested for significance, the null hypothesis being that there is no difference between the two percentages p_1 and p_2 in the population from which the sample was drawn. The alternative hypothesis is that the two brands have different shares of the market. The survey results also show that p_{12} = eight per cent of men had bought both brands 1 and 2 in the previous three months. To calculate the standard error the three relevant percentages, $p_1 = 25$ per cent, $p_2 = 20$ per cent and $p_{12} = 8$ per cent, are converted to the three proportions 0.25, 0.20, and 0.08 respectively.

Standard error $(p_1 - p_2)$

$$= \sqrt{\tfrac{1}{2000}[(0.25 \times 0.75) + (0.2 \times 0.8) + 2(\{0.25 \times 0.2\} - 0.08)]}$$
$$= 0.0120 = 1.20 \text{ per cent.}$$

The actual difference $p_1 - p_2 = 25$ per cent $- 20$ per cent $= 5$ per cent is 4.17 times its standard error. The ratio is higher than the value 3.29 needed to be significant at the 0.1 per cent level, and it can be concluded that a real difference exists in the population, from which the sample of $n = 2000$ men was selected.

The Chi-Square Test. Two-way classification tables usually form a prominent part of the results from a market survey. A typical example is given below, based on $n = 650$ housewives.

| *Purchasing habits* | Social class | | | |
	AB	*C1*	*C2DE*	Total
Brand A bought most often	35	72	172	279
Brand B bought most often	21	62	164	247
Brand C bought most often	14	26	84	124
Total	70	160	420	650

When both the row classifications and the column classifications are independent, i.e., a respondent can be in only one cell of the table, the differences in the cell frequencies may be tested for significance by using the chi-square test. This test enables one to say whether the observed cell frequencies are in agreement with the frequencies expected when the null hypothesis is true. The formula for computing the test criterion is best explained in terms of an example.

Example. The above data on 650 housewives will be used in this example. The null hypothesis to be tested is that the brand shares are all equal for the three social classes and that differences observed in the above sample data reflect only sampling variation. This unknown distribution of brand shares is best estimated by pooling the data for the three social classes. This is given by the total column in the above table. If the null hypothesis is true then each column (social class grouping) will have its row (brand) frequencies in the same ratio as the total column's row frequencies. It is thus possible to work out an expected frequency for each cell of the table. This may be most easily done by using the following rule. The expected frequency for a given cell is obtained by multiplying its row total by its column total and dividing the result by the grand total. Thus for the cell 'brand A/social class AB' the expected frequency is:

$$E = \frac{279 \times 70}{650} = 30.0.$$

The data is reproduced below with each expected frequency (E) being given in brackets next to its observed frequency (O).

Social class

	AB	C1	C2DE	Total
Brand A	35(30.0)	72(68.7)	172(180.3)	279
Brand B	21(26.6)	62(60.8)	164(159.6)	247
Brand C	14(13.4)	26(30.5)	84(80.1)	124
	70	160	420	650

It will be noted that the expected frequencies add down and across to the column and row totals respectively. The next step in the test is to calculate the test criterion:

$$\chi^2 = \sum \frac{(O - E)^2}{E}$$

where O denotes observed frequency and E denotes expected frequency and the summation is over all cells of the data. This quantity χ^2 will not have a normally distributed sampling distribution like previously-discussed test statistics. It will be distributed, when the null hypothesis is true, like another well known statistical distribution, the chi-square distribution. The calculation of χ^2 for this example is given below.

O	E	$(O - E)$	$(O - E)^2$	$\dfrac{(O - E)^2}{E}$
35	30.0	5.0	25.00	1.83
21	26.6	−5.6	31.36	1.18
14	13.4	0.6	0.36	0.03
72	68.7	3.3	10.89	0.16
62	60.8	1.2	1.44	0.02
26	30.5	−4.5	20.25	0.66
172	180.3	−8.3	68.89	0.38
164	159.6	4.4	19.36	0.12
84	80.1	3.9	15.21	0.19

$$\chi^2 = \sum \frac{(O - E)^2}{E} = \overline{3.57}$$

The chi-square distribution does not have a fixed shape like the normal distribution but takes many forms dependent on a quantity known as its *degrees of freedom*. In the context of a multi-cell table, or contingency table as it is often called, the degrees of freedom are calculated as $df = (r - 1)(c - 1)$ where r is the number of rows and c is the number of columns. In this case $df = (3 - 1)(3 - 1) = 4$. Table 12.2 gives, for various degrees of freedom, the values that χ^2 must attain to be significant at certain levels. For $df =$ four degrees of freedom χ^2 must be 9.49 or greater to be significant at the five per cent level. The observed value of $\chi^2 = 3.57$ falls well short of this value, so this data gives no evidence to doubt the null hypothesis that purchasing habits are the same for all three social class groupings.

284

The quantity χ^2 has a distribution like the chi-square distribution only when the expected frequencies (E) are large. How large, is a matter of opinion and conflicting advice is often given in statistical texts. For tables with more than one degree of freedom, Cochran[2] suggests that less than 20 per cent of the cells in the table should have expected frequencies less than five and that no cells in the table should have E less than one. If the data do not meet these restrictions, then row and/or column classifications may be combined until the expected frequencies are of sufficient size. The merging of rows or columns must only be done, however, if the resulting classifications are meaningful. The calculation of χ^2 is done using discrete numbers whereas the chi-square distribution is a continuous distribution. If the calculation of χ^2 includes what is known as *Yate's correction for continuity*, then it approximates much better to the chi-square distribution, especially with small expected frequencies. The correction consists of adding a half to

Table 12.2   Table of significant values of chi-square*

df	\multicolumn{15}{c}{Probability under H_0 that $X^2 \geq$ chi-square}
	0.99	0.98	0.95	0.90	0.80	0.70	0.50	0.30	0.20	0.10	0.05	0.02	0.01	0.001
1	0.00016	0.00063	0.0039	0.016	0.064	0.15	0.46	1.07	1.64	2.71	3.84	5.41	6.64	10.83
2	0.02	0.04	0.10	0.21	0.45	0.71	1.39	2.41	3.22	4.60	5.99	7.82	9.21	13.82
3	0.12	0.18	0.35	0.58	1.00	1.42	2.37	3.66	4.64	6.25	7.82	9.84	11.34	16.27
4	0.30	0.43	0.71	1.06	1.65	2.20	3.36	4.88	5.99	7.78	9.49	11.67	13.28	18.46
5	0.55	0.75	1.14	1.61	2.34	3.00	4.35	6.06	7.29	9.24	11.07	13.39	15.09	20.52
6	0.87	1.13	1.64	2.20	3.07	3.83	5.35	7.23	8.56	10.64	12.59	15.03	16.81	22.46
7	1.24	1.56	2.17	2.83	3.82	4.67	6.35	8.38	9.80	12.02	14.07	16.62	18.48	24.32
8	1.65	2.03	2.73	3.49	4.59	5.53	7.34	9.52	11.03	13.36	15.51	18.17	20.09	26.12
9	2.09	2.53	3.32	4.17	5.38	6.39	8.34	10.66	12.24	14.68	16.92	19.68	21.67	27.88
10	2.56	3.06	3.94	4.86	6.18	7.27	9.34	11.78	13.44	15.99	18.31	21.16	23.21	29.59
11	3.05	3.61	4.58	5.58	6.99	8.15	10.34	12.90	14.63	17.28	19.68	22.62	24.72	31.26
12	3.57	4.18	5.23	6.30	7.81	9.03	11.34	14.01	15.81	18.55	21.03	24.05	26.22	32.91
13	4.11	4.76	5.89	7.04	8.63	9.93	12.34	15.12	16.98	19.81	22.36	25.47	27.69	34.53
14	4.66	5.37	6.57	7.79	9.47	10.82	13.34	16.22	18.15	21.06	23.68	26.87	29.14	36.12
15	5.23	5.98	7.26	8.55	10.31	11.72	14.34	17.32	19.31	22.31	25.00	28.26	30.58	37.70
16	5.81	6.61	7.96	9.31	11.15	12.62	15.34	18.42	20.46	23.54	26.30	29.63	32.00	39.29
17	6.41	7.26	8.67	10.08	12.00	13.53	16.34	19.51	21.62	24.77	27.59	31.00	33.41	40.75
18	7.02	7.91	9.39	10.86	12.86	14.44	17.34	20.60	22.76	25.99	28.87	32.35	34.80	42.31
19	7.63	8.57	10.12	11.65	13.72	15.35	18.34	21.69	23.90	27.20	30.14	33.69	36.19	43.82
20	8.26	9.24	10.85	12.44	14.58	16.27	19.34	22.78	25.04	28.41	31.41	35.02	37.57	45.32
21	8.90	9.92	11.59	13.24	15.44	17.18	20.34	23.86	26.17	29.62	32.67	36.34	38.93	46.80
22	9.54	10.60	12.34	14.04	16.31	18.10	21.24	24.94	27.30	30.81	33.92	37.66	40.29	48.27
23	10.20	11.29	13.09	14.85	17.19	19.02	22.34	26.02	28.43	32.01	35.17	38.97	41.64	49.73
24	10.86	11.99	13.85	15.66	18.06	19.94	23.34	27.10	29.55	33.20	36.42	40.27	42.98	51.18
25	11.52	12.70	14.61	16.47	18.94	20.87	24.34	28.17	30.68	34.38	37.65	41.57	44.31	52.62
26	12.20	13.41	15.38	17.29	19.82	21.79	25.34	29.25	31.80	35.56	38.88	42.86	45.64	54.05
27	12.88	14.12	16.15	18.11	20.70	22.72	26.34	30.32	32.91	36.74	40.11	44.14	46.96	55.48
28	13.56	14.85	16.93	18.94	21.59	23.65	27.34	31.39	34.03	37.92	41.34	45.42	48.28	56.89
29	14.26	15.57	17.71	19.77	22.48	24.58	28.34	32.46	35.14	39.09	42.56	46.69	49.59	58.30
30	14.95	16.31	18.49	20.60	23.36	25.51	29.34	33.53	36.25	40.26	43.77	47.96	50.89	59.70

* Table 12.2 is abridged from Table IV of Fisher and Yates: *Statistical tables for biological, agricultural, and medical research*, published by Oliver and Boyd Ltd., Edinburgh by permission of the authors and publishers.

each negative value of $(O - E)$ and subtracting a half from each positive value of $(O - E)$.

In the case of 2×2 two-way classification tables the formula for χ^2 takes a special form. Denoting the four cells of a 2×2 table by the letters a, b, c, d, we have

		Total
a	b	$a + b$
c	d	$c + d$
$a + c$	$b + d$	n $= a + b + c + d.$

The formula for χ^2, including the correction for continuity, then becomes:

$$\chi^2 = \frac{n(|ad - bc| - n/2)^2}{(a + b)(c + d)(a + c)(b + d)} \quad \text{with one degree of freedom.}$$

The vertical lines enclosing the expression $ad - bc$ mean that the positive value of the expression must be taken, irrespective of whether it turns out to be positive or negative.

Example. The following data was collected from a random sample of $n = 100$ women.

	Social class		
	ABC1	C2DE	Total
Owners of sewing machines	23	13	36
Non-owners	12	52	64
	35	65	100

The null hypothesis to be tested is that the ownership of sewing machines is at the same level for both social class groupings. The alternative hypothesis is that the ownership levels are different:

$$\chi^2 = \frac{100[|(23)(52) - (13)(12)| - \frac{100}{2}]^2}{(36)(64)(35)(65)} = 18.7.$$

Table 12.2 shows that for one degree of freedom the value $\chi^2 = 18.7$ is significant at the 0.1 per cent level, and on the evidence of this data it must be concluded that the ownership levels are different for the two social class groupings. The ownership levels are, for $ABC1$ equal to $p_1 = \frac{23}{35} = 65.7$ per cent and for $C2DE$ equal to $p_2 = \frac{13}{65} = 20.0$ per cent. They have been put in percentage form to indicate that the chi-square test for 2×2 tables is equivalent to the test of two independent percentages given above.

McNemar's Test. This test is useful for 2×2 tables where the data has come from matched samples. The term matched samples includes those cases where each respondent in one sample is matched, on a number of criteria, to a respondent in a second sample, and also the case where the same sample of respondents is interviewed twice. The data from such 2×2 tables may often be presented, as below, in a form which might suggest that the ordinary chi-square test is applicable. This example shows the results of interviewing the same sample of respondents twelve months after a previous interview, about ownership of refrigerators.

	Interview 1	Interview 2
Refrigerator Owners	a	b
Non-owners	c	d
	$a + c$	$b + d$

It is incorrect to treat the two interviews as two independent samples and do a chi-square test to see whether the proportion of owners has increased or decreased. It is necessary to examine the changes from the first interview to the second.

		First interview		
		Owner	Non-owner	Total
Second	Owner	e	f	b
interview	Non-owner	g	h	d
	Total	a	c	$n = a + c = b + d.$

It is important to notice that all that has been done is to recast the data in a different form. The marginal totals (a, b, c, d) of the 'changes' table correspond to the same values $a, b, c,$ and d in the previous table. To test the null hypothesis that the proportion of owners has neither increased nor decreased it is only necessary to consider the cell values f and g, as these are the only two cells that contribute to any change. If the null hypothesis is true the total number of respondents who change their ownership status will be evenly divided between these two cells. Thus, the expected value E for both these two cells is $(f + g)/2$. Having obtained observed and expected frequencies for these two cells, as given below, the usual formula for χ^2 may now be applied to this data.

	Observed (O)	Expected (E)
Non-owner to owner	f	$\dfrac{f + g}{2}$
Owner to non-owner	g	$\dfrac{f + g}{2}$
Total	$f + g$	

$$\chi^2 = \sum \frac{(O - E)^2}{E}$$

$$\chi^2 = \frac{[f - (f + g)/2]^2}{(f + g)/2} + \frac{[g - (f + g)/2]^2}{(f + g)/2}$$

$$\chi^2 = \frac{(f - g)^2}{f + g} \qquad \text{with one degree of freedom.}$$

With a correction for continuity, the formula becomes:

$$\chi^2 = \frac{(|f - g| - 1)^2}{f + g}.$$

Table 12.2 of significant values of χ^2 may, therefore, be used to test the validity of the null hypothesis.

Example. A random sample of $n = 500$ motorists are interviewed, before a new advertising campaign for motoring magazine A, to estimate the proportion who regularly read the magazine. The same 500 motorists are re-interviewed some time after the campaign is finished and the following data is obtained.

		First interview		
		Readers	*Non-readers*	Total
Second	Readers	203	66	269
interview	Non-readers	41	190	231
	Total	244	256	500

The null hypothesis is that there has been no change in the readership level, this being tested against the alternative hypothesis that some change has taken place. The test criterion is calculated as:

$$\chi^2 = \frac{(|66 - 41| - 1)^2}{66 + 41} = \frac{(24)^2}{107} = 5.38.$$

Reference to Table 12.2 shows that, for one degree of freedom, $\chi^2 = 5.38$ is significant at the five per cent level. The data suggests that there has been a real change in the readership percentage for magazine A.

Tests on Ranked Data

Testing rating scales

(a) *The Kolmogorov-Smirnov Test For Two Independent Samples*

Semantic rating scales are extensively used by market researchers. An example of such a scale would be:

(a) very good quality;
(b) good quality;
(c) neither good not bad quality;
(d) bad quality;
(e) very bad quality.

This scale represents a non-numerical ranking of the attribute 'quality'. The Kolmogorov-Smirnov test assumes that underlying this scale is a hypothetical numerical measuring scale, to which the five statements approximate. In a later section actual numbers will be attached to each position on such scales, and more powerful statistical tests will be carried out, involving assumptions about the underlying numerical scale.

The Kolmogorov-Smirnov test may be used to compare two sets of percentages on the same rating scale obtained from two independent samples. The test consists of cumulating the percentages for each sample separately, and finding the maximum difference between any two cumulative percentages at any of the positions on the scale. This maximum difference may be compared against known theoretical values to judge its significance.

Example. A random sample of $n_1 = 200$ men and an independent random sample of $n_2 = 200$ women were asked to assess a new brand of sherry in terms of its sweetness/dryness. The results of the test were as follows.

	Men (per cent)	Women (per cent)
Very sweet	18.5	15.0
Sweet	22.5	17.5
Neither sweet nor dry	29.0	25.0
Dry	20.0	22.5
Very dry	10.0	20.0

The null hypothesis to be tested is that there is no difference in assessment by men and women, against the alternative hypothesis that there are some differences. This gives a two-tailed test. Denoting the percentages for men by p_1 and for women by p_2 the calculation of the maximum difference D between the cumulated percentages proceeds as below.

p_1	p_2	Cumulative $p_1 = A$	Cumulative $p_2 = B$	$D = |A - B|$
18.5	15.0	18.5	15.0	3.5
22.5	17.5	41.0	32.5	8.5
29.0	25.0	70.0	57.5	12.5
20.0	22.5	90.0	80.0	10.0
10.0	20.0	100.0	100.0	—

In a two-tailed test the maximum *positive* difference $D = |A - B|$ is taken as the test criterion irrespective of whether the difference is positive or negative. In this example, $D = 12.5$. The significant values of D for two samples of size n_1 and n_2 are shown below. The sample value of D must equal or exceed these values to be significant at a given level.

Significance level	Significant value of D
(per cent)	$\sqrt{\dfrac{n_1 + n_2}{n_1 n_2}}$ times:
10	122
5	136
1	163
0.1	195

Using the five per cent significance level it is calculated that D must equal or exceed the value,

$$D = 136 \sqrt{\frac{200 + 200}{200 \times 200}} = 13.6.$$

The sample value of $D = 12.5$ is less than this, and therefore this data leads to the conclusion that there is no difference in the assessment of the new sherry by men and women.

For this particular significance test a one-tailed test will also be given, as the significance testing procedure differs from that of a two-tailed test. The null hypothesis will now be tested against the alternative hypothesis that men rate the product sweeter than do women. The calculation of the test statistic D is the same as for the two-tailed test, except that the sign of D in the last column of the above calculations is retained. If A is greater than B, then D is positive, and if B is greater than A then D is negative. The maximum value of D, in the direction predicted by the alternative hypothesis, is taken as the test statistic. In the present example this means considering only *positive* values of D, which would indicate men rating the product sweeter. In the one-tailed test the calculated value of D must be equal to or greater than:

$$\chi^2 = 4D^2 \left[\frac{n_1 n_2}{n_1 + n_2} \right]$$

a quantity which has the chi-square distribution with two degrees of freedom, when D is expressed as a proportion and not as a percentage. In the example $D = 12.5$ per cent or 0.125 as a proportion and χ^2 is found to be equal to:

$$\chi^2 = 4(0.125)^2 \left[\frac{200 \times 200}{200 + 200} \right] = 6.25.$$

Table 12.2 of the significance points of the chi-square distribution shows that for two degrees of freedom $\chi^2 = 5.99$ would be significant at the five per cent level. The calculated value of $\chi^2 = 6.25$ is greater than this and it may be argued that the data support the alternative hypothesis that men judge the new sherry to be sweeter than do women. This result is different from that obtained previously by using a two-tailed test, and illustrates the point that a one-tailed test is always better at rejecting the null hypothesis than a two-tailed test.

(b) The Sign Test For Two Matched Samples

The 'sign test' may be used in a number of market research contexts, but here it is demonstrated in the situation where two matched samples of respondents rate two items, or where the same sample of respondents rates both items. The results are often presented in survey reports in a form which give the impression that the Kolmogorov-Smirnov test for two independent samples is appropriate. An example of this would be where $n = 200$ men were asked to rate two improved versions, X and Y, of an existing after-shave lotion. The data would probably be presented as below, in terms of frequencies and percentages.

	Version X	per cent	Version Y	per cent
Like very much	82	(41.0)	50	(25.0)
Like	57	(28.5)	70	(35.0)
Neither like nor dislike	29	(14.5)	40	(20.0)
Dislike	18	(9.0)	30	(15.0)
Dislike very much	14	(7.0)	10	(5.0)
	200	(100.0)	200	(100.0)

As the samples are matched a different approach is needed, which involves presenting one rating analysed by the other in the form of a two-way table. The sign test is then applied to some of the cells of this two-way table.

Example. The data below show the results obtained by analysing version X ratings against version Y ratings in the example on after-shave lotion.

		Rating on version X					
		Like very much	Like	Neither like nor dislike	Dislike	Dislike very much	Total
	Like very much	20	20	4	4	2	50
Rating	Like	30	20	10	5	5	70
on	Neither	18	10	8	3	1	40
version Y	Dislike	10	7	5	4	4	30
	Dislike very much	4	0	2	2	2	10
	Total	82	57	29	18	14	200

The null hypothesis is that there is no difference in the ratings for the two versions, and this will be tested against the alternative hypothesis that one or other of the two new versions is better liked. If the null hypothesis is true then the number of men rating X more favourably than Y on the scale ought to be the same as the number of men rating Y more favourably than X. Usually those rating X above Y are denoted by a $+$ sign and those rating Y above X by a $-$ sign, and this is how the sign test gets its name. The test consists of comparing the observed numbers rating X above and below Y with their expected frequencies. The test criterion turns out to be identical to the criterion of McNemars test.

	Observed	Expected
Number rating X above Y ($+$)	f	$\dfrac{f+g}{2}$
Number rating X below Y ($-$)	g	$\dfrac{f+g}{2}$
	$\overline{f+g}$	

$$\chi^2 = \frac{(|f-g|-1)^2}{f+g} \quad \text{with one degree of freedom.}$$

In the example the number rating X above Y is obtained by summing the frequencies in the lower triangle of the above two-way table and the number rating Y above X is obtained from the sum of the frequencies in the upper triangle. Those men giving equal ratings are not used in the test, but the size of this group should be taken into account when interpreting the result of the significance test. Two summations give $f = 88$ and $g = 58$.

$$\chi^2 = \frac{(|88-58|-1)^2}{88+58} = 5.76.$$

From Table 12.2 of the chi-square distribution with one degree of freedom it can be seen that a value of 5.76 is significant at the two per cent level. The observed differences in the two ratings do not appear to be due to sampling fluctuations, and the data suggest that version X is the better product.

Testing numerical rankings

A technique that is often used in market research, especially in product tests, is for respondents to be shown a number of objects and asked to rank them (1st, 2nd, 3rd, . . . etc.,) in order of preference or acceptability. Special methods have been developed to test the significance of the results from data ranked in this way.

(a) *Ranking of Two Objects—Paired Comparisons*

In paired comparison tests objects are presented in pairs to respondents. The respondent is asked to state which object he prefers, i.e., he ranks them first and second. If more than two objects are to be tested it is possible to arrange that every respondent makes a judgement on all possible pairs. This situation is known as a 'balanced paired comparison experiment' or 'round robin'. In practice, respondents do not always consider all possible pairs of objects but only compare some pairs. Even so, it is possible to arrange that each pair of objects is judged by the same number of respondents. If the number of objects being tested is denoted by t and n measurements are made on each possible pair, then the total number of possible pairs is given by:

$$\frac{t(t-1)}{2};$$

and the total judgements or rankings will be:

$$\frac{nt(t-1)}{2}.$$

When comparing two objects, say A_1 and A_2, a score of one will be given to the preferred object and a score of zero to the object not preferred.

	Object		
	A_1	A_2	
Respondent 1	1	0	A_1 preferred to A_2
Respondent 2	0	1	A_2 preferred to A_1
Respondent 3	1	0	A_1 preferred to A_2
Respondent 4	1	0	A_1 preferred to A_2
	$a_1 = 3$	$a_2 = 1$	

The total score a_i for each of the t objects is used for testing the significance of paired comparison data.

Usually, this type of test is run to determine which objects are preferred overall, and in particular to find the 'best' object. This aim may be accomplished by comparing pairs of scores a_i and a_j on objects A_i and A_j for significant differences. Unfortunately, if the number of objects in the test is large, so is the number of possible pairs and therefore if a large number of significance tests are carried out on the data the probability of obtaining an apparently significant difference just by chance, will be quite high. To guard against this the data are examined by an *overall test of significance* to see whether the scores $a_1 \, a_2 \, a_3 \cdots$ etc., as a set are significantly different. The test criterion is given by the expression:

$$D = \frac{4\left[\sum a_i^2 - \dfrac{tn^2(t-1)^2}{4}\right]}{nt}.$$

This quantity has the chi-square distribution with $(t - 1)$ degrees of freedom. If this test gives a significant result at the chosen significance level, it indicates that some significant differences between scores exist. Individual pairs of scores may then be tested for significant differences by using the so-called *least significant difference* criterion defined by:

$$m = 1.96 \sqrt{\frac{nt}{2} + \frac{1}{2}}.$$

Any pair of scores whose difference is equal to or greater than m may be declared significant at the five per cent level. Replacing 1.96 by 2.58 or 3.29 gives equivalent criteria at the 1 per cent and 0.1 per cent levels respectively.

Example. $n = 60$ respondents were asked to do paired comparisons on all possible pairs of $t = 5$ types of biscuit, each respondent making $t(t - 1)/2 = 10$ judgements. The total scores for each biscuit were:

$$a_1 = 132; \qquad a_2 = 102; \qquad a_3 = 178; \qquad a_4 = 48; \qquad a_5 = 140.$$

Squaring the scores for each biscuit gives:

$$a_1{}^2 = 17\,424; \quad a_2{}^2 = 10\,404; \quad a_3{}^2 = 31\,684; \quad a_4{}^2 = 2304; \quad a_5{}^2 = 19\,600.$$

Summing these squared scores $\sum a_i{}^2 = 81\,416$

$$D = \frac{4\left[81\,416 - \dfrac{5(60)^2(4)^2}{4} \right]}{(60)(5)} = 125.55.$$

With $t - 1 = 4$ degrees of freedom, Table 12.2 of percentage points of the chi-square distribution shows that at the 0.1 per cent level D has to be 18.46 or greater to be significant. The computed value of $D = 125.55$ is therefore very highly significant and indicates that real differences between biscuits' scores do exist. Using the least significance difference criterion at the five per cent significance level the critical value is:

$$m = 1.96 \sqrt{\frac{60 \times 5}{2} + \frac{1}{2}} = 24.51.$$

Any difference in scores equal to or greater than 24.51 may be declared significantly different at the five per cent level. However, it must be remembered that not too many significance tests should be carried out on the same set of data. Strictly speaking, one ought to test for significance only those pairs which are thought, before the experiment is carried out, to be a comparison of interest and not on pairs of scores which, when inspecting the data, just happen to look if they might be significant. It is quite likely that the object with the highest score will be significantly different from the one with

294

the lowest score even when the null hypothesis of no differences between any scores, is true. Further analyses on paired comparison data are given by David[3]. Among these is a special version for paired comparisons of a technique known as *analysis of variance*, which will be described later in this chapter. It uses a seven-point rating scale of preferences scored from $+3$ to -3 and allows for the effect of order of presentation of objects to respondents. This special version of the technique is due to Scheffé and the interested reader may consult his original article[4] for details.

(b)   Ranking of Three or More Objects

If a number of objects are to be compared, and the objects have obvious differences, then it is better to get respondents to do an overall ranking of all the objects instead of doing a number of paired comparisons. When t objects have been ranked by n respondents it is possible to test whether there is any agreement between respondents ranking by calculating *Kendall's Coefficient of Concordance* (W) and testing its significance. If significant agreement is found, it is possible to obtain the order of preference or acceptability of the objects. A description of the calculation of W is best done in the context of an example.

Example.   A random sample of $n = 100$ housewives are asked to rank $t = 4$ new designs for a breakfast cereal packet. The results of such ranking tests are usually given in the following form:

Cereal packet designs

Rank	*A*	*B*	*C*	*D*
1	40	10	25	25
2	30	20	40	10
3	20	30	25	25
4	10	40	10	40
	100	100	100	100

A design ranked first is given a score of 1, a design ranked second a score of 2 and so on. First calculate the sum of ranks R_i for each design:

$$R_A = (40 \times 1) + (30 \times 2) + (20 \times 3) + (10 \times 4) = 200.$$

Similarly,

$$R_B = 300; \qquad R_C = 220; \qquad R_D = 280.$$

Then calculate the average sum of ranks, $\bar{R}$:

$$\bar{R} = \frac{200 + 300 + 220 + 280}{4} = 250.$$

295

Next, compute $S = \sum (R_i - \bar{R})^2$

R_i	$R_i - \bar{R}$	$(R_i - \bar{R})^2$
200	-50	2500
300	50	2500
220	-30	900
280	30	900
		$\overline{6800} = S$

S is the sum of squares of the deviations of the individual R_i scores from their average $\bar{R}$. If all respondents were in complete agreement, S would be equal to:

$$S = \frac{n^2(t^3 - t)}{12}.$$

Kendall's W is the ratio of the observed value of S to its theoretical counterpart:

$$W = \frac{12S}{n^2(t^3 - t)} = \frac{12 \times 6800}{(100)^2(4^3 - 4)} = 0.136.$$

The coefficient W may vary from $W = 0$, when all respondents are ranking at random, to $W = +1$, indicating complete agreement between respondents. To test whether W is significantly different from zero, use has to be made of tables of significant values of a statistical distribution known as the F distribution. Table 12.3 gives the five per cent and one per cent level values for this distribution, from which it will be seen that two values of degrees of freedom are required to specify significant values of F. It can be shown that a transformation of W given by:

$$F = \frac{(n - 1)W}{1 - W}$$

will have the F distribution with degrees of freedom approximately equal to:

$$V_1 = t - 1 \quad \text{and} \quad V_2 = (n - 1)V_1.$$

In the example,

$$F = \frac{(100 - 1)0.136}{0.864} = 15.6$$

with $V_1 = 4 - 1 = 3$ and $V_2 = 99 \times 3 = 297$ degrees of freedom. Reference to Table 12.3 of the F distribution reveals that the calculated value of $F = 15.6$ is at least significant at the one per cent level. There appears to be a small but real agreement between respondents in their ranking of the new packet designs.

The rank order of acceptability of the new designs is given, when W has been found to be significant, by the individual sum of ranks R_i for each design. A low score indicates a high preference and a high score suggests a low level of acceptability. To test whether one design is ranked significantly higher than another the sign test, previously described, may be used. If design B is to be compared with design C in the above example, the following two-way table involving the ranks of these two designs must be produced.

Ranking of design B

		1	*2*	*3*	*4*	Total
	1	0	5	10	10	25
Ranking of design C	2	5	0	25	10	40
	3	3	12	0	10	25
	4	2	3	5	0	10
Total		10	20	40	30	100

the number of times C ranked above B $(+)$ = 70;
the number of times B ranked above C $(-)$ = 30.

$$\chi^2 = \frac{(|70 - 30| - 1)^2}{70 + 30} = 15.21 \text{ with one degree of freedom.}$$

Looking up Table 12.2 of the chi-square distribution for one degree of freedom shows that $\chi^2 = 15.21$ is significant at the 0.1 per cent level. Design C is significantly preferred to design B by respondents.

Tests on Measured Data

Testing the difference between the means of two independent samples

A frequent comparison, that is needed when assessing the results of a market research survey, is that between the means of two rating scales, where the scales have been given simple numerical scores. As explained earlier, if one is prepared to assume that the scores represent meaningful values on an underlying continuous distribution, then the test about to be described, which is applicable only to measured data, may be used. As an example of how more than one type of significance test may be used on the same set of data, the data previously used in describing the Kolmogorov-Smirnov test will be examined again for significance. This time a scoring system will be attached to the scale positions, and the frequencies are used in place of the percentages.

Rating on new brand of sherry

	Score	*Men*	*Women*
Very Sweet	+2	37	30
Sweet	+1	45	35
Neither Sweet nor Dry	0	58	50
Dry	−1	40	45
Very Dry	−2	20	40
		$n_1 = 200$	$n_2 = 200$

The main assumption being made is that scoring system is an interval scale and that the numerical distances between the scale positions are valid. The Kolmogorov-Smirnov test makes no such assumption.

To test the difference between two means $\bar{x}_1$ and $\bar{x}_2$ based on two independent samples of size n_1 and n_2 it is necessary to calculate the variance of each set of data. From the two variances s_1^2 and s_2^2 the standard error of the difference between two means is calculated as:

$$\text{Standard error } (\bar{x}_1 - \bar{x}_2) = \sqrt{s^2 \left[\frac{n_1 + n_2}{n_1 \times n_2} \right]}$$

where s^2 is a pooled estimate of the variance based on both samples

$$s^2 = \frac{\sum f_1(x_1 - \bar{x}_1)^2 + \sum f_2(x_2 - \bar{x}_2)^2}{(n_1 - 1) + (n_2 - 1)}.$$

This average value of the variance is used as this test assumes that the two samples come from populations where the variance is equal. The null hypothesis usually states that there is no difference in the means. If this is true then the quantity:

$$Z = \frac{\bar{x}_1 - \bar{x}_2}{\text{standard error } (\bar{x}_1 - \bar{x}_2)}$$

will have the normal distribution (except when the sample sizes are very small). Tables of the normal distribution may, therefore, be used to test the significance of Z calculated from the two samples.

Example. The data on sherry is used in the example calculations given below. Subscripts 1 and 2 in the formulae refer to the sample of men and women respectively.

Score

$(x_1$ or $x_2)$	f_1	f_2	$f_1 x_1$	$f_2 x_2$	$(x_1 - \bar{x}_1)$	$(x_1 - \bar{x}_1)^2$	$f_1(x_1 - \bar{x}_1)^2$
+2	37	30	74	60	1.805	3.2580	120.5460
+1	45	35	45	35	0.805	0.6480	29.1600
0	58	50	0	0	-0.195	0.0380	2.2040
-1	40	45	-40	-45	-1.195	1.4280	57.1200
-2	20	40	-40	-80	-2.195	4.8180	96.3600
	200	200	39	-30			305.3900

$(x_2 - \bar{x}_2)$	$(x_2 - \bar{x}_2)^2$	$f_2(x_2 - \bar{x}_2)^2$
2.150	4.6225	138.6750
1.150	1.3225	46.2875
0.150	0.0225	1.1250
-0.850	0.7225	32.5125
-1.850	3.4225	136.9000
		355.5000

$$\bar{x}_1 = \frac{\sum f_1 x_1}{n_1} = \frac{39}{200} = 0.195 \qquad \bar{x}_2 = \frac{\sum f_2 x_2}{n_2} = \frac{-30}{200} = -0.150$$

$$s^2 = \frac{305.39 + 355.50}{199 + 199} = 1.661$$

$$\text{Standard error } (\bar{x}_1 - \bar{x}_2) = \sqrt{1.661 \left[\frac{200 + 200}{200 \times 200} \right]} = \sqrt{0.01661} = 0.1288$$

$$Z = \frac{\bar{x}_1 - \bar{x}_2}{\text{standard error } (\bar{x}_1 - \bar{x}_2)} = \frac{0.195 - (-0.150)}{0.1288} = 2.68.$$

Table 12.1 may be used to determine the significance level obtained by a difference in means which is equal to $Z = 2.68$ standard errors. Such a value is greater than the 2.58 standard errors needed for the result to be significant at the one per cent level but less than 3.29 standard errors needed for one per cent significance. It is actually significant at the 0.74 per cent level. The conclusion which leads from this significance test is that men rate the new sherry to be more sweet than do women.

When scores are attached to the semantic rating scales used in market research and the data is assumed to have the properties of measured data, significance tests such as the one just described may be used to evaluate differences. The gain in doing so may be seen by considering the results of the present significance test on the sherry data along with the analysis of the same data using the Kolmogorov-Smirnov test. This latter test was unable to detect any significant differences between men and women's ratings, whereas the present test between the two means was able to show that a real difference was present. On the debit side the two-means test requires a lot more calculations than does the Kolmogorov-Smirov test. However, most modern computer programs for survey analysis have facilities for automatically calculating means, variances, standard deviations and standard errors for scales which have been scored.

Testing the difference between the means of two matched samples

When the same sample of respondents rates two separate items or rates the same item on two separate occasions, the ensuing data is often presented in a form which may suggest that the test for two independent means may be employed. That test, if applied to such matched sample data, would give too few significant results due to the matching. The correct test for this situation will now be described using the data on after-shave lotion previously analysed by means of the sign test. This data consisted of a sample of $n = 200$ men rating two new versions, X and Y, of an existing after-shave lotion, by means of a semantic scale. It will give another example of how ranked data may, if certain assumptions are made, be treated as measured data by attaching a numerical scoring system to the scale positions. The scoring used in the example will be:

	Score
Like very much	5
Like	4
Neither like nor dislike	3
Dislike	2
Dislike very much	1

The matched sample test uses the two-way table, presented previously, of version X's score (denoted by x_1) analysed by the score for version Y (denoted by x_2). From this table the difference in scores, $d = x_1 - x_2$ may be calculated and a frequency distribution of the d values can be formed. If the null hypothesis that there is no difference in the ratings of the two versions is true, then the expected or mean difference score $(\bar{d})$ would be zero, with a standard error of:

$$\text{Standard error } (\bar{d}) = \frac{s_d}{\sqrt{n}},$$

where s_d = the standard deviation of the difference scores,

$$d = x_1 - x_2.$$

The null hypothesis that $\bar{d} = 0$ may be tested by calculating the criterion:

$$Z = \frac{\bar{d} - 0}{\text{standard error } (\bar{d})} = \frac{\bar{d}\sqrt{n}}{s_d}.$$

Z will follow a normal distribution, when the sample is not too small, and Table 12.1 may be used to evaluate the significance level.

Example. Scoring the two-way table of version X's ratings against the ratings on version Y gives the following table.

		Rating on version X (x_1 score)					
		5	4	3	2	1	Total men
Rating	5	20	20	4	4	2	50
on	4	30	20	10	5	5	70
version Y	3	⑱	10	8	3	1	40
(x_2 score)	2	10	⑦	5	4	4	30
	1	4	0	②	2	2	10
Total men		82	57	29	18	14	200

From this table a frequency distribution of difference scores is easily obtained; for instance, the score $d = x_1 - x_2 = +2$ is obtained from the cells circled in the above table.

$d = x_1 - x_2$	f	fd	$(d - \bar{d})$	$(d - \bar{d})^2$	$f(d - \bar{d})^2$
$+4$	4	16	3.725	13.876	55.504
$+3$	10	30	2.725	7.426	74.260
$+2$	27	54	1.725	2.976	80.352
$+1$	47	47	0.725	0.526	24.722
0	54	0	-0.275	0.076	4.104
-1	37	-37	-1.275	1.626	60.162
-2	10	-20	-2.275	5.176	51.760
-3	9	-27	-3.275	10.726	96.534
-4	2	-8	-4.275	18.276	36.552
	200	$+55$			483.950

$$\bar{d} = \frac{\sum fd}{\sum f} = \frac{+55}{200} = +0.275;$$

$$s_d = \sqrt{\frac{\sum f(d - \bar{d})^2}{\sum f - 1}} = \sqrt{\frac{483.950}{199}} = \sqrt{2.432} = 1.56;$$

$$\text{Standard error } (\bar{d}) = \frac{s_d}{\sqrt{n}} = \frac{1.56}{\sqrt{200}} = 0.110;$$

$$Z = \frac{\bar{d}}{\text{standard error } (\bar{d})} = \frac{+0.275}{0.110} = 2.50.$$

The calculated mean $\bar{d} = 0.275$ is 2.50 standard errors distant from the hypothesized mean of zero. Such a deviation is almost equal to the 2.58 standard errors needed to be significant at the one per cent level. It is in fact, significant at the 1.24 per cent level. The sign test applied to this data gave a result which was just significant at the two per cent level according to Table 12.2 of the chi-square distribution.

Testing the difference between the means of three or more independent samples—the analysis of variance

A comparison of arithmetic means from several samples is often required when interpreting survey results. It is not good statistical practice to proceed immediately to carry out a number of individual significance tests on pairs of sample means. It is better first to do an overall test of the null hypothesis that the populations, from which all the samples have been selected, have identical means. The appropriate test for doing this is the F test. To carry out the test it is necessary to use a technique known as *analysis of variance* in which the total variance of all the data values in all the samples is split into two additive parts, that due to variance between samples and that due to variance within samples. The within sample variance in this case is equivalent to the pooled variance used previously, when testing two independent means. When these two parts of the variance, which are called

301

Table 12.3 *Significant values*

v_2 \ v_1	5% points of F									
	1	2	3	4	5	6	8	12	24	∞
1	161.4	199.5	215.7	224.6	230.2	234.0	238.9	243.9	249.0	254.3
2	18.51	19.00	19.16	19.25	19.30	19.33	19.37	19.41	19.45	19.50
3	10.13	9.55	9.28	9.12	9.01	8.94	8.84	8.74	8.64	8.53
4	7.71	6.94	6.59	6.39	6.26	6.16	6.04	5.91	5.77	5.63
5	6.61	5.79	5.41	5.19	5.05	4.95	4.82	4.68	4.53	4.36
6	5.99	5.14	4.76	4.53	4.39	4.28	4.15	4.00	3.84	3.67
7	5.59	4.74	4.35	4.12	3.97	3.87	3.73	3.57	3.41	3.23
8	5.32	4.46	4.07	3.84	3.69	3.58	3.44	3.28	3.12	2.93
9	5.12	4.26	3.86	3.63	3.48	3.37	3.23	3.07	2.90	2.71
10	4.96	4.10	3.71	3.48	3.33	3.22	3.07	2.91	2.74	2.54
11	4.84	3.98	3.59	3.36	3.20	3.09	2.95	2.79	2.61	2.40
12	4.75	3.88	3.49	3.26	3.11	3.00	2.85	2.69	2.50	2.30
13	4.67	3.80	3.41	3.18	3.02	2.92	2.77	2.60	2.42	2.21
14	4.60	3.74	3.34	3.11	2.96	2.85	2.70	2.53	2.35	2.13
15	4.54	3.68	3.29	3.06	2.90	2.79	2.64	2.48	2.29	2.07
16	4.49	3.63	3.24	3.01	2.85	2.74	2.59	2.42	2.24	2.01
17	4.45	3.59	3.20	2.96	2.81	2.70	2.55	2.38	2.19	1.96
18	4.41	3.55	3.16	2.93	2.77	2.66	2.51	2.34	2.15	1.92
19	4.38	3.52	3.13	2.90	2.74	2.63	2.48	2.31	2.11	1.88
20	4.35	3.49	3.10	2.87	2.71	2.60	2.45	2.28	2.08	1.84
22	4.30	3.44	3.05	2.82	2.66	2.55	2.40	2.23	2.03	1.78
24	4.26	3.40	3.01	2.78	2.62	2.51	2.36	2.18	1.98	1.73
26	4.22	3.37	2.98	2.74	2.59	2.47	2.32	2.15	1.95	1.69
28	4.20	3.34	2.95	2.71	2.56	2.44	2.29	2.12	1.91	1.65
30	4.17	3.32	2.92	2.69	2.53	2.42	2.27	2.09	1.89	1.62
40	4.08	3.23	2.84	2.61	2.45	2.34	2.18	2.00	1.79	1.51
60	4.00	3.15	2.76	2.52	2.37	2.25	2.10	1.92	1.70	1.39
120	3.92	3.07	2.68	2.45	2.29	2.17	2.02	1.83	1.61	1.25
∞	3.84	2.99	2.60	2.37	2.21	2.09	1.94	1.75	1.52	1.00

Table 12.3 is abridged from Table V of Fisher and Yates: *Statistical Tables for Biological, Agricultural and*

mean squares, have been calculated, their ratio F given by:

$$F = \frac{\text{between samples mean square}}{\text{within samples mean square}}$$

will follow a statistical distribution known as the F distribution, when the null hypothesis is true. Table 12.3, which gives significant values of F, may be used to test whether the between samples mean square is larger than the within samples mean square. If the calculated value of F is found to be significant then it may be concluded that differences between the means exist.

Example. Three samples of young men ($n_1 = 138$), middle-aged men ($n_2 = 112$) and old men ($n_3 = 137$) were asked to rate a new beer on a five point scale of bitterness/sweetness. The results of the test are given opposite. The total variance has been previously defined as:

$$s^2 = \frac{\sum f(x - \bar{x})^2}{n - 1}$$

The numerator in this expression is known as the total sum of squares, and

302

v_1	1 % points of F									
v_2	1	2	3	4	5	6	8	12	24	∞
1	4052	4999	5403	5625	5764	5859	5981	6106	6234	6366
2	98.49	99.00	99.17	99.25	99.30	99.33	99.36	99.42	99.46	99.50
3	34.12	30.81	29.46	28.71	28.24	27.91	27.49	27.05	26.60	26.12
4	21.20	18.00	16.69	15.98	15.52	15.21	14.80	14.37	13.93	13.46
5	16.26	13.27	12.06	11.39	10.97	10.67	10.29	9.89	9.47	9.02
6	13.74	10.92	9.78	9.15	8.75	8.47	8.10	7.72	7.31	6.88
7	12.25	9.55	8.45	7.85	7.46	7.19	6.84	6.47	6.07	5.65
8	11.26	8.65	7.59	7.01	6.63	6.37	6.03	5.67	5.28	4.86
9	10.56	8.02	6.99	6.42	6.06	5.80	5.47	5.11	4.73	4.31
10	10.04	7.56	6.55	5.99	5.64	5.39	5.06	4.71	4.33	3.91
11	9.65	7.20	6.22	5.67	5.32	5.07	4.74	4.40	4.02	3.60
12	9.33	6.93	5.95	5.41	5.06	4.82	4.50	4.16	3.78	3.36
13	9.07	6.70	5.74	5.20	4.86	4.62	4.30	3.96	3.59	3.16
14	8.86	6.51	5.56	5.03	4.69	4.46	4.14	3.80	3.43	3.00
15	8.68	6.36	5.42	4.89	4.56	4.32	4.00	3.67	3.29	2.87
16	8.53	6.23	5.29	4.77	4.44	4.20	3.89	3.55	3.18	2.75
17	8.40	6.11	5.18	4.67	4.34	4.10	3.79	3.45	3.08	2.65
18	8.28	6.01	5.09	4.58	4.25	4.01	3.71	3.37	3.00	2.57
19	8.18	5.93	5.01	4.50	4.17	3.94	3.63	3.30	2.92	2.49
20	8.10	5.85	4.94	4.43	4.10	3.87	3.56	3.23	2.86	2.42
22	7.94	5.72	4.82	4.31	3.99	3.76	3.45	3.12	2.75	2.31
24	7.82	5.61	4.72	4.22	3.90	3.67	3.36	3.03	2.66	2.21
26	7.72	5.53	4.64	4.14	3.82	3.59	3.29	2.96	2.58	2.13
28	7.64	5.45	4.57	4.07	3.75	3.53	3.23	2.90	2.52	2.06
30	7.56	5.39	4.51	4.02	3.70	3.47	3.17	2.84	2.47	2.01
40	7.31	5.18	4.31	3.83	3.51	3.29	2.99	2.66	2.29	1.80
60	7.08	4.98	4.13	3.65	3.34	3.12	2.82	2.50	2.12	1.60
120	6.85	4.79	3.95	3.48	3.17	2.96	2.66	2.34	1.95	1.38
∞	6.64	4.60	3.78	3.32	3.02	2.80	2.51	2.18	1.79	1.00

Medical Research, published by Oliver and Boyd, Ltd., Edinburgh, by permission of the authors and publishers.

Scale	Score x	Young f_1	Middle-aged f_2	Old f_3
Very bitter	5	21	11	14
Fairly bitter	4	46	29	22
Neither bitter nor sweet	3	37	47	35
Fairly sweet	2	22	18	38
Very sweet	1	12	7	28
		$n_1 = \overline{138}$	$n_2 = \overline{112}$	$n_3 = \overline{137}$ $\quad n = 387$

it is this quantity which is split into two parts, as below:

(a) square all $n = 387$ data values and sum them to give A.

$$A = (5^2 \times 21) + (4^2 \times 46) + \cdots + (1^2 \times 28) = 4132;$$

(b) sum all $n = 387$ data values and square this total to give T^2.

$$T^2 = [(5 \times 21) + (4 \times 46) + \cdots + (1 \times 28)]^2 = (1178)^2 = 1\,387\,684;$$

303

(c) divide T^2 by the total sample size n to give the so-called correction factor $C = T^2/n$

$$C = \frac{1\,387\,684}{387} = 3585.75;$$

(d) sum the data values for each sample to give T_1, T_2, and T_3

$$T_1 = (5 \times 21) + (4 \times 46) + \cdots + (1 \times 12) = 456$$

similarly: $\qquad T_2 = 355 \qquad T_3 = 367$

(e) calculate the quantity B given by:

$$B = \frac{T_1^{\,2}}{n_1} + \frac{T_2^{\,2}}{n_2} + \frac{T_3^{\,2}}{n_3} = \frac{(456)^2}{138} + \frac{(355)^2}{112} + \frac{(367)^2}{137} = 3615.13$$

The total sum of squares is given by $A - C = 4132 - 3585.75 = 546.25$.

The between samples sum of squares is given by $B - C$

$$= 3615.13 - 3585.75 = 29.38.$$

The within samples sum of squares is given by $A - B$

$$= 4132 - 3615.13 = 516.87.$$

The calculations are summarized in the following analysis of variance table.

Source of variation	Sum of squares	Degrees of freedom	Mean square	F
Between samples (age groups)	29.38	2	14.690	10.91
Within samples	516.87	384	1.346	
Total	546.25	386		

Just as the total sum of squares is divided by total sample size less one ($n - 1 = 386$) to give the variance, so the between samples mean square is obtained by dividing its sum of squares by the number of samples less one ($3 - 1 = 2$). These divisors are known as degrees of freedom and, like the sums of squares, are additive. The degrees of freedom for the within samples mean square is, therefore, obtained by difference. If the null hypothesis of equal means is true, the expected value of the ratio of the two mean squares will be $F = 1$. The calculated value of $F = 10.91$ with $V_1 = 2$ and $V_2 = 384$ degrees of freedom may be assessed for significance by referring it to Table 12.3. For $V_1 = 2$ and $V_2 = \infty$, F must exceed 4.60 to be significant at the one per cent level. The calculated value $F = 10.91$ is therefore significant and it may be concluded that differences in means do exist between age groups.

After finding a significant value of F, one is now justified in comparing pairs of means for significance using the test for two independent sample means given previously. If the number of samples is large, then so is the number of pairs of means that can be tested, and this leads to some of the comparisons being significant just by chance, as explained in the section on paired comparisons. *Multiple comparison tests* have been developed to overcome this and a good summary of them is given in the book by Snedecor and Cochran[5].

The analysis of variance described above was concerned with data classified in one way only, i.e., by age. Often, data appears in a two-way table, e.g., age by sex, or in multi-way tables. The technique of analysis of variance may be applied to such data to highlight the effects of the various classifications and the interaction between them. A full treatment of this is beyond the scope of this chapter and the reader is referred to chapters 10, 11, 12, and 16 of Snedecor and Cochran[5], the latter chapter giving an account of analysis of variance as applied to percentage data. A related technique to analysis of variance is the *analysis of covariance*. It enables comparisons between classifications to be made using analysis of variance when the effect of an unwanted classification has been eliminated. Details of how to use this technique may be obtained from chapter 14 of Snedecor and Cochran[5].

Some General Points on Significance Testing

Significance tests on small samples

When the data collected is based on small samples, many of the significance tests given in this chapter need modifying or replacing by special alternative tests. As a rough rule it is recommended that, if the sample size is $n = 50$ or larger, the tests given may be all applied without serious error. On this point, it is worth mentioning that the first two tests given for measured data are often referred to as 'the t-test for two independent sample means' and 'the paired t-test for two matched sample means'. This is because the significance test criteria Z, in both cases, will follow a statistical distribution known as the t distribution. This distribution which is applicable for small samples becomes more and more like the shape of the normal distribution as the sample size increases. The convergence may be illustrated by considering the number of standard errors difference that are needed between two means to achieve a five per cent significance level. In the case of large samples, where the normal distribution is appropriate, the value is 1.96. For small samples leading to the t distribution, a value of 2.04 is required for $n = 30$ and 2.00 for $n = 60$. This shows that the normal distribution may be used for samples of $n = 50$ or more in such significance tests.

Interpretation of significant results

The fact that a survey result is found, by carrying out a statistical significance test, to be significant often leads to confusion when such a result is presented to people unfamiliar with research methodology. The layman, when told that something is significant, often assumes that the researcher considers the result to be 'important'. As explained in this chapter, such an inference is not necessarily true. In statistical terms, if, for example, a difference between two percentages is declared significant, it simply means that this difference, no matter whether it is a *large* or *small* difference, cannot be explained by sampling errors. With very large samples, where the sampling distributions of the null and alternative hypotheses will have small standard errors, small differences in percentages will be significant. Whether these small differences are important to the researcher and his client depends on the subject matter of the survey, previous survey results and any number of other practical considerations. The example that follows gives some idea in one particular case how small differences in percentages may be viewed. A random sample of 1000 housewives owning washing machine brand A is found to contain 48 per cent who claim to be 'very pleased' with the machine. A further random sample of 1000, who own brand B, contains 56 per cent who are 'very pleased'. The difference in percentages 56 − 48 per cent = 8 per cent is comparatively small and might be regarded as unimportant, even though it is a statistically significant difference. However, if it is known from previous surveys with samples of 1000 that differences between brands of washing machine are always insignificant, then the observed difference may be thought of as being an important finding.

This chapter has been presented in terms of simple random sampling. Most surveys use more complicated sampling methods where the standard errors are usually larger than the standard error formulae given here. The amount by which they are larger is known as the *design factor*. In those cases above where a standard error has been given, this standard error should be increased by the design factor of the survey being analysed, when carrying out a significance test.

On this point about simple random sampling it is difficult to give much advice to users of quota samples. Strictly speaking, it is not possible to calculate sampling errors and, therefore, carry out significance tests on data from quota samples. In practice, researchers quite often assume that the data is as if it had come from a random sample and proceed to carry out significance tests as described above. The limited research that has been done into quota sampling methods indicates that, in some cases, the sampling errors may be higher than for random sampling. For this reason, some researchers increase the standard error by an arbitrary factor such as 1.5 or 2.0 when carrying out significance tests on quota sample data.

Appendix A

The chances are 95 in 100 that the percentage being estimated by the survey lies within a range equal to the observed percentage plus or minus the number of percentage points shown in the table.

Sampling errors on percentages in survey reports

Observed percentage	Sample size						
	100	250	500	750	1000	1500	2000
	$\pm\%$	$\pm\%$	$\pm\%$	$\pm\%$	$\pm\%$	$\pm\%$	$\pm\%$
50	9.8	6.2	4.4	3.6	3.1	2.5	2.2
40 or 60	9.6	6.1	4.2	3.5	3.0	2.5	2.1
30 or 70	9.0	5.7	4.0	3.3	2.7	2.3	2.0
20 or 80	7.8	5.0	3.5	2.9	2.5	2.0	1.8
10 or 90	5.9	3.7	2.6	2.2	1.9	1.5	1.3

The usual formula for sampling errors of simple random sampling given below, was used in the calculations.

$$\pm 1.96 \sqrt{\frac{P(100 - P)}{n}} \quad \text{where} \quad \begin{aligned} P &= \text{the observed percentage,} \\ n &= \text{the sample size.} \end{aligned}$$

Appendix B

Significant differences between survey percentages

The following five tables may be used to decide whether observed differences between two survey percentages are statistically significant at the five per cent level.

How to use the tables

To compare two percentages p_1 per cent and p_2 per cent based on sample sizes of n_1 and n_2 respectively, where n_1 is the smaller sample size:

(a) if the two sample sizes are approximately equal, calculate the average of p_1 per cent and p_2 per cent

$$p\% = \frac{p_1\% + p_2\%}{2};$$

if the two sample sizes are very different calculate

$$p\% = \frac{n_1 p_1\% + n_2 p_2\%}{n_1 + n_2};$$

307

(b) look up the table corresponding to $p\%$ (the table closest to $p\%$);
(c) find the cell of the table corresponding to n_1 and n_2, approximately;
(d) the observed difference between the two percentages p_1 per cent and p_2 per cent must be equal to or greater than the value given in this cell to be significant at the five per cent level.

Example. Is a value of $p_1 = 46$ per cent based on a sample of $n_1 = 500$ significantly different from a value p_2 per cent $= 54$ per cent based on a sample of $n_2 = 500$?

As the sample sizes are equal, $p\% = (54\% + 46\%)/2 = 50$ per cent.

The first table corresponding to $p = 50$ per cent shows that for $n_1 = n_2 = 500$ the observed difference must be 7.4 per cent or greater to be significant.

The observed difference of $54 - 46$ per cent $= 8$ per cent is thus significant.

Differences needed between two percentages around 50 per cent to be significant at the five per cent level.

$$p = 50 \text{ per cent.}$$

Sample size n_2	Sample size n_1						
	100	250	500	750	1000	1500	2000
	%	%	%	%	%	%	%
100	13.8						
250	11.6	8.8					
500	10.7	7.6	6.2				
750	10.4	7.2	5.7	5.1			
1000	10.3	6.9	5.4	4.7	4.4		
1500	10.1	6.7	5.1	4.4	4.0	3.6	
2000	10.0	6.6	4.9	4.2	3.8	3.4	3.1

Differences needed between two percentages around 40 or 60 per cent to be significant at the five per cent level.

$$p = 40 \text{ or } 60 \text{ per cent.}$$

	Sample size n_1						
	100	250	500	750	1000	1500	2000
Sample size n_2	%	%	%	%	%	%	%
100	13.6						
250	11.4	8.6					
500	10.5	7.4	6.1				
750	10.2	7.0	5.5	5.0			
1000	10.1	6.8	5.2	4.6	4.3		
1500	9.9	6.6	5.0	4.3	3.9	3.5	
2000	9.8	6.4	4.8	4.1	3.7	3.3	3.0

Differences needed between two percentages around 30 or 70 per cent to be significant at the five per cent level.

$$p = 30 \text{ or } 70 \text{ per cent.}$$

	Sample size n_1						
	100	250	500	750	1000	1500	2000
Sample size n_2	%	%	%	%	%	%	%
100	12.7						
250	10.6	8.0					
500	9.8	7.0	5.7				
750	9.6	6.6	5.2	4.6			
1000	9.4	6.3	4.9	4.3	4.0		
1500	9.3	6.1	4.6	4.0	3.7	3.3	
2000	9.2	6.0	4.5	3.8	3.5	3.1	2.8

Differences needed between two percentages around 20 or 80 per cent to be significant at the five per cent level.

$p = 20$ or 80 per cent.

Sample size n_2	Sample size n_1						
	100	250	500	750	1000	1500	2000
	%	%	%	%	%	%	%
100	11.1						
250	9.3	7.0					
500	8.6	6.1	5.0				
750	8.3	5.7	4.5	4.1			
1000	8.2	5.6	4.3	3.8	3.5		
1500	8.1	5.3	4.1	3.5	3.2	2.9	
2000	8.0	5.3	3.9	3.4	3.0	2.7	2.5

Differences needed between two percentages around 10 or 90 per cent to be significant at the five per cent level.

$p = 10$ or 90 per cent.

Sample size n_2	Sample size n_1						
	100	250	500	750	1000	1500	2000
	%	%	%	%	%	%	%
100	8.3						
250	7.0	5.3					
500	6.4	4.5	3.7				
750	6.3	4.3	3.4	3.0			
1000	6.2	4.2	3.2	2.8	2.6		
1500	6.1	4.0	3.0	2.6	2.4	2.2	
2000	6.0	3.9	2.9	2.5	2.3	2.0	1.9

References

1. STUART, A. Standard Errors for Percentages, *Journal of the Royal Statistical Society*, Series C, Applied Statistics, **12**, No. 2, pp. 87–101, 1963.
2. COCHRAN, W. G. Some Methods for Strengthening the Common χ^2 tests, *Biometrics*, **10**, pp. 417–451, 1964.
3. DAVID, H. A. *The Method of Paired Comparisons*, Charles Griffin and Co. Ltd.
4. SCHEFFÉ, H. An Analysis of Variance for Paired Comparisons, *Journal of The American Statistical Association*, **47**, pp. 381–400, 1952.
5. SNEDECOR, G. W. and COCHRAN, W. G. *Statistical Methods (Sixth Edition)*, The Iowa State University Press.

Suggested Further Reading

FERBER, R. *Statistical Techniques in Market Research*, McGraw-Hill Book Company

QUENOUILLE, M. H. *Introductory Statistics*, Pergamon Press.

MOOD, A. M. and GRAYBILL, F. A. *Introduction to the Theory of Statistics*, McGraw Hill Book Company.

MAXWELL, A. E. *Analysing Qualitative Data*, Methuen and Co., Ltd.

SIEGEL, S. *Non-Parametric Statistics for the Behavioural Sciences*, McGraw Hill Book Company.

QUENOUILLE, M. H. *Rapid Statistical Calculations*, Charles Griffin and Co. Ltd.

KENDALL, M. G. *Rank Correlation Methods*, Charles Griffin and Co., Ltd.

13. Multivariate analysis of market research data

C. Holmes

Marketing is a complex process. It involves the evaluation of many different variables and the ways in which they inter-relate in the marketing 'mix'. In order to try and make sense of a mass of data measured on a sample drawn from a population, more and more reliance is being placed on the use of a variety of statistical techniques. Some of these techniques such as correlation analysis, are relatively well established; others, such as canonical analysis and cluster analysis, are not so well known, and their potentialities in terms of their problem solving abilities are only just being realized.

Statistical techniques which simultaneously examine the relationships between many variables are known as 'multivariate statistical procedures'. A major contributing factor to the upsurge of interest in this area has largely been due to advancements made in computer technology.

Most multivariate techniques require an immense number of calculations which, whilst not beyond the resources of clerks and adding machines, are more quickly and economically carried out by computer.

It is not my intention in this chapter to dwell at large on the theoretical properties underlying the basis of the varying types of multivariate procedures. The inclusion of statistical and mathematical formulae will be kept to a minimum. References to the appropriate literature will be quoted for the interested reader to pursue at his leisure. The main aim is to present a somewhat simplified overview of a rather complex subject matter in as non-mathematical a manner as possible.

It is useful to consider some of the typical practical problems with which multivariate analysis is concerned. Some may be well known and well documented, others may be of a specialist nature; all are pertinent to the field of market research:

(a) in a survey of television viewing a 'dependent' variable, quantity of viewing, is measured. A hypothesis is formed that this may be predicted by such variables as age, education, readership, etc. *Regression analysis* would assist in the construction of a model to fit the data. Variations in the parameters of the model would enable changes in viewing to be predicted;

(b) in an attitudinal survey about various companies and their products, it is of interest to examine the relationships not only between correlations within the battery of 'company' rating scales and within the battery of 'product' rating scales, but also the relationships between the two data matrices. *Canonical analysis* could provide an insight into the way the two sets of data are inter-related;

(c) results are available relating salesmen's performances over various activities together with training observations and results. It is required to produce, from these data, criteria to evaluate whether salesmen may be classified into specific groups. The use of *discriminant analysis* will assist in this problem as it attempts to maximize the probability of correct assignment to groups;

(d) from the results of repertory grids a large battery of semantic attitudinal scales is drawn up and administered to a sample of the population of, say 'cake-mix' users. Straightforward correlation analysis is applied to the results but the matrix of correlation coefficients is too large to facilitate an 'understanding' of the data. The researcher seeks to find a certain kind of organization in the data to identify fundamental and meaningful dimensions in the inter-relationships. *Principal components* and *factor analysis* might be used to explore the underlying dimensionality of the data;

(e) a list of a hundred towns (qualifying on certain issues) is drawn up as potentials for test marketing operations. Statistics relating to population, retail sales, readership, etc., are collected. A limited number of towns are required to be representative of national characteristics. In what way can they be chosen? The application of some form of *numerical taxonomy* (*cluster analysis*) might reveal distinct homogeneous sub-groups of towns. The selection of one town from each group would ensure that each strata is represented in the overall test-marketing mix.

These, then, are just a few examples of marketing problems where the use of multivariate analysis may assist in finding the answers. It must be stressed however, that the techniques of multivariate analysis are not able to solve problems by themselves. It is not good enough to have masses and masses of doubtful data, consult a text-book for an appropriate technique and feed the lot into a computer. You may be lucky enough to get an answer that 'makes sense', but if the original data is not the 'right' kind of data then you will not get the 'right' kind of answer. In fact, the use of multivariate analysis makes it all the more imperative to consider the hypothesis-making and question-forming stages of the research. To quote Collins[1]: 'Multivariate analysis systems make ever-increasing demands upon the question designer, the question poser and the question answerer. Questionnaires become not only lengthy but extremely monotonous. With so many analysis techniques based upon the search for non-random patterning of responses, boredom is clearly a major problem'.

It is not within the scope of this chapter to dwell at large on issues like these but, nevertheless, they are important and should not be overlooked.

Dependence or Interdependence

So to the actual subject itself. What is multivariate analysis? It is broadly concerned with the *relationships* between sets of dependent variables.

Kendall[2] in a very clear exposition of the subject discerns two main branches of the multivariate tree, and subdivides multivariate analysis into whether we are concerned with dependence or inter-dependence.

Dependence

In this type of problem we are concerned with the way in which one or more (so-called criterion) dependent variables, often chosen by us or dictated to us by the problem *depends* on the other (so-called independent) variables. The simplest example of 'dependence' analysis is the regression of one variable on others often in the form:

$$y = a + b_1x_1 + b_2x_2 + \cdots + b_nx_n.$$

An often quoted example of a multiple linear regression is the prediction of university degree results from the so-called independent variables (number of 'O'-levels, 'A'-level passes and so on). The phrase, so-called independent variables is a choice one, since they are often genuinely correlated or they are fortuitously correlated in the data sample.

Interdependence

The second branch is that of interdependence: here we are not concerned with any criterion variables, but only with the relationship of a set of variables amongst themselves. No variable is selected to be of special interest. Correlation analysis is a clear example of this part of the subject.

Correlation Analysis

Since multivariate analysis is concerned with the inter-relationships between variables, the starting points of most analyses begin with the way in which the variables correlate (or co-vary) with each other. A useful way of considering the various manipulations that can be carried out on data is to visualize the end results of a survey in the form of a data matrix (Fig. 13.1).

Whatever the subject matter of the research we can visualize it in this row-by-column tabulation. It is convenient at this stage to look upon the columns as variables and the rows as respondents. By considering each pair of columns separately we can see how each pair of variables correlate.

314

VARIATES (Responses)

OBSERVATIONS (Respondents)

	x_1	x_2	x_3	• • • •	x_i	• • • •	x_p
1	x_{11}	x_{21}	x_{31}	• • • •	5	• • • •	x_{p1}
2	x_{12}	x_{22}	x_{32}	• • • •	4	• • • •	x_{p2}
3	x_{13}	x_{23}	x_{33}		6		•
4	x_{14}	x_{24}	x_{34}		7		•
5	x_{15}	x_{25}	x_{35}		2		•
•	•	•	•		•		•
•	•	•	•		•		•
•	•	•	•		•		•
•	•	•	•		•		•
•	•	•	•		•		•
•	•	•	•		•		•
n	x_{1n}	x_{2n}	x_{3n}	• • • •	3	• • • •	x_{pn}

Fig. 13.1. *Data Matrix:* Generally x_{ij} stands for the jth observation on the ith variable. Thus, the column headed x_i could refer to a rating scale and, as an example, hypothetical ratings are illustrated for respondents.

The most widely used measure of correlation is the Pearson 'product moment coefficient of correlation'. It is a coefficient ranging from -1 through zero, to $+1$ and is a measure of the degree of *linear* association between two variables. We can illustrate varying degrees of correlation by means of a simple scatter diagram (Fig. 13.2). Positive correlation (Fig. 13.2(a)) means that increasing values of variable y are associated with increasing values of variable x and vice-versa. Negative correlation (Fig. 13.2(b)) indicates that increasing values of x are associated with decreasing values of y. Zero correlation implies that there is no linear association between the two variables (although there could, of course, be a non-linear relationship). Essentially, Pearson's correlation coefficient, r

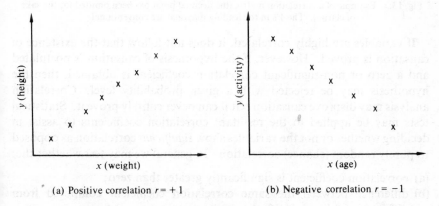

(a) Positive correlation $r = +1$ (b) Negative correlation $r = -1$

Fig. 13.2. Examples of scatter diagrams.

between two variables x and y is:

$$r = \frac{\text{covariance } (x \cdot y)}{\sqrt{[\text{variance } (x)][\text{variance } (y)]}}$$

where

$$\text{covariance } (x \cdot y) = \frac{1}{n} \sum (x - \bar{x})(y - \bar{y})$$

and the variances are as defined in chapter 12.

From the data matrix we can calculate the respective correlation coefficients for each pair of variables across all sample members. The resultant correlation matrix (Fig. 13.3) is a useful starter in seeking relationships between variables. A. S. C. Ehrenberg[3] in a robust attack on factor analysts considers that in many cases the 'look at it' approach is equal to the more so-called 'sophisticated' types of analyses. However, it is increasingly difficult to sort out relationships since as the number of variables grows, the number of correlation coefficients increases rapidly. (For n variables, there are $n(c)2 = n(n - 1)/2$ correlation coefficients.)

		1	2	3	4	5	6	7	8
	1	100	+31	−50	00	−35	−70	+40	−87
	2	+31	100	+37	−56	+21	+17	+10	−25
	3	−50	+37	100	+34	+40	−70	+25	−37
VARIABLES	4	00	−56	+34	100	−35	+45	+27	−55
	5	−35	+21	+40	−35	100	+05	−97	−43
	6	−70	+17	−70	+45	+05	100	+10	−17
	7	+40	+10	+25	+27	−97	+19	100	+24
	8	−87	−25	−37	−55	−43	−17	+24	100

Fig. 13.3. Example of a correlation matrix (the decimal point has been omitted for the sake of clarity). The 1's in the leading diagonal are conventional.

If variables are highly correlated, it does not follow that the existence of causation is proved. However, if the hypothesis of causation is postulated and a zero or non-significant correlation coefficient is obtained, then the hypothesis may be rejected with a given probability level. Correlation analysis may disprove causation but it can never entirely prove it. Statistical tests may be applied to the resultant correlation coefficients to assist in deciding whether or not the variables show *significant* correlation as opposed to purely random (chance) correlation. In general we may test whether the:

(a) correlation coefficient is significantly greater than zero;
(b) difference between the same correlation coefficient computed from different samples is significant.

In addition to Pearson's product moment correlation coefficient there are a number of 'non-parametric' measures, such as Spearman's rank and Kendall's tau which are often used on data which is not distributed normally, or where the measurement level achieved is only up to an 'ordinal' scale. For details of these and other coefficients the reader is advised to consult Siegel[4].

Principal Components Analysis (PCA)

In the statistical analysis of relationships between variables it is often important that the variables are uncorrelated (orthogonal) with one another. This is particularly true in multiple regression techniques and in the interpretation of factors in factor analysis. The method of principal components analysis is a technique for obtaining new 'artificial' variables which are uncorrelated with one another. It is, therefore, a useful mathematical device as well as being central to the generally accepted method of carrying out factor analysis. Both Kendall[2] and Hope[5] describe the technique mathematically and it is only intended here to describe the mechanics of principal components analysis briefly.

Algebraic Visualization. If one considers the diagonal terms of the covariance matrix (or the standardized correlation matrix with '1's' in the leading diagonal) then the sum of the diagonal terms represents the total variance of the data sample. This total variance can be split up into N latent roots each of which has an eigenvector associated with it. The eigenvectors generate a set of principal components each of which has a variance associated with it equal to its latent root.

Geometric Visualization. Another way of visualizing principal components is to consider the data sample plotted in N—dimensional space. We may, for example, plot measurements made on three variables, say, height, weight, and breadth as in Fig. 13.4. The first principal component is directed along the main long axis of the cigar-shaped cluster. Having extracted this component, then the second principal component is along the next longest axial direction of the cluster, orthogonal to the first, and so on.

The main attraction of principal components analysis is that the components are extracted in descending order of the amount of total variance each one accounts for. There are as many components as there are original variables and the sum of the variances of all the principal components equals the sum of the variances of the original variables. In very simple terms, we may think of the principal components as weighted combinations of all the original variables. If we start with three variables, X_1, X_2, and X_3, then the three principal components, C_1, C_2, and C_3 are given by

$$C_1 = W_{11}X_1 + W_{12}X_2 + W_{13}X_3$$
$$C_2 = W_{21}X_1 + W_{22}X_2 + W_{23}X_3$$
$$C_3 = W_{31}X_1 + W_{32}X_2 + W_{33}X_3$$

where W is a numerical weight determined by the analysis; (they are also termed the 'loadings' of the variables on the components). In practical terms, it is usually found that the first few components account for a large proportion (often in the range 70 to 90 per cent) of the total variance. In certain circumstances the researcher ignores the remaining components in any further analyses and, thus, achieves a significant gain in data-reduction.

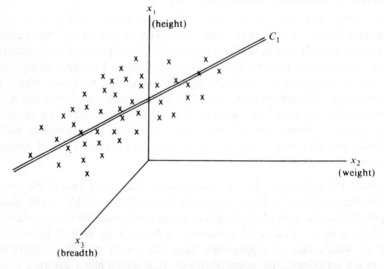

Fig. 13.4. Geometric visualization of the first principal component.

Since each component is a weighted combination of the original variables, it is possible to calculate for each person (or object) in the sample a score on each component. Thus, not only does principal components analysis enable us to find out the basic dimensionality of our data, it allows the facilitation of further analyses to be made on scores which are measured on orthogonal dimensions.

Summary

Principal components analysis

Principal component analysis is a technique which examines the correlations between variables and contributes to an understanding of the dimensionality of the data. The important property concerning the extraction of components in order of diminishing variance facilitates a data reduction process and, consequently, the elimination of variables which contribute little information. By calculating scores for the components, individuals may be mapped in n dimensional space. A practical drawback with principal components analysis is that the components are rarely interpretable in a marketing sense.

318

Examples of principal component analysis

(a) *Test Market Locations*

Christopher[6] utilized principal components analysis in an attempt to classify towns into homogeneous clusters. Information was collected for thirty towns considered suitable for test marketing operations. A set of mutually independent factors were extracted using principal components analysis and towns were then clustered according to their scores on the factors.

(b) *Stratification of Local Authority Areas*

Holmes[7] similarly carried out experimental work relating to local authority areas in Yorkshire and Humberside. One hundred and forty local authority areas were analysed over seven variables using principal components

Table 13.1. *The first three principal components for local authority areas in the West Riding of Yorkshire conurbations*

Variables	C1	C2	C3
% SEG 1–4 + 13*	−85	70	54
% Labour vote	34	−37	43
Population density	−07	17	−71
% Car-owning households	04	45	04
% Owner-occupiers	−27	−37	−12
Occupation density	27	02	−05
Rateable value	−06	05	10
Variance	54.1%	16.6%	11.7%

* This statistic computed from 1966 sample census of population is the percentage of economically active and retired males aged 15 and over employed as professional workers, employers and managers.

analysis. Three independent components were found to account for over 70 per cent of the total variance. Table 13.1 sets out the principal components analysis loading matrix for the first three components for local authority areas in the West Riding of Yorkshire conurbation. Whilst the components are not easily interpretable, the writer utilized the local authority area scores on the first component (accounting for over half the variance) to rank, and subsequently clustered the local authority areas. This exercise was an attempt at optimal stratification for use in the selection of primary sampling units.

Factor Analysis

A concise history and the development of factor analysis may be found in Harman[8]. Factor analysis embraces a set of statistical techniques which seek to analyse the intercorrelations within a set of variables. Developed originally by psychologists—amongst the early pioneers were such distinguished theorists as Spearman, Burt, Kelley, Thurstone, Holzinger and Thomson—factor analysis has gone through a controversial and turbulent history. To quote Cooley and Lohnes[9], 'Each pioneer seemed to feel his procedure was *the* method of factor analysis. Only recently have students of factor analysis begun to see that the different procedures are suitable for different purposes and usually involve different assumptions regarding the nature of human attributes'.

Factor analysis model

Factor analysis is different from principal components analysis (although the latter is often a prerequisite to the former) in that the factor analysis model attempts to describe the data in terms of a model with a number of new variables called 'factors', *less* in number than the original variables. The simplest formulation of the model is that the total variance in the data can be split into two parts, that due to the common factors and that due to residual factors, thus:

total variance (V) = var. (factors) + residual variance.

In contrast to the principal components analysis model, the factor analysis model for three variables and two factors may be written mathematically as

$$X_1 = W_{11}F_1 + W_{12}F_2 + d_1R_1$$
$$X_2 = W_{21}F_1 + W_{22}F_2 \qquad + d_2R_2$$
$$X_3 = W_{31}F_1 + W_{32}F_2 \qquad\qquad + d_2R_3$$

where X_1, X_2, X_3 are the original variables; F_1, F_2, are the common factors, R_1, R_2, R_3 are the residual (sometimes known as the unique) factors. The coefficients, W and d are frequently referred to as the loadings. Explained in words, the factor analysis model assumes that each variable may be represented as a linear sum of a number of orthogonal factors, usually less in number than the number of original variables, plus a specific residual factor unique to that variable. In other words, a hypothesis is formed that the total variance of a variable is made up of:

(a) a proportion of variance which the variable shares (or has in common) with other variables;
(b) an amount of residual (unique) variance which is uncorrelated with other variables.

Communality

The proportion of variance that is common to other variables is known as the *communality* of the original variables and is calculated as the sum of the squares of the coefficients (loadings) associated with the m common factors. This estimate of communality, strictly speaking, requires to be inserted in the leading diagonal of the correlation matrix but this cannot be achieved until the factor solution is obtained. This seemingly circular problem is resolved by estimating the communalities, carrying out a trial factor solution, re-adjusting the communality estimates and so on. The most widely used method of estimating communalities is the utilization of the squared multiple correlation between the variable and the remaining $(n - 1)$ variables. It is worth noting that the problem of communalities is only acute in the case of small data matrices. In practice, it has been found that the larger the order of the correlation matrix the less it matters what values appear in the leading diagonal.

The most common methods of obtaining factor solutions are the 'principal factor solution' and the 'maximum likelihood solution'. Neither method will be explained here and the interested are directed to Cooley and Lohnes[9] for the former and Lawley and Maxwell[10] for details of the latter. The principal factor solution, based as it is on principal components analysis has the important property that it produces factors in order of the amount of variance they explain. The maximum likelihood solution is probably more efficient and does not require any estimation of communalities although the number of factors required has to be stipulated in advance.

How many factors?

The problem of how many factors to extract has plagued factor analysts for many years but with advanced computer technology it is less of a problem today. There are, basically, two criteria for deciding on how many factors to retain:

(a) statistical;
(b) marketing meaningfullness.

Amongst the statistical criteria is the widely adopted Kaiser's[11] rule of retaining factors whose latent roots are greater than one. However, statistical considerations alone are not entirely satisfactory and in most market research studies the meaning and interpretability of the retained factors plays an important part in the decision process. A factor contributing only a small portion of variance may not be statistically important but it may prove a good discriminator for, say, degree of purchase.

Rotation

We now touch upon, what perhaps has caused most controversy in the history of factor analysis, that of rotation of the factors. The rotation problem arises because of the indeterminancy of factor solutions. It is a mathematical fact that, given a set of correlations between variables, the estimating of the factor equations is fundamentally indeterminate, that is to say, that the loading of the variables in the estimating equations may be chosen in an infinite number of ways, consistent with the observed correlations. Over the years, therefore, certain criteria have been established to limit the factor analysis solutions. The accepted criteria in the determination of new reference axes is Thurstone's[12] properties of 'simple structure'. The aim in rotating axes is to enable the factors to be more meaningfully interpretable. Amongst the many proposed solutions, two have stood the test of time, namely Varimax and/or Promax. The Varimax rotation still requires the restriction that the axes are orthogonal (uncorrelated) to one another. Promax, developed by Hendrickson and White[13] is an acceptable extension of Varimax such that the axes are allowed to become non-orthogonal or oblique (correlated). Over several studies, the writer finds that Promax usually gives the same factor structure but is slightly more interpretable. When the factor solution is oblique, knowledge of the degree with which the factors correlate with one another is required. A disadvantage of an oblique solution is that further analysis (such as cluster analysis) may prove to be more difficult to handle. Interpretability is gained at the expense of statistical simplicity.

Factor scores

A 'factor score' may be estimated for each respondent for each factor. These may be averaged for any sub-group in much the same way as ordinary rating scales. Thus, a typical factor analysis may involve 80 rating scales which produce some 10 to 12 dimensions (factors). On each factor we can estimate scores for rated products, brands, services, etc., which together with breakdowns by purchasing behaviour, age, social grade, etc., can provide useful marketing information. Charting methods such as simple 'profile charts' and two and three dimensional maps assist in the interpretation stage. Hill[14] gives clear examples of single and two dimensional charts whilst Hope[5] devotes a chapter to 'spherical maps'.

Summary

Factor analysis

Factor analysis is a technique for finding a set of dimensions latent in a set of variables. Conceptually it differs from principal components analysis in that the model hypothesizes that the variables may be represented in fewer than n dimensions, although the former is often used to assist in the factor solution. When utilized in conjunction with further forms of analysis such as multiple regression, the technique is useful for identifying likely variables (or likely composites of variables, the factors) which contribute most to predicting the dependent variable(s). Finally, factor scores may be estimated so that persons may be measured on concepts which may not be directly measurable themselves (e.g., a general evaluative concept).

Example of factor analysis

Frost[15] gave a clear example of factor analysis applied to seven point rating scales. 750 television viewers rated 58 statements on two programmes they had watched. In total, 61 programmes were rated in this way rotated randomly between the respondents, and the resultant factor analysis gave the following nine factors:

(a) general evaluation;
(b) information;
(c) romance;
(d) violence;
(e) conventionality;
(f) scale of production;
(g) noise/activity;
(h) acceptability;
(i) humour.

As Frost points out, 'It should be noted that whilst names have been attached to these factors, this has been done simply for ease of reference and that the proper interpretation of a factor is to be found amongst the individual attitude scales which have substantial loadings upon it. Thus, for example, Factor 2 called 'information' in fact describes a dimension of viewer differentiation which has at one end programmes which tend to have much scientific interest, which make the viewer think and which convey educational information and which has at the other end programmes which contain little scientific interest which encourage the viewer to relax being of a less informative and generally more entertaining type'.

Frost utilized these nine dimensions to compute programme attitude ratings covered in the survey. An example in the paper illustrates that programmes like 'Man Alive' and 'The Power Game' score highly on the 'information' factor whilst 'Juke Box Jury' 'Black & White Minstrels' and 'The Monkees' are to be found, not surprisingly, at the 'little scientific interest' end. 'These typical results', Frost concluded, 'confirm our original interpretation of this factor as being a dimension which differentiated between educational programmes and entertainment programmes'.

Numerical Taxonomy

Cluster analysis

An integral part of the analysis of market research surveys is that of *classification*. Traditionally, analysis has been of the uni- or bi-variate kind; i.e., analysis by age, social grade, products bought, etc., and by combination of suchlike variables. Since data are collected for many variables, it seems logical that we should attempt to classify our respondents over many variables. The analytical procedures designed for this purpose of simultaneously assessing respondents over many variables may be subsumed under the heading of 'numerical taxonomy', the principles of which are clearly set out by Sokal and Sneath[16]. The term 'cluster analysis' strictly refers to part of the taxonomic procedure but has come into general usage to mean classification usually in a market segmentation context. Numerical taxonomy has,

323

as its objective, the classification usually of persons, but not necessarily always so, such that persons within a cluster or group are more alike each other with respect to the measured variables than persons outside the cluster. If definite clusters exist then they may be described in terms of their 'profiles' and utilized as breakdowns in similar fashion to the traditional classification systems such as age within social grade.

Mechanics of numerical taxonomy

Figure 13.5 illustrates the steps required in the taxonomic process. Neither 'sample selection' and 'measurement' will be dealt with here since they

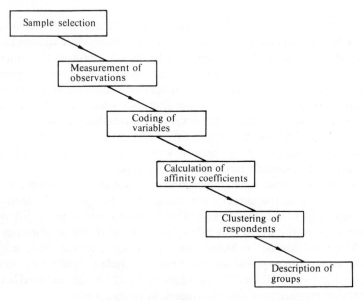

Fig. 13.5. Flowchart describing the steps involved in numerical taxonomy as applied to market research.

are topics common to all types of multivariate analysis and, in any case, are dealt with elsewhere. Before proceeding to discuss the remaining steps it is worthwhile to reconsider the data matrix (Fig. 13.1) and the possible ways of analysing it. Traditional methods of analysis have always been based on the relationships *between the variables across the respondents*. Analysis of this kind leads to a clustering of variables and is known as 'R-technique'. However, there is another way of looking at the data matrix, and that is to look at the relationships *between respondents across the variables*, known as 'Q-technique'[17].

Coding of characters

Once the information required has been measured on a sample of respondents, a coding operation is required before it is possible to calculate measures of

324

affinity. Basically, their are three different kinds of measurement:

(a) dichotomous characters (1:0 data);
(b) multi-state characters, of a *quantitative* nature;
(c) multi-state characters, of a *qualitative* nature.

The latter type of measurement presents the greatest problems and Sokal and Sneath[16] comment on the potential dangers involved in the coding process.

Calculation of affinities

The next step is to calculate estimates of affinity (similarity) between each pair of respondents so as to form an affinity matrix. The three basic measures available are:

(a) *Similarity coefficients.* These types of coefficients are mainly used in conjunction with dichotomous measurements (1:0 data). Essentially, a similarity coefficient expresses the number of 'matching' attributes respondents have in relation to the total number of comparisons. A coefficient is calculated for every pair of respondents. Figure 13.6 illustrates how a similarity coefficient may be computed using the familiar 2 × 2 layout. The most common similarity coefficients range from zero (non-similar) to one for perfect matching. Further examples of similarity coefficients are discussed by Joyce and Channon[17].

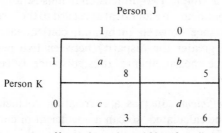

Person J

	1	0
Person K 1	a 8	b 5
0	c 3	d 6

$N = a+b+c+d=$ total No. of attributes

(a) S_{JK} $\dfrac{a}{a+b+c} = \dfrac{8}{16} = 0.50$;

(b) S_{JK} $\dfrac{a}{N} = \dfrac{8}{22} = 0.36$

Fig. 13.6 Example of the calculation of two different similarity coefficients. The interpretation of the 2 × 2 table is as follows: code 1 for possession of an attribute; 0 for non-possession. Thus, comparing person *J* to person *K* in the numerical example—they each match on possessing eight attributes, person *K* possesses five attributes which person *J* does not, person *J* possesses three attributes which person *K* does not and neither person possesses six similar attributes.

(b) *Distance coefficients.* Measures of distance are based on a geometric model, and in special cases are related to similarity coefficients. The most common distance measurement is:

$$d_{jk} = \left[\frac{\sum (x_{ij} - x_{ik})^2}{N} \right]^{1/2}$$

x_{ij} is person j's score on the ith variable and x_{ik} is person k's score on the ith variable, and N = No. of variables.

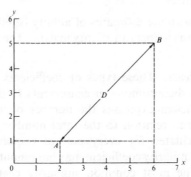

Fig. 13.7. Illustration of the calculation of a distance coefficient in two dimensional space.

Figure 13.7 gives a simple two-dimensional illustration of the 'distance' concept. If the respondents are identical as regard to the measured characteristics then the distance between them and, consequently, the coefficient will be zero. The greater the disparity between two persons, the larger will be the distance measurement; thus, distance is complementary to similarity.

(c) *Correlation coefficient.* Just as a correlation coefficient between two variables may be calculated, so can a coefficient of correlation between two persons. This is an alternative method to the distance coefficient for handling quantitative data. Inglis and Johnson[18] in a studied paper on the developments in and the analyses of multivariate survey data consider that a distance measurement is often preferable since, conceptually, it measures distances between people more powerfully.

Cluster analysis

Having computed some form of affinity coefficient, the next step is to group together those respondents who are most similar to each other. In a paper read to a MRS course on 'segmentation analysis', Emmett[19] reviewed the new methods of 'clustering' and 'clumping'. Essentially, 'clustering' involves the formation of trial sets of clusters which are continually modified by successive iterations. The 'clumping' methods require the establishment of basic 'clumps', e.g., the two 'nearest' points, which are added to by the addition of nearest neighbours.

An appropriate method of clustering similarity coefficients appears to be that of 'average linkage'[16] whilst Scientific Control Systems Ltd,[20] and Cybernetics Research Consultants Ltd,[21] describe programs in their Users Guide to Cluster Analysis, based on successive iterations from trial solutions which are appropriate when using distance coefficients.

Naming the groups

Once the researcher is satisfied with the cluster solution the resultant groups can be tested for homogeneity using a variety of statistical tests including Holzingers B coefficient. The salient features of each cluster require to be summarized and described in terms of the variables/attributes involved in the analysis. As in factor analysis names may be attached to each cluster for ease of reference but, again, care is required to ensure that any 'shorthand' descriptions used are not later misinterpreted. The charting of simple 'profile charts' is a useful summarizing aid.

Summary

Numerical taxonomy

Numerical taxonomy embraces a group of techniques which seek to statistically segment a sample of respondents into homogeneous groups with respect to several variables/attributes. When we are not testing prior hypotheses or where the problem is one of seeking patterns, of looking for natural groupings in the data, then taxonometric procedures may assist.

Examples of numerical taxonomy

(a) *Political Party—Scientific Control Systems Limited*

Morgan and Purnell[22] report on a cluster analysis using factor scores derived from a battery of attitudinal scales relating to elector's attitudes to political issues. Four factors were obtained and factor scores were estimated for each of 500 electors. A ten-cluster solution was considered to be the most appropriate. Each cluster was 'subjectively' named as follows:

Cluster No.	Name	Sample size
1	High Tory	45
2	Me first	34
3	Whig	36
4	Labour (little England)	70
5	Meritocrat	46
6	Me first (anti-Europe)	57
7	'One nation' Tories	44
8	Left-wing Labour	42
9	Meritocrat (pro-Europe)	43
10	Right-wing Labour	83

One of the aims of this case-study was to see whether or not a 'new' political party could be discovered—a position analagous to seeking a new product. A program NEMO seeks to describe the existing products in a market in an n-dimensional product attribute space. The object of the analysis is to look for a point in the space which defines a new product which is as different as possible from existing ones.

(b) *Subjective Clustering of Television Programme Similarities*

Several papers in the Journal of the Market Research Society[23] concerned clustering procedures of television programmes. An interesting paper by Green, Carmone and Fox[24] described the methodology and application of subjective clustering of television programmes. Briefly, this procedure entails respondents sorting into groups various stimuli (television programmes). One of the analyses reported is that of respondent configuration. For each pair of respondents a distance measure was computed, based on the degree of agreement in the pair's clustering of programmes. The resultant distance maxtrix was submitted to a multi-dimensional scaling program. Whilst the authors report little relationships between the subjective clusters and other certain predictor variables such as demographic and socio-economic variables, the technique is mentioned here as being of particular interest in the area of defining markets and sub-groups in markets.

Multiple Regression Analysis

Multiple regression analysis is a technique for estimating the relationship between one 'dependent' variable and a number of so-called 'independent' variables. Since the technique is concerned with relationship—the way in which the variables are associated with one another—it is not unlike correlation analysis. Indeed, in practice both correlation coefficients and regression equations are generally desired in the same problem. The essential difference is that *regression analysis* is concerned with dependence; one (or more) variable is selected for study and we are concerned to find out whether the magnitude of the variable can be *predicted* from knowledge about the independent variables. *Correlation analysis* is concerned with the degree of association between sets of observations.

Simple linear regression

Let us consider the simplest case of regression i.e., the way in which one variable may be related (and hence predicted) by another. A useful first step in such a problem is to draw a 'scatter diagram' (see Fig. 13.2). A line of 'best fit' through the points may be drawn visually. If there is a high degree of correlation between the variables then for any given value of x (weight) we can predict the likely value of y (height). Mathematically, we may predict y (height) by the equation;

$$y = a + bx$$

where a is the y-axis intercept and b is the slope of the line. The parameters a and b are known as the regression coefficients and they are chosen so as to minimize the sums of squares of the deviations from the regression line. This method is known as the 'least-squares' method. a is estimated by $\bar{y}$ and b is estimated by:

$$b = \frac{\text{covariance } (x \cdot y)}{\text{var } (x)} \left[\text{or } \frac{\sum xy}{\sum x^2} \text{ when } x \text{ and } y \text{ are standardized} \right].$$

Multiple regression

Multiple regression analysis is merely an extension of the simple case. Again, there is one dependent variable, but a number of 'independent' variables are used to try and explain the variations of the dependent variable. The addition of more independent variables means that the mathematical model can portray more realistically real life situations. It is rare that only one variable influences another. In a complex marketing situation, variation in sales may be associated with many factors, such as amount spent on advertising, distribution levels, national prosperity, etc.

The linear model for multiple regression is:

$$y = a + b_1 x_1 + b_2 x_2 + \cdots + b_p x_p$$

where x is the independent variables and b the rate of change of the dependent variable y in each of the independent variables when the other independent variables are held constant. They are often called the *partial regression coefficients* and their estimation is carried out in similar fashion to the simple linear regression case. The mathematics is more complicated but the principle is unchanged, i.e., the coefficients are chosen so as to minimize the residual sums of squares. Those interested should consult almost any intermediate statistical text-book for details of the theory and Ferber[25] gives practical examples with detailed worksheets for simple cases. As the number of independent variables increases the computational aspect is considerable. Perhaps the best existing commercial computer programs are those developed by Scientific Controls Systems Ltd. Beale, Kendall and Mann have made very notable contributions to the development of multiple regression. They offer two main alternative programs. One is optimum in that it produces the best possible sets of independent variables. The other is a less expensive procedure which, however, does not guarantee an optimum solution.

Summary

Multiple regression

The main use of regression analysis is the setting up of equations to provide estimators for the prediction of a predetermined variable. It is only appropriate when the criterion variable is continuous (such as quantity of sales, percentage of market share). With care, the regression equation may assist in interpretation—but the problem here is one of the collinearities which usually exist in the so-called 'independent set of variables'.

Example of multiple regression

Multiple regression is, perhaps, one of the most common statistical techniques used in marketing and yet, unfortunately, few case histories are available in the literature. This is probably because the greatest use of multiple regression is in the sales forcasting area, i.e., given sales data and a set of sales determinants such as economic data, household information, a fore-casting model may be set up. The effect of changes in the parameters of such a model may be estimated by regression techniques.

Frank and Boyd[27] studied each of 44 grocery products (the dependent variable) and the way in which the proportion of product purchases related to nine household socio-economic characteristics and five measures of purchasing behaviour (independent variables). They found little association between household socio-economic or total consumption characteristics and *private* brand purchasing. The significant relationships which emerged were the obvious ones, such as, households with members that shop in grocery stores with substantial private brand stocks spend a higher per-centage of their purchases on private brands.

Canonical Correlation

Canonical correlation procedures are designed to measure simultaneously the relationships between several dependent variables and several independent variables, all measured on the same set of persons (or objects). It is, therefore, a further extension of multiple regression, the main difference being that, whereas in multiple regression we have only one dependent variable, in canonical analysis we have more than one. Canonical analysis works in the following way. The variables are split into two sets, a set of criterion (dependent) variables and a set of predictor (independent) variables. Sets of coefficients are calculated such that the correlation between the weighted sum of the criterion variables has the maximum correlation with the weighted sum of the predictor variables. This equation is the first canonical regression equation. It is analogous to a principal component in that it maximizes correlation and thus facilitates prediction. A second canonical regression line is then found orthogonal to the first and yet has maximum correlation between the two (new) equations. There are as many canonical regression equations as there are variables in the smallest set.

Tests of significance may be applied to the resultant canonical correlations and one hopes that the first few will be large and the remainder negligible. To date the writer knows of only one published example of canonical analysis in a marketing context[26]. It is considered that, as computing facilities become more available, the potentialities of applying canonical analysis to marketing problems will be realized.

Example of canonical correlation

For a detailed discussion of the statistical theory underlying canonical analysis the reader should refer to Cooley and Lohnes[9] who also give an example which uses the technique to test general hypotheses that relate two sets of variables. The example is concerned with a set of seven predictor variables which are scores on scales relating to early home environment, e.g., how close was respondent to mother and father in childhood. The criterion variables are scores relating to the respondents present orientation towards people, e.g., degree of curiosity expressed towards people. Those interested may consult the reference for actual results. A basic conclusion was that early home environment is related to orientation towards people and that the primary antecedent is early experience of social activities.

Multiple Discriminant Analysis

We are often concerned with the ability to predict a person's response given a set of different measurements about this person. We may wish to predict which car a person will buy from knowledge about his past ownership, his present situation and say, his attitudes to cars in general. Discriminant analysis and in general, multiple discriminant analysis is a technique for classifying persons into one group or another given certain information which is correlated with a multichotomous attribute.

In discrimination, the classes are predetermined and we are concerned with allocating a person to one of several classes. In the simplest case, that of two classes, the following example illustrates the technique. Suppose we have two groups of persons, purchasers and non-purchasers, and we have information for each person regarding attitudes, behaviour, socio-economics characteristics, etc. A discriminant function may be calculated by defining a new variable, 'propensity to purchase', as a weighted sum of the attitude, etc., variables. Assume we only have two pieces of attitude information, then we can plot the data as shown in Fig. 13.8. The discriminant function attempts to predict, by considering the weighted score for each person whether or not he is more likely to be a purchaser or a non-purchaser. The problem is one of drawing the boundary so as to minimize the probability of misclassification.

Sequential Dichotomization Techniques

One of the earliest new classification methods was developed by Belson[28], who was primarily interested in attempting to find the best combination of independent variables which would predict a 'dependent' variable. The

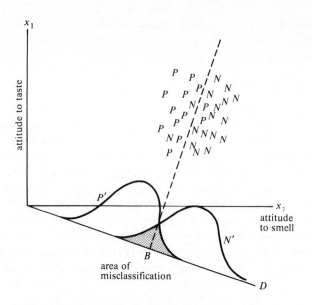

Fig. 13.8. Discrimination analysis: example in two dimensions. Purchasers (P) and non-purchasers (N) are plotted on two dimension x_1 and x_2. A discriminant analysis generates a score (D), based on the two attitude scores. The problem is one of where to draw the boundary (B) so as to minimize the probability of misclassification (shaded area). Predictions may be made for 'new' observations by allocating persons to one or other side of the boundary by considering the score generated by the discriminant function.

'Belson sort' procedure examined all alternative dichotomizations of a sample to discover those which were significant predictors and then went on to examine in a sequential fashion the best combinations of independent variables. At each stage in the splitting process, chi-square values are calculated to test the predictive performance of the chosen dichotomies (Fig. 13.9).

Automatic Interaction Detection

This is a technique for dividing a sample into groups on the basis of demographics or other variables, again splitting on one variable at a time. The method arose because the authors, Sonquist and Morgan[29] were concerned with the inadequacy of simple cross-tabulations to reveal the complex interactions in survey data. It is similar to the Belson sort, splitting on one variable at a time except that the criterion for retaining the discriminating variables is based on analysis of variance. The first predictive variable is that which maximizes the between group variance and minimizes the within group variances.

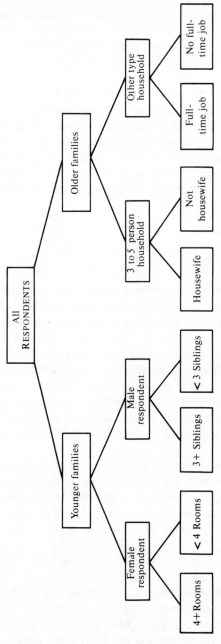

Fig. 13.9. Example of **Belson Sort** reproduced with permission of Dr W. A. Belson. Matching and Prediction on the Principle of Biological Classification. The criterion variable in this case is the degree to which individuals participate with others in the home, i.e., joint activity. For simplicity's sake further dichotomization has been excluded in the example.

Non-Metric Multi-Dimensional Scaling

The latest developments in multivariate statistics are concerned with the relative low level degree of measurements achieved in market research data. Much of the data collected by researchers is of the nominal or ordinal kind (non-metric) and in the past, analysts have indiscriminately applied the techniques described in this chapter which assume the conditions of metric measurement.

Statistical techniques are now available which require only non-metric data and yet yield results which are of metric scaling. These techniques may be subsumed under the heading of 'non-metric multi-dimensional scaling'. An interesting paper which would serve as an introduction to this current development is by Neidell[30]. In this paper, Neidell introduces the notion of developing a multi-dimensional attribute space from a uni-dimensional data bank consisting of inter-object non-metric relationships.

Multivariate Analysis

Concluding remarks

Inevitably this chapter on multivariate analysis can only touch the surface of the subject. It is hoped that the references provided will enable both specialist and non-specialist seeking to widen their knowledge in this complex field to a greater understanding of multi-dimensional space. Increasing use is being made of techniques like factor analysis, multiple regression, and so on, often in inappropriate situations on data that are not amenable to such analyses. The market researcher, faced with such a toolbag of techniques must be familar enough with the subject to utilize the right techniques. The mathematician/statistician must, likewise, appreciate the research problems and use techniques not for themselves but for their problem-solving capabilities.

The latest developments concerning *non-metric* multi-dimensional scaling are likely to continue with the awareness by analysts of the inadequacy of present day data input. It is to be hoped that the introduction of 'time-sharing computers and the advancement of higher level programming languages will enable researchers to utilize multivariate techniques to great advantage.

The initial head-on plunge into new techniques and methodologies is always to be expected. As Green and Frank[31] point out; 'Despite the inevitable misapplication of techniques and over-selling (with the consequent failure to live up to expectations), the fact remains that quantitative and behavioural science are here to stay'. Multivariate analysis as an important sector of quantitative science should not be ignored simply because of its apparent complexities.

References

1. COLLINS, M. A. Three Approaches to a Multi-dimensional Problem, *Journal of the Market Research Society*, **11**, 3, 1969.
2. KENDALL, M. G. *A Course in Multivariate Analysis, Introduction*, Chas. Griffin, 1965.
3. EHRENBERG, A. S. C. Some Queries to Factor Analysts, *The Statistician*, **13**, 4, 1963.
4. SIEGEL, S. Measures of Correlation and their Tests of Significance, *Non-parametric Statistics for the Behavioral Sciences*, McGraw-Hill, New York, 1956.
5. HOPE, K. Principal Components, *Methods of Multivariate Analysis*, University of London Press, 1968.
6. CHRISTOPHER, M. A. *A Cluster Analysis of Towns in England and Wales according to their Suitability for Test Market Locations*, University of Bradford Research Project Series in Marketing, 1969.
7. HOLMES, C. Construction and Stratification of a Sampling Frame of Primary Sampling Units, *The Statistician*, **19**, 1, 1969.
8. HARMAN, H. H. Foundation of Factor Analysis, *Modern Factor Analysis*, Second edition, University of Chicago Press, 1967.
9. COOLEY, W. W. and LOHNES, P. R. Factor Analysis, *Multivariate Procedures for the Behavioral Sciences*, Wiley, New York, 1962.
10. LAWLEY, D. N. and MAXWELL, A. E. *Factor Analysis as a Statistical Method*, Butterworth, 1963.
11. KAISER, H. F. *Comments in Communality and the Number of Factors*, Read at Conference, Washington University, St. Louis, 1960.
12. THURSTONE, L. L. *Multiple Factor Analysis*, University of Chicago Press, 1947.
13. HENDRICKSON, A. E. and WHITE, P. O. PROMAX—A Quick Method for Rotation to Simple Structure, *British Journal of Statistical Psychology*, **17**, Part 1, 1964.
14. HILL, P. B. Multivariate Analysis—What Payoff for the Marketing Man?, *Journal of the Market Research Society*, **12**, 3, 1970.
15. FROST, W. A. K. The Development of a Technique for TV Programme Assessment, *Journal of the Market Research Society*, **11**, 1, 1969.
16. SOKAL, R. R. and SNEATH, P. H. A. *Principles of Numerical Taxonomy*, W. H. Freeman, 1963.
17. JOYCE, T. and CHANNON, C. Classifying Market Survey Respondents, *Applied Statistics*, **XV**, 3, 1966.
18. INGLIS, J. and JOHNSON, D. Some Observations on and Developments in the Analysis of Multivatiate Survey Data, *Journal of the Market Research Society*, **12**, 2, 1970.
19. EMMETT, B. P. The Exploration of Inter-relationships in Survey Data, *Journal of the Market Research Society*, **10**, 2, 1968.
20. *Users Guide to Cluster Analysis Program*, Scientific Control Systems Ltd.
21. *CRC Cluster Analysis Program*, Cybernetics Research Consultants Ltd.
22. MORGAN, N. and PURNELL, J. M. Isolating Openings for New Products in a Multi-Dimensional Space, *Journal of the Market Research Society*, **11**, 3, 1969.
23. *Journal of the Market Research Society*, **11**, 1, 1969.
24. GREEN, P. E., CARMONE, F. J., and FOX, L. B. Television Programme Similarities: An Application of Subjective Clustering, *Journal of the Market Research Society*, **11**, 1, 1969.
25. FERBER, R. Multiple Correlation Techniques, *Market Research*, McGraw-Hill, New York, 1949.
26. GREEN, P. E., HALBERT, M. H., and ROBINSON, P. J. Canonical Analysis: An Exposition and Illustrative Application, *Journal of Marketing Research*, **3**, Feb., 1966.
27. FRANK, R. E. and BOYD, H. W. Are private—brand—prone Grocery Customers Really Different?, *Journal of Advertising Research*, **5**, 4, 1965.
28. BELSON, W. A. Principle of Biological Classification, *Applied Statistics*, **VIII**, 2, 1959.
29. SONQUIST, J. A. and MORGAN, J. N. *The Detection of Interaction Effects*, Monograph 35, Survey Research Center, University of Michigan.
30. NEIDELL, L. A. The Use of Non-metric Multi-dimensional Scaling in Marketing Analysis, *Journal of Marketing*, **33**, Oct., 1969.
31. GREEN, P. E. and FRANK, R. F. *A Manager's Guide to Marketing Research*, Wiley, New York, 1967.

Part II. Use of consumer market research

Section 3 Consumer research applications

Introduction

The role of market research is to make marketing operations more efficient and profitable, by improving the quality of planning and decision taking. This is the only way in which market research can justify itself. The following chapters, therefore, illustrate how the research tools described earlier are applied to various problems encountered in marketing.

There are many different definitions of marketing: economic, physical, organizational, even psychological. We will not attempt yet another for the purposes of this section. Enough to say that market research is involved with all those activities which are directed towards helping an organization to supply, as efficiently and profitably as possible, goods or services designed so as to satisfy identified consumer needs. This is not intended to be a precise or comprehensive statement of what market research is about. It is, even so, a very broad one. Its implications are not restricted to distribution and selling activities but cover many aspects of production and, indeed, of company policy generally. Market research is not exclusively the preserve of the marketing man. It has increasingly drawn in the laboratory scientist, the production manager, finance and personnel departments and others. This is brought out very clearly in, for example, the chapters on product development and on corporate image research. The contributions which follow reflect this broad view of market research.

In planning these chapters we had in mind a structure of the marketing process which explains their sequence. Like all such structures it is greatly over-simplified, but the reader may find it helpful to know the pattern. This is illustrated in Fig. Intro. 1, the bracketed figures being the chapter numbers. There are two additional chapters which do not fit so neatly into the pattern: the more specialized but very important field of financial research (21), and the broader and growing field of international market research (22).

There are four comments to make about this approach. First, the total material, to be manageable, has to be divided under several sub-headings, i.e., chapters. This is inevitable but artificial; and it would be positively dangerous if, in real life, the different problems were treated as though in watertight compartments. A successful brand does *not* consist simply of a

340

formula plus a price plus a pack plus an advertisement plus . . . etc., where each of these elements has been developed in isolation. The whole is (or certainly should be) far greater than the sum of its parts. The various elements of the marketing mix, therefore, have to be interrelated and tested together at various stages. This point is emphasized at several points in these chapters. The principle is absolutely basic to successful brand marketing; but it is still depressingly often ignored.

Second, market research and brand development does not often proceed in a neat and tidy time sequence from a study of market opportunities to the national launch of a new brand. It tends to involve a process of continual rethinking and adjustment of plans as more information becomes available. The elements of the marketing mix, and sometimes even the brand concept itself, may have to be modified as we progress towards the stage of market testing. This may mean going back on an earlier stage of market research and retesting.

Third, much of the following material is presented in the context of developing a *new* brand. This is the clearest, and in many respects the most comprehensive, method of illustrating the way in which market research is applied. Obviously, a great deal of market research is concerned with *existing* brands, particularly in recycling them to give them a new lease of life in changing and heavily competitive markets. The principles discussed in these chapters apply to such brands also, although not all the steps described will be needed. Probably the major difference is that an existing brand will

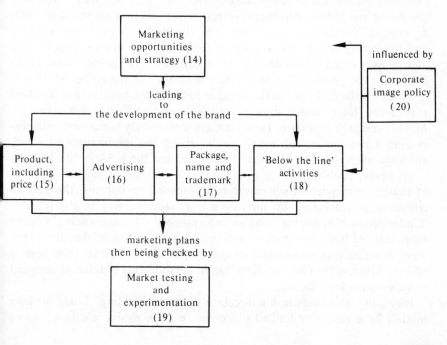

normally have an established personality or image as far as consumers are concerned. This may sometimes be weak, and quite possibly be one we wish to change, but our research approach must take account of it, for in the market-place the existing image will condition consumers' views about any new developments (product, advertising or other) which we may plan for the brand. As chapter 15 points out, 'blind' testing can be particularly misleading in this context.

Finally, a substantial part, perhaps approaching a third, of the total expenditure on market research in the UK is devoted to market measurement (retail audits, consumer purchasing panels and barometers of different kinds). This is necessary both for drawing up plans and monitoring progress in existing markets and also to provide certain key background data for investigating possible new markets. Earlier chapters have described these techniques and discussed several of their key applications. The following chapters, therefore, do not make much reference to the more descriptive, background planning aspects of market measurement and similar research, since the latter's value in dealing with various marketing problems should already be clear.

One other general comment is worth making. Much of the discussion in these chapters concentrates on the problems of frequently bought consumer goods. Even so, a lot of what is said will apply equally to durable goods and to services, although some of the detailed mechanics of the research have to be adapted to fit the special characteristics of these products.

Over the last fifteen years, market research has moved from a stance of *providing information* to one of *solving problems*. This shift reflects not only the raised sights (and ambitions) of researchers themselves but also wider agreement that market research must be directed towards decision taking and marketing action. One aspect of this is that far more research briefs and plans nowadays include not only a discussion of the marketing background to the problem but also a clear statement of the action which will be based on the findings. In the extreme case this can be an action standard of the form, 'If the findings show A, we will take action X; if B, then action Y'. Market research reports in their turn are increasingly concerned with discussing action instead of merely summarizing the information collected, although even now the UK tends to lag behind the USA in this respect.

However, 'problem solving' does not by any means cover all the objectives of market research. Much research is intended to improve the general efficiency of marketing by increasing our *understanding* of the market. 'Understanding' is *not* the same as 'information'. 'Understanding' implies knowledge of both the structure and the dynamics of the market and of the ways in which marketing activities achieve, or fail to achieve, their desired effects. Much of the research described in the following chapters is designed to secure such knowledge.

Inevitably, this leads in the direction of model building. Some of these models have relatively limited objectives, e.g., in media selection. More complex ones deal with issues such as consumer decision processes: how *does* a consumer come to choose a particular brand on a given occasion? Work of this kind is often aimed particularly at helping researchers themselves to improve their research approach and methods. The most ambitious models, however, attempt to reproduce the mechanism of the market as a whole (or at least substantial parts of it), often with a view to providing facilities for market simulation where marketing experiments can be carried out inside the computer. At this point, it becomes difficult to draw any clear boundary between market research and other disciplines such as operational research.

The major contribution of market research in this area has probably been its emphasis on the value of studying the attitudes and behaviour of consumers *individually*, particularly through panels. This 'micro' approach contrasts with the longer-established 'macro' approaches which involve studying consumers in the mass. Here, market research has ultimately much more to offer than econometric techniques in improving our understanding of markets.

Another point at which market research tends to cross a boundary is in its concern with information as such. The higher-flying comments of the last paragraphs should not distract attention from this important, if less glamorous, function. In looking at what market research has to offer we must remember that it is one among several sources of data. Within a company, market research information has to be integrated with sales data, trade statistics and much other material. Increasingly, therefore, we have as users to think of total management information systems into which market research data must be fitted. We also have to find better ways of getting the relevant information (and only this) to the right people at the appropriate time quickly, clearly and concisely. This is another perspective against which to consider the material discussed in the next chapters.

The fact that market research is not the only source of market knowledge introduces a further issue. Knowledge normally costs money (and time). This is certainly the case with knowledge obtained through research. We should therefore weigh the cost of the additional knowledge to be gained through a particular research project against the pay-off (extra profit) we might expect to obtain as a result of having this knowledge. This is very much more easily said than done. It involves calculations not only of cost and potential pay-off but also of risk and the probability of different research and marketing outcomes. There is a field of statistics—Decision Theory, based on Bayesian statistics—which attempts to get to grips with this type of problem. So far, very little practical work has been done (rather more in the USA than in the UK) in applying this to the buying of market research. However, the problem is so important that we shall inevitably have to try to use this or some similar approach more effectively during the next few years: reference is made to it in chapter 19.

As market research has developed further and further away from the simple 'nose-counting' of its early days, so the problem of effective communication between market researchers and their clients has also increased. When dealing with the more sophisticated approaches now available (such as those described in chapter 14) the user of research may need to understand at least the principles of quite complex techniques if he is to make good use of their findings. He may, on occasion, even have to rethink his own basic marketing approach, e.g., when considering market segmentation studies. This is a challenge to both researcher and user. The researcher must try to explain his methods and findings simply and directly, avoiding jargon as far as he can, but the user must also build his half of the bridge. He can no longer expect to cope adequately with market research (or with other modern marketing techniques) on the basis of a short briefing plus a skimming of the report's summary of findings. The subject need not be abstruse, except in its most specialized technical aspects, but it has to be worked at if it is to be applied effectively.

The following chapters aim to help with this, although they cannot hope to deal with all aspects of the topics discussed. They will be the more useful if the earlier, more technical chapters have also been studied and if some of the books and articles referred to are subsequently followed up for more detailed information on subjects of interest.

John Downham

14. Segmenting and constructing markets

Tony Lunn

During the past decade or so, market segmentation has emerged as a central concept in consumer research. It is often defined as a *research technique*, as a type of survey, say, or a method of data analysis: and it has, in fact, been the focal point of major advances in research technology, especially in the field of multi-variate analysis. However, simultaneously with its growth in popularity, segmentation has become a somewhat ambiguous concept, associated with a diversity of analysis techniques, e.g., cluster analysis, sequential dichotomization[1], with attempts to find new ways of classifying consumers[2], and with a variety of different kinds of research approach, e.g., market description studies[3], market structure studies[4] and contextual mapping[5]. The position taken in this chapter is that segmentation is more aptly defined in its original sense, namely as an *approach to marketing*. This approach may be summarized as the philosophy whereby products are directed at specific target groups of consumers rather than at the total population, a philosophy that has gained considerable influence in the post war era[6].

In a recent publication[7] the author attempted an overview of some prominent research issues in market segmentation. The purpose here is to outline the present position more from the marketing standpoint, with particular emphasis upon problems and applications. The marketing man is often faced, nowadays, with bewildering volumes of data, gathered from mammoth surveys, and analysed by highly abstruse techniques. There is a danger of both marketing men and researchers becoming lost in a forest of complexity; of the former seeking panaceas, and, inevitably, becoming disillusioned, and of the latter becoming entranced by methodological niceties. In the present chapter it is hoped to illustrate how even the most sophisticated techniques can have clear and practical applications for both long term planning and day to day decisions.

Given the ubiquity of the segmentation concept, some of the points discussed below are also dealt with elsewhere in the book, usually in greater detail. This applies both to research techniques, e.g., the chapters by Sampson, Morton-Williams and Holmes and to applications, e.g., those by Greenhalgh and Brown. The topic has generated a voluminous literature, some of which is listed in the references at the end of the chapter.

Some Marketing Considerations

General

Segmentation is a new term but an old concept. Manufacturers have long been aware that certain products are bought mainly by certain types of people: gold watches and tonic wines are obvious examples. Again, take the motor car market. A Model T Ford and a vintage Bentley are just as illustrative of market segmentation as are contemporary cars such as the Ford Capri and the Austin Maxi. Nevertheless, much of this early segmentation was accidental, i.e., the product was launched with no clear target group in mind, but, by its nature, turned out to attract certain types of people: or, if not accidental, the marketing action was often highly speculative: target groups were based mainly upon intuition, and described rather vaguely in such phrases as, 'The modern woman who cares for her children'.

The main difference today is that segmentation policies are pursued much more purposefully, and are applied to a much wider range of product fields. This development can be attributed to a number of inter-related factors, some of which are outlined below.

First, as a result of fundamental changes in society, purchasing is becoming more discretionary and less concerned simply with the necessities of daily life. The most important changes for marketing men are the growth of affluence and the rising level of education. These have been accompanied by increasing social mobility and by an erosion of traditional class-determined patterns of behaviour: the typist, like the deb, can afford to express her personality through the latest fashions; the factory worker may take his holiday in Majorca. As the constraints of income have eased and the traditional social constraints have ceased to apply, individual patterns of requirements have flourished. The result has been an ever-widening range of consumer tastes and needs for the marketing man to satisfy. Thus, in an era of social change, manufacturers are paying much more attention to consumer differences in their general planning. This consumer-orientation is a matter of necessity in an era of mass production and mass marketing, when the financial penalties of failure to market the right kinds of goods and services can be ruinous.

Second, the whole climate of marketing has become much more 'scientific'. The individual entrepreneur is being replaced by teams of specialists: product life-cycles are more carefully planned and monitored: manufacturers

346

are increasingly concerned with maintaining complementary ranges of products within any one area, and also with diversifying into related areas.

Third, the increasing sophistication of technological development in the physical sciences has been increasingly harnessed for the production of consumer goods, e.g., frozen foods, hi-fi radios, disposable clothes. But the resultant new products rarely meet with instant and universal acceptance. Many may be dead-ends. To be successful, a new product type usually has to make its appeal, at least initially, to a particular market segment, perhaps broadening its appeal to wider elements of the population as time goes by. Frozen foods provide a case in point.

Fourth, the combination of technological development and mass marketing has meant that basic physical products in certain fields have become almost uniform in composition and scarcely distinguishable by the consumer. As a result, marketing men have sought to establish clearer identities for specific brands, e.g., toilet soaps are given different perfumes and colours, toothpastes special ingredients such as fluoride and so on. These extra product characteristics may well offer to the consumer benefits over and above the basic function of the product. A particular toilet soap may offer cosmetic benefits, a gold fountain pen may act as a status symbol, Scandinavian cutlery may satisfy a need to feel up to date. In some product fields secondary benefits of this kind have become the primary reason for purchase: pop art watches may be valued more as fashion accessories than as time-pieces; the majority of Virginian tobacco cigarettes are indistinguishable on blind product tests, yet often command striking preferences in their branded form. Discussion of this fourth point makes it important to distinguish between at least three levels of segmentation, namely where:

(a) totally different *product types* are produced for different consumer needs, e.g., toothpaste rather than some alternative means of cleaning teeth;
(b) different *product variants* are produced within the same overall type, e.g., special benefits such as fluoride are built in;
(c) different *brands* are produced within the same specific product variant.

Fifth, a further corollary of mass production has been the neglect of certain minority tastes. These tastes have often been identified in product concept research[8], and have subsequently formed the basis of new product developments. The growth of delicatessen and health food product ranges provides a contemporary illustration.

Sixth, recent years have seen an interdependence between developments in marketing thinking—which have led to demands for more detailed descriptions of consumers—and developments in research techniques, which have themselves opened up wider possibilities for marketing action. At a time when complex data analyses can be carried out with increasing speed and economy by computers, marketing men have much sharper tools at their disposal for the implementation of segmentation policies.

347

To summarize the effects of these changes: there has been a growing recognition that consumers may differ in ways that are exploitable by marketing activity, and that to concentrate upon producing 'universal products' for the 'average consumer' is to run the risk of missing significant marketing opportunities. Increasingly, therefore, marketing men have become concerned to identify target groups of consumers with distinctive patterns of needs, to develop products with the appropriate benefits, and to promote and distribute these products in optimum ways.

Different types of marketing problem

It was pointed out earlier that segmentation is essentially an approach to marketing. As such, it can provide the cornerstone for a company's total planning. It helps to set the basic objectives for the whole marketing operation, and to indicate strategies for implementing these objectives. There are, of course, many different kinds of marketing objectives and strategies, which, in turn, give rise to different types of segmentation problem. It is important to distinguish between these. The particular problem posed will determine the kind of research necessary, including the sort of data that will be most relevant, and the ways in which the data should be analysed. A number of prominent types of marketing problem are listed below, and are referred to again later in the chapter.

(a) *Defining the Market*

This has become an increasingly important question in recent years. Consumers do not necessarily perceive the market in the same way as do manufacturers. From the consumer's standpoint, a market may be thought of as a set of products (or brands) which are considered equally suitable for the same need—or set of needs. These products may come from product fields which manufacturers would treat as quite distinct. In a recent project, for instance, the main substitutes for a particular type of frozen food were not rival brands in the field, but two quite different kinds of tinned food on the one hand, and poached eggs on toast on the other. That is, the consumer's product field concept may range quite widely. Moreover, the repertoire of brands he considers suitable for a particular need will not necessarily include all the brands from any one field[40].

(b) *To Rationalize Policies for Existing Brands and Products*

This problem can be posed at two levels. At one level are questions of optimum strategies for specific brands (or products) marketed by the company. A variety of questions arise, such as how can market share be maintained or improved; how can inroads be made into the position of competitive brands; how best can the brand be protected from competitive activity; and so on. In the light of research, attempts may be made to increase the purchasing of current buyers, to convert buyers of competing brands, or to attract new buyers to the product field.

348

The second level is discussed under the third objective, namely:

(c) *To position Ranges of Brands and of Product Varieties*

This point was referred to earlier. Where in a given market there are different segments of consumers with differing needs, a company is well advised to market its brands in such a way that in total they satisfy as many as possible of the more important segments, at the same time minimising direct competition between the company's own brands as far as any one segment is concerned. The same point applies to ranges of product varieties.

(d) *To Identify Gaps in the Market Which Offer New Product Opportunities*

Here the object is to identify consumer segments whose needs (at least in their eyes) are not being adequately met by any existing brand. These needs may be met by launching a totally new brand (or product) or by modifying an existing one[8,9].

Underlying all four types of problem is the equally fundamental one of competition. Segmentation studies usually include amongst their objectives the location and specification of competition from rival manufacturers. Resultant marketing strategies may, of course, be essentially defensive—particularly in relation to new entries in the market—or more aggressive in nature.

Segmentation and Research Developments

It has been emphasized that segmentation is essentially an approach to marketing rather than a research technique but that it has, nevertheless, stimulated a variety of developments in consumer research. Some of these are discussed below under two main headings: criteria for defining market segments and research methodology. A third major issue will also be dealt with, namely the growing distinction between consumer and product segmentation. In summary, the former places chief emphasis upon ways in which people can be grouped in terms of their requirements; the latter upon ways in which products can be grouped in terms of the benefits they offer. These have often been represented as rival approaches[10]. They are, however, better viewed as complementary.

For ease of exposition, the following subsections on criteria and methodology are written from the standpoint of consumer segmentation: then comes a discussion of product segmentation, and the final subsection discusses relationships between the two approaches.

Segmentation criteria

Requirements from Criteria

Market segmentation is disaggregative in nature. It was pointed out above that for the marketing man to produce a 'universal product' for the 'average consumer' is to run the risk of missing important marketing opportunities.

Likewise, for the researcher to represent data in aggregate form rather than analysed by relevant variables is to provide information that may well be misleading. These variables are often referred to as segmentation criteria.

But what types of criteria are relevant? This will depend upon the particular market being examined. There are, however, a number of general considerations determining relevance; namely that criteria should:

(a) discriminate between consumers themselves;
(b) pick out differences in market patterns;
(c) increase the understanding of the market, particularly by indicating consumer needs;
(d) be fully exploitable in practice.

The fourth requirement implies that the criteria should be fully understandable by marketing and advertising men, that they should be the kind of variable that marketing men feel they can influence (unlike some of the more esoteric characteristics that have sometimes figured in segmentation projects), that they should be feasible to measure under normal market research circumstances and that they should, if possible, be related to differences in media and shopping habits in order to guide media strategies and distribution policies.

Different Kinds of Criteria

Consumers, and markets, can be described from an almost unlimited number of standpoints. The possibilities of several quite different kinds of variable have been examined in recent years. Those most commonly used in segmentation are outlined below, roughly in the order in which they have attained prominence*.

'Historically, perhaps the first type to exist was *geographic* segmentation. Small manufacturers who wished to limit their investments, or whose distribution channels were not large enough to cover the entire country, segmented the US market, in effect, by selling their products only in certain areas'[11]. Haley's comments apply to many countries other than the US. Indeed, segmentation by region is by no means uncommon even today.

Perhaps the most popular form of segmentation has been in terms of *demographic* characteristics. A comprehensive list, covering 13 countries, is given in a recent paper[12]. They include sex, age, occupation, income, social class, and household composition. These characteristics have become the basic terms in which many marketing men and researchers think about the consumer. This is reasonable up to a point. Demographic variables describe important aspects of people's circumstances which give rise to purchasing needs. They also act as moderators upon the translation of these needs into behaviour, e.g., a low income household may have expensive tastes, but little prospect of indulging them. Moreover, because they have been

---

* For a further discussion, see references 7 and 42.

studied over a long period of time, their relationships with other market factors, such as media patterns, have become well known. They have, however, been subjected to considerable criticism in recent years, mainly through lack of brand discrimination, and because giving as they do only indirect reflections of consumer needs, they are of limited value in the formulation of marketing strategies. Some of this criticism may be overcome by a more critical and imaginative treatment of demographic criteria. Attempts to find new ways of measuring social class have met with little success. Indeed, they have suggested the diminishing relevance to marketing of social class as traditionally defined. A growing emphasis upon education, however, and upon the life cycle concept—a composite of variables such as length of marriage and age of children—are showing promise.

The term 'demographic' is itself somewhat ambiguous. And there are a number of additional ways of describing the consumer's *background and social environment* which may prove valuable for segmentation policies. These include the possession of complementary products. An obvious example is the relationship between the ownership of a refrigerator and frozen food purchasing. For a useful list of such variables, see a paper by Agostini[13].

There are many products which either cater for, or are affected by, the consumer's *physical* attributes, e.g., skin and hair texture; and such characteristics are being increasingly used in segmentation.

The most straightforward way of classifying consumers is in terms of their behaviour, e.g., heaviness of buying in a product field, brand purchasing within product fields, different ways of using the same product. *Behavioural* segmentation has often been advocated as a simple and logical policy. The 'heavy-half' theory popularized by Twedt[14] for instance, argues that granted that in many product fields, 50 per cent of the consumers account for 80 per cent of consumption, these high-volume groups should command maximum marketing effort.

There are, however, two strong arguments against taking this reasoning too far. They are given by Haley[11], and Frank[15]. The former points out that people do not always buy products for the same reasons. Consequently, some heavy buyers may be better prospects than others. The latter points out that, in any case, the heavy half is already the heavy half, and may offer little scope for expansion. These arguments should not be taken to imply that behavioural variables have little part to play in segmentation; on the contrary, they have a great part to play. Moreover, as the author has pointed out elsewhere[7], the increase in our knowledge of buyer behaviour, stemming from the work of Ehrenberg, Kuehn, Massy and others, has considerable value for marketing in general and segmentation in particular. The reader is particularly recommended to a recent book[16], which shows a highly imaginative treatment of behavioural variables. Another interesting approach is that of backward segmentation[17]. In summary, this involves factor analysing purchasing patterns across a variety of product fields, in the search for patterns of complementary and substitutable products[18]. Wells suggests three main applications of this approach. To:

(a) stimulate ideas and guide future research;
(b) simplify marketing strategies, e.g., by suggesting common policies of couponing and distribution for related products;
(c) increase understanding by stimulating researchers to question why sets of products group together as they do.

The most promising development of the past decade has been segmentation by *psychological* characteristics. This has been accelerated by advances in psychometrics, which allow such variables to be measured effectively in day to day market research projects. Illustrations of psychological segmentation are given below. Suffice it to say here that relevant psychological variables differ in both nature and generality. They range, for instance, from specific product field requirements such as a need for powerful acceleration in motor cars, to more general traits such as traditionalism and economy mindedness. The latter are relevant to purchasing across a wide range of product fields. In a recent project the writer carried out factor and cluster analysis on responses to 60 such general traits on four separate samples of 500 housewives. The results have identified a small number of general consumer personality variables, which appear to reflect fundamental purchasing mechanisms, and also suggest the existence of about a dozen basic consumer types.

When psychological variables were first introduced to segmentation, the tendency was to use general personality characteristics, such as extroversion and neutroticism, borrowed *a priori* from clinical and general psychology[2,16]. Not surprisingly, the results of applying these in market research have proved disappointing. The most recent trend has been towards deriving measures of specific consumer requirements in the product field in question. Other kinds of psychological variables may be relevant on occasions, e.g., shopping and budgeting styles, general interests and certain aspects of general personality, such as self-esteem, self-confidence and willingness to take risks. So may wider aspects of life-style.

In a slightly different sense, *media* habits may also be thought of as segmentation criteria. Once the decision has been made to direct a product at a specific target group, selective media scheduling becomes an important concomitant of the total marketing plan. The problems associated with media are discussed in the final section of this chapter, and are also touched upon later in chapter 23.

Changes in Approach to Deriving Criteria

The previous section discussed some of the main criteria used in past and present segmentation research. There have been three main changes in researchers' approach to deriving these criteria. First, there has been a move from an essentially *a priori* to an empirical approach. That is to say, through the use of a stage of qualitative exploration (see below under Research

Methodology), criteria are increasingly tailor-made for particular markets, rather than imposed on the basis of researchers' preconceptions. Second, there has been an increasing emphasis upon *explanatory* criteria, which provide a direct measurement of consumer needs and motives. Third, there has been a move away from the search for one single kind of variable, a search which dominated much of the early work on segmentation. It has been recognized that purchasing behaviour is determined by a multiplicity of factors, some of them being 'internal' to the consumer such as her specific needs and general attitudes, others being 'external' to the consumer, e.g., her background and circumstances, and the situation in which the product is purchased and used. Consequently, segmentation projects are increasingly concerned with using *multiple* criteria, i.e., with including all kinds of variables that might be relevant to the particular market.

Segmentation and research methodology

It has been pointed out that marketing problems giving rise to segmentation studies are of different kinds, and that the nature of the specific problem will determine the methodology to be adopted. There is no best technique, or set of techniques, for all circumstances. It is, nevertheless, possible to map out a broad sequence of stages applicable to most consumer segmentation projects. Four characteristic stages are:

(a) background clarification;
(b) qualitative exploration;
(c) developing measuring instruments;
(d) defining target groups.

This does not mean that all projects must pass inexorably through all four stages or that additional stages may not, on occasions, be appropriate. These four do, however, provide a useful means of categorizing consumer segmentation methodology.

Stage 1. Background Clarification. The first stage in a segmentation project, as in any other major research activity, should be a thorough review of all existing knowledge and assumptions about the market. Most of this will probably consist of desk research. Information reviewed may vary from the findings of past motivation research to purchasing patterns derived from consumer panel records. Prominent issues will probably include:

(a) the nature of the market—is it expanding or contracting?
(b) the number of brands in the market and their respective shares;
(c) any rising or falling trends shown by individual brands;
(d) the proportion of the population buying the product, and the frequency of purchase;
(e) ways in which the product is used.

This information may, in itself, lead to hypotheses about the nature of the market and its basic mechanisms, which will help to guide subsequent research stages. It may also identify distinct behavioural subgroups which will provide a valuable focus for qualitative exploration (see stage 2).

This is a crucial stage with respect to the relationship between client and researcher. Discussions between the two parties can lay the foundation for the mutual understanding which is a prerequisite of a successful segmentation project (see final section of this chapter).

A useful example of how a behavioural analysis can help to set the scene for subsequent research is given by Winkler[19], with reference to the German toilet soap market. One finding reported by Winkler is the close correspondence between behavioural analyses of consumer panel data and consumer ratings of brand similarities. The same point is made by Stefflre[4]; and in several recent R.B.L. projects, small-scale analysis of consumer similarity and preference data have provided valuable supplementary indications of market structure. (See also p. 370.)

Stage 2. Qualitative Exploration. This stage is often the cornerstone of the entire segmentation project. It has, however, been neglected all too often in the published literature, and also tends to be devalued by researchers whose particular skills and predilections are towards quantitative methods (see stage 3). The author's position is clear. Having identified, at stage 1, the main behavioural patterns in the market, it is then important to explore the various factors determining or influencing these patterns. Behavioural data may, in itself, suggest hypotheses, but it is only by a thorough stage of qualitative research that these hypotheses can be fully pursued and amplified.

The techniques of qualitative research have been described by Sampson in chapter 1. Any or all of these may be appropriate to an individual segmentation project. The author goes along with Sampson in deploring the recent tendency by some researchers to over-emphasize the value of the Kelly Repertory Grid. Strict adherence to Kelly triads, for instance, at the expense of respondent free-association guided by skilled probing interviewing, may lead to the omission of some of the more fundamental psychological characteristics. Such variables are invaluable both for current advertising themes and also as a source of new product concepts.

The objectives of this second stage can be summarized as to:

(a) build up a set of hypotheses about the consumer characteristics relevant to purchasing in the market;
(b) develop a feel for the language used by consumers holding these characteristics, in order to guide the development of attitude scales and other appropriate measuring instruments (see chapter 4).

This qualitative stage may not always be carried out as one complete phase. Hypotheses may be progressively refined and developed during successive waves of interviews; some interviews may be carried out on the population at large, others on specific behavioural subgroups of particular relevance to the problem.

354

Stage 3. Developing Measuring Instruments. Content analysis of the interviews and other procedures used at stage 2 will have provided a set of hypotheses about the main forces relevant to consumer behaviour in the market. The next stage is to express these forces in quantitative form, i.e., to develop appropriate measuring instruments so that they can be applied feasibly in day to day market research enquiries. This stage is especially important for psychological variables, whether specific consumer requirements or more general attitudes. Ways of translating attitude dimensions into sets of statements are discussed in chapter 4. Techniques for analysing the responses to these statements, such as factor analysis, are described in chapter 13 and by the author[7]. Amongst the issues discussed in the latter is the crucial one of *how many* factors to extract from a given set of items. It is pointed out that there is not necessarily a single best factor solution, and that a variety of guides are available to help the researcher to select the best number of factors for the problem in question.

The objectives at this stage are basically three-fold. To:

(a) confirm or modify the nature and number of consumer characteristics already hypothesized;
(b) clarify the meaning of each characteristic in terms of the statements that link together in practice, and also of those that do not;
(c) produce subsets of statements that will serve as measuring instruments for each characteristic.

Measurement problems are not, of course, confined to psychological variables. Concepts such as income and life-cycle, or behaviour in relation to 'prestige products' and 'socially embarrassing' activities, may all involve the creation of special questions and indicies. To give just two illustrations of cases where factor analysis helped to clarify the picture originally provided by qualitative exploration. The first is from a study of the confectionery market, carried out several years ago, where twelve general attitude dimensions had been indicated by the qualitative research, and where sets of statements had been derived for each dimension. There were some 80 statements in all, to which a representative sample of 300 adults responded on a five-point agree/disagree scale. The twelve dimensions were labelled:

(a) sweet-toothedness;
(b) weight consciousness;
(c) conservatism;
(d) extravagance;
(e) compulsive eating;
(f) activity;
(g) gregariousness;
(h) preoccupation with personal appearance;
(i) social self-consciousness;
(j) impatience/impulsiveness;

(k) self-indulgence;
(l) ability to plan ahead.

Responses to the 80 statements were factor analysed. A final solution of eight attitude dimensions was arrived at, comprising 40 statements in total. Basically, the first six dimensions listed above were confirmed. Several of the second six, however, were shown to merge with other dimensions, to produce the following picture:

(a) sweet-toothedness;
(b) weight consciousness;
(c) conservatism;
(d) extravagance;
(e) compulsive eating;
(f) activity;
(g) self-organization;
(h) self-consciousness.

This picture was confirmed in a further factor analysis in a follow-up stage involving a sample of 2000 adults. As will be shown later, the eight dimensions helped to define important market segments.

The second illustration is from a study of general attitudes towards thrift. Initial qualitative exploration had suggested one broad dimension. Twelve statements were drawn up. Factor analysis of these revealed two separate dimensions, namely economy-mindedness and bargain-seeking. Further qualitative research carried out on high and low scorers on each of these two scales indicated that up to five separate attitudes were involved, namely economy-mindedness, extravagance, quality-consciousness, bargain-seeking and price-consciousness. Appropriate statements were derived for each dimension. Factor analysis confirmed the picture but indicated that bargain-seeking and price-consciousness were so closely related as to be scarcely worth separating in practice.

This picture has been confirmed in subsequent factor analyses, and the four separate attitudes to economy have played a valuable part in many segmentation projects.

Stage 4. Defining Target Groups. This stage provides the culmination of the previous three. Having identified the seemingly most relevant variables in the product field, and having developed new measuring instruments where necessary, the objective is now to pinpoint target groups on whom to concentrate maximum marketing effort. A search is made for subgroups of consumers who are as similar as possible to each other in terms of important characteristics, and who are, in the same respects, as different as possible from consumers in other subgroups. The techniques employed here have undergone radical development in recent years, and will undoubtedly advance still further in the future. At the risk of oversimplification, it is

356

possible to distinguish four main historical phases of development in this area:

(a) simple cross-tabulations;
(b) regression-type techniques;
(c) sequential dichotomization;
(d) cluster analysis.

In the first, researchers simply examined cross-tabulations between pairs of variables, e.g., the tendency to go on a packaged holiday to Europe would be analysed separately by age, social class, income, adventurousness, and so on. This approach is most appropriate when only a few variables are being analysed. Take the position in the floor polish market eight years ago. There were two main product types: wax polish, a long-established product which, amongst other characteristics, demanded considerable effort on the part of the user; liquid, no-rub polish, a relative newcomer, and very much a labour-saving product. Over the past few years, wax polish had been on the decline, and liquid on the ascendancy.

The client had a brand in each type. He wondered whether the position of his wax brand might be improved by giving it more of the characteristics of a no-rub polish. No help had come from analyses by demographic variables, which failed to show any differentiation between buyers of the two types. However, a scale measuring the extent to which women are traditional or modern minded in their approach to housework was developed specially for this market. As shown in Fig. 14.1 this scale neatly segmented the market,

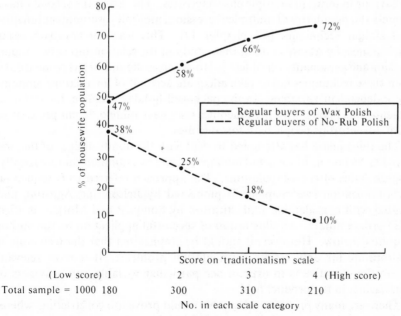

Fig. 14.1. Score on traditionalism scale.

357

clearly discriminating between buyers of the two types of polish. In the light of further analyses of the traditionalism scale, the client reversed the previous policy decision for his wax brand. Instead, through changes in both product characteristics, e.g., perfume and advertising, he further emphasized its current characteristics. Likewise, he re-emphasized the labour-saving and other characteristics of his liquid brand. The wax brand subsequently increased its share, and maintained its sales volume despite the continuing decline of this market, and the liquid brand improved its share in the other market, which continued to expand. Moreover, an attempt by a competitor to launch a brand combining the characteristics of the two product types was a failure.

Cross-tabulations run into difficulties when several segmentation criteria are important. Take the packaged holiday case referred to earlier. Let us assume that there was a marked positive relationship with adventurousness and income. An inference might then be made about the existence of a target group for this kind of holiday amongst, say, highly adventurous people with a high level of income. The inference is, however, invalid. It can only be made through carrying out a cross-tabulation, with the two characteristics interlaced; and there is, of course, for practical reasons, a strict upper limit to the number of such cross-tabulations that are feasible, especially when three or more variables appear to be relevant.

There has, however, been a growing awareness that consumer behaviour is determined by a multiplicity of factors, some combining to precipitate or reinforce it, others to deter it and, consequently, of the need to analyse behaviour in terms of multiple characteristics. This led to the second phase, namely the popularity of multiple regression, multiple discriminant function and similar techniques (see chapter 13). This was the approach used, for instance, by Massy et al, in their study of the relationship between purchasing and personality variables[16]. However, as the author has pointed out[7], even these techniques fail to take adequate account of interactions amongst the independent variables. In the packaged holiday example, for instance, adventurous people with high incomes may have quite different preferences from adventurous people with low incomes.

The third phase has attempted to deal with the disadvantages of the first two, i.e., by taking into account interaction, and by examining 'automatically' a large series of cross-tabulations. The approach referred to is sequential dichotomization (see chapter 13) pioneered by Belson and Agostini, and treated with considerable sophistication by Sonquist and Morgan in their AID programme[22]. An illustration of successful application by the author is quoted below. However, it should be emphasized that the technique is appropriate for only certain segmentation problems. It is most relevant where the objective is to explain one particular variable, say heaviness of purchasing, in the product field.

There are many problems where this would prove too constricting, where, for instance, the objective is to examine the basic need structure in the market, or to define target groups from amongst the most important consumer characteristics, *without* gearing these groups to one particular variable. Here the collection of techniques known as cluster or profile analysis (see chapter 13) are more relevant. These constitute the fourth phase of development and have, in fact, become the most popular current type of methodology in market segmentation.

The search for target groups may well be carried out on the data collected at stage 3, i.e., where a sample of between 150 to 300 respondents will be interviewed with the main purpose of developing attitude scales, etc. It is, however, more customary to use a large and fully representative sample. The size and nature of the sample will be determined by the sorts of consideration discussed in chapter 3.

Let us assume, for simplicity, that the data collected on our full-scale sample is of five kinds:

(a) demographics;
(b) specific consumer needs in the product field;
(c) specific attitudes to the various brands in the market, i.e., brand image data;
(d) more general values and attitudes;
(e) consumer behaviour such as brand purchasing and usage.

In the light of the above, it is unlikely that cross-tabulations or regression techniques will be used, at least initally, but a decision will have to be made between sequential dichotomization and cluster analysis.

An instance where the former method seemed more appropriate was in the confectionery project referred to at stage 2. The main marketing problem posed had been to provide a description of current purchasing in the product field, with a view to guiding strategies for reinforcing existing buyers, and suggesting ideas for new product development. The sample of 2000 respondents was roughly divided into two equal halves on the basis of heaviness of purchasing in the field. An AID analysis was run, using all independent variables considered relevant. Ten clear subgroups of consumers were identified. Only three will be described here. The first, which contained 12 per cent of the sample, contained 85 per cent heavy buyers and 15 per cent light buyers, compared with 50–50 in the total sample. It was defined in terms of four main characteristics:

(a) sweet-toothedness;
(b) low conservatism;
(c) highly compulsive eaters;
(d) D.E. social class.

It portrayed the typical buyer of the product in question and was used by marketing and advertising men to reinforce current purchasing. The group turned out to have distinguishing habits of buying the product at certain types of outlet, a finding which guided distribution policy.

By contrast, a second group, consisting of 11 per cent of the sample, had a very low propensity to purchase, namely 21–79. The defining characteristics of this group—low sweet-toothedness, low activity, older respondents without children—indicated that it was unlikely to respond to marketing action, and should, therefore, not be given special attention.

Particularly interesting was a third group, comprising 20 per cent of the total sample, which had a buying propensity of 55–45. Some of the characteristics of this group, e.g., their low sweet-toothedness, strongly deterred them from purchasing; other characteristics, e.g., the fact that that they were predominantly young married couples with children, and of D.E. social class, were factors which might be expected to encourage purchase. This was a group sufficiently large to be of interest from the marketing point of view; and analysis of their requirements guided the development of a totally new confectionery product which among its other characteristics, was designed to be less sweet than other variants in this sector of the product field.

For most segmentation problems, however, cluster analysis is the most appropriate means of treating the data, at least initially. A key decision to be made then concerns which variables should be included in the cluster analysis itself, and which should be used subsequently in building up profiles of the groups obtained. Various positions have been adopted by different researchers.

One extreme approach is to cluster respondents in terms of all available data, including behavioural variables and attitudes towards brands. This approach, although comprehensive, may lead to difficulties in interpretation: the groups produced may be something of a hotchpotch, rather than clearly delineated descriptions of people. The second extreme involves clustering respondents only on data directly representing specific consumer needs. This has the advantage of clarity and precision, but may often be too limited.

Several years of experience with cluster analysis suggest that it is difficult to lay down hard and fast rules. There is no single, absolute way of looking at a market. In some recent segmentation projects guided by the author, data has been cluster analysed more than once, using different variables, e.g., specific needs only the first time, general attitudes the second and both sets of data the third time. On each occasion fresh and valuable light has been thrown upon the market. As always, much depends upon the purpose of the study. For instance, where the main objective is guidance concerning the *physical* development of existing products, specific consumer needs are probably most suitable; where *advertising* themes are sought, or insights for new product concepts, more general attitude variables assume greater importance.

With the above provisos, a sound general principle is to omit behavioural and brand image data from the cluster analysis, and to concentrate upon characteristics describing the consumer and his circumstances, e.g., general attitudes and values, specific needs, and demographic variables, and to

360

select any variables of this kind which exploratory work has indicated will interact with each other to influence behaviour.

A number of detailed but important methodological issues surround the choice and treatment of input data for cluster analysis. A major issue is whether the same analysis can include both continuous, e.g., general attitude, non-continuous, e.g., sex, and categorical, e.g., age data. There are theoretical grounds for assuming that the inclusion of data of such different kinds will produce distorted results; in particular, that the categorical data will swamp the remainder, and play an artificially high part in cluster formation[23]. This issue has been tested out in several studies in which cluster analyses have been run under different conditions: the results suggested that this fear is not realized in practice. Other such issues include the question of whether the variables should be allowed to be correlated, whether they should be normalized to zero mean unit variance, and whether individual items should be given different weights.

It was pointed out above, in referring to input data, that there is no unique way of looking at a market. This also applies to the number of groups that should be extracted from a cluster analysis. In fact, the various methods all allow us to inspect a *range* of cluster solutions. They either start with each individual respondent, progressively combining those who are most similar, until, say, only two groups of respondents remain; or they start with the total sample and break it down into progressively smaller subgroups. The issue of selecting the optimum set of subgroups can prove a taxing one for researchers. A number of criteria can be brought to bear on the problem. First, *size;* there is a limit to the number of groups which marketing men can seriously consider: moreover, once a cluster contains less than a certain minimum proportion of respondents, it ceases to be of marketing interest. The minimum proportion acceptable will vary with the product field; for instance, five per cent of the population of cigarette smokers is an acceptable level, whereas five per cent of the owners of dishwashers is not. Second, *homogeneity;* that is, at certain levels of generality, clusters may become too diffuse. Criteria have been suggested[24] for assessing the tightness or compactness of clusters. These can be at each level of a cluster solution. Third, *meaningfulness;* inspection of a range of cluster solutions usually leads one to reject several on grounds of interpretability. They just don't ring true; they are not describing real people. Fourth, *discrimination;* the most valuable cluster solution is generally considered to be that which discriminates consumer behaviour most sharply. This is true up to a point, but clusters which do not distinguish between current purchasing patterns may also be valuable to the extent to which they indicate sets of needs currently uncatered for, i.e., where they indicate marketing opportunity groups.

Cluster analysis provides a convenient means of describing subgroups of consumers in terms of shared characteristics. It should be borne in mind, however, that these groupings are not fixed entities with rigid boundaries.

They are relative, not absolute. Products directed at one particular group may be expected to attract sales from other adjacent groups—those which are most similar to it in terms of key characteristics. Furthermore, within a given cluster, individuals will usually vary in their strength of membership: some will be central, hard-core members; others will be more peripheral. It is not uncommon to find certain respondents who are so peripheral to all clusters that they are better removed from the analysis altogether and treated as non-classifiable. In a recent study of a specialist market, cluster analysis of the total sample proved hard to interpret, but a very clear set of groups was revealed once 25 per cent of the sample, all outliers, had been removed from the analysis.

In the context of the relativity of clusters, it should also be pointed out that cluster membership may change over time, either because the clusters themselves change, e.g., different combinations of needs become relevant, as happened to the detergent market after the launch of enzyme products; or individuals themselves may change, perhaps developing different needs with changes in their background circumstances.

Cluster analysis of consumers is a relatively recent development in market segmentation, and manufacturers are still, understandably, reluctant to allow the results of their projects to be published in detail. However, published examples are starting to appear. Heller[25] describes a project where consumers in the automobile market were grouped in terms of both relatively general attitudes:

(a) attitudes towards travel;
(b) social activities and mobility;
(c) attitudes towards highway safety;
(d) liberalism—conservatism;
(e) self-image;
(f) attitudes towards automobile buying and maintainance;
(g) driving habits and patterns.

Also, more specific consumer requirements from automobiles:

(a) styling;
(b) size;
(c) economy;
(d) driving characteristics;
(e) special features;
(f) prestige factors.

Four groupings were produced. First, a group of consumers who like to travel a lot in their car and are generally safe drivers. They take good care of their car and they are not at all economy minded. They require large cars and are not overly concerned about style, power or speed. Second, a group which does not like to travel a lot by car. They are socially active and fairly reckless, being unconcerned about safety, care of their car and conservative behaviour. They desire a car that is stylish, has power and speed. Third, a group which tends to be socially inactive, conservative and economy oriented. They are unconcerned about automotive styling, power, speed or the size of their car. Fourth, a group of drivers who are primarily interested in a conservative car that is expensive but stylish, powerful, fast and roomy. Their view of travel is neutral, they are neither socially active nor inactive and they care little about their car or about safety.

Sherak[26], quotes a detailed description of consumer segments in the American beer market, based on such variables as benefits to be found in the 'ideal' beer, e.g., quality, prestige, smoothness, youthful image, mildness, robustness, dryness; and also more general personal characteristics, e.g., gregariousness, self-consciousness, price-orientation, masculinity. Nine clusters were identified, three of which he labelled 'The Sociables', 'The Rugged Individualists' and 'Light beer drinkers'.

The definitions of groupings such as these are based in part on the variables included in the cluster analysis, in part on additional personal characteristics against which the clusters are cross-analysed, and which provide extra profile data. This data may be obtained in successive stages, as illustrated below.

Some recent research in a motor-product market clustered 1000 respondents in terms of five types of variable—general attitudes, specific needs, demographic variables, description of car, and behaviour in relation to the product in question. Nine clusters were produced. Figure 14.2 indicates

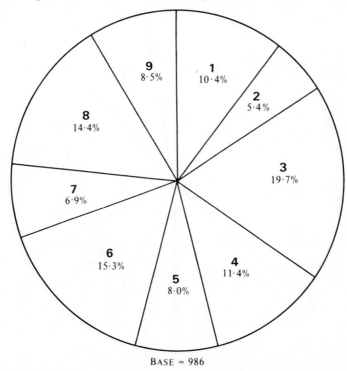

BASE = 986

Fig. 14.2. The nine clusters.

the proportion of respondents coming into each cluster. Unfortunately, it has not been possible to publish descriptions of the clusters.

The main purpose of the study was to show where the client's brands were positioned *vis-a-vis* competitive brands, in order to suggest both aggressive and defensive advertising strategies, and to indicate gaps for a new brand launch. The first cross-analysis gave brand shares for each cluster. Substantial brand discrimination was obtained (see, e.g., Figs. 14.3 and 14.4). This information in itself suggested a number of marketing and advertising strategies. Further analyses incorporating brand image data sharpened the picture of the structure of the market, including the strengths and weaknesses of the various brands within each cluster.

The next step was to attempt to determine the relative importance of the consumer needs indicated to be salient to the particular decision. It has increasingly been recognized by researchers that consumer needs are not all equally important for brand choice. Relative importance cannot be obtained directly from analysis of cluster characteristics alone. These characteristics only show the extent to which members of the cluster deviate from the general population. A technique that has been extensively employed

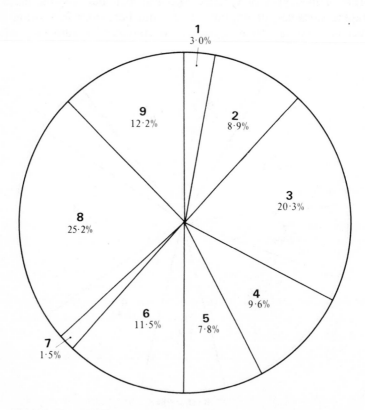

Fig. 14.3. Brand 'A' (Base = those claiming Brand 'A' as usual brand = 270).

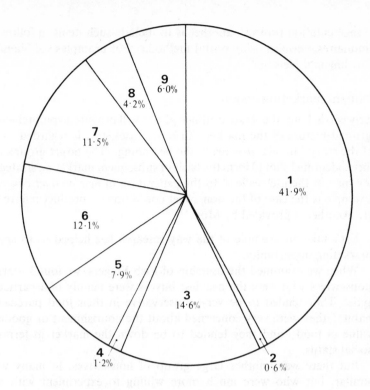

Fig. 14.4. Brand 'B' (Base = those claiming Brand 'B' as usual brand = 165).

for this purpose is the St. James Model developed in the UK by Hendrickson[27,28] (see also chapter 2). Its use in the motorist project quoted here was of considerable value in indicating which particular aspects should be given prime marketing effort within each cluster. One result of the total study was that the client's two existing brands were more clearly directed into different clusters, in each case by reinforcing the appeal to one cluster, and aiming the brand at an adjacent cluster with many similar needs. In addition, a new brand launch was aimed at two clusters in which no existing brand had established a dominant position.

The research approach outlined so far will have helped marketing men decide which clusters should be regarded as target groups. The purchasing and brand image profiles of different clusters will have played a major part in this; so will the hypotheses developed at the behavioural classification and qualitative exploration stages. An acid test, however, is the likely *responsiveness* of the various clusters to proposed marketing and advertising strategies. The importance of assessing responsiveness has been recognized by researchers for some time[29]; but the step has often been neglected in practice. One way of proceeding is to include items designed to assess consumers' reactions to specific product concepts in the main questionnaire of the segmentation project: another is to include such items in follow-up questionnaires, perhaps using postal methods. For examples see Sherak[26] and Cowling and Nelson[30].

Subsequent marketing action

Properly carried out, the stages outlined above will provide a comprehensive background picture of the market. In some cases, this is regarded as the end of the story. In fact, it is really the beginning. The target groups that have been identified should form the basis of subsequent marketing strategies.

They may in themselves lead to the generation of *new product concepts*. One example is the case of the non-sweet confectionery product referred to earlier. Another is provided by Moss[31]:

> Let's take an example of the way research has helped us to spot a marketing opportunity.
>
> When we examined the usership of Fish Fingers, we found that the housewives who were the heaviest buyers were mainly of a particular type. They tended to be very conservative in their food purchasing habits; they were very concerned about the nourishment or goodness value of food; and they tended to be down the market in terms of social status.
>
> But there was another large group of housewives, in many ways similar, but who were much more willing to experiment with new products, and were much less concerned about the nourishment value of food.
>
> To them, tastiness was all important. Compared with the first group, these people tended to be either light or non-users of Fish Fingers. The research seemed to suggest that there was an opportunity to sell the second group an entirely new and novel fish product—a product that was very tasty but concerned itself less with nourishment value. This seemed likely at first to get a high level of trial, because we would be appealing particularly to the experimentalists.

The result was the launch of Crispy Cod Fries.

In addition, these groups should now figure at the centre of research designed to test the effectiveness of marketing strategies. It is the ratings, attitudes and preferences of the target group that matter, not those of the population in general. This applies to product concept tests, product tests, advertising copy tests, brand image research, media research, and so on.

Product Segmentation

The discussion so far has concentrated on consumer segmentation, with particular reference to the identification of target groups. During recent years, however, researchers have paid increasing attention to a different, if related, concept, which has become known as product segmentation.

A paper by Barnett[10] is a useful reference. This outlines a particular methodological approach which has attained some popularity in the US and gives an account of the reasons for its development. At the same time this paper provides in itself an example of the fallacious reasoning of those who regard product segmentation as a rival or alternative to consumer segmentation.

Barnett discusses some traditional consumer segmentation criteria e.g., demographic and personality variables, points out that none of these, individually, have shown much success in brand discrimination and goes on to argue that researchers should concentrate instead on deriving product-field-specific criteria by which consumers themselves distinguish between brands and products. So far so good, with certain reservations; but he then goes on to imply that researchers should turn away from grouping consumers and should, instead, confine their efforts to grouping brands and products. Here the logic breaks down. Barnett's critique of traditional approaches is just as effectively answered by the developments in consumer segmentation outlined above, namely, that the criteria elicited should be relevant to the product field in question, and that techniques such as cluster analysis should be used to deal with the multiple influences on consumer behaviour. It is just as valuable to cluster consumers in terms of their requirements from product-field-specific variables as it is to cluster products in terms of the extent to which they are perceived to satisfy these requirements. The criticism being made here is not of the value of clustering products, which is, in fact, illustrated below, but of the extreme position exemplified by Barnett's paper. A more balanced view would concede that both consumer and product segmentation are valuable, often for different kinds of. marketing problem. The former is essential for questions about the *kind* of consumers who should be appealed to. It can throw light upon *brand positioning* through examining which brands are bought by the same types of people and can also indicate *new product opportunities* by identifying clusters of consumers whose pattern of needs is not currently being closely matched by existing products.

Product segmentation, too, can identify gaps for new product opportunities. However, its other major value is in market definition. It was pointed out earlier (p. 348) that consumers do not always perceive markets in the same way as do manufacturers. Consequently, it is important, for market planning, to establish which brands and products are seen as substitutable. Manufacturers can then check which brands or products are competing with each other and in which respects, and whether there are any sections of the market where they might usefully reposition a brand—either to attack competition, or to fill a current gap.

Turning to methodology, there are at present two main approaches to product segmentation, one used mainly in the US, the other mainly in the UK. The latter is a logical extension of traditional brand image research. The basic methodology closely resembles that used for consumer segmentation, as described above. Consumers are asked to rate a selection of brands or products along a series of double-ended scales, e.g.,

Soothes the skin . . . . . . irritates the skin

Makes you feel more feminine . . . . . . doesn't make you feel more feminine.

Preferably, the phraseology of these scales, like those used in consumer segmentation, will be based on qualitative research (stage 2 above). In many cases, individual scales will have been selected, by factor analysis or similar procedures (stage 3), as instances of underlying attitude dimensions, such as medication or cosmetic-benefit.

The simplest analysis is to compare the various brands or products along each factor, e.g., set of highly correlated scales, separately. The 'ideal' brand, say, for a particular usage occasion, may be used as a yardstick, as below.

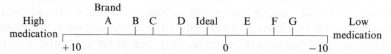

This step can provide valuable diagnostic information in its own right. It is more illuminating, however, to compare brand ratings on pairs of factors. Where possible, each pairing is taken in turn. Figure 14.5 gives an illustration. This second step portrays a series of 'contextual maps' of the product field, which provide:

(a) an indication of which brands are competitive in the sense that consumers perceive them as closely substitutable—in this case, brands B and C;

(b) market gaps, in that no brands are judged by consumers to provide this particular combination of characteristics—in this case the combination of high medication and low cosmetic benefits.

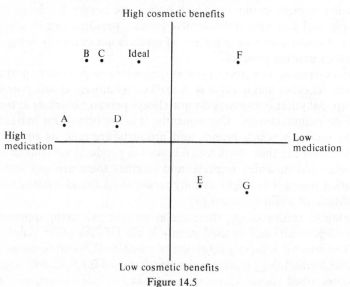

Figure 14.5

If products have been rated on a relatively small number of factors, say three or four, it is relatively easy to examine contextual maps for all possible pairs. In many projects, however, more factors will have been included; quite often more than ten. Here, it is no longer feasible to inspect all the maps. A further problem is that each pairing deals with only part of the total information. Full knowledge about both substitutability and gaps can come only from a procedure which attempts to examine data from several factors simultaneously.

The final step, therefore, is to use cluster analysis to summarize the total set of ratings for all the brands. One approach to this is through the 'Nemo' programme which deliberately searches for gaps in the total brand space[32,33]. This procedure also attempts to assess the viability of possible new products, by examining how many people each would attract, and from which products they would gain market share. Another is to base the cluster analysis on actual brand ratings. This has been carried out successfully in research guided by the writer on a number of occasions, using a cluster analysis programme[34].* An example is given below from a food market project.

The main research objective was to guide marketing and advertising planning by showing how each of the client's products fitted into the wider context of all the products competing for the housewife's attention at certain meal occasions. Some twenty products were selected as characteristic of the meal occasion in question, most were manufactured products, but others were home produced alternatives; some were essentially 'hot-served' products, others 'cold'; some were fruit-based, others savoury. Ninety scales were elicited (stage 2) and reduced to twelve factors (stage 3), using a pilot sample of 300 housewives. A sample of 1000 housewives rated the twenty products on the twelve scales. The cluster analysis progressively combined the twenty products into two main groupings. Each grouping, from the nineteen product solution to the two, was examined for its defining characteristics.

The four cluster solution was judged to be the most meaningful, and was also the most compact, statistically (see Consumer Segmentation above). One finding was that four out of the five client products came into the same cluster, a grouping which was, on the whole, assessed rather unfavourably by consumers. Several leads, in both product development and advertising terms, were obtained for repositioning two of the client's existing products, and for launching two totally new products.

The second main approach to product segmentation has, at the time of writing, been used mainly in the US. The objectives are very much the same, but the specific techniques are quite different. The 'UK approach' uses

---

* There is reason to believe that small numbers of objects, such as brands or products, are better grouped by 'clumping' rather than 'clustering' methods[35]. Experimentation on this issue is currently being carried out in market research circles.

similar methods to consumer segmentation, e.g., factor and cluster analysis; and bases the product groupings upon attribute ratings. By contrast, the 'US approach' uses multi-dimensional scaling methods, and bases product groupings upon overall judgments of similarity. The two best known variants of this approach are those of Stefflre[4] and Green[20,36]. Stefflre has produced a six-stage routine, defining what he calls a 'market structure study', which ends with the generation and evaluation of promising new products. The writings of Green and his colleagues indicate that they have explored fewer commercial problems than Stefflre; but they have experimented with a wider variety of methods. These have included 'joint-space' programmes which open up one possibility of continuing consumer and product segmentation (see below).

Despite their detailed differences, the UK and US approaches may well produce similar results in practice. However, no findings of systematic comparisons between the two have been published at the time of writing this chapter.

Linking Consumer and Product Segmentation

Like many aspects of research, consumer and product segmentation are better regarded as complementary rather than competitive. Each can throw light on a different aspect of the market. An illustration of this was provided by a recent study of the food market. The research involved the four stages of consumer segmentation described above, as well as product segmentation, in which the various brands in the market were clustered in terms of empirically derived attribute ratings. Two findings of the consumer segmentation are of particular interest. First, research failed to confirm certain strongly-held marketing convictions. It was assumed that the market was roughly divided into nourishment and economy segments, and that consumers would be grouped accordingly. Cluster analysis on specific consumer requirements failed to find any evidence of this. A number of clusters were, in fact, identified, but they had very different characteristics to those hypothesized by the marketing team; moreover, they did not show any distinctive patterns of brand usage. Second, when the cluster analysis was re-run with the addition of more general attitudes, a much clearer picture emerged. The clusters were more readily identifiable as 'real people', and showed pronounced discrimination between current brands. This illustrates the value of characteristics additional to product specific requirements, a point ignored by some researchers. The nature of these clusters, combined with the importance weights of the product attributes established by the St James Model[27], formed the basis of the re-launch of two existing client brands and stimulated thinking for two possible new brands. It is worth adding that the two re-launched brands achieved significant differences in product, pack and copy tests, within the target clusters and in terms of the attitude dimensions selected as most important.

Returning to the first point, the product segmentation did, in fact, confirm the marketing presuppositions in one respect. The twelve brands in the market grouped together into two clusters, one a mainly nourishment cluster, and the other a mainly economic one, defined in each case by distinctive attribute ratings. The point of this comparison is that the manufacturers had been successful in their policies: brands in this market were perceived in the intended ways; but their success had not had a full marketing pay-off, for the benefits conveyed did not correspond to consumer needs as revealed by the consumer segmentation analysis.

The whole area of linking consumer and product segmentation presents an important challenge to researchers. One means of attempting this is to superimpose actual and ideal brand clusters in the same spatial representation. An excellent example is given by Sherak[26]. A variety of instances can also be found in Green's publications[20,36]. Another means is to carry out product clustering *within* previously established consumer segments.

Some General Research Issues

A few comments of a more general nature before leaving this section on methodology. First, although in itself a relatively simple concept, segmentation has been the focus of a highly sophisticated series of research developments. Some of the techniques such as factor and cluster analysis are now widely used in consumer research; their strengths and weaknesses are well known. Others, such as the various 'non-metric' techniques[36], are still at a more speculative stage. Further experimentation can be expected to resolve some of the outstanding issues surrounding these methods. For the moment they are better regarded as supplements to rather than replacements for the more traditional 'metric' methods[43].

Second, this wealth of different approaches may sometimes lead to a certain feeling of arbitrariness; to a fear that quite different marketing inferences might have been drawn had other techniques been used. But, as was pointed out earlier in the chapter different techniques have different properties and underlying models, and should, strictly speaking, only be applied to problems and data which meet the assumptions of these models. See also references 7, 21 and 37. Moreover, it is often possible to cross check the results of any one technique by the use of another, e.g., by the combined use of qualitative and quantitative methods in attitude research[3,37].

Third, different marketing problems require different types of analysis techniques. Here the writer echoes the warning given by Holmes in chapter 13 about the dangers of standard packages. The marketing man should be wary of the researcher who encounters him armed with an all-purpose set of segmentation procedures.

Fourth, the very complexity of segmentation methodology can lead to a total rejection by marketing men in favour of a much more simple approach. One school of thought, for instance, confines research for new product development to the following three stages:

(a) group discussions;
(b) the development of new concepts in the light of these group discussions;
(c) an assessment, on a national sample, of the proportions of the population responding favourably to each concept.

Such an approach may sometimes be justified, for instance, if budgets are tight; but the marketing man should be aware that he is adopting a rudimentary, hit and miss approach. For his medium term strategic planning he will derive much more value from identifying consumer groups of varying potential defined by the needs they are seeking to fulfil by purchasing in the product field, and also from the richer assessment of the competitive situation which a segmentation study provides. Moreover, it is important to regard projects of the kind described in this chapter as contributing towards banks of data which can be used for re-analysis on several occasions.

A final, more specific research issue concerns the 'ideal brand' concept. This has been referred to several times in this chapter. It is widely used as an anchor point on semantic differential scales, and as an index of specific consumer requirements; for instance, as illustrated on page 368, respondents can be asked to rate not only particular brands but also 'the ideal brand' in terms say of cosmetic properties. Many researchers hold considerable misgivings about this concept. It is thought to be rather artificial and prone to ambiguity—what exactly does the respondent understand by an 'ideal' brand, something purely fanciful or something highly desirable but 'realistic'? Moreover, there are many product fields where a respondent might be expected to have several ideals, according to the mood or usage occasion: for instance, would it be helpful or meaningful to ask a woman to conceptualize her ideal dress?

In practice, however, the concept appears to work well. And in two unpublished studies known to the writer where it was compared to a more elaborate and indirect method of assessing consumer requirements, the results provided by the two methods were very similar. It should, however, only be used in contexts where it is meaningful, and care should be taken in the interview to provide a precise, operational definition to the respondent, thus minimizing dangers of ambiguity. Furthermore, it is better regarded as a reference point indicating consumer needs on specific attributes, rather than as a general concept in itself. That is, we are not asking consumers to describe their 'ideal' brand in a total sense.

Segmentation, Models and Theory

This chapter has emphasized the need for an empirical approach to market segmentation studies. It is equally important that these projects should be guided by appropriate theories and models of consumer behaviour. Discussion of these goes beyond the scope of this chapter (see, however, chapter 2). To make just two brief points. First, there is a need for a systematic assessment of the relative importance of different segmentation criteria. We are still a long way from a comprehensive method for achieving this. The St James Model[27], adaptations of Fishbein's attitude theories[30], and more recently, Causal Path Analysis[38], are illustrative of approaches with potential, although the first two are currently restricted both in the concepts they include and in the type of input data they can handle, and the potential of the third for market research problems has not yet been explored.

Second, attempts to develop appropriate models of this kind should, ideally, be guided by an understanding of consumer decision processes and of how these processes are influenced by market forces. A segmentation study can only provide a snapshot of the market at any one period of time. For a full understanding, and for effective marketing action, we require a consideration of the changes that take place over time. Some highly relevant insights can be found in the work of Nicosia[39] and Howard and Sheth[40] amongst others[44].

Conclusion

There is still considerable scope for improvement in segmentation methodology. However, in some respects, it has already outrun the practical value being derived by marketing and advertising men. This final section summarizes some problems arising from—or inhibiting—the application of this type of project.

First, there is still a basic suspicion by some marketing men of the whole segmentation philosophy. To focus upon specific target groups seems to imply a deliberate rejection of certain sections of the market. This is really a question of facing up to the issues raised earlier under 'Some Marketing Considerations'. Consumers do have different needs, and there is more to be gained from identifying and catering for these needs than from ignoring them. Moreover, as pointed out elsewhere, segmentation is not always a matter of focussing down. Certain products may start with a minority appeal, and steadily capture sales from large sections of the population. In this context, the author has already suggested 'market construction' as a more positive term from the marketing standpoint one, which does more justice to the range of marketing activity than can stem from a 'segmentation' project. Hence the title of this chapter. From the research standpoint, 'market description' or 'market structure' might be preferred to the term segmentation.

Second, some of the early segmentation studies produced disappointing results. Little discrimination was achieved at brand level, or even, at times, at product level. The picture has improved considerably with the incorporation of less restricted input data and more appropriate analysis techniques. At the same time, there are circumstances where it would be unrealistic to expect clear-cut results. For instance, consumers may be largely homogeneous in terms of determinant needs in the market; there may be considerable overlap in brand purchasing (although it must be remembered that quite different motivations may underly similar purchasing behaviour); where involvement in the product field is low purchasing may be more a matter of chance or of easily changed habit than of strongly motivated habit or conviction; and finally, there may have been little systematic marketing or advertising policy in the past in terms of either established or even hypothesised consumer needs.

Third, given the volume and complexity of segmentation research findings, a particular strain is placed upon client credibility and client-researcher relationships. Undoubtedly, it is important for marketing and advertising men to be involved in and committed to a segmentation project from the outset, to understand its possibilities and limitations, and to specify the problems they expect it to illuminate. It cannot be emphasized too often or too strongly that a client should commission a problem-solving project, not a set of techniques. Ideally, close liaison between client and researcher will be maintained throughout the project, and special attention will be given by the researcher to the ways in which the data is presented and communicated. A variety of devices can be brought to bear here[41]. Effective use can also be made of cartoons, pen-portraits, and other visual aids. The company research officer has a crucial role to play. Hill[5] provides an admirable illustration of this point, with reference to several recent applications by Birds Eye. His paper gives several valuable examples of the practical value of segmentation research.

Fourth, there is a danger of getting carried away by enthusiasm, of attempting over-fine segmentation of the population or of expecting more than is feasible given the current stage of technical development.

Fifth, media constraints still present a problem. Some marketing people feel that segmentation projects are only of value where the target groups identified have distinctive readership or viewing patterns, thus laying the foundation for differential media scheduling. This is a somewhat extreme position. Absence of distinctive media profiles does not lessen the purchasing potential of a target group, or its value in product development and copy formulation. Research on selective perception suggests that consumers will respond to information that is congruent with their needs and filter out that which is not. At the same time, media problems undoubtedly help marketing men to extract the fullest possible value from research.

The position in the UK is complicated by the dominance of television as an advertising medium. It is complicated in two ways. First, because of the nature of the activity, there is less likely to be a relationship between viewing habits and product-related characteristics than is the case with, say readership. That is to say, magazines and newspapers are themselves likely to have much more distinctive consumer profiles and these profiles are much more likely to be related to purchasing. This is especially the case with special interest products such as baby items, health foods, gardening equipment; but, second, even where distinctive and product-relevant viewing profiles can be located, it will not necessarily be considered feasible or economical to buy on a selective basis. For a fuller exposition of this issue, see chapter 23.

Discovering distinctive media profiles is complicated by the recent trends in segmentation criteria described earlier in this chapter. In the days when demographic variables formed the major criteria it was relatively easy to find corresponding media profiles, but these chances have lessened as target group definitions have become increasingly tailor-made for specific markets. However, the discovery of fundamental psychological or life-style variables, relevant to a wide range of product fields, is emerging as a strong possibility, and would open up promising avenues for media.

Sixth, there are still issues to be resolved in identifying target groups quickly and cheaply in everyday market research projects, where there is little opportunity for extensive batteries of questions. A method currently under experimentation requires respondents to allocate themselves to profiles, based on cluster analysis descriptions.

Finally, the question of change. It was pointed out in the previous section that a segmentation project produces a static picture. There is, however, a need to be aware of and to anticipate market changes. This may be helped both by the use of motivational variables as segmentation criteria, and also by reference to theories and models of buyer behaviour. The crucial point is to recognize that target group profiles are not fixed for all time. Markets evolve naturally: they may also be changed by manufacturers. Segmentation and construction projects can indicate some of the means for achieving this.

References

1. HOLMES, C. Chapter 13, WORCESTER (Ed.) *Consumer Market Research Handbook*, McGraw-Hill, 1972.
2. LUNN, J. A. Psychological Classification, *The Journal of the Market Research Society*, **8**, 3, July, 1966, pp. 161–173.
3. LUNN, J. A. Perspectives in Attitude Research, *Journal of the Market Research Society*, **11**, 3.
4. STEFFLRE, V. Market Structure Studies: New Products for Old Markets, FRANK, BASS *et al.*, (Eds.), *Applications of the Sciences in Marketing Management*, Wiley, New York, 1968.
5. HILL, P. B. Multivariate Analysis—What Payoff for the Marketing Man? *Journal of the Market Research Society*, **12**, 3, July, 1970.
6. SMITH, W. Product Differentiation and Market Segmentation as Alternative Marketing Strategies, *Journal of Marketing*, July, 1956.
7. LUNN, J. A. Market Segmentation—an Overview, AUCAMP, J. (Ed.) *The Effective Use of Market Research*, Stapel Press, 1972.
8. GREENHALGH, C. Chapter 15, WORCESTER (Ed.) *Consumer Market Research Handbook*, McGraw-Hill, 1972.
9. GOLBY, C. New Product Development, PYM, D. (Ed.) *Industrial Society*, Penguin Books, 1968.
10. BARNETT, N. L. Beyond Market Segmentation, *Harvard Business Review*, Jan.–Feb., 1969.
11. HALEY, R. I. Benefit Segmentation: a Decision-oriented Research Tool, *Journal of Marketing*, **32**, pp. 30–35, July 1968.

12. BROADBENT, S. and MASSON, P. Informant Classification in Media and Product Surveys, *Admap*, Jan., 1969.
13. AGOSTINI, J. M. New Criteria for Classifying Informants in Market Research and Media Strategy, *Admap.*, **3**, 9, 1967.
14. TWEDT, D. W. How Important to Marketing Strategy is the 'Heavy Half' Theory? *Journal of Marketing*, **28**, 1, 1964.
15. FRANK, R. E. *But the Heavy Half is Already the Heavy Half*, Paper presented to the American Marketing Association's Conference in Philadelphia, June 17–19, 1968.
16. MASSY, W. F., FRANK, R. J., and LODAHL, T. M. *Purchasing Behaviour and Personal Attributes*, University of Pennsylvania Press, Philadelphia, 1968.
17. WELLS, W. D. *Patterns of Consumer Behaviour*, Unpublished manuscript, University of Chicago, 1967.
18. BASS, F. M., PESSEMEIR, E. A., and TIGART, D. J. Complementary and Substitute Patterns of Purchasing and Use, *Journal of Advertising Research*, **9**, 2, 1969.
19. WINKLER, A. Problems in Connection with the Use of Segmentation Methods with Examples from the Field of Consumer Goods, DURAND, J. (Ed.) *Market Segmentation*, papers from the conference organized by ADETEM, Paris, March, 1969.
20. GREEN, P. E., HALBERT, M. H., and ROBINSON, P. J. Perception and Preference Mapping on the Analysis of Marketing Behaviour, ADLER, L. and CRESPI, I. (Eds.) *Attitude Research on the Rocks*, American Marketing Association, 1968.
21. LUNN, J. A. New Techniques in Consumer Research, PYM, D. (Ed.) *Industrial Society*, Penguin Books, 1968.
22. SONQUIST, J. A. and MORGAN, J. N. *The Detection of Interaction Effects*, Monograph No. 35, Survey Research Centre, University of Michigan, 1964.
23. NUNNALY, J. *Psychometric Theory*, McGraw-Hill, 1967.
24. KOGAN, M. and WALLACE, J. C. A New Coefficient for Cluster Discrimination, *Australian Journal of Psychology*, **6**, 1969.
25. HELLER, H. E. Defining Target Markets by their Attitude Profiles, ADLER, L. and CRESPI, I. (Eds.), *Attitude Research on the Rocks*, American Marketing Association, 1968.
26. SHERAK, B. A Beer Segmentation and Brand Mapping Study, DURAND, J. (Ed.) *Market Segmentation*, papers from the conference organized by ADETEM, Paris, March, 1969.
27. HENDRICKSON, A. E. *Choice Behaviour and Advertising: A Theory and Two Models*, paper read at the Admap World Advertising Workshop, Southampton, October 18–22, 1967.
28. MCDONALD, C. D. P. How to Decide between Attitude Models, *Admap*, **6**, 6.
29. FRANK, R. E. Market Segmentation Research: Findings and Implications, FRANK, BASS et al. (Eds.) *Applications of the Sciences in Marketing Management*, Wiley, New York, 1968.
30. COWLING, A. B. and NELSON, E. H. *Predicting Effects of Change*, paper given at MRS Annual Conference, Brighton.
31. MOSS, M. *A Marketing Man's View of Research*, paper given at MRS Annual Conference, Brighton, 1967.
32. MORGAN, N. and PURNELL, J. M. Isolating Openings for New Products in a Multi-dimensional Space, *Journal of the Market Research Society*, **11**, 3, pp. 245–266, 1969.
33. THORNTON, C. *Researching New Product Openings in Multi-dimensional Space*, paper given at MRS Annual Conference, 1970.
34. *The CRC Cluster Analysis Programme*, Cybernetics Research Consultants Ltd.
35. SOKAL, R. R. and SNEATH, P. H. A. *Principles of Numerical Taxonomy*, Freeman and Co., 1963.
36. GREEN, P. E. and CARMONE, F. J. Marketing Applications of Non-metric Scaling Methods, *Operational Research Quarterly*, **21**, 1970.
37. LUNN, J. A. *Attitudes and Behaviour in Consumer Research: a Re-appraisal*, Proceedings of ESOMAR Seminar on Attitude and Motivation Research, 1970.
38. CHRISTOPHER, M. G. and ELLIOTT, C. K. Causal Path Analysis in Market Research, *Journal of the Market Research Society*, **12**, 2, April, 1970.
39. NICOSIA, F. M. *Consumer Decision Processes*, Prentice-Hall, New Jersey, 1968.
40. HOWARD, J. A. and SHETH, J. N. *The Theory of Buyer Behaviour*, Wiley, New York, 1969.
41. TWIGG, J. and WOLFE, A. Problems of Communicating the Results of Market Segmentation Studies, *Journal of the Market Research Society*, **10**, 4, pp. 264–278, Oct., 1968.
42. LUNN, J. A. Consumer Classification in the 1970s. Paper to be given at ESOMAR Conference on Market Segmentation, Belgium, May 1972.

376

43. WARWICK, K. M. Statistical Data Processing. In FERBER, R. (Ed.) *Handbook of Marketing Research*, McGraw-Hill, New York, in press.
44. LUNN, J. A. *A Review of Consumer Decision Process Models*, paper given at ESOMAR Conference, Helsinki, August 1971.
45. HALEY, R. I. Beyond Benefit Segmentation, *Journal of Advertising Research*, August 1971.

15.   Research for new product development

Colin Greenhalgh

It would be convenient, not only for the purposes of this chapter but also for marketing companies generally, if new products were developed by a logical step-by-step approach—by surmounting a succession of hurdles which remained constant from product to product, so that new product development could be 'learned by rote'. The facts, of course, are quite the opposite. The majority of new products are developed by a series of fairly unordered steps, the order and the degree of attention paid to each varying from company to company and from project to project.

There are many reasons for this lack of formality. Principal amongst these are the:

(a) large contribution which is undoubtedly made by sheer creativity to most new products which have much chance of success;
(b) interaction of all the elements in the total 'marketing mix' (product, price, pack, name, advertising, etc.);
(c) cost and timescale pressures which are ever present in most competitive situations.

Nevertheless, despite the difficulty of pursuing a thoroughly logical procedure, in practice it is well to have one constantly in mind, to avoid going too far off the charted course. This chapter, therefore, is written in terms of such a formal structure, though it is recognized that, once studied, this may well often have to be amended in the face of practical difficulties.

Coverage

Many of the steps in a new product programme are ones in which market research has no part to play. Several publications are available to take the reader through all these stages[1,2,3]: we are concentrating here on the contribution of consumer research to new product development, and are only describing those other, non-research, elements to the extent to which it is necessary to put the whole into context.

It is also essentially restricted to low unit price, pre-packed and branded consumer goods (colloquially 'cheap things bought often'). In other words, even within the context of consumer goods, it excludes specific discussion of durables and services. The major contribution of market research to new product development has, so far, undoubtedly been in this area of consumer non-durables, but marketers and researchers working in the area of durables, services (and even industrial goods) will certainly find much of relevance here and will, no doubt, amend and adapt the techniques described when necessary.

Finally, the research contributions described in this chapter stop short of the market-place (whether national, test market or mini-test market) because these later stages are dealt with in chapter 19. It also precludes detailed discussion of elements of the marketing mix except the central ones of new product concepts, new products themselves and their price. This is not to say that the other necessary elements—packaging, name, advertising, etc.—are less crucial to ultimate success, but that they also are covered elsewhere, in chapters 16 and 17.

Why New Products?

It is, perhaps, worthwhile dwelling for one moment on why new product development is so important in the first place, and why so much market research effort is devoted to this particular end-use.

Mass-marketed products undoubtedly go through a life cycle[1]. The exact shape of the life cycle is irrelevant; its length is certainly very variable from product to product, but it is almost axiomatic that any product will eventually start to decline in the face of competition and changing consumer needs. Various devices can be resorted to to postpone the effects of this decline on profits, e.g., a cut in advertising or increase in price. Such devices, however, are generally self-defeating in the long run. More promising is 're-cycling', i.e., finding and promoting new uses for the product, attacking new segments of the market, or straight product improvements designed to hold up sales in the face of the inevitable life cycle; in other words, 'product development'. Even product development, however, will wear thin in the long run and profits will start to decline.

It follows that most companies need to develop new products regularly, so as to phase in their profit contributions as those on existing products start to decline. The new products which are developed may be new brands in an existing product group, they may be 'new, new products', of which the like has never been seen before, or they may be range extensions, companion brands to existing company products. Which of these they turn out to be is for the new product programme, allied with the necessary research, to determine.

It is for these reasons, though—that the changing demands of consumers, allied with the spur of competition, forces innovation on most companies—that new product development is so vitally important to the prosperity and, even, survival of most companies.

Generating New Product Concepts

While 'product concept' is a term which is often used at the initial 'ideas' stage of a new product programme, there is no universally accepted definition of what a concept is. One definition which is quoted in the literature is, 'A description in words of a product: the vocabulary employed should be non-evaluative and descriptive'[4]. This would not seem to cover all cases however. For one thing, many concepts (particularly in the non-durable consumer goods markets which we are considering here) cannot be adequately conveyed in *non-evaluative* words, if they can be conveyed in words at all. These are the concepts which depend, not so much on what the end product looks like or what it does, but on the way people feel about it. The justification for a new toilet soap, for instance, may be, 'A soap which contains an ingredient which will eliminate blemishes and recapture the skin's natural softness'. It may be that a more profitable starting-point, however, is that of, 'A soap which makes you feel young again!'

The most important characteristic of successful concepts is probably that they are based on the *consumer's* point of view, that they express what consumer benefits will be offered, what consumer needs will be satisfied, even if this means they cannot be expressed in words at all! Perhaps a fairer definition, if a definition is needed at all, would be that a concept expresses the 'essentials of the product idea—that collection of consumer benefits by which it differs from other available products and which are believed to be essential to its portrayal to enable it to achieve its desired position in its target market'.

Where do new product ideas come from?

The majority of new product ideas are generated in one or more of the following ways[3,5]. The task of consumer research is to take its appropriate place amongst these different sources:

(a) creative flair;
(b) R & D (Research & Development) breakthroughs;
(c) deliberate search procedures:
    (i) non-consumer based,
    (ii) consumer based;
(d) deliberate invention:
    (i) non-consumer based,
    (ii) consumer based.

While there is no reliable evidence on the relative effectiveness of these different sources in generating *successful* product ideas, it is likely that the continuing growth of the marketing philosophy in British industry will result in an increasing proportion of new product ideas being directly consumer based. Therefore, while all these sources will be briefly described in this section, the particular contribution of consumer research will be stressed.

Creative Flair

Marketing men, advertising agency people—particularly those in 'creative' jobs—salesmen, laboratory workers—all are likely to think of new product ideas out of the blue—'I wonder what consumers would think if we gave them . . .?' This creative flair is not, however, necessarily accidental and it can be cultivated and stimulated in various ways. One of these is deliberately to expose such people to consumers and to relevant consumer research. If a copywriter attends group discussions on an existing product group, it exposes him to the possibility that a chance remark may suggest the germ of a new idea. If an R & D scientist reads the detailed results of a product test, it increases the chances that he will spot a new way of satisfying a minority segment of the market.

Doing consumer research at all—almost any type of consumer research—exposes the lively minds of marketing, advertising and technical people to consumers' behaviour, attitudes, needs and aspirations and increases the chances of a *relevant* creative breakthrough.

R and D Breakthroughs

Another very fruitful source of new product ideas is undoubtedly investment in R & D. Sometimes, though rarely in the type of packaged consumer goods which we are considering here, these ideas are the result of basic research in the natural sciences; more often they come from the accidental or deliberate application of well-known technologies and processes in new areas.

The major contribution of consumer research is probably in keeping the R & D technologists, and those who direct their efforts, constantly aware of consumers' needs. In this way the company's R & D effort can be directed into the potentially most rewarding areas and ideas for new product breakthroughs, when they occur, will be more readily recognized.

Deliberate Searches. These are broadly of two types. Those which are:

(a) conducted amongst and about consumers and are therefore, to a greater or lesser extent, consumer research based;
(b) not amongst and about consumers.

We will take the latter (historically the more usual) first.

Non-consumer Based Searches

These differ in kind from 'flair' and 'breakthroughs', in that there is a conscious effort to go out and look for possibilities, not to wait for them to arrive 'out of the blue'. Such searches include:

(a) routine vetting of the UK market for new entrants to copy, or improve on;
(b) routine observation of the UK market for potential growth areas;
(c) perhaps more productively—similar observation of overseas markets;
(d) reading of technical periodicals and journals;
(e) regular searches of the register of patent applications;
(f) gap and spectrum analysis.

(The latter has much in common with gap analysis based on consumer attitude surveys (see below). In this context, however, it refers to a conscious search for gaps in product technology rather than in consumers' perceived image characteristics[1].)

Consumer Based Searches

Probably the cheapest and simplest search procedure amongst consumers is the regular vetting of correspondence on existing products; though, in truth, new product ideas from this source will generally be very unformed and needing astute recognition and nurturing.

In the area of more formal and *research* based attempts to find new product ideas, the first is quite straightforward. It is simply to read previous qualitative and quantitative research (usership and attitude studies, product tests, advertising tests, etc.), very comprehensively and with a very detailed eye, in a conscious attempt to look for openings via, for instance, likes and dislikes of existing products. However, the odds are that, if consumer research is to be increasingly productive in generating new product ideas, it will be through 'tailor made' studies. Four techniques are worth describing.

Qualitative Research

This involves the use of group discussions and individual depth interview, to explore consumers' behaviour, attitudes and needs in a product group or a particular need-area (see chapter 1). Being qualitative, the research can be comprehensive and reasonably exhaustive and, in this way, unsatisfied needs and aspirations can be looked for. Once found, these needs can become the starting-point for a deliberate attempt at new concept invention.

The reasons for using qualitative research are (a) that, at this stage, we are only searching for possible ideas, not to evaluate their potential, and (b) that most of the markets we shall be looking at are already highly developed—latent needs will be lurking beneath the surface, to be patiently winkled out, by discursive questioning. 'Qualitative' research, however, is not necessarily synonymous with 'small scale' research. If our marketing criteria are such that we are prepared to look for latent needs in a very small segment of the total market, then we may well have to employ substantial sample sizes, minimizing the cost of researching the interesting segment by filtering out the remainder at an early stage of the recruiting procedure. As long as we know in advance how the potentially interesting segment will be defined!

A development of qualitative research which has sometimes been used for suggesting new product ideas is 'action studies'[3]. These generally take the form of very detailed studies of consumers' behaviour in a need area of interest to the manufacturer. A panel of women, for instance, might keep a detailed diary of their use of toiletry and cosmetic products over a period or a sample of housewives might be filmed throughout a working day in their kitchens. These records can be used to draw conclusions about possible needs or, more productively, they can be used as recall aids when informants are subsequently interviewed in depth about their feelings and frustrations at each point in the 'action'. These are merely devices to increase the chances of latent needs being recognized; any other productive or cost-effective device is open to the researcher at this ideas generating stage (providing, of course, it complies with the accepted professional and ethical standards).

Quantitative, Structured Research

This is the next logical progression to the use of previous research to look for possible new product ideas. If the company has no, or inadequate, previous research, in a market or 'need-area' in which it is currently interested, then it might consider it worth its while to specially commission usership and attitude studies, product tests on existing brands and so on. Then, of course, to use these as previously described, to sift and search for new product possibilities. However, such specially commissioned research may be something of an exception and a luxury *for this basic, inventive purpose*. (It must be clearly distinguished from the very frequent use of market surveys after the product idea is available, to optimize the way in which the new product is to be marketed.) Structured consumer research may be productive of product ideas if one needs it for other purposes anyway and, obviously, it is then very cost-effective. But if one wishes to specially commission research to generate new ideas, then the odds are that qualitative research will be more productive, £ for £, than larger yet, inevitably, more limited structured research.

Gap Analysis of Existing Products

There are several variants on consumer based gap analysis[7-13]. In general, a representative sample of consumers in a broadly defined target group is interviewed about existing products in a broadly defined market. ('Broadly defined', in both cases, because the end-product of this whole search procedure may well be a concept which has the potential to attract new types of users to the product group. Such a concept may be at, or beyond, the fringe of existing products and existing consumers.) The vital information collected in these interviews is consumers' evaluation of the existing products along relevant attitudinal dimensions, i.e., their 'image' of each product (see chapter 14). Appropriate multivariate techniques are used to analyse this image data and to 'look for gaps' (see chapter 13). These gaps are empty spaces in the multi-dimensional attitude space, where no existing product represents a particular set of attitudinal characteristics as seen by a significant segment of the population covered. Such gaps in the attitude space represent potential areas for the positioning of a new product with significant appeal. They *are* only potential areas at this stage, because such a procedure inevitably throws up obvious but impractical gaps (e.g., a cheaper product than any existing brand, but using only the highest quality ingredients), and 'nonsense' gaps (an expensive product using poor quality ingredients). Such gaps are thrown up simply because no manufacturer is able (or would be foolish enough) to market such a product: their existence is no great disadvantage in the research because they can easily be eliminated on sight.

Since most consumer markets have a substantial number of relevant attitudinal dimensions, certainly if they are sufficiently broadly defined, such a gap analysis will often throw up a large number of attitudinal gaps. Each of these could, if wished, be subjected to the next (evaluation) stage of the new product programme, but the available gap analysis techniques often have built-in devices for ranking the gaps in approximate order of their potential[7,8,14] so that the least interesting can be passed over without further ado.

Market Segmentation

Market segmentation[13,15] can, perhaps, be conveniently visualized as a gap analysis of consumers, rather than a gap analysis of products. Data about the market of interest is collected from a large and representative sample of the possible target group, very much as above. There tends, however, to be a greater emphasis on descriptive information about the consumers themselves; demographic, personality, behaviour in the relevant need-area, and attitudes to the need-area itself. Appropriate multi-variate techniques enable the consumers to be clustered into groups which are homogeneous within themselves, but as different from each other as possible, in terms of the descriptive and attitudinal data collected about them. Simple tabulation of existing product-use and attitudes for each of these clusters can now help to identify significant segments of consumers who appear to have a (possibly latent) unsatisfied need. Examples are quoted in the literature; one such might be, say, 'Elderly women who worry about their health, who believe that a particular ailment can be cured and not just relieved, but also believe that existing remedies might not be entirely safe'. If, in addition, a high proportion of this hypothetical segment currently uses no proprietary medicine (or has very fragmented brand-use—another way of saying their *needs* appear not to be very effectively met by currently available products), then they would appear to present the necessary potential for a possible new product.

384

By drawing an 'Identi-kit picture' of potential market segments, such a technique clearly goes a long way to suggesting possible product concepts which might attract those segments.

Deliberate Invention. The final stage is to move from techniques which are designed to 'search' for possible openings (which a minimum of deduction must then fill) to those which actively set out to *invent* the product idea itself. As before, the more usual of these are not basically consumer based. Others, possibly insignificant at this time, do derive from consumer research based techniques.

Non-consumer Based Invention

Perhaps the three most common attempts at deliberate invention are:—

(a) asking R & D people, inside or outside the company, to 'invent something';
(b) suggestion schemes amongst employees;
(c) 'brain-storming' amongst employees and other groups.

A newer development is that of 'synectics'[16]. This is a form of high-powered brain-storming which brings together experts from several different, and apparently unrelated, disciplines and, by making them aware of the nature of the creative process, attempts to turn them into highly original inventors. Synectics has not been much used in the marketing of everyday products (whose success does not often depend on the solution of difficult technical problems) but it is a technique which may well be adapted to such areas as time goes by.

Consumer Based Invention

Getting consumers themselves to invent products is by no means easy. Attempts which have been made tend to be qualitative in nature and in scale. At their simplest they involve brain-storming in a group discussion context. All the evidence, however, is that consumers are not very productive or inventive when being handled in this way.

A few practitioners have attempted to go rather further and to apply such knowledge as we have about creative processes to ordinary consumers— even to try the full synectics approach. From their attempts, they claim to have at least learnt how to *encourage* inventiveness in consumers; for instance, Sampson[17] says that the principal lessons are:

(a) not to expect consumers to spell out potential new products in all their detail, but to get ideas to the prototype stage where they can be recognized and carried forward by experts;
(b) to allow much more time than for conventional group discussions and, even, to hold repeat sessions;
(c) to have materials and props available, rather than expecting informants to discuss too much in the abstract;

385

(d) not to hope for much *technical* inventiveness from ordinary consumers, even in a synectics environment.

Conclusions on this stage: generating concepts

These, then, are the principal sources which have generally been used to generate new product ideas. It is for the individual manufacturer to decide how comprehensive he can afford to be in setting up such facilities. In doing so, however, he should remember two things. The first is that, despite what the future may hold, the vast majority of new product ideas do not, at present, derive from specially commissioned consumer research. They tend to derive from existing research, creative flair, R & D breakthroughs and searches (more or less formal) of home and overseas markets[5]. The principal contribution of consumer research is to act as a catalyst, to prompt creativity and to help the recognition of valuable ideas when they are otherwise suggested.

The second thing is that none of the above procedures can produce a unique or 'best' new concept in a particular product area. Several of these procedures, e.g., searches, gap analysis, will almost certainly produce several different ideas. It is the principal function of the next stage to evaluate concepts and to sort the more promising from the less promising.

Evaluating and Developing New Product Concepts

When new product concepts have been generated, by whatever means, they need to be:

(a) evaluated;
(b) developed.

'Evaluation', in its turn, has two meanings. First, assuming there is more than one possible concept to pursue, putting them into a likely order of interest, so that the available management time, R & D expense and financial investment (which are never unlimited) can be devoted to the most promising ideas. Second, determining whether the best, or the only one, of these concepts deserve time and money put against them at all.

Then, these new concepts need 'developing', because no new product will be complete and optimal in every respect as it comes straight off the 'ideas production line'. It will need rounding-out: some aspects to be pronounced, others to be suppressed or amended, before it stands a good chance of success in the market-place. The marketing man will also need guidance at an early stage, about which segments of the total available market appear to offer the easiest target including, for instance, which competing products might be most profitably attacked; and which concept will best complement, rather than compete with, existing company products. Such 'diagnostic' information is all part of the development of the new product concept, before the manufacturer gets down to the serious job of

386

specifying the physical product, its packaging, advertising and other detailed elements of the marketing mix.

Initial screening

The first stage of the evaluation process has, again, little or nothing to do with consumers or consumer research. It is the stage of 'initial screening'[1,2,3,18]. Is the potential new product compatible with the company's strategic aims? Is it compatible with its financial objectives? Is it compatible with company know-how? Are there any legal constraints to its marketing? Is it compatible with plans for the sales force?, and so on. While this initial screening is a vital stage in weeding out concepts which never could lead to marketable products *for this company at this time*, it does not generally involve consumer research and is not, therefore, expanded on here.

Evaluating new product concepts

After initial screening, new product concepts are generally evaluated in the context of a 'concept test'; but, bearing in mind that what is required is often just 'a steer'—a rough idea for the marketing man whether he should recommend going on or not—consumer research can sometimes help in quicker and cheaper ways. A very simple behavioural check (perhaps two or three questions on an omnibus survey) can, maybe, demonstrate that the available market is nothing like big enough to support the potential new product at a level which would be acceptable to the manufacturer. (A typical example might be a new medicine, where a simple check might demonstrate that the number of sufferers in the market could never support a product which was compatible with the company's financial objectives.) In rejecting a potential new product on these grounds, however, it is vital to ensure that there is no question of a blinkered approach; that there is no possibility of stretching the proposed product to encompass more interesting and extensive end-uses.

Concept Testing[1,3,19,20]

Useful though a simple usership check or, even, a full usership and attitude survey into the existing market, may be in its own right—for general 'orientation' throughout the whole of the development programme—the majority of new product concepts will *not* be amenable to evaluation in such a quick and easy way; some form of concept test will generally be called for.

Concept tests provide guidance in all four of the areas listed above:

(a) which of these ideas looks most interesting?
(b) does it (do they) warrant further investment of time and money?
(c) in what ways can it (they) be further developed?
(d) which segments of the market look most interesting to aim for?

If these are the *aims* of concept testing, however, a discussion of particular *techniques* must embrace the following main headings:

(a) in what form the concepts are exposed;
(b) to whom;
(c) where;
(d) in what particular research design;
(e) what questions are asked.

How are the Concepts Exposed? The expression of the concept(s) to be tested can vary, at one extreme, from simple oral statements (sometimes tape recorded for uniformity from interview to interview) through written statements ('words on cards') and line drawings, to dummy packs and mock advertisements (press or video-taped television). If there is no heavy investment involved, or if a 'cribbed' product will do, the dummy pack might even contain a close approximation to the real product, as it is envisaged at this stage. It goes without saying that this is an ideal way to express the physical elements of the concept if it is possible.

It is widely argued (the 'holistic' argument, as opposed to the 'atomistic'[21,22]) that the saleability of a product depends so much on the *interaction* between different elements of the total marketing mix, that the nearer we can get to testing 'the whole thing' the less likely we are to make errors in predicting the success or failure of new concepts. However, carried to its logical conclusion the holistic approach introduces three major difficulties into the research design. That:

(a) any testing short of the market-place (with real advertising, real media, actual retail outlets, point-of-sale material etc.,) may produce wrong answers;
(b) component parts of the marketing mix cannot be developed and tested independently;
(c) *every* element in the marketing mix must be optimally executed before *anything* can be tested.

In other words, the holistic approach would argue that the concept itself cannot be evaluated until all the other elements of the marketing mix have been optimally developed and yet, if *anything* needs to be changed after this initial evaluation, then *everything else* might have to be changed and re-evaluated because of their interactions.

While such a thoroughgoing holistic approach is not universally accepted, there would seem to be fairly wide agreement that the diametrically opposed atomistic approach can lead to serious errors, certainly in products where the 'communication' elements are likely to play a large part. The most practical approach would seem to be to build into the concept testing stage those elements which are necessary to convey the proposed new product idea adequately (bearing in mind its possible novelty and uniqueness) and seem likely to interact significantly. And to leave out those which, on judgment, are unlikely to interact to any significant extent. This would

388

suggest that the concept test should often include:

(a) the emotional aura surrounding the product, as well as its functional claims;
(b) the creative execution up to a fairly advanced stage;
(c) its expression in the chosen main medium;
(d) and (very possibly) its proposed name, price, etc.

This would argue, in such cases, for expressing the concept in a fairly finished advertisement. In other cases, we can probably get near enough by using a mock pack alone and, in rare cases, a new product idea may be so functional that 'words on cards' will be adequate. No hard and fast rule can be laid down. Much depends on the perceived risk in missing out some elements of the marketing mix which could significantly affect consumers' evaluation of the proposed new product, against the costs and time involved in building these other elements into the initial concept testing stage.

To Whom is the Test Administered? Quite simply, the test should be administered to a representative sample of the target market. This should be defined as those consumers who are likely to have any part in affecting the purchase decision: it would probably, for instance, include the users of many day-to-day products as well as the housewife purchasers. The target market should certainly not be defined too restrictively, however. Bearing in mind that one of the objectives of most concept tests is to provide guidance on how the product might be developed, and on which segments of the market it will mostly appeal to[15], it is highly desirable to include in the sample all consumers who could be in the market for the proposed product— perhaps in an amended and improved version. (Then, of course, it becomes necessary to analyse the results by relevant characteristics of the testers—demographic, current behaviour, attitudes to this need-area, etc.—to establish the acceptability of the concept to different segments, their likes and dislikes and so on.)

Some researchers believe that in-depth, qualitative, concept testing[23] on small samples is likely to be more helpful than straightforward quantitative testing, certainly for diagnostic purposes if not for quantitative evaluation, and, indeed, there is often a strong case for both. For such tests, the participants are often recruited purposively and they might comprise, for instance, heavy users of the product group, recent brand switchers, known innovators, extreme acceptors and extreme rejectors of the new concept, without too much regard to strict representative sampling.

Where is the Test Administered? Usually this is 'in-home' (sometimes by post) but the use of video-taped commercials to express the concept often necessitates 'in-theatre' testing (very much as for pre-testing advertisements themselves)[24]. And 'in-depth' qualitative testing often implies the use of group discussions in a typical discussion room.

In What Research Design? If there is only one concept to be evaluated then there is little problem about research design: it has to be monadic (with rare exceptions (see below)). It is well to remember, however, that no known method of concept testing can forecast the absolute viability of a new product idea, i.e., whether or not it will make a profit, nor even what level of sales it is likely to achieve. Therefore, the only reliable uses of monadic test designs for *evaluative purposes* are to ask:

(a) is the idea so utterly rejected by testers that it is highly unlikely to be viable at all (even to a minority segment)? (In truth, however, this is a very rare finding for any sensible idea which has passed initial screening);
(b) how does it compare with other concepts which have also been tested monadically in the past? (This implies really comparing like with like, in a comparable research design, with comparable questions.)

If there were plenty of such comparable cases from the past which had subsequently been marketed, then we would have 'normative' data to set the latest concept against; but it is unlikely that much normative data of this type exists. Individual manufacturers may have accumulated such norms for particular product groups but, in general, it is not possible for most concept testers to refer to past data and to say, 'This new concept achieves such-and-such a score, therefore the product should sell so much'.

However, if several new product ideas are to be evaluated at the same time, then it is possible to use well-known research designs such as matched monadic tests, paired comparisons, complete ranking, etc., (see chapter 2), with a reasonable degree of confidence. It goes without saying that such tests should still be trying to compare like with reasonable like. Indeed, as with all tests, concept testing is probably on safest ground when it is trying to choose between alternative *treatments* of the same basic idea, different creative claims, different end-uses, different prices etc.[24], than between different basic ideas.

Occasionally, new concepts are tested against existing marketed products. Theoretically, this does build in the necessary point of reference to predict an approximate level of sales in the market-place, but such a procedure is obviously of very doubtful value if the existing product is known to testers; like is not, then, being compared with like. It could, however, be of real value in those rare cases where the test can be conducted amongst a universe to whom the existing product is itself new: e.g., the existing product may still be in test market, so that it can be used as a new concept but with a known level of sales, in other parts of the country.

What Questions Are Asked? The questions that are asked in a concept test, as in any piece of research, depend on the marketer's informational needs. But there are pitfalls to be avoided in thinking that concept tests are more definitive than (given our present knowledge) they can be.

For the evaluative aspects of concept tests it is certainly necessary to ask

390

one (or more) questions which will provide a measure of 'overall acceptability', an index of saleability. Such questions can range from simple rating questions, 'How would you describe this product: excellent/very good/good/?'; through propensity to purchase, 'How likely are you to buy this product at 15p?'; to mock purchasing situations, 'Would you like to buy a pack for 15p?' A danger to avoid, however, is that of rejecting the concept because of the stated price at which it was put into the test. Price is, after all, one element of the marketing mix and the proposed new product may well be marketable at other prices, something which could be tested by putting alternative prices into the test.

The most important point about such questions, even those of a mock purchase nature, is that they cannot be used blithely to predict sales. Any test is a highly artificial, heightened situation and quite unlike real life. Therefore, their major use must be for comparative purposes and, for this, they should be as comparable as possible from test to test within a given product group.

In the case of straightforward comparative testing, particularly paired comparisons, rankings, etc., the problem of meaningful questions is eased. Any sensible questioning technique would probably be acceptable, e.g., 'Which of these products would you be most interested in trying?', and the usual arguments for using the most *discriminating* questions would apply.

The diagnostic questions which can be asked in a concept test are of almost infinite variety. Standard questionnaires have much in common with those of advertisement testing, i.e., in studying:

(a) comprehension of the new concept;
(b) perception of its attributes (particularly its differences from existing products);
(c) its believability (as a possible new product);
(d) its perceived advantages and disadvantages, again with particular reference to existing products;
(e) its ratings on relevant specific attribute scales, to establish its strong and weak points;
(f) what situations it might be used in;
(g) how often/much at a time;
(h) which existing products it might replace.

One would say that it is in these *diagnostic* areas that qualitative concept testing mainly comes into its own and ingenious techniques are often used for learning how best to develop the new product idea. A typical example is 'word-of-mouth chains'[23] in which successive informants pass on the idea to each other in their own words, and discuss it together, their conversations being tape-recorded and subsequently analysed. This is sometimes found to provide new insights into the most promising appeals of the potential new product. And, of course, if this diagnostic evidence is to be used constructively to *develop* the new concept, it must be ploughed back and be re-evaluated. Quite often, this results in a to-and-fro procedure—test, evaluate, diagnose, develop, re-test—with the marketing man 'carrying on a dialogue' with his potential consumers.

Another Method of Evaluating New Product Concepts

Recent advances in concept testing[11,14] depend less on asking consumers directly what they think of the possible new concepts, and more on asking them to provide ratings relative to existing brands and, sometimes, relative to an 'ideal' product. They are rated along the image dimensions which are known to be relevant in their market: indeed, such techniques are often directly derived from the gap analysis which may have invented the new concepts in the first place.

The alternative concepts are now evaluated by their nearness, in the image space, to the ideal product and/or to their distance from existing brands in the market. The number and the characteristics of the consumers they could hope to attract are deduced by the relative distance between each concept and each existing product in the image space. One particularly interesting example of such a linked invention and concept test—the invention of a new political party—has been written up by Morgan and Purnell[9].

A postscript

It is probably worthwhile to stress three final points. The first is that concept testing has never been *proved*, at least in any general sense, to provide a *valid* technique for predicting the success (even the relative success) of new product ideas. It has this, however, in common with most other techniques in the market researcher's battery in the present stage of our knowledge. Many researchers would claim that, because of the complexity of the real market-place and the interaction of content and execution (particularly in advertising) concept testing never will be completely validated.

Second, despite one or two interesting experiments in extended-use concept tests[20], current methods essentially measure 'first-time interest'. The long term success of most products undoubtedly depends on their ability to generate repeat purchase and this, in its turn, must be due to something more than simple propensity to try. Perhaps 'first-time interest' *is* highly correlated with 'long-term persuasiveness' but some evidence to this effect would be consoling.

Third, these limitations are probably well known to most users of concept tests. Generally their problem is to 'screen out' obvious failures from a wealth of possible new product concepts, certainly if they are using really productive sources for new ideas. They want to avoid putting more time and money than is absolutely necessary against too many concepts which are going to be failures anyway, no matter how well they are handled by R & D, advertising etc., and, despite the lack of evidence, they feel confident that concept testing does effectively screen out most of the real failures—even if, occasionally, a baby may be thrown away with the bathwater.

Evaluating and Developing New Products

In our idealized model of the new product process we have, at this stage, an idea (or ideas) which we believe to have potential saleability but which must be *developed* into a physical product before there is anything available to test. This first stage of development will tend to be in the laboratory, the R & D chemists, engineers, designers turning an agreed blueprint, based on the concept testing stage, into something physical.

Business analysis

This laboratory development is often an expensive process, both in terms of management time and out-of-pocket expenditure. For this reason, a full 'business analysis' is often undertaken at this stage of the programme[1,2,3]. The marketing man has the benefit of a fully developed product concept and is to turn this into a complete business proposition—forecast sales, cost of goods, advertising, selling and other marketing costs (and, therefore, anticipated profit), proposed channels for distribution, advertising strategy, etc., etc. Only on agreement of this business analysis can he expect to get top management approval to invest in physical product development.

Product Testing[1,3,25,26]

Once there is a physical product to 'evaluate' and 'develop', the almost invariable way of tackling this is by product testing. As with most types of research the exact boundaries of product testing are somewhat vaguely determined but, as a working definition, we can say that a representative sample of the target group will be exposed to the physical product under more-or-less controlled conditions, will use it, to a greater or lesser extent, under more-or-less realistic conditions, and will then express their opinions about it in a more-or-less structured way.

A great deal of what has been said of concept testing is entirely analogous here. Product testing, too, has two basically different purposes, to:

(a) evaluate;
(b) develop.

However, there *are* differences in emphasis which often affect research design. At this stage of the programme, the manufacturer will generally have focussed onto one or a very limited number of new product concepts. Everything up to this point (initial screening, concept testing, business analysis) will have served to weed out many non-runners so that projects which are still under serious consideration at this stage are probably *intended* to be put on sale (even if only in a test market).

'Evaluation', then, is generally to help decide whether or not to proceed with a project at all, rather than to compare and rank basically different products; in other words, to help to make simple go/no-go/amend decisions.

'Development' still has the purpose of rounding-out, determining the strengths and weaknesses of the prototype product, amending and adjusting its weak points and (unless the concept testing stage managed to do it exactly—which would be unusual) determining which segments of the market are best attacked. Often, too, it is aimed to provide R & D guidance as much as marketing guidance: not only to *suggest* changes in physical character- istics but to *choose* between alternatives—different strengths, flavours, perfumes, colours, shapes. The manufacturer's aim is to market the optimum combination of product attributes (compatible with manufacturing costs) and, as such, product testing is frequently a dialogue between the consumer and the R & D man, albeit via the marketing man. In summary, then, the areas in which product tests provide guidance are:

(a) does the potential new product (now in its physical form) live up to its concept, which has already been shown to be potentially saleable?;
(b) does it warrant further investment of time and money?;
(c) which of several alternative treatments is likely to be most successful?;
(d) in what ways can it be further improved?;
(e) (if there is still any doubt) which segments of the market look most interesting to aim for?

As for concept testing, discussion of particular product testing techniques must embrace the following main headings:

(a) in what form the product is exposed;
(b) to whom;
(c) with what instructions;
(d) where;
(e) in what particular research design;
(f) what questions are asked.

How are the Products Exposed? For the major purpose of evaluation, it is highly desirable that the product itself be tested in a reasonably complete form under reasonably realistic conditions. But we are really involved in the holistic *v* atomistic dilemma again—whether a product can be correctly evaluated unless it is surrounded by *all* the other elements in the total market- ing mix, including specifically the communications elements.

Again, there is no categoric solution to this dilemma, though it would still seem that a thorough-going atomistic approach could lead to serious errors in some cases, e.g., the packaging of many day-to-day products certainly contributes a great deal to their acceptability to consumers, both in practical and aesthetic terms. It is quite likely that a test product placed in an unsuitable and unpleasing package would be misleadingly assessed by testers, no matter how acceptable they found the product itself.

On the other hand, it is also true that many of the elements of the total marketing mix cannot be faithfully reproduced except in the real market-place. The only sensible solution would seem to be much as for concept testing, namely to build into the test those elements which are necessary to convey the product and its performance adequately (bearing in mind its possible novelty and uniqueness) and seem likely to interact significantly. [27]

As a broad generalization, then, the elements which it is often found necessary to put into the test include a reasonable approximation to the final packaging, and enough copy (on the package and/or contained in accompanying material) to make clear the benefits which will be claimed for the product. This copy will, of course, itself be based on the developed concept from the preceding concept testing stages. As the product itself moves from the 'functional' towards the 'emotional' e.g., from a staple food towards a luxury cosmetic, so the creative execution of the claims becomes of greater significance in expressing the product benefits. It may become necessary to execute a finished pack design, to accompany the test product with a mock advertisement, even to give it the aura of a suggested price, in order to be confident that the product has a realistic chance to 'express its point of view' in the test.

Conversely, if the communications elements become overwhelmingly important, it may be that the product itself becomes almost an irrelevancy—any competent formulation, e.g., an exact copy of an existing brand, may perform as well as any other. In extreme cases, there might even be a case for getting the communications elements right, by concept, advertisement, name and pack testing, and then going straight into the market-place without product testing at all.

A particular problem in deciding what to include in the test is whether to use the proposed brand name or not, whether to test 'blind' or 'branded'. Bearing in mind that we are considering potential new products here, and not accepted brands, it is probable that in many cases the name serves a relatively unimportant part in 'expressing' the product and has little interaction with other elements of the marketing mix, so that it is not generally essential to include it. Having said which, it is generally difficult to convey the other creative elements *without* a name. Since the name itself costs very little to develop it will frequently be included as a peg to hang the package and mock advertisements on. In some cases, indeed, judgement may suggest that the name *is* an important conditioning element in its own right and then it is essential that it be included if consumer acceptability is to be reliably assessed. The most obvious example is where the new product is an extension to an existing, familiar brand range. Perhaps the manufacturer's name is more often important in this respect than the proposed brand name itself.

Testing for 'development' purposes may result in different conclusions about how the product is exposed. For example, we may have established that a potential new product is sufficiently well evaluated to be worth putting into a test market. Before that crucial step, however, we will normally want to develop the optimum formulation including, say, finding the colour which is most consonant with our proposed gentleness claim. We *could* continue to test alternative colours accompanied with copy claims which say 'gentleness' and then establish which colour produces the highest overall acceptability of the test product. It is equally valid, however, and is often more discriminating, to test the alternative colours without any promotional claims but asking the testers (amongst other things) which they found to be most gentle.

To Whom is the Test Administered? Again, the test should be administered to a representative sample of the target market. However, it may now be possible to specify the target market in rather more specific terms; that, indeed, was probably one of the objectives of the previous concept testing stage. Care should still be taken, however, not to recruit too restrictively for fear of eliminating potential consumers who would find the product acceptable if it were amended in accordance with their opinions as expressed in the test. Testing is often to provide guidance on which segments of the market the product will appeal to most, *including* consumers who might become users if it were amended in certain ways.

Unlike concept testing, in most cases there is probably little point in testing a new product, in use, on people who are expected to be purchasers but not users, e.g., on housewives who buy for their husbands. The original concept and its presentation may well be highly relevant to such purchasers but the performance of the product *in use* probably is not (except at second-hand).

With What Test Instructions? The instructions to testers should say, simply but unambiguously, what they are expected to do with the product. Therefore, they generally embrace the essence of the instructions which will accompany the marketed product, *less* any unnecessary 'blurb' but *plus* any additional clarification for the purpose of the test itself. For instance, the marketed product may eventually say, 'Whenever you feel jaded and under the weather, a teaspoonful of delicious X, stirred into a glass of cold water, will give you that get-up-and-go feeling'. The comparable product test instructions will probably say something like, 'Use this product whenever you feel a little tired and would like a refreshing drink during the next week. Please try, in any case, to take it at least once during that time. To prepare, stir one teaspoonful into a glass of cold water'.

There is one particular trap to avoid in writing product test instructions. Testers are generally very co-operative and will try to do just what they are asked. If one of the developmental objects of the test is to encourage experimentation and provide information on different ways testers find of using the product (different end-uses, different modes of preparation) then they should be clearly invited in the instructions to experiment. For instance, in the example above, by adding statements such as, 'Stir one teaspoonful, or more or less according to taste, into a glass of cold water'; 'Use it also on other occasions when you feel like a drink'. Otherwise, the test will stand in danger of simply demonstrating that the product was used as specified in the test instructions and consumers in the real market-place will probably not feel so constrained.

For some developmental purposes, particularly for choosing the optimum treatment of one factor in the new product, a full in-use test is not always judged necessary. It may be that a 'sniff test' is adequate for choosing a perfume, a 'look-and-handle test' for choosing a shape and a 'taste test' for choosing a flavour[27]. While advising caution in the use of such truncated tests—the physical attributes of a product can interact substantially and 'snap judgements' may sometimes be misleading—such tests clearly simplify the instructions which are given to testers, simply to 'please smell this' or 'please taste this'.

The length of time over which participants in full in-use tests should be invited to use the products is, however, a problem too. The pressures are often to produce a result quickly. Against this should be set the fact that many products are used infrequently 'in real life', or take some time to use up, while opinions can and do change after continued trials. A flavour or perfume which was initially acceptable can pall after repeated exposure. Yet all the evidence is that the majority of successful products depend for their long term health on achieving adequate repeat purchase over several years. Certainly, it must be a danger to base important decisions about a potential new product on an unrealistically short test period and, if in doubt, the researcher should always veer towards extending the period rather than curtailing it, even if this means providing a supply of samples for each individual.

Where is the Test Administered?   In-use tests are almost always administered in-home, unless there is something very specific to the product which makes this inappropriate. Even products which are used out of the home (handbag cosmetics, alcoholic drinks, etc.,) are generally placed and testers re-interviewed in their homes, because this is the most efficient way to contact and re-interview a representative sample of testers.

It is not unusual, however, for in-use product tests to be conducted by post, since relatively simple questionnaires are often involved. Some organizations have standing panels specifically recruited to test products by post in this way[27]. Since the panel members get an element of practice in completing tests, and appreciate the supply of test products, response rates can be much higher than with other postal research. However, since conditioning is a latent problem with all panels, product testing panels are probably particularly well-suited for developmental purposes, choosing between alternatives etc., but should be used with caution for absolute evaluation.

Sniff, look and handle, and flavour tests are often conducted, for economy, in a 'hall test' situation, where a sample of testers is invited into a test room, e.g., a church hall, an advertisement testing theatre or a specially equipped test van, and exposed to the test on production line principles. Apart from the limited exposure to the test products in these circumstances, however, we must bear in mind that it is an artifically controlled exposure, fixed as to time of day, methods of preparation, etc., and this could possibly be a distorting influence. On the whole, such hall tests should probably be restricted to screening tests, to eliminate the obvious failures amongst a number of alternatives.

In What Research Design? Once again, we must distinguish between evaluation and development. For the former, we shall be attempting to put a measure to the likely success of a single test product. All that was said above about monadic concept tests will, therefore, apply here, and particularly the lack of normative data for projecting results to the market-place[27]. However, unless a product is really 'new, new', it can more often be tested against an existing brand. Whilst it is difficult to take an existing product and express its basic *concept* in truly 'blind' form (except in the rare case where it is still only on sale in part of the country), it is much easier to repack a competitive *product* so that this does effectively become 'blind'. Provided the product itself does not have peculiarly recognizable physical characteristics then 'like' will reasonably well be being compared with 'like' and we shall have *some* sort of benchmark against which to judge the test results.

Having settled on a suitable bench mark of this type (or more than one, if that is possible, to increase the reliability with which the results can be interpreted), then paired comparisons or complete ranking can generally be used for establishing relative preferences. Sometimes, however (see below), it is desirable or necessary to use matched monadic designs despite their lower sensitivity.

Turning to research designs for developmental purposes, simple diagnostic information—strong points, weak points, suggestions for improvement— are a natural byproduct of all test designs and are simply a function of asking relevant questions about each test product. To choose, however, between different treatments of one or more factors in the product calls for careful consideration of research design.

First, this is one of the few cases where we usually are testing like with like in most relevant respects. Even if the different treatments would be given different creative support, this can be built into the test design with supporting pack material or mock advertisements. Therefore, the relative evaluation of one variant against another probably does reliably predict relative market-place performance.

Second, paired and other side-by-side comparisons are generally more discriminating for a given research expenditure than matched monadic tests. This is the case both statistically, in the sense that sampling errors are reduced by making the comparisons within each tester rather than between sub-samples, and psychologically, in the sense that a tester can often express a preference when he would give identical scores on independent rating scales.

398

Some researchers argue that paired comparisons ought *never* to be used, because products are used monadically in real life. While this argument is important in relation to evaluation testing, it would not seem to be a particular cause for concern in development testing. Most testing of the latter type is only to determine the *direction* of preferences (which variant is most preferred, which next, etc.,) and it must be rare for the test design actually to reverse the direction of a preference [27].

Occasionally, paired comparisons do have drawbacks peculiar to the product under test or to the particular circumstances and objectives of the test. It may not be possible, for instance, at least within a sensible timescale, to test two alternatives on an equal footing. The first medicine may cure the ailment, so that there is no opportunity to test the second realistically. The first application of a cleaning product may remove the dirt for good. Even if the use of the first test product does not make the second irrelevant, it may so affect the condition of the test material that the second cannot be tested under comparable conditions. Ingenuity can sometimes overcome these difficulties, for instance by dividing the test material into two and using one product on each half. In some cases, however, there are no ingenious solutions to such problems and then a matched monadic design is inevitable.

Sometimes, too, particularly in tests which involve several elements of the 'marketing mix', the researcher will judge that there is something inherent in the alternatives to be tested which could make paired comparisons invalid. This is usually because of the danger of consumers being too 'sensitive' or too 'rational' in the test situation. As an extreme example: a 'marketing mix' test which included a statement of alternative retail prices might tempt consumers to choose the more expensive product in a paired comparison situation ('because it must be better quality') where, in a monadic situation, therefore being oblivious of the price differential, they might choose the cheaper (because, in truth, they judged it to be better value). Similar situations could arise with other elements of the marketing mix, e.g., with particular product claims which lend themselves to a degree of rationality or sensitivity on the testers' part which *would not exist* in the parallel marketing situation.

No *general* rules about this can be laid down. The researcher must be on his guard to recommend paired comparisons or complete ranking, for their greater sensitivity, where they are practicable and are not likely to distort the results, but to recommend a matched monadic design where one tester cannot sensibly use more than one test product or where a multi-product design might actually distort the results as they would relate to 'real life'.

It should go without saying that, whatever research design is chosen as appropriate for a particular test, full use should be made of the principles of experimental design (see chapter 2) to get the maximum information for a given research expenditure. If several different factors in a product are to be explored, say, colour, flavour and perfume, it is not only more cost-effective to test all the variants at once in a factorial design, but information can be obtained which might not otherwise be available. Information on the interactions between the different factors—flavour and perfume, perhaps—allows the optimum *combination* of these to be marketed and not a simple addition which might be less than optimum.

What Questions are Asked?   The form of the questionnaire for most product tests follows fairly uniform lines. There is usually a measure of overall acceptability which, in the case of monadic tests, will be similar to those used in concept testing, described earlier. Just as with concept tests, the answers to such questions cannot be used directly to predict sales. Their major use is, again, for comparative purposes, if possible against an existing brand for normative data. As before, they should be made as comparable as possible from test to test within a given product group.

Side-by-side testing—paired comparisons and ranking tests—eases the problem of designing sensitive and reliable questions and any sensible comparative questioning technique is likely to be acceptable. 'Which product did you prefer?', is probably as sensitive and valid as anything, but some researchers prefer to bring the decision nearer to the market-place by asking, for instance, 'Which of these products would you be most likely to buy for 12p?' Unless there is likely to be an *interaction* between the variants being tested and the price at which they might be sold, it seems unlikely that such a device adds anything to the validity of the test.

However, mock purchase situations are sometimes introduced further into the test design[28]. Since the long-term health of most products depends on their level of sustainable repeat purchase, an offer is made to sell another pack (or packs) of the product at the end of the in-use test. The reasoning is that the proportion of testers who do purchase will approximate to the proportion who will repeat purchase in the market place. This is an ingenious and promising use of product tests which comes very close to mini-test marketing (see chapter 19), but it has again to be admitted that there is, as yet, very little published evidence that such tests do, in fact, predict subsequent market place performance.

After appropriate overall acceptability questions, most product tests then go on to ask diagnostic questions of the type, 'Why did you prefer that product? What did you like about it? What did you think were its good points? Was there anything you disliked about it? Any other way in which it could be improved?', and so on. There will also usually be preference or ratings questions, as appropriate, on specific attributes of the test product(s), 'Which of the two products did you prefer for its flavour?', or, 'How would you rate this product for its flavour—excellent/very good, etc?'. These, too, will sometimes be followed by more specifically diagnostic questions, 'Why did you prefer that one for its flavour?'.

While these specific attribute questions can prove of great value in suggesting where to look for product improvements and even, in some cases, for determining 'the winner', like many other measures they must be treated with caution. Some effort will have to be made to attach relative importance weights to the different attributes asked about. This may have been attempted at an earlier stage of the new product programme, as part of the basic market survey, etc.[29] It may also be built-in to the product test design itself but, often, it must be based on nothing more sophisticated than asking informants about the relative importance of each attribute to them.

It is also obvious that large 'halo effects' exist in product testing. The test variant which is preferred overall will often also be preferred on every individual attribute, including those on which it does not, in fact, differ from the other variants. Various analytical devices have been tried for eliminating halo effects, e.g., simplified forms of regression analysis. But, in the present stage of our knowledge, the most defensible procedure to isolate the effects of different attributes on overall evaluation, should it be necessary, is to build the different treatments of these attributes into a factorial test design in the first place.

A different problem to do with specific attribute questions is that of semantics. It is very important to ensure, for instance, so far as possible, that the attributes described in the questionnaire mean the same thing to typical consumers as they do to R & D technologists and others. The term 'bitter', for example, clearly means different things to different people. Much has been written about the necessity for prior qualitative research into the relevant semantics and reference should be made to the relevant papers[30].

The final questions, as with concept testing, will often deal with the way consumers perceive this particular new product—what situations it might be used in, how much at a time, etc., etc. These can obviously be catered for as appropriate within each specific test.

Two final comments on product testing

What has been described so far has been, on the whole, quantitative product testing, i.e., the design of tests in which numbers can reliably be attached to the results. *Qualitative* product testing can also be very valuable. Sometimes this is conducted on independent samples of testers; sometimes on the same testers, say, those who expressed extreme favour or disfavour with the new product in a quantitative test. In either case, the test procedures are much the same, except that sample sizes are generally much smaller (for cost reasons) and the final interview is much more discursive and unstructured. Such qualitative testing can prove valuable for gaining insights into product performance which more structured tests cannot do, and for suggesting product and creative leads which might not otherwise have been forthcoming.

Sometimes, the concept testing and product testing stages are collapsed into one, by placing a test product with the sample of consumers who have just carried out the concept test. While such a procedure can save research costs it can also have limitations and potential dangers. Diagnostic leads from the concept test obviously cannot be taken into account in designing the test product itself. The converse is also true: the test product must be exposed in the context of the original 'unrefined' concept, without the benefit of any improvements in presentation which might have resulted from a prior concept test. There is everything to be said for testing a new product in the context of its claims but two separate stages of concept and product testing would seem to be both safer and more productive.

Pricing New Products

As stressed earlier, the product itself is only one element, although a vital one, in the total marketing mix. Development and testing techniques for the more important of the other elements—name, packaging, advertising—are described in chapters 16 and 17. There is one element, however, which is so vital to the whole *business proposition* that it must be considered almost as basic as the concept and the product itself; namely, its price. Indeed, so basic is price that it will almost certainly have been built into the much earlier concept testing and business analysis, because it is only by converting anticipated sales into approximate revenue that management could evaluate the whole project at that stage. However, despite the fact that an approximate unit price must have been in mind at a very early stage of the project, there will probably be a need later in the development process to refine and firm up on this price.

How is price determined?[31]

Techniques for determining an optimum retail price ahead of actual marketing are probably sketchier than for any other element of the marketing mix. (Controlled experiments to choose between a number of alternative prices can be conducted in the market-place (see chapter 19) but we are only concerned here with what can be done before actually putting the product on sale, even on a 'mini' scale.) As a result, retail prices are very often determined as a fixed mark-up on the cost of goods (or cost of sales)[3]. Such a procedure, however, though it may limit the possibility of loss, is unlikely to result in an optimally profitable price. There is certainly evidence that a 'just' price, from the consumer's point of view, has little relationship to the manufacturer's costs and, indeed, why should it when these costs are generally not known to consumers?

An Examination of the Ruling Price Structure[1]

When a new product is going into an existing market, or even into peripheral competition with existing products, its price must bear *some* relationship to competition. Exactly what relationship is up to the manufacturer to decide in the light of his marketing strategy. He may have decided, on judgement or, better still, in the light of his research into the existing market, that he wishes his new product to be seen as relatively premium-priced. Then an examination of existing brands, their retail prices and brand shares, will obviously help to set his own lower limit. (Also, clearly, vice versa if his intention is to be seen as relatively cut-price.)

Occasionally, the manufacturer may feel that the ruling price structure determines his own price exactly; perhaps all brands sell at one price and he cannot afford to be different.

Such an examination still, to some extent, begs the question because the decision, to be seen as premium-priced, cut-price or average-priced is, in itself, a pricing decision, and *marginal* differences in price can affect volume off-take and, therefore, profit significantly. Therefore, the manufacturer of a new product would usually like assistance in determining its price fairly exactly, not in the sort of broad range which an examination of the ruling price structure generally affords. What assistance, then, *can* research provide?

Propensity to Purchase

Price questions are often asked as an integral part of concept and product tests[1,3], as indicated earlier in this chapter. Generally, they are of the type, 'What do you think you would be prepared to pay for a 4 oz size of this product?', or, 'Do you think you would buy a 4 oz size of this product for 12p?'. Sometimes, too, they are asked as rating questions, 'How likely would you be to buy a 4 oz size of this product for 12p; very likely, fairly likely?' etc.

It is dangerous, however, to apply the answers to such questions, as they stand, directly to 'real life'. Consumers probably tend spontaneously to understate the price at which a new product will subsequently establish itself in the market-place; in other words, a smaller proportion tends to nominate the market price than will actually become regular purchasers at that price. Yet, perversely, when the question is asked the other way the evidence is that a much *greater* proportion tend to claim to be interested at a nominated price than ultimately do buy regularly at that price.

In order to get over these difficulties, some researchers have used actual selling situations at the end of product tests (and even at the end of concept tests) by offering to sell another pack to the tester. It has been suggested that, if appended to a realistic product test, the proportion of testers purchasing a further sample of the product at a given price may be a reasonable predictor of *repeat* purchase, which is the major determinant of off-take in the long-run[28].

What would certainly improve predictions from test situations to real life would be reliable normative data to build into an 'aiming-off' formula. While some companies and some researchers may claim to have such a formula it is safe to say that there are none generally available which have been validated for a wide variety of product groups. Predictions based on such formulae will usually need, therefore, to be treated with great caution.

Propensity to purchase questions (and mock selling situations) are probably on safer ground when they are simply intended to choose between two or more alternatives. In such cases it is obviously nonsensical to ask testers whether they would rather purchase a given product for $12\frac{1}{2}$p or 15p; matched samples faced with the alternative prices is the appropriate research design to use. Clearly, such tests are much more reliable for predicting which price is likely to sell more and which less than in attaching precise magnitudes to the difference, but even if this only eliminates some options before market testing, it may prove to be very worthwhile. It also goes without saying that the nearer the test product can be to an 'as marketed' situation (including its packaging and advertising) the more reliable such a test is likely to be, since price undoubtedly creates an 'image' of its own which may well interact with other elements in the mix.

Developments of Propensity to Purchase

Gabor and Granger[32] have suggested two developments on simple 'propensities to purchase'. In the first variant, which is said to be more relevant to completely new products, a representative sample of the target group is shown a sample of the proposed product either in illustrative, conceptual form or, better, in its physical form. Each tester is asked whether or not he would be prepared to buy at each of a range of prices, up to about nine in number, from one which is obviously too high to one which is obviously too low, asked in random order. For those prices at which he would not buy, he is also asked why; because it appears too expensive or because quality might be suspect? The summation of this data over the total sample gives the proportion prepared to buy at each discrete point within the range and, from this, appropriate pay-off calculations can be made.

In the second variant, which is said to be more relevant to a new entrant in an existing product group, each tester is asked what would be the most he would be prepared to pay, and the least, before he would begin to suspect the quality of the product. A cumulative calculation then enables the demand curve to be calculated at all points between the most and the least that any tester says he would pay.

These extensions of simple propensity to purchase do not avoid all the difficulties referred to earlier, but obviously provide more comprehensive data for choosing between all possible prices and, since they produce a continuous curve, certainly demonstrate which particular price *ought* to be optimal. They also demonstrate the sharp peaks and troughs which are typical of 'natural' and 'threshold' prices (5p, $9\frac{1}{2}$p, etc.,) and the plateaux which occur between prices. Whether or not the demand curve as it stands is truly predictive of the market-place for potential new products, there must be a strong presumption that such *patterns* have some relevance to reality, i.e., that sharp troughs should be avoided, that it is more profitable to price at the expensive end of a plateau rather than just 'over the edge', at its lower end. This, at least, may enable the manufacturer to find a localized

404

optimum price when the range has already been limited in other ways, e.g., by the cost of goods or ruling price structure.

One important limitation of all such pricing techniques must, however, be stressed. A new product with a new-style marketing mix, e.g., enzyme detergents, may on occasion markedly change consumers' expectations of, and judgements about, what constitutes a suitable price in a particular product field. The techniques referred to above tend, in the main, to provide answers based on the current market price structure, and (especially at the concept stage) do not easily cope with innovations which may upset this.

Re-Cycling [3, 27]

As indicated at the beginning of this chapter, a process which frequently goes on in parallel to new product development is the re-cycling of existing brands, i.e., the attempt to prolong their profitable life by finding new uses, attacking new segments of the market, reinforcing existing appeals or incorporating new ones, and generally combating competitive and other market changes. This may involve making product and pack improvements, using more persuasive advertising claims, altering the price and other marketing activities.

Of course, devices such as these designed to increase or maintain profits are the *constant* preoccupation of marketing men, but we are concerned here with something more than a new copy line, a revamped pack design, a revised trade price structure or increased advertising expenditure. Re-cycling, to warrant the title, implies a significant change in what is on offer *in the consumer's terms*, together with a thoroughgoing examination of all the other elements of the marketing mix to ensure that they optimize on that change, whatever it is. The really significant change, therefore, will generally be in the product itself (or, occasionally, in its packaging where this is an important element of the product) and/or in its creative claims and 'positioning'. An example of the former would be the development of instant coffees into their accelerated freeze-dried form; of the latter, the repositioning of foot-soaking salts as a general bath additive.

Similarities with new product development

Expressed in this way it is clear that re-cycling has a very great deal in common with new product development. Every product, even an accepted brand, has a 'concept': to re-cycle, it may be necessary to *generate* a new concept for the brand, to *evaluate* and *develop* this new concept, and then to *evaluate* and *develop* the product itself in the context of this concept.

The first really major difference between re-cycling and new product development, however, is that some of these stages may not be appropriate in any given case and they may, therefore, be eliminated. It may, for instance, be decided that the basic concept (and all that this implies in creative treatment) should be unaltered. What is really required is a radical product improvement. Maybe what was the 'whitest' washing powder is now only 'white' compared with its competitors—then we might go straight to the product development and product testing stages.

Maybe the product itself cannot easily, or economically, be reformulated; what is needed is that it should be repositioned. Then it will be necessary to generate, test and develop a new concept for the brand, and although the product itself will almost certainly need to be *evaluated* in the context of its proposed new concept, product development will be irrelevant.

What is needed from the marketing man and the researcher is that they think of their re-cycled brand *as though* it were a completely new project, eliminating only those stages in our idealized programme which are clearly inappropriate or unnecessary.

Branded and Blind Tests[27]

There are, however, two other major differences between re-cycling and new products. One is that, as far as the consumer is concerned, existing brands already have a wealth of associations from the full range of marketing elements which have been deployed in their support, pack, name, price, advertising, promotion, etc. Since it will be impossible to divorce the re-cycled product from these associations it will often prove not only desirable but also necessary to carry out concept and product tests in a 'branded' rather than a 'blind' form.

The principle for the researcher to remember is basically the same as that for new products. If the new element being tested—concept or product—is likely to interact with other existing elements of the marketing mix (and in this case it most often is) then these other elements should be introduced into the test. At the very least this frequently involves the introduction of the brand name because of all its prior associations.

Research Design

The third major difference is that of research design. Re-cycling of an existing brand implies that there is almost always a built-in 'norm', namely the brand as it is now. Instead, therefore, of often having great problems in evaluating the proposed new concept or new product in any absolute sense, this becomes comparatively easy; it can be evaluated against its current self. Many more of the tests in such a programme will, therefore, be paired comparisons or (in the circumstances described earlier) matched monadic tests against the current brand. Even if such a norm does not permit a prediction of absolute consumer off-take it does help in making a reasonably reliable 'more–less–or about the same' projection. Such testing does not, of course, necessarily remove the requirement also to test against competition; we will often still need to check that improvements to our own brand have gone sufficiently far to match, and preferably beat, the competitor's brand.

Companion Brands

One special case of re-cycling is that of range or variety extensions or companion products, in which increased sales and profits are derived not from the existing product (though that may well benefit in the process) but by adding new products under the umbrella of the same brand name.

Companion brand development has so much in common with completely new brands that the test programme outlined above may well be adopted in its entirety. There are, perhaps, two special considerations. In the first place, the brand name, with all its associations with the existing product, is vital. In this respect, the companion brand is in much the same position as the re-cycled product and its correct evaluation by consumers may well depend on the use of branded tests. Second, the introduction of a companion brand may well have a 'kick-back' effect—either good or bad—on the parent product. It is highly desirable to try, through research, to anticipate this effect, because of the importance of the existing product; the techniques for doing so are not appropriate to this chapter but are, indeed, very much akin to those of advertising research on existing brands.

Conclusion

The outline programme described in this chapter has been very much idealized. Apart from the fact that several important elements of the marketing mix have been left to elsewhere in this book, a new product programme will rarely be so logically pursued 'in real life'. At the simplest the whole programme will often *start* with a product—from R & D or from overseas—rather than starting with a search for product ideas. The structure of the programme can, however, easily be adapted. The important thing is to understand the two underlying functions which all of this research is designed to perform.

The first is to *understand* consumers better, in their total relationship to the proposed new product. This basic understanding, often a by-product of other research, acts as a general 'orientation' and constantly conditions the activities to do with the development of a new product, in directions which are favourable rather than unfavourable.

The second underlying function is to provide a series of checks, along the line, that all the elements of the marketing mix are satisfying the original concept, and the 'blueprint' which was derived from it, in a *consistent* way. Even if the whole research programme cannot be 'holistic', it is certainly desirable that each element is pulling in the same direction, towards the ideal specification rather than (perhaps unwittingly) away from it. In other words, a programme of research and testing acts like a compass on a strange journey, a constant source of reference that the new product is not straying too far away from its intended path.

References

1. KRAUSHAR, P. M. *New Products and Diversification*, Business Books Ltd., 1969.
2. SMITH-WARDEN LTD. *Product Assessment Decision Series*, 1968.
3. WOOD, J. F. New Product Development, *Admap*, **3**, 1–10, 1967.
4. FROST, W. A. K. *New Product Concept Research: Getting Started*, unpublished, Market Research Society Course on Concept Testing, 1968.
5. GREENHALGH, C. *Generating New Product Ideas: a Review Paper*, ESOMAR, 1971.
6. GOODYEAR, J. R. Qualitative Research Studies. In AUCAMP, J. (Ed.), *The Effective Use of Market Research*, Staples Press, 1971.
7. CLEMENS, N. J. S. and THORNTON, C. Evaluating Non-Existent Products, *Admap*, **4**, 5, 1968.
8. O'MULLOY, J. B. Research and the Development of New Products, *Admap*, **5**, 8, 1969.
9. MORGAN, N. and PURNELL, J. M. Isolating Openings for New Products, *Journal of the Market Research Society*, **11**, 3, 1969.
10. FIELD, J. G. *The Study of Preferences in Market Research*, ESOMAR, 1967.
11. ROTHMAN, L. J. and TATE, B. Research Techniques for Minority or Maniple Marketing. In *Research in Marketing*, Market Research Society, 1964.
12. STEFFLRE, V. Market Structure Studies: New Products for Old Markets. In BASS, F. *et al.* (Eds.), *Applications of the Sciences in Marketing Management*, Wiley, New York, 1968.
13. CLUNIES-ROSS, C. Different Uses of Market Segmentation. In AUCAMP, J. (Ed.), *The Effective Use of Market Research*, Staples Press, 1971.
14. THORNTON, C. *Ranking New Product Openings in Multi-Dimensional Space*, Market Research Society Conference, 1970.
15. SKELLY, F. and NELSON, E. H. Market Segmentation and New Product Development, *Scientific Business*, **4**, 13, 1966.
16. GORDON, W. J. J. *Synectics*, Harper and Row, 1961.
17. SAMPSON, P. Can Consumers Create New Products? *Journal of the Market Research Society*, **12**, 1, 1970.
18. WILSON, A. Selecting New Products for Development, *Scientific Business*, **1**, 3, 1963.
19. SHERAK, B. *Testing New Product Ideas*, ESOMAR, 1966.
20. THORNTON, C. *Concept Testing*, unpublished, University of Bradford Management Centre Course on Creating and Marketing New Products, 1969.
21. KING, S. J. How Useful is Proposition Testing? *Advertising Quarterly*, Winter 1965/66.
22. LOVELL, M. R. C., JOHNS, S., and RAMPLEY, B. The Pre-Testing of Press Advertisements, *Admap*, **4**, 3, 1968.
23. CAFFYN, J. M. *Concept Testing*, unpublished, Market Research Society Course on Research for New, New Products, 1968.
24. CAFFYN, J. M. and LOYD, A. *Predicting Effects of Brand Name and Consumer Proposition on Consumer Purchase Decisions: A Case History*, ESOMAR 1968.
25. COLLINS, M. Product Testing. In AUCAMP, J. (Ed.), *The Effective Use of Market Research*, Staples Press, 1971.
26. CLARKE, T. J. Product Testing in New Product Development, *Journal of the Market Research Society*, **9**, 3, 1967.
27. PENNY, J. C., HUNT, I. M., and TWYMAN, W. A. *Product Testing Methodology in Relation to Marketing Problems: a Review*, ESOMAR, 1971.
28. SMULIAN, P. A. *Testing the Product*, unpublished, Market Research Society Course on Research for New, New Products, 1968.
29. HENDRICKSON, A. E. *Choice Behaviour and Advertising: A Theory and Two Models* (*The St. James Model*), unpublished, Admap World Advertising Workshop, 1967.
30. KONDOS, A. and CLUNIES-ROSS, C. *Sources of Bias in Sensory Evaluations as Applied to Food and Beverages*, ESOMAR, 1966.
31. TAYLOR, B. and WILLS, G. *Pricing Strategy*, Staples Press, 1969.
32. GABOR, A. and GRANGER, G. The Pricing of New Products. In TAYLOR, B. and WILLS, G., (Eds.), *Pricing Strategy*, Staples Press, 1969.

Further Reading

ASHTON, D., GOTHAM, R., and WILLS, G. Conditions Favourable to Product Innovation, *Scientific Business*, **3**, 9, 1965.

408

AUCAMP, J. (Ed.) *The Effective Use of Market Research*, Staples Press, 1971.
Especially ROYDS (LONDON) LTD. *The Role of Research in a New Product Launch.*
BINGHAM, J. S. (Ed.) *British Cases in Marketing*, Business Books Ltd., 1969.
Especially WRIGHT, A. T. Quaker Puffed Wheat: The Re-birth of a Brand.
USHER, J. N. The Updating of Andrews.
SAMUELS, I. The Launch of Kerrygold Butter.
COOKLIN, L. Rumalade: a Cautionary Tale.
CORAM, T. (Ed.), *Cases in Marketing and Marketing Research*, Crosby, Lockwood, 1969.
Especially WILLS, G. The Reading Evening Post.
HAYHURST, R. Thomas Hall Ltd. *The Alpine Launch.*
GILES, G. B. *Case Studies in Marketing*, Macdonald and Evans, 1967.
Especially Cadbury Bros. Ltd. Cakes: A Major Diversification.
Beecham Food and Drink Division. Pie-fillings: Development and Test Market Problems.
GOLBY, C. New Product Development. In PYM, D. (Ed.), *Industrial Society: Social Sciences in Management*, Penguin Books, 1968.
LEDUC, R. *How to Launch a New Product*, Crosby, Lockwood, 1966.
McIVER, C. *Marketing*, Business Publications, 1959.
Especially Developing a New Product.
RODGER, L. W. *Marketing in a Competitive Economy*, Hutchinson, 1965.
Especially Managing the Product Planning Function.

16. Advertising research

Mark Lovell

This chapter examines research into *advertising*. Although media researchers regard much of their work as 'advertising research', media research generally is left to the next section. Anyone engaged in advertising research presupposes that there is, in fact, something about advertising that *can* be studied, and is worth studying. From time to time, in a given instance, he may question either assumption. Researchers who have limited contact with advertising research often voice these questions, critically, for various reasons.

Given the total amount of money spent on advertising, it must, logically, pay people handsomely to conduct research into it, but attempts to hold various factors under experimental control, in order to isolate the effects of advertising, prompt two lines of argument against this.

First, that a campaign should influence the consumer's mind, in the face of heavy competition for attention, is important, but we are unlikely to know *how* important it is, relative to other factors. Why not simply judge that the direction of the advertising is right, examine the expected advertising/ sales ratio to find a reasonable level of pressure, and assume that all will go more or less according to plan? Why try to calculate what may be incalculable?

Second, markets change, as to consumers, products, needs, and interests, but the advertising scene in a product field can change more quickly, more dramatically than anything else. This tends to make advertising research data *historical*. Does it do any more, then, than satisfy academic curiosity?

Advertising researchers have been known to touch the extremes of confidence and despair. Assurances have been given from time to time that a particular technique, or interpreter, has been proved beyond reasonable doubt to provide utterly reliable indications of advertising effectiveness. This has applied to pre-tests and post-tests alike, but no sooner has the new sun appeared over the horizon, than clouds of doubt have blotted it out. There is then a reaction, which can be summed up in the words by Peat and

De Vos as a statement of 'Murphy's Law': 'If something can go wrong with advertising research, it will'. Someone with a new technique, then, appears little better off than a huckster preparing bottles of cure-all medicine in his cellars.

A presentation of advertising research results can sometimes be notable for this individual feature: cynical eyebrows are raised not only at explanations of what preliminary depth interviews suggest but also at percentages indicating differences of 'shifts' based on respectably-sized samples. The terms of reference are suspect; the context of the interview is suspect; the questions are suspect; the analysis is suspect; the people, even, are suspect.

Why cannot the research world develop, agree, and validate set procedures for advertising research? Advertisers, and some advertising agencies, have often demanded this. It is good that they do so. The result is progress, up to a point. To expect a complete answer, however, is unrealistic. *Why* this should be so, is important. Formalization of advertising research is difficult because:

(a) advertising itself works in different ways—*or* achieves a range of effects with varying degrees of emphasis;
(b) the marketing context within which advertising is expected to work is itself variable—between brands and products and over time;
(c) the demands placed on advertising research vary, according to the interest of the parties concerned;
(d) the relevance of certain survey data (whether collected in a pre-test or in a campaign evaluation study) to the end results of advertising is a matter of dispute.

These factors need to be looked at separately, before proceeding to techniques.

(a) *Advertising Theory*

The case has often been put that anyone who is doing research into advertising must consider, first of all, how advertising works; i.e., he must have some theory or model in his mind, and his research activity should be consistent with that theory. It seems, on the surface, a sensible requirement.

There have been several attempts to systematize advertising theory. Step-wise models have been constructed, like these:

AIDA—Attention
Interest
Desire
Action.

What AIDA suggests is that advertising works by inducing each of these four effects in sequence.

A slightly more complex scheme was put forward by Colley in the early 'sixties';

DAGMAR = Defining Advertising Goals
for Measured Advertising
Results.

The steps up which advertising was expected to take the consumer corresponded to:

Awareness	*Comprehension*	*Conviction*	*Action*
(of existence of brand or product)	(of what the product is, and will do)	(mental preparedness to purchase)	

It seems straightforward. A consumer needs first to be made aware of the brand and what it is; then there is understanding of its advantages, its characteristics; 'conviction' is a matter of persuasion that the brand delivers these goods and that he wants them; 'action' speaks for itself.

The big problem is that step-wise models of this kind do not take time and experience into account. Various studies, particularly of buyer profile and buying pattern data, have pointed to one main finding—that much advertising effort that can be judged to be successful succeeds by virtue of marginally increasing the frequency of purchase of the brand among consumers who already have experience of it. A further finding is that attitude changes are not necessarily measurable when this advertising effect occurs. There are situations, in fact, where the progression shown in Fig. 16.1 seems to be

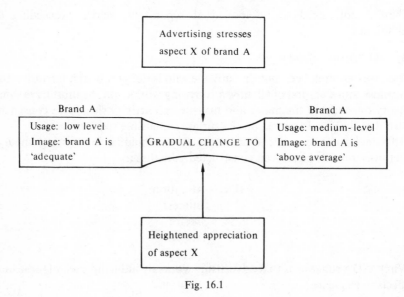

Fig. 16.1

412

more likely. In this situation, it may be very difficult to observe subtle differences in attitude, until after the increased usage has developed into a strong trend of which the consumer is conscious.

There are, of course, special cases, such as product launches, or when advertising is being put behind a near-dormant brand for the first time, that make DAGMAR seem much more realistic. Here, advertising must develop awareness, understanding of what is special about the brand, and so forth, but even then, the various stages of a DAGMAR progression may happen all at once; and the item 'conviction' in an impulse purchase will be something very elusive by contrast with a consumer durable buying situation. Time, competition and other marketing support make advertising seem even more complex in its ways than any of the above models suggest.

Time. Advertising input is rarely, if ever, separate from a stream of past and future activity. Reactions to a new campaign are conditioned by past advertising.

Competition. A competitive market means competitive advertising. One brand's claims are not judged in limbo. There is *other* advertising, *other* promotion.

Other Marketing Support. If a campaign succeeds in sales terms—how far was it the work of a banded offer, or the advertising that told people about it? (This point is expanded below.)

In our present state of knowledge, there is no reason why a particular advertising theory should be regarded as central to all or even most advertising research. There are, in fact, good reasons why only a very flexible theory could be regarded as allowing for many different cases. This makes the experienced researcher more likely to be eclectic than systematic.

(b) The Marketing Context

The point has been made above that advertising does not happen in a vacuum. Special provision may have to be made to study other influences, in parallel with the analysis of how a particular 'above the line' campaign has performed. The success or otherwise, for example, of that campaign may be affected by the extent to which promises about a reformulation of the brand are borne out by experience of it. Copy tests combined with product tests may be one means, before the event, of seeing that results are in line with expectations raised. During and after the campaign, comparisons between trialists and non-trialists may be necessary. This argues a need to choose or adapt advertising research techniques according to the circumstances of the market. Even where standard methods are used, judgement may have to be applied as to what the resulting figures mean. This applies both to the question of whether a particular score is 'good' or 'bad'—and to the problem of disentangling the elements that have produced such a score.

413

(c) *What People Demand from Advertising Research*

Sometimes the purpose of an advertising research study seems to undergo changes, as it moves from planning to presentation. This has encouraged some researchers to analyse the motives behind particular tests. Here is a list of possible reasons, any number of which may be operative when a research brief is delivered:

(a) information about advertising that is developed; about possible improvements to advertising; about the market (as a substitute for formal consumer research);

(b) justification to make sure one's judgement has been right;

(c) conformity e.g., because the managing director is expecting it to be done;

(d) litigation to settle an argument;

(e) in search of a weapon to use against the agency.

The interesting section is 'information'. It is enough to recognize the others when they occur.

Information is required by different people at different stages. In the early stages of creative development, the value of advertising research lies mainly in providing the creative team with indications of advantages and disadvantages in particular approaches and in presenting data about consumers' comments on the product field, the brand, past advertising, etc., that helps the team *create* approaches.

When finished advertising is being pre-tested, most clients will want some indication of its absolute value. The account executive may want the same. A choice may have to be made—in which case all parties will want research that is sensitive enough to discriminate between reactions to alternative advertisements. The creative team will be interested in evaluation but will usually want to know more about *why* a particular effect has been achieved.

When a campaign is being tested in the field, other specialist needs may have to be catered for. Whoever is responsible for marketing and media planning will be concerned to know what sort of response function data is available. That is to say, how many exposures to the advertising are required to get the consumer to register, understand, or buy something?

The emphasis put on special information needs in advertising research will vary according to the nature of the individuals involved, and the efficiency of the communications that connect them. Not everyone will see the same value in the data he is given. The researcher must be aware of how this affects his brief, and plan accordingly.

(d) *Relevance of Advertising Research Measures*

A great deal, still, has to be taken on trust. Commonsense suggests that, if after heavy advertising pressure, there is still no demonstrable awareness of a new brand's name, something is likely to be wrong with the creative content; but if there is moderate awareness, how much *latent* awareness is there that may be raised to the surface by sight of the product at point of sale? How good are question and answer methods at uncovering the amount and the value of material that has been registered as a result of advertising?

There is a lot of evidence, from psychologists as well as from market researchers, to suggest that the deeper you dig the more you will find. Dig deeper, then; but the more intensive the interview, the smaller are the chances that it will be administered in a standard way.

Awareness data should be treated as symptoms, not achievements in themselves. Those claiming they first learned about a newly launched brand when they saw it on display, might or might not have noticed it if advertising had not helped. A new campaign for a well-known brand may, paradoxically, remind some consumers of previous advertising, raising a question mark against figures for 'claimed' and 'proved' advertising recall alike. Irrespective of what may be the most sensitive or the fairest way to gauge awareness and recall, it has been claimed by some that neither of these measures has much relevance anyway. When advertising is very successful indeed, awareness is usually high along with most other measures. At the other extreme, one of the features of a dead loss is lack of any evidence that anyone has noticed the campaign. Between the extremes, however, recall data can mean practically anything. For a fuller exposition see Lovell and Lannon[1].

Some attempts have been made to observe what kind of measures, in pre-tests or in post-tests, have results that correlate well with sales change data in test markets, where other marketing factors can be kept more or less constant. The most sensitive and stable measures and the best predictors are those which prove to be the most useful *on average*. They will not be appropriate in every case[2].

The more that is known about question forms and interview situations, the greater the choice seems to be for the individual who is planning and interpreting a particular advertising study.

Who Does What

If standardization is suspect, the responsibility for briefing, planning, and making sure that what gets presented in the end is what people need to know, quite apart from being accurate, is all the greater. The past decade can be looked upon as one in which individual advertising research experts have evolved and who adapt and choose from the techniques available. This is a move away from a more technique-oriented era, in which advertising researchers tended to be made use of by organizations who had pet systems. It is also very different, however, from what might be called the 'age of the wizards', in the 'fifties', when advertising research was often the province of an intuitive virtuoso whose analogies were drawn from Viennese consulting rooms. The advertising researcher today knows that there are various kinds of evidence, which can be gathered in different ways, and he judges their relevance and importance according to marketing circumstances.

He can be found in four places:

(a) in an advertising agency;
(b) in a research agency;
(c) in an advertiser's research department;
(d) on his own, as an independent consultant.

The proportion on the client side (the third category) is growing, only slowly. The biggest increase has been in the fourth category. This analysis is important because it has an effect on communications, which are crucial if advertising research is to be meaningful, understood, and acted upon.

Table 16.1   *Communication in advertising research*

Advertising agency

A Research executive — is responsible for day-to-day communication with creative team. Plans internal work, to B's brief. Plans formal work jointly with D (or E); and with F (or G) as required, by agreement with D (or E).

B Creative team — asks A for help; gets answers from A, and (by arrangement) from F and G.

C Account executive — observes that communications are working. Combines with B and E to deliver brief for formal pre-tests, and post-testing.

Advertiser

D Research executive — liaises with A to ensure advertising research fits without duplication into overall research programme. Discusses with A plans and results; commissioning work from F and G; presentations to C and E.

E Brand manager — draws on D's advice for briefing input; for considering interpretation of results.

Independent research consultant

F — may be retained by A or D, either continuously or 'ad hoc'. He may do planning; perform small-scale work; provide objective assessment of large-scale work.

Research agency

G Advertising research specialist — as F; but conducts large-scale work as well.

A communications system is suggested in Table 16.1. It works, but it is expensive, in that it demands the presence of certain people whose time is valuable. It may, of course, save time and money in the long run. Alternatives can be worked out by doubling-up certain of the functions.

Problem Analysis

A careful distinction often needs to be drawn between two things:

(a) creative strategy, the effects that advertising is intended to have on the consumer;

(b) creative tactics, how the creative team intends a specific advertisement to work.

Failure to observe the differences between these two is often at the root of any frustration that follows a presentation of copy test results. It also thickens the blanket of fog that may surround the advertising component in a test market study.

416

An example of this difference is afforded by a television campaign for Cadbury's Bournville chocolate. The *strategy* included, as one of the basic advertising aims, the need to make the brand distinctive and have an individual appeal. A campaign was developed (see Fig. 16.2) in which the creative *tactic* was to develop an identity for Bournville as being reserved, 'For Adults Only'. This, arguably, would be consistent with the 'mature taste' that Bournville enthusiasts accredited it with. The campaign development stood or fell by the extent to which it could induce consumers to associate the slogan with Bournville, in an appreciative way, that reflected an acceptance of the imagery as fitting the product. Whether or not this would mean that the campaign would succeed in strategic terms is another question.

The brief for pre-testing was to examine reactions to a pilot film, to aid understanding of how strong a link between the brand and the slogan would appear after one exposure. 'Strong' here meant two things: frequency of association and interpretation of this in terms of the taste characteristic. Pre-testing suggested that the pilot film, at least, met the aim.

Research into the evaluation of the campaign had a very different brief: how far is increased consumption of Bournville associated with awareness of the slogan? Do those who include the brand more often among their confectionery purchases tend to be those who have had the greatest exposure to the advertising? . . . who regard its advertising as more distinctive? How does this group interpret the slogan? Is what they interpret relevant to them and is it appreciated? Again, the results justified the campaign and it ran a long time.

The point of the example is to underline that certain aspects of the campaign evaluation brief *could* have been put into the pre-test brief. This might have shown, for example, that, after exposure to this film, very few were prepared to regard Bournville very differently from the way they looked at it before. This is because with a well-known brand the response to advertising must be understood to be gradual. A good campaign *could* have come under suspicion; an irrelevant part of a pre-test *could* have condemned it to be jettisoned.

Pre-testing—At Different Stages

A pre-test may happen once in the development of a campaign or there may be a pre-testing programme. There may be cases where preliminary work on rough creative material is ruled out because of a conviction that the kind of advertising envisaged demands finished or near-finished treatment if it is to have any appreciable effect on the consumer. A similar case can be made out against testing at an early stage on the grounds that reactions to rough material may be misleading. The two arguments are not quite the same. When this happens, the campaign may be discussed with the advertising researcher who is required to give his views, based on other research or experience of the brand, of the campaign's likely success. This may be

Fig. 16.2
Reproduced with permission of Leo Burnett-LPE Ltd.

useful or not, depending on the people concerned: but it should be recognized that it is discussion, *not* research.

The preliminary stages of a pre-test programme are often explorations of basically different advertising approaches. The term 'concept test' is sometimes used in this context, except by those who have taken a public stand against formalized concept testing, in which case they may use other phrases to describe the same thing.

The problems of concept testing are very real. The main ones can be stated briefly. The essence of a concept may be easy to describe, logically, on a plain piece of card but it may seem very bald; it may provoke the response, 'So what?' among the same people who would react positively to an emotionally-loaded presentation of it. How, then, do you interpret the 'So what?' Any attempt to present concepts in forms that approximate to advertising, on the other hand, may lead to difficulties in disentangling response to the concept and response to the treatment. There is both the difficulty of deciding what constitutes a meaningful but undistracting illustration to the claim, and the difficulty of avoiding an interview situation where the informant has clear-cut but misguided ideas that his job is to improve advertising.

Nevertheless, many find it useful to put a rough advertising treatment in front of some consumers and analyse their reactions in order to assess the viability of an advertising platform or approach. The data is, perhaps, no different from any other advertising research data, in that it requires interpretation to sort out what influences are at work. There is a question of degree of obscurity, however: this makes it more often a matter for qualitative research, and for psychologists, than for using a pre-coded questionnaire. Disagreement among advertising researchers is often, therefore, about the value of certain people, e.g., 'Is *X really* objective?', rather than about techniques.

Some believe that concept research is of most use when the primary features of the possible campaigns are rational, rather than emotional. The point here is that the strength of an effective rational theme is more likely to be apparent despite crude representation, since it depends on logic. An emotional theme may depend on the suspension of logic, and it may only be by use of elaborate professional treatment that the right mood for this can be established. (Of course, very little advertising is *entirely* rational or *entirely* emotional.)

A second limiting point sometimes made is that valuable negative information is more likely to emerge from concept testing than any meaningful indication of the degree to which an idea may be a good one. That is to say, concept testing is allowed the credit for pointing out what probably won't work, and saying why; but sorting out the good from the average is another matter. This is the territory of opinion. Practitioners will disagree about how positive, as well as about how sensitive or accurate, concept test work can be.

Fig. 16.3A
Reproduced with permission of Leo Burnett-LPE Ltd.

MOTORWAY PETROL
gives you A1 performance on B class roads

So there you are.

Doing your Graham Hill bit along your favourite stretch of empty country road.

And screeeeeeech!

You're stuck—just here the road measures 12 feet across and that hay cart measures 10.

Well sit back and stop biting your fingernails.

Just thank your lucky stars you were smart enough to fill up with National 99. The Motorway Petrol.

You want to show that horse and cart a clean pair of heels?

Fine.

When the time comes just put your foot down. National 99 will respond immediately.

National 99 makes the most of your horsepower, at all times, at all speeds, because it has three gear-changes in it.

1st gear: Butane for smooth first-time starting.

2nd gear: Iso-Pentane for that snappy burst of acceleration to zoom you past the old horse and cart.

3rd gear: Iso-Octane for breezing your car along in the sweet sixties. For hours on end.

So, now you won't be surprised to hear that 9 out of 10 cars go better on National 99.

Whether on highways or byeways.

No other 4-star petrol gives you more octanes for your money than National 99 (some have only 97 octanes). National 99 may cost a penny or two more in the beginning.

But when you snap past that old hay cart you know you're getting better value in the end.

National 99
The Motorway Petrol

Fig. 16.3B
Reproduced with permission of Leo Burnett-LPE Ltd.

Fig. 16.3C
Reproduced with permission of Leo Burnett-LPE Ltd.

The development of an advertising campaign for National Benzole petrol is a case in point. In 1968, a new campaign was prepared with the purpose of projecting National as a big, dynamic brand, a technological leader in tune with modern idiom, having a recognizable style of its own. Any number of advertising platforms, in theory, could achieve this. In practice, the limitations imposed by the nature of the target market, by the need to avoid territory pre-empted by other brands, by the need to demonstrate consistency of tone with past advertising and by what is permissible as a claim for differentiating a petrol brand from others, are severe. The advertising concept for National needed to be new, distinctive, re-echoing past success, making desirable points, and above suspicion; all at once. The task of advertising concept research was, therefore, as much one of suggesting *how* a concept might best be developed, as *whether* it should be encouraged at all. Figure 16.3 shows three press ad layouts. These were tested in parallel with pilot film material to investigate the concept. 'National is the Motorway Petrol' ought, basically, to make an association. Was this association in which the fastest, most modern, most technically admired means of road travel was pre-empted for the brand, desirable, noteworthy and without danger? What possible aspects of the association were likely to work hardest for National?

Layout A shows an attempt to provide a technological background to the motorway claim. Layout B shows a 'human interest' approach in stressing that the 'motorway petrol' is right irrespective of the road, picking up a commonly experienced motoring situation. Layout C makes a dramatic, if imprecise announcement of the 'motorway' theme.

Consumer reactions in group discussions suggested that, despite criticism of certain aspects of motorways, motorists admired them and acknowledged their superiority and necessity, but the argument attempted in Layout A aroused suspicion. Building the campaign around one octane rating (99) was also limiting. Further concept work suggested that *any* logical approach was likely to be self-defeating. Motorists appreciated a sense of power and 'motorway performance' that appealed to them in Layout C. If they were not made to work it out, they did not query it. The attempt to widen the motorway theme in Layout B merely achieved bathos. This underlined the importance of capitalizing on the dynamic aspects of motorways, to achieve interest and meaningful association. Concessions to normality were resented.

Television commercials were created and produced with the concept research in mind. Figure 16.4 shows stills from these films, which aimed at an emotional rather than a rational declaration of the superiority of 'the Motorway Petrol'.

Subsequent research showed that the campaign had registered very strongly with the target market; and that National buyers, in particular, spoke of 'the Motorway Petrol'. This illustrates the point that concept research must be directed towards development opportunities of a concept,

Fig. 16.4

Reproduced with permission of Leo Burnett-LPE Ltd

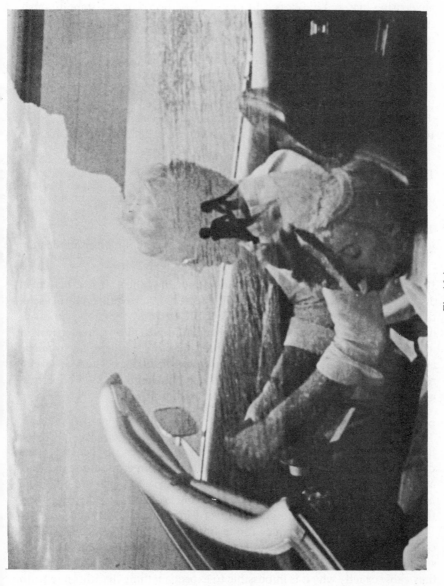

Fig. 16.4
Reproduced with permission of Leo Burnett-LPE Ltd.

in order to aid judgement about the viability of the concept itself. Putting up a sheet of paper with 'National is the Motorway Petrol' on it would have put research informants into an intolerable situation if asked to react to it.

Once a campaign theme has been established—tested or not—the advertising material developed from it may be tested in any state of finish. At this point it is worth observing that advertising researchers (as in the case of product development research) incline to either end of this spectrum:

Holistic ———————————— Atomistic

The more 'holistic' they are, the more likely they will be to:
(a) test only finished material;
(b) test campaigns, rather than individual advertisements;
(c) examine specific elements using techniques that allow breadth of expression of consumer reactions.

The more 'atomistic' they are, the more often they will:

(a) test individual advertisements, as individual queries arise, using material in any state of finish;
(b) test headlines, illustrations, other details;
(c) examine specific elements using techniques that allow precise reflection of effect of those elements in consumer reactions.

It is not necessarily *bad* to be more one than the other. It is a matter of dispute which research approach will succeed in providing more useful diagnostic data that can help improve creative work. Possibly, however, it is easier to observe cases where a holistic approach allows greater insight into the real business of advertising than it is to see where an atomistic approach has a clear advantage. Questions of detail, e.g., which of several recipes attract sufficient interest to warrant including in a food advertisement?, tend to be those at which the atomist shines.

Pre-testing Techniques

Several techniques are common to market research in general. The depth interview, group discussion, the use of structured questionnaires, are all involved in advertising research, but scarcely need separate comment here. This chapter will concentrate only on features of such basic tools that require specific attention in the advertising context.

For convenience, techniques for testing television commercials will be covered separately from press and other media. There are first, however, some considerations which apply in all cases. These are stressed, because they show exactly why it is impossible to expect anything like absolute truth from any of the techniques outlined here. Figure 16.5 shows the relationships between the actual situation—consumers (C^1) actually exposed to real advertising (S^1) in its media context (M^1), and reacting to it (R^1)—and the pre-test. Any broken line indicates a relationship that will vary in

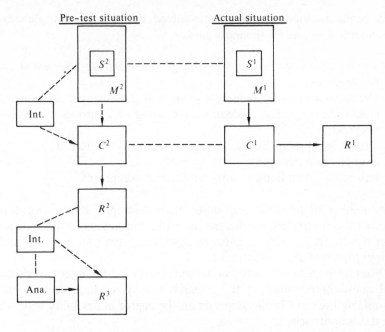

Fig. 16.5

Note: The point at issue in pre-testing is the extent to which R^3 is an aid towards calculating R^1. This figure shows the influences and possible differences, that can make the relationship between R^3 and R^1 uncertain.

C^2 is a sample selected to be representative of C^1. S^2 is advertising that may be in any state of finish. M^2 could be a theatre test, or a folder, etc... Int. (interviewer) is an important component of the exposure to test advertisements. Both Int. and Ana. (Analyst) mediate the direct response to S^2, (which is R^2) and record and/or interpret it as R^3.

closeness; a broken arrow shows that there is an influence by one factor on another, that also varies in nature and strength.

It is rather unlikely that the pre-test result will show *how* successful the advertising will prove, but what one can demand from pre-testing is direction, with a rough indication of extent—other things being equal.

Television Commercial Tests

The first problem in a television commercial test is to show the material to the pre-test informants. Arranging for the right equipment to be in the right place is not always straightforward. It is always possible to hire machinery to project 35 mm, 16 mm, or videotape films, but some apparatus is bulkier, noisier or more expensive than others. Sometimes, it makes sense to test a film in doublehead form, so that changes can be made before going to the expense of getting married prints: unless the film is put onto videotape, this can be a severe limitation on where, physically, the test can be held. It pays to plan everything *well in advance*.

Once the question of equipment is solved, the place needs to be chosen. The alternatives are, for the most part:

(a) a theatre (or large hall) in which large audiences can be exposed to the commercial;
(b) a room in a studio or agency, allowing use of permanent equipment and special features, e.g., videotape recording of a group discussion in progress;
(c) a room in a private house, to which informants are invited;
(d) a mobile unit (test van);
(e) informants' own homes, using moviematic equipment.

A number of research companies have developed systems for testing television commercials, in theatres or halls, but anyone can organize his own theatre tests, using a fieldwork agency to recruit an audience and to supply projector and projectionist.

What happens at a theatre test depends on the kind of interview situation and questions favoured by the research agency or the executive who is organizing the test. It also depends on the degree of flexibility with which the test is approached.

The sample size has an influence on what can be done. Small audiences of, say, 12 to 50 have been split up into groups, after exposure to the commercials, and separate group discussions in separate rooms conducted. Alternatively, this size of audience can be considered a 'large group', in which informants use self-completion questionnaires, and are then led by an interviewer into discussion. When there is disagreement, the interviewer can ask the informants to write down their personal views or to give a show of hands or to use Votometer machines.

Some research companies have theatre test systems in which standard questions are used nearly every time, with a number of 'slots' allowed for specific questions that refer directly to aspects of one test commercial. By analysing the results of many such tests, norms have been developed against which the scores achieved by individual test commercials can be compared. Because some types of commercial perform better than others on certain measures, and because the target market varies in the precision with which it is defined, e.g., 'analgesic users' as opposed to 'all adults', norms can be built up for product fields, or market segments, and used for comparison as well. Most companies nowadays favour having a range of standard measures within each test. Those who buy tests of this kind appreciate the fact that there is a combination of the standard and the specific. Comparison with the norms they see as supplying a perspective against which to examine individual features of the commercial.

Critics will be found to say that a norm has, in fact, little relevance. This is because the commercials for a product field may have been made for products at very different points in their life cycle, and with very different creative aims in mind, both at the strategic and the tactical level. How far any standard question can be relevant to many such aims is a matter for conjecture. The average of different commercials' scores is unlikely to be *more* relevant.

Many advertising researchers at this point in time are likely to be suspicious of any comparisons against norms, except in those cases where the question seems to measure something that coincides precisely with a creative aim and where the brand's own past commercials have contributed most of the normative data. This avoids the problem of nobody knowing when they are comparing like with like.

The search for a single measure that discriminates infallibly between commercials in terms of their overall selling effectiveness has long occupied the minds of researchers. The ground is strewn with the remains of systems that have been promoted on this basis. There is no reason whatever why such a measure should exist anyway; the problems of relating R^3 to R^1 (see Fig. 16.5) suggest that evaluation must be complex, and must be relative to a specific advertising context.

One alternative to standard questions for quantified pre-tests has been to make use of brand image batteries. This can mean administering attitude scales before and after exposure to the commercial. The scales may be established in advance, separately, for each product field (sometimes for each brand) as being those which are critical for choice between brands. Comparison between the rating scales before and after exposure can be both evaluative and diagnostic. Objections to this practice centre on the question of how attitude formation *really* happens. Attitudes to well-established brands, in particular, are unlikely to change after one 30 second commercial. When informants react to scales the second time round, they may mislead by trying to be helpful.

Brand image questions can be useful in pre-tests, more so for lesser known brands, but comparison ought to be between measures taken on separate, matched samples, which is expensive.

Many of the measures used in theatre tests are dependent on recall; or on informants' verbalized explanations of what has been shown to them; e.g.: 'What did the advertisement say about brand A?' or, 'What was the main point that the advertisement was trying to get across?'

Answers to this kind of question certainly have a significance, but one which varies with the advertisement being tested and which requires interpretation. Recall *as such* has been shown to bear little relationship to advertising success, but the *kind* of recall may be important. Such questions are dependent, to some extent, on informants' ability to verbalize their impressions. Some people are more articulate than others, or more imaginative. The nature of the target market, and samples drawn from it, obviously affects the answers that result; but so does the nature of the advertisements. Jingles, slogans, with obvious meanings, are easily repeatable, but consumers may well be deriving the desired information and emotional colour from a television commercial that lacks these recall aids without being able to put these into the neat, elegant language of the creative *rationale*.

Several techniques have been developed to avoid this kind of problem. In one of these, informants are asked to note down what were the main thoughts that occurred to them while they saw each separate section of a commercial. Analysis shows whether the thought processes that the creative team imagined would be set in motion were, in fact, forthcoming. Supplementary questions check on whether informants agree that they were given a particular communication, or not. The technique involves showing the commercials in small 'reminder' sections, as well as in their complete form. This yields a mass of diagnostic data, but criticisms are made that the way of showing commercials in pieces is so unnatural that reactions to them among the audience are suspect. In a sense, this is a development of a very simple research situation, whereby spontaneous reactions to a commercial shown to a small audience are noted, probed and analysed in detail.

Some theatre test operators have maintained that the large screen required in most theatres gives a false impression of how a commercial will appear on most people's television screens. They have divided large rooms into sections, each served by television sets with normal size screens. There is no published data on this point, but theoretically, a close-up of, say, an eating shot on a large screen might detract from the appeal of a food commercial. Occasionally minor details that are unobtrusive on a small screen seem to make a stronger impression on a large one.

While colour television is still very restricted, the use of colour in television commercial tests runs the risk of making the fact of colour more impressive than the point of the advertisement. In time this will, no doubt, change.

Theatre tests organized for quantified research have been criticized for the unrepresentativeness of the samples who appear there. A considerable proportion, varying according to incentive, of those who are invited refuse to come. An extension of this point is that those people who *do* attend may be rather unsociable people, who ordinarily have little evening life. The kind of products and commercials that appeal to them may be different than if a strict probability sample is involved.

Taking the test to the people is the obvious alternative to invitation to a theatre. Mobile units, which can go to any suburb they please to pick up any kind of sample, have an obvious appeal from this point of view. A large number of small-scale sessions can be held in them throughout the day, so that the system bears economic comparison with theatre tests. The measures applied may be exactly the same. The differences are mainly a matter of interview atmosphere and the fact that there can be closer supervision.

Private houses are sometimes preferred for television commercial tests, because this is closer to normal viewing conditions; but trying to achieve greater reality in this way is an expensive business unless one limits oneself to small-scale qualitative work.

Distrust of the meaning of question-and-answer data has driven some researchers to want physiological measures. These may be applied in a theatre, or a mobile unit, but they are mainly used in laboratories. Their basic purpose is to provide objective indications, that are not subject to interpretation, of the extent to which an informant is emotionally aroused by a commercial. Either the total effect of the whole commercial is observed or the separate effects of the constituent parts as well.

The psychogalvanometer, which provides a measure of the sweat response—an autonomic indicator of emotional arousal—is the tool most often used. In the US an eye camera was developed to measure pupil dilation, another autonomic indicator. The latter, it was argued forcibly for some years, was superior to similar devices for two main reasons—sensitivity and direction. Very precise, minute measurements make it possible to have fine discrimination between reactions to successive parts of a commercial. At the same time, the *nature* of this particular response encouraged some to consider that it showed direction, i.e., not just emotional arousal was being measured, but *desirable* reaction which could be related to likelihood of purchase behaviour. A bigger response to brand A's pack, after exposure to a commercial, suggested to them that the consumer was wanting to see more of it (with pupils dilated) because he was now more in favour of buying it. Efforts to substantiate this suggest that whatever diagnostic value the tool may have the evaluative promise that it held out has not really been fulfilled.

Physiological psychologists have noted that different people react emotionally in different unconscious ways, e.g., some turn white with anger, others red. A polygraph is an instrument developed to account for this by taking a range of arousal measures, including galvanic skin response and pupil dilation. The costs are, needless to say, very considerable. It seems likely to remain a matter more for experiment than for consistent commercial use.

At this time, experiments are proceeding with a machine that measures the tension in the eyebrow while people observe commercials. It seems unduly pessimistic to assume that this will go the way of the eye observation camera, but we still seem to be a long way from a physiological technique in which one is entirely confident, and which seems to be useful and economic in most pre-testing circumstances.

An alternative objective measure is to test on a large scale, near a supermarket, and offer informants money-off coupons which can only be used there. A matched control panel needs to be interviewed. Even with fast-moving consumer goods, such a test can be very slow, and very insensitive. Unexpected re-interview with commercial test informants, or signing them up for diary panels, might be more fruitful avenues.

An on-air pre-test demands small, localized operations if it is not to be a contradiction in terms. In the UK (as opposed to the US) it is impossible to have subdivisions that are smaller than a television area, *or* that extend over space where overlap is ruled out, e.g., Dover transmitter. On-air pre-tests can be arranged in Border Television Areas, where only a small, but reasonably representative, section of the population will be exposed to the test commercial. Consumer research services are available for evaluation.

Press Advertising Tests

There is a problem of definition of pre-testing that tends to occur more when press advertisements are being discussed. What, exactly, constitutes a 'pre-test' as opposed to a 'post-test'?

The standpoint taken here is that 'pre-testing' may include any situation in which a deliberately restricted proportion of the target population is exposed to the advertising. This includes cases where a magazine or newspaper actually appears, with the advertisement inside it, provided this is on a restricted scale. (The point here is that a check of advertising is being carried out prior to putting the bulk of media expenditure behind it.)

(a) *Folder Test*

Probably the most frequently-used technique of pre-testing a press advertisement is to expose the sample of informants to an advertisement included in a folder containing control advertisements. The classical version of this is described below, but in passing it should be mentioned that there are several variations. The first of these is where specially prepared copies of magazines are used for the same purpose as the folder. The main advantage claimed for this procedure is that the advertisement appears in a natural, rather than a contrived, context. It also becomes possible for the informant to consider the advertisement in a more realistic situation, e.g., the magazine may be substituted for his normal magazine in a particular week, when it is left to be read at home for a period of time before the second interview. Another variation is where a folder, as such, is not used but a number of advertisements are shown to the informant, divorced from the media context, and the informant's reactions are observed.

In a sense, these two variations represent a deliberate movement in opposite directions: towards greater realism in the research situation, and away from it, in order to concentrate attention on particular items. The advantages of either approach are matters of dispute. Some claim that greater realism in the research situation allows for greater meangingfulness in informants' response. Others argue that realism is illusory in the context of advertising research, because getting insight into likely reactions to advertisements depends, to some extent, on focussing attention.

A typical folder test will proceed as follows. Informants are allowed to look through a folder containing press advertisements. Included among them is a test advertisement. The folder should preferably be not too bulky, so it can be flicked through easily and the state of finish of all the advertisements should be roughly similar. It is sometimes claimed that only advertisements of comparable size or nature (black and white with black and white,

432

or colour with colour, etc.,) should appear in the folder. In fact, this seems less important than that the kind of advertisement included should be calculated to have roughly comparable appeal in terms of subject matter and style to the target group. At the same time, it is obviously undesirable to have all the control advertisements in black and white, and only the test advertisement in colour. At this stage, the informants should not realize which is the test advertisement. Sometimes the interviewer will be instructed to pay attention to the amount of time spent looking at each advertisement. Occasionally, a time limit is imposed for looking at each advertisement but this procedure has been known, on occasions, to unnerve informants. Allowing the informant to browse through *ad lib* seems better practice. The folder is then withdrawn, and informants are asked a variety of questions, usually designed to elicit evidence of 'impact', 'involvement', 'interest', and the like. These questions are often favoured: 'We have only time to talk about two or three of these advertisements. Which would you prefer to discuss?', or, 'People sometimes like to turn back to a particular advertisement and have a closer look at it. Do you feel that about any of these? Which?' The questionnaire may often proceed: 'Which products can you remember seeing advertised here? Can you remember the brand name?'

The importance and relevance of these and other questions depends very much on which aspects of the advertisement are being researched, and what they are intended to do. This is particularly to be borne in mind when considering questions about the message received, e.g.: 'What was the main point of the advertisement for . . . ?'

A check list of adjectives is sometimes offered to the informant. This aims at getting evidence of the *kind* of message received, and the way in which it has been received. Informants may be asked, for example, to choose from a list including 'convincing', 'attractive', 'childish', etc. In themselves, the choices of adjective may be puzzling, bearing in mind that different people read words differently; therefore, reasons for choice of adjectives are often probed.

At some point in the interview, some kind of recall question, demanding playback of detail, is often included. The extent, or often the nature, of the recall of details may not in itself tell very much. It may, however, indicate the degree to which, in the short term, an advertisement tends to dominate attention or to be swamped by other advertising. It can also suggest which features of an advertisement are dominant; but careful interpretation is needed here, because some features may be simply easier to describe than others.

(b) *Coupon Response*

Arrangements can be made for advertisements to be included in local media, or in restricted issues of national media, in order to check how the advertising would work *in situ*. As opposed to relying on consumer research to show what the results are, behavioural measures can be used. The main ones in this group are:

(a) coupon response—redemption at local shops;
(b) coupon response—sent to advertiser/agency;
(c) 'hidden offer'.

These measures are valuable only to the extent that the behaviour itself is the result that the creative work is designed to achieve. It is easy to visualize a short-term effect being contrived, possibly among consumers outside the target, which risks cheapening expectations of the products among the best long-term prospects.

The total number of people who send in coupons from couponed advertisements may give an impression of precision in advertising evaluation that is entirely illusory. Where durables or services are concerned, it is the total number of conversions that is of interest. It is one thing to encourage twice as many to send in coupons for a brochure or a salesman's visit; it is another to do so without leading to disappointment. Relying on conversion data makes the assumption that the brochure and the salesman are standard items, with a fixed value. This may not be true.

When coupon response is a matter of detaching a coupon and handing it over as part-payment for the brand, certain other considerations apply. Some housewives collect coupons of this kind, as a matter of principle. They are continuously defraying the costs of their basic household purchases. In the shops they need to get the brand name right, but beyond this, they are simply thinking in terms of commodity. Further, if premium pricing means anything for a brand, this technique may affect the brand image particularly badly. There is also the question of 'malredemption' whereby retailers accept coupons indiscriminately, without strict reference to the brands concerned.

'Hidden offers' are said to provide evidence that consumers have really penetrated as far as the body copy. (A coupon, of course, may just have been seen as a coupon.) Insofar as the consumer must have read deep into the advertisement in order to know that the offer exists, and how to get it, this is a fair assumption; but the principle that some people are more likely than others to be 'offer-hunters' is still an influence on results.

There is one variation that should be mentioned, i.e., research that is organized into much department store advertising, without often being described as such. Multiple advertisements, drawing people's attention to a series of bargains available at the time, can be varied so that they include different combinations of bargains. Some combinations are then proved to be better at getting people into the store to make a purchase.

Some have found that these measures distinguish better between *media* than between the advertisements themselves. This is an important consideration for interpretation. All these measures are best regarded as telling part, but not all, of the story. Qualitative research among matched groups of coupon senders—those who are converted into buyers and those who are

434

not—can often indicate far more about the advertisement's *role* and *how* the advertisement played it.

(c) *Laboratory Methods*

The equipment used to make physiological measurements discussed under 'Television Commercial Tests' (p. 427) is used for testing press advertisements too. The same comments apply. Tachistoscopes are also used to determine the thresholds at which features of one or more press advertisements are registered. Two points can be of interest here—the degree of legibility, or recognition that the advertisement is for brand 'A', and the *order* in which certain features are recognized.

There are few things as unlike real media contexts as a tachistoscope, which is a large box used for exposing material for small, controlled periods of time. If it suggests or confirms, however, that an advertisement is not communicating identity, or a basic point, efficiently, then its evidence needs to be considered alongside data from more 'natural' sources.

The eye movement camera (as opposed to the eye observation camera used for measuring pupil dilation) is capable of showing *how* people look at advertisements. It traces the path taken by the eye when it passes over a printed page. Some media owners have found it useful as an indicator of how people read magazines, but consistent use on individual advertisements seems unlikely, outside special experimental programmes.

Post-testing

There is little point in describing all the pitfalls to be avoided in consumer surveys, which are covered elsewhere. Essentially, post-testing tends to be a matter of finding out, by means of 'ad hoc' consumer survey work, what effects of advertising can be found among consumers. For anyone to want to do this, he must have good reasons for supposing that other, simpler steps that could be taken will not give all the information necessary. These simpler steps include:

(a) counting sales changes, retail audit;
(b) coupon return analysis;
(c) playback from sales force;
(d) consumer audit;
(e) standardized post-test services.

Sales data, in the final analysis, must be relevant, but the point has already been made that advertising is one of many things contributing to sales and that the relationship between these factors is more likely to be dynamic than additive. It is like testing fertilizer by observing whether the flowers come up big and strong from a packet of seeds. If the results are good, perhaps the product (the seeds) is so good that advertising (fertilizer) is scarcely necessary. Comparison with what happened last year, with a different fertilizer, is difficult, because the weather conditions may have been different. The metaphor can be extended indefinitely.

Coupon returns have their limitations, which have been discussed in the previous section. The opinions of the sales force are subject to remarkable bias.

Consumer audit data is a half-way house between retail audit work and sample surveys. The Television Consumer Audit in this country is organized in such a way that there is objective recording of purchases made, among large, representative samples. This audit of purchases can be broken down by area, or looked at over time, depending on how the examination of advertising effect is required. Several research agencies offer broadly similar services.

Analysis of any changes in user profile, and brand switching can be made and these can be related to probability of advertising exposure. For the latter special questions may be required. Data on price paid and promotion up-take can be collected, which gives an idea of below the line influence. This kind of information goes considerably further than simply counting the cases that leave the factory but it still gives no indication as to what may be going on in the consumer's mind, to the brand's advantage or disadvantage, as a result of advertising. A campaign may compare well or badly with *competitive efforts*. Unless consumers are interviewed, we cannot know. This gap, it has been claimed, can be filled by standardized post-test services, such as 'reading and noting' studies—press—and 24-hour recall studies—television. In fact, they are, in the author's view, quite inadequate for anything but a very superficial reading. This argument is based on experience, as well as on what have been shown to be the severe limitations of recall data apparent from the literature.

Very often the worst aspect about planning a post-test for the researcher is matching the practical need for speedy information to aid forward planning, and the likelihood of getting meaningful results while the campaign is still new. The timing of a post-test must take into account:

(a) how much advertising pressure is being put behind the brand—in absolute terms and in relation to competitive activity?;
(b) over what period is the money being spent?;
(c) when was there advertising behind the brand before?, at what level?, on the same theme?;
(d) how far is advertising trying to introduce a new thought, about new or generally reformulated products? How far is it a matter of trying to amend the image of a well entrenched product, which has near commodity status?;
(e) what is the repurchase rate for the product?

All these points, which are obviously interrelated, can decide whether a clear picture is likely to emerge from survey work done earlier or later. Most researchers tend to advise later research. They do so for a number of

436

reasons. They are less sanguine, as a rule, about the chances of consumers really seeing a product in a new light, when that product has already been around a long time. They also prefer to judge a campaign once they have seen how appreciation of the product in use ties in with expectations derived from advertising; for this, it helps if time has been allowed for a repurchase rate to establish itself. The classical approach is to conduct identical checks before and after a campaign appears. This allows one to evaluate how much progress has been made. There are problems, however, in that several factors may not be the same, before and after the campaign break. The product may be seasonal or dependent on epidemic conditions, etc. The sales force activity may be heightened by the campaign. Competitors may have started to retaliate. This makes it desirable, in some cases, to have a control area, as below.

	Pre-campaign	*After campaign break*
Test area	Check 1^A	Check 2^A
Control area	Check 1^B	Check 2^B

Some prefer to take the rest of the country as the 'control' on the principle that a particular control area may be rendered unsuitable half-way through the test, by competitive activity.

Sometimes, no pre-check is possible, because the decision to post-test comes too late. In this case, a control area is most desirable. Long-term effects, or campaign wear-out, can be studied by repeating post-checks.

What to measure? Recall measures will certainly figure among what is measured, although relatively uncomplicated things such as purchase, and the presence of the brand in the pantry, etc., can also be covered. These question areas are sometimes useful:

(a) brand saliency (first mentions of brand when product field is mentioned);
(b) spontaneous awareness (any mentions of brand);
(c) prompted awareness (recognition of brand);
(d) trial and repurchase (for new brands);
(e) purchase and frequency of purchase (established brands);
(f) spontaneous awareness of advertising;
(g) prompted awareness of advertising;
(h) detailed recall of advertising;
(i) impressions of the advertising;
(j) brand image questions;
(k) attitudes to purchase (possibly using 'constant sum' technique);
(l) media exposure data.

A long questionnaire already, and no mention has yet been made of specific questions that may be important to establish the penetration of a particular campaign, e.g., 'How does brand 'A' compare for price against brand 'B'?

Is it more, or less expensive, do you think?', where an economy platform has been used. The optimum question order must be expected to vary.

Some of the questions above, it has been suggested, are better indicators than others that a campaign has succeeded, or is succeeding, in increasing sales—'brand saliency', 'spontaneous advertising awareness', and 'constant sum' have support here, e.g., Axelrod[2]. Certain useful cross-analyses stick out a mile. Ability to recall advertising detail can be usefully crossed with trial, repurchase, and intentions to purchase. 'Brand image' can be crossed with 'frequency of purchase' groups. The value of this is fairly obvious.

A lot can also be done with media exposure data. Given analyses of media questions a series of cells can be built up as follows:

Likelihood of advertising experience:

Definition:	*Very high*	*High*	*Medium*	*Medium/ Light*	*Light/ None*
Television	Watches ITV every night	Watches ITV 4–5 nights a week	Etc.	Etc.	Etc.
Press	Reads daily two out of three publications on schedule	Reads daily one publication on schedule; occasionally sees others	Etc.	Etc.	Etc.

These groups can be considered separately on such questions as 'brand saliency', 'advertising awareness', etc. Figure 16.6 shows two very simple

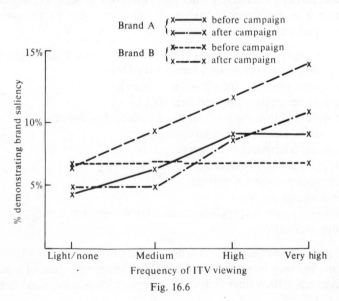

Fig. 16.6

examples of the value of this. The example assumes that 'brand saliency' is a crucial measure, as it may be for a fragmented market. Brand 'A' has achieved no significant increase in brand saliency, given that heavier ITV viewers were very much aware of it already. Both the media choice and the creative content need to be critically examined. Brand 'B' has fared better. The fact that the response function seems to be linear could be important. Briefly, this suggests that the *more* advertising received, the *greater* the effect. One implication could be that greater advertising pressure would be useful.

The story is still incomplete, however. Large-scale quantified work usually yields hypotheses about advertising effects, e.g., 'Those who were exposed to the advertising message were made aware of the brand, but not of its advantages; this is reflected in disinclination to purchase it'. The paradox of advertising research is that one is often forced, then, to go below the surface and examine hypotheses by means of qualitative work. Campaign evaluation studies can often be considered as establishing which sub-groups need intensive interviewing. This stands much conventional market research procedure on its head but advertising research is territory where the practitioner needs to develop and follow his own rules.

Two further approaches to campaign evaluation deserve attention. The first is to have a continuous survey checking on a brand's performance. This makes use of measures that relate to the effect that advertising is supposed to have on long-term promotional objectives. The second involves having panels that are set up on a permanent basis, in which there is built-in experimental control over media exposure. Both systems lend themselves to syndicated services, because of the high costs.

Most large research agencies nowadays offer a continuous survey (or one that is repeated at regular, frequent intervals). Some of these are specifically angled towards advertising post-tests, but most omnibus surveys can be adapted to a similar purpose.

It is often useful to observe the progress of a brand's advertising penetration, compared with other brands' performances, and broken out by usage and media exposure groups. Standardization of interviews means it is easier to note significant changes over time.

To be satisfied with standardization presupposes that one is confident that certain questions, repeated every few months, will continue to get at reactions to a brand's advertising in the most meaningful way, despite campaign changes, and possibly altered strategy. For some brands, in some situations, this may, almost, be the case, but to understand what a specific campaign is achieving, it is usually necessary to add specific questions. The same argument can be applied to the standardization of the sample.

While many advertisers will find it easier and cheaper to buy into a continuous survey, say, twice a year, to get data of this kind on brand saliency, awareness, comprehension of messages, brand image, and so forth, a larger advertiser with a number of brands often reaches a different solution. This is to buy fieldwork direct, at appropriate intervals, from a fieldwork agency. The sample will be structured to suit his purposes, and there is no risk of 'interference' from questions on other advertisers' product fields.

The second approach does not, at the time of writing, exist in the UK, although in the next decade it can be predicted that something of the kind may become available to the advertising research world here. It involves setting up matched panels of homes within the *same* geographical area and controlling their reception of advertising (primarily television, but in one case press also), so that the effects can be measured of exposing comparable groups of homes to alternative advertising. This system, which is now well-established in the US, is described at rather greater length on pages 489 to 490. The principle of the system seems above criticism, provided there is accurate panel matching (in terms of shopping behaviour and access to different outlets, as well as demographics) *and* provided the test area is typical. Control of media exposures will never be perfect so long as people visit each other, but this is a minor problem.

Preliminary experience in the US suggests that a lot of time is needed before getting clear-cut measurable results, even in markets which have the reputation of changing quite rapidly. It is probably fair to say that researchers are still learning to use this tool, and to know which campaigns in which market situations can reasonably be tested with it.

Advertising Research Programme

There is no perfect advertising research programme, but here is an example of one, taken from work done to re-launch Silvikrin Shampoo in the UK in 1966–8, which introduces many of the points made in this chapter.

In 1968 Silvikrin Shampoo was re-launched as a range of shampoos based on natural ingredients, called 'The New Naturals'. The outline of research is given below.

(a) Summer 1966. Concept of 'New Naturals' tested on small scale in group discussions.

(b) Winter 1966. Reactions to 'New Naturals' concept (adapted since summer, 1966) tested on larger scale, in parallel with tests of optimum balance of shampoo variants, names and packs.
(1967. Product and packaging development).

(c) Winter 1967/8. Tests of four advertising approaches for the 'New Naturals' introduction.

(d) Spring 1968 In light of the above, two press advertisements in finished form. (One 15-second announcement commercial was also prepared, using the features that came out best in winter 1967/8). These press ads were tested on a small scale.

(e) Summer 1968. Tested on a large scale, in a folder test, against other toiletry and cosmetic advertising.
(Autumn 1968. Advertising broke (national launch). Mainly press and television in support.)

(f) Autumn 1968/70. Tests of further individual press advertisements, featuring each shampoo variant separately. Mostly small-scale, to check for negatives and appropriateness to specific hair types; occasional larger-scale tests to check the strength of the continuing campaign.

(g) Spring 1969. Large-scale national usage and penetration study, checking inter-relationships of:
brand use;
advertising awareness;
understanding of 'New Naturals' theme;
appreciation of 'New Naturals' theme;
media exposure.

The length of time spanned by this whole programme is a function of the fact that the re-launch involved a re-vamping of the whole brand. The right formulations, colours, bottles, and names for each of the four Silvikrin variants—'Natural', 'Protein', 'Lemon and Lime', and 'Almond Cream'—had to be developed in parallel. As the creative work was developed, it had to take into account any new turn taken in the presentation of the range.

The first stage showed that the idea of the 'New Naturals', as a means of reintroducing a well-known brand, was arresting, intriguing, and pleasing to the target market. The natural ingredients featured seemed to carry considerable promise, and were consistent with the brand image idea, 'beauty through health' (see original concept board in Fig. 16.7). The work in the winter of 1966 (b) confirmed this impression. It also showed which names, colours, packs were consistent with the promise of the 'New Naturals' theme, and which were not.

The 'Natural' theme inspired four creative routes, one of which is illustrated in Fig. 16.7. Of these, one featured a headline 'Once Upon a Time', recalling the days of childhood when hair was naturally attractive. This had significant negatives for some women, who saw it as a reminder of advancing years, and was abandoned; but the one illustrated in Fig. 16.7 'Silvikrin Goes Natural', combined emotional arousal with communication and appreciation. The other two were workmanlike, rather than inspired.

Figure 16.8 shows the two advertisements that were tested at (d) and (e). Both were significantly more likely to arouse comment, interest, and remarks suggesting relevance to consumer need than the other advertisements tested in the folders at (e). Further, they succeeded in securing the attention and enthusiasm of both the younger and the older parts of the target market, which earlier creative work had never quite succeeded in achieving. The sales results of the re-launch thoroughly vindicated the

441

Fig. 16.7

442

Fig. 16.7
Reproduced with permission of Leo Burnett-LPE Ltd.

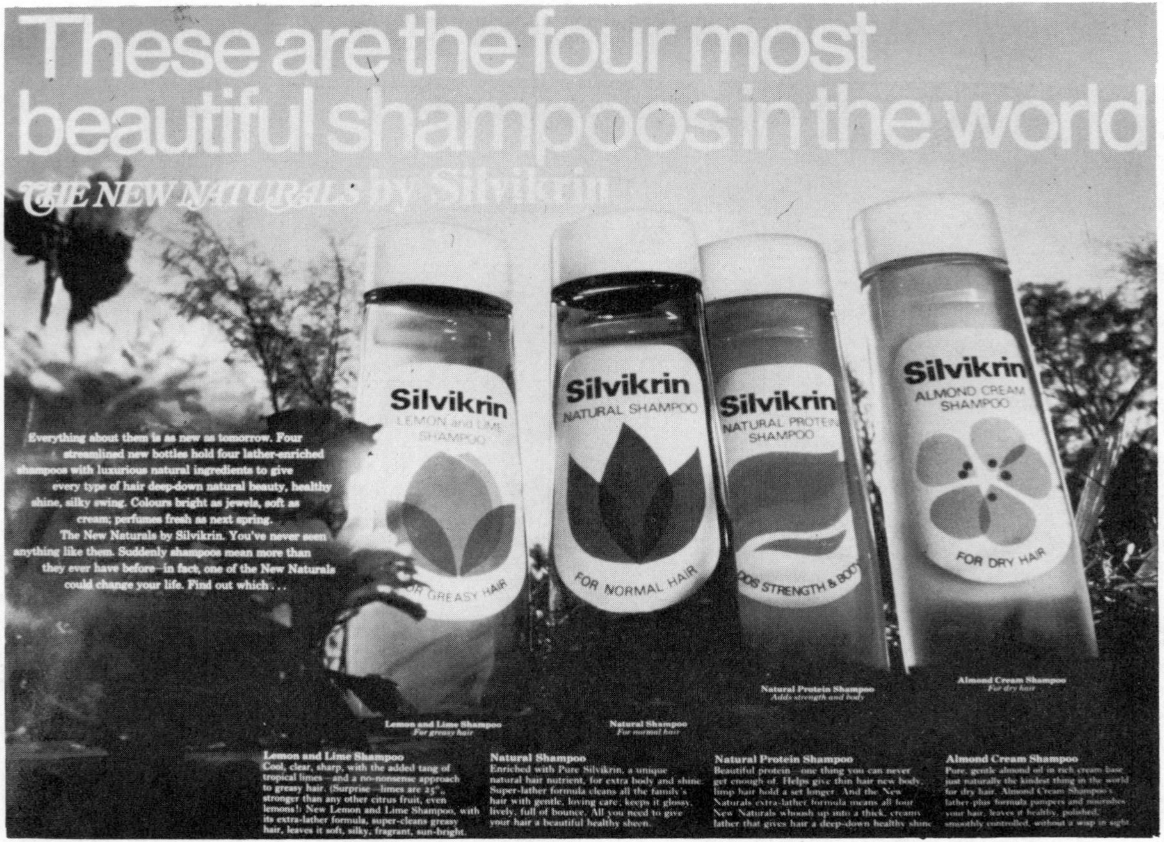
These are the four most beautiful shampoos in the world
THE NEW NATURALS by Silvikrin
Everything about them is as new as tomorrow. Four streamlined new bottles hold four lather-enriched shampoos with luxurious natural ingredients to give every type of hair deep-down natural beauty, healthy shine, silky swing. Colours bright as jewels, soft as cream; perfumes fresh as next spring.
The New Naturals by Silvikrin. You've never seen anything like them. Suddenly shampoos mean more than they ever have before—in fact, one of the New Naturals could change your life. Find out which . . .
Silvikrin LEMON and LIME SHAMPOO
Silvikrin NATURAL SHAMPOO FOR NORMAL HAIR
Silvikrin NATURAL PROTEIN SHAMPOO
Silvikrin ALMOND CREAM SHAMPOO FOR DRY HAIR
Lemon and Lime Shampoo For greasy hair
Natural Shampoo For normal hair
Natural Protein Shampoo Adds strength and body
Almond Cream Shampoo For dry hair
Lemon and Lime Shampoo
Cool, clear, sharp, with the added tang of tropical limes—and a no-nonsense approach to greasy hair. (Surprise—limes are 25% stronger than any other citrus fruit, even lemons!) New Lemon and Lime Shampoo, with its extra-lather formula, super-cleans greasy hair, leaves it soft, silky, fragrant, sun-bright.
Natural Shampoo
Enriched with Pure Silvikrin, a unique natural hair nutrient, for extra body and shine. Super-lather formula cleans all the family's hair with gentle, loving care, keeps it glossy, lively, full of bounce. All you need to give your hair a beautiful healthy sheen.
Natural Protein Shampoo
Beautiful protein—one thing you can never get enough of. Helps give thin hair new body, limp hair hold a set longer. And the New Naturals extra-lather formula means all four New Naturals whoosh up into a thick, creamy lather that gives hair a deep-down healthy shine.
Almond Cream Shampoo
Pure, gentle almond oil in rich cream base, just naturally the kindest thing in the world for dry hair. Almond Cream Shampoo's lather-plus formula pampers and nourishes your hair, leaves it healthy, polished, smoothly controlled, without a wisp in sight.

Fig. 16.8

Fig. 16.8
Reproduced with permission of Leo Burnett-LPE Ltd.

whole operation. The close inter-relationship of all factors in the marketing mix made it extremely difficult to apportion results to causes. (Note that the original concept research was as much product concept as advertising concept research.) The comparison of awareness, usage and media exposure in the post-campaign evaluation at (g), however, showed that advertising must have played a considerable part.

References

1. LOVELL, M. R. C. and LANNON, J. M. *Difficulties with Recall*, ESOMAR, WAPOR Congress, August, 1967.
2. AXELROD, J. N. Attitude Measures that Predict Purchase. *Journal of Advertising Research*, March, 1968.

Bibliography

NB. The divisions between 'Theoretical' and 'Practical' are arbitrary, and signify degree, rather than category.

Theoretical

APPEL, V. and BLUM, M. Ad Recognition and Respondent Set. *Journal of Advertising Research*, **1**, 4, June, 1961.
DEMBAR, W. N. *Psychology of Perception.* Holt, New York, 1965.
HASKINS, J. B. Factual Recall as a Measure of Advertising Effectiveness. *Journal of Advertising Research*, **4**, 1, March, 1964.
JOYCE, T. *What do we Know about the Way Advertising Works?* ESOMAR Seminar 1967.
KING, S. How Useful is Proposition Testing? *Advertising Quarterly*, Winter 1965/6.
KRUGMANN, H. E. The Measurement of Advertising Involvement. *Public Opinion Quarterly*, Winter 1966–67.
LEAVITT, C. *Classic Models of Communication Effects and Innovations in These Models*, Annual Conference of American Association for Public Opinion Research, May, 1970.
LOVELL, M. R. C. and LANNON, J. M. *Difficulties with Recall*, ESOMAR WAPOR Congress, August 1967.
LOVELL, M. R. C., JOHNS, S. and RAMPLEY, B. Pre-testing Press Advertisements. The Thomson awards for Advertising. *Research*, 1967.
LUCAS, D. B. The ABC's of ARF's PARM. *Journal of Marketing*, July, 1960.
MORGENSZTERN, A. *How to Determine the Optimum Screening Frequency of a Movie Commercial.* ESOMAR, 1967.
WELLS, W. D. How Chronic Overclaimers Distort Survey Findings. *Journal of Advertising Research*, **3**, 2, June, 1963.

Practical

AXELROD, J. N. Attitude Measures that Predict Purchase. *Journal of Advertising Research*, March, 1968.
BUCHANAN, D. I. How Interest in the Product Affects Recall: Print Ads. vs. Commercials. *Journal of Advertising Research*, March, 1964.
CAFFYN, J. M. and BROWN, N. A. *The Application of Psychological Ironmongery to Commercial Problems.* ESOMAR Congress, 1964.
HESS, E. Attitudes and Pupil Size. *Scientific American*, April, 1965.
KING, S. Can Research Evaluate the Creative Content of Advertising? *ADMAP*, June 1967.
KONIG, G., LAKASCHUS, C., and LOVELL, M. R. C. *The Measurement of Pupil Dilation as a Market Research Tool.* ESOMAR-WAPOR Congress, Sept., 1965.

SEGNIT, S. and BROADBENT, S. R. *Area Tests and Consumer Surveys to Measure Advertising Effectiveness.* ESOMAR Congress, 1970.

STARCH, D. Measuring the Effect of Advertising on Sales. (5 articles) *Printers Ink*, Mar.–May, 1964.

WINICK, C. Three Measures of the Advertising Value of Media Context. *Journal of Advertising Research*, **2**, 2, June, 1962.

WOOD, J. F. Pre-testing the Advertising, *ADMAP*, September, 1967.

17. Packaging and symbolic communication

William Schlackman and John Dillon

This chapter attempts to present a way of looking at the problem of packaging, name testing and symbol research. It is not meant to be an exhaustive discussion of all the methods that are available for such research. This can be established through additional reading on the topic. Some of the sources for this are provided in the bibliography but this is by no means exhaustive.

While there may be various methods not indicated in this chapter of tackling the problems which we have outlined, it would be fair to say that the conceptual framework which has been provided as a means of looking at the problem has proved to have empirical validity in day to day marketing activity. Hopefully, there will be readers who can improve on the suggested methods. Undoubtedly, in time, useful procedures will be developed which substantially supplant those methods indicated in this chapter. However, the framework within which methodology has to develop is unlikely to change unless the marketing environment changes and this is not likely to happen except over a long period of time.

For the most part, the material for this chapter has been prepared out of the experience which the first author has accumulated over a period of fifteen years, both in the US and in the UK. The section which deals with perceptual (visual) factors has been prepared by Dr. John Dillon, who has been directly involved over recent years with the problems discussed in this particular section. The chapter stresses the idea that all research on the problems of packaging and symbols must be related to marketing criteria. There is no such thing as a good package or a bad one in the absence of a criterion which can be used as the basis of evaluation. The criterion is related not only to the marketing strategy of a given brand, which is always critical, but to the marketing environment in which the brand must live. This is also true with regard to symbols. This chapter sets out to show how this principle is operative and how research can deal with the main issues.

The Package

A package is the key vehicle in the passage of a product from the manufactured state to the point of consumption. The package can, therefore, be an effective vehicle which facilitates distribution or it can be a defective vehicle which fails in some way in the distribution cycle.

When we speak of the distribution cycle we refer to the package's function in the various phases of the marketing process. Because each product has a character of its own and because merchandizing and marketing of given products will vary, the criteria for a successful package will, to some extent, vary as well. Understanding the nature of the distribution requirements of the various stages, in depth, conditions the research that will be needed. Hence, it is not realistic to suggest that there is a standard or fixed technique in researching a package. Flexibility in thought and procedure is required to resolve specific issues that will emerge in the distribution cycle. This, however, is not meant to deny the existence of certain general criteria which all packs share at the consumer level.

In order to design the right kind of package for a product one must know and understand, in addition to other facts, the distribution cycle of the particular product as well as its physical characteristics. In past years, heavy emphasis was placed on the physical characteristics of the product. This has logically resulted in measurements of size, weight, hardness, temperature, alkalinity of materials, 'machineability' and many other physical characteristics of a package geared to ensure production efficiency and prolong the product's shelf life. However, the package requirements from the viewpoint of both the trade and the consumer are also important.

Retailers

With regard to retailers there are many functional considerations one should determine through research during the design planning stage. There is much evidence to suggest that if a package fails to meet the retailer's needs he will behave in such a way that distribution of the product will be severely inhibited. He may not display the product or he may discourage consumers from making a purchase, or he may simply not carry the product because its packaging creates too many problems for him.

There are a number of general characteristics to be borne in mind but, ultimately, one might usefully survey a representative cross-section of retailers to discover their requirements. Broadly speaking, we may conceive of a number of research areas which we shall put in terms of questions:

(a) what kind of package will be most convenient for retailers to stock and maintain in an orderly fashion?;
(b) what kind of package will minimize the expensive cost of handling?;
(c) what kind of package will minimize breakage and pilferage?;
(d) what sizes and shapes will fit into his display arrangements?; and, in

conjunction with this, what kinds of point-of-purchase display racks and assistance will be welcomed?;

(e) what kind of package does the retailer have faith in from the viewpoint of what he thinks consumers will buy?;

(f) with what types of packs currently on the market has he experienced difficulty?;

(g) what are his personal preferences and how do these influence his buying practices?

Before one designs a package which will meet the needs at this stage of the distribution process, one should have the answers to these questions. A successful deodorant package, for example, which was selling well met with retailer resistance because it occupied too much space on the display counters. The result was that retailers only displayed a small number of packages. Because it was a good turnover item, the customers frequently missed it on the counters. Changing the package size enabled the company to have more packages displayed and, at the same time, satisfied the retailers.

The Consumer

Although the research questions and methods on the wholesaler and retailer level present certain complexities, the most challenging question to be answered by far—and certainly the most critical—is the role of the package as it relates to consumer behaviour. *The package is not simply a functional carrier of the product but is intrinsically continuous with the meanings the consumer attaches to the product.* The package design is a key factor influencing the image of the product and brand. As in the case of retailers, it is first necessary to determine, preferably through careful investigation, what the package will be required to do at this stage of the distribution process. Here, one must know:

(a) will the package be sold on a self-service basis or not?;

(b) will it act as a container for the product within the home or simply be discarded?;

(c) is the product an impulse item or a planned purchase?;

(d) in what units do consumers prefer to buy?;

(e) where is the package kept in the home?, on the table, in a store bin?, etc.;

(f) what are the brand imagery requirements in selling the brand?

These are a few of the simple questions that should be examined with regard to designing a good package for consumers, for how the consumer will buy and use the product will dictate the design direction. The responsibility of the market researcher in the early stage is to provide the designers with this type of basic information.

At this point it is useful to bear in mind that researchers cannot create designs. Research should not be a design function. Attempts at using

450

research as a way of getting consumers to give specific design concepts have almost always failed. During the criterion stage of research the researcher should provide the designers with a comprehensive and sensitive understanding of the problem so that the designers can maximize their ingenuity in solving the problem. Research can never be a substitute for creative effort. In a study for a hosiery manufacturer, for example, it was found that the brand was rarely displayed on a self-merchandizing shelf, but that consumers frequently saved the package for storage of personal items. In conjunction with this, it was also found that in shopping for this product the first contact the consumer had was with the inner wrapper of the package when offered before her eyes by the sales assistant. This indicated two important directions for design. It:

(a) was relatively unimportant to have an 'impact' design (rapid recognition) but it was most important that the package have a pleasing feminine quality which would look attractive in a lady's boudoir;
(b) pointed to the need of having a luxurious transfer design on the inner wrapping because that was the first thing the consumer saw at the point of purchase; her first judgement of the product was influenced by the tissue sheet on the inside.

In a study for a large producer of eyedrops, it was found that frequent users of the product usually carried it in a glove compartment or in handbags but the pack was awkward and many women thought it was inconvenient and unattractive. A new single unit package dispenser was developed which was also attractive.

In the past, drug manufacturers—particularly of vitamin pills—found that the packaging which was used frequently created reluctance to use it at meal times due to the old-fashioned medicinal-looking containers. One manufacturer created a completely new design for the various nutritive supplements he sold. These bottles were made to look like attractive condiment jars. Housewives enjoyed keeping them not in the medicine chest but on the table with flowers and salt shakers. Such a redesign created more interest in the product.

The brief examples given above illustrate how the package can be a powerful selling tool. The packet can contribute to overcoming barriers to product consumption and provide greater satisfaction in use. In this planning area the role of the market researcher is critical. By thoroughly understanding the dynamics of the 'consumer/product' interaction he can provide the designer with directions which will enable the creative people to produce packages which will effectively help the marketing of the product. Often, in these research areas, statistical procedures of study are not required. Understanding derived through qualitative research procedures is sufficient.

The marketing performance characteristics of a package require serious attention. Here, we should think in terms of three dimensions of importance in the marketing process as it relates to the package, the:

(a) *subjective mental* features as a vehicle of communication with the consumer;

(b) *functional* features of the package as it meets both the retailers' needs and the needs of the consumer;

(c) *visual* structure—speed and clarity of perception.

The Package and the Unplanned Purchase

Self-service and effective packaging, both interdependent developments of recent years, have opened up a new type of selling phenomenon. This change has expanded markets and drastically changed merchandizing concepts. We refer to the whole area of the unplanned purchase. This is sometimes referred to as the impulse sale. Actually, only a fraction of the unplanned purchases are purely impulse, in the sense that no apparent need for the product exists but that which is nurtured at the point of sale. Most unplanned purchases are purchases made where the consumer is reminded of a need for the product by seeing the package at the point of sale. Unplanned purchases account for a substantial proportion of buying in some product fields, although of all the unplanned purchases only a minor part are based solely on impulse.

Today, stores with a wide variety of merchandise (particularly supermarkets distributing with self-service techniques) encourage the consumer to shop without a prescribed list for purchase. One survey found that only nine per cent of shoppers tested actually had a written shopping list with them. Most of the shoppers stated that they usually walk through the aisles and get what they 'need'. (This word 'need' should be put in clearly labelled quotation marks.) This suggests that, in assessing the features of importance for research on a package, one should know the extent to which it is an impulse item.

Subjective mental factors

The package projects the brand image. People buy products for the promise of the gratifications offered and *these gratifications are not simply physical but emotional and social as well.*

The package, seen as clothing for the product, must communicate in visual symbols the promise that what is within the container will fulfil these satisfactions. In order to do this, it is first necessary to know the buying habits, usage patterns, attitudes, and motives of consumers with regard to the product and brand. Once this is done, one is in a position to establish the criteria on which the designer can fruitfully start to work.

The package is one vehicle in the marketing and advertising programme. In a sense, design planning research is not significantly different from research in these broader areas of marketing and advertising, although its focus may be somewhat different.

The most critical consideration is the degree to which the package activates

452

purchase behaviour. If, for example, you are selling ice cream and you want to create an aura of 'abundance' and 'traditional qualities', it would be necessary to measure the degree to which the package does, in fact, induce this image. By using motivational procedures which include depth interviews and projective tests it is possible with a relatively high degree of accuracy to determine the image projected by the package. An example relates to a brand of dandruff remover. Here, it was found that, although women were the most frequent users and invariably those who bought the product, men used the product as well. However, the package being used was extremely feminine and many potential male users were reluctant to use the brand. With these factors in mind, the company dropped the use of a flower pattern but retained all the other design elements. This made the package less feminine and tended to make the product less cosmetic in its appearance. This simple change resulted in increased usage by men while, at the same time, holding its female users. The symbolic cues of a package can influence judgements about the taste and other physical characteristics of a product. It can also suggest the character of the product, who uses it and, sometimes, when the product would be used. In this way the packet can define the psychological character of the brand. Since the consumption of products in our culture satisfies not only physical requirements but also psycho-social needs, correct manipulation of the symbolic cues can help to create consumer satisfactions and make a major contribution to the marketing effort. Most of the packaging research done today concentrates on this aspect of a pack's performance. A number of examples of how this can be done usefully are given below.

Concept Association Tests

The most common procedure used to deal with this aspect of the problem is what might be described as the 'Concept Association Test'. This is a projective test procedure in which the respondent links concepts with the packet. There are a number of versions that can be used in research terms but the principle is usually the same, depending to some extent on the context of the research. In a non-directive type interview, for example, there would be little structure. The respondent might simply be asked to free associate to the packet, i.e., simply relay all the thoughts that come to mind as he/she looks at the packet or in slightly more structured form to *imagine*:

(a) the kind of product that would be in the packet;
(b) the kind of people who might use it or not use it;
(c) where the product might be used and seen;
(d) types of shops in which it would be sold.

Still within the framework of an unstructured interview the respondent may be required to make up a story involving the stimulus pack, or make-believe that the pack is a person and describe what sort of person the pack would be. All these procedures are projective in nature and based on associative procedures. This type of research principle is easily extended to quantitative surveys.

There are several procedures one can use in doing the quantitative association tests. The two primary methods are:

(a) assessing the pack individually, usually using a scaling procedure;
(b) using a forced choice method from a number of designs.

The forced choice has been found useful when one needs to obtain significant differences between alternative packs. This is perhaps a more direct way of establishing their relative standing. However, it has a serious and significant weakness in that a consumer will never be confronted with the designs that fail in the research. Hence, there is artificiality in the exercise, since performance against *competition* is a central issue.

It is often important to see how a new design stacks up in imagery profile terms to competition that it will meet in the market. Simultaneous exposure of competition with each test design is useful. This procedure requires the use of matched samples for each alternative design as it is compared with competition. However, since the competitors have a well-established image the results of this test may be biased against the new design (an unknown compared to a known, etc.,). This research design done monadically, however, is useful in that we emerge with a score for each design against its normal competition and the relative imagery effectiveness of the designs can be seen. One answers the question, 'Given the image we want to create which one of the proposed designs does best against competition?'.

In carrying out such association tests quantitatively we have found it useful before exposing all the alternative designs to do the competition test as outlined. At the conclusion of this phase we then expose all the alternative designs and use the forced choice procedure. To illustrate this we show below the results of a pack test for a hairdressing product.

Example. General imagery was ascertained in two different display contexts. Respondents were first shown one of three test packs, 'K' or 'L' or 'T', and the packs of the three competing brands, Nos. 1, 2, and 3. In the second stage they were shown 'K'–'L'–'T' test packs and the current pack 'N', but no competitive packs. The dimensions used were the same on both the occasions. The findings are shown in Tables 17.1 and 17.2.

The Pseudo-product Test Procedure

As mentioned earlier, experience has shown that the symbolic cues on a pack design will influence the perception of the product. This is especially true in the case of food and other such products involving ingestion. This is an important phenomenon in the marketing of such products, since reliance on blind product tests alone does not reveal how the packaging will influence the consumers' judgement of the product. In these instances

Table 17.1 *General imagery in comparison with competing brands (competition test)*

	'K'	'L'	'T'	Average No. 1	Average No. 2	Average No. 3
Base numbers	205	196	203	604	604	604
Best quality haircream	% 34	% 30	% 25	% 14	% 50	% 7
Most attractive pack	42	39	32	6	52	5
Contains most haircream	9	31	25	61	10	7
Most up-to-date	67	64	55	3	33	2
Most difficult pack to use	51	28	37	18	9	34
Least greasy haircream	32	24	19	11	44	18
Costs the most	25	30	27	7	60	6
Would make hair look natural	26	30	20	14	49	10

The respondents were shown competitive packs 1, 2 and 3, plus test pack 'K' or 'L' or 'T'. They were asked to select out of the four the best quality haircream, the most attractive pack, etc.

the pseudo-product test procedure is ideally suited to evaluate symbolic influences on product judgement. The method consists of either double placement or sequential placements *of the same product* but in alternative pack designs. In our experience, allowing respondents to act as their own control, i.e., by testing and comparing more than one pack, is superior to the monadic design for this purpose.

Since the manufacturer usually has a clear idea of the desirable characteristics for the product and as he knows which sectors of the market the product is aimed at, the dimensions for measurement are normally predetermined. A simple illustration is from a beverage study where two alternative labels were studied. A sample of 200 who were drinkers of the beverage were recruited. These were people drinking normally a mild version of the beverage. The client who was not currently a producer of such a version wanted to launch a new brand into this section of the market.

Table 17.2 *General imagery among test packs (forced choice)*

	'K'	'L	'T'	'N'	
Base Number	604	604	604	604	
	%	%	%	%	%
Best quality haircream	34	27	10	29	100
Most attractive	46	25	8	21	100
Contains most haircream	5	31	22	42	100
Most up-to-date	59	19	7	15	100
Most difficult pack to use	48	13	15	24	100
Least greasy haircream	42	20	13	25	100
Costs the most	35	34	14	17	100
Would make hair look natural	34	25	12	29	100

The respondents were shown the three test packs and the current pack 'N'. They were asked which of these had the best quality haircream, etc.

The problem was to indicate which of two alternative labels would be most appropriate.

The same product formulation was presented in two differently labelled bottles 'M'–'L', (it was a simultaneous double placement test). Respondents were instructed to use one bottle first and, on completion, to use the second bottle. This sequential instruction was rotated from respondent to respondent in 'M'–'L'—'L'–'M' order. Respondents were simply told that they should consume the product and that the interviewer would return in four days and ask them some questions about their experience.

The results from pseudo-product tests are often dramatic, as in this case. Consumers experience differences where chemically and physiologically no differences could possibly exist. Here are some results from the pack test.

	'L'	'M'	Don't know	'N' = 200 Total (%)
Product found most acceptable	20	75	5	100
Product which was mild	25	65	10	100
Product most bitter	70	28	2	100

This very brief abstract illustrates a clear difference in the perceptions of the same product presented with two varying labels. Version 'M' moves the product more effectively in the direction of the marketing intention than does 'L'.

Functional Considerations

Another trend in recent years relates to the entire concept of convenience in marketing. Functional innovations in packaging which facilitate actual product usage are welcomed by consumers. Consumers are learning to expect effective, convenient packaging from manufacturers and when they do not get it they may express hostility toward the brand. In your own experience as a consumer, think of all the times you had difficulty opening a can or bottle. Try to remember how aggravated you got. Then multiply your experience by thousands and you can easily realize the sales effects such experiences can create for a given manufacturer.

The familiar closure problem, however, is only one of the many in the area of usage. Consider such things as: slippery glass bottles that break in the bathroom while shaving, bulky bottles, and cartons that cannot be easily disposed of and bottles which are cumbersome to use.

Packages which overcome such problems are attractive to consumers. Packages which go beyond problem solving and make it even easier for the consumer become an even more important brand differential. Through research in the usage pattern area, it is possible to locate such consumer difficulties and even uncover new directions which will facilitate usage. One familiar example is crushproof 'flip-top boxes' for cigarettes which have been well received in the UK due to their functional characteristics.

Measuring Functional Considerations Using Placement Tests

The functional features of a pack are best studied under in-use conditions. This research is best presented in a way which avoids any concentration on the pack as such by the respondent at the time of placement and usage. A useful procedure is to conduct a sequential pseudo-product test research design. The product is kept constant while the package construction varies in each placement. Unlabelled packets are used to eliminate 'symbolic interference' and brand bias.

Example. This study comprised a package construction test for a hand-rolling tobacco, in which two alternative types of construction were compared. These are referred to, for convenience, by the code letters 'R' and 'T'. These two packs were tested upon a total of 200 men who smoked brand 'Y' as their usual brand. The two packs were placed with informants, separately and in sequence, with the placement order rotated; informants were allowed two days to smoke the tobacco, and then were called upon and interviewed to find their reactions. At the end of the test, when the informants had tried both packs, they were asked to express a preference between them, and to give reasons for this. This emerged as follows.

| | $N = 200$ |
Preferences between the packs*	%
Prefer pack 'R'	31
Prefer pack 'T'	68

There was no difference in these preferences when one considered the size of pack normally bought by the informants; over the range half-ounce, one-ounce, and two-ounce usual pack, there was the same pattern of preference.

When asked the *reason* for their preferences, the informants replied as follows.

Reasons for pack preferences*

Bases = informants who preferred each pack.

	Prefer 'R' %	Prefer 'T' %
Just like it, for no particular reason	2	4
Easier to open	7	43
Easier to get at the tobacco	4	31
Better sealed	26	2
Easier to reseal	9	6
Keeps the tobacco fresh	42	10
A stronger pack	19	8
Easier to use	0	9

* Open-ended question—does not add up to 100%.

These comments on the reason for preferring one pack or the other centred upon two aspects of the packs, *convenience* and *protection*. The informants seemed mainly concerned with either one or the other of these aspects: those who were convenience-oriented preferred pack 'T' and those who were protection-oriented preferred pack 'R'.

Measuring the visual factors

With the increasing importance of self-service merchandizing, creating pack displays which will easily be singled out by the consumer has become an important criterion in packaging success. However, measuring this dimension in a meaningful way is difficult. And the methodology involved in such studies is somewhat complex and difficult to handle.

One primary aim in this phase of research is to establish the extent to which a pack will 'stand-out' in a visual display. There are other 'identification' factors such as legibility and brand recognition. These latter factors are of significance but they should not be confused with the problem of 'stand-out', as they often are.

Now, let us look at the sequence of visual events (a fuller description of this line of argument will be found in a paper by Dillon, 1969). For the sake of simplicity, we will imagine that the viewer has her eyes closed, and we will examine the sequence as she opens her eyes and thereafter.

The viewer is suddenly bombarded by the light coming from the total display. At that moment, each item is competing with each other item in the display for the viewer's attention. Where the viewer's attention goes is influenced by several factors. However, it is possible to control for a number of these factors in the test situation so that the critical factor—the effective contrast between each item and its background, i.e., other items in the display—is the one measured by the test.

Let us call this immediate, attention-capturing stage 'visual stage 1'. What happens next? The viewer's eye will stay on the item which has now caught her attention for an indefinite time, during which her brain (at least) will begin and continue to process the information transmitted by the pack; and then her eye may move to another item in the display. Let us call the stage at which she is *processing* the information transmitted by the first item to which her eye has moved 'visual stage 2' and the later event(s) 'visual stage 3'. This is a simplified model of the situation for the purposes of our argument. We can summarize the sequence as follows.

Visual stage 1: viewer's attention goes to one item
in the display;

Visual stage 2: viewer processes the information
transmitted by that item;

Visual stage 3: further events occur.

In stand-out research we are trying to measure *simply what happens at visual stage 1*, i.e., how well the test pack competes with its competitors in terms of catching the viewer's attention.

It may be noted that *as visual stage 2 progresses* the viewer will begin to be able to identify the brand, the manufacturer, the (projected) product characteristics, etc., and she will be reacting to what we might call the imagery properties (of the pack, the brand, as described elsewhere). Using questions relating to brand identification as a measure thus presupposes *both* visual stages 1 and 2. Since in most tachistoscopic* measures the respondent is required to report what she saw, these do not adequately measure 'stand-out' as it has here been defined. To measure stand-out it has been found that a 'find time' method is most useful. It has several advantages in addition to its relevance; for example, it avoids certain procedural problems and it is sensitive. However, tachistoscopes are usefully employed when visual stage 2 information represents the research objective. The most common instance of this is when one wants to establish the ease of brand identification.

Another device which has sometimes been used for packaging research is the eye camera, measuring where the eye is focussed from moment to moment. However, this has proved to be of little value in market research generally, and its application in the area of packaging has similarly been discouraging. There are three main problems associated with its use. First, where the eye is fixated does not reliably indicate what the person is in fact perceiving. Second, the equipment tends to be cumbersome to use (and unpopular with respondents). Third, data analysis is time-consuming and costly.

The Find Time Procedure

The procedure is a variation on what is known as 'disjunctive reaction time'. In essence, the respondent has to search for an item in each of a series of displays, knowing that it will sometimes be in a given display, and sometimes not. If she finds it, she gives one response; as soon as she decides that it is not there, she gives an alternative response (which is normally ignored, but which could also be taken into account). One is measuring how long it takes to find a pack when it is there. Prior to the main task each respondent should be tested for normal vision (with glasses if worn), and undertakes a practice run in an unrelated product area and series of displays.

Let us say there are two test variants, 'A1' and 'A2'. These might be two (competitive) current packs, a current design and a proposed new design, or two possible designs for a new product. The type of display should correspond to the actual market environment—gondolas, counter tops, counter units, dump bins, display stands, window displays, etc. Also, two

---

* A tachistoscope is a mechanical or electronic device for exposing stimuli (packs, advertisements, etc.), to a viewer for strictly controlled (brief) periods of time.

or more different types of display, e.g., supermarket gondola plus chemist's counter top, can be used in the one series.

Although the number is arbitrary, a frequent pattern is to use six displays with a given test item *present* (in six different positions, with detailed control over the pack adjacencies from display to display) plus three displays with the given test item *absent*. A separate closely matched group of, say, 50 people will see each different series (of nine displays). One series will differ from the other *only in respect of the test variant* which appears (in six out of the nine displays).

After screening and the practice run, each respondent (individually) is shown her particular test item and is allowed to familiarize herself with it as she wishes, and she has it in front of her during the rest of the session. She is instructed to press one of two small response keys (situated immediately beneath her fingers) as soon as she sees the test item in a display (speed being emphasized), *or* to press the other response key as soon as she decides that the test item is not in the display.

Each display is projected by means of a pre-loaded, pre-focussed, automatic projector (the order of test item present/absent being determined by the experimenter in advance), which is electronically linked with a timer, a light (to keep illumination constant between and within trials), and the two response keys. Exposure time continues from the start of the projection (which starts the timer) until either response key is pressed. Colour coded lights indicate which key was pressed. The timer is stopped by the operation of either response key. Having recorded the reaction time (or 'find time' as it is often called) and reset the timer, the start button is pressed to start the next display (and the clock, putting out the light simultaneously).

The basic data is six reaction times per respondent to the presence of that respondent's test item when it is in the displays, subject to about two per cent known response error. With 50 people per test item, we have 300 measures of how long it takes to find each test item, and this amount of data of this power is more than adequate to provide robust evidence of differences (or otherwise) between the test items. Being parametric in form, the data can have a 't' test applied to it. Perhaps the central virtue of the test, apart from its sensitivity in terms of discrimination between test items, lies in the fact that it appears to overcome, or at least minimize, the 'familiarity bias' found in tachistoscopic methods. Examples follow of both 'stand-out' and 'identification' problems.

Example of 'Stand-out' Problem. The aim in this research was to assess two variations of a new pack design for a confectionery product in terms of stand-out effectiveness relative to the current pack. The research involved the use of the find time technique. The test material comprised:

(a) variation 1 of a new pack;
(b) variation 2 of a new pack;
(c) the current pack 'P'.

Table 17.3 *Stand-out results*

Packs	Mean reaction times	t-test value	Significance level
'V2' Current 'P'	1.77 s 1.59 s	1.99	Not significant
'V1' Current 'P'	1.98 s 1.59 s	3.71	P < 0.001
'V2' 'V1'	1.77 s 1.98 s	2.05	P < 0.05

The total sample of 150 respondents was split into three quota-matched sub-samples of 50 respondents each, corresponding to the three test items. After visual screening, and a full practice run, each respondent was given the test pack appropriate to his/her sub-sample. He was then shown, sequentially, a series of nine slides showing displays of confectionery items. In six of these displays the test pack *was* present and in the other three displays it *was not* present. The respondent was required to press one or other of two response keys, according to whether or not he found the test item present in the display. The length of time taken to find the test pack when it *was* present comprised the data for this research, summarized in Table 17.3. The 'V2' packet was thus significantly better in stand-out than 'V1' at the five per cent level. However, there was no significant difference between 'V2' and the current pack, which was also significantly better than 'V1' at the 0.1 per cent level.

Example of Identification Problem. The aim of the research was to provide some measurement of the:

(a) visibility of a rectangular panel introduced onto the main display face of a frozen food brand package;
(b) relative visibility and legibility of the various components of the message contained within that panel.

The method employed in the research was a tachistoscopic procedure (sample size 36) in which each respondent was first familiarized with the normal current carton, i.e., one *not* bearing the panel which was the subject of the research. The woman was given the carton to hold and study, and the major design elements of the pack were pointed out to her. The respondent was then told that she was about to be shown a similar pack 'for just a very short space of time' and would be asked to say if she saw anything on that pack which was in any way different from the carton she just studied. The test pack, bearing the rectangular panel, was then exposed to the respondent in a series of controlled-time exposures, by means of a mirror tachistoscope. Eight progressively longer controlled-time exposures were used, ranging from 10 ms ($\frac{1}{100}$ of a second) to 2000 ms (2 s). After each exposure the respondent was asked to say what, if any, difference she saw in the test pack, compared with the initial prompt pack, and her responses were recorded verbatim. Responses were probed to ensure that maximum available data emerged after each exposure. If, at the conclusion of the full series of eight controlled-time tests, the respondent had not fully verbalized the message contained on the panel, the test pack was exposed to her for such a period of time as was necessary for her to do so. This constitutes the ninth (infinity) trial on the table of results included in Table 17.4.

Table 17.4 Summary of responses. Trial at which design component/element first mentioned

Sample base: 36		Design Component Code (see key below)						
Trial No.	Controlled time exposure	A	B	C	D	E	F	G
		No.	No.	No.	No.	No.	No.	No.
1	10 ms	—	—	—	—	—	—	—
2	20 ms	1	—	—	—	—	—	—
3	50 ms	4	—	1	2	—	—	—
4	100 ms	9	2	—	2	—	—	—
5	200 ms	12	8	3	3	—	—	—
6	500 ms	5	8	6	3	—	—	—
7	1000 ms	1	6	3	6	4	8	—
8	2000 ms	—	3	1	3	12	4	11
9	infinity	—	—	—	—	—	—	25
Total responses on each design component		32	27	14	19	16	12	36
Median score—in trials		4.17	5.44	5.5	5.83	7.66	6.75	—

Key to coding of design components:
Noting of, reference to . . .
A difference from prompt pack/panel mentioned
B design motif in panel, i.e., stylized flower
C red/red lettering in panel
D blue/blue lettering in panel
E actual phrase 'Free Gifts'
F actual slogan
G identification/verbalization of total message

The panel introduced onto the display face of the test pack contained the message 'Free Gifts' in red lettering and a slogan in blue lettering. It also contained a central stylized flower design motif. The results are shown in Table 17.4. Of the total sample of 36 respondents, 32, or 89 per cent, registered their awareness of the test panel, by shape, position on pack, etc., as not having been present in the prompt pack. The most readily noticed and remarked feature of the panel was its stylized flower design motif. Rather more respondents registered awareness of some blue lettering in the panel than those mentioning the red lettering (although these produced essentially the same median score related to speed of perception). However, rather more respondents deciphered the red rather than the blue lettering, as a prelude to verbalizing the total message, even though they did so somewhat more slowly. Only about 30 per cent of the entire sample of respondents were able to decipher the *total* message at the maximum operable time exposure of two seconds.

462

In summary the findings of this research suggested that, although the test panel, as a total unit, made its presence known widely and promptly, its ability to communicate a message was relatively poor within the terms of normal tachistoscopic procedures. Within the panel, the stylized flower design motif appeared to be the most visible and, therefore, the dominant element. The blue lettering appeared to be more *visible* than the red in this particular design context, but less *legible*. (However, this last point must be considered in the light of the longer phrase and, perhaps, less familiar words involved in the blue print, compared with the simpler 'Free Gifts' in red.)

Name Testing

Is testing a name really a worthwhile exercise? Some marketing men have disputed this point on the grounds that any name given advertising backing can be made effective. And many examples of names meaningless in themselves can be cited where the brands in fact are highly successful. In some cases the names themselves would on the surface appear to be detrimental in marketing.

One may conclude from this that in all probability the name itself is not a key factor in marketing. Success might be achieved without it. Yet an ineffective name or one which is inappropriate represents a significant handicap at least in the early stages of a brand's marketing life. Assuming that other factors in the product mix are right an inappropriate name places a burden on the total effort while one that communicates effectively will facilitate the marketing process.

The criteria for an effective name

The manner in which we research the name problem is to some extent conditioned by the criteria by which we are to judge its value. One might usefully delineate two types of criteria:

(a) general;
(b) specific.

General Criteria

Here we may list a number of factors one would ideally like in any brand name:

(a) easy to pronounce;
(b) suggestive of the product class;
(c) easy to recognize quickly;
(d) easy to recall;
(e) not spontaneously associated with negative ideas;
(f) not associated with other products;
(g) not previously registered by another company.

Specific Criteria

Specific criteria are those dimensions one would like to communicate by the name in terms of the way in which one intends to position the brand within the market. Such ideas are usually related to the findings of previous market surveys and, more especially, the findings from motivational types of studies. Hence, for example, in a study for a shampoo manufacturer who wanted to position a brand in the cosmetic shampoo side of the market, in addition to the general criteria cited he wanted the name to suggest *beauty*, *softness*, *lightness*, *romance*, and *luxury*.

In sharp contrast, a washing machine manufacturer wanted to suggest *durability*, *engineering quality*, *speed*, *modernity*, and *reliability*.

Methods of researching the problem

As a rule, research itself is not effective in generating specific names for testing. However, background research does provide specific criterion information which is useful to the marketing executives and advertising agencies in their efforts at building up a preliminary list of names.

In our experience, one usually starts with a very long list of possible names which as a rule is too exhaustive to test. Hence, short-listing procedures are required. More often than not this step is conducted on the basis of judgment, though there is no reason, budget allowing, why the names should not be short-listed by means of a simple open-ended word association test for the entire list. At this point, it is as well to check-out the short list to ensure that no name is submitted to further testing which has previously been registered by a competitor or another company. A good deal of money and effort can be spent only to find at the end of it all that prior registration makes it impossible to use the winning name.

Testing the Short List

Pronunciation. Respondents can be asked to read aloud from a printed list the various names. Two features of the act can be usefully observed. First, the relative ease or difficulty the respondent encounters in saying the name aloud. Second, an indication can be made by the interviewer as to where the accent falls. Ideally, one likes a name which will usually be asked for in the same way.

Association Tests

One of the most useful procedures in name testing is the use of free association. The procedure consists of simply saying the name aloud to the respondent and asking him to give you all the thoughts and ideas that occur to him. Experience suggests that it is a good idea first to give the respondent a few words not related to the test by way of practice trials. Practice trials are important in that they familiarize the respondent with the task and serve as a learning experience for an act which many ordinary people find unusual.

A further useful preliminary procedure is to give examples of what you want the respondent to do. Hence a typical introduction to the question might be, 'I'm going to say a number of words to you one at a time. After each word I say I want you to tell me the first word or thought that pops into your mind; for example, if I say *"hot"* you might say *"cold"*; if I say *"sweet"* you might say *"bitter"*. Alright, now when I say ————— what pops into your mind?' (It is at this point that the trial or warm-up words are introduced.)

Two types of information should be recorded. First, though less important, is the amount of time (using a stopwatch) that the respondent takes in responding. Second, the actual verbatim response.

An analysis of the time it takes to respond may be significant. An average response time is worked out for the entire list. This is compared with the mean time for each name. If a name yields a time factor which is significantly larger than average it gives reason for concern because very slow reaction times are usually indicative of blocking or emotional complexes of an unconscious nature. However, by far the most important feature of this part of the test, is the content analysis. Here one can determine the extent to which the name induces:

(a) positive/negative tendencies;
(b) imagery which may be related or unrelated;
(c) spontaneous product expectancies if such emerge.

In this type of research, rotation of name presentation from respondent to respondent is particularly important, since it is known that the responses to some extent will be influenced by the previous stimuli.

After eliciting spontaneous associations to the names we have found it useful to get respondents to anticipate the kind of product that each name might represent. Here it is best to start with open-ended procedures, e.g., 'Some of the words I've read out to you are in fact names for products. Now for each name I read out to you could you try to guess what product or products it might be a name for?'. After a question on product anticipation using open-ended procedures one might repeat the question requiring the respondent to select from a list the product that each name might represent. (It is as well to point out to the respondent that he can use the same product on the list more than once if he so desires.)

Anticipated Imagery

By far the most important aspect in name research is to establish the kind of imagery that the name in itself will elicit in terms of the specific criteria discussed previously. At this point a forced choice type of association test similar to the procedure in packaging research might be employed. The respondent is told that all the names describe different brands in a particular product class. He is given a printed list of the brand names and asked to guess which of the names is most likely to be high on each of a series of attributes. As has been pointed out elsewhere one can use *rank-order* or *rating scale* procedures in these quantitative association methods. However, we are inclined to favour in name tests either rank-order or single forced choice procedures. Analysis of this data will give the researcher and client a good indication of the extent to which the test names will contribute to the desired imagery profile for the brand.

The Name in Configural Context

It is at this point that name testing merges into the area of packaging research. While the name as such may be suggestive of various ideas which are relevant, and while it may be easy to pronounce, the actual logo-style used and context in which it will appear will have a bearing on how the name will be perceived. Once a name has been selected it will usually be treated differently on alternative pack designs. In addition to testing packs with the name simply as part of the total configuration (as described in this chapter generally) it is useful to look at the name treatment specifically. Hence while we believe that 'visual find-time' for the pack in its competitive environment is critical, it is also useful to look more specifically at how easy or difficult it is to recognize the brand name as it appears on each alternative (by using a tachistoscope test).

Testing Corporate Trade-Marks

Research in this area usually falls into two types:

(a) evaluating existing symbols;
(b) appraising new symbols.

Existing corporate symbols

In studying existing corporate symbols that have been used by a company for a number of years three key dimensions must be taken into consideration:

(a) penetration, i.e., how familiar the relevant public is with the symbol;
(b) appropriateness, the extent to which ideas communicated by the symbol are associated with the attributes the company wishes to communicate about itself;
(c) visual properties, the visual properties of the design in terms of stand-out (impact).

We have discussed in the course of this chapter a number of methods in packaging and name research which are also relevant in testing a symbol. As we discuss each of these dimensions the reader's attention will be drawn to research procedures previously described where such reference is appropriate.

Penetration Evaluation. This problem is best dealt with by means of representative samples of the relevant publics with which the company is concerned. Here, we have found that unaided and aided re-call procedures are most useful to establish the extent to which the symbol has become associated in the public mind with the company. The method usually consists, first, of getting the respondents to describe in words what the trademark looks like for each of a series of companies, one of which is the client organization. Second, the aided re-call section consists of exposing to the sample a series of actual trademarks and requiring the respondent to name the company with which each trademark is identified.

Measuring Appropriateness. The procedures here are similar to techniques described elsewhere. Various forms of association methods are adequate to deal with this problem.

Measuring Visual Strength. 'Find-time' procedures are particularly useful in this case and it is useful to run the experiment not only for the client's trademark but for competitors' as well.

The stimulus environment material may vary depending upon where the trademark is usually placed, e.g., the respondent is given a copy of the trademark to look at and he is instructed to push the timing device when he thinks he has seen it in a display of several trademarks. One might use a montage of trademarks from letterheads as the stimulus material. Rotations, and sequences involving the presence or absence of the trademark, can be varied as one would do in packaging experiments described elsewhere (see p 460).

The Relationship between the Key Variables

The three variables just discussed may be taken into consideration together in planning the company policy with regard to its trademark. Conceptually, the relationship between the three variables may be described as shown below. (What will constitute a high or low score will depend on the subjective criteria set by the management. Since absolute values cannot be assigned meaningfully it is as well to look at the results relative to trademarks for other companies.)

+ = high

− = low

	1	2	3	4	5	6	7	8
Penetration	+	−	+	−	−	−	+	+
Appropriateness	+	−	−	+	−	+	−	+
Visual strength	+	−	−	+	+	−	+	−

These are the ways a company trademark may stand on the three dimensions. The indications suggested in each case might be as follows.

Case No.

1   No change is indicated in the trademark.

2   An entirely new trademark is indicated.

3   The trademark should be revamped but preserving cues of familiarity.

4   The trademark should not be revamped but used more widely/effectively (in promotional activity, perhaps).

5   The trademark requires modification and wider promotion.

6   As above but with action on visual clarity.

7   Redesign retaining strong visual elements.

8   Improve visual clarity of trademark.

Bibliography

1. Books

ADLER, M. K. *Marketing and Market Research*, 1967 (see section p. 277, Package Tests Are Fashionable: refers to visual instrumentation and other psychological and physiological tests).

AGNEW, H. E. and HOUGHTON, D. *Marketing Policies*, 1951, 2nd edition (see p. 363, chapter 17 Package Sales Tests).

CORAM, T. (ed.) *Cases in Marketing and Marketing Research*, 1969 (see section 11, p. 92, David Greig Package Designs contributed by Gordon Wills from article in *Packaging*, Jan. 1967).

GILMER, VON HALLER. *Psychology*, 1970.

HEPNER, H. W. *Advertising—Creative Communication with Consumers*, 1964 (see pp. 199–201, 205–206).

LEDUC, R. *How to Launch a New Product*, 1966 (see p. 61 for package-testing).

LE GRAND, Y. *Form and Space Vision*, 1967 (see chapter 10 pp. 158–177, Movements to the Eye, for discussion of different types of experimental method in this connection, including instruments and apparatus; also findings).

RODGER, L. W. *Marketing in a Competitive Economy*, 1965 (see p. 120, ratings chart, p. 124 section on Test Marketing. Text and charts include package research under product research).

2. On packaging

INSTITUTE OF PACKAGING. *Fundamentals of Packaging*, 1962.

GRAY, M., CBE RDI FSIA, Senior partner Design Research Unit. *Package Design*, 1955 (chapter 2, The Science of Distribution).

GUSS, L. M. *Packaging Is Marketing*, AMA Inc., 1967.

JONES, H. *Planned Packaging*, 1950 (see chapter 17, p. 89, The Value of Research).

PILDITCH, J. *The Silent Salesman*, 1961 (see chapter 7, When to Use Research, pp. 82–95).

3. On motivational and visual research.

BERLYNE, D. E. *Conflict Arousal and Curiosity*, 1960.

CHESKIN, L. *Basis for marketing decision through controlled motivation research*, 1962.
    Color for Profit, 1951.
    Colours and what they can do, 1951.
    Why People Buy, 1960.

CIRLOT. *A Dictionary of Symbols*, Eng. trans., 1962.

DICHTER, E. *The Strategy of Desire*, 1960.
    Handbook of Consumer Motivations, 1964.

HOGG, J. *Psychology and the Visual Arts, selected readings*, 1969.
LEHNER, E. *Symbols, Signs and Signets*, 1950.
VERNON, M. D. (Ed.) *Experiments in Visual Perception: selected readings*, 2nd Edn., 1970.

Articles, Papers, Pamphlets

Articles and papers

BERLYNE, D. E. Conflict and Information Theory Variables as Determinants of Human Perceptual Curiosity. *J. Exp. Psychol.*, **53**, 1957.

BERLYNE, D. E. Influence of Complexity and Novelty in Visual Figures on Orienting Responses. *J. Exp. Psychol.*, **55**, 1958.

BERLYNE, D. E. Complexity and Incongruity Variables as Determinants of Exploratory Choice and Evaluative Ratings. *Canad. J. Psychol.*, **17**, 1963.

BERLYNE, D. E., CRAW, M. A., SALAPATER, P. H., and LEWIS, J. L. Novelty, Complexity, Incongruity, Extrinsic Motivation and the GSR. *J. Exp. Psychol.*, **66**, 1963.

BERLYNE, D. E. and PECKHAM, S. The Semantic Differential and Other Measures of Reaction to Visual Complexity. *Canad. J. Psychol.*, **20**, 1966.

DILLON, P. J. *The Tachistoscopic Falacy: a Case of Invalid Research*, paper given to Market Research Society Annual Conference (UK), March 1969.

ENOCH, J. M. Effect of the Size of a Complex Display upon Visual Search. *J. Opt. Soc. Amer.*, **49**, 1959. (Use of 'opthalmograph unit'.)

FORD, A., WHITE, C. J., and LICHTENSTEIN, M. Analysis of Eye-movements during Free Search, *J. Opt. Soc. Amer.*, **49**, 1959. (Use of electrodes, cathode ray oscilloscope and automatic camera to obtain electro-oculographic plots of eyeball movements.)

FLETCHER, R. and MABEY, B. Effects of Set and Expectation in Tachistoscope Testing, *Admap*, January 1970.

GOULD, J. D. and SCHAFFER, A. Eye-movement Patterns in Scanning Numeric Displays, *Perceptual and Motor Skills*, **20**, 1965. (Excerpt from this comprises reading twenty-four from M. D. Vernon *Experiments in Visual Perception*, q.v.)

JAHODA, G. Sex Differences in Preference for Shapes: a Cross-Cultural Replication, *Brit. J. Psychol.*, **47**, 1956.

MACKWORTH, J. F. and MACKWORTH, N. H. Eye Fixations Recorded on Changing Visual Scenes by the Television Eye-market. *J. Opt. Soc. Amer.*, **48**, 1958. (Use of television camera to record the position of a man's gaze, use of second television camera to record scene he is looking at, and television monitor showing same scene; total composite eye-scene picture recorded with motion-picture camera; primarily intended for use with moving display.)

MACKWORTH, N. H. and LLEWELLYN-THOMAS, E. Head-mounted Eye-market Camera, *J. Opt. Soc. Amer.*, **52**, 1962. (Device consists of a small movie camera and a periscope that transmits a spot of light reflected from the eye.)

NEISSER, U. Decision without Reaction Time: Experiments in Visual Scanning. *Amer. J. Psychol.*, **76**, 1963.

POTTER, J. Packaging Research: Is It Adequate? *Advertisers Weekly*, 21 July 1967.

ROCHE, M., LODGE, G., and YASIN, J. A Pre-test Market Programme. *Admap*, April 1970.

SCHLACKMAN, W. Evaluating the Pack Design in Marketing. *Scientific Business*, 1963.

TINKER, M. Recent studies of Eye Movements in Reading, *Psychol. Bull.*, **55**, 1958.

2. Pamphlets

(a) *AMA Management Bulletins*

Especially:

No. 53, 1964: *The Package: Key Components of Marketing Strategy*. Articles by Murphy and Gee.

No. 96, 1967. *The Uses of Imagination in Packaging*. Articles by Siebel, Hoffman, and Solomon.

No. 106, 1968. *Consumer Oriented Packaging*. Articles by Goldberg, Mahaney, Friedman, and Wuerther.

No. 118, 1968. *Effective Beverage Marketing through Better Packaging.* Articles by Glazier and Bergwall.

(b) *Other Publications*

AMA Management Report No. 65, 1961. *The Power of Packaging.* See Part III, Consumer Packaging, articles by Barksdale and Thomas.

AMA Packaging Series No. 53, 1957. *Marketing Research Reports on Packaging.* Articles by Nielsen and Trelogan.

Institute of Packaging Advisory Service Report No. 350, 1960. *Fundamentals of Packaging.*

How Much Value can be Added by Packaging? *Journal of Marketing*, Jan. 1968.

The Coming Battle of the Packages, *Sales Management*, 4 May 1962.

18.   Research on 'below the line' expenditure

Martin Simmons

This chapter deals with the contribution of research, both in the planning and evaluation, of 'below the line' activity. Any definition of 'below the line' assumes a false dichotomy since many promotions are dependent on media advertising. This would be so, for example, when reduced offers are backed by national press advertising. In the current context 'below the line' expenditure is defined to include the following, whether or not they are supported by media advertising:

(a) any in-store promotional activity to the consumer such as premium offers, reduced price offers, stamps and coupons, competitions and banded packs;
(b) any trade incentives or discounts to the retailer;
(c) all display material whether in support of specific promotions or not;
(d) any point-of-sale aids such as leaflets, brochures, store demonstrations;
(e) any direct promotion to the consumer such as couponing or free samples.

Expenditure on items such as sales force incentive schemes and sponsorships is excluded for the purpose of this chapter.

The Growth of 'Below the Line' Expenditure

There are three trends in British retailing which have placed increasing emphasis on 'below the line' activity. The first is the development of self-service techniques, especially in the grocery trade. Self-service retailing now accounts for 70 per cent of grocery turnover and is becoming increasingly important in other retail outlets such as chemists, confectioners, hardware stores and off-licences. Any self-service operation lends itself naturally to 'below the line' activity. The manufacturer has to ensure that his goods are noticed and subsequently purchased. The second trend is the increasing concentration of retail trade into a fewer number of outlets, e.g., in this country there are around 130 000 grocers; 24 000 of these are self-service stores accounting for nearly three-quarters of the total grocery trade, and 3000 of these are supermarkets taking up over one-third. This means that about two per cent of stores account for over one-third of the grocery trade. Manufacturers now spend vast sums of money to secure a favourable position at the point-of-sale particularly at these key outlets. The third trend is the ever-increasing range of brands from which the consumer has to choose. To identify his brand from the competition, the manufacturer resorts to varied forms of promotion apart from media advertising.

There are no validated figures for the size, in monetary terms, of 'below the line' activity but the growth has been substantial in the last decade. One estimate of expenditure on display material alone was £36 million in 1965. In 1970, expenditure is likely to have exceeded £80 million. In five years, expenditure on display material has more than doubled. If all 'below the line' activity is included, expenditure probably exceeds that of media advertising and is generally agreed to be in the range of £350 to £450 million per annum.

Planning 'Below the Line' Activity

The problems facing an advertiser in planning his 'below the line' activity can be classified into four broad categories:

(a) *Budget allocation*—he has to decide for, possibly, a range of products on the optimum allocation of limited resources. What part of his promotional expenditure should be made on television, press, and other media and what part should be spent 'below the line'?

(b) *Setting promotional objectives*—what exactly is the aim of the promotional activity? It is necessary to distinguish between retail objectives which can be regarded as 'intermediate' such as increasing shelf space, and final consumer objectives which are 'ultimate' in the sense of actual sales;

(c) *Pre-testing*—the next problem involves pre-testing the promotional plan in order to evaluate its likely success, or which of several possible tactics should be adopted. In practice, this normally means pre-testing the components of the promotional plan, i.e., the individual promotions;

(d) *Post-assessment*—having decided on a certain level and form of 'below the line' expenditure, how effective has this been? The manufacturer will want to assess whether or not his objectives have been achieved.

The allocation of budgets for 'below the line' expenditure is often not planned on any scientific basis. Because of the difficulty of creating a marked division above and below the line, there is a tendency to consider an overall promotional budget. Then portions are hived off for 'below the line' activity as and when needed. This philosophy is encouraged by the reluctance of some advertising agents to fit 'below the line' into their services and functions. J. Wood has recently stated the case: 'Part of the problem is that promotional activity does not fit neatly into the recognised triumvirate of account, creative, and media group'[1]. Ranjit Chib in a recent article in Ad Weekly, had this to say about the question: 'The total marketing budget for a product/brand is found to be usually related to its anticipated gross sales and thereby to the profit it is likely to generate. The first thing to come out of the marketing budget is media expenditure, with below-the-line activity something of a poor relation. Where below-the-line activity is regarded as important, it can be fixed as a definite proportion of the marketing budget. The point is, however, that it still has to fit into the budget rather than help determine it. This can be extremely wasteful from the manufacturer's point of view'[2].

Budget allocation and the setting of promotional objectives for 'below the line' activity are inseparably linked, and equally liable to neglect in forward planning. Many marketing executives would have difficulty if asked to define exactly what a specific promotion is designed to achieve. It can be argued that the aim of any promotional activity is to increase sales, either short-term or long-term. The advantage of more precise objectives is that they can determine the most appropriate promotional techniques to be used. Some examples of possible promotional objectives and techniques are shown below.

Promotional objective	Technique
(a) To encourage consumer trial of a new product or pack size.	Product sampling.
(b) To clear old stock prior to brand re-launch or main promotional campaign.	Consumer offer, e.g., plastic daffodils for two packs.
(c) To widen retail distribution prior to commencement of media advertising.	Trade discounts.
(d) To obtain prime display position in key outlets.	Trade bonusing backed by special display units.
(e) To maintain display space in key outlets.	Self-liquidating consumer offer.
(f) To encourage consumer purchasing across a range of, e.g., soup flavours.	Money-back consumer offer, e.g., 20p postal order for five packs of different flavours.
(g) To emphasize a new variety, e.g., a flavour of soup.	As above, requiring two of the packs to be of the new flavour.
(h) To combat competitive pressure; blocking the competition.	Price cuts.
(i) To stimulate repeat purchasing.	On-pack coupon, i.e., money off on next purchase.
(j) To widen consumer interest in a brand.	Competition.

The Contribution of Research

While many stages of marketing activity are scientifically planned and researched, the influences on consumer purchasing have been widely neglected at perhaps the most vital point of all, the point of sale. 'A survey on point of sale, carried out in November, 1966 by Industrial Facts and Forecasting on behalf of Abbey Goodman Display Limited revealed that fewer than one company in ten has ever assessed point of sale effectiveness on any systematic basis[3]. Relatively little research has been conducted on promotional activity despite the fact that 'below the line' expenditure now rivals traditional media in size. Decisions still tend to be based on experience, competitive activity and on hunch. Some reasons for the slow development of research into promotional activity are:

(a) lack of clear promotional objectives to measure;
(b) vested interests; i.e., those with the function of promotional planning at advertiser and agency level resisting the entry of research into a traditionally creative area;
(c) the 'ad hoc' nature of many aspects of promotional activity which does not allow for long-term conclusions to be drawn for future promotional planning;
(d) the apparent limitations of time and confidentiality when pre-testing any parts of a promotional plan. This is due to the tight schedules (or lack of forward planning) operating and the fear of any 'leak' to the competition.

There are also doubts about the validity of research on promotional activity coupled with the failure of research agencies to develop and convincingly market appropriate techniques. These techniques, their applications and their limitations are described under the following headings:

(a) budget allocation;
(b) pre-testing;
(c) post-assessment.

Research: Budget Allocation

The problem here is what part of advertising expenditure should be made 'below the line' or, more specifically, on point-of-sale activities. Research has contributed very little to this decision and certainly no available technique can give an exact figure for the appropriation to be allocated to point-of-sale activities. The decision is clearly not a simple matter of statistics. Media advertising is often an important strategic weapon to use with retailers to gain distribution. Also point-of-sale advertising can act as a reminder of a message previously got across by other media. We are back to the extreme difficulty of introducing an artificial line between media and other promotional activity. Nevertheless, a premise which is gaining acceptance is that point-of-sale activities should be concentrated on product groups where the impulse sector is high. That is where the brand, and often the product purchased, is decided inside the store. Research can contribute by assessing the magnitude of the impulse sector. Shoppers can be interviewed before and immediately after purchase.

The expenditure on a product can then be divided into four sectors:

(a) *Specifically planned*—product and brand known before the shopper arrives at the store;
(b) *Substituted*—specifically planned but brand substituted in the store;
(c) *Generally planned*—the shopper knew the product, but not the brand, before arriving at the store;
(d) *Unplanned*—the shopper had no intention of buying the product when arriving at the store.

This information establishes the relative influence on the purchase of store factors. Research conducted by the Gallup Poll in conjunction with the Association of Point of Sale Advertising in 1968 showed the level of impulse purchasing across a range of products illustrated in Table 18.1. A limitation of this method is that it can only be applied to 'quick-moving' product categories, otherwise the expense of interviewing shoppers at the retail outlets is prohibitively expensive. For less frequently purchased products, research methods relying on a reconstruction of buying behaviour at a single-call interview can be used to establish the importance of impulse buying. Before deciding how much to spend at the point of sale, it seems

Table 18.1

	Product expenditure	Specifically planned	Substituted	Generally planned	Unplanned	Impulse sector
Breakfast cereals	100	52	19	13	16	48
Brown bread	100	38	10	24	28	62
Butter	100	65	13	13	9	35
Cakes and pastries	100	17	4	37	42	83
Canned cat food	100	61	11	17	11	39
Canned dog food	100	62	9	18	11	38
Canned milk pudding	100	45	6	17	32	55
Canned soup	100	55	10	12	23	45
Chocolate confectionery	100	16	5	29	50	84
Frozen foods:						
Burgers	100	45	5	11	39	55
Fish fillets	100	43	5	24	28	57
Fish fingers	100	43	7	21	29	57
Green beans	100	45	5	18	32	55
Mousse	100	39	2	16	43	61
Peas	100	61	4	18	17	39
Instant coffee	100	59	9	12	20	41
Instant milk powder	100	60	4	5	31	40
Margarine	100	73	6	10	11	27
Meat and vegetable extract	100	48	8	6	38	52
Paper handkerchiefs	100	18	20	25	37	82
Paper kitchen towels	100	48	12	23	17	52
Soft tissue toilet rolls	100	33	9	29	28	67
Tea (not tea bags)	100	70	8	9	13	30

relevant for a manufacturer at least to find out what part of brand expenditure is decided there. This information can only be used as a broad guideline, indicating whether more attention is warranted to 'below the line' activities in a particular market or not. It can be used to avoid the situation where 60 per cent of consumer brand decision is made at the point-of-sale, and 15 per cent of the promotional budget is spent 'below the line' and vice versa.

Another consideration on budget allocation is whether the brand is growing, static or declining. With a growing brand, promotions have an element of investment in encouraging trial and, thereafter, repurchase. With static or declining brands, this is unlikely to be true and promotions may have to justify themselves in terms of short-term payoff. A further factor determining 'below the line' expenditure is the marketing situation. Again, there is an investment element in a new product launch or a major product relaunch, compared with the continuing activities connected with an ongoing brand.

Research Pre-testing

There are various techniques which exist for pre-testing either with the consumer or the retail store the likely success of promotional activity. These tests can be carried out on a wide variety of materials ranging from verbal concepts to actual examples of the promotion. These techniques can be classified into:

(a) group discussions;
(b) hall tests;
(c) van tests;
(d) mini-van tests;
(e) postal and door to door tests;
(f) pre-testing the advertising of promotions;
(g) in-store tests.

The first six of these methods are consumer based for the very good reason that they tend to be easy, quick and cheap to operate. They are designed to give a reliable indication of the relative levels of likely consumer acceptance of a given set of promotional ideas or propositions. This may be further divided into two parts, first which is the most likely to succeed of a list of possible ideas and, second, how successful is the best one likely to be.

Group discussions. Before considering any kind of quantitative research, a company will often make use of a group discussion with their likely target group to test concepts and ideas. Groups may be used to:

(a) glean ideas for promotions which could warrant further consideration and research;
(b) assess which of several promotional ideas should be pursued, and which should be discounted as completely unacceptable.

Group discussions should be used only as a first filter and never interpreted as a final quantified result.

Hall Tests. Hall tests can be used to sort out which one is the most likely to succeed out of several similar possibilities. The hall test would usually be employed to pre-test such offers as free gifts, extra-size packs, on and in-pack premiums, and with-pack premiums. The methodology usually involves bringing a sample of target consumers into a hall or theatre and asking them to rate alternative offers in rank order. Briefly, the procedure of hall tests to pre-screen promotional items is as follows: a ranking of, say, six possible items, consumers are invited to take part at the hall on a particular day; the interviewers ask the respondents which items they like best, which second best and so on, and which they would not be interested in at all. The sample size is usually 100 to 150 which is sufficient to indicate the favourably and unfavourably considered. In the items to be tested it is advisable to include a control item, an item that has performed well in the past and, consequently, will give a relative measure of success and failure. The following points need to be built in to the test for the results to be of value:

(a) a maximum of eight items—large numbers would confuse the housewife and produce distorted ranking;
(b) the items to be tested should be of a similar cost to give the company a basis for decision;
(c) items should be of a similar nature—gimmicky items should not be tested against practical ones. Although the housewife may prefer the gimmicky items, she will be reluctant to admit so in the interview situation;
(d) only certain types of promotional ideas may be tested in the hall test. Money-off offers, for instance, will always be ranked the highest alongside other ideas.

The hall test may also be used effectively to test differing designs of the same proposed offer, e.g., drinking glasses or table mats.

Van Tests. In this instance a motorized caravan can be parked in a busy shopping area. Respondents would then be invited into the van to take part in similar tests to those carried out in hall tests. The advantage over the hall test for this technique is that larger samples of respondents can be obtained for the same field costs.

Mini-van Tests. A more sophisticated method has recently been set up in this country by Research Bureau Ltd. Promoted items are sold through vans calling at panels of homes and the extent of buying each promotion is recorded to assess their likely success. One important aspect of the mini-van is that it sets out to provide as closely as possible an actual retail sales situation within which activities such as promotions can be tested. To that extent, it is similar to store testing.

Postal and Door to Door Tests. The postal method consists of a panel of consumers to which the promotional offer is sent by post. It is then possible to assess the likely success of an offer or the relative success of offers by recording the extent to which the panel members buy the offer or offers. Information would also be collected on the types of consumers who are liable to take up a particular offer. This type of test does not necessarily have to be carried out by post. It is possible, for example, to place by distributing door to door and then measure the effects of couponing, sampling etc., by recording returns or by re-interview.

Pre-testing the Advertising of Promotions. It is useful before embarking on a large scale promotion to pre-test supporting advertising and display material which may have an effect on the success or failure of a promotion. The aim of this is two-fold. Is the:

(a) advertising and what it has to say readily understood?;
(b) approach attracting the target consumers?

Tests can be carried out with consumers to assess these aims and can check whether the advertising is likely to have an adverse effect on the brand's image, even though it may persuade people to buy in the short-term. These tests may involve using the same pre-testing techniques as for ordinary display advertising (referred to in another chapter).

In-store Tests. In-store tests are offered by a number of research companies in this country. The in-store test is a natural progression from hall tests and van tests, in that the items for offer that did well in these tests may now be put on the market-place. This will provide a useful indicator in a realistic situation of likely market sales. There are two main methods which can be employed both based on the technique of retail auditing:

(a) two panels of stores, one with the promotion or particular activity that is being tested and the other panel as a control. The success of the promoted item is measured by the sales achieved compared with the control item;
(b) alternatively, the two items (promoted and control item) are rotated within the same panel of stores. This reduces any error which may arise from using two matching panels. The disadvantage is the extra administrative work involved in switching the items so that both are tested in the same store within the test period.

In-store tests, unlike hall tests, can also be used to assess the effect of price changes, different shelf space allocations, changes in display material and variations in display position. The tests can involve a particular promotional activity versus no promotion, e.g., a banded pack tested against the normal marketing situation. Or they can involve an assessment of two possible promotions, e.g., two different self liquidators, or $1\frac{1}{2}$p off tested against 1p off normal price. Most forms of promotional activity can be tested in-store but there are certain limits. It is not possible to take account, in the pre-test

478

situation, of promotions which, when they go national, are going to get media backing. The test, if carried out, cannot measure the influence of television or press support. It is also difficult to pre-test competitions and contests, since this involves giving away the prizes which can result in an expensive piece of research. Additionally, the main practical problem in these tests is to ensure that all other variables are controlled throughout its duration. It is essential that each test item is examined in exactly equal competitive situations. To achieve this, complex designs have been developed using, for example, Latin squares. These are more complicated to administer but achieve a tighter control of outside variables.

Research: Post-assessment

The case for not assessing the effect of promotional activity is that it cannot be measured quantitatively because there exist in the market-place too many other variables which are difficult to isolate. This is a somewhat defeatist attitude emphasizing the problems and dismissing any possible solutions. Provided the objectives are clearly defined, measures can be found to assess their achievement. Outside variables may blur any assessment but allowance can be made for them, where necessary, in the interpretation.

Rather than have no assessment of promotional activity, it is preferable to develop research techniques whilst recognizing their uses and limitations. As in pre-testing of promotional activity the research methods are retail and consumer based.

Store checks. Measures of effectiveness obtained from store checks can include the:

(a) penetration achieved by the promoted product in the retail outlet, i.e., the number of stores handling the product;
(b) shelf space achieved by the promoted product in relation to competitive brands;
(c) penetration of display material; and its type and position.

All these statistics are relevant to a manufacturer who wants to assess his return on point-of-sale investment.

Retail Audits. All the above data can be obtained from retail audits. Additionally, sales data is collected from retail audits providing accurate information over specific time periods. However, identifying the sale of promoted items is generally very difficult because the timing of the retail checks may not fit in with the promotional activity, while competing promotions may overlap.

Consumer Research. Consumer research on aspects of 'below the line' activity must not be considered as an alternative to retail research. The retail research can be used effectively to answer a number of important questions on distribution, sales and stock cover but it provides no information about the target audience. It then becomes necessary to research the important questions of, for instance, who are the buyers taking up the promotion?, are they existing or new buyers?, will they or have they repeated their purchase of this brand or product?, is there an increase in the rate of buying per buyer resulting from the promotion?, how did buyers come to take up the promotion in the first place?, does the promotion affect the shopper's attitude towards the brand? These are some of the numerous questions that the manufacturer will ask when planning his promotional strategy and the consumer techniques available at the present time can, and do, provide some of the answers.

Consumer Panels. The consumer panel is one of the more important methods of obtaining the relevant data and has a great advantage over other methods in that the information is continuous over time. Parfitt and McGloughlin[4] have described the use of consumer panels in evaluating promotional activity. They state that the consumer panel is suited for three basic reasons. It:

(a) measures consumer purchasing behaviour accurately and sensitively;
(b) measures this on a continuous basis to gain information over time;
(c) is possible to ascertain accurate information on when purchases are made.

However, they also outline the practical difficulties involved which may obscure the relationship between promotional activity and sales. Again, three factors are basically involved:

(a) consumer purchasing behaviour is extremely complex in that individual rates of buying a product may be changing continuously in what appears a relatively static market;
(b) competitive activity may have a blurring effect and for one brand individual promotions can and do overlap with each other. This makes it more difficult to isolate the effect of a particular promotion;
(c) the objective of a promotion as in advertising may not be to increase sales in the short-term but rather to maintain a share or halt a declining share of the market.

It may be relevant to measure the extent of repeat purchasing some time after the promotion to establish whether the initial purchase has been followed up by a repeat purchase, and the relationship of repeat buying by 'new' buyers to those original buyers already using the brand. This can be observed from consumer panel data. The model developed by Ehrenberg and Goodhardt[5] is based on a theoretical framework. Basically, it states that in a 'stationary' market the average rate of buying per buyer is constant. The model takes actual sales and predicts what would have happened without the promotion. The difference is the effect of the promotion. As Barnes, McDonald and Tuck[6] point out, the limitation of this method is that it can only be applied in 'stationary' markets, and in a market undergoing change a control panel would be needed. One advantage of this method is that it eliminates the necessity of controlled experiments and consequently reduces the expense.

Impulse Buying. The share that a brand achieves of impulse purchases is largely determined by its point-of-sale activities—its retail distribution, shelf space, display, pricing and other promotional activities[7]. One measure, therefore, of the success of these activities is the share taken by a brand of impulse purchases in the product category. Expenditure on a product group can be segmented as described earlier. We can look at the brand's position in the two broad sectors of the market—the planned sector and the impulse sector where the brand is decided in the store; for example, a brand may have a 24 per cent share of the impulse sector. This can be taken as a benchmark *prior* to promotional activity; and a similar look can be taken at the market at a later date to assess the brand share of impulse purchases *after* the promotional campaign. The advantage of this technique is that it removes the planned sector, which is largely dictated by media advertising, from any evaluation. This argument is rather tenuous in markets where promotional activity is supported by media advertising.

Appraisal and Limitations of these Techniques

Pre-testing

The qualitative and quantitative research outlined should be regarded as a means, despite their limitations, of reducing the risk of failure. A relatively small expenditure on research, prior to embarking on the expense of the promotional campaign, can enhance the likelihood of success. The consumer and retail pre-tests are complementary rather than competitive in the sense that ideas and offers that have been successfully screened in group discussions, hall tests and van tests may then be tested in stores. The limitations of consumer pre-tests are:

(a) the methods do not really measure what is likely quantitatively to take place in the actual market situation. They cover preferences and attitudes but should not be used to forecast potential sales;
(b) they cannot be used for certain types of promotional activity, e.g., price changes, display positions, shelf space allocation, etc.

The limitations of in-store pre-tests are:

(a) they are difficult to control;
(b) they tell you nothing about the consumer, e.g., whether the promotion is attracting new buyers or people who would have bought it anyway. This limitation can sometimes be overcome by linking in-store consumer interviews to the test;

(c) there is also a limit to the type of promotional activity that can be tested, as described earlier.

Despite these limitations, the present pre-test methods do go a long way in helping the manufacturer to assess the likely success or failure of promotional activity. It is a small price to pay for what could turn out to be an expensive failure.

Post-assessment

The main problem in any post-assessment of promotional activity is that of isolating all other variables such as seasonal effect and competitor activity. Controls can sometimes be set up but these are normally expensive and not always appropriate. The practical answer to this problem is to deal with outside variables in the interpretation of the results, making due allowances according to the particular circumstances.

The retail audit has limitations:

(a) the timing of a retail audit, e.g., bi-monthly may not fit in with the promotional activity. Promotions often last only two to four weeks;
(b) retail audits are highly organized and inflexible. It may be impractical or expensive to adapt an ongoing service to the specific needs of promotional assessment;
(c) retail audits provide no information about the consumer, e.g., on repeat buying behaviour.

Consumer panels do not provide information on certain in-store activity, e.g.:

(a) retail distribution;
(b) display penetration;
(c) the penetration achieved by a promotion.

The objectives of the promotional activity and the criteria for success must, therefore, be defined. The criteria taken determine whether retail checks, consumer panels or both are appropriate to measure the effect.

Future Development

The future contribution of research to 'below the line' planning and evaluation is dependent on several factors. First, clearly defined promotional objectives and criteria for measuring success are needed. Second, forward planning should allow for a research programme and so avoid the current limitations of time and money which often bear no relation to the sums being risked on promotional activity. Third, researchers need both to improve their present techniques and to extend them into areas which are currently under researched.

Some possibilities for research development are as follows.

Shelf Space Allocation.   What is the relationship between shelf space and brand share? It would be very useful for a manufacturer or a retailer to be able to assess what shelf space he requires to achieve a target level of sales. The evidence of some work carried out suggests that in high impulse markets shelf space tends to equate with brand share or, putting it very simply, to get 20 per cent brand share you need 20 per cent of shelf space. In low impulse markets however, e.g., margarine, a high brand share can be achieved with a relatively low share of shelf space. In such markets, consumer brand loyalty is high and impulse purchasing is low. The shopper knows what she wants before she gets to the store and the manufacturer must get his brand across at that stage. In the store, the manufacturer does not necessarily require shelf space exactly pro rata to brand share provided his brand is currently one of the leaders. Shelf space allocation requires a great deal of researching and could be rewarding.

Data Bank.   Another important question (the answer to which depends upon the particular situation at the time and also the creative aspect) is what type of promotion seems to work best for particular objectives in a particular product field? If a sufficient backlog of information were available about different types of promotional activity in different product fields, it would be possible to draw some useful conclusions about what type of promotion seems to achieve a particular objective best.

Trade Reaction.   Research can also help to avoid waste by getting trade reaction to a new promotion at an early stage. Many promotions have failed, not because of lack of appeal to the consumer, but because the trade would not accept them. Too often this is found out when large sums of money have already been spent.

References

1. WOOD, J. Below What Line? *Admap*, June 1968.
2. CHIB, R. Promotions a Challenge to the Researcher. *Ad Weekly*, 25 July 1969.
3. SIMMONS, M. Evaluating Promotions: a New Syndicated Method. *Advertising Management*, Feb. 1968.
4. PARFITT, J. and McGLOUGHLIN, I. The Use of Consumer Panels in the Evaluation of Promotions. *Admap*, Dec. 1968.
5. EHRENBERG, A. S. C. and GOODHARDT, G. J. *Evaluating a Consumer Deal.* Extracts from a case-study for the J. Walter Thompson Co.
6. BARNES, M. C. J., McDONALD, C. D. P., and TUCK, R. T. J. *Evaluating 'Below the Line' Expenditure.* The Thomson Medals and Awards for Advertising Research, 1969.
7. SIMMONS, M. Point-of-sale Advertising. *Journal of the Market Research Society*, **10**, 2.

Bibliography

SAMPSON, P. and HOOPER, B. *Evaluating 'Below the Line' Expenditure.* The Thomson Medals and Awards for Advertising Research, 1969.
KENNEDY, R. W. Merchandising and Point-of-Sale Evaluation. *Advertising Management*, April 1968.
SIMMONS, M. *Research in Merchandising.*

WEBER, J. H. Can the Results of Sales Promotion be Predicted? *Journal of Marketing*, Jan. 1963.

Retailer Attitudes to Promotions. *The Grocer*, 6 July 1968.

HEARNE, J. J. Does 'Below the Line' Promotion Pay? *The Financial Times*, 4 July 1968.

ALTMAN, W. The Point of Point-of-Sale. *Marketing*, March 1969.

CHRISTOPHER, M. The Whys and Wherefores of Below the Line. *The Financial Times*, 3 July 1969.

Buyers Attitudes to Below-the-Line. *The Grocer*, 1 June 1968.

WILLETT, R. P. and KOLLAT, D. T. Customer Impulse Purchasing Behaviour: Some Research Notes and a Reply. *Journal of Marketing Research*, V.

HOOFNAGLE, W. S. Experimental Designs in Measuring the Effectiveness of Promotion. *Journal of Marketing Research*, 11, May 1965.

19. Market testing and experimentation

John Davis

One major function of market research is to provide a feedback of information from the market to the manufacturer or distributor. This information shows the state the market is in as a result of the marketing strategies currently being applied to the various competing brands. Taken together with other relevant data, such as the observations and impressions of the executives concerned, this provides the basis on which the company can take its decisions about continuing or changing the strategies for its existing brands, or developing strategies for new brands.

As long as the possible alternative strategies remain mostly within the company's existing field of experience, the likely outcome of changing from one strategy to another can sometimes be assessed sufficiently accurately for the purpose of making a decision *without* conducting extensive additional research. It may be possible to base the decision on judgment alone, but more often it will be necessary to supplement this by various types of pre-testing research. However, problems can still arise even where the company knows the field well and, once it moves outside its existing range of experience, pre-testing is very unlikely to provide a sufficient guide to the likely results of introducing a given change into the market. The company will then need to carry out some form of market testing or experimentation in order to gain the additional experience required to make its marketing decisions, in some cases merely to form an initial assessment of whether a project is worth carrying further; in other cases major planning and investment decisions may depend on the results. Some may be concerned with comparing the relative effects of two or more alternative courses of action open to a company, others only with assessing the effects of a single proposed course of action. Projections of the scale of effects in a wider market may be required, or merely a 'better, no-change, worse' result. A whole new product and its marketing plan may be involved in a test-launch, or only a single factor in the marketing mix of an existing product.

The difference between this type of experimentation and the various forms of pre-testing is that the changes and innovations are generally introduced into the market through the normal channels of communication or distribution—through normal advertising media and retail stores. Any effects are then measured among a population who have been exposed to the media and who have made their preference and purchasing decisions in the normal way. Experimenting under these conditions is generally expensive, and there is a marked rise in costs as a project moves out of the pre-testing stage into a marketing experiment. As a result of this step in costs, a number of attempts have been made to provide 'mini-testing' marketing facilities which, while sacrificing some of the benefits of full-scale testing, provide the means of obtaining some key information and measurements at much lower costs. One development has been the establishment of panels of housewives who are visited by a mobile shop or van and from which they can make purchases of a range of foods and household products. By calling on the same housewives regularly through time and recording their purchases on each occasion, details of their buying patterns, and any alterations in them through an experimental change or innovation, can be built up. Hence, for a comparatively small outlay on stocks and research a manufacturer can gain information on such key factors as the rate of repurchase among triers of a new product. While the results may not be adequate to provide a firm forecast for the total market, they will indicate whether the project is worth proceeding with in its present form, either through immediate introduction or through more extensive testing in the market. Similar limited testing facilities are also available among retail outlets, special panels of stores being set up in which to experiment with new products, pricing, etc.

The remainder of this chapter is concerned with the principles and problems of the more general larger-scale forms of marketing experiments, but as will be seen later, considerations of the costs and risks involved may frequently indicate the advisability of moving through some form of initial exploration before becoming committed to a major experiment.

Practicability of Testing

With some projects a company may not have the option of testing in the market, since production or other constraints may preclude the possibility of introducing the proposed changes into only some parts of a market in advance of a total market decision. It may, for example, be impossible to produce a new product in quantities sufficient to supply a test area without building a plant capable of producing on a national basis; or of adapting the style or design of an existing product without changing the whole output. It may be impossible, because of overlapping and interlocking channels of distribution, to vary trade terms or prices within test areas without serious repercussions on the total market, and so on.

The competitive situation in a market may frequently inhibit any experimentation, because this will reveal company planning or product formulation. Competitors may then react and, if the time necessary to take counter-activity or even copy the product is short, be the first to launch on the wider market. In any case, much of the experience to be gained from an experiment by one company can be frequently acquired by competitors if they merely observe and measure the effects for themselves. One advantage of some forms of mini-testing referred to above is that they preclude competitive access to the results.

If such problems cannot be overcome then the possibilities of mounting specific experiments do not exist. For the purposes of this chapter, however, it is assumed that an experiment is not precluded by such constraints.

Definition of the Problem

Seldom is the initial request for an experiment or test framed in a way that can lead to an effective plan. Frequently a great deal of questionning has to be done to establish the proper objectives of the experiment, and to quantify them sufficiently to determine such factors as the scale of the experiment or the precision required in the results. A client, for example, recently asked for help in designing an experiment to see whether a proposed display stand would be worth introducing into stores. The first question was whether the experiment was to cover the rate of trade acceptance and use of the stand, and possibly its life expectancy, or whether it should only cover the in-store effect of the stand when it was there. This is a vital planning question, since an experiment of the first type would have involved normal distribution through the sales force, large numbers of the stands, and heavy expenditure on display checks and store audits. The second type of experiment could have been carried out, in this market, with two matched panels of 20 stores and 20 display stands, and for a modest expenditure on auditing. The question had not previously been considered explicitly by the group concerned, and discussion immediately showed that some members were expecting only an in-store test; others, the wider experiment.

A major problem area concerns the precision and type of results required, and the uses to which they are to be put. A simple feasibility study to assess whether some project holds sufficient promise for further limited investment in it should not be allowed to become large or elaborate. At the other end of the scale, an experimental launch from which estimates are to be made of the likely effects in a wider market must be mounted with a great deal of careful planning, executed under properly managed conditions and measured in ways which will provide the required data. Dangers frequently arise when a modest experiment, designed perhaps merely to assess certain aspects of a complex situation, is then expected to provide forecasts for which it was not originally intended.

Examination of Existing Experience

Given that any experiment is a means of gaining experience, before any experiment is undertaken the question should be posed whether additional experience is necessary in order to arrive at an adequate decision. Because of the costs involved in a major marketing experiment, it should only be considered as a last resort when all other means of reaching a firm decision have failed. Consequently, before an experiment is started a rigorous reassessment of all available data and experience should be made, including the subjective assessments of those who know the market, to establish the range of the possible profits or losses which might arise from the marketing activity under consideration. Not infrequently this rigorous assessment based on existing experience shows that the entire range of possible results is profitable, or that the entire range is unprofitable. The latter result must mean that testing the project in its present form will be a waste of time and resources which would be better spent on some other activity. The former result (that all outcomes of the project would be profitable) should lead to immediate marketing without testing if the proposed course of action can only take one form, but there may still remain a need for experimenting if there is scope for variations in the project which would lead to different levels of profitability. If the optimum level cannot be prejudged but there are marked differences between the optimum level and other levels, further investigation of the value of experimenting is needed. If a manufacturer of a packaged product, for example, is considering whether or not to add a 3 lb pack above his existing range of sizes, and all assessments of the outcome are profitable, there is no point in an experiment. If, however, he is considering the more open question of introducing a new larger pack which could take one of a range of sizes, there might still be a case for experimenting in the market to get as near as possible to the most profitable new size.

Where the expected range of possible outcomes shows that some will be profitable but some will lead to losses, the company has three options.

First, introduce the course of action fully into the market in the hope of success, but with the risk of losses. Experience is then gained after the events.

Second, experiment by introducing the proposed course of action into one or more small parts of the proposed market, thus limiting the risks while experience is acquired, but at some cost. These costs may well include the loss of profits through delaying the introduction of a beneficial change into the wider market or the losses through the sacrifice of any lead time the company has achieved or even pre-emption by a competitor.

Third, postpone or shelve the project, thus avoiding the risk of direct losses through failure, but accepting the risks that profits are being forgone through delay, and may be lost altogether through pre-emption.

At this stage we assume a decision to test, and examine some of the problems involved.

Types of Experimental Design

Basically, the normal principles of experimental design as described by Rothman in chapter 2, apply to marketing experiments, although there are frequently some practical limitations which prevent the full application of some more complex designs. Hence, experimental designs tend to be simple 'before and after' or 'side by side' designs, and generally without replication, so that each treatment and control appears only in a single area.

In 'before and after' experiments the relevant results are measured in the selected area before and after the introduction of the innovation or change, and comparisons are made between the readings. Since other conditions in the market may cause changes beyond those due to the experiment itself, a control area (in which the experimental measurements are made but no experimental action is taken) is normally needed to arrive at a sound interpretation of the results. Hence, even simple 'before and after' experiments tend to become comparative or 'side by side' experiments anyway. Not infrequently a control area can be found among marketing areas already being measured and analysed in normal continuous research.

Comparative tests, where the relative merits of two or more different 'treatments' are to be assessed, call for designs in which the treatments can be run side by side in different areas although there is no need for the selected areas to be contiguous. To avoid wrong conclusions a control area free of any experimental stimulus is again needed, as one recent set of results showed. Here, the introduction of two experimental methods of promotion into separate areas was followed by uniform increases in sales of about 10 per cent. Without further information the conclusion would have appeared to be that the introduction of either method into the market would be beneficial. Fortunately, a control was used, because this showed a rise in sales of the same magnitude but without any experimental stimulus. Some other factor, in this case probably the weather, was affecting the market, and this could only be detected, at least in the short-run, by the inclusion of a control area in the design of the experiment.

Because the individual areas used in experiments, whether towns, television areas or other units, may vary in their initial pre-test states and in their reactions to an experiment, the ideal design of any type calls for the placing of each experimental treatment in a number of areas. This is particularly so in comparative tests. However, in the great majority of marketing experiments such replication of the design is not administratively or financially possible, and operations are limited to single areas. This is a condition which generally has to be accepted—although every opportunity should be taken to use multi-area designs—but it should never be forgotten. To some extent, and given adequate background data, some of the risks involved in single-area tests can be reduced in the later stages leading to forecasts (referred to later in this chapter) but this again is only a poor substitute for proper multi-area testing.

An alternative method of attempting to overcome the problems posed by the variability of sales or other factors between areas has been to create facilities for mounting some types of tests with the different treatments, or treatment and control, within the same geographic area or market. The most widely known of these is probably the Advertising Laboratory operated in Milwaukee, USA. There, by split-running and controlling the distribution of newspapers in the city, and by the use of 'muters' to cut out reception of certain commercials in panels of television homes, matched panels of people living close together in the same general environment can be subjected to different advertisements or campaigns. Any effects on their purchasing patterns can then be measured and they will be free of any inherent 'between-area' differences. The Ad-Lab closed in 1971.

Similar, and somewhat more closely controlled, facilities for television testing have been developed in other cities in the US, making use of the Community Antenna Television (CATV) systems and their associated cables distributing the in-coming signals to sets in homes. By running 'split' (parallel) cables to service alternate blocks or homes and using appropriate signal generators and switchgear, a manufacturer can have his normal commercial cut out of some fraction of homes throughout the city and an experimental commercial substituted. Measurements of effects follow using the usual methods, comparing the results from the matched panels of homes receiving the alternative commercials.

So far, for a number of reasons, including legal problems, these methods are not available in the UK although several possibilities are under study at the time of writing. It is, however, to be hoped that these difficulties can be overcome, because in appropriate circumstances the facility of being able to run two different commercials or campaigns within the same community affords a far more powerful experimental design than the use of geographically separate areas.

The Scale of Experiments

Three main sets of factors operate to determine the appropriate scale for an experiment. These are the physical requirements to mount the experiment at all, the research requirements to provide adequate measurements, and the risks and costs of success or failure.

Physical requirements include such factors as availability of advertising media, the use of administratively coherent sales or depot areas, or that the experimental areas shall absorb a given proportion of capacity if production or packaging lines have to be modified to provide the necessary material. Such factors may place either upper or lower limits to the scale of an experiment, and may, on occasion, rule out the possibility of an experiment of the desired type. Thus, an experimental launch heavily dependent on television advertising may not be possible if available production facilities could only supply a few dozen stores.

490

The *research requirements* will set lower limits to the scale in terms of the number of areas needed and the populations of consumers or stores within them. Hence, they will depend on the extent to which the market varies between areas, on the current or expected levels of distribution and consumer usage, the magnitude of any expected changes or results, and the precision with which the results are to be measured.

Where the research requirements call for experimentation on a scale above the limits set by the physical factors, then the experiment must either be abandoned or its objectives modified. On the other hand, the research need not, and often should not, cover the whole area into which the experimental stimulus is introduced; e.g., in test-launching a new product using television in the area covered by a single transmitter, it will normally be considered necessary to allow—if not impossible to prevent—distribution of the product to extend to the limits of transmission. If, then, research measurements are carried out over the whole transmission area, and this includes some overlap areas, the results will be diluted through the inclusion of outer areas in which the advertising is not achieving full impact. Hence, the research should be limited to the primary area, however far distribution may be carried.

The *risks and costs* of success or failure seldom receive the attention they merit in planning the scale of an experiment. The costs of research usually receive some attention, and they can normally be estimated in advance from quotations, whether for 'ad hoc' work or for the use of the increasing number of packaged facilities. Such costs tend to depend far more on the design of the experiment than on the scale or the sizes of the areas used.

There are two other sets of possible costs, one of which will have been incurred by the end of the experiment (although in certain cases the costs may prove negligible). If the experiment leads to the project being introduced into the wider market, then there may have been some *loss of profits* during the period in which the project was held back from the main market awaiting the test results and a decision. This is not inevitable, e.g., when a test launch is carried out using pilot plant production and where the timing of the main launch depends on the completion of production facilities already under construction irrespective of the test; but whenever the introduction into a market of a profitable project is held back by the decision to test, there will be some loss of profits chargeable against the costs of the test. Taking time to test projects which are profitable always costs profits; but these opportunity costs can be reduced by carrying out the experiment and, thus, avoiding this loss of profits, in a wider area.

Conversely, if the test results lead to the project being abandoned there will generally be *pull-out costs*. In some cases, such as in a test of a revised television schedule which has not affected media or production costs and which has failed to move the market share away from the line it would normally have followed, these may be insignificant. However, if the same experiment had led to a fall in market share, there would have been some loss of profits during the test and for such time afterwards as it took the market share to recover, plus the costs of any additional efforts put into the area to aid recovery. With test launches which fail, there may be considerable losses on plant and equipment, on materials and labour, and such costs as cleaning-up operations and uplifting stock in the areas used. These pull-out costs can be reduced by keeping the size of the experimental areas as *small* as other requirements permit.

It follows that, where the project is believed to have a high probability of succeeding, the ultimate costs of testing may be reduced by allowing the sizes of the areas used to increase. Where a project is believed to have a high probability of failure the area involved should be kept to a minimum or key factors in the situation tested first on some more limited basis.

In some cases a rolling launch, in which the project is introduced through time into successive marketing areas across the country, may be the appropriate form for an 'experiment'. A company may be certain of gaining a profit, for example, from a new product if production is geared to the right level. Underproduction may kill the market, overproduction may kill the profit, and there may be a wide range between the available estimates of the upper and lower limits of potential sales. In these circumstances, if other factors are favourable, a logical plan would be to install capacity to meet the lowest estimated total sales level, and to launch in a part of the market which could still be adequately supplied if the highest level of demand was reached. Treatment of this area as an experiment would then provide the data for planning any necessary expansion of production as the product was 'rolled-out' into the remainder of the market. As a corollary to this, if for other reasons concerned with production, manpower, cash-flow or whatever, a rolling launch is imposed on the marketing planning then, again, the patterns of development in the initial areas should be researched in the same way as for a test launch, to provide bases for forecasting and indications of failings or weaknesses in the marketing processes.

The Selection of Areas

The problem of selecting areas to be used in marketing experiments presents some difficulties. In an ideal situation the major market would be divided into areas on some suitable basis, and an adequate number of areas for use in the experiment and the control would be drawn at random. Unfortunately, this ideal method can seldom, if ever, be applied to marketing experiments for two major reasons. The first is that many of the areas which would appear as natural sub-units of the market are for one reason or another not suitable for particular experiments, e.g., in any experiment using television advertising in the UK the natural sub-units of the market tend to be the respective areas covered by the various transmitters, of which there have been fourteen in the VHF network. Some of these fourteen contain too large

492

a part of the population to be generally economic as test areas, and they may put too large a slice of the market at risk in the event of a failure. Hence, they must often be excluded. Other areas may exhibit other characteristics which would make them unsuitable for use in particular tests. Consequently, it is frequently found that only three or four may remain which can be classified as suitable. Even when towns are considered as test areas, by the time that a number have been rejected because they are too large or too small, or possess other features deemed unsatisfactory, the number remaining can again be very small.

The second reason is that random selection of the single areas within which most testing is conducted, or even two or three areas in exceptional cases, is too 'chancy' to be acceptable. The selection of only one or two areas at random for a test to be carried out once only does not allow the chance factors in random sampling to operate effectively. Hence, it becomes preferable to sample on a purposive basis, selecting each area for what it is known to be or to contain.

Logically, this leads to attempts to select areas for use in experiments and controls which are typical of the wider market, and which reflect within themselves the major characteristics of the wider market. This can be extended where more than a single area is used, to selecting one typical of the north, one typical of the south, one hard-water area and one soft, and so on. In practice, however, it is doubtful whether there is a completely typical area in any market, because even after the usual comparisons have been made on demographic or economic bases it may still be found that particular relevant market parameters differ in the area from any 'national' pattern. Normally, then, the most that can be done is to ensure that the areas finally selected for an experiment are not widely atypical, and then to cope with moderate degrees of atypicality through more sophisticated methods of interpretation and projection.

In some situations where there is a choice between a number of areas, such as towns of medium size, some form of cluster analysis may be useful (see chapter 13). This has been used to divide towns into groups with similar characteristics, and one set of such clusters has been devised and published by Christopher[1]. If, then, a spread of towns is required to provide a range of results from a single set of experimental conditions introduced into a range of different environments, this can be achieved by selection from as many of the different groups as the resources permit. On the other hand, when comparing two or more alternative projects, or selecting pairs of towns for experimental and control use, selection is made *within* the groups.

It is worth mentioning that a wide range of test market research and other facilities is offered by media owners in the UK, sometimes at specially favourable rates to users of the media concerned. Lists of such facilities available are published from time to time by the media owners themselves, by trade journals and advertising agencies.

493

Timing

Many tests and experiments suffer from being run over too short a time. Often, this is a condition imposed by other considerations, but not infrequently it arises from an inadequate appreciation of the time which may be needed for a project to produce an effect on the market at all or, having produced one, to reach a stable level. Where a new product is introduced into a market or where some additional activity is added to an existing marketing programme, it is frequently found that sales will move to an initial level from which they subsequently decline before stabilizing. If, then, the experiment or the measurements associated with it are discontinued prematurely the final readings will still be above the stable level and misleading results may be obtained. An analysis of 141 test markets in the UK and USA, for example, carried out by the AC Nielsen Co., suggests that, after the first six months of testing, the chance of adequately predicting the final test market share (achieved at the end of 12 to 18 months) is only about 1 in 2. This rises to about 2 in 3 after eight months of testing. In the opposite situation, where some factor is being removed from a marketing programme or is being diminished, such as the advertising appropriation or the frequency of representatives' calls, there can be an inertia effect, and the market can continue unchanged for some considerable time before any movement can be observed. In one case there was an interval of fifteen months between the complete withdrawal of advertising for an established brand and any fall in market share in the test areas.

When both sets of factors may occur together, as in experiments where one type of activity is substituted for another, extreme care is needed in interpretation and in deciding when an experiment can be terminated. If the benefits of introducing the new type of activity appear quickly and before any detrimental effects from removing the old activity, sales or other measures will show a rise irrespective of the real strengths of the two activities. Conversely, if removing the current activity leads quickly to a detrimental effect but it takes time for the effects of the new activity to appear, early sets of measurements will show falls from the previous level. In either case, the initial results may be seriously misleading and time must be allowed for the position to stabilize. In the ideal situation, apart from using a suitable area as a control in which the existing activity will continue unchanged, a further area should be utilized in which the existing activity is removed and not replaced by the new one, in order to observe the decay of the current activity effect. This, however, may be too drastic a solution to be acceptable.

Apart from endeavouring to ensure that adequate time is allowed for experimentation two further points relating to the time factor should be considered during the planning and execution of the research. The first is concerned with saving time by making provision for projections from the early results to provide estimates of the way the market is likely to move in subsequent periods. For consumer goods, such projections are based on

494

analyses of the build-up of penetration of the product concerned (either from scratch in the case of a new product or from base levels for existing products) and of the repeat buying patterns among buyers of the product concerned. For details the reader is referred to chapter 7.

The second point is that the experiment and its associated research and measurement should continue in the test areas after any decision to introduce the project into a wider area is taken. Then some warning will be obtained should any detrimental movement occur in the market at a later stage, and appropriate action can be initiated. There is also a supplementary benefit from such a procedure, in that the experimental areas may then be used for further experiments for which they are uniquely suitable, such as testing the second year's advertising for a new product in an area which has already completed its first year, or in testing other forms of follow-up activity.

Projections, Predictions, and Forecasts

The problem of converting the results observed in an experiment in a limited area into an assessment of what can be expected to happen if the project is introduced into the wider market is one of the most critical in marketing experimentation.

There is a range of experiments in which it may not be a vital concern, as in early feasibility studies of a new project or in some forms of pilot marketing where the emphasis is on ensuring that the more mechanical aspects of an operation will work efficiently. Even in those cases, however, where the development of wider market estimates may not have been part of the original brief, demands for some form of estimate will almost inevitably be made at later stages in the operation. In other cases the development of estimates of the likely effects of introducing the proposed course of action into a wider market is a prime requirement.

It is useful to differentiate between projection and prediction, and between the results of these processes and a forecast.

Projections are essentially simple means of obtaining estimates from test results. A brand share of x per cent in a test launch is merely projected to an estimate that x per cent of the wider market will be obtained; a rise in sales of y points as a result of an experimental promotion is projected to a rise of y points nationally, and so on. Straight projection is easy, but highly fallible, because there is an underlying assumption that 'all other things' will remain equal. Almost inevitably differences will be found between test areas and the wider market in such factors as demographic characteristics and the size of the target group, the existing penetration and rates of consumption of the product group, market shares of existing brands, shop populations, media coverage and so forth. These and other factors will tend to render the simple processes of projection inaccurate.

Predictions are the result of more complex series of calculations, in which some attempt is made to take account of the factors which vary between the test area and the wider market. An attempt is made to construct a 'model' of the situation in the experimental area from the relationships found between the level of sales, or whatever criterion is being used, and the other market factors such as the demographic structure of the population, the store population, the shares held by competing brands before and after the experiment and so forth. Once these relationships are established in the test area, then predictions of the likely results in a wider market can be calculated by inserting the wider market values of the other factors into the relationships. One simple model which has proved useful is based on calculations of the proportionate changes in existing brand shares before and after a test launch. The predicted new brand share is then calculated by applying these proportionate changes to the wider market shares held by the existing brands. and subtracting from 100 per cent.

If x_o, y_o, are the market shares held by brands X, Y, in the test area prior to the test; x_1, x_1, are the test area brand shares after the test; X_o, Y_o, are the wider market shares of X, Y, when the new brand is introduced there; then T, the expected wider market share of the test brand is given by:

$$T = 100 - \left(\frac{x_1}{x_o} \cdot X_o + \frac{y_1}{y_o} \cdot Y_o + \cdots \right) \text{ per cent.}$$

Normally, only simple models can be built up from the results of a single experiment because data to quantify many of the possible relationships is lacking. Where, however, a company has been able to bring together larger amounts of data, either from experiments or from observations in the main market, and to establish relationships between the main marketing factors and the levels of sales, the resulting marketing models can be invaluable not only in the interpretation of the results but in the planning stages of experiments as well.

A *forecast* should be developed from the projections or predictions as a joint effort between the research team and the marketing team involved. At this stage the whole history of the experiment should be reviewed and allowance made in the forecast so far as possible for any factors which may have detracted from the integrity of the experiment—difficulties in maintaining supplies, the effects of competitive activity, problems with major multiple organizations and so forth. Beyond this, there may be elements in the situation whose effects are wholly 'unpredictable' however sophisticated a model may be used, such as knowledge that a new competitive product is to be launched, and allowance for such factors can only be made at this final stage of turning projections or predictions into forecasts.

One point which is often overlooked in forecasting from the effects of test launches or other experiments is that a time element should be incorporated. This is because the forecast needed for the main operation should be pitched at some point in the future, while the information on which it is based is inevitably historic. Failure to take due note of time trends has led

496

to significant differences between projections and results in the past, and the need to have information on movements outside the test area, in other parts of the main market, calls for the establishment and measurement of a control—a factor which is often left out of the design of experimental launches.

It follows that, since results from test areas may not be related to the results likely to occur in a wider market by a simple relationship, comparisons between the results of different strategies tested in separate areas should only be made after forecasting to a national level. There is always the risk that, if comparisons are made between raw area results, different conclusions may be drawn. The only safe procedure is to produce forecasts from each individually before comparing the results, in order to remove as far as possible any specific area influences.

Establishing the Appropriate Test Conditions

The application of experience gained in experiments to wider markets or at later periods depends for its justification on the experience being valid. To be valid the experience must, among other things, have been generated under appropriate conditions, and setting up such appropriate conditions is probably one of the more difficult aspects of many marketing experiments.

In bald terms, the object of experiments is to create in a small area a prescribed set of conditions. In a full scale experiment this normally means establishing as nearly as possible the conditions under which the project will be introduced into a wider market, in order to measure the effects. In the most complex case of an experimental launch this involves introducing the proposed product with the proposed advertising material used in the proposed media, and backed by promotions, offers, the activities of the sales force and any other factors at appropriate levels. If the experiment is to succeed it is necessary to look at each of these factors carefully to see precisely what is needed in the test areas and what can be achieved.

With the physical factors, such as the product or the pack, achieving comparability with what will be marketed on a wider scale may not be difficult—although it is not always easy. The product from a pilot plant may differ in some ways from the product which will eventually come off the main production line. An imported product used in anticipation of setting up a production line domestically may differ in its formulation, in the nature of the ingredients, in the form of packaging, or even only in the fact that it may bear the name of the country of origin, but any of these factors could be significant in affecting results achieved.

With advertising and promotion, the material to be used in the wider market may already be available for use in the test area, although even here the media selection problems may make changes necessary. The increase in split run facilities among newspapers and of tipping-in and other facilities among magazines is reducing the extent of such problems, but they still exist for many experiments and should always be looked for. With television advertising the problem appears simple, but this is deceptive and it is a good example of how an apparently simple solution to the problems arising in experiments can be damaging.

Consider an experimental launch in which television is the only form of advertising and the national appropriation has been set at £300 000 for the first six months. The problem is to assess the advertising appropriate to a test area containing, say, five per cent of the population. One approach is to put five per cent of the appropriation into the test area but this, of course, will take no account of variations in 'costs per thousand' between stations. A second approach is to put into the test area the national schedule of advertising which would be run in the event of a wider launch. However, because of the ways in which companies allocate their budgets after taking account of differences in card rates and other conditions between television areas, there may not be a 'national' schedule as such but only a series of differing area schedules. If there *is* a national schedule, or if an approximation to one can be constructed, this achieves comparability between the test area and the expected national pattern in terms of transmitted advertising —but still not necessarily the national pattern in terms of received advertising or opportunities to see. There appear to be quite marked differences between viewing habits in different parts of the country so that to attempt to set up a pattern of received advertising which will be 'typical' it is necessary to consider the reach and frequency schedule which is being aimed at on a national basis, and to reproduce this in the test area.

Even if comparability is achieved on this basis it may still leave problems unsolved, because of the relationship between the advertising for the experimental brand in the test area and advertising for brands already existing in the market. If there are area variations in the weights of advertising generated by competition it is quite possible that, whereas on a national basis the effort put behind the new product X may leave it below the effort put behind existing product A but above that for existing product B, variations in spending by A and B between areas may provide a quite different set of relationships in the test area. The main point is that a very detailed approach to the establishment of the appropriate experimental conditions is needed, not only in the media field but in others as well, both in an attempt to set up an appropriate set of test conditions, and also in order to know how far the conditions actually achieved may depart from the ideal and may need to be specifically allowed for in forecasting.

Beyond setting up the appropriate conditions at the beginning of an experiment, it is necessary to maintain them during its life. This involves such factors as ensuring that the sales effort is not unduly augmented either by the activities of the personnel normally working in the area, or by the attention or the visits paid to an area by head office personnel, acting on the best of motives of gaining experience but possibly influencing the experiment in some way at the same time. Hence, rigid discipline must be maintained over any company activities which might impinge on the experimental results.

Outside the company other factors may come into operation. The general effects of exogenous factors should have been catered for by setting up an adequate system of control areas in designing the experiment. Beyond this, however, competition may introduce counter activities into the test area which may affect the results. To maintain the integrity of the experiment these activities must be carefully monitored and appropriate action taken. If, for example, a new launch is countered in the test area by increased advertising or other activity on the part of competitors, this may, in fact, enhance the value of the test operation if it is the type of activity which is to be expected on a wider scale in a wider launch. Further, if in the wider launch plan a contingency reserve has been set aside for use should such counter activity develop, then it is logical to use similar appropriate resources in the test area for this purpose.

However, if the counter activity mounted by competitors is specifically aimed at wrecking the test, such as flooding the area with coupons or samples or advertising on a scale which could not be supported nationally, then it may be necessary to abandon any hope of obtaining a projectable result from the test area, and to proceed as seems best with more limited objectives; for example, competitive couponing or sampling may have so distorted the market that any immediate estimate of brand share is unlikely to be valid but it may still be possible to gain a great deal of useful information from the test. Valid data may still be obtainable on the extent of awareness of the new product, the comprehension of the content of the advertising, the types of people who have bought and, in particular, the repeat buying patterns of those who have tried the new product at all. Some of these measures may have become suspect as a result of the competitive activity but almost certainly something can be gained from any test, whatever the interference, and any opportunities of gaining useful information should be taken rather than allow the whole operation to be written off.

This raises a point on the advisability of attempting to interfere in tests run by other manufacturers. In general, it would appear that far more is gained by watching and measuring the test oneself, and possibly using it in order to test any logical counter activities, rather than by becoming involved in a wrecking exercise.

The Cost-effectiveness of Experimenting

While there are numerous cases where hindsight shows that prior experimentation would have enabled a company to avoid losses incurred in launching some unsuccessful project, there are also many examples to be found where experiments were needlessly undertaken with a subsequent increase in costs or loss of profits. One large company, since taken over by another, for years prided itself that it never took a major decision without proper experimentation, and time after time it lost heavily because competitors had pre-empted the market by the time the experiments were completed. The problem of whether a particular experiment will justify the full range of costs involved is therefore vital.

The first requirement is for the likely range of outcomes of launching the project to be assessed in the light of existing knowledge and experience, together with assessments of the probabilities of the various outcomes occurring. Some such assessments are normally made anyway in considering a new project, although few take the process as far as attaching probabilities to the outcomes. This, however, is easily achieved by, in effect, carrying out an opinion survey among executives who know the project and the market, and deriving mean assessments of the probabilities, weighted perhaps to allow for different degrees of experience (or different weights of authority).

The outcomes normally need to be assessed in terms of profits or losses. In some cases, any effects resulting from the project will be immediate and of short duration, such as with a short-term promotion in a market with little brand loyalty. The effects will .ppear within a limited period and there will be little carry-over into the future, and there is little difficulty in putting a profit figure onto any set of market conditions which may arise. At the other extreme, if the project is one of launching a new brand which may be expected to have a life of some years ahead of it, it may be preferable to discount future profits in some way to provide figures of current net worth.

Where the assessed range of outcomes shows some probabilities of profits and some of losses if the project is put directly into the market, the first point to consider is the size of the maximum loss and its assessed probability of occurrance. If the loss is one which the company, the marketing group, or the executives within it, could not survive, then the only logical options open are to 'test' or 'abandon', irrespective of all other factors. If the maximum loss would not be crippling in this way, then all three options of 'launch now', 'test', or 'abandon' are still open and further calculation is required.

The next stage is to consider whether a test operation would lead to a more precise assessment of the range of outcomes, allowing for the problems of measurement and forecasting. Measurements can be made more precise by increasing sample sizes at a cost, and forecasts can be made more firm by increasing the number of areas into which the experiment is introduced, but again at a price. If the original assessments of possible outcomes were based on solid information and experience, the range may already be so narrow that further testing may do little to provide additional information. On the other hand, if existing experience is sketchy and the possible range of outcomes developed is wide, then even a simple experiment may help in refining the estimates of outcome.

The problem of balancing the costs and the benefits of market testing is one of Bayesian Statistics, and a full discussion is beyond the scope of this chapter. For the general theory readers should consult Schlaifer[2], and for an application to market experiments, Davis[3].

In essence, the procedure involves balancing the costs against the improvement in the probability of avoiding losses or of gaining profits, as a result of testing. Hence, apart from the estimated outcomes and their probabilities, calculations of the costs already mentioned are needed, and some estimate of the accuracy likely to be attained by the possible methods of testing and forecasting. In many cases, where experimentation could proceed at more than one level, separate calculations need to be made covering the various options open to the company.

If the whole range of assessed outcomes is profitable two situations arise. On the one hand, if the investment required to introduce the project will remain flexible and can be adjusted to meet the market requirements as they develop, then clearly there is no point in incurring the costs of a separate test operation. An immediate launch, nationally or on a rolling base, is logical. On the other hand, if there are severe penalties involved should planning and investment proceed on a level which is not subsequently matched by market performance—even though that performance in itself would have been profitable had it been properly planned for—then testing may be called for. Thus, an achievement of selling 400 000 cases of a product a year in a market may be profitable if the whole planning was on the basis of achieving that level, but it may prove to be *un*profitable if the original planning and investment was based on achieving a level of 800 000 cases. This is a further complication which can be brought into the calculations if required.

Exploratory Experiments

In the past, it has probably been true to say that most market experiments have been carried out to secure information relating to some specific immediate problem—whether a new product will gain a viable share of a market, a new campaign will increase sales, changes in an appropriation will be profitable, and so forth. With many aspects of marketing this is the only way in which experiments can be conducted at all, because until the new product has been formulated and its marketing mix agreed, or until a new campaign has been developed or a new pack designed, there is nothing to experiment with. On the other hand, there are some areas of marketing in which useful experience can be gained through exploratory experiments at almost any time and added to the company's fund of knowledge for future use. Such areas include the level of the advertising appropriation, the way it is allocated between media, the ways in which it is scheduled; the representative journey cycles and the frequencies of calling on customers of various types; the effects of display bonuses and so forth. With these factors it is not necessary to wait until a particular decision has to be taken before beginning to collect experience by introducing planned changes into different parts of the market and measuring their effects. This type of experimentation becomes more important if the company is attempting to build marketing models, when all too frequently it is found that some factor which may well have a bearing on sales or profitability has hitherto been running at a steady level so that no information can be gained about the effects of variations from a study of past data. In these fields, then, it is possible to anticipate needs for experience and to carry out a comparatively inexpensive programme of experiments accumulating the information through time, either in order to increase the running efficiency of an operation or to be able to provide more specific data when faced with future problems.

Collecting Data

Linked with this is the idea that whenever any changes are made in the way a product is being marketed—whether in limited areas or on a total market basis—as much relevant information as possible should be collected. In general, most marketing experiments suffer from a lack of resources applied to the collection of data. The results of test launches, appropriation tests, campaign tests and so on, too often tend to be assessed only in terms of changes in retail sales measured through some form of store panel. Such measurements may be adequate to answer the immediate direct question of whether the test produces beneficial results or not, but they fail to cover two other vital aspects.

The first is that if the experiment does not generate an improved level of sales or profitability then unless the failure is due to some in-store conditions such as a lack of distribution, there will be no information to show where the marketing process broke down. If, for example, in an experimental launch only store audit data has been collected, there will be no means of diagnosing many possible causes of failure—or even of detecting weaknesses in a project which is in most respects successful. There will be no way of knowing whether the advertising failed to achieve attention or to create awareness; whether awareness was created but interest in the product did not develop; or even whether adequate numbers of the population did, in fact, buy the product but did not repeat their purchases. Thus, even though some of these measures may not be needed in order to assess the profitability of the project they are vital in any attempt at diagnosing weaknesses or causes of failure.

Second, in a more general way, the lack of this type of information, whether collected during experiments or when changes are introduced into wider markets, means that our knowledge of marketing is more restricted than it need be. There is, for example, little information about the way in which awareness of a new product or of a new advertising campaign develops. Too often, research in this area is merely confined to a single 'ad hoc' survey some weeks or months after the launch which will then show some existing single measure of awareness. There will, however, be no indication of whether the level found has only just been reached, whether it was reached some time earlier and has merely been held since, or whether the level has been higher in the past and is now declining. It is also then difficult to assess whether the achieved level is a satisfactory one or not. Increasing the amount of research to collect this information will, of course, involve additional expenditure in most cases, but this need not be unduly high. Against this the benefit of being able to plan future launch advertising against a more secure knowledge of the way in which awareness develops could well lead to significant increases in the efficiency of such operations.

Any collection of additional data beyond that necessary to assess and interpret the results of the particular experiment must, however, be done within the context of the experiment itself. Attempts to use or modify an experiment being run for a specific purpose, in order to test some other quite different factor at the same time, must normally be resisted. The bits and pieces tacked on are likely to jeopardize the main experiment. However, arranging for a more comprehensive set of measurements to be made within the context of the experiment should normally enhance the value of the results as well as adding to the company's fund of experience.

Summary

To sum up: marketing experiments need to be carefully designed and measured in order to answer the questions being posed—and this applies whether the experiments relate to immediate problems or are being mounted in order to gain long term experience. Before embarking on any experiment, four basic questions should be answered:

(a) is it possible to get the information required in this experiment from any other source, such as re-analysis of existing data, comparisons with other markets, or the accumulated experience of the company?;
(b) given what is already known about this situation will an experiment add to that experience in a way which will lead to a better-based decision?;
(c) will the benefit expected from the better decision be sufficient to cover the costs of the experiment, taking account of the full range of costs which may be incurred?;
(d) if this experiment is run can it be used as a source of other useful information and experience?

When an experiment or test is to be run four major considerations should be covered as far as is possible:

(a) the experiment should, wherever possible, be conducted in more than a single area;
(b) the integrity of the experiment must be established and maintained, and all decisions relating to the way it is handled operationally must be made in the light of the objectives and needs of the experimental situation;

(c) adequate time should be allowed for the effects of the changes to be developed and to reach stable levels;

(d) an adequate amount of measurement should be undertaken, not merely to provide measures of performance, but also to provide for diagnosis of the causes of weaknesses or failure and to increase the general understanding of the market.

References

1. CHRISTOPHER, M. *A Cluster Analysis of towns in England and Wales according to their suitability for test market locations.* University of Bradford Management Centre, 1969.
2. SCHLAIFER, R. *Probability and Statistics for Business Decisions.* McGraw-Hill, New York 1959.
3. DAVIS, E. J. Experimental Marketing, Nelson, 1970.

Further Reading

GOLD, J. A. Testing Test Market Predictions, *Journal of Marketing Research*, August, 1964.

GREEN, P. E. and FRANK, R. E. Bayesian statistics and marketing research. *Journal of the Royal Statistical Society*, Series C, **XV3,** November 1966.

PARFITT, J. H. and COLLINS, B. J. K. The use of Consumer Panels for brand-share prediction. *Journal of Marketing Research*, May 1968.

PYMONT, B. C. *The Development and Application of a New Micro Market Testing Technique.* ESOMAR Congress Papers, 1970.

WILLS, G. Cost Benefit of a Test Market. *Management Decision*, Winter 1967.

Measuring the Odds in Test Marketing. *The Nielsen Researcher* (Oxford Edition), **9,** 1, 1968.

The Advertiser's Guide to Media Marketing and Merchandising Services, Supplement to *Advertising and Marketing Management*, Feb. 1970.

20. Corporate image research

Robert Worcester

What has corporate image research to do with consumer market research? This question can be answered in three ways. First, many companies use a well known and well respected corporate identity to support their marketing effort and, as such, use their image as a 'launch-pad' for new product introductions. Second, because while corporate image research is perhaps out of the mainstream of the average market research manager's usual activity, nonetheless the market research manager is the one to whom public relations will turn for a study amongst the general public and personnel will turn for assistance on an employee attitude study, as will others for research into their areas of interest. Third, the social responsibility of business is becoming ever more increasingly a factor to be contended with. Companies who fail the test of good corporate citizenship are likely to be called to task by the public in many ways—by fall-off in sales, lower price earnings ratios for their shares, possibly by difficulty in recruiting staff and in other ways.

In succeeding sections, this chapter defines and puts into perspective the role of corporate image, discusses a number of the 'publics' of concern to the company, and describes how corporate image research is conducted.

The Four Image Categories

Over the last three decades, a great deal of research has been carried out into the images of companies, institutions, products, and brands. It may be said that generally there are four major categories of image influences. There is the *image of the product class* as a whole, *the image of the brand* as opposed to other brands within the product class, *the image of users* of the brand, and the *corporate image* of the company that stands behind the brand[1]. Of course, there are other influences at work on image as well, such as the time and place that the product or service might be used.

Research has shown that the crucial image influences sometimes occur in one of these dimensions and sometimes in another. This situation varies from product class to product class, brand to brand and company to company. Substantial variance also occurs during the life-cycle of a product of some manufacturers; witness the prominence given the corporate identity of Proctor and Gamble during the first eighteen months of their new product introductions in America.

The product class image is that collection of image attributes shared by all the brands of a particular product class, such as motor vehicles, cigarettes, textiles or a certain sort of machine tool. Every class and product exists for a reason, meets certain needs and desires, plays a certain role in the lives of its users, is associated with certain kinds of people and competes directly or indirectly with other product classes in various ways, most often for disposable income, increasingly frequently for leisure time.

Brand images are the unique characteristics of a brand that distinguish it from others. These include how, and how well, the brand is seen as fulfilling the functions of the product class, its appearance and style, package, price, and the degree to which it is believed to be economical and of good value.

Alan Brien's comment in Punch some time ago related brand images to the third category of image, the brand user image. He said,

> When I was a boy, men would talk about their cigarettes as they now talk about their cars. Brand loyalty was as strong as class loyalty and the two were often linked. Park Drive, de Reske, Black Cat, Balkan Sobraine, Passing Clouds—they were clues in a detective story. It was possible to deduce the sex, the income, the accent, even the favourite fantasies of the last person to dump a fag in your ashtray just by reading off its name. For a gent to be discovered smoking Woodbines was as suspicious as a tramp lighting up a fresh cigar[2].

Especially when there are few clear and demonstrable functional differences among brands, brand user images can be crucial to a brand's success.

The fourth source of image is that of the corporation or other institution that stands behind the product or service. This includes the company's general familiarity and favourability and many specific corporate image attributes that can be categorized as relating to product reputation, customer relations, employer role, ethical reputation, and others.

In 1967, David Lowe Watson set out a theory of advertising based on the concept of a set of relationships between the buyer, the 'personality' of the brand, and the 'personality' of the seller, or company[3]. This theory, he suggested, is more useful than standard advertising theories because it can satisfactorily account for a number of discrepancies between existing theory and empirical observations.

Lowe Watson provided a model that distinguished three key factors involved in effective advertising: a customer's image of the company, his image of the product, and his perception of the advertising. He said that the company image is related to advertising effectiveness and this underscores the concept of 'total communication' which includes the co-ordination of policy in every part of the company's communications activity, advertising, sales promotion, packaging, product planning, public relations, and corporate identification. He concluded that the advertiser who can build up a strong and favourable relationship with his customers will establish a fund of goodwill from which he can derive future benefits. These benefits include not only a greater readiness on the part of the customer to pay attention to his advertising, and a predisposition to put a favourable interpretation on the message received but also a favourable attitude toward the product itself and expectation of satisfactory product performance and a greater willingness to try a new product.

The late Leo Burnett was quoted as saying, 'We feel that proliferation of brands and mergers have brought on a growing need for corporate advertising. No brand can be given the support it needs and corporate identity is becoming more important as a seal of approval'[4]; and in speaking about industrial purchasing, William Paterson of Tube Investments said, 'The reputation of the company is an important factor and it is in this area that subjective decisions tend to be made'[5].

Definition of corporate image

What is a corporate image? Corporate image may be defined as 'the net result of interaction of all experiences, impressions, beliefs, feelings, and knowledge people have about a company'. The sources of image are extensive. These include the product, its packaging, both product and corporate advertising, distribution, and promotion patterns. Also, all the other manifestations of its communications, such as its letterhead, brochures, public relations, the impressions left by the company's employees and salesmen, its factories, offices, lorries and the activities of the industry in which the company operates also frequently have important effects on the corporate image. Opinions of other people and messages from competing companies also play an important role in forming a person's image of a company.

The role of the corporate image

A strong corporate image influences the predisposition to buy a company's products, speak favourably of it, believe its statements, apply for a job with it, and the like. It is important for industrial goods companies with listed shares. It is important to companies seeking highly technical staff in a tight staff availability situation. It is important to a consumer goods company whose very life is dependent on successful new product introductions. Just how important it is to a consumer goods company is illustrated by these recent findings that show that a sizeable proportion of the British public are less than enthusiastic about any new product, and yet show faith and trust in companies they feel they know well.

	Agree	Disagree
'I *never* buy products made by companies I have never heard of'	(37%)	53%
'New brands on the market are usually improvements on the old established brands'	37%	(41%)
'Old established companies make the best products'	(48%)	32%
'A company that has a good reputation would not sell poor products'	(75%)	16%

Fig. 20.1. Market & Opinion Research International Cooperative Corporate Image Study, Autumn, 1969. National Probability Sample of 1991 Adults in Great Britain.

And how important a company's reputation is to a housewife's propensity to try new products is shown by research which found women 14 per cent more likely to try a new product from 'Heinz' than from 'a large (unspecified) food company'.

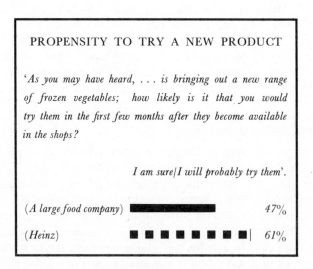

Fig. 20.2. Split sample of 1072 adult women in Great Britain. National Probability Sample. Market & Opinion Research International Cooperative Corporate Image Study, Spring, 1970.

Obviously, if corporate image can assist new product introductions and the marketing of products and services generally, it is necessary to see that consumers link the company's brand names with the company name.

That image relates to propensity to apply for a job was recently illustrated by findings from a survey of final year male undergraduates at universities throughout the UK. Eleven organizations recruiting at the universities were studied in detail and it was found that the students' *favourability* ranking directly paralleled the rank order of *interest in a job* with the organizations.*

The Corporate 'Publics'

Any company has a number of masters who must be served. The prime public of concern to every manager is the customer. Certainly without the customer the company must fail; but there are a number of other groups without which the company could not live, much less prosper, and chief among these are the company's employees. Yet there must be literally thousands of consumer research studies conducted each year for every study conducted amongst employees, or even, if the truth be known, amongst *all* of the other corporate 'publics' put together. The company 'publics' generally include:

(a) consumers;
(b) shareholders;
(c) the 'city';
(d) opinion leaders;
(e) potential employees;
(f) community;
(g) suppliers;
(h) the 'trade';
(i) employees
   (i) management;
   (ii) sales force;
   (iii) administrative staff;
   (iv) scientists and engineers;
   (v) production workers.

Consumers. Much that has been said above, and will be said in the pages that follow and in other chapters, relates to work with consumers, yet so often, as Lowe Watson has pointed out, the relationship the consumer feels with a company is overlooked or ignored.

There is considerable variability in the image influences that determine the brand commitment of the consumer. Each product field differs in the way in which brands are discerned and in the criteria that consumers use

---

* Market & Opinion Research International—Co-operative Careers Research Study, 1970; 935 interviews with final-year male undergraduates at universities throughout the British Isles.

to compare brands. Conducting corporate image research to determine the effect of an image on a brand, the researcher seeks to determine the image of the company that stands behind the brand as differentiated apart from the companies that provide other brands; for example, 'the company that makes these brands of breakfast cereals is constantly doing research to improve its products' is in a stronger position than, 'the company that makes these brands of breakfast cereals really doesn't care about its customers'.

As Pilditch put it in his excellent book,

> The pertinent question is not when to adopt the brand policy, but how to see this in corporate terms. In the soap business, the archetypal product or brand structure, an important change is taking place.
> Marketing men have thought in the past that the brand name was the important thing to get across. They felt that the company making the brand was unimportant, and didn't help sell the product. Who cares who makes Tide as long as Tide has what the shoppers want?
> This view is now less strongly held. In front of the author now is a bottle of Square Deal Quix. Which is the brand name? In a prominent place it states: "A Lever Product—guaranteed". Below it is written: "Lever quality and performance guaranteed or your money back" . . . .
> A corporation needs to become well known in the interests of attracting shareholders and employees, and developing good relations generally. Three points emerge. First, the relationship between brand and corporate identity is being reassessed. Second, the requirements of a corporate identity are different from those of a brand. This difference must be understood and preserved, and, the problem of relating the two will then be much easier to solve. Third, relationships must vary to suit the situation, particularly the comparative strength of brand name to corporate name, the ubiquity of the corporate name, and the appropriateness of the product to the corporate identity[6].

Another use is in product compatibility research. This type of study determines whether a new product is compatible with the company's existing image. Where it is not, different brand names are often used so that these names will *not* be identified with the company. Where it is, the company can use the corporate name to help sell the product. Research can help determine the compatibility of prospective new products with established brand and corporate names.

Corporate image research may also be used to uncover new products people think are compatible with an established corporate name which may not be those that management expects. Consumers judge product compatibility from a personal point of view that may differ drastically from that of the manufacturer. The manufacturer may reason that he should keep within his special areas of manufacturing competence. Consumers may see this in a different light entirely.

510

Shareholders and the 'City'. These groups are receiving increasing attention from companies in recent years. While consumer research techniques in the main apply, there are special problems one may encounter in researching these publics. The next chapter is devoted to financial relations research.

Opinion Leaders. Much misleading work has been done in the name of opinion leader research in the past. Many studies of AB men have purported to represent opinion leaders' opinions. Yet for all the work that has been done in this area, none has shown that there is any constant segment of the public that can truly be termed 'opinion leaders'. Other studies have been conducted with parliamentarians, the press, with business executives, and even with clergy, in the belief that they are in a position to mould public opinion *and so they are* but what is most often forgotten is that this ability to mould public opinion varies enormously, depending on the subject. The big businessman, for instance, may wield enormous influence among his contacts when he recommends an industrial product, or a share to buy; he may also influence the son of a friend seeking career advice; but it is unlikely his word on washing powders or washing machines or even for whom to vote, would swing much weight, for the thing that is often over-looked in this sort of study is the selective perceptions of those led, and selective indeed they are.

Precise sample selection and careful attention to ensure full and comprehensive interviews (nearly always personal if to be most useful) is of prime importance. A key is the thought that the most valuable image study, probably by a factor of ten, is the second one, after the facts have been obtained from a first study and action has been taken based on the facts uncovered. It is necessary to structure the study so it may be replicated a year or two hence. This requires questionnaire construction that will enable comparisons to be made and more attention to sampling than 'ten of those and twenty of those'.

Potential Employees. Potential employees generally fall into three categories: executive, university, and staff. In each category there are a number of factors that affect the two elements of successful recruitment, attracting appropriate applicants and convincing the desired applicants to 'sign up'. Factors potential employees consider important to know about a company, media they value and remuneration expectations may be researched. Hundreds of thousands of pounds are spent each year on recruitment activities, yet the amount of research to improve the effectiveness of recruiting is practically nil.

Community Studies. Consumers, employees, potential employees, opinion leaders, a prime source of shareholders, suppliers, and others gather in the community in which the company is located. Some companies have looked at residents of these local areas as a separate audience to be researched. Especially interesting to factory managers and other executives concerned with community relations are social issues and the concept of corporate citizenship. Do the townspeople regard the company's offices and factories as assets or liabilities? Is the company blamed for pollution? Is the company regarded as a good place to work? If not, why not? These and many other areas of general interest become especially relevant in communities in which the company is a major force.

Suppliers. Another audience of importance often overlooked is the company's suppliers. A few companies have realized that if they can help their suppliers serve them more economically and effectively, the company will itself reap rewards in lower prices, better delivery and service, and generally more effective purchasing.

The 'Trade'. Other important, but also often overlooked, links in the chain are the company's distributors, dealers, or agents. These are, to many companies, the only contact with consumers, and yet often go unresearched. Within the trade, corporate image—dealer relations, delivery practices, payment policies, and the like—are very important and sometimes the key to success or failure. This is a group usually easily, if not inexpensively, researched. As in any 'image' study, it is most valuable done periodically, so that the effect of changes that occur can be reliably measured over time.

Employees. And finally, employees. How much 'upward communication' is there? Management attention is overwhelmingly devoted to telling employees what to do and rarely listens to what employees, at all levels, think about the company and how it can be made more effective. As a letter to the Editor of the Financial Times[7] put it,

> However much it spends on the introduction of modern management techniques and up to date equipment and machinery, a company still depends for its success in the end on recruiting and holding sufficient staff of the right calibre at all levels from the boardroom to the shop floor. In these days, this can be a difficult enough process without the added drawback of a poor employer image. Anyone who has had anything to do with the operation of confidential reply or box number services must be able to compile a list of firms to which candidates frequently request their applications should not be forwarded. In the closer knit professional groups, a whisper on the grapevine can mean death to successful recruitment. How many companies even take the trouble to find out what their employees think about them—as employers? The attitude survey technique is still too little used. Perhaps some employers prefer not to know just how bad their image is. Sometimes, no doubt, the bad employer's image is a deserved one in which case the remedy lies elsewhere than in improved communications; but employers who take more trouble in talking (by word of mouth or in print) to their employees in a language they can understand, who take pains not to create mystery where none exists, will find the

rewards in terms of improved recruitment and reduced staff turnover are well worth the trust and effort.

Yet few companies have made employee attitude measurements a regular aspect of their research programme.

The Context of Corporate Reputations

The detailed image profile of a company or organization as seen by external publics can best be understood within the perspective of overall attitudes towards business; attitudes towards specific industries, not only the industry in which the client is involved but other industries as well; and then towards the client company versus its competitors and in the context of many companies, some better known and some less well known. Images cannot be studied in a vacuum. All images are relative and must be comparative.

Union Carbide, a large chemical company in the US, began measuring its corporate reputation with the American public in 1957. For four years they saw almost no change in their level of awareness. In 1961 they took a number of steps to increase the level of familiarity among the American people. Included among these steps were the identification of several consumer product lines having sterling brand images as 'a product of Union Carbide', and a consistent corporate identity programme. In addition, they embarked on a heavy programme of corporate image advertising, especially on television. By 1969 they had increased the portion of the population that had heard of them to 85 per cent, an increase of 30 percentage points. It might be interesting to note that during the same period their level of favourability, i.e., those people who consider them very or mostly favourably, increased from 36 per cent to 60 per cent of the American public.

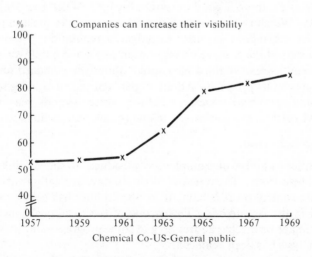

Fig. 20.3. Opinion Research Corporation Data.

513

That favourability increases with familiarity is an important finding indeed to a company with a low level of public awareness. Companies are most highly regarded by those that know them best. Over half (59 per cent) of those who say they are very familiar with 14 companies studied in 1969 said they had a very favourable opinion of them, whereas only 15 per cent of those who were least familiar with them held very favourable opinions. To be relatively better liked than known is possible but it is a swim against a very strong tide.

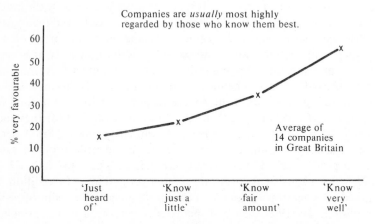

Fig. 20.4. Market & Opinion Research International, 1991 interviews, National Probability Sample of all adults in Great Britain, Cooperative Corporate Image Study, Autumn, 1969.

The ingredients of corporate image

What goes to make up a good corporate image? When the British public were asked, 'Which two or three things do you consider most important to know about a company in order to judge its reputation?', about a third talked in terms of the company's reputation as a good employer and being fair to its employees. A third also spoke about the standard and quality and reliability of its products. About 10 per cent talked about good service to public and customers, honesty, reliability, price of goods, reasonable and competitive pricing, the company's management, and its financial stability.

Image and behaviour

In this chapter a number of examples are introduced to suggest links between image and behaviour. The research methodology for relating variables that conceivably control overt behaviour to one another has been considerably developed in the last decade. This is one of the basic problems to which corporate image research is addressed and some progress along experimental lines of analysis has been achieved.

Variables which were related to behaviour included data on ratings of the

514

company's products, support for public relations platform objectives, corporate symbol recognition, data on recent purchases of the company's products and recommendation of the company's products to others. Multiple regression analysis techniques were used to rank corporate image measures and other variables in terms of their relationship to action. The most closely related image measurement to recent purchases of the company's brands was not the company's product reputation image as might have been supposed but the customer treatment image. The same image dimensions related to those who had recommended the company's products. On the other hand, willingness to listen to a company spokesman on an issue was most closely associated with having a favourable attitude towards big business.

The actions people take with respect to a company depend on far more than whether or not they like or dislike the company. Yet complex and subconscious as a person's feelings and beliefs about a company may be, they can yet often be synthesized into ranked data that may be examined statistically. Images differ from company to company in important ways. While they are undoubtedly rooted in general value systems, each company has its own strengths and weaknesses among various segments of the population. With objectively measured knowledge of corporate strengths and weaknesses, companies can organize their efforts in appropriate directions, capitalizing on their strengths and, where possible, identifying and taking steps to correct their weaknesses.

One of the most useful findings from a study of corporate image is where the facts of the situation contradict the image. One large, very well known and well respected British company has a price earnings ratio far below where its management believes it ought to be. In fact, it is a well diversified and reasonably profitable company. Yet nine out of ten AB British men think of it as selling only one product and that product is traditionally a low profit item. Thus, the company has a blueprint for communications action based on objective knowledge of the facts, *as seen through the eyes of the shareholding public.*

How to do it

Corporate images don't exist in a vacuum; they are affected by the company's activities, its industry's image and by information from competing companies. All images are comparative; therefore, wherever possible, and this means in most studies of corporate 'publics', one must study a company's image in the context of other companies. This, in the case of image studies of 'publics' outside the company itself, leads to the development of syndicated studies and the dual advantage of the reduction in the demands made on the public under study and the price to the client.

There are cooperative surveys sponsored by a number of market research organizations. These include semi-annual surveys of corporate image amongst the general public and annual corporate image surveys amongst

AB men and final-year male undergraduates in universities. Also, technical staff recruitment surveys are undertaken periodically, as are various trade surveys. One source of information about these is the annual Recent Research Summary, published formerly by Advertisers' Weekly. Employee attitude studies are more difficult in that comparative studies are impossible (except of course over time) without access to data collected from a cross-section of other studies and, as yet, no agency has done enough work in this area in the UK to provide a sufficiently broad data base of 'normative' information.

As there are a number of special considerations as to the methodology of internal studies, it may be useful to devote a few paragraphs to how employee attitude studies are carried out. Further reference to this type of work is found in William Schlackman's paper[8] and in a recent article in *International Management*[9] magazine.

The goal of an employee attitude survey is to produce an accurate and detailed picture of employee satisfactions as well as their dissatisfactions, their knowledge and understanding of the company and its operations, any 'road blocks' which may be limiting employee productivity, reactions to company communications and the like.

It is important, whenever possible, to have access to previous studies which have developed data on important aspects of employee attitudes and thinking. These accumulated results can serve as norms against which to judge survey results in any given company.

In order to develop the necessary understanding of the specific company's employee relations practices and objectives, to discuss current operating problems and to explore employees' ideas as to 'what the survey really should cover', the research agency normally conducts preliminary interviews with members of management and representatives of all groups to be surveyed.

Depending on such factors as the geographical dispersion, levels to be included, the number of employees who can be taken off the job for the survey and the budget available for obtaining and processing the data, the procedure may be as follows.

Survey all employees—a survey based on 100 per cent coverage takes maximum advantage of the morale-building potential of employee attitude research. It also permits detailed analysis of results department by department or unit by unit and an analysis of the thinking of small groups of employees whose functions or problems may be deemed especially important. Ideally, all employees at a single location, of like job classification, should participate in the survey. If half are sampled, the half that are selected tend to say, 'Why pick on me?' and the half that are left out say 'Don't my opinions count?'.

Survey a representative sample of employees—the sample can be so planned that an adequate number of interviews is obtained from both supervisory and non-supervisory employees and that enough interviews are taken in major departments to permit separate analysis of the results for key employee groups.

Some employee surveys have been very satisfactorily carried out by mail. In 1968, a survey of 900 district managers of a large insurance company was conducted by mail and received a 91 per cent response rate.

The following list suggests possible questioning areas that might be considered:

(a) how is the company regarded as a place to work?;
(b) how do employees regard their supervisors?;
(c) what do employees think of the employee benefits provided for them?;
(d) how do employees evaluate the various methods of communication used by the company?;
(e) what is the attitude toward promotion practices and policies?;
(f) how do employees feel about job security?;
(g) how do employees appraise working conditions?;
(h) what is the extent of employees' knowledge of important economic facts?;
(i) what is the appraisal of the management of the company?

In addition to this type of question, the survey should include some questions that give employees the opportunity to say, in their own words, whatever is on their minds.

Also included on the questionnaire are background questions designed to permit analysis of replies of various groups of employees. Frequently, special tabulations are made by departments, sex, length of service, occupation, location, etc. This detailed type of analysis enables the company to isolate sources of dissatisfaction wherever they exist. Results are reported only for groups of employees, of course, not for individuals.

Conclusion

Corporate image research differs from most other forms of market research being carried out here today because it is at the same time both tactical and strategic. It is geared both to finding out gaps between the facts as they are and as people believe them to be—immediately actionable—and to pointing the way for the future.

Corporate image research can take many forms among the 'publics' under research. Corporate image research can be carried out with all 'publics' of interest to a corporation, all 'publics' having influence over its destiny, including consumers, employees, potential employees, the plant community, parliamentarians, opinion leaders, shareholders, and so on.

The importance of the corporate image is just beginning to be felt here. It will become even more important in the future than it is today. It is the responsibility of research to help management to understand and measure its importance and effect on the future.

References

1. MACLEOD, J. S. *The Marketing Power of Brand and Corporate Images*, Opinion Research Corporation, Dec. 1961.
2. BRIAN, A. Pleasure. *Punch*, 648, 22 Oct. 1969.
3. LOWE WATSON, D. *Advertising and the Buyer/Seller Relationship*. IPA Thesis Competion, 1967.
4. BURNETT, L. Advertising. *The New York Times*, 14 Dec. 1969.
5. PATERSON, W. Try to Use the Same Language. *IAM*, 12–14, June, 1970.
6. PILDITCH, J. *Communication by Design*. McGraw-Hill, 1970.
7. ROBERTS, L. D. Letter to the Editor, *The Financial Times*, 19 Mar. 1970.
8. SCHLACKMAN, W., THORNLEY, R., and VULLIAMY, J. *The Hartcliffe Project—A Progress Report of a Sociological Study in Environmental Planning*. Conference Papers, Market Research Society, 87–109, Mar. 1970.
9. MACKENZIE, E. What Do Your Employees Think? *International Management*, Mar. 1971.

21. Market research in the financial field

Michael Burrows

'Financial research' may be most simply defined as 'all market research survey work concerned with matters affecting the financial community'. For a variety of reasons, some practical and some emotional, the financial community made comparatively little use of market research until recently. However, the situation is changing rapidly, as the City itself is changing, in response to the increasing influence of the 'professional investor' (the insurance companies' investment manager etc.) and the highly numerate investment analysts. There is also, among insurance companies, unit trusts and merchant bankers, a growing awareness of, and interest in, new marketing methods—often involving a more direct approach to the public or to potential customers, the development of new services, and the need for more effective advertising and promotional campaigns. Moreover, the financial community is being subjected to the constant pressures of increasing costs and growing competition which, as in industry, encourages the growth of larger units, which in turn need a more 'professional' management structure. Against this background, it is not surprising to find that financial research is one of the more rapidly growing segments of the market research business, continually throwing up new problems and new opportunities.

Research Problems

The range of problems that may be encountered in the field of financial research may be divided into three broad categories, as follows.

First, factors affecting the portfolio investment decisions of both professional and private shareholders including, for example,

(a) how investment managers judge the 'quality of management' in a company, and the 'personality of the chief executive'; or what influences

519

private shareholders to invest in government stocks, unit trusts, building societies or the shares of individual public companies;

(b) factual data about individual companies or sectors of industry for use by investment analysts. This is usually a very different type of work, more akin to industrial research than the problems described in the above paragraph which are, perhaps, of a more fundamental, qualitative, attitudinal nature. Problems may be concerned primarily with long term forecasts of the demand for industrial products, the degree of competition and the prospects for profit, the scope for rationalization or mergers, the import/export situation, and, perhaps most important, brand share data which may indicate which companies are on the up and which are failing;

(c) the collection and analysis of market research data for general forecasting purposes, in order to confirm or modify statistical forecasts in accordance with the degree of optimism existing among consumers or in industry.

Second, factors affecting the use made of the services offered by City firms concerned with banking, insurance, or brokerage, e.g., what influences a public company to use one bank rather than another? Why do the institutional investors use one stockbroker rather than another? Why do people use one insurance company or invest in one unit trust rather than another and how can they best be influenced to change?

Third, corporate communications including,

(a) factors affecting the 'image' of a company. In all matters affecting finance a firm's reputation and standing is of prime importance and, indeed, a company's continued existence may depend upon its reputation if it becomes involved in a disputed takeover bid. One may be concerned with either an industrial company's reputation in the City, or a bank's reputation in industry, or even a foreign bank's reputation with other banks in the City from which it may expect its business to come;

(b) readership and advertising research insofar as it affects the financial community, e.g., what do stockbrokers read in the train on their way to the City, and before the market opens? Who reads the Chairmen's statements advertised in the press? How best can one reach private shareholders or investment managers during a takeover bid?

It is, of course, always easier to delineate problems than to solve them, and the rest of this chapter is concerned with, first, a discussion of some of the problems common to most financial research surveys, including sampling, contact and interviewing, quantitative and qualitative analyses; and then, more specific notes on recent developments and some of the major issues encountered in each of the three fields of research outlined above.

Sampling

The sampling problem is usually unique to each survey, but there are certain basic works of reference which should provide at least the basis of a sampling frame, although they may each have their limitations, as explained in the paragraphs that follow.

First, the Stock Exchange Yearbook provides a basic list of stockbrokers but the most recent volume must be used, because the number is shrinking quite rapidly. In 1969, 194 were located in London, 149 in Scotland and the major provincial centres, and 73 elsewhere, often in seaside residential towns. London probably accounts for about 75 per cent of the business, but the attitudes and opinions of non-City firms are often quite markedly different. Those located 'elsewhere' are generally small, with very low overheads, but they may be important in the case of, say, a unit trust survey. Firms may be stratified by the number of partners they have: this is not perfect and there are major discrepancies but it provides a reasonable basis for analysis.

Second, the Stock Exchange Yearbook also contains a formidable list of institutions—banks and insurance companies etc.—but many of them are quite small offices of foreign banks, and must have only limited investment interests. There are probably only about 175 to 300 effective institutional investors and their identification is mainly dependent upon personal knowledge.

Third, in many surveys, particularly those concerned with takeover bids and 'financial' corporate image studies, the views of the 20 City editors of the major daily, evening, Sunday, and weekly journals may be of prime importance because of their persuasive influence upon influential City opinion, particularly their morning and evening 'captive' train readership audiences.

Fourth, the Financial Times Actuaries' Index includes 625 major British public companies, conveniently divided into 41 groups and sub-groups, such as building materials, breweries and banks, etc. Together, these firms account for 80 per cent of the market value of all British quoted companies and about 60 per cent of UK manufacturing capacity. Its main limitation is that the major subsidiaries of foreign firms, such as Ford, IBM and Alcan etc., are excluded, as are the major private companies such as David Brown and Pilkington's.

Finally, for larger universes, as in industrial surveys, one may go to Dun & Bradstreet's 'Guide to Key British Enterprises', which lists the largest 15 000 firms or to Kompass, which includes most firms with more than 50 employees and those who are members of the CBI.

The names and addresses of all private shareholders are, of course, listed in Companies House, and for a small fee a representative sample may be compiled. This is useful in the case of a takeover bid when there is a need to interview the shareholders of a particular company, but if the requirement is to interview shareholders—or unit trust holders—in general, it is usually cheaper to ask an identifying question on a continuous omnibus survey, with a view to re-interviewing an appropriate sample in a second phase operation.

Contact and Interviewing

Respondents in the financial community generally, as in industry, are usually busy, brusque, and highly intelligent. As a universe it is probable that the professionals in the City suffer fools less gladly than any other groups of respondents interviewed, but if the subject interests them, and if the interviewer is well-briefed, sensitive and intelligent, they are more courteous, better informed and more helpful than most people.

During a recent survey among senior investment managers, a response rate of 90 per cent was obtained, which is better than one would expect from either an average group of housewives or AB class men as a whole. The subject was of particular interest to them, but the markets were quite busy and this response rate was much better than anticipated. The questionnaire guide had been carefully designed, and piloted, to keep the interview down to 40 minutes, which was thought to be the limit of a busy man's tolerance, but in fact many of the discussions ran on to 90 minutes, and even 2 hours, in spite of explicit instructions to interviewers to 'get out before they became a bore'.

In these situations the quality and character of the interviewer is of fundamental importance, and there is persuasive evidence that, even in the City, an intelligent, mature, and experienced female is far superior to a male! It seems that, in the City as elsewhere, men tend to judge men instantly, instinctively and usually unflatteringly—'a young demo', 'a drunken has-been', or a 'retired colonel' etc.—and respondents become quickly bored. By contrast an intelligent, sympathetic woman, who has, perhaps, had previous experience in commerce or the academic world may listen more sensitively, probe more delicately and record what she hears more objectively, perhaps because she has fewer preconceived opinions. Good male interviewers can be very good but they are not easy to find or to keep, as interviewers, for long.

The danger in financial research, as in the industrial field, is that the very small number of potential respondents will become over-interviewed, and permanently alienated by over-persistent, ill-briefed, dull interviewers struggling through a long, highly structured questionnaire more suitably designed for pet food purchasers.

There are certain situations, such as takeover bids, where it is quite unnecessary to waste respondents' time with lengthy personal interviews. City people are accustomed to doing much of their business by telephone, and are usually quite ready to spend ten minutes discussing the factors affecting a particular bid situation, or the effect of a recent counter-offer: but it is often helpful if respondents have met the interviewer previously, or at least have been interviewed, without antagonism, by the research agency on some previous occasion.

Whom to Interview

Perhaps the major problem in any survey concerned with City services, such as banking, is deciding whom to interview (as in many industrial research surveys). One may, for example, telephone a large company and ask to speak to 'the person who takes the responsibility for export trade insurance matters': eventually one should get through to an export manager or an insurance manager or perhaps a shipping manager, depending on the firm's organization and job titles (no two firms seem to call the man doing the same job by the same title: or if they have the same title their responsibility and status may vary enormously from company to company). However, one's problems are then by no means at an end, because the person who takes important day to day decisions about insurance or shipping problems may not be the person who takes the responsibility for a major change of policy: this could well become a boardroom decision, powerfully affected by the views of the finance director or the company secretary (whose responsibilities and status may again vary considerably from company to company).

One solution is to interview the person contacted by telephone; and then to ask who else might be concerned with a major policy change of the type outlined, and then who might finally decide if there was a conflict of opinion within the company on the subject. This final referee is probably as near to the decision maker in that company as one can get, and a final five minute interview with him, if it can be arranged, is often of the greatest value.

Quantitative and Qualitative Analyses

Most clients in the financial field are numerate by nature, and they tend to be more impressed by percentages than by qualitative comment and interpretation; therefore, in spite of the comparatively small universe, it is usually desirable to interview at least 100 respondents, which allows perhaps two or three breakdowns, for example, London versus The Rest; those aged under 45 versus the over 45; large, medium, and small scale stockbrokers (according to number of partners or investment analysts) etc. In theory there might seem to be a large standard error involved in small samples, but in practice 100 interviews may cover a substantial part of the total universe involved, so that the problem is less than it appears.

In order to provide a sensible statistical framework for analysis, it may be necessary to evolve a simple code list—sometimes merely 'favourable', 'unfavourable', 'mixed', 'indecisive/no comment'—upon which answers can be quickly and cheaply coded, punched, and run through the computer to provide a quantified framework for an essentially qualitative analysis of opinions and facts influencing investment decisions, etc. The questionnaire guide must, however, also be designed so that at least the main points of any significant answers can be recorded by the interviewer, so that a research executive can subsequently go through the interview notes and pick out quotations which illustrate, qualitatively, the tenor of respondents' replies and the emphasis with which they express their preferences or prejudices. This is a task that requires considerable skill, experience, and patience: the best interviewers' work can be reduced to platitudes by an unimaginative commentator, or worse still biased by an injudicious selection of quotations. In this sense, the success or failure of most surveys may depend ultimately upon the quality of the commentator, and the skill and patience with which he 'de-briefs' his interviewers.

At this final stage it may also become evident that the report could be strengthened by further statistical analyses, but simple hand tabulation will usually satisfy the requirement; and there is seldom a need for additional, more sophisticated computer work unless considerably more than 100 interviews are available for analysis.

Recent Research Work

Development problems

(a) *Factors Affecting Portfolio Investment Decisions*

As regards institutional investors two surveys have been published: 'the GEC bid for AEI' (published by J. Walter Thompson) and the 'Professional Investor' (published by the 'Investors Chronicle').

The 'GEC bid' survey was conducted in January/February 1968, about two months after the event, and was mainly concerned with the factors influencing institutional investors to support one firm rather than the other, and to enquire into City readership habits. One of the most interesting tables, which may merit reproduction yet again, showed the four major factors influencing investment decisions to be:

	Stock-Brokers	*Institutional Investors*	*Private Shareholders*
Factor rated as important:			
Quality of management team	36%	35%	38%
Profit potential (over next two years)	31%	25%	53%
Profit record (over past five years)	11%	25%	36%
Personality of chief executive	20%	12%	27%

524

To the numerate such a table may have a certain plausibility, but in fact the argument tends to go round in a circle. 'How do you estimate future profits'? Partly at least by reference to past profits. 'How do you judge the quality of management'? Partly at least by the past profit record. Similarly, 'How do you judge the quality of the chief executive'? Again, quite frequently, by his profit record—'Arnie Weinstock must be good: look at his record'. The last few years, and months, however, have seen several examples of men with a brilliant record who have made a miscalculation or over-reached themselves and been unhorsed as a result. A research man must feel instinctively that some more objective criteria could, or should, be developed which would at least give some early warning signals when matters were going astray, or the chief executives were moving from the 'dynamic' category to the 'eccentric' or 'megalomanic' classification.

In a rather different field, a series of unpublished surveys has been conducted recently into factors affecting the ownership of unit trust holdings, and attitudes towards insurance and savings generally. In addition the results of two large scale sample surveys have been published which contain a wealth of detailed factual data[1,2], but many questions remain unanswered: notably perhaps why only about eight per cent of the adult population invest in unit trusts, and why so comparatively few people can name a unit trust company as compared with, say, a building society; and why building societies were so much preferred to unit trusts by young people in 1970.

Special problems arise when conducting research during an actual takeover situation, when the usual problem is to identify the major factors affecting the outcome and to monitor changes of opinion as they occur, almost from day to day, in a variety of different audiences.

Thus in one major bid 'battle' one research company (BMRB) was asked to launch seven separate surveys in seven days among financial editors, stockbrokers, and institutional investors, bank managers, shareholders, customers, university appointment boards, and the company's own staff. Daily reports were supplied each day at about 5 p.m. for consideration that evening and at the following morning's executive committee meeting.

On another occasion the research company was asked to interview 20 shareholders a day (in practice it was usually each evening): the results were telephoned in on the following morning, hand tabulated, commented on, printed and delivered each day by 5 p.m., so that the results of bids, counter-bids, and press conferences could be monitored day by day. Within 48 hours a sample of 40 was available, which built up at a rate of 20 a day, until the next phase of the 'battle' was signalled by a new bid or counter-bid.

The most surprising result of such surveys is the general antipathy among small private shareholders to takeover bidders, who are often described as 'brash', 'arrogant', 'conceited', 'young' men. This may of course be attributable to the fact that in a typical British 'blue chip' company, 65 per cent of the shareholders may be over 55, 60 per cent women; 40 per cent may have held their shares for over 10 years, and probably a third have had the shares 'left' or given to them. Even so it is surprising to find how reluctant many shareholders are to see 'their' company taken over, despite the financial benefits that they stand to gain.

Factual data for investment analysts

Comparatively little research is as yet commissioned by investment analysts, who usually prefer to collect their own data and to visit companies themselves. In some ways this is surprising, because market research agencies are generally much closer to the consumer and service industries than is the City, and usually have a great deal of background information and library facilities at their disposal which few broking firms could equal. Firms in the consumer and service industries do of course account for about one third of the 500 in the Financial Times actuaries' index. However, at least two major syndicated services deserve mention. The first is Taylor Nelson's 'business opinions' survey, from which some of the major results are printed monthly, in statistical form, in the Financial Times; but in addition monthly reports are circulated, on a confidential basis, to a limited number of stock-brokers and financial institutions: these are based on interviews conducted at regular intervals at a senior management level and designed primarily to pick up *changes* in management attitudes, from industry to industry, from company to company, and from year to year. Changing attitudes may be signalled by a variety of signs ranging from a change of managing director to the appointment of a finance director, the rationalization of production facilities (and an improved turnover/personnel ratio), the introduction of management consultants, or a change of advertising agents (in the case of consumer goods).

On a larger scale—and more closely concerned with the consumer goods industries—is the City edition of BMRB's 'target group index'. This is a quarterly volume, based on the analysis of about 6500 self-completion questionnaires covering the usage of all types of consumer goods and services (including holiday plans, shopping habits, and unit trust holdings etc.) and expenditure on a wide range of durables and clothing, which is designed to show in which product fields demand is increasing or decreasing, and which brands are expanding and which are contracting. Brands are then indexed to companies, so that one can see at a glance how a company like Boots is faring across a range of product fields. Ideally, a company should have an expanding share of a number of expanding markets: a firm can, of course, lose money expanding a market share, but, in the longer term, it is almost impossible to increase profits while losing out in a major market (vide the old BMC). In the consumer goods field one can, of course, also check advertising expenditure, and as this is one of the major variables in costs, one should be able to assess the trend of UK profits—at least well enough to question a company's chairman with pertinency.

Research data for forecasting purposes

Probably the most sophisticated forecasting being done in the financial field is being conducted by Donald Gomme Research Associates Ltd. with the assistance of Scientific Control Systems (CEIR). It was fully described in a paper read to the Royal Statistical Society, in April 1969, by Professor Kendell, Gomme and Coen. As a result of a great deal of complex mathematical analysis, using techniques made possible by large computers, it has been demonstrated that a number of indices, lagged on events which occurred several years ago, plus a statistically computed confidence factor, can forecast movement on the stock market and did, in fact, predict the extent and the timing of the 1969/70 break in London, and on Wall Street, with remarkable accuracy. This work is now being supported by a number of major City institutions, who have found it to be a valuable guide to longer term investment decisions.

From a marketing research point of view one may, however, be more immediately concerned with the application of survey data to statistical forecasts, and there is an accumulation of evidence to suggest that confidence levels in the City or industry, which are measurable, can be correlated in some way with the movement of stock market prices and the demand for financial services as well as industrial products.

The CBI and its predecessor the FBI have been producing tri-annual reports on the state of business confidence since 1958 and these are taken into account by government departments, economists, and industrialists (reference to this work are included in 'Economic Trends', September, 1965; 'Applied Economics', August, 1969; and the NIES review, May, 1970).

The more recent 'business opinions' survey conducted by the Taylor Nelson Group is printed monthly in the Financial Times: experiments to illustrate its predictive value have been encouraging and were reported to the 10th CIRET Conference in Brussels in September, 1970. Meanwhile, in the field of consumer durables the Gallup Poll have been collecting data on 'intentions to purchase' durables and the attitudes of consumers to the economy over the period 1959–1970. Heald, of the London Business School, presented a paper on this work to the Institute of Management Sciences and the Operational Research Society in July, 1970. An Index of Consumer Confidence is derived with the aid of a principal component analysis from five attitudes questions. The Index is incorporated into an econometric model and is shown to have a useful predictive value up to six to nine months ahead.

BMRB has also been following the work done at Michigan University, collecting data from a cross-section of the public asking them whether they are better or worse off than a year ago and whether or not they expect things to improve. The analysis of past data shows that by these methods statistical forecasts of new car registrations or advertising expenditure might be improved up to 24 months ahead. The timing of the 1966 stock market fall,

527

which was primarily attributable to internal (British) factors, was predicted, but the 1970 break which closely mirrored Wall Street's behaviour would probably not have been picked up by any internal predictors.

Echoing Gilbert and Sullivan it can be said that, 'A forecaster's lot is not a happy one', but one is persuaded that further research along these lines is merited, and that the 'areas of uncertainty' are being steadily diminished as a result of the continuous, painstaking research work being undertaken by a variety of academic and commercial organizations.

(b) *Research into Services Provided by the Financial Community*

The City and other financial centres in Britain provide a wide range of services including banking, insurance, brokerage, merchanting of all kinds and money management. An intricate network of agents, brokers, bankers and discount houses has developed over centuries which make the City of London in many ways unique. Some have better adapted to changing conditions than others; but attempts to alter established methods in advance of demand can cause difficulties.

An example of this was an attempt to alter established insurance procedures for containerized traffic: there is general agreement that containerization reduces pilferage and damage to goods in transit, and it seemed logical to offer a standard rate of insurance for such traffic; but this was calculated to be higher than existing rates for large companies with a good insurance record, and there was a loss of flexibility which caused the scheme to be shelved. This is the type of problem that can be surveyed by a competent agency with an experienced research staff, but most City firms would probably still be reluctant to entrust such a problem to a non-City research agency, for fear of alienating potential clients by wasting their time with superficial questions. They can only be reassured, over a period of time, by competent, imaginative, and constructive research work conscientiously undertaken.

A major development in this field during the last two years has been NOP Market Research's development of two major syndicated surveys each based on random samples of 25 000 personal interviews. The first covers both savings habits and private investment patterns; the second measures both behavioural and attitudinal aspects of the private insurance market. This latter has been recently supported by a syndicated, qualitative study amongst insurance brokers. More simplified quantitative data allied to readership and viewing habits is of course also covered in the 'Target Group Index', which was described earlier.

More recently, KBMS, in association with the 'Investors Chronicle', have launched the 'British Savings and Investment Opinion Index': a quarterly survey among ABC1 men designed to measure attitudes towards forms of investment and 'awareness of' major companies involved in the field of unit trusts and building societies, etc.

528

(c) *Corporate Communications*

Major developments have been taking place in the field of corporate communications during the last five years, as more companies have come to appreciate that their reputation, or 'image', is of prime importance in all matters affecting finance and that the continued existence of the company (and the career prospects of its senior executives) may be at hazard if the firm becomes involved in a takeover bid. A sound 'corporate image' will, of course, also greatly assist the marketing staff to sell more goods and introduce new products, the personnel department to recruit and retain managers and staff at reasonable salaries, as well as all those who have dealings with the government, local authorities, the unions and the press, over matters ranging from planning permission to pollution. This aspect of the problem is dealt with at greater length in chapter 20.

As regards a company's 'corporate image' in the City a very great deal depends upon its profit record, which as was explained earlier (in connection with the 'GEC bid' report) powerfully influences the City's views on a company's future earnings, the quality of its management and the effectiveness of its chief executive. It follows that the main determinant of a company's reputation in financial circles is its profit (or loss) figures, but companies do also have a powerful opportunity to communicate with professional and private investors through the medium of the annual chairman's statement and by discussions with individual stockbrokers and merchant bankers.

A recent survey showed that a surprisingly large proportion of company directors felt it quite wrong that a firm should try to influence its share price on the stock market, which, it was said, was quite irrelevant to the proper conduct of the company's business. In many cases stockbrokers' visits were regarded as a nuisance, and primary factors governing the drafting of the chairmen's annual statement were that nothing should be given away to competitors and that no leverage should be given to the executive staff, the unions, suppliers, customers, the PIB, the Monopolies Commission or the Board of Trade to expect higher bonuses or pay, or better bargains or lower prices, etc. Such negative attitudes, however, may be counter-productive, because there is some evidence that private shareholders, at least, and some advisers, including bank managers and solicitors, and stockbrokers, are instinctively attracted towards companies like Marks and Spencers, Beechams, and Boots which have established a reputation for quality and sensitivity to public opinion. Indeed, it can be argued that it is only companies that have established a reputation for social responsibility that can steadily raise their prices and their profits without public outcry and government interference and this could be of increasing importance in the years ahead, if governments struggle to control wage-cost inflation and rising unemployment by an intensification of prices-and-incomes policies.

It follows that if a company has a policy for developing and projecting its 'image', then it should also assess the effectiveness of that policy by regularly measuring its own standing and reputation against that of its major competitors, or comparably sized firms, in the financial field as well as in the spheres of customer relationships, personnel recruitment, etc.

Readership and Advertising Research

Financial advertising varies enormously in scale and content from the announcement of company results and the chairman's statement to 'offer' and unit trust advertisements and corporate advertising beamed at the financial community. It is necessary to discuss each in turn because they differ so widely. As regards chairmen's statements a great deal of research still needs to be done. It used to be traditional for the chairmen of major companies, particularly the banks, to print their statement in full in the leading financial journals. Insofar as these statements were often the company's considered views on the state of the country's economy this was, and still is, useful, because in paid space a chairman's views cannot be distorted, edited or ignored. However, in recent years, it has become customary for some companies to limit their annual advertisement to a few headlines covering profits, major changes and prospects. One may argue that this more commercial approach may have gone too far, and that a valuable promotional opportunity may often be being discarded too lightly, often, it seems, because the advertising and drafting of the chairman's statement is the responsibility of the company secretary rather than, say, the advertising manager or a director concerned with marketing or sales who might take a broader view of the issues involved.

The research problem is not only to identify the various target audiences for statements of this kind but also to determine how best they may be influenced. A basic difficulty is that one part of the audience is highly numerate and is basically only interested in the profit and turnover figures, analysed in as much detail as possible, and the prospects, preferably expressed in numerate terms; but the wider audience, ranging from Members of Parliament to elderly private shareholders and employees, may not be very numerate and they primarily want to be reassured, or persuaded that they are concerned with a company which is large, but humane; profitable, technically advanced and efficiently run but socially responsible (not surprisingly, survey results show that, under such headings, Marks and Spencer and Sainsbury rate very well with all sections of the community).

Turning to 'offers' (company prospectuses, etc.) and unit trust advertising, one is immediately restricted by the legal requirements which are largely responsible for the tone and format of those formidable advertisements which fill the City pages when the market is rising, but perhaps market research could, and should, be used to test the effectiveness of such advertising and the relative impact of advertising and direct mail.

In the case of unit trust advertising, in particular, the case for further research work seems persuasive, because only about 20 per cent of their

530

income is derived from the 'instant response' to City page advertising i.e., the money received within days in direct response to a unit trust advertisement. The bulk of their money therefore comes from regular weekly or monthly payments, often linked with an insurance policy or via a bank, perhaps influenced by the 'point of sale' material available in most banks.

Further research might well show that more promotion or more advertising in the popular dailies and the women's weeklies could substantially increase this market, particularly if rational arguments could be developed for investing when the market is historically low rather than pulling in the money as the market rises to a peak (thereby inevitably creating groups of dissatisfied customers soured by any subsequent market fall).

The whole subject of unit trust advertising was discussed quite fully at the Advertising Association Conference in May, 1970, and again at the Unitholder's second conference on 'Unit Trust and Money Management' (June, 1970) and no doubt will have been subjected to further analysis by the time this book is published. At present only about eight per cent of all adults hold unit trusts, as compared with 39 per cent who have Premium Bonds and 29 per cent who have a National Savings Bank account: the differences are large, and seem certain to attract more research and analysis.

The third area for research in this field is more concerned with conventional readership or 'reading and noting' studies. Readership surveys are probably the most rigorously controlled of all market research work done: an effective survey will almost certainly require the imprimatur of the IPA, who will need to be satisfied that a survey has been based upon a statistically valid sampling frame and the use of the exact JICNARS phraseology (see chapter 24) to ensure comparability with other surveys. However, stockbrokers and investment managers tend to read, or look at, a very large number of publications, and therefore the JICNARS questions need to be supplemented by questions about the relative 'authoritativeness' attributed to each journal read, and also about reading habits. Is a paper bought privately or by the firm? Is it read at home, on the train or in the office? Is it read early in the day or, perhaps, days later on an office circulation list?

The 'GEC bid' report drew particular attention to the importance of morning train readership and the influence that certain commentators, notably 'Lex' in the Financial Times, have upon morning investment conferences and opening prices, even if they form only the basis for discussion between partners or brokers and investment managers. Two quotations from that report may illustrate the point: 'I have 25 minutes in the train: I allow 5 for idle chatter and 20 for the F.T.'; 'I would sack any analyst who had not read Lex by the time the market opened'.

Conclusions

Financial research covers a wide range of subjects—none of which have been adequately investigated as yet: indeed, very little had been done at all until five years ago; but there is every reason to believe that the demand for such work will grow rapidly in the future as investors, the City institutions and the brokers become more professionalized and better able to handle— and put to profitable use—the flow of information that can be fed to them.

References

1. *How does Britain save?* The Stock Exchange Council, 1966.
2. *Savings and Investments*. The Building Societies Association, 1969.

22. International market research

Lucy Law Webster

International Marketing Styles and Research Tactics

International selling is organized in a number of ways. There is a continuum ranging from direct exporting to supranational marketing. The approach which most firms use is direct exporting and practically all firms which sell abroad do at least some direct exporting. Many firms with local management in various countries are also engaged in international marketing; they sell internationally from a number of centres. When a company has several centres of real initiative around the world which are used as a basis for supranational planning one has the *most* global approach; this can be called supranational marketing.

Each of the patterns in this continuum affects the points of decision at which marketing research is relevant. Research for direct exports is usually planned and used from head office. Companies with separate marketing operations in various countries tend to plan and use research in each place with occasional efforts at coordination. Even supranational companies take most decisions on a national or regional basis, but here there is often a real attempt at a world framework of systematic planning. These varied styles of international marketing set the stage for international market research.

Two main tactical approaches to international marketing are often used in series to complement each other. The empirical experimental approach is used to test what happens in one or a few countries before moving outward to more countries. The global scanning approach makes broad comparisons between countries which allow for systematic decisions on where to try or to emphasize a particular product or policy. It is often useful to alternate between these two complementary approaches. Since costs dictate that one cannot examine everything everywhere at once, the use of one or both of these approaches is essential.

Special Aspects of International Market Research

All the market research techniques and objectives described in other chapters of this book can in principle be used in any one country, and also in any group of countries. This is only limited by the market research skills available, which will be discussed later. Thus, all the varied aims of market research are also potential aims of international market research. However, there are other additional aims and requirements when market research is international—when it covers more than one country or when it is conceived in one country and conducted in another.

International market research is often needed to obtain information which is *already* available to the manufacturer about his home market. In the home market a manufacturer has a fuller grasp of the role his product fills than he does abroad; many things one knows at home are only hypotheses abroad. It is thus desirable to use market research deliberately and systematically in many cases where background knowledge and experience might suffice in the home market.

In the home market, to take a typical example, a manufacturer of electrical appliances would probably know whether or not any market existed for gift-packaged electric hair dryers; but if he wanted to sell such a product abroad, one early and deliberate step would be to go and see, or commission someone else to see, whether any gift-packaged hair dryer is sold and within what price range. If it is found that none are sold in a number of countries, the next step is to learn why—just because no one had thought to launch such a product, or for adequate reasons which would make it unprofitable for him to try? Such questions can often be answered by fairly simple market research, but it is essential that they be answered.

It is equally important to ask the right questions, e.g., it is important for anyone concerned with the direct export of cars to the status-conscious US with its powerful cars to know that:

(a) dirty cars are normal and that very few cars are kept clean and polished;
(b) almost no one drives at more than 70 mph (but that the car must be able to accelerate to 70 mph within a few moments of joining a motorway).

To obtain such information is easy, but to perceive that it must be obtained is often difficult. It is only by deliberately and continually questioning assumptions about his marketing ideas that an exporter can be sure he is not missing information which is critical for the success of his product.

Often the process of undertaking market research at more stages than one would in the home market, involves looking at many countries. This can be a very simple scanning process: e.g., to know whether a particular type of product exists, or to know whether there are regulations which make it impracticable to launch a particular product. Such knowledge often makes it possible to distinguish priority markets on which attention can then be focused.

534

Thus, an initial global scanning study can precede a country by country series of sequential studies. Having found certain priority markets, one wants to examine them closely; but beyond that, in international market research, one needs to come to some view on the extent to which the findings in the priority countries can be expected to generalize to any other countries.

The sequential approach

Many branches of social science, and market research in particular, have been notable for their failure to build up a body of generalizable knowledge which fits together into any empirically based theory. This fact has tended to give market researchers very little faith in the possibilities of extrapolation from one situation to another or from one country to another. The tendency has been to do a new survey for each new problem. Gradually this tendency is changing.

In international market research it would be prohibitively wasteful to tackle each problem everywhere at once. Consequently, the two tactical approaches mentioned have developed: scanning to look at relatively few problems globally, and selecting to look at a few countries more closely. In either case the process of using the results *necessitates* some view as to how the results generalize. The question as to how far, if at all, one ought to generalize from one country to another thus requires careful consideration. First, we might ask a more limited question.

Are there countries in which the facts of a larger world region might be represented in miniscule? The short answer is almost certainly, 'No'. However, if we think of a particular product field, or a particular part of a product field, the answer might well be, 'Yes'. Or even if a whole country would not normally represent a region even on relatively few variables, it is usefully likely that a special segment of a country's population *would* represent a similar segment of other adjacent populations; for example, if the market structure of different flavour preferences of a food product is similar in two countries, then the acceptance which one finds for a new flavour in one country will in most cases recur in the second country. Then, also, if we look at countries across time it is widely held that certain countries provide indicators in certain respects of what will happen in other countries several years later; but *which* countries provide what kinds of information on what products and habits is difficult to specify. Thus, if a matrix of information is built up over time and across a number of countries or sub-country market segments, one can gradually learn what types of findings generalize across countries and across time.

Although such a systematic scheme of multi-country investigation has only been tried to a limited extent by a few companies, steps in this general direction are taken quite often. It is normal to do fairly intensive market research in a few countries and then consider whether research in further countries is required. To decide whether to proceed to other countries necessitates—at least implicitly—various judgements: whether the research suggests anything of use for any marketing action; and if so, whether similar action might be taken now or later elsewhere; and whether any decisions for action based on extrapolation require further research either now or later.

When intensive research in a few countries has been preceded by scanning market research across the universe of countries of interest, the presence or absence of common indicators helps one assess how far the intensive research is generalizable. Another basis for assessing projectability is the extent to which the intensive findings themselves indicate variability or lack of variability between the countries thus studied. If, for example, scanning research has shown certain types of general homogeneity across, say, eight countries, and intensive research in four of these countries then shows that these four countries are essentially the *same* on all variables relevant to a given product field, one can make many projections to the additional four countries. If, on the other hand, the four countries' intensive research had come up with two or more patterns of results, fewer, if any, projections would be possible.

Products vary in the extent to which a single product is acceptable in different countries, e.g., the markets for detergents often do not vary greatly in many countries. Very similar products can be sold across a range of countries. On the other hand, the market for a food such as soup varies considerably, in terms of the type of soup that is acceptable, in flavours within type, and even in terms of the functions for which soups are used.

If the sequential approach to international market research is taken to its logical conclusion, several results follow. First, it is best to use the sequential approach after an earlier scanning survey. This provides information for deciding which particular countries should be taken first in the intensive sequential research and it provides indicators of the relationship between these countries and the others of interest. Second, once engaged in intensive country by country studies, one should tackle countries one or two at a time, stopping as soon as the results begin producing homogeneous patterns. In other words, once certain results start to come out the same in country after country, one can begin to deduce that these results will project to additional countries without going through the whole research process. Third, the data collected in the earlier scanning study should be used to form judgements on which findings can and cannot be projected. Fourth, one can test this projectability by carrying out *small-scale* checks in additional countries in order to confirm that there are no radical differences from the patterns found previously.

The global approach

We have mentioned the global approach in connection with scanning studies. Another equally important application of this approach is to examine a group of countries which might be treated as an operational unit, if certain kinds of homogeneity are found to exist. Thus, the global approach can be used for surveys which cover some four to eight countries with the approximate scale of research normally used to study one country by itself. Insofar as the heterogeneity of, say, the European Common Market is not much greater than that of France on the variables one wishes to study, thus far it is practicable to use a sample for the EEC which is not much greater than that one would use for France taken alone. Thus, some 2000 to 4000 interviews can be an adequate basis for certain types of surveys covering a whole world region.

If in a particular product field one already knows that certain types of homogeneity exist across several countries, this sort of 3000 interview multi-country survey is particularly relevant. However, even if one knows very little to begin with, it is often better to conduct *one* multi-country study of 2000 to 4000 interviews than to launch into one of 2000 to 4000 interviews in *each* of five or six countries. The multi-country survey on the scale normally used for a national survey will provide usable data on those variables which prove to be reasonably homogeneous and it will also point up those topics which require further, more detailed, investigation. In such a multi-country survey, each country is treated roughly as a region would be treated within a national survey. Some analyses can be broken down by region and others can be split in other ways. When such analyses indicate that more useful results would be obtained if one could look at detailed breakdowns within each country, then this is a sign that it would be useful to carry out further research.

The sort of multi-country survey indicated here is primarily an alternative to the country by country sequential approach in that it can readily follow directly after a wide-scanning initial study. Whether the sequential or global approach is more appropriate depends upon the sorts of alternative decisions that can result from the research. If the decisions can only be multi-national in that any smaller market would be inadequate, then multi-country data is required. Alternatively, if the action contemplated depends on precise knowledge of one or two individual countries, then the sequential approach is appropriate. In reality, various combinations of imperfectly perceived marketing alternatives must be weighed against each other to decide which approach is better. The important point to remember is that whichever approach is taken, one can go on to collect more data at the next stage. With the sequential approach one goes on to investigate further countries. With the global approach one goes on to fill in in detail those countries where fuller knowledge is required.

Market boundaries

Most international research studies are organized by country and by groups of countries. These are the boundaries which at the start of a project everyone has most clearly in mind and, of course, many of the realities of marketing are actually organized on a national basis. Predominantly, linguistic and media boundaries follow national boundaries. It is notable, therefore, but not of very great general marketing significance, that certain German and Austrian television stations are viewed outside the country of transmission, and a few Swiss and German periodicals are read quite widely abroad, and that Flemish speaking Belgians use Dutch media. Although there are many such facts—in Latin America, in the Middle East, and in Southern Asia, as well as in Europe—such facts do not change the basic pattern of reality: predominantly, languages are spoken within countries or groups of countries and media are used in the originating country. Channels of distribution such as retail chains are mainly organized on a national basis. Also, national legal requirements often mean that marketing activities have to vary from country to country. Market research institutes are also predominantly organized by country, and although fieldwork can be commissioned for all of Benelux or for all of Scandinavia, the research company itself almost always organizes fieldwork country by country.

Nonetheless there are exceptions to this traditional national pattern. Subtle cultural patterns are emerging—based both on the history that preceded existing national boundaries and on the different rates and styles of current technologically-based change. If one thinks in terms of market segmentation, the segments that prove to have importance often cut across countries. Various supra-national geographical patterns have been indicated, especially within Europe: e.g., it is well known that purchasing patterns in northern Italy are, in many regards, more like those in countries to the north of Italy than those in the south of Italy. Yves Fournis has suggested that with European unity a wealthy industrial conglomerate will develop along the axis of the Rhine Valley, encompassing Benelux, north eastern France, the Ruhr, Lyons, and running through to the Milan area. If such a region does develop, one might look for differentiation between the patterns of behaviour and purchasing which exist within this region as compared with those in parts of the same countries outside this region.

A more immediate hypothesis cutting across countries has been suggested by Mark Abrams who has described three Europes. He refers to the 'new Europe' of such big cities as Stockholm, Paris, London, Hamburg, and environs, combined with such high-density population areas as Switzerland and north west Italy. His second 'emerging Europe' lies in the semi-urbanized hinterlands of southern France, northern Italy, and south west Germany, for example. And a third area, 'old Europe', of international marketing significance only in that it may be excluded, is the difficult farming lands of for example Spain, Portugal, and north west Scotland.

As we discover which groups of people actually do behave similarly with regard to particular products, the patterns that transcend boundaries can refine various country by country working approximations of reality. Such information would be invaluable to refine any matrix of country by country data.

538

Organizing International Market Research

In some 20 countries throughout western Europe, north America, and in Japan and Australia, the amount of market research done is similar to that in Britain, relative to the commercial activity of each country. There are also a further 20 or so countries (in eastern Europe, Latin America, the Middle East, and southern Asia) where at least one or two locally-based market research firms carry out many of the types of studies found in Britain. On the other hand, the prevalence of top-quality work varies from country to country, e.g., there are very few countries where it is possible to get sophisticated segmentation studies carried out effectively, and in many countries such studies must be closely guided and controlled from outside. Also, there are groups of countries in which the organization and control of fieldwork is not reliable. Even if we examine the countries which are most highly developed in market research, we find certain differences of emphasis in expertise. This means that it is generally more difficult to obtain good market research in another country than in one's own country, even when the work there is on average just as good.

There are various ways to organize market research abroad. In countries where the facilities and skills are sparse or non-existent, it is necessary to set up or have specially set up on one's behalf all the market research facilities required. This must include recruiting and training local interviewers, and organizing sampling procedures. Both of these steps often create problems. Recruiting appropriate interviewers can be especially difficult, e.g., if one must interview women in a strict Muslim country: the informants can only speak to other women, but women should not properly do that sort of job. The local educated minority can often come to the rescue in such a situation. From this minority, interviewers can be drawn. Also, the minority which is most fully educated is to some extent bi-cultural, and can thus provide various types of people who can help the international researcher come to grips with the local situation.

Countries which lack market research firms often lack reliable demographic data, and thus sampling problems arise. Here government officials or academic staff at schools or colleges can help in various ways, e.g., detailed maps or detailed aerial reconnaissance data can sometimes be obtained through such sources and provide the basis for a sampling procedure.

Even in countries where certain local market research facilities do exist, some market researchers from abroad prefer to train their own local interviewers and do their own sampling. This procedure is most reasonable when special techniques are required. While it is sometimes appropriate to organize the details of a study directly, however, it is not sensible to ignore local talent. Any questionnaire which has been designed with the skills of a psychologist or an economist, for example, should, if possible, be discussed with the help of a local psychologist or economist before it is used. Also, in finding and training interviewers and in sampling it is usually extremely unwise to neglect to consult any local professional or technical advisors who are available. Whether such advice is best found inside or outside a local market research institute is of secondary importance, but it usually helps communication to deal with people who have some understanding of market research.

In the last analysis effective communication is essential. It is usually difficult, if not almost impossible, for a foreign researcher adequately to communicate directly with the actual informant. The exception to this is in some studies of an elite group or a top management population where the researcher and informant share a common international language and culture. Normally, some form of intermediary is needed for communication. Often the choice before the researcher is whether to communicate himself with a local researcher who will then arrange interviews as agreed, or alternatively to have one's own fieldwork-control personnel train local fieldwork-control staff who will then arrange whatever is agreed. In principle, it would seem that it is better for the cross-cultural communication to take place at the highest educational level possible. However, most international researchers have had at least one experience of non-communication at the research planning level; and it can be argued that the cross-cultural communication should take place at the most routine and systematized level possible. In practice, it is best to communicate and to check and recheck the effectiveness of the communication at *several* levels. It is essential to organize international research in such a way that all major steps can be checked.

When market research is organized locally, and closely controlled by an international research specialist, it *is* possible to verify at various levels and at various stages of a project that effective communication has taken place. To do this one must communicate at both the conceptual and also at the technical level. At the conceptual level the local research executive must be fully briefed to understand the survey aims as well as the international researcher, but also the international research co-ordinator must directly inspect and control all the technical details of interviewing and of sampling. Control here does not, of course, mean day to day control, but it does mean sufficient inspection at the critical stages to ensure that what is being done is what has been agreed. The object of such inspection is not primarily to check for dishonesty, which in many countries is relatively rare, but to check for misunderstandings and for inefficiencies arising from inadequate facilities; these are common. The sort of control indicated here is expensive. It may at times be more expensive than doing the whole job directly without the help of any local market research firm. But using local experience should not be viewed as a short cut but as an investment in coming to grips with the nuances of the market.

Research which is conceived and controlled in one country and executed with the help of local market research firms in other countries can be arranged in two alternative ways. The market researcher of a manufacturing company may commission and supervise the research in each country directly. Alternatively, an international market research firm can fill this function for the manufacturing company.

It is sometimes assumed that an international market research chain will, simply by virtue of being international, be able to co-ordinate a multi-country study without having someone explicitly go through the processes of control indicated above. In fact, co-ordination does not happen automatically. International market research chains are groups of companies (usually one per country) which work together on multi-national projects. Sometimes, the companies in a chain are, in part, jointly owned. Even in those few cases where the joint ownership is appreciable, the number of joint multi-country projects is but a small fraction of the business in each country. Nonetheless, research chains can offer some common experience, and the opportunities for multi-national planning and for common analysis provide certain advantages to the user. Some of the same advantages, plus others, can be obtained by using research companies or consultants which have experience of international co-ordination but which are not connected with any particular research chain. However, because co-ordination does not happen automatically, *any* research firm or group, regardless of its structure, will need to provide some one person to be responsible for the processes of international control described earlier. Likewise, if a manufacturing firm wishes to undertake international market research, directly co-ordinated by its own internal personnel, it must be sure that one person has adequate time and authority to provide the required control. It does not much matter whether the appointed co-ordinator of an international study is employed by the manufacturing company concerned or by an international market research firm or consultant, but it matters greatly that he exist.

Applying techniques in international research

As already indicated, there are cultural factors which make almost any type of market research difficult in some countries. Other cultural factors limit the types of research which it is practicable to attempt, e.g., the social mores in countries where retailers normally try to cheat the tax inspector make it extremely difficult if not impossible to collect reliable retail audit data. Likewise, product placement tests for many types of product are not equally acceptable in all countries. Thus, surveys must be designed to take account of differences in culture and mores. Also, educational and cultural differences affect the ways respondents understand the concept of a survey and the content of survey questions, and the level of co-operation possible. Such considerations affect the length of a questionnaire and the types of questions which should be used. There is no substitute for local knowledge (sometimes plus experimentation) to sort out these problems. One must, therefore, be discriminating in selecting the survey techniques which are both relevant and usable in the countries concerned. Even here there are problems which have to be solved at the planning stage. It is worth referring briefly to questions of translation and questionnaire wording, and problems of sampling.

Translation is possible; it is possible to write questions in different languages so that they have the same meaning, but it is important that the sameness of meaning be assessed by someone who knows the local culture, and who understands the aims of the survey and the questionnaire as well as the literal meaning of the words involved. Even when the questions do have literally the same meaning, differential interpretation and response is still possible in different countries. However, we should not overstress this point. Within a region such as Europe which has some common cultural and linguistic heritage, the problems of differential interpretation of questions with the same wording may often be no greater between countries than it normally is between regions within a single country.

Just as word by word translation does not necessarily produce a questionnaire with the same meaning in different languages, the parrot-like copying of sampling procedures need not produce comparable samples. It is often necessary to use random sampling procedures in one country and quota sampling in another to get samples which are equally valid and, therefore, most likely to produce comparable results.

Conclusion

The process of obtaining comparable results from different countries in international research thus involves several precautions. First, one must clearly avoid using any techniques which experience or knowledge suggest would not work in one or more of the survey countries. Next, one must use types of questions and wording which will communicate equally effectively, and one must use reliable sampling procedures. However, all such precautions are subject to the risk of error, e.g., a sampling system which seems to be of known reliability may in a particular country be found to contain unanticipated built-in biases. In order to check for such errors and correct for them, the multi-stage approach to international market research is again extremely valuable. By using the global approach and the sequential approach one after the other, and by building up over time a matrix of knowledge about many countries, it is then possible to gradually develop a reliable understanding of a large number of markets and of how they compare.

References

CARSON, D. *International Marketing, A Comparative Systems Approach*, Wiley, New York, 1967.
Glossary of Technical Terms for Market Researchers. The European Society of Opinion and Market Research, 1969.

Multi-country Research, The European Society of Opinion and Market Research, Seminar, 1971.

FAYERWEATHER, J. *International Marketing*, Prentice-Hall, New York, 1965.

HESS, J. M., and CATEORA, P. R. *International Marketing*, Richard D. Irwin, 1966.

LEIGHTON, D. S. R. *International Marketing, Text and Cases*, McGraw-Hill, New York, 1966.

LIANDER, B. *Comparative Analysis for International Marketing*, Marketing Science Institute with Allyn and Bacon.

MILLARD, P. Information for Marketing Outside the United Kingdom, *Sources of UK Marketing Information* by Gordon Wills, Nelson, 1969.

RYANS, J. K. JR. and BAKER, J. C. *World Marketing, A Multinational Approach*, Wiley, New York, 1967.

THOMAS, J. *International Marketing Management, Readings in Systems and Method*, Houghton Mifflin, 1969.

Section 4. Media research

Introduction

Media research is mainly concerned with the size, composition and reactions of audiences to different advertising vehicles—press, television, posters, cinema, radio, etc. It also concerns the vehicles themselves in terms of how readers/viewers regard the actual publication on programmes. Cost efficiency in media selection ideally depends on securing accurate estimates of the sort of sales response one could hope to achieve for a given outlay among the various media opportunities available. This ideal is rarely achieved because the 'response function' is one of the most difficult factors that researchers are called upon to isolate and measure. Most media men have to be satisfied by seeking to achieve minimum costs in reaching the relevant target audience either in terms of product/demographics or more subtle psychological segmentation factors.

The media covered herein are press, television, and posters, each in separate chapters, and radio and cinema research combined. Press and television are obvious candidates in terms of the sheer size of research expenditure and data that they generate.

Among the less sizeable media, that of posters has been selected as a field presenting unique research problems, whereas cinema and radio, while being important media, do not offer technical problems that are quite so far divorced from those of press and television.

There are several important reasons why 'media research' merits a separate section in a book on market research. Media research is used widely, constantly and intensively and there is a very high degree of similarity in the objects and methods among the users in the continuous effort by advertisers and their agencies to secure maximum value per pound spent in allocating their advertising appropriations both between and within media. Similarly, calibration of his audience or readership is the essential basis of any sales effort by a media owner. Accordingly, media research is one of the largest single areas of market research expenditure.

As a result of the above factors, media research (with the possible exception of the political polls) is the most generally scrutinized area of market research. Most media research is widely circulated as a direct result of the joint industry committees that have been set up to govern press and television research in Britain and privately commissioned media research projects are invariably published in attempts to convince advertisers and their agents of the particular merits of, say, one publication versus others. Media research is also widely employed as a source of basic market data and demographic information and for dividing the country up into realistic marketing areas. Few other types of research come under this type of informed, users' scrutiny. And for this reason the standards achieved tend to set the pace for the market research profession.

Ideally, one would wish for directly comparable techniques for assessing the value of different media, but this has so far eluded both the methodology and the cash resources of the industry. The reader will note in the following chapters the way in which the feasibility of measurement (both technical and financial) has produced quite different ways of calibrating media. This particularly applies to comparisons between press and television. Thus, basic press research is typically based on large, national samples with relatively infrequent reporting periods compared with small regional samples with weekly reporting of minute by minute data in the case of television.

The pitfall of assuming that because the research monitoring systems are so dissimilar that this necessarily indicates fundamental differences in the way that the respective audiences react to the media must be avoided; one often hears, for example, such statements as: Press is a stable medium, whereas television is highly volatile. In fact, such remarks tend to reflect the systems of measurement we have developed rather than the true nature of the media. If one had a technique that scrutinized readers as constantly and minutely as meters scrutinize television sets—ignoring presence and attention for the moment—it is highly likely that press would be proved to be just as 'volatile' as television.

Another general question that the reader should consider is that of the cost efficiency of media research. Are we spending too much on what *can* be measured, as opposed to devoting more time, effort and money on that part of the iceberg beneath the surface? Very little work, for example, has been done on inter media effectiveness compared with the enormous volume of intra media research.

The marginal efficiency of extra media data in terms of the cost of obtaining it is another question for the reader to ponder.

In the early days of the move from simple circulation data to readership data based on market research, the research payoff was manifestly obvious and large in terms of improved advertising efficiency. We now seem to be at a stage in media research where many potential avenues of enquiry, while of considerable theoretical interest, have much less attractive potential in terms of cost effectiveness. One suspects that reading intensity measures could be cited as an example here. Possibly the most important step for media research to take over the next decade is to evaluate the uses of the data much more stringently. To date, the emphasis has rested heavily on getting as much data as possible—some would think too much data now that computer processing has made the marginal cost of extra tabulations so low.

A. B. De Vos

23. Print media research

Michael Brown

Objectives and Applications

This chapter is concerned with research into print media in the sense of newspapers and magazines, whether aimed at a wide, general audience or a narrower, more specialized one. This introductory section comprises, first, a brief review of the several purposes to which research in this area is put and, second, a synopsis of the order and content of the other parts of the chapter.

Media research is often interpreted as being synonymous with audience measurement, particularly in the case of newspapers and magazines and, further, as providing data solely of relevance to advertising agencies or, in some cases, for direct use by the advertisers whose accounts they handle. Both of these concepts are oversimplifications. From the point of view of the advertiser or his agency, the requirement from research into any medium is to provide information that will assist both in choice between media— between newspapers and magazines, for example, or between magazines and television—and as regards intra-media choice; the selection, for instance, of individual advertising vehicles, such as the 'Daily Express' or 'Woman's Own'. The criterion of both inter- and intra-media choice will be, at base, one of cost-effectiveness: a relation between the price of using a particular advertising medium and the 'effects' of the campaign concerned, however defined.

The contribution of media choice itself to the overall variation in effectiveness, from campaign to campaign, is a matter of opinion and contention, rather than one of fact; some authors[1] would rate the creative content of advertising ten times as important a factor as media selection. However, insofar as the media element is certainly not completely negligible, one factor of obvious relevance to effectiveness is the size and nature of the audience delivered by an advertising schedule. At the same time, to enumerate the audience that has opportunity to come into contact with advertisements is far from providing a complete assessment of a campaign's likely results. There are thus many other aspects of 'effectiveness' beyond audience size and composition and some of these fall into the proper area of media research.

Turning to the publisher's viewpoint, the advertisement department of a newspaper or magazine will, in common with the advertiser and agency, require from print media research data on audiences and other criteria of effectiveness; the difference in application of the results is the self-evident one that the publisher will be seeking to demonstrate a competitive advantage for his vehicle *vis-à-vis* others, both generally and in relation to the particular marketing and advertising briefs of a potential client. However, the publisher has also other interests, since he is operating in a situation of joint supply in two markets: not only is he selling advertising space or a potential audience, but also his actual newspaper or magazine to readers. He thus requires marketing research, in all its aspects, which treats the publication as being just as much a 'product' as any other one. Under this heading may be included investigation of readers' preference for and reaction to editorial material—a particular form, relevant to media, of 'product content' research.

Within the total area of media research, there are thus a number of measurement requirements, some overlapping, from advertisers, agencies, and media owners. The next section of this chapter covers audience measurement; after consideration of the relevant concepts, research methods and problems in the measurement of issue, page, and advertisement audiences are discussed. The section ends with a review of the sub-groups identified in audience research—demographic, attitudinal, and behavioural including, under the latter heading, audience breakdowns by product/brand purchasing and the research requirements of 'single source' and integrated data.

The third section turns to the use of audience measurement and other data as input to computer programs designed either to construct print media schedules or forecast their performance on certain prespecified criteria. The objectives, broad lines of development, advantages, and limitations of such programs are described, but full, mathematical treatment of methods is outside the scope of the section.

In the fourth section, criteria of newspaper and magazine advertising effectiveness other than audience measurements are discussed. Requirements and difficulties peculiar to media research are highlighted, fuller treatment of relevant techniques being provided in other chapters.

The final section deals with the applications of market and marketing research to print media as a product field and to individual newspapers and magazines as 'brands', rather than as advertising vehicles or providers of audiences.

Audience Measurement

Audience concepts

Given that the overall requirement in the implementation of any advertising brief is to achieve optimum cost-effectiveness, a sub-objective is to select advertising vehicles in such a way that the size and nature of the audience, and the pattern of their opportunities for contact with the advertisements is 'best', on some agreed set of criteria. There thus exists a need for audience measurement, so that the performance of alternative schedules, on these criteria, may be evaluated; but before dealing with the practical problems involved, it is necessary to consider what is implied by 'audience'.

Issue audience may be defined as the number and kinds of individuals that come into contact with either a specific issue of a given newspaper or magazine or with the 'average' issue. People counted within the issue audience are often referred to, loosely, as 'readers' and their total is frequently labelled the 'readership' of the publication concerned. Further, being an issue reader is said to provide an 'opportunity to see' (ots) an advertisement carried by the issue. Any definition of issue audience is essentially an operational one, as will be seen below; but irrespective of the exact definition selected, it will not reflect differences, within the total issue readership, between individuals and occasions as regards the amount that is read or looked at *within* the issue. A narrower definition thus exists of the *page* (or double-page spread) *audience* as comprising the number of people who look at anything on a page or spread, or on the 'average' one.

Being counted within the page audience obviously confers on an individual a higher probability of contact with an actual advertisement than does merely being a member of the issue audience. However, it is possible to refine the concept yet further and define, as falling within the *advertisement audience*, those people who have contact with the ad itself.

The main points to note from the brief discussion of audience concepts above are two: their exists a hierarchy of increasingly narrow definitions; but at each level—whether issue, page, or advertisement—the interpretation of 'contact' is not an unambiguous one.

Issue Audience

Having dealt briefly with basic audience concepts, attention is now turned to the practical problems of issue audience measurement. The simplification is first made below of assuming a 'black and white' division between those individuals who are and are not issue readers. The refinement of recognizing probabilities of issue contact other than 0 or 1 is introduced later.

Average Issue Readership. Although the audience for a specific issue of a newspaper or magazine can be and sometimes is measured, by far the more frequent research objective is to provide an unbiased estimate of the audience for the average issue of the vehicle. Meeting this requirement raises two essential problems: defining 'readership', in the sense of contact with an issue; and selecting an appropriate data-collection method.

As already noted, *any* definition of issue readership is operational; there is no absolute standard against which it may be assessed whether a person is or is not a reader. As an example, the National Readership Survey takes a reader to be a respondent who claims to have read or looked at any copy of the newspaper or magazine concerned, anywhere, within a period equal to the publication interval of the title prior to the date of interview. (That is to say, a reader has to have seen a daily paper on the day before the date of interview, a Sunday paper or a weekly magazine within the seven days ending on the day before the interview, and so on.)

Three points within this NRS definition serve to illustrate the contention that 'readership' is not an absolute concept. First, a respondent qualifies as a reader irrespective of the proportion of an issue they have seen at all and of whether they have read intently or merely glanced. In fact, people labelled as 'readers' in the NRS sense do have a high probability of having looked at the average page within an issue, as experimental work preceding the 1968 Survey[2] shows; but it is possible to count within the average issue audience only those with some 'proved' level of 'within the issue' reading intensity.

Second, the NRS definition allows readership of current and outdated issues to count equally; but it is possible, if it is relevant to the application of the research, to consider only those reading occasions which occur within some set interval of an issue going on sale producing, naturally, a numerically different estimate of average issue audience.

Third, NRS readers are not necessarily those who actually purchased the newspaper or magazine—they may equally be people, within or beyond the purchaser's household, to whom the issue was passed on; nor, to be counted within the average issue audience, must they have read the issue concerned at home or in some other, specified, circumstances. Clearly, audience definitions may be framed which take a different view on these points.

Turning to research techniques relevant to average issue audience measurement, a first, major choice lies between recall and recognition methods. The National Readership Survey approach is basically to rely on respondents' recall of newspaper or magazine reading occasions. Whilst this method allows, amongst other advantages, standardized questions to be asked, within one survey, regarding a large number of titles, it also has deficiencies. For a number of reasons, underclaiming, overclaiming, and the displacement in time of a reading occasion in the respondent's mind all occur; evidence from Belsen's work[3] is to be noted. However, the biases resulting from faulty recall of reading behaviour may often be within acceptable limits. If recall is to be used, the further question arises of whether it should be prompted and, if so, to what degree. The NRS utilizes, as prompts, reproductions (reduced in size) of publications' mastheads, i.e., their titles, in the type style used on the cover or front page. However, there are many examples of average issue readership measurement using other forms of prompt—including just the names of the newspapers and magazines, whether shown to the respondent or only read out—or none at all. Formal evidence of the effect on the level of readership claims from varying the style of recall aid is very limited. Completely open, unprompted questioning, however, certainly tends to result in underclaiming of issue contact, particularly for titles which the respondent sees infrequently or irregularly. Recognition methods provide a complete contrast to relying on people's recall of previous reading behaviour. In their typical form (as more widely used in the US than in Europe or the UK), they involve showing the respondent an issue of the publication concerned and asking them to glance through it before stating whether they have looked at it before the interview.

Whilst it may appear that recognition-based readership claims will be more reliable than those based on recall, the former technique brings its own drawbacks. Its demand on interview time and on the amount of material physically to be carried by the interviewer are considerable; these problems are only partly alleviated by using, in place of complete issues, 'stripped-down' ones containing, hopefully, just sufficient pages for the respondent to be able to say, unambiguously, whether they have looked into it previously. Further, the age of issue to be used is not simple to determine. If it is very recent, the audience it will accumulate, through the mechanism of pass-on readership, may not have 'grown' to its limit by the time of the survey. If, on the other hand, an 'old' issue is used in an attempt to circumvent this problem, respondents will have increased difficulty in saying definitely that they have or have not read it some time ago.

In parallel with the choice between recall and recognition approaches, there are options of average issue readership measurement via personal interviews, telephone contact and self-administered questionnaire. Whilst readership research has, very largely, grown up in a face to face personal interview setting, there is a growing volume of evidence that satisfactory estimates can be obtained from self-administered questionnaires; comparisons between NRS results and those from the Target Group Index[4] provide an example. At the same time, once questioning is beyond an interviewer's direct control, there may be problems in adequately conveying to a respondent the precise definition of 'readership' that is being employed; in what prompts may be used; or in controlling the order in which the respondent answers similar questions on different publications. This last point is important since, from personal interview data at least, there is evidence that estimates of average issue readership depend on the position of the publication within the interview sequence.

Readership measurement by telephone interviewing is by no means impossible, although this particular data collection technique has had limited use in the media area in the UK. Apart from sampling problems imposed by the low absolute penetration of telephone ownership and its skewness, it would not be easy to maintain respondent interest throughout a lengthy, largely repetitive readership covering many newspapers and magazines. Further, prompting is self-evidently limited to verbal naming of titles.

Turning to another dimension of research design, the majority of readership surveys tend to provide either 'once-off' estimates or regularly published reports, in the latter case derived from fresh samples on each occasion. However, panel techniques may also be employed[5].

It is beyond the scope of this chapter to consider at length the numerous special problems that may apply in specific cases of issue readership measurement. However, a note must be added regarding publication with narrow and specialized audiences. Here, in the interests of sampling economy, it is not uncommon practice to obtain self-completed data on a sample drawn from a magazine's list of subscribers, or to insert a questionnaire in all copies of a particular issue. Whilst there is nothing intrinsically wrong in a well-conducted readership survey by mail—given that, with or without follow-up, a satisfactory response rate can be obtained—the characteristics of readers who choose to return a questionnaire inserted in the actual publication can often be markedly different from those of its total audience. Further, pass-on readership clearly cannot be directly measured in any 'one copy, one questionnaire' design.

As a final point in relation to average issue audience measurement, it is to be noted that, non-response errors apart, the particular National Readership Survey method cannot produce a completely unbiased estimate. This situation arises through the phenomena of 'replicated' and 'parallel' readership. Respectively, these are the cases where one person reads a given issue within each of two or more different publication intervals; and where one person, within one publication interval, looks at two or more different issues (a publication interval being the time span from one publication date for a given title to the next one). Replicated readership leads to overestimation of average issue readership; in effect, two or more reading events by the person concerned each have a chance of being 'counted' when, in fact, only one issue and one reader is involved. Parallel readership, by contrast, tends to bias a readership estimate downwards. Two or more contacts with different issues are involved, but they will be counted as one only.

The net effect of these biases may not be large and their elimination, while possible, would involve a much more complex research approach. A very full treatment is provided by the published papers submitted for the Thomson 1962 awards[6].

Reading Frequency. The discussion, in the section above, of issue audience measurement has been on the basis of an oversimplified assumption that a given individual is either in or out of an audience; that is to say, the picture has been one of a population divided on a black and white basis into 'readers' and 'non-readers' of this or that publication. In fact, of course, the situation includes shades of grey. For a particular newspaper or magazine, there will be a group who, to all intents and purposes, never come into contact with it; another set of people who see virtually every issue; and, in between, those who are irregular readers to a greater or lesser degree.

The probability that an individual has of contact with the 'average' issue has come to be known colloquially as his or her *reading frequency* for the title concerned. The importance of measuring reading frequency lies in the fact that readership research results are used not only to forecast the potential audience for one insertion in one issue but, more generally, to investigate the full pattern of contacts arising from a schedule of several insertions in one or more publications. This pattern will depend intimately on the reading frequencies involved. Consider, say, five issues of one magazine, having an average issue audience of one million. On the simplifying assumption of there existing only 'readers' and 'non-readers', each of the million will see five issues and the remainder of the population none. On the more realistic model of issue-contact probabilities other than zero or one occurring, somewhat more than one million people will read at least one issue, because the audience from issue to issue will not comprise always exactly the same individuals. On the other hand, the average number of issues read, amongst those who see any, will now be less than five.

There are at least three distinguishable approaches to reading frequency measurement. First, consistent questions on issue readership can be repeated twice or more to the same individuals in a panel context. As previously discussed, this will normally involve a self-administered question-nair depending on respondents' recollections of historical reading occasions. Recognition of distinct issues will not normally be involved. Note, therefore, that it will not in general be known whether a given individual's claim, for example, of two reading events in relation to two successive publication intervals relates to the two issues respectively current in these periods, to some other two issues or, indeed, to the same issue. The panel approach to reading frequency estimation has, in practice, been little employed in the UK outside the work by Attwood. A much fuller consideration of its possibilities and limitations than is given here is provided by the Thomson award papers[7] on the general problem of panel use in audience measurement.

As a second method, recognition can be relied on: a respondent can be asked, in a single interview research design, which of each of a number of issues of a newspaper or magazine they have seen. The previous comments on the limitations of the recognition method apply here also, in particular the sheer logistics of the interviewer carrying several issues of each of a number of titles.

Third, and most commonly, as regards UK or European practice, a reader may be asked, in effect, to make a subjective estimate of their usual reading frequency. In the National Readership Survey, for example, with the aid of a prompt card, a respondent is asked which of a number of illus-trative frequencies best apply to their usual behaviour; for a daily newspaper, the choices provided are between 6, 5, 4, 3, 2, 1, 'less than 1' and no issues, out of 6. In France and several other countries, a verbal scale rather than a numerical one is employed, e.g., a person may be asked whether he sees 'every issue' of a title or reads it 'fairly often', 'occasionally' or 'never'.

The difference between the use of a numerical and a verbal scale is not so great as may at first appear. The intention in both instances is to segment the population in such a way that within-group differences in true frequency of issue-contact are smaller than between-groups ones. Responses to a verbal scale have, clearly, to be given a quantitative meaning; but so, in fact, have those on a numerical scale. Answers here cannot be taken at face value; individuals, generally speaking, tend to *over*estimate their reading frequency, so that a claim to see 'six issues out of six' implies, in fact, a probability of contact with the average issue not of one but of some smaller number.

In the NRS case, the scale of reading frequency is 'calibrated' by use of the data on average issue readership obtained in the same interview; e.g., if, for some weekly magazine or Sunday newspaper, 90 per cent of those claiming to see four out of four issues actually qualify as 'average issue readers' on the definition used, then the *adult probability*, as it is termed, for this group will be taken as 0.9. It will be noted that there is an implicit assumption that the true reading frequency is the same for all respondents making a given frequency claim. The developmental work behind the NRS scale and its application are fully dealt with by Corlett[8].

It is equally possible, of course, to give numerical values to each position on some frequency of reading scale by research quite separate from the readership survey in which the scale is to be employed; e.g., a verbal scale might be put to the individuals providing readership data on a panel.

As noted earlier, the practical application of reading frequency data involves using it to forecast the pattern of contacts over several issues and publications. With panel data, individuals' claims of issue contact in successive periods may be used directly for this purpose, assuming only that the pattern of claimed reading actually observed is stable over time. With NRS–type information—providing, in essence, average probabilities for groups of individuals—further assumptions are involved, principally that successive issue contacts for a given individual are independent events. Given such an assumption then if, say, the adult probability for some group and title is 0.6, the Binomial Theorem can be employed to calculate distributions such as:

Number of issues read	Probability
3 out of 3	$1 \times (0.6)^3$
2 out of 3	$3 \times (0.6)^2 \times (1.0 - 0.6)$
1 out of 3	$3 \times (0.6) \times (1.0 - 0.6)^2$
0 out of 3	$(1 - 0.6)^3$.

To obtain the forecast pattern of issue contacts resulting from a schedule, calculations of the above type would have to be performed, person by person, for each newspaper or magazine involved and the results then accumulated. Clearly, this is a time-consuming process, even in computer terms. A number of mathematical techniques have thus been developed which approximate, with adequate accuracy, the results of a full binomial expansion.

A full treatment of these short-cut approaches to obtaining a frequency distribution of issue contacts is beyond the scope of this chapter. However, it is to be noted that there are calculation techniques which achieve the same objective without the use of frequency of reading data at all, utilizing, typically, only average issue readership figures and the degrees of audience overlap between publications taken two or three at a time. The best known formulae of this type are attributed to Metheringham[9]. An improved version of his original technique is utilized in one of the UK sets of computer-media programs[10].

Spread, Page, and Advertisement Audiences

If an individual qualifies as a reader of the average issue, or of a particular issue, of a newspaper or magazine, this clearly confers on him a better chance of contact with an actual advertisement in that issue than would be the case if he were outside the audience for the publication. However, only wide limits can be set on the probability of such ad contact actually occurring: even if they see an issue, some people will read more of its contents, some less. Given that the media selection objective is essentially to put an advertisement economically before a relevant group of people, a more refined measurement than issue audience seems desirable. Exactly the same two basic problems occur here as have already been noted in relation to issue audience: selecting a workable operational definition that is sensible in relation to the basic concept; and devising the best technique for measuring an audience against this definition. It is convenient to consider these problems first in relation to the audience for a particular page of a newspaper or magazine.

Conceptually, the audience for a page comprises those individuals for whom, at some time, the page was in their perceptual field, i.e., those who were in a position to perceive some particular item on it or, colloquially, had 'open eyes in front of the page'. Unfortunately, it is extremely difficult to frame an *operational* definition, suitable for large-scale audience measurement use, which well mirrors this concept. On the one hand, evidence may be sought merely that a given page in a publication has been opened, using the 'glue-spot technique', first introduced many years ago[11]. Here, a small spot of glue, hopefully imperceptible to the reader, fixes together each pair of pages near their edge. Copies specially prepared in this way are placed with a sample of people and collected again after a period. A person is then counted within the audience for a pair of pages if the glue seal between them is found to have been broken. Setting aside the practical difficulties of neither making the glue spot so weak as likely to be broken accidentally nor so strong as to interfere with normal reading behaviour, the technique is clearly more studied to limited-scale use. It is artificial to the extent that the respondent will be receiving the copy to be measured in an 'abnormal' way. It is necessary to check that the issue has only been handled by the respondent between placement and recall interviews. Finally and most importantly, the evidence is, literally, of a pair of pages having been opened—whether or not as a prelude to the reader giving attention to anything on them is not known just from the glue-spot break.

On the other hand, far more complex, observational techniques may be employed; e.g., it is possible to take a continuous record on film of a respondent in a reading situation—unavoidably, a somewhat artificial one—that can show not only which pages were opened and for how long but also the direction of gaze in relation to the page. Equipment for this purpose, originally developed in Germany, is currently in use in the UK by the British Market Research Bureau. The technique is known as the Direct Eye Movement Observation System (DEMOS) and is referred to again below.

Whilst it may be possible, by such approaches, to obtain relatively direct evidence of page contact, on a small scale or under 'laboratory' conditions, survey measurement of page audience has, in practice, come largely to rely on an operational definition where a respondent is counted as within the audience if, on their own report, they have looked at one or more items on the page in question. For this purpose, unprompted *recall* is little used; to ask a respondent, without the use of any recall aids at all, what items they remember having read or looked at will produce generally low scores and ambiguous data, in view of the peripheral importance to the reader of many reading events. Instead, *recognition* is largely employed. In Gallup's Field Readership Index, for example, having established that respondents claim to have seen a particular issue at all, they are taken through it page by page and asked to indicate each item—whether editorial or advertisement, text or illustration—that they have previously looked at. *Page traffic* is then defined at the proportion of the issue audience claiming one or more items on the page in question.

There is little doubt that, unavoidably, the recognition approach leads to some bias in page audience estimation. In the interview situation, there may be strong internal pressures on a respondent to report, even if it can be recalled, not exactly what he or she did when previously looking at the issue—which is the answer sought—but what they think they did or think they 'ought' to have done. Faced with a dominant item on a page which now seems unavoidable to the eye, it is not easy to say, 'I didn't look at it'. Equally, reading some items may seem less socially desirable to the respondent than other ones: comic strips (or, for that matter, advertisements) as against leading articles. To this extent, to deduce page contact from *claimed* self-exposure to an item on it is far from straightforward.

There is another approach to page audience measurement, distinct from the recognition technique just discussed. Here, a respondent is presented with some form of scale indicating degrees of thorough or less thorough reading within the issue of a particular title and asked to choose that scale position which best describes their own behaviour. The scale itself can take a number of forms. In the National Readership Survey, a pictorial scale is currently in use. It shows six simple line drawings of issues, having varying proportions of their pages shown in a second colour; the scale positions are labelled, ordinally, from 'A' to 'F'. However, many other formulations are possible; some of them were investigated in the developmental research proceeding the introduction of the NRS Scale[12]. People might be asked, for example, how many pages out of ten they look at on average or, in verbal rather than numerical terms, whether they read 'all' of an issue, 'most', 'some', or 'little'.

Irrespective of the exact form of scale employed, this technique will require actual numerical values of probability of contact with the average page to be ascribed to each scale position, if the data is to be of practical use in choosing between print media vehicles in planning schedules. In the National Readership Survey case, the scale of reading intensity has been 'calibrated' (so far for groups of publications only rather than individual titles) by taking a page traffic measurement amongst people opting for each of the scale positions, but using a postal survey rather than personal interview approach[13].

It will be seen that there is an important difference between deriving page audience data from claims of what was read or looked at previously and using a scaling approach of the type just described. The former is applicable to one or more specific issues; the latter can use questions phrased in relation to a respondent's 'usual' behaviour. This raises a basic problem in the application of the data, if it is desired to forecast the probability of contact between a given person and the 'average' page in a particular publication: it is likely that not only will people differ between themselves in the amount they 'usually' read of this newspaper or that magazine, but also that, for any one reader and title, the amount they look at will vary from issue to issue, dependent on content and reading circumstances.

So far, the discussion of this section has been entirely in terms of *page* audience. However, the various measurement methods touched on can equally well produce data in relation to the double-page spread formed by two facing pages; and operational definitions of 'spread audience' follow naturally from those for 'pages'. Indeed, it has been strongly argued that the spread is the more natural unit in relation to audience measurement, in the sense that it is difficult to imagine a reader having no opportunity to perceive an item on a given page if the evidence is that they have focussed some attention on the facing one. In fact, the validity of this argument may be seen very much to depend on definitions of 'reading' and 'attention'. All too little is known about the mechanisms of perceptual organization of complex stimuli as applied to newspaper and magazine pages. However, it does seem likely that a large amount of scanning—probably subliminal—will be involved before the eye fixes on this or that item. Thus, everything on a double-page spread may have been 'seen' in a subconscious sense; but the items later reported—quite honestly—as 'looked at' may be far fewer. This point brings one directly to the final topic of this section—measurement of audiences not for issues or spreads or pages, but for advertisements themselves.

It is to be stressed immediately that this subject lies on the borderline of 'media research' in the sense taken throughout this chapter. *Post facto*, the number and sorts of people whose knowledge, attitudes or opinions have been modified by anything transferred to them from a particular advertisement will heavily depend on its content—its product or brand subject, the ideas the advertisement expresses and the way it expresses them. This variation of advertisement audience with ad content is not the province of media research. There are, however, a number of 'media' variables which *are* relevant at this level. An advertisement's size, absolutely or relative to the page; its position on the page; the position of the page in the issue; whether the page is left- or right-hand; whether the ad faces or is amongst other advertisements; surrounded by a margin or 'bled' to the edge of the page; and whether it is in monochrome or colour are all characteristics which may, in principle at least, affect the size of an advertisement's audience and render it distinguishable from the audience for the page on which it appears.

Conceptual and operational definitions offer even more difficulty at this stage than before. In terms of '*opportunity* to see', the advertisement audience is virtually equivalent to that for the page carrying it; refinement must invoke some idea of communication. Whilst the principle may be to count only within the ad audience those potentially affected by it, the practice is far more difficult; what cut-off point of behaviour in relation to the advertisement should be taken, and how is unbiased evidence of this behaviour then to be obtained?

In practice, methods already mentioned are the ones in use. Unaided recall of advertisements read can be employed. For an exhaustive treatment of comparisons of recall and recognition results, the reader is referred to the Advertising Research Foundation's Printed Advertisement Rating Methods (PARM) study[14]. Regarding recognition methods themselves, the Field Readership Index referred to above has the measurement of claimed readership of individual advertisements as a prime objective, its page traffic results being a byproduct. Here, reported ad contact is researched at three levels, respondents being categorized on whether they claim to have 'noted' the advertisement, to have 'read most' of its text and to have registered the brand name concerned.

As already noted, claims regarding previous advertisement reading behaviour are not unbiased, and the work reported by Fletcher[15] with the DEMOS equipment well illustrates the difficulties.

In conclusion, it is to be stressed that the techniques currently in use for measuring contact with advertisements have primarily been developed for assessing the apparent, comparative effectiveness of the ads themselves, as influenced by their content and its creative expression. Quite apart from the difficulties of definition and technique, considerable reprocessing of the data is needed to render it of relevance to media decisions; e.g., noting scores from many individual advertisements may be examined to see if the effects of such factors as ad size may be partialled out. Work by the Agencies Research Consortium in the UK has had as its objective development of more immediately 'media-oriented' ad audience research, although to date it has introduced no basic changes to the recognition method.

Audience Classification

A Rationale of Audience Breakdowns. In the preceeding sections, the concentration has been on the measurement of a total audience—whether for the average issue, a page or an advertisement. However, the sub-groups which are to be examined within this total are of considerable importance; and their identification may call for considerably more than gathering straightforward 'classification' data in the usual sense of that term.

There are two basic concepts which underlie the need for audience breakdowns. First, people differ between themselves in their value as prospects to a given advertiser. This leads to a search for criteria which meaningfully segment the population both as regards their actual or potential purchasing behaviour and also in respect of their contact with media and vehicles.

Second, the effectiveness of a particular campaign may be thought to depend—holding creative content constant—on the vehicle which carries it. This variation, again, may derive from the characteristics of the audience and of their interaction with the newspaper or magazine.

Demographic Classification. The most commonly occurring audience breakdowns utilize demographic criteria, including sex; age; socio-economic class; marital status; household size and composition; employment status and geographical area. The collection of data on these criteria does not call for special comment here, except in two cases.

The objective of any socio-economic classification is to group individuals in a clear-cut and unambiguous manner into segments which may be expected to display differing patterns of consumption of goods and services. Such an objective is difficult to meet in practice. A simple, robust, reproducible coding framework for social class is hard to find. The categories developed by the National Readership Survey are based on employment, combining basic data on job-type with information on size of firm and status within it. Reasonably stable results are produced but the method is still criticized. These difficulties, combined with the limited discrimination between socio-economic classes in purchasing behaviour in many fields may lead to a decline in the use of the criterion.

Regarding age, there is a school of thought that favours replacing age group classification with stages in the life cycle. However, there has yet been little if any move in this direction as regards day by day audience classification practice in the UK. The greater utility of the 'life-cycle' segmentation in relation to purchasing behaviour has also been questioned.

560

Attitudinal Classification. The demographic breakdowns of print media audiences covered briefly above have, as their basic objective, the identification of population sub-groups with varying actual or potential behaviour in the market-place. However, on turning to attitudinal classification of audiences, both of the two distinct concepts noted in the beginning of this section are relevant. On the one hand, brand or product-oriented attitudes of members of the audience of a newspaper or magazine may be measured. Such criteria may yield a more meaningful segmentation of the population than demographics alone can provide, in terms of 'value as prospects' for a given campaign; and it will be desired to ascertain media coverage within the attitudinally-defined segments.

Within the last few years, there have been considerable advances both in quantitative attitudinal measurement techniques for market research purposes and in market segmentation methods based on such data. Despite this progress, however, there has been very limited introduction, so far, of attitudinal classification into print media research, at least as regards syndicated or other generally available work as distinct from private surveys. One likely reason is that, quite apart from many remaining difficulties on the prediction of *future* purchasing behaviour from measurement of attitudes, in the cases where some success has been achieved by an advertiser in developing measures of demonstrable relevance to his market, the scales in question will have tended to be specific rather than general. By contrast, the objective of much print media research is to provide market-actionable data to a wide variety of users, operating in many different product fields. Few attitudinal scales are likely both to be general enough to offer 'something for everybody' yet also 'sharp' enough to provide actionable data in specific marketing and advertising planning instances. There may be exceptions: conservatism versus experimentalism (as affecting behaviour towards new brands) or attitudes to price may be cases in point. The Target Group Index[16] provides instances of including general attitudinal, as well as demographic, audience classification.

There is, in fact, another consideration relevant to classification of audiences in attitudinal terms. Such data can certainly provide a 'richer' portrait of an audience group; and 'pen portraits' of this or that set of readers are to be welcomed in a situation where media selection decisions, increasingly, jointly involve both creative considerations and viewpoints equally with 'traditional' media department opinions.

So far, the attitudinal measurements discussed have been market-oriented; but quite separately, attitudes to vehicles—to newspaper and magazines themselves—are measured. The thought here is that, in addition to behavioural aspects of the interaction between a reader and a print-media vehicle, what the audience thinks of and feels towards the publication is of importance to the likely effect on them of advertising it carries.

The classification of audiences according to the 'image' the medium or vehicle presents to them is, again, limited at present to isolated cases rather

561

than being general practice. Examples of measurement of perceptions of newspapers or magazines on such dimensions as their prestige, sophistication and modernity are provided by the work of the National Magazine Company[17], the Evening Newspaper Advertising Bureau[18] and TV Times[19].

One particular instance of 'attitudes to media' has received quite considerable attention, though more in Europe than the UK. It argues in favour of a generalized dimension of a reader's 'involvement' with a newspaper or magazine and thus of the importance they attach to it. A common question format here is to ask how vital it would be to a reader if he or she could not obtain a particular title—the so-called 'regret at loss' question. A related idea is to classify readers according to their claimed strength of interest in each of a number of product areas and activities, on the argument that the higher their interest in a given subject the better prospect a person is for advertising on that topic.

In conclusion, it seems a reasonable assumption that readers hold definable attitudes towards print media vehicles, largely (though not wholly) determined by their perceptions of the contents of the various publications. Whether, as a result, the editorial environment in which an advertisement appears has a material bearing on its effectiveness is, at present, a more debatable point. Research in support of this contention—and thus justifying attitudes-to-media classification—is limited. Experiments by Winnick[20] are often cited but, as Broadbent[21] has pointed out, the evidence they provide is not strong.

Behavioural Classification. Just as in the previous section, there are two separate aspects to the classification of members of an audience in terms of behaviour. On the one hand, measurement of a person's behaviour towards a particular newspaper or magazine may be used as an indicator of the likely effectiveness of an advertisement it contains. On the other hand, the 'behaviour' in question may be in the market-place and of importance in grading people as more or less valuable advertising targets.

Under the first of these headings, the dividing line between attitudes to media vehicles and behaviour towards the same publications is a narrow one; e.g., measures of a person's 'involvement' with a particular magazine or newspaper, or of the importance they attach to it, or of their interest in its editorial contents will correlate highly with many of the behavioural criteria dealt with below. A danger to be avoided, therefore, in media research design and the application of its results, is the use of a number of audience classifications as if they each provided independent evidence of vehicles' values when, in fact, their information is largely redundant.

Apart from actual criteria of issue, page, or ad contact, dealt with above, a common behavioural measure is of claimed time spent reading, usually in relation to the 'average' issue and thus asked about in terms of habitual behaviour. Whilst usually seen as an indicator of probability of advertisement exposure, reading time is equally a likely correlate of the importance the reader attaches to the title and thus, possibly, of the degree to which its editorial authority 'rubs-off' on advertisements.

Adding another dimension to people's reading behaviour is a measurement of the number of separate occasions a particular issue is looked at. (This criterion is to be distinguished from reading frequency, where the concept is one of regularity of contact taken across *different* issues.) Apart from observational techniques—impracticable economically and otherwise on other than a small scale—readers' recall of their previous reading behaviour must be relied on. This in turn normally limits research to the measurement of the number of different dates on which a particular issue was looked at and leads to 'readings days' becoming the shorthand term. The measure was pioneered in the US; UK example is provided by 'Radio Times' work[22].

Next, the reading locale may be measured by asking, for example, whether the newspaper or magazine concerned was read 'at home', 'during a journey to work', 'at work', and so on. Similarly, the time of day when reading took place may be questioned. The common rationale in both cases is that the circumstances surrounding a reading event, such as the degree of distraction or relaxation or concurrent preoccupations of the reader are of likely relevance to the effectiveness of advertising in general or of a particular campaign carried by a vehicle.

Finally in this list of aspects of behaviour towards a newspaper or magazine, audience members may be classified according to how they acquire it: whether it is delivered to their home and if so whether wholly or mainly for them or for some other member of their household; or, if not delivered, whether copies are personally purchased by a respondent or passed on to him or her.

Data of this kind have relevance for circulation marketing problems of a publication treated as a 'brand', discussed later in this chapter. In the present context, the justification of the measure is again that being a 'primary' reader of a publication is likely to be a correlate of a person's general attitude to it and thus of the effect on him of advertising it contains.

The above paragraphs have listed various aspects of people's behaviour towards newspapers and magazines that may identify meaningful audience sub-groups. In a print media survey, it will also be common practice to collect at least relatively simple data on respondents' contact with other media, such as television, radio, or the cinema. The objective here is not so much to provide audience estimates in their own right (which may better be achieved by research techniques tailored to the task) but again to allow breakdowns of the readership of publications which are relevant to print media selection, e.g., to demonstrate the penetration of a particular magazine amongst those who view little commercial television.

Turning, now, to the other area of behavioural classification of audiences mentioned at the head of this section, demographic and attitudinal measurements noted earlier provide indirect evidence of whether a reader is a better or worse prospect from an advertiser's viewpoint, as regards their present or prospective purchasing behaviour. Self-evidently, readers may also be classified directly in terms of what they buy. This subject of integrated data (integrated in the sense of providing both media contact and purchasing behaviour information on the same individual) is a wide one and only a few salient points can be covered here.

First, the two sets of information can literally both be measured on each of a sample of individuals, in which case the data is not only integrated but also 'single source'. Alternatively, separate media and market research can be conducted and then the data 'married'. This technique depends on locating a set of classification criteria, common to the two surveys which, collectively, correlate highly either with behaviour towards media or towards products and brands. On this basis, appropriate purchasing characteristics can, for example, be ascribed to each individual in the other, media survey. Examples of single-source data are provided, in this country, by BMRB's Target Group Index and by the US Brand Rating Index. Integrated data obtained by 'marriage' has not been largely developed in Britain, but in France Agostini has undertaken considerable work[23].

Next, as regards single source data, the number of technique alternatives is large. In principle, at least, any appropriate audience measurement method can be linked to any one of several approaches to collecting purchasing data, including single contact versus continuous (panel) reporting and personal interview versus self-completion questionnaires.

Third and last, the limitations as well as apparent advantages of integrated data are to be recognized. Being able to classify media survey respondents in terms of their purchasing behaviour does not of itself solve previously existing problems of whether vehicles should be so selected as to reach heavy or light buyers of a product, buyers or non-buyers of a brand. Again, readers' purchasing behaviour may often be inferred with adequate accuracy on the basis of indirect classifications, e.g., demographic ones, although by no means always so[24]. Fine distinctions between newspapers and magazines in terms of the buying behaviour of their respective audiences may, in practice, be swamped by gross difference in their advertising rates, as largely dictated by the sizes of their total audiences.

Schedule Construction and Evaluation Programs

Program types and objectives

In parallel with the refinement of audience measurement methods, a notable feature of the media research scene in the last decade has been the development and application of computer programs which take as their input, partly or wholly, the data discussed in earlier sections of this chapter. Whilst such programs are usable, in principle, in relation to any measured advertising medium, in practice they have related most frequently to newspapers and magazines and therefore should be briefly covered here, although the subject is by now a wide one, with a very considerable literature.

Media programs may be divided according to objective into two groups. First, *evaluation programs* take as input an existing schedule or schedules of insertions in a number of vehicles and provide, as output, measures of schedule performance—notably full data on the pattern of contacts that should be produced and indices of the 'effectiveness' of this pattern.

Construction programs by contrast have, as input, audience data and much other information and produce an actual schedule on the basis of given instructions and assumptions. The term 'optimization' (of schedule selection) has been and is still often applied to these routines. It is more accurate to regard them as producing, within stated constraints, a selection of vehicles and numbers of insertions in each of them which is 'best', if at all, only under the assumptions made. Further, the schedule can often be guaranteed to be no more than 'very close to the best', for technical reasons of the programming method employed.

In the next section, the input requirements and calculation methods of these programs are described, in bare outline only. No detailed comparisons between programs are drawn, but several general reviews are available[25,26,27,28]. A later section turns to some consideration of the advantages and limitations of their use.

Methods

It is convenient to consider first schedule construction programs, although it is to be stressed that evaluation routines are, almost certainly, finding wider day by day use at present, at least in the UK.

The first input requirement is a list of *candidate vehicles* from amongst which a schedule is to be selected. Different programs will accept lists of varying lengths. For each vehicle, the cost of the size or sizes of insertion associated with it is to be specified. Some programs are able to take series discounts into consideration. The audience data included in the input will usually relate to issue contact, often but not invariably in the form of reading frequencies. It is required for each population sub-group to which the program is instructed to ascribe a different 'value'. Unless the schedule is to be constructed on the assumption that all people are equal in their worth as prospects for the advertising concerned, a full set of *market weights* is to be specified, comprising the relative values—whether based on assumption or measurement—of each type of individual to be separately considered by the program. Such groups may be identified by any classification covered by the audience research data used, but are most commonly demographic ones. Some programs require the user to specify weights separately for each criterion he nominates—to say, for example, that upper social class individuals are twice as valuable to him as lower class ones and that, separately, younger people should carry three times the weight of older ones. Other input formats may call for weights for groups identified by interlaced criteria; thus, for instance, a figure might be attached to mothers with children under 16 living in the south east and to other mutually exclusive groups similarly defined.

Quite separately from market weights, most construction program inputs will allow the optional use of *media weights*, which are quantative expressions of the varying values the program user attaches to a contact between one individual and the different vehicles within the candidate list. In the calculations the computer subsequently performs, these media weights are almost always treated mathematically as probabilities; but in fact they may reflect either of two different concepts.

On the one hand, a media weight may express the probability of advertisement contact (or, at least, of opportunity of such contact) conditional on contact with an issue of the vehicle. Clearly, data on page traffic, or its correlates such as time spent reading, could be utilized to provide weights in this sense. On the other hand, a media weight may be an attempt to express a judgement on the relative strength of impact delivered to a reader by exposure to an advertisement in one vehicle rather than another; e.g., it might be felt that the editorial authority of some magazines was greater than others, that this 'rubbed off' on their advertising and, therefore, that the former should be given higher media weights.

Data input requirements are completed by a statement of the budget available for the schedule to be constructed—some programs will call for a single figure, others a range—and by a set of constraints which limit the pattern of insertions the program may choose. These may be partly 'environmental' in the sense that, for example, if a rule of 'one insertion per issue' is being followed and the schedule period is a year, the computer must be instructed that there are only 52 issues of a weekly magazine available for selection; or constraints may again reflect purely the program user's wishes that, say, no more than half of the total budget is to be expended in one media group.

Given the type of input data outlined above, the objective of a construction program is then to arrive at a schedule which is permissable within the constraints laid down and is also 'best', in some sense, amongst all feasible alternatives. This simple statement of the problem raises three basic issues: what criterion is to be nominated, against which any given schedule may be evaluated? How is this evaluation to be achieved in practice? And how is the program to arrive at a candidate schedule for evaluation?

The type of criterion most commonly adopted is the weighted number of contacts a schedule delivers for given expenditure. The weighting involved comprises the varying values of individuals as advertising prospects, as expressed in market weights; the differing worth of contacts effected by this vehicle against that one, or media weights; and, usually, a third weighting expressing a view that successive contacts with a given individual are not of uniform value. This last-mentioned set of weights is termed, collectively, a

566

response function: a numerical expression of the marginal or cumulative value of the first, second, third . . . contact with a given individual. It may be in-built into a program; or it may be variable at the user's choice and form part of the required input. Different response functions may be chosen to reflect viewpoints that the first, tenth, and hundredth impact are of just the same value; that several impacts are necessary to gain any effect at all but that, beyond this critical point, nothing is added by further ones; that cumulative effect rises slowly at first with number of contacts, then more rapidly and later tails off once more; or that early impacts in a series are the relatively most forceful, diminishing returns then applying.

In evaluating any given schedule against such a criterion of market, media, and response function weighted impacts, a program's central task is to calculate a frequency distribution of issue contacts—to calculate the numbers of people, in total or within relevant sub-categories, seeing varying numbers of issues. Here two basic approaches are possible. First, the program can consider each individual in a population (or more strictly, each member of a sample of that population) in relation to each vehicle concerned and 'decide' on the basis of the data provided (reading frequency information, for example) whether a contact will or will not occur. This *simulation* approach may use up much program running time where a large sample and many vehicles are involved. Alternatively, a program may estimate a distribution of contacts, through the use of appropriate formulae, by considering reading patterns for the population or group as a whole, rather than one by one; this technique has come to be known as the '*formula*' approach.

Turning to the third essential problem, even given a meaningful criterion on which schedules' values can be compared and a calculation method for such evaluation, a program has still to arrive at a feasible schedule in the first place; and, even given the very high calculation speeds which attain, it will not be economically practicable to generate and evaluate every one of the myriad alternative sets of vehicles and numbers of insertions that derive from even a short candidate list.

A common approach is to build up the 'best' schedule in a series of steps. Such a *stepwise* program first ranks candidate vehicles on a value for money basis, comparing market and media weighted audiences with costs; selects the most economical; examines the value-weighted patterns of contacts formed by this first insertion combined with each possible addition to it; again makes a choice on value against cost; and so continues until the budget is exhausted.

Any form of such a procedure is properly subject to the criticism that it cannot be guaranteed to produce a schedule which is optimum. However, the shortfall is likely to be small and can be further reduced by refinements which allow the deletion of insertions as well as their addition or permit the program, in effect, to 'look back' and compare, in terms of value, the point it has currently reached with branches of its path that it rejected earlier.

The discussion of this section has, so far, been entirely in terms of schedule construction programs, but it will be seen that the essential problems of evaluating an existing schedule have also been covered. The calculation of a frequency distribution of contacts, together with the application of market, media, and, probably, response function weights are, on the one hand, intermediate stages in most 'optimization' routines but are equally the core of evaluation programs.

Advantages and limitations in program use

The period which saw the first introduction of computer programs for the construction or evaluation of print media schedules was characterized by considerable over-claiming of resultant benefits; but subsequently and currently, the gains from the use of the computer remain hotly debated. This section summarizes some few points on both sides of the argument. A longer and very balanced review is provided by Broadbent[29].

It is unquestionable that computer use permits fast, numerically accurate comparative consideration of far more schedules, permissable within the budgetary and other constraints, than could ever be reviewed by manual means within economic time and cost limits. Equally, a program may 'consider' simultaneously a large number of factors held to be relevant to a schedule's value. However, the program of itself adds nothing to the logic of its constructor. What factors are to be considered and how they are to be traded off the one against the other must be specified in its instructions. There is no genie in the hardware bottle, only a totally obedient, incredibly fast-working slave. Further, 'garbage in, garbage out' is no empty truism. If the logic of the program's construction or the quality of the input data are indefensible, so will be the output. Even so, the availability of only limited data is no argument against using sophisticated analysis techniques on it.

The two areas of input information most frequently criticized are media weights and response functions. It is properly said that, in relation both to the contribution of vehicle environment to advertisement impact and to the marginal effect of successive impacts, judgement must currently largely stand in for knowledge.

On the first of these areas, if any 'qualitative' factor, beyond intrinsically quantitative audience and cost data, would be taken into account in selection of advertising vehicles by non-computer means, it seems hardly logical to ignore it when writing a program. At the same time, the hard task has to be undertaken of turning generalized 'feelings' about relative media values into overt, quantified judgements the computer can note.

As regards response functions, the advent of the computer has merely given a name to a problem existing long previously. Every hand-constructed schedule for which reaching many people was traded-off, to some purposeful degree, against contacting a smaller audience more frequently concealed an opinion on the planner's part regarding the relationship between cumulative number of impacts and cumulative 'effect'.

In relation of both these areas of 'doubtful' input, it is to be noted that computer use allows—and should ideally always include—investigation of the effect on the schedule constructed or evaluated of varying the assumptions that have been made. Such sensitivity analysis cannot answer the question of whether this media weight or that response function, assigned on judgement, is 'right' or 'wrong'; but it can indicate, quickly and relatively inexpensively, how critically dependent a particular media decision is or is not on some unmeasured factor.

Finally, there are those who are happier only to use the computer to evaluate, rather than to construct schedules and who, further, stop short at weighted distributions of impacts; they point out the uncertainties of whether (for mathematical reasons) a strictly 'optimum' schedule can be arrived at, and stress the non-knowledge regarding response functions. The counter-arguments are that a handful of trial schedules constructed outside the computer can, equally, not be guaranteed to contain the 'best', or even 'nearly best' one possible; and that two or more tables of the numbers of people subject to varying levels of contact can only be compared when, for example, '70 per cent receiving eight opportunities to see' and '60 per cent with 10 ots each' can be put on a common denominator. This reduction to common coinage involves, inevitably, a response function concept.

Measuring Print Media Effectiveness

Media effect and content effect

This section is concerned with the measurement of the effectiveness, as advertising vehicles, of media at large and newspapers or magazines in particular.

Taking a mass media advertising campaign as a whole, it is neither theoretically desirable nor practically possible to separate its effect (however 'effect' is defined) as between contributions from the content of the campaign—the advertising theme and its creative expression—and from the media in which that content appears.

On the theoretical point, the contributions to effectiveness of advertising content and media vehicles are unlikely to be straightforwardly additive; they will interact. Even holding advertised brand and audience constant, a given medium or set of vehicles may be more effective carrying one campaign than another. Hence, any concept of a fixed 'pecking order' of media effects, irrespective of mode of advertising use, is somewhat sterile.

On the practical point, media effectiveness cannot be measured *in vacuo;* an actual campaign, or advertising created for test purposes must enter into the research. The ability then to generalize from one particular set of circumstances to the intrinsic, forecastable value of the medium under test is limited by a total lack of any comprehensive model of 'how advertising works'.

These somewhat pessimistic comments are intended to point up some overall limitations of media effectiveness measurement. The following paragraphs firstly review criteria of 'effect' and then comment on some aspects of research design and method. These are not explored in depth since many of the relevant points are covered in other chapters of this handbook.

Effectiveness criteria

One half of the problem of media effectiveness research is the question 'what to measure?' There exists a continuum of variables which may be utilized. In one direction this runs from data which is relatively easy and inexpensive to collect to more complex and more costly measurements. Unfortunately, however, the ranking of measures in terms of relevance runs in the opposite direction.

At the one extreme lies a measurement of consumers' purchases or of retail sales. Given that the objective of advertising, and thus of the use of some particular medium or vehicle, is to increase or maintain sales, there is no doubt here of relevance. (The admitted fact that achieved sales will depend on many other factors besides advertising complicates research design and interpretation but is not, *per se*, a reason for measuring achievement against some other criterion only.) However, accurate purchases' or sales' measurement are costly. Manufacturers' deliveries may, occasionally, be an adequate substitute, given no complications of alternative distribution channels, varying stock levels or inability to break out delivery figures just for the area required.

Midway in the continuum lie measures of attitudes to the brand advertised and of their change. Research costs *may* be lower than for sales' measurement, although very considerable developmental work may be involved if relevant attitudinal dimensions have to be established from scratch and scales for their measurement built up and tested. The major question is, however, of relevance, since the link between attitudinal change and subsequent purchasing behaviour is far from unequivocably established.

Questions in the general area of communications effects are the easiest to formulate and probably the least expensive to administer; they include recall and recognition of product, brand name, attributes and copy points. Unfortunately, an individual's knowledge of an advertised brand or its campaign is but tenuously connected to his behaviour towards it in the market-place. The relevance of communications measures is thus considered the lowest of those here mentioned.

Effectiveness research design

In parallel with the choice of criterion measure discussed above, research into media effectiveness can be conducted under controlled 'laboratory' conditions, at some cost, unavoidably, of realism, or in the field. The latter alternative subdivides according to whether data is collected in parallel with an ongoing advertising campaign or whether a special pattern of exposure is imposed for experimental purposes.

'Laboratory' scale research may constrain costs and allow at least some of the many unwanted, confounding variables to be controlled. It will typically involve exposing relatively small samples of individuals to advertising in the vehicle or vehicles under test and taking measures on these people of the chosen 'effect' variable. A simple 'before and after' measurement approach is often used but more complex experimental designs may be introduced. An example of this general category of media research is provided in work by the 'Daily Mirror' aiming to demonstrate its effectiveness relative to that of television[30].

The main limitations of 'laboratory' work are two-fold. First, the conditions of exposure to the media vehicles concerned and of contact with the test advertising are often far different from those naturally occurring and, if a comparison of widely dissimilar media is involved, the bias thus introduced regarding their relative 'effectiveness' may not easily be assessed. Second, the measures that may be taken obviously stop short of any actual expression of brand preference in the market-place.

Turning to field research, one approach to effectiveness measurement in the context of a normal, ongoing campaign is to monitor both levels of exposure and 'effect' amongst the same sample of individuals. At the analysis stage, weight of purchasing of the advertised brand of changes in attitudes towards it, for example, may then be compared as between a sub-sample with low numbers of ots and a group exposed to many issues. Whilst some success has been reported with such a method[31], there is a major danger to be avoided in confusing correlation with causation when interpreting the results. Even if high levels of 'effect' are found to be associated with high exposure, it is quite possible for some third variable to be responsible, which predicates both 'effect' and exposure. More commonly, the advertising plan will be tailored to research requirements. The simplest design will be to run a press schedule in one area only, and to take measurements of the chosen variable(s) before and after the advertising period. The problem of other uncontrolled factors also affecting the observed difference between the 'before' and 'after' readings leads naturally to the addition of parallel research in another control area, in which there is no advertising. This device cannot, however, solve the problem completely; in general, neither will it be known what other factors is it important to take account of, nor in practice will it be possible to select two areas which are comparable in all aspects thought likely to be relevant. More complex experimental designs may, therefore, be sought (as discussed in chapter 2), using several areas and allowing statistical estimation of the contributory effects of the actual media being researched, of between-area differences, of time effects, and residual factors. An example of an elaborate experimental project, aiming to compare the effectiveness of magazines and television, is provided in American work by General Foods[32].

Another practical problem in the application of experimental designs to print media effectiveness measurement is that the regions available will be dictated by the areas in which part or all of the circulation of a newspaper falls, which may not be ideal, in size or nature, on research grounds. (It is to be noted that experiments *are* possible with national media since, increasingly, regional editions are available as a regular facility or by special arrangement.)

One alternative to using naturally occuring circulation areas for experimental purposes is to so arrange matters that, amongst two otherwise comparable samples, one receives copies of a publication containing a test advertisement and the other sees issues which are apparently similar but do not, in fact, carry the campaign. The method of achieving this result will depend on the realism demanded and the level of permissible costs: an extra advertisement may just be 'tipped-in' or, at much greater trouble and expense, a whole section of four or more pages may be 'doctored'. Whilst unwanted inter-personal and inter-regional differences may thus be eliminated, it will be administratively extremely difficult to supply specially prepared copies through normal trade channels. The artificiality may have to be accepted of having respondents receive the test publication other than by the delivery to the home or purchase at a newsagent as would normally be the case.

Finally, the use of coupons or keyed write-in addresses as a means of evaluating media vehicles is to be noted. The analysis only of enquiries resulting in actual sales may be preferable to looking just at total enquiries received by the advertiser. Clearly, a *media* comparison properly results only from the use of the same couponed or keyed advertisement in two or more newspapers or magazines. Note that, as in virtually all attempts to evaluate media effectiveness under 'real-life' conditions, the overall level of coupon response actually derives from the combined effect of many factors, including the size and nature of the issue audience, intensity of reading within the issue, the contents of the advertisement itself and interaction between vehicle and ad.

This section has provided a very brief overview of some approaches to print media effectiveness assessment. A useful further summary of American methods and case-histories has been published by the National Industrial Conference Board[33].

Circulation Marketing Research

Introduction

The research problems and methods discussed so far in this chapter have been concerned almost entirely with newspapers and magazines viewed as advertising vehicles. However, as already noted, a publisher is often operating in a situation of joint supply. He derives income not only from offering an audience, or opportunities for advertisement contact, but also from selling actual copies to readers. Clearly, the relative importance of the two markets will vary from case to case. At the one extreme, a free sheet or controlled circulation magazine depends entirely on advertisement revenue. At the other there are periodicals (although few, if any, now, in the consumer area) carrying no advertising and deriving all income from copy sales. In practice, in the UK at least, less research effort is devoted to publications as 'brands' in their own right than as advertising vehicles; but some mention is to be made of the techniques relevant to the former.

Note that the concept of a newspaper or magazine as a 'brand' is often questioned, on the argument that 'product content' is entirely variable from issue to issue. However, a publication is unquestionably seen by its readers as a continuing entity: and those needs which a title seeks to satisfy are no more impermanent than for other fields.

Circulation market measurement

Nearly all newspapers and magazines provide a figure of their net sales. Often, this will be one endorsed by the Audit Bureau of Circulation (ABC), a body calling for sales' returns in a set format and carrying out spot-checks of publishers' internal auditing procedures. ABC figures usually relate to a net sales' average struck over all publishing days in a six months' period; monthly data is also published, in arrears. Some publishers not in membership of the ABC will appoint their own auditors to produce net sales figures, or offer merely a 'publishers statement' of their sales. Audited circulations lie somewhere between ex-factory sales data for other product fields and a true, unbiased estimate of net consumer offtake. They do take into account not only the quantities of copies supplied to the trade, but also the numbers unsold and returned for credit. However, in the UK at present, newspapers are *not*, in general, supplied ex-publisher on a 'sale or return' (SOR) basis; and whether SOR applies to a magazine, either as a permanent feature or a limited period, will vary from case to case.

There is a further complication to audited circulation figures. Even if SOR applies, the promptness and speed with which unsold copies are returned through the trade channels will vary. However, an audited figure for a given period will be based on ex-publisher supplies for that month or months and on returned copies recorded in that same period, but representing outdated issues of varying age. Thus the audited figure may well provide a biased estimate of short-term variations in net consumer offtake. The problem can, of course, be overcome, at some trouble and expense, by sorting returned copies according to their cover date.

It is to be noted that ABC and similar figures provide, in this country, total sales data only. The parallel American returns go into considerable detail on geographical and other breakdowns.

Seeking fuller information on sales to, or purchases by, the final consumer of newspapers and magazines, there are at present no continuous, generally available measurement services analogous to those for many other product fields. However, techniques employed in other areas can be applied—with some modifications—and are in use by some publishers on a limited or experimental basis.

Purchase data can be derived both from single-contact surveys (either using personal interviews or self-administered questionnaires) or by panel techniques. Two problem areas are to be noted. First, the casual, irregular purchase of a particular title will not be a highly memorable event to a respondent. Second, publications are acquired through more than one channel. Separate questioning may be required to cover copies received on direct subscription from a publisher (of negligible proportions in this country, save for some few magazines); copies delivered to a household by a news-agent; copies purchased at a retail outlet—whether newsagent, station bookstall, other type of shop or street vendor; and copies passed on by an initial purchaser to someone else. Loose questionning can lead to copies in this last category erroneously being counted more than once.

Retail audits are also possible with, again, some special problems attaching to newspapers or magazines as product fields. Street sales will be un-measured if the universe sampled is only of newsagents and bookstalls. Newsagents' normal recording of 'deliveries' may need to be specially supplemented, particularly where they receive supplies not only from wholesalers but also by publishers' representatives 'filling-in' their additional requirements. Far more than in other product fields, 'outdated stock'—yesterday's newspapers, for example—are waste and will normally be disposed of unrecorded. Finally, if sales' data is required issue by issue, the audit period becomes as short as a week or a day for some publications, which would clearly lead to astronomical costs if a normal stock-check approach were used. However, self-completion of a questionnaire by the retailer may be employed.

Research for publication launches

Formal test marketing of a major new newspaper or consumer magazine hardly ever takes place. Editorial, production and distribution economics are such that 'first copy' costs are high and pilot-scale production hardly feasible. This is not to say, of course, that 'dummy' issues are not produced, both for early circulation to advertisers and agencies and, sometimes, to gauge reaction to a new title from the wholesale and retail trade. Short of full-scale test marketing, however, the publisher can apply much of the methodology of other areas of consumer research to measuring prospective demand before committing himself to a new publication. An example is provided by research for Thomson Regional Newspapers[34].

'Product' and pricing research

The individual newspaper or magazine, as much as any other brand, has definable 'product content' in the shape of the news, comment, fiction, and features it carries. The actual items vary from issue to issue, but the satisfied

574

reader is, nonetheless, buying a mix with a consistent shape imposed on it by editorial policy. Systematic product content research is relatively little applied to print media; a strong journalistic tradition makes more for a producer-oriented outlook than a marketing one. However, relevant evidence can be obtained.

Post facto investigation of claimed readership of individual items, discussed above, points to their apparent relative interest to different segments of a publication's readership. Reasons for an individual pursuing this item but ignoring that one can be probed by direct questioning, with the usual caveats that some degree of rationalization will be unavoidable. More elaborately, a market segmention approach can be applied to mapping the consumer needs that print media satisfy.

The 'make-up' of a newspaper or magazine—the style and arrangement of its content on and through its pages—is in many ways the analogue of packaging in other fields. Again, research techniques used in other areas may be applied to measure the legibility of a particular typeface or the brand image conveyed by a magazine's cover design. Examples of research in this area that are generally available are few; some have been summarized by the American Newspaper Publishers Association Foundation[35].

Finally, in this section, the special problems of pricing research may be mentioned. For British newspapers and magazines, resale price maintenance is the invariable rule so that experimental manipulation of cover prices for research purposes is not practicable; questioning on readers' attitudes to present or prospective prices must be relied on. The limitation is perhaps not a critical one, since print media do not occupy an essential 'price-market', nor is pricing used as an aggressive marketing weapon, being largely determined, at least for newspapers, on a 'cost-plus' basis.

References

1. EPHRON, E. H. Some Observations on Media Planning in the United States, *Admap*, **6**, 1, 1970.
2. *Development Research for the 1968 National Readership Survey*, Joint Industry Committee for National Readership Surveys, 1968.
3. BELSON, W. A. *Studies in Readership*, Business Publications, 1962.
4. Introduction, Comparisons with Other Data, *Target Group Index*, British Market Research Bureau Ltd., 1969.
5. SMITH, H. A. The Use of Panels for the Collection of Readership Data, *The Thomson Medals and Awards for Media Research 1966*, Thomson Organization, 1967;
   AGOSTINI, J. M., *ibid*. The Possible Role of Readership Panels in Media Research and Media Planning;
   JOYCE, T. and BIRD, M., *ibid*. The Use of Panels for the Collection of Readership Data;
   PARFITT, J. H., *ibid*. The Use of Panels for the Collection of Readership and Other Data.
6. NOELLE-NEUMANN, E. Winning Paper, *The Roy Thomson Medals and Awards for Media Research 1962*, Thomson Organization, 1962;
   JONES, H. J. M., SCHLAEPPI, A. C., NUTTALL, C. G. F., and AGOSTINI, J. M., *ibid*. other published papers, untitled.
7. SMITH, H. A. and others, *op. cit.*
8. CORLETT, T. *An Introduction to the Use and Interpretation of Reading Frequency Data*, Institute of Practitioners in Advertising, 1967.

575

9. METHERINGHAM, R. A. Measuring the Net Cumulative Coverage of a Print Campaign, Journal of Advertising Research, **4**, 4, 1964.
10. SHEPHERD-SMITH, N. H. Computers and the Advertising Agency: A Practical Approach, *Admap*, **5**, 9, 1969.
11. LUCAS, D. B. and BRITT, S. H. Exposure of Advertisements, *Measuring Advertising Effectiveness*, McGraw-Hill, New York, 1963.
12. *Development Research for the 1968 National Readership Survey, op. cit.*
13. *Reading Intensity Scale: Interim Report on Calibration*, Joint Industry Committee for National Readership Surveys, 1970.
14. *A Study of Printed Advertisement Rating Methods*, Advertising Research Foundation, 1956.
15. FLETCHER, R. *Reading Behaviour Reconsidered*, ESOMAR-WAPOR Congress, 1969.
16. *The Target Group Index*, British Market Research Bureau Ltd., 1969.
17. National Magazine Co. Ltd. *Markets and Media*, 1969.
18. *A Qualitative Study of Regional Evening Newspapers*, Evening Newspaper Advertising Bureau Ltd., 1963.
19. Qualitative Media Assessments, *TV Times*, 1967.
20. WINICK, C. Three Measures of the Advertising Value of Media Context, *Journal of Advertising Research*, **2**, 2, 1962.
21. BROADBENT, S. R. and SEGNIT, S. Beyond Cost per Thousand—an Examination of Media Weights, *The Thomson Medals and Awards for Advertising Research 1968*, Thomson Organization, 1968.
22. Page Traffic and Page Frequency of Three Leading Publications, *Radio Times*, 1965.
23. AGOSTINI, J. M. The Marriage of Data from Various Surveys: an Expedient or a Unique Way to Make Progress, *Admap*, **3**, 9, 1967.
24. JOYCE, T. YES—or How the TGI can Help You, *Admap*, **6**, 1, 1970.
25. BROADBENT, S. R. Media Planning and Computers by 1970, *The Thomson Medals and Awards for Media Research 1965*, Thomson Organization, 1966.
26. GENSCH, D. H. Computer Models in Advertising Media Selection, *Journal of Marketing Research*, **5**, 1968.
27. BROWN, M. M. Media Selection Models Compared and Contrasted, *Admap*, **4**, 10, 1968.
28. Media Research Group, Media Model Comparison, *Admap*, **5**, 3, 1969.
29. BROADBENT, S. How to Approach the Computer, *Spending Advertising Money*, Business Books, 1970.
30. CAFFYN, J. *Experimental Intermedia Studies*, Twelfth Annual Conference, Market Research Society, 1969.
31. MCDONALD, C. D. P. *ibid. Relationships between Advertising Exposure and Purchasing Behaviour.*
32. A Major Advertiser Tests the Effectiveness of General Magazines and Television, *Admap*, **6**, 4, 1970.
33. WOLFE, H. D., BROWN, J. K., CLARK THOMPSON, G., and GREENBERG, H. *Evaluating Media*, (Business Policy Study, No. 121), National Industrial Conference Board Inc., 1966.
34. MOONEY, P. B. and WICKS, A. *The Use of Market Research in the Launching of a New Evening Newspaper—a Case History*, Market Research Society Annual Conference, 1967.
35. BUSH, C. F. (Ed.) *News Research for Better Newspapers*, American Newspaper Publishers Association Foundation, Vol. 1, 1966; Vol. 2, 1967; Vol. 3, 1968; Vol. 4, 1969.

24. Television media research

W. A. Twyman

The Background to Television Media Research in the UK

In the UK, there are three television services—ITV, BBC1, and BBC2. Of these, ITV and BBC1 are shown on 405-line VHF which is received by over 90 per cent of households currently. All services are now transmitted on 625-line UHF, but the present stage of transmitter building means that UHF services are received by over 50 per cent of households. Colour transmissions for all services are on UHF only and about two per cent of households have colour sets; reception of both UHF and colour is increasing.

The British Broadcasting Corporation controls BBC1 and BBC2 which carry no advertising. These stations provide largely a national service with only small and infrequent regional variations. The BBC's present charter expires in 1976.

The Independent Television Authority administers ITV through its appointed contractors. There are fourteen ITV areas with one contractor for each, except London where the franchise is divided into Monday to Friday 7 p.m. and Friday 7 p.m. to Sunday. Some contractors have recently announced combined sales operations and further amalgamations are possible. The existing contracts expire in 1974 but are likely to be extended to 1976. The basic organization of British television is then open to change from 1976.

Each of the fifteen ITV programme companies is financed by the sale of advertising time. No more advertising than seven minutes in a clock hour and an average of six minutes per hour may be screened. Commercials are shown in breaks separate from programme material, but these breaks can occur within and between the programmes. Commercial breaks contain several commercials. The most common spot length is 30 seconds, others are 15 seconds and 60 seconds, rarely longer. Slides of five, seven, and ten seconds are also used.

Commercial spots may be bought in a number of ways in regard to transmission time. At one extreme 'guaranteed home impressions' schemes leave no control over timing with the buyer except a broad period of some weeks. The measured home audiences to the spots shown are added together to check that the booked target number of impressions has been delivered. 'Run of week', with day and exact time unspecifiable, and various package opportunities give slightly more control over timing in that the week is specified. The basic rate cards allow booking by time segments, which vary greatly in length (peak time being three hours or more) and by the specific day. A further surcharge is needed to fix the exact break in which the spot will fall and another to fix the position in the break. The buyer's control of timing may, therefore, range from within two or three weeks down to a matter of a few seconds, paying an increasing premium for greater precision.

The general classes of segments to be bought and some further details of timing will be determined by a media plan. The pattern of spots so laid down may have been designed to meet some overall requirement of total coverage and frequency of exposure for the schedule.

Within the limits specified by the media plan, the time-buying operation seeks to get the most target audience impressions per pound spent.

Time-buying is a very dynamic process with bookings made months in advance gradually being made more precise by negotiation as transmission day approaches and more research information becomes available. The times at which spots are likely to be transmitted are available from the programme company even where a surcharge has not been paid. Spots can then be moved to where it is forecast that more favourable ratings will occur. This movement can be made up until two days before transmission. Movement to more favourable times will depend on speed, negotiating skill and sometimes preparedness to pay the fixing surcharge if not already paid.

Given that the range of impressions per pound is considerable within segments, it is reasonable to suppose that a good time-buying operation can achieve advantages in value for money on a scale not easily demonstrable in relation to other aspects of advertising effort.

All this evaluation in buying and selling of television advertising time is based on the use of research estimates of television audiences. Whilst it is not easy to sort out historically the causal relationships between research and television selling and buying systems, it is clear that once a selling and buying system exists, it establishes certain requirements from the research system. In the present case for the UK, these are:

(a) regional samples providing actionable data in each region but the more accurate where most money is at stake;
(b) data which include an audience for each individual advertisement. This leads to minute by minute recording;
(c) data which enable decisions to be made in terms of reaching advertising target groups;

(d) continuous reporting by the same sample over long periods of time (panels), so that cumulative coverage and frequency of impact can be estimated for whole schedules of spots spread over time;

(e) fast reporting to enable the most recent and relevant research figures to be used in last minute time-buying negotiations.

Whether the cost of collecting and using this continuous minute by minute data is compensated for by greater advertising efficiency is difficult to evaluate. It is hard to simulate decision making with alternative forms of data, because competent decision makers have an accumulated experience of decision making from the current form of data. It is even harder to define and quantify advertising efficiency in the present state of knowledge about advertising.

Research for programming can be required both to establish how far a service's programmes are being seen (there is undeniably competition between BBC and ITV in this respect), and how much programmes are enjoyed by their target audience, which may be a minority group. Obviously, size of audience is an indicator of enjoyment, but not reliably, because audience size depends also on timing and competition. Programming requirements for audience size measurements are likely to be met by any system which satisfies the more complex advertising requirement. The additional needs for programme research in greater depth are likely to be met outside this system.

Spot advertising is the only legal form of television advertising in the UK, and the growing form of television advertising in the USA. The form of television advertising in other European countries can be found in a BBTA publication[1].

The US, with its complex of big networks and small regional stations, sponsorship of programmes and spot advertising, has generated conditions where a number of different companies have offered various forms of audience measurement, sometimes in parallel and competing services.

Since sample sizes required for a given accuracy do not decrease with decreasing population, but total wealth of the market does, the economics of mass media measurement systems are more precarious in smaller countries. In the UK there is now only one comprehensive metered service operating under an industry contract formerly held by TAM (Television Audience Measurement Ltd) and now held by AGB (Audits of Great Britain Ltd) from mid 1968 to 1974. (An account of this history of television research in the UK is given[2].) JICTAR (Joint Industry Committee for Television Advertising Research) is the industry body controlling the contract. JICTAR is formed by the combination of three classes of organization with an interest in Independent Television, namely programme companies, advertisers, and advertising agencies, working through their representative associations.

JICTAR, operating through its committee, secretariat and consultants, is responsible for collecting the research requirements of its members, formulating the research system which will meet these requirements, preparing a specification for the system and awarding a contract to a research company to operate the specification. The system is currently based on continuously reporting meter and diary panels in all ITV regions.

One effect of the 'industry contract' is that there is one set of figures for all transmissions universally accepted as the basis for buying and selling television advertisement time. It is unlikely that a parallel comprehensive system would now be commercially viable. In addition to the industry ratings system, smaller scale research about television audiences also occurs for a number of special purposes and is conducted by a variety of research companies. Examples are the linking of television exposure to marketing data, or obtaining measurements about the television audience not available from the JICTAR system, such as presence in commercial breaks or attitudes and reactions to programmes.

Studies of audience behaviour in greater depth than the 'head counting' or 'probable exposure' level have not so far had a great deal of commercial potential either in Europe or in the US, except on an experimental basis. This is probably because such work is costly and it is difficult to achieve the universally acceptable aims and definitions necessary for financial viability. This difficulty in turn arises from lack of knowledge of advertising processes, there being no easy way to attach value to different levels of attention or involvement. As knowledge about advertising increases, so may the demand for greater 'in depth' studies of media exposure.

Again, following the US[3], the demand for media data linked to marketing data has increased in the UK. There have been surveys very much for this purpose such as AMPS (All Media and Product Survey)[4,5] and TGI (Target Group Index)[6] and an increasing amount of media data collected from consumer panels. The general trend has been towards such media data getting more and more elaborate and comparable to the main media data collection systems. Whilst the gap is still widest in the case of television, since meters are expensive to run, there have been suggestions and discussions concerning the possible integration of product and media data collection including television. Whether this occurs depends upon the future demonstration of marketing benefits and on cost savings arising from such a change. (For a fuller discussion of these questions see[7,8].)

Another effect of an industry contract has been the very high degree of methodological scrutiny and checking to which television audience research has been subjected. A number of studies have looked at aspects of validity[9,10] and there is a continuing programme of investigation into both methods of collecting data and their usefulness[11,12].

Quite separate from research conducted in relation to advertising or for ITV programming there is the BBC research system. This is financed, controlled, collected, and used almost exclusively by the BBC through their own audience research department. Although there is much in common between the two bodies of data collected for the ITV and BBC sides of television, they have not so far been collected and presented in ways which maximize their equivalence or comparability. This situation could change if the organization of the BBC and ITV services were greatly altered in 1976. The BBC covers its radio audiences in its daily broadcasting audience measurement system. This involves aided recall applied to the previous day's viewing and listening, with a fresh sample interviewed each day. The BBC also undertakes its own investigations into audience reactions and other special programming questions.

In conclusion, the form of the mainstream of television media research for ITV has been fairly stable over a number of years in the UK, relying on a meter and diary system for counting heads with some special studies for other purposes. Forces which may change this stability are rising research costs, increased understanding of how the use of data affects decisions and how advertising works, changes in methods of handling data such as increasing computerization and, finally, changes in the nature of media and marketing. The timing of all these forces of change is difficult to forecast. Some are discussed again at the end of the chapter.

The Measurement of TV Set Ownership, Station Reception and Definition of Station Areas

Purpose of the data

The measurement of set ownership and reception arises in two types of situation. There is the research problem of defining the media sources to which an individual or household is potentially exposed. This may be necessary for a number of reasons, e.g., in order to relate their media exposure potential to other aspects of their behaviour or merely as a sample stratification control.

The second situation is that of defining the coverage of a television station. This also involves measuring the reception potential of individuals and households but may involve the further stage of making judgements about populations of individuals, such as administrative districts.

In the UK, an ITV station is created by the allocation of one or more transmitters to a programme company which is then responsible for both programming and collecting revenue by the sale of television advertising time. The coverage of the station is one basis of selling time and its definition an important research problem.

There are three aspects of defining an ITV station's coverage:

(a) fixing the potential audience for a station. This means measuring the number of people or households effectively receiving the station and their characteristics;
(b) defining the areas to be sampled for audience measurement. Theoretically, there need be no geographical limits. Since coverage of a station generally does have geographical limits and because of marketing needs,

Fig. 24.1
(Reproduced with the permission of JICTAR/HMSO/Map Productions).

it has been usual to associate the media measurement with a formally defined area;

(c) defining the area covered by the station. This can be used for various marketing purposes such as distribution of the advertiser's brand in a regional campaign.

These three functions could be satisfied by three different definitions. Potential audience could be independent of area whilst audience measurement could be limited to an area of dense reception and the marketing area based on another criterion. In fact, within the JICTAR system only one set of ITV areas (overlapping) are published; those current at mid 1970 are shown in Fig. 24.1. The potential audience for an ITV area is limited to a count within that ITV area. This area is sampled for the viewing research panels. This common solution to the three functions has created some strains. Some advertisers feel that the boundaries overlap too much for distribution purposes and devise their own different marketing areas sometimes from their own research. These problems barely exist for the BBC which is not concerned with marketing products and does not have clearly separated regional services.

Methods of measuring station reception

Asking the Respondent. In an 'out of home' interview an individual can be asked if his household has a television set and which stations can be received. It is generally felt that respondents are unreliable in identifying ITV stations where there is any doubt as to which ITV station or stations could be received. It is possible, however, to use aided recall to establish which set of programmes have been viewed. This still leaves open which alternative services were available and could be viewed.

Interviewer-Assessed Picture Quality. The JICTAR system, through AGB, and previously TAM, has measured reception by households, with an interviewer physically examining the set with the householder present and switching between the possible stations. A criterion of quality of reception is applied by trained interviewers. JICTAR currently uses a six-point scale defined by photographs and descriptions.

Respondent-Assessed Picture Quality. Similar information to that obtainable by interviewers has been asked for experimentally by post with the aim of reducing costs. The respondent is required to check the television set (by contrast with attempts to recall reception possibilities in a street interview). A comparison of answers with subsequent interviewer data has been carried out by AGB for a limited overlap situation. No overall biases were found in the postal technique. For individual households, reception and non-reception were generally accurately reported as was the quality of reception, with a few exceptions around the middle of the scale.

A further check of this postal technique has been considered by JICTAR

583

under the more complex conditions of UHF and where several ITV services can be received. There is, however, a difficulty in that complexity of reception sources is increasing over the next few years which means either delaying a further test or carrying out several tests at intervals.

Interviewer Check on Respondent-Assessed Channel Preferences. An interviewer calling on a household may check the reception capabilities of the set and then ask the respondent questions about his viewing habits. This is concerned with the problem of respondent classification rather than just reception measurement. This extension has been regarded as particularly important in relation to the situation where two ITV stations could be received. If one ITV station were strongly preferred, there could be arguments for counting that home as 'belonging' to one ITV station's potential audience and not to two.

A recent study for JICTAR by AGB examine the viewing records of most panel homes who receive two ITV stations. These were checked against their answers to the question, 'Out of every 10 hours watching ITV how many hours would you and your family watch each of the ITV transmitters?' This form of question contrasts with that on the National Readership Survey which, after asking whether ITV is received on more than one channel number on the set, then reads, 'Which ITV station do you (generally) watch if you are watching ITV?'

The conclusions from the JICTAR study were that classification of viewers as belonging to one ITV station and not another, when in fact they can receive two, is not meaningful for about 40 per cent of households because they do view both. A forced choice question hides this fact, although the station viewed a majority of times can be identified verbally in 80 per cent of cases if an interviewer is asking the question whilst checking the set. Asking the question away from the set relies on memory of station identifications or of channel numbers and becomes increasingly unreliable with the development of UHF. For the moment this means two forms of tuning per station and UHF is often tuned on a scale rather than having a discrete switch per channel.

Measuring Viewing Habits. Having established that a household's television set can receive more than one ITV station, any audience measurement technique can then be applied to establish whether stations are viewed in practice. This could then be used as a basis for classifying the household as 'belonging' to one or both stations. This procedure is clearly more elaborate and expensive than asking questions. To be at all useful, such a procedure would have to be quick, possibly measuring a week's viewing by diary or aided recall. Such a sampling of viewing may give an atypical result for some households although in another context Buck & West[13] have shown that total ITV viewing weight is consistent for four out of five consecutive weeks. Comparisons have not been made for choice between ITV stations.

584

Overall Comments. Measuring a household's television set reception capability is reasonably unambiguous if carried out by a competent interviewer checking the television set, although there may be difficulties when new reception possibilities are just opening up. It is getting increasingly difficult to measure reception possibilities without either the interviewer or the respondent checking the set.

For some purposes there may be a need to classify a respondent in terms of ITV stations habitually viewed rather than available to view, where more than one ITV station is received. It is not possible to allocate all households to just one ITV station; some who receive two view both and some view both about equally. Separate classification of individuals other than the housewife within households has not been examined but might have some meaning in multi-set households.

Possible approaches to household classification are asking a viewing allocation question or measuring a sample period of viewing, probably in both cases using the housewife as the respondent. Both approaches would correctly show some households as belonging to more than one ITV station and both would probably involve some inaccuracies of classification for the remainder. These shortcomings have to be evaluated in the light of the purpose of classification.

Methods of defining television areas

The previous section dealt with methods of measuring the television services available to an individual or household. It showed that some households were almost certain to be classed as receiving more than one ITV station.

An ITV area can be defined by a list of the smaller population units which are included, such as administrative districts. Defining an area, therefore, involves making decisions about possible districts; accepting or rejecting them on some criterion. Such criteria have tended to be based on the proportion of homes effectively covered by a station. It is conceptually possible to define separate areas for UHF and VHF or for colour but this has not been considered necessary so far and the combined effects of UHF and VHF transmitters are taken as the basis for area definitions.

The current JICTAR criterion for defining an ITV station area is that a district is included if 15 per cent or more of the households have sets capable of receiving that station from whatever source. Station areas overlap because a district may have 15 per cent of homes receiving each of two or more ITV stations. It is possible (although unlikely) for a district to be in two ITV station areas without any homes receiving two ITV stations. There could just be 15 per cent of homes receiving station A and another 15 per cent receiving station B.

In practice, there will be some receiving station A *and* B. Even if a classification method is found to reduce the number of these, for example, by referring to viewing habits as discussed above, this would still not necessarily greatly reduce overlap. Some possible alternative approaches to deciding whether a district should be included in an ITV area are listed in the following sections.

Inclusion of a District if a Fixed Percentage of Homes in the District Receive or View that Station. A representative sample is surveyed for the district. A decision is made about each home sampled. This could be on the criterion of reception or on actual viewing habits if the latter was acceptable. Each home is therefore classified as covered by the station or not. For a long time the criterion of 15 per cent has been used for industry ITV areas; if at least 15 per cent of the sample district can receive (or view) the station then the district is included. This criterion could be raised to reduce overlap. However, TAM in 1966 reviewed some limited data and concluded that an increase to 30 per cent would make little difference to overlap because density of reception fell off very sharply. The advent of UHF transmitters mixed with VHF may have changed this but there have been no further checks.

Inclusion of a District Based on ITV Station Received or Viewed by a Majority of Homes. This approach has not been tried but is a way in which overlap could be eliminated. One effect would be that some ITV viewing would go unrecorded and this would seem unsuitable as a basis for a measurement system.

Publication of Reception and Viewing Densities for Each District. This is a form of publication of data, not undertaken at the moment in the UK although used in the USA, which would enable marketing decisions to be taken about any district without referring to any fixed or permanent concept of a boundary. In so far as marketing requirements are often conflicting it has some advantages but in the UK the present level of JICTAR surveys would not yield data on enough districts to make this possible without grouping districts together.

Definition of Areas by Minimum Signal Strength Boundaries. For technical purposes authorities responsible for transmitters publish maps showing a contour defining the extent of a certain level of measured signal strength. How far this corresponds to a true reception boundary depends on alignment of aerials which in turn is affected by the history of services available to the area. Signal strength contours have been used in the UK to define the reception areas until true reception surveys have been completed.

Sampling in Relation to the Measurement of Television Reception. All JICTAR surveys relating to reception and potential audiences have been multi-stage random samples of households but with the personal interview usually conducted with the housewife. Minimum sample sizes of 1000 have been used for surveying in order to establish the potential audience for a total ITV area whose boundary is already defined. These are known as 'establishment surveys'.

For 'boundary surveys', each administrative district in question is sampled separately. Many districts may need to be surveyed and a decision made on each. The districts will often be at the periphery of ITV areas, and away from the main centres of population. This would make it unlikely that samples for any other survey purposes could be used.

Some years ago, TAM developed a sequential sampling procedure for determining whether or not a district qualifies for inclusion within an ITV area boundary. This involves surveying an initial minimum sample, usually 50. If the percentage of reception found can be regarded as above or below the criterion percentage at a pre-set level of confidence then the decision to include or exclude the district is taken at that stage. Otherwise, further samples are taken until the decision can be made at the pre-set level of confidence. This ensures considerable savings in sample sizes for districts with very high or low densities of reception. This method can only be used where the object of the survey is to make a decision about including a district rather than measure its absolute density of reception.

Systems of data collection in the UK

The definition of ITV areas and the establishment of potential audiences only occurs under the JICTAR system described below[14]. Other surveys do, however, involve establishing which media sources an individual receives and these are discussed briefly.

JICTAR. Establishment surveys to measure potential audiences for all ITV stations are carried out at a minimum of one per annum, usually referring to January. These surveys are carried out in conjunction with the AGB Home Audit whose prime purpose is the measurement of ownership of consumer durables. This survey interviews a multi-stage random sample of 35 000 households per quarter of which 25 per cent are new contacts, each household being interviewed in four quarters. The JICTAR surveys are based on some 24 000 interviews in 530 administrative districts using one half of the AGB Home Audit sample and augmenting this in certain ITV areas where the sample would otherwise fall below 1000, and in Northern Ireland which is not included in the Home Audit. Sample sizes of areas, therefore, range from the minimum of 1000 up to about 5000 in the London ITV area.

The television reception capabilities and detailed demographic data are obtained for all households. These establishment surveys provide:

(a) the size and nature of potential audiences to television stations;
(b) targets for the various characteristics by which the television viewing panels are stratified;
(c) a master sample from which television viewing panels are selected.

Boundary surveys are conducted when JICTAR subscribers agree that they are necessary. For established areas this is infrequently. The growth of UHF, however, means that new transmitters are changing the reception pattern. A guide to the effects of new transmitters has always been possible by monitoring the activities of television dealers. This has recently been set up more formally so that a panel of television dealers within the transmission range of a new transmitter are questioned at intervals so that it can be established when installation or adjustment activity after the opening of the transmitter has decreased sufficiently to warrant trying to define a stable reception area.

Defining a whole new boundary may require 5000 to 10 000 interviews, depending on the number of districts needing to be surveyed and the interviews required by the sequential sampling procedure.

Following a change in reception possibilities, in addition to boundary checks, it may be necessary to conduct special surveys of overlap areas to supplement existing establishment information and provide new estimates of potential audience.

Other Research Sources Measuring Reception and Television Ownership. The NRS asks its respondents which BBC and ITV services can be received. Where two or more ITV stations are received the respondent is asked which ITV station is generally watched. Asking questions without a physical check of the set may become more unreliable as station tuning complexities increase. Nevertheless, this source can be analysed for data on television reception.

Product/media surveys such as AMPS and TGI and various 'ad hoc' surveys, ask about television stations received, again without a physical check on the set.

The Attwood and TCA consumer panels both publish product-media data from time to time which requires some measurement of reception capabilities of panel members. With a panel home the opportunities exist for a physical check of the television set if necessary.

Various surveys may establish ownership of a television set among other durables, and other surveys may use declared ability to receive ITV as a stratification control.

Methods of establishing television reception vary so widely that it cannot be assumed that an 'ITV viewer' has a common basis of definition between surveys.

Techniques and Sources of Measurement for Broad Viewing Habits or Average Media Exposure Probabilities

Purpose of the data

In the longer term planning of future advertising campaigns, having identified those people who are the target market, it is necessary to establish which are the media vehicles by which they are most economically reached. This is often done by a narrowing down process; making decisions about whether

588

to use television and press, then which broad categories and, finally, which specific vehicles. Computerized media selection models would enable decisions to be made across a mass of vehicles from different media all at once, were it not for the lack of knowledge about the relative value of different kinds of media exposure. Such lack of knowledge presents an equal problem for the stage by stage approach, too, but the greater opportunity for making personal judgements may make this a more efficient way of using unquantified experience and certainly more reassuringly conceals lack of fundamental knowledge about media values.

Either approach generates a need for data relating to an individual which represents a prediction about his behaviour in terms relatable to his probability of exposure to the medium. It is likely that the more computerized the media selection process the more precisely defined in terms of vehicle, (i.e., timing in the case of television), the media exposure probability will have to be expressed.

As has already been pointed out, the biggest television research effort goes into the ratings service which obtains a continuous historical record of an individual's viewing. This continuous record can be condensed into probabilities of viewing the medium, defined with any level of precision; within a week, within an evening, within a certain time class or within a programme. Limitations to using this approach are cost, need for access to JICTAR basic data, and the fact that only a restricted range of information is available about the individuals on the panel, mainly their basic demographic characteristics.

Data about peoples' purchasing habits is frequently used to define marketing opportunities and target groups. The question of how to reach these target groups then leads to making simplified media measurements on product surveys and consumer panels. The suggestion has been made that detailed media and detailed product data could all be collected from a single source[7,8].

This section discusses methods of obtaining, for an individual, broader estimates of probability of exposure to television, mainly other than by collecting a detailed historical record of all viewing. These measures can be used either to link product and media data or as a stratification control in surveys where television exposure may be relevant. These methods may also be used in studies where the aim is to relate probability of exposure to the medium to some other attitudinal or behavioural variable.

Methods and sources of measuring broad viewing habits or television exposure probabilities

Derivation from Detailed Viewing Records. If detailed viewing records are routinely available, which is likely to be from the JICTAR panel in the UK, then viewing probabilities can be computed for a class of individuals for a single occasion of viewing or for a single individual averaged over a number of possible occasions of viewing, e.g., viewing three weeks out of four on

Monday at 7 p.m. gives a probability of 0.75 for that individual. Looking at a number of individuals like him could give a further average and a distribution of probabilities. This sort of calculation can be made by companies who can put JICTAR basic data tapes through a computer. No purchasing or other media data will be known about the individuals. It is, however, possible to combine viewing data like this with other forms of data via demographic characteristics using various data marriage systems[15,16].

It is also possible to obtain detailed viewing records for a short time period from respondents for whom purchasing or other information is available. Television diaries for a single week's viewing, for example, are completed by housewives in ITV homes on the Attwood Consumer Panels about every six months. On the TCA Panels a seven-day aided-recall survey is carried out on panel housewives three times a year. These techniques are discussed in the section below dealing with the measurement of audiences for time segments, programmes, and advertisements. In both cases the data obtained are used almost exclusively to classify housewives into the three viewing categories; heavy, medium, and light ITV viewers. This kind of intermittent collection of viewing records precludes the use of meters and generally less is known about their validity which is also discussed below. It is arguable, however, that if only broad classifications are to be used these may be accurate enough even though the precise details of viewing might be at fault. Some findings reported by Buck and Taylor[17] suggest that seven-day aided-recall as used by the TCA gives classifications as consistent as JICTAR data whilst producing overall higher levels of viewing.

Use of Questioning Techniques for General Classification by Weight of Viewing. Something like a standard set of questions to establish a weight of viewing classification has been developed over recent years. The first version of the questions appeared in AMPS (All Media and Product Survey)[18] carried out by Research Services for AMPSAC which yielded some partial validation based on comparing this claimed level of viewing with other viewing records obtained from the same people. A version of the questions was adopted by the NRS and by JICTAR where they were later slightly modified. Similar questions are also used in BMRB's Target Group Index (TGI).

The form and use of the questions by JICTAR are as follows:

Question one. How often do you watch television these days?

In answer the respondent indicates whether it is nearer to seven days, six, five, three or four, one, or two, or less often per week.

Question two. On a day when you watch, for about how many hours on average do you watch television?

In answer the respondent selects an answer from a scale running from 'none', 'over one and up to two', 'over two up to three', etc., etc., to 'over nine'.

590

Question three. About how many hours out of every ten that you watch television would you say that you watched ITV?

The respondent replies on a similar scale to question two with a zero and ten positions.

JICTAR applies this question on establishment surveys and for each respondent multiplies out the replies to the three questions to form claimed hours of ITV viewing. All respondents (housewives) in an ITV area can then be put into rank order, divided into equal thirds and thus defined as 'heavy', 'medium', or 'light' ITV viewers. The cut-off points could be used to classify other viewers outside the survey for that area and period. Such a procedure is bound to have a limited correspondence with actual viewing levels but can still be useful (see below) if it correlates at all.

AGB have compared the claimed viewing classification with actual viewing for a number of television panels. A typical result is shown in Table 24.1.

Table 24.1   *Comparison of weight of viewing classifications obtained from questions and from viewing records*

		Classification based on weight of viewing questions Percentage of Lancashire housewives		
		Heavy	Medium	Light
Classification based	Heavy	54	28	18
on actual ITV	Medium	34	32	32
viewing	Light	12	40	50
TOTAL		100%	100%	100%

Source: JICTAR/AGB
Lancashire Housewives four weeks ending 16 March 1969.

As is inevitable with categorization, if the basic figures are fairly continuous, there is bound to be a certain amount of blurring between adjacent categories. The correlation between the two sets of data is about 0.4 and there are about 10 per cent extreme misclassifications. Thus the correspondence between weight of viewing classifications obtained by questions and those obtained by measurement is only a rough one. The question answers are nevertheless useful if used with an awareness of their limitations. The main justification for their use is that they can be used when other methods are impossible on a short interview.

The terms 'heavy', 'medium', and 'light' viewers are used in many media contexts. Despite some standardization there are a number of slightly different bases of definition.

In comparing results from different surveys therefore it is worth checking whether the classification:

(a) relates to ITV (one station) or TV (all stations) viewing;
(b) is based on a household, housewife, or individual;
(c) is derived from actual viewing records and for which period;

(d) or from questions, and if so which;

(e) and how the classifications were derived from the viewing data or questions.

The Use of Questioning Techniques for Obtaining Segment Exposure Probabilities. The broad classifications mentioned above just give a general indication of media availability. Of more precise use in media planning and buying are probabilities of exposure relating to bookable units of the medium, like time segments. This is, of course, the prime purpose of the basic ratings system. Such segment data have sometimes been obtained in conjunction with product purchasing data. The TGI, using a long self-completion questionnaire, in addition to asking weight of viewing questions and which ITV station is usually viewed, also asks more detailed questions. Respondents are asked about their usual viewing for hourly time segments for Saturdays, Sundays, and weekdays (one fifth of the sample covering each weekday). They are also asked for major programmes, frequency of viewing in the average month and whether seen in the last seven days. This kind of data differs from the measurements in the following section in that it is mostly asking about usual behaviour rather than for a record of actual viewing. This form of television data is analogous to much data collected about press readership. No validation experiment has been carried out on this technique. This approach could still be useful in indicating relative probabilities even if absolute viewing levels were distorted, as they probably are when people record usual behaviour.

The Measurement of Audiences for Time Segments, Programmes, and Advertisements

Purpose of data

Regular data on audience size are collected under the JICTAR contract for those concerned with ITV both for advertising and programming purposes and by the BBC for programming alone. The emphasis in this chapter is upon advertising purposes but the total range of methodology common to both is considered here.

Although the concept of audience size sounds unambiguous there is a problem in deciding how to define an individual as part of the audience to some piece of a transmission. Does the individual just have to be present in the room with the set on, or should some attempt be made to include attention in the definition? How much of the piece of transmission does the individual have to have 'viewed' (however defined) in order to count as in the audience? Techniques vary as to how audiences are defined which often leads to problems of non-comparability of data.

It is generally felt that standard audience measurement techniques such as the meter-diary system are measuring something close to presence in the room with the set on. To probe further into behavioural attention requires special questioning. This has generated a class of 'attention studies' which have been experimental rather than regular sources of data collection.

Units of measurement can be time-based, expressed in minutes, quarter hours, or averages of separate minute readings, or content-based, covering commercials, breaks, programmes, or parts of programmes. Sometimes, the technique determines this basis, as with meters which must measure by time, but some techniques can be adapted to cover any unit. Within a single unit of measurement the quantity criterion may vary both intentionally and in how the viewer interprets instructions. The most commonly used approach is to ask viewers to count themselves as viewing if they cover more than half a quarter-hour or programme. On this basis, measured audience levels disregard brief absences from the room. Such absences could, however, cover some commercials under the industry quarter-hour measurement system. This has led to a sub-class of audience measurement work concerned with establishing presence levels during commercial breaks and seeking to relate these to conventionally measured quarter-hour data.

Techniques of measuring audiences for time segments, programmes and advertisements

In the sections below, techniques have been reviewed separately followed by discussion of some common problems.

Interviewing: Coincidental: Personal. It is perhaps appropriate that this is the first technique discussed since it is the one which has been regarded generally as the most artifact-free and therefore used as an expensive yardstick in validation studies.

In its simplest form, the coincidental technique makes a measurement of viewing at a given time by knocking on the door of an individual's home at that time and asking whether the individual (and perhaps other household members) had the set on and were viewing at the time of the knock. In this simplest form it is clearly an expensive technique, one interview yielding a measurement for just an instant of television transmission time. There is also a major problem for the technique in that it is not reasonable to knock on doors after about 9.30 p.m. in the summer and perhaps earlier in winter. This again makes for use of the technique for methodological purposes rather than routine data collection. There are a number of further questions about the coincidental technique which require discussion and have to be settled in the light of the aim of the survey and pilot work.

First, it is obviously efficient to keep evening interviews short and to maximize the number of effective calls an interviewer can make. This inevitably means clustering which should be done as carefully as possible. It also means that it may be worthwhile to split the survey into two stages. At the first enumeration stage, by day, a sample of households is interviewed to establish which can receive the appropriate television services and their demographic details. The second call, therefore, can be confined to the true universe for the study and questioning limited to who was viewing what. It has been possible to conduct these interviews at about eight per hour[9]. Clearly, the home should not be forewarned at the first interview that a check will be made on their viewing later.

Second, there is a problem about what exact time period the interview covers. Unless all interviewers are issued with special watches it may be difficult to keep to precise timing. This makes it a difficult technique to use in relation to commercials if time alone is to be relied upon and no reference made to what is on the screen.

There is a choice as to whether viewing is asked about, or just presence in the room. If respondents are questioned about other behaviour such as reading or ironing, as in attention studies, they may give an answer which really covers, say, the last five minutes since these activities may be discontinuous.

Third, a decision is necessary as to how to treat refusals and non-contacts. Refusals at a second stage are rare if previously contacted respondents are interviewed. Ignoring refusals equates their behaviour with cooperators. An ARF study in the USA[19] found that refusals on a one-stage survey had different (lower) viewing levels than co-operators but this may not be a general rule.

Non-contacts, or a sample of them, can be called back on the next day to check whether they were out or viewing and not answering the door. The latter occurs to a small extent. It can be measured on a sub-sample and total figures adjusted accordingly.

The problems of coincidental interviewing and practical solutions are well displayed in an industry study by TAM[9] and one by BMRB[20].

Interviewing: Coincidental: Telephone. Coincidental interviewing about television by telephone is the norm in the US and almost unknown in the UK, where the level of telephone ownership is felt to be so low as to bias samples in relation to television viewing.

The absolute accuracy of normal telephone coincidental interviewing in the US was challenged in CONTAM Study No. 4[21] where it was found to slightly underestimate ratings. This study showed that results could vary with training and supervision of interviewers, procedural rules for dealing with contact difficulties, and rules for interpreting non-contacts. Telephone interviewing will undoubtedly increase in the UK as the proportion of telephone ownership increases. It is not known whether present telephone owners differ in viewing behaviour from demographically similar non-owners. If they did not, then telephone interviewing would be possible if some means could be found for obtaining, economically, samples balanced to match the television universe.

Interviewing: Near-Coincidental: Personal. This approach consists of making what is almost a normal coincidental interview and questioning back over the recent viewing periods. Interviews covering the last hour of viewing

594

conducted during evening viewing time have been used in the past by LPE[22] and TAM[23]. A version of this technique was developed in an industry study by BMRB for the IPA and ISBA[10,20] where the objective was to measure presence in commercial breaks. The difficulty of precise timing was overcome by scheduling calls just after a commercial break, checking at the interview that the break had just occurred and then effectively carrying out aided recall backwards over the last three commercial breaks and intervening programming. This procedure is best illustrated diagrammatically as in Fig. 24.2.

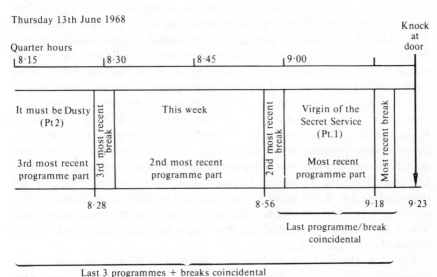

Fig. 24.2. The interview obtaining near-coincidental data.

Each successive break and programme segment asked about involves a longer memory span. The validity of this approach was supported by the fact that there were not significant differences between results for the same break or programme, whether asked one, two, or three back in time. The viewing levels reported, where comparable, were consistent with TAM data published at the time. One study may not represent conclusive proof of validity for the technique. Nevertheless this seems a promising way of getting more than one minute's data from a call during viewing time. It appears to be the most viable way of studying presence in commercial breaks at present. It is, however, subject to the limitation that it cannot be used late at night and is still relatively costly.

Interviewing: Recall: Aided and Unaided, Next Day and Seven Day. A variety of media research problems are approached through various kinds of recall techniques.

First, next-day recall of specific commercials is used as a kind of on-air advertising testing procedure and according to circumstances may be

595

attempting to measure attention and communication aspects of the advertisement. This is really advertising effectiveness research.

Second, next-day aided recall was used by the London Press Exchange in 1961 in some experimental studies to measure the behaviour of audiences to television advertisements[22]. This next-morning recall technique involved showing a programme sheet with ITV and BBC programmes laid out side by side on a time scale, the ITV list showing where the commercial breaks came. Respondents indicated which programmes they had viewed and were then taken through the list with careful probing as to when they started and stopped and whether they saw the commercial breaks. After rating their liking for the programmes seen, they were then asked for each commercial break what their behaviour had been at the time, classified into a number of possible activities. This sounds a difficult matter to recall from the previous evening. The LPE studies compared results from this technique with those from similar questions asked of a different sample on the actual evening of viewing and covering the most recent hour of viewing. Housewives in the morning recalled consistently less activity during breaks than those asked in the evening. The various kinds of activities were reported in similar proportions from evening or morning. Men, however, reported slightly more activity during commercials in the morning and there were some noticeable but non-significant differences in kinds of activity reported. Despite the optimism of the LPE reports these and other differences between next morning re-call and evening re-call suggests that more methodological work would be needed before findings from 'next morning data' could be interpreted with confidence.

Third, another technique which was used in the LPE studies, hopefully as a measure of attention to commercials, was based on the ability of programme viewers to identify commercials that had appeared from a list containing three commercials shown and three not shown in a particular break. For a commercial break this yields measures of correct responses for true commercials and for false commercials and a 'no decision' score.

Results from the technique were also compared from evening and morning interviews. There were more 'no decision' responses from next morning data, but of the decisions made the proportions correct were mostly similarly related to factors like time, reported viewing behaviour and interest in programme, whether from evening or morning interviews. The use of these recognition procedures in relation to commercials seem promising but has not had the necessary methodological development since the LPE studies.

Fourth, 'next-day aided recall' designed to cover all transmission times in a comprehensive service measuring audience size is used by the BBC[24]. Interviewers ask first about yesterday's radio listening and then about television viewing. Television viewing is probed from a list of programmes and start times for available services shown side by side. A programme is counted as viewed if the viewer claims to have seen more than half of it. A quota sample is interviewed in public places or at home.

A version of 'next-day aided recall' tested in the TAM Comparison Survey[9] used simplified displays of programmes taken from the programme magazines printed out side by side in the questionnaire. The respondent was taken through the programmes but viewing was recorded on the questionnaire by quarter hours. This technique, using a random sample, was close to the coincidental results in the TAM Comparison Survey in peak time but significantly under-reported in early time (5.30 p.m. to 7 p.m.). This result has been interpreted as suggesting that a technique relying on memory may be less accurate when covering periods of low attention or less distinctive programmes.

BBC data has correlated well with JICTAR data[11] although the systems have never produced exactly similarly defined statistics, so that absolute levels can never be compared.

Fifth, 'seven-day aided recall' is one of the most economical techniques in that a whole week's viewing is collected at a single interview. Each informant is taken back over programme aids such as the programme magazines or some derivation from them and questioned more closely about exact timing. The viewing record can be completed by the interviewer in terms of quarter hours or half hours viewed. This technique was used by Granada Television in 1959/60, studied in the TAM Comparison Survey 1961, and used by Marplan for JICTAR 1962/64 to produce data on more demographic groups than the meter-diary service. The technique is currently used intermittently with TCA panels to establish housewife weight of viewing classifications. The technique has been surrounded by controversy, heated because seven-day aided recall appeared to offer a cheaper alternative to more expensive industry services and arising from the possibility of interpreting limited validation evidence in alternative ways.

Extensive, if somewhat perplexing, discussion of seven-day recall is given by Ehrenberg[11,25]. Evidence and interpretation from various sources is conflicting and discussed a little in a section below. A reasonable conclusion would appear to be that the data need not generally get any worse over the seven days as the recall period gets longer, but that the technique does report relatively low-levels of viewing in early time and possible off-peak time generally. The suggestion of over-reporting in peak time depends on whether one expects exact correspondence with coincidental interviewing. The technique has produced slightly different deviations from the JICTAR meter-diary data on different groups of surveys suggesting some sensitivity to small variations in procedure.

A recall aid, discussed by Simmons[26], with considerable potential for methodological work is a series of story-boards which can show the progress of transmissions through programmes and breaks.

Meter Recording of Set Switching. The most comprehensive form of meter is a device which, when fitted to a television set records, with precise timing, to which channel the set is tuned when switched on.

Such a meter needs to be capable of recording an increasing number of channels and adaptable to changing structure of television sets particularly in relation to switching and tuning, and to be robust and attractive. The meter currently used in the JICTAR systems is AGB's SETMETER (Fig. 24.3). A different approach is used in the INTOMETER in use in Holland where a signal within the station's transmission signal is recorded by the meter if received. Other meters are in use in different parts of the world.

Fig. 24.3
(Reproduced with the permission of AGB Ltd.).

Designing, developing, and mass producing trouble-free meters is a costly capital investment with design the least of the problems. This clearly limits the amount of commercial competition to operate meter services although JICTAR will actually own its present meters. No doubt meters will become smaller but they are unlikely to become cheaper. Other areas of development include how the data recorded by the meter are collected and processed. The original 'TAMmeters' produced spools of track-marked tapes collected weekly by interviewers. More recent meters have tapes detachable by the housewife, posted by her and read by machines. An obvious next stage is the direct transmission of the data from the home by line to the data processing unit. Surprisingly enough, such systems were developed in the UK by TAM and Nielsen in the late 'fifties' but were not commercially viable. As facilities for direct transmission of information increase an on-line meter system producing instantaneous ratings may become a possibility. A fuller description of some current meters is given by Webb[27].

Meters have a double role in audience research methodology:

(a) to produce a precise time record of the channels to which the set is tuned. There are two components—the timing of switching and the identification of the channel;
(b) as a monitoring device used in conjunction with diaries. This also works in two ways—the 'on' and 'off' records serve as a check against diary keeping and the presence of the meter has a psychological incentive value in that the household knows that some check is being made. The set switching record also relieves diary keepers of the need to identify the channel viewed.

The records of set running which the meter produces make it usable on its own although 'audiences' could only be expressed in terms of sets tuned. The graphs currently produced under the JICTAR systems are in this form. Set switching data are, in fact, a useful way of looking at audiences because that is where the main variation arises.

Set switching data could be used in conjunction with 'people data' from another source, although if the latter were collected continuously it is difficult to see what advantage there would be in collecting it separately unless larger samples were used for more breakdowns or the meter panel was required to keep other records such as purchasing diaries.

Meters eliminate virtually all possible sources of error in recording set switching. The only possible bias that might be created is that panel members know the correct time, but the clock faces could be eliminated if this seemed important.

Meters discussed in this section so far do not include devices which merely record total set usage which is only of use as a partial monitoring device for diaries. These include the Nielsen/TAM Recordimeter and AGB's Metrilog used currently in the Channel Isles.

Diaries: Fully Monitored. These are diaries used with meters where the meter records set switching and channel. The individual records only viewing in the room with the set on and has no need to identify channel. Furthermore, if the individual completes the records totally from his imagination or fading memory the disparity with the meter record is immediately noticed and an interviewer can visit. In the present JICTAR system the diaries are read by machine and their data checked against and incorporated with meter records within the computer. This kind of system checked well against coincidental interviewing in the TAM Comparison

Survey[9]. It is the only validated technique which must be immune to problems from the increasing complexity of services available since the respondent does not record what he is viewing, only when he is viewing.

The current JICTAR diaries have separate pages for each individual in the household and for guests and cover each quarter hour of transmissions. The diaries for the household are posted in weekly with the meter tape.

Individuals ideally mark their diaries when they start and finish viewing sessions filling in the quarter hours in between. In practice, they may well fill in their diaries more in arrears than that, although grosser malpractices are eliminated by being part of a monitored supervised panel. Any attempt to get individuals to punch their viewing onto the meter tape, however, would be likely to fail since once having forgotten to record they could not redeem themselves from memory. Some of present diary recording is undoubtedly recall but the important thing is that it produces validated accurate answers.

Being a set-based technique, one set of diaries and one meter is required for each set in a home.

Diaries: Partially Monitored. Diaries can be used in conjunction with devices like the Recordimeter or Metrilog which record total set usage in coded form which the respondent notes down. This provides a check on his other recording good enough to indicate serious malpractice in diary keeping and the incentive value probably improves upon this. This kind of technique was closest to coincidental interviewing in the simple ITV–BBC situation in the TAM Comparison Survey. This form of diary, however, requires that individuals record which channel the set is tuned to as well as when they are viewing, usually by quarter hours. New problems may arise as reception possibilities become more numerous and difficult to distinguish. Whilst it seems likely that panel members could be trained to record channel accurately, further validation would be advisable before using the technique more widely in the UK multi-channel situation. Again, one set of diaries will be required for each television set in the home.

Diaries: Unmonitored. Unmonitored diaries are potentially the cheapest form of audience research particularly if they could be used by post.

Diaries can take a variety of forms. Somehow, the respondent must indicate the channel viewed and minimally the start and finish times of viewing sessions. Some possible formats include the following.

(a) *Time-Scale Diaries*

The channel to which the set is tuned can be recorded on one scale with further columns to be marked by individuals present, or individuals may indicate channel by the column used. Basically these diaries would be like the successful Recordimeter diaries without the Recordimeter. All entries are recorded on grids representing time units, usually quarter hours. No strict validation exercise has been conducted. The AMPS survey used time-based unmonitored diaries[4,18,28] and the results were reasonably close to TAM data from metered diaries. There could be problems with more complex reception possibilities.

(b) *Start and Finish Time Diaries*

This form of diary has been used in the USA by ARB[29] and experimentally in the UK by AGB. The respondent records the start and finish times of viewing sessions, i.e., when the set is turned to and then from a channel the name of which has to be entered in another column. Individuals present can be recorded in separate columns. Data from the ARB system in the US has in the past correlated well with the Nielsen meter/diary data[30,31]. This form of diary apparently gives minute by minute data although probably misses brief absences. It seems quite a promising layout particularly as it has succeeded in US multi-channel conditions. Further validation would be necessary in the UK.

(c) *Programme Diaries*

These diaries show the titles of programme parts for the services obtainable. There will be errors due to last minute programme changes. This form of diary is probably the most attractive for the viewer. It has been used, mainly for obtaining classification data, on the Attwood Consumer Panels.

(d) *Programme-Break Diaries*

This, at one time, seemed the most economical and promising technique for establishing presence in commercial breaks with possible extensions to cover attention.

Programme and break diaries have been used by TAM[23] and BMRB[32] and have produced very meaningful-looking results showing how the pattern of viewing varied between programmes and breaks. That technique, using the format shown in Fig. 24.4 was subjected to a rigorous programme of validation through an IPA and ISBA industry group with BMRB as the research company[10,20]. The pilot stages involved the identification of certain 'wrong-looking' completion syndromes, with later evening calls on those homes to see how they were keeping their diaries. This established a number of patterns which should be rejected, some arising from completion in advance as well as the more conventional completion in arrears.

On the main study the diary results were checked against coincidental data.

Surprisingly, in view of the success of other unmonitored diaries, the viewing levels recorded by the diary were much too high compared with coincidental data which were in line with TAMmeter diary results. Furthermore, many of the most interesting findings from this kind of diary appeared to be artifacts. Whether such a diary could succeed if monitored by a meter and with greater training and supervision of respondents is untested.

Observers. An experimental approach to studying viewing behaviour in depth is for someone present in the room during viewing to record the behaviour of the others present. This has been done by RBL[33] placing selected interviewers in the homes of a television viewing sample for two consecutive evenings. Much useful information was obtained about family activities in relation to viewing although there must have been an influence on the behaviour observed.

The experimental TAM study with programme break diaries[23] asked other members of the household to complete the diary about the housewife where this was possible, otherwise she completed it herself.

TUESDAY   Early evening
11th June   up to 7.30 p.m.

Office use   16.1 17.4 18.1

1. Have you viewed any of these television stations during this part of the evening in your own home?

NORTHERN ITV	Yes ✔ / No	**BBC 1**	Yes ✔ / No
OTHER ITV	Yes / No ✔	**BBC 2**	Yes / No ✔

2. If you do view any television at home during this part of the evening, please complete the diary below, placing a tick in one of the five columns (A, B, C, D or E) for each programme part and commercial break listed.

BBC 1

HAVE YOU VIEWED ON BBC 1:—

		A All	B Most	C About half	D Not much	E None	Office Use
4.40	Jackanory					✔	20.
4.55	Deputy Dawg					✔	21.
5.15	Tom Tom					✔	22.
5.20	All Change					✔	23.
5.45	The Magic Roundabout					✔	24.
5.50	The News	✔					25.
5.55	Look North	✔					26.
6.15	Whicker's World			✔			27.
7.05	Z Cars					✔	28.

BBC 2

HAVE YOU VIEWED ON BBC 2:—

		A All	B Most	C About half	D Not much	E None	Office Use
7.05	Bonjour Francoise					✔	33.

Fig. 24.4. A programme/break diary.

NORTHERN ITV

HAVE YOU VIEWED ON NORTHERN ITV:—

		A	B	C	D	E	Office Use
		All	Most	About half	Not much	None	
.40	Thunderbirds Part 1					✓	41.
	Commercial Break					✓	42.
	Thunderbirds Part 2					✓	43.
.05	Felix The Cat					✓	44.
.10	World Of Life					✓	45.
	Commercial Break					✓	46.
.20	Come Here Often Part 1					✓	47.
	Commercial Break					✓	48.
	Come Here Often Part 2					✓	49.
	Commercial Break					✓	50.
.55	News					✓	51.
.05	Northern News					✓	52.
	Commercial Break					✓	53.
.10	New Faces					✓	54.
	Commercial Break					✓	55.
.30	All Our Yesterdays			✓			56.
	Commercial Break		✓				57.
.00	Turn Of Fate Part 1	✓					58.
	Commercial Break				✓		59.
	Turn Of Fate Part 2	✓					60.
	Commercial Break	✓					61.

A number of studies in the US have recruited interviewers, sometimes students, to observe their own families, whilst viewing[34,35]. Another study by CBS[36] on television and press was concerned with the advertising effectiveness of specific advertisements and the observations were to record exposure rather than conditions of viewing.

The use of observers runs the risk of getting either atypical behaviour or atypical samples. The technique can be used, however, to get information otherwise inaccessible. It thus has considerable potential where the inevitable atypicalities can be discounted or allowed for.

Cameras. Cameras can be used with a television set to take pictures of the viewing audience and the screen itself via a mirror. This can be arranged to occur at time intervals or be triggered by some transmitting device. It could thus cover commercial breaks, or rather a sample of them because a picture covers a short exposure time compared with most television measurements. Problems associated with the technique are similar to those for observers. It is likely that co-operation rates would be low and that respondent behaviour may be affected by the presence of the camera even if it can be turned off. There is the further problem of interpretation of the pictures. A brief observation of how people watch television is revealing; they instantaneously pass through a wide range of postures in attentive behaviour which overlaps with inattentive behaviour. The camera obviously records presence versus absence unambiguously and may have some methodological applications. An account of some experimental work in the US is given by Allen[37].

Detectors. Detection machinery is capable of registering that the television set is on from the outside of a house. The technique has been used by the ARF in the US as a means of establishing whether refusals and non-contacts in a coincidental survey had their television sets switched on[19]. The machine used had limitations in that it could only be used unambiguously for detached houses. This would seem to be a technique with a clear but very limited methodological potentiality.

Validity of Television Audience Research Techniques. It is unfortunate that techniques which have never been subjected to any validation test are used with more confidence than those which have been tested and found to have perhaps only limited faults.

The biggest study was the TAM Comparison Survey in 1961, sponsored by an industry committee. This survey was, in many ways, a model of planning and compared against coincidental interviewing, TAMmeter monitored diaries, Recordimeter-monitored diaries, 'one-day' and 'seven-day aided recall', all on sample sizes of 500 households per quarter hour comparison.

The recall methods showed under-reporting in early evening. For peak time, all the techniques deviated in the same direction, i.e., above the coincidental level, but the recall slightly more than the diary methods. Thus, if the comparisons are made with the coincidental survey the recall methods show most significant differences, the interpretation made in the report. If, however, the main techniques are compared among themselves, there are few significant differences between them, the interpretation offered by Ehrenberg[25]. Logically, being averages of instantaneous readings and, therefore, depleted by all brief absences, the coincidental ratings should be lower than those from the other techniques which are based on seeing more than half of the units measured and, therefore, not depleted by some brief absences. Thus, the results of all techniques should have been higher than those for coincidental interviews by an unknown amount and they were higher for peak time. This, perhaps, leaves as the only certain finding that the recall techniques were under-reporting in early evening. There are other possible adjustments which can be made to the data to cover definition differences[38].

The foregoing discussion illustrates the difficulty of establishing validity unambiguously even with a large, expensive, and well-planned study. A further limitation on this study was that, because of the enormous commitment of coincidental interviewing (500 interviews per quarter hour added up to nearly 9000 interviews per evening), only three evenings could be covered and between 5.30 p.m. and 9.30 p.m. It so happened that ITV ratings graphs on those evenings were fairly smooth and no exceptional programmes occurred. Thus, nothing is known about the techniques in relation to late evening, sharply changing audience levels, or unusual programmes. Other gaps in our knowledge include children's viewing. The TAM Comparison Survey covered only adults. Most techniques are used with children, sometimes with adults reporting. The validity of some of these procedures seems somewhat unlikely for the youngest age groups.

For the UK, any technique, apart from those using meters for channel identification, may well be affected by changing reception possibilities. For some time there may be, in parallel, VHF services which the viewer switches between, and UHF services (perhaps exactly the same as VHF plus BBC-2 but perhaps with a different ITV service) which are tuned rather than switched. In the UK, compared with the US, station signs are not so prominent and ITV stations are very much alike at peak-time because of networking. Thus, even US evidence on validity in multi-choice situations, whilst reassuring, is not acceptable without question in the UK. This does not mean that all techniques other than meters are hopeless in a multi-channel situation, just that they need testing.

. A further UK validation study was the IPA and ISBA Television Audience Presence Research in 1968 carried out by BMRB[20]. Many of the findings have already been mentioned. This study, concerned with more detailed measurements than normal ratings research, supported near-coincidental interviewing and largely invalidated the programme-break diaries. This result is a salutary one for market research because the data from the invalidated technique had a lot of 'face validity', i.e., they supported widely held views. The truth, if that is what was established, was much less interesting. For this study, too, there could be well be some alternative interpretation of the coincidental findings.

In the US a programme of validation work has been conducted for CONTAM[21,30], an industry group representing broadcasters. There have been four studies so far. Number one showed that sampling theory applied to audience measurement which, although enjoyable, seemed to be a large hammer to crack an opened nut. Number two compared Nielsen meter panel data and ARB diary sample data and found them basically in agreement. This implied that there were no conditioning effects on the Nielsen panel and no other mechanical fieldwork errors unless they cancelled out. Number three demonstrated a bias in audience size estimates because of non-co-operation, discussed below. Number four examined the telephone coincidental technique and has already been discussed. Some smaller scale validation studies are reported by Simmons[26].

Thus, large scale methodological and validation studies normally seem to occur with industry backing, and are very expensive. Even the best validation studies raise some problems of interpretation and absolute validity is largely a myth. In practice, many techniques are either accepted on 'face validity', which can be dangerous, or because their results compare well with those of other techniques which may have some validation support.

Emphasis has been laid here upon the limited knowledge about the validity of many of these techniques. Validity, however, is most usefully considered relatively and more is known about techniques in television audience research than in most areas of market research and the methodological problems to be solved are probably slightly easier.

Panel Controls, Sample Design, and Special Problems in Television Audience Research. The running of panels and designing of samples are topics dealt with elsewhere in this book. The present discussion concerns some problems particularly related to television research.

(a) *Conditioning and Running-in*

What little evidence there is, suggests that conditioning is not a problem with meter-diary systems. Newly recruited Recordimeter samples gave similar results to existing TAMmeter panels and both matched the coincidental results[9]. Similarly, long-running Nielsen panels gave similar results to fresh ARB samples in CONTAM[30]. A Nielsen study[39] and a number of 'ad hoc' survey results which match panel data also confirm these findings.

Related to conditioning is the question of running-in periods for diaries. *A priori* it could be rationalized that diaries are kept most conscientiously when people are fresh to it and they then tire *or* that people have to learn to fill in diaries and are best after a running-in period *or* that people behave atypically at first and then settle down. The evidence is scanty and conflicting. Unmonitored diaries run by BMRB[40] and Research Services for AMPS[28] showed consistency over their first twelve and eight weeks respectively. This was taken as evidence against the need for running-in periods. JICTAR experience has been, however, that monitored diary results on long running panels are sensitive to contact with interviewers and instructions, e.g., in relation to the recording of guest viewing. The high levels obtained by IPA/ISBA programme/break diaries also support the view that diaries are more sensitive to format and procedures than had been believed. The only deduction one can make from a mixture of evidence is that individual cases need testing.

(b) *Co-operation Biases, Panel Controls, and Stratifications*

A number of studies in the USA[30,39,41] have shown that co-operators in samples and panels in television audience research view more than non co-operators. The amount varies with study and co-operation rate. The effect may be partly compensated for by substitution procedures involving stratification controls.

JICTAR has adopted a stratification procedure which applies a control by weight of viewing classification. On establishment surveys respondent housewives are asked the questions discussed on page 590 and divided into equal 'heavy', 'medium', and 'light' ITV viewing thirds. Recruitment to the viewing panels is equally divided between these thirds. At the initial sign-up of the AGB panels it was found that response rate increased with viewing weight classification. Overall it varied between 65 per cent to 75 per cent of households originally selected for the AGB Home Audit. It was possible to compare viewing level results on the panel *with* the viewing control operating, against what would have happened *without* the viewing control. For one area it seemed that ratings would have been some five per cent higher without the control. Table 24.2 shows how demographically similar groups viewed more in the initial sign-up group *without* the weight of viewing balance than in the final balanced panel *with* the weight of viewing control. Other ITV areas examined showed less effect but in the same direction.

Table 24.2 *ITV viewing hours with and without weight of viewing control*
(week ending 24 November, 1968: Midlands Area)

	With/without children		Social class		No. in household			Age of housewife		
	with	without	ABC1	C3DE	1–2	3	3	−35	35–64	65+
S/U (without control)	19.3	18.5	14.1	20.5	16.8	21.2	19.7	17.9	20.2	17.0
Total balanced panel	18.9	17.1	13.3	19.6	15.1	20.1	19.4	17.7	18.9	15.9

Source: JICTAR/AGB

It was shown earlier on page 591 that the weight of viewing classifications only roughly correlated to viewing. This section demonstrates how an imperfect measure can, nevertheless, be useful. Even an irrelevant stratification correctly applied cannot be harmful[42]. These first results of controlling a panel by a direct forecast of what it is supposed to be measuring seem promising.

In JICTAR panels normal demographic controls are applied (for a full list see JICTAR[14]) marginally and interlaced.

The BBC reported in 1961[43] that terminal education age was associated with ITV and BBC preferences which makes it an appropriate control. Other stratification controls used by JICTAR include reception capabilities and geographical location in relation to ITV areas.

There may be value in some form of multivariate analysis of television viewing which would group people by the similarities in certain aspects of their viewing behaviour and provide other data about the groups. This might establish either groups of people or factors which were as meaningful as the heavy viewing syndrome and which could be used as a basis for stratification controls, perhaps in place of some of the less effective demographic controls.

It is also important to establish more about biases not only at the sign-up but arising from differential dropout with panels. For various reasons the

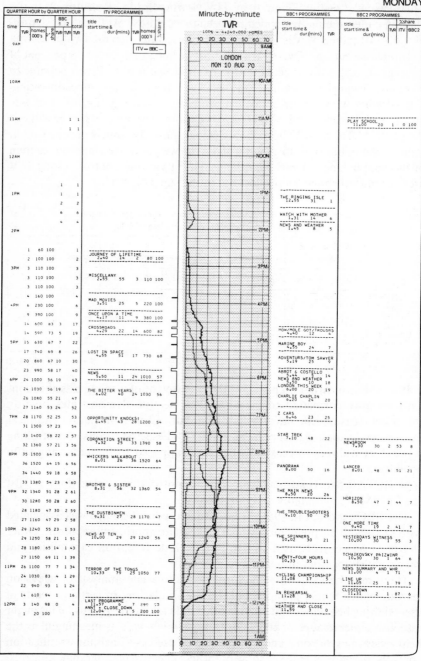

Fig. 24.5
(Reproduced with permission of JICTAR).

total turnover of JICTAR panels is about 25 per cent per annum. The first drop-outs from AGB were biased towards heavier viewers cancelling some of the signing bias. Perhaps the evidence suggesting lack of conditioning also supports the view that differential drop-out in panels does not cause much atypicality.

Systems of research in the UK

Much of the methodology of various research systems operative in the UK have already been described. The two continuous research systems concerned with audience size are controlled by JICTAR and the BBC.

JICTAR's present contract is placed with AGB and expires in 1974. ITV areas are defined by boundary surveys when necessary. Establishment surveys measuring the potential audiences in ITV areas are carried out at least once a year, currently referring to January. This data collection is fully integrated with the AGB Home Audit, using multi-stage stratified random samples. Sample sizes range from 5000 in London down to a minimum of 1000. From the establishment survey samples, and matching them on the stratification control characteristics, the viewing panels are selected. Net reporting panel sizes range from 350 households, nearly 1000 people, in London to minimum sizes of 100 households and around 300 people. The net panels are selected weekly and balanced from gross panels some 15 per cent higher to allow for unavailability of records for any reason. Each household member has a meter and diary for each set in the home. Recording is continuous and by all family members, meter tape and diaries being posted in weekly on Mondays. Interviewers call for the purpose of diary re-education when necessary and at least every six weeks, for general contact, and collect records in times of postal breakdown. Weekly reports start appearing within a week following receipt of records.

The reports show charts as in Fig. 24.5 for all areas and days. Programme and quarter hour audiences are shown. For commercial breaks costs per thousand homes, adults, housewives, men, women, and children are compared with the previous four-week average. All commercials shown are listed chronologically with their audiences and by brands in product groups. Thrice-yearly reports show quarter-hour data for more detailed audience composition groups. Data are also supplied to users on tapes and special analysis facilities available. The most frequently-used special analyses show the coverage and frequency of viewing by a target group for schedules of spot times covering several weeks. These are based on the continuous records for individuals.

A fuller description of the JICTAR system is available in the JICTAR Reference Manual[14] and elsewhere[7].

JICTAR carries out only audience size measurements and relevant methodological work.

The BBC audience size measurement system is based on a continuous fieldwork operation interviewing a national quota sample of 2250 individuals aged five years and over, per day. Interviewers ask about listening and viewing on the previous day. Television viewing involves a degree of aided recall from the interviewer's programme log with the respondent proceeding chronologically through the evening.

Reports issued for internal BBC use include a daily barometer of viewing showing percentages of the UK population viewing BBC-1, BBC-2, ITV networks and some regional ITV programmes. Daily charts show nationally BBC-1 versus ITV overall, and are likely to cover BBC-2 in the future. A weekly bulletin summarizes trends in viewing and findings of special interest.

The BBC also measures audience reaction to programmes and conducts and commissions 'ad hoc' studies on a variety of topics. A description of the BBC systems and methods is available[24].

The two systems, JICTAR and BBC, are often presented to the outside world as in conflict because the much publicized audience share figures are higher for the BBC from the BBC system than from JICTAR. In fact, the figures represent different things as well as coming from different systems. The BBC data are based on individuals in all homes for certain time periods whilst JICTAR figures refer to set usage in ITV homes for all time periods.

BBC fieldwork involves the interviewers identifying themselves as from the BBC and using quota sampling. Both these aspects are felt by the BBC, on the basis of some experimental work, not to affect results.

Despite differences in total levels, BBC share figures show the same trends as JICTAR data and BBC ratings, insofar as they can be compared, correlate quite well with those of JICTAR[11].

No other continuous research systems exist in the UK. Work on audience behaviour in the form of presence and attention has been experimental. Audience reaction data for ITV has been run for an experimental panel recently (see p. 615). For a while, the TAM TVQ system (pp. 614 and 615) was produced regularly and bought by the ITA, some programme companies and advertising agencies.

As has been mentioned, there has been discussion about integrating the JICTAR system with other research systems[8] but there are no concrete proposals as yet.

The Measurement of Responses to Television Viewing

Purpose of the data

The most fundamental response to a television transmission is watching some of it. The measurement of exposure to television transmissions has been the subject of previous sections. This section is concerned with other forms of response mostly dependent on having seen transmissions. Some of them are already dealt with in other chapters and are, therefore, only briefly referred to here.

The purposes of measuring the further responses to transmissions viewed depend naturally on the purposes of the transmissions and these may sometimes become complex to define.

An advertiser initiates transmission of advertisements ultimately to increase his profits against what they would have been without advertising. He may think that this will be achieved through some intermediate and more readily measureable sub-goals such as attention to his advertisement, the communication and understanding of his advertising message, retention of certain facts, the change of certain attitudes and the formation of 'intentions to buy' his brand. Whilst it is likely that advertising can *sometimes* work this way it is clear that it does not *always* work this way (see chapter 17). Nevertheless, this is the easiest way to study advertising effects so that, whether appropriate or not, advertisers sometimes adopt this approach. Advertisers may also attempt the more difficult task of relating sales to media exposure.

Those making and screening programmes have complex aims to fulfil according to the basis of their legal franchises. In simplified terms these aims amount to satisfying certain requirements which the public has, for entertainment, news, information, education, and special personal interests.

Defining these requirements in terms of who has them, how important they are and how they might be met for different people, is such an overwhelming task that it has largely discouraged any attempts at comprehensive research. If requirements can be deduced from other research, or merely hypothesized, in terms such as entertainment, information, etc., then respondents can be asked to score programmes on scales based on these 'requirements'. This gives some impression of the way in which programmes are being received. The simplest form of this research is to apply a simple scale of liking to all programmes. Thereafter one can progress from a few to many scales. It is also possible to attempt to simplify the problems by creating a programme typology[44] and a viewer typology[45]. This whole area is, of course, an application of the methodology of attitude research fully discussed elsewhere in this book. Only some special points of relevance to the medium are therefore mentioned here.

In addition to checking how far programmes meet rather general overall requirements, there may be occasions when a study in greater depth is needed on the impact of a specific programme or series. This may be to check achievement of the detailed aims of the programme-maker, such as the comprehensibility of a documentary and the communication of certain information.

The advertiser, too, may have an interest in programme research because he feels it will enable him to predict where the highest target audiences are or because he believes that attitude to programmes influences reception of advertising material.

Responses to television are also of interest to those other than originators of programmes and advertisements such as sociologists, psychologists, educationalists, and politicians. All that has been discussed so far could be of interest to this group. Additionally, they may be concerned with broader problems such as the effects on beliefs, attitudes, and behaviour within the community, which go beyond the programmes and products advertised. The influence of the media on violence is a much discussed example. Social scientists are also interested in establishing general principles of communication. Whilst most of this work is outside the scope of this chapter, it is suggested that, viewed selectively, it has considerable heuristic value for the development of media and advertising research. There are, therefore, three reasons why this section deals with a vastly complicated and interesting area only briefly:

(a) this area is really only bordering on that covered by the definition of media research adopted for this book;
(b) the methodology is largely not peculiar to television and is therefore discussed elsewhere in this book;
(c) much of the work done in this area in the UK is unpublished and the total volume is smaller than for research into audience size and media exposure.

The response to advertising

Aspects of Advertising to be Studied. There are a number of decisions which an advertiser has to make about using the medium which can be broadly classified under the headings of 'content, volume, and patterning'.

Content is usually studied for individual commercials in the form of some pre- or post-testing of an individual advertisement discussed in chapter 17. Little systematic research is done by advertisers on looking for principles of communication. More use could be made of more general work on communications theory, reviewed by Tannenbaum and Greenberg[46], much of which has been unsystematically assimilated in the general background knowledge of advertisement producers.

Most advertising research in the form of pre-testing examines responses to single advertisements. How much money an advertiser should spend is a question which cannot be answered directly by research. Ideally, a market model should be capable of showing the return in profits of money spent on advertising. In practice, budgets are fixed in a variety of ways (Broadbent[47], chapter 8).

Return for advertising money could be deduced if the average response of an individual to each possible number of exposures were known, together with the number of individuals likely to see each number of exposures. This amounts to combining an absolute response function and the expected frequency of exposure distribution. Once an advertising budget is fixed, even a relative response function (one that shows the *relative* value of each number of exposures) would be useful. Unfortunately, it has proved difficult to establish even relative response functions and some assumptions have to be made on limited evidence. This area has been thoroughly reviewed by Broadbent[47,48].

A closely related problem is that of choosing between ways of using the medium in terms of the way spots are patterned in time. Are they more effective close together or spaced, for example? A further aspect of advertising strategy is the length of advertisement to be used. Both choices really depend on establishing the factors which change the nature of the response function. They may be, however, solved independently of establishing the response functions if the effects of patterning or spot length are simple and do not interact with repetition.

Studies of all the aspects of advertising effectiveness have some problems in common relating to experimental design. All possible theoretical designs for evaluating the effects of mass communication have been critically reviewed by Haskins in an Advertising Research Foundation Monograph[49].

Measuring Sales. Evaluation of alternative advertising strategies in terms of sales is, in practice, exceedingly difficult as some of the previous references will make clear. There are a number of approaches, only some of which will be mentioned briefly here.

(a) Using Historical Consumer Panel Data

Consumer panels yield purchasing data all the time. It is, therefore, possible to try to relate sales volumes or brand shares to concurrent or past advertising expenditure by regression analyses. A programme of research for the BBTA[50] suggested that different models are necessary for different markets. Even a model with some general applicability across markets would not necessarily sort out the causality in the relationship.

(b) In-market Experiments

An advertiser can vary his advertising strategy either between different time periods in the same area or different areas in the same time period. The problems here are lack of controlled identical conditions in the two periods or areas, and uncertainty concerning over what period the effects should be measured. For these reasons, the results of such experiments are often inconclusive and advertisers seldom publish them. Segnit and Broadbent[51] give one case-history and show how understanding of this kind of experiment can be improved by using consumer surveys where the respondent's media exposure was estimated as well as her purchasing behaviour and awareness.

(c) Advertising Laboratory Experiments

The best controlled design reviewed by Haskins[49] is what he called the 'controlled field experiment'. This is the situation where purchasing is measurable in as near to real-life conditions as possible for two matched populations identical in every way except in the advertising input they receive. In the US this has been achieved for television, either by having alternative cables serving two panels in the same district and their input differing only in respect to the advertising experiments, or by use of muting

613

devices which block out some part of the advertising transmissions on either panel leaving a blank screen. Experience with one system in the US has been reviewed by Adler and Kuehn[52]. This approach can be used theoretically to study alternative contents, volumes of advertising, and length of patterning strategies. A major limitation on the approach is that it can be used only for effects big enough to show above the noise level of the sampling error of economically viable panels. Another problem is in deciding over what period to study the advertising effects. It appears, from what little has been published so far, that findings are likely to be specific to marketing situations and therefore cannot be immediately reduced into the simplest rules like 'always cluster spots'. No form of this kind of experimental system has yet started in the UK. Despite the difficulties mentioned, this does appear to be the most powerful design for studying the response to advertising.

Measuring Intermediate Advertising Effects

(a) *In-home, On-air*

Measurements of attention triggered by individual advertisements in-home are not really attempted. Recall, measuring the combined result of attention, understanding and retention, is however, used following on-air transmissions. Similarly, the progressive effectiveness of campaigns is often judged by a sequence of measures of attitudes or 'intentions to buy'. If these measures are acceptable they can be used in any time-period or area experiment with advertising strategies and in an advertising laboratory situation.

(b) *Out-of-home Testing*

The majority of pre-testing is conducted in theatres, coaches, and testing centres. This provides proper control over exposure conditions at the expense of realism. The passive privacy of the normal home viewing is exchanged for an involved, forced-attention, observed situation. In these conditions only intermediate measures can be used unless respondents are drawn from a panel or followed-up afterwards. These forms of advertising research are discussed in chapter 16.

Measuring General Responses to Advertising

Advertisers have concentrated on studying the effects of individual commercials and have seldom looked at the overall attitudes to advertising. An exception is a group of studies published by the IPA and reported by Treasure and Joyce[53] which include a comparison of attitudes to Press and television advertising, reactions of audiences under different survey conditions and data from a variety of analyses derived from theatre testing a large number of commercials.

The response to programmes

Deducing Reactions from Audience Size. It is easy to assume that, because many people watch a programme, that it must be enjoyed more than a programme seen by fewer people. A similar deduction may be made that people watch the kind of programmes they like. These hypotheses are only rather weakly justified. The mismatch between what people like and what they view arises from the following reasons:

(a) people cannot watch all the programmes they would like very much because
    (i) other people sometimes determine what is viewed,
    (ii) the programmes may not be at a convenient time,
    (iii) the programmes may clash with something liked on another channel;
(b) people sometimes watch programmes they like less because
    (i) other people sometimes determine what is viewed,
    (ii) they may want to watch television and there may be nothing on any channel which they like very much,
    (iii) they may watch a programme because it follows or precedes one they like.

Despite these problems, deductions can be made from ratings research about the popularity of programmes but they are likely to be in very general terms.

Measuring Reactions to Programmes

(a) *TVQ*

During 1964, TAM introduced an approach to measuring simple audience reaction, based on a service operating in the US, TVQ. The TVQ system used postal questionnaires with lists of programmes against which people indicated whether they were familiar with the programme and how they rated it on a five-point verbal scale—'one of my favourites', 'very good', 'good', 'fair', 'poor'. Such data helped to explain ratings but were not such a strong predictor as had been hoped, probably due to the reasons for the liking and viewing mismatch suggested above. The data nevertheless represented a measure of enjoyment independent of ratings which could be of use to the programmer. It was sometimes suggested that one universal liking scale was not appropriate to the different kinds of programmes screened. People, however, do see programmes as part of a single presentation rather than shown in categories. The TVQ service ran for several years and was bought by the ITA and by several programme companies and for an experimental period by some advertising agencies.

(b) *The ITA Research Programme and TOP*

The ITA commissioned a programme of exploratory research in 1967/8 ending in a pilot panel operation in London for a limited period. This has been fully described by Frost[54]. The programme started by seeking the terms in which viewers described programmes using the Repertory Grid technique (Kelly triads). The constructs obtained were converted into seven-point semantic differential scales. These were then applied to programmes by another sample and the results factor analysed. This yielded

615

nine factors upon which any programme could be rated. A programme typology was then built up by cluster analysis. Following this pilot work in autumn 1969 a further large-scale pilot study, covering three areas over six months, was commissioned by the ITA and ITV programme companies from a consortium, Television Opinion Panel Ltd (TOP). A variation on the earlier procedure was used to establish eleven factors and a general evaluation factor. Programmes were again clustered and the importance of factors within cluster determined in some cases. Panels of 300 in each of three areas then reported fortnightly by mail on the programmes they chose to view. The data covered an appreciation index for all programmes, detailed factor scales for a limited list, spontaneous comments and, occasionally, special questions.

A full discussion of TOP and some examples of its applications to programme scheduling is given by Haldane[55]. Another approach to forming a programme typology is given by Kirsch and Banks[56] and a viewer typology in terms of programmes liked by Rothman and Rauta[45].

(c) *BBC Research*

The BBC has for some time collected audience reaction data from a 'viewing panel'. This comprises some 2000 people recruited from those interviewed on the daily listening and viewing survey and reporting weekly by postal questionnaire. Respondents are asked to comment only on programmes seen in the normal course of viewing. The questionnaire covers both detailed aspects of the programme's content and evaluations on a number of dimensions such as 'funny-unfunny', 'entertaining-boring'. This service is described by the BBC in their booklet[24].

(d) *Other Research*

ITV programme companies, the ITA and the BBC all carry out surveys concerned with aspects of individual programmes or classes of programmes. These are seldom published but do not represent any unique methodological problems.

One point which should be emphasized is the need to talk about programmes in the viewers' terms. Viewers cannot be relied upon to understand classifications such as 'ITV play' which are obvious to programme planners and market researchers.

Measuring the Understanding of Television Programmes and their Immediate Effects

A programme originator may wish to establish how far his programme has been understood and whether it achieves some particular aim. A range of techniques is open to him including group discussion and survey interviews. This area has been thoroughly discussed with case histories by Belson[57], sections two and three.

Measuring What People Require from Television

This question can be approached on a number of levels. At the most general level, establishing the interests and habits and knowledge of the population provides background material for programme planning. Studies of this kind are again reviewed by Belson[57], section one. A large scale study has been published by the BBC[58].

Reaction to existing programmes can also provide some guidance as to needs but it may be difficult to generate new ideas this way. Emmett[59] discussing this problem quotes Galbraith on a related area, '. . . only a few goods serve needs that are made known to the individual by the palpable discomfort that is felt in their absence'. This is true of television programmes and means that it is very difficult to get people to report directly what they want in terms other than existing programmes. An approach used by the ITA has been described on p. 615 whereby viewers' own constructs for programmes were elicited by triadic interviews. It must then be assumed that a person's constructs reflect his requirements and the scales then developed are at least related to requirements. The concept of the ideal programme in various categories can be used[55]. If viewer typologies are formed then requirement groups can be identified[45]. The problem of translating this data into policy decisions is a formidable one and some very exploratory suggestions are made by Emmett[59]. A related series of studies in the US were reported by Steiner[34].

At the most detailed level, research may be needed for planning a particular programme or series which is intended to communicate certain facts or attitudes. Belson[57] reviews techniques and case histories.

In the US a modification of TVQ technique has been used on new programme ideas by the Home Testing Institute[60]. One might expect this to be the more meaningful the more the programmes tested resembled existing programmes.

Response to Programmes in Relation to Advertising

An advertiser would be interested in any programme reaction data which could be used as a basis for predicting ratings. It is probable that no reaction data would do this perfectly because of factors affecting his viewing other than an individual's preference, i.e., timing, competition, and other people.

There has been some evidence that attitudes to the surrounding programme context are correlated with some measures of commercial effectiveness. There may be different principles at work with sponsorship, where attitude to programme can represent attitude to message source, compared with spot advertising in the UK, where the commercials are clearly unrelated to the programmes and seen as interrupting them[53]. With spot advertising it seems likely that the mediating link is reduced activity competing for attention or even enhanced probability of staying in the room during the break rather than any kind of editorial mood rub-off. The source of the

617

effect remains to be demonstrated. That there is an effect, although some-times a weak one, is shown by studies by TAM[23] and Unilever[61] whilst a number of US studies are briefly mentioned by Bogart[62] and some recent data reported by Corlett and Richardson[63]. Generally, those liking a programme viewed show higher levels of behavioural attention and/or re-call than those liking it less and viewing it.

Establishing principles of communication and studying the social effects of television

This title covers the general body of 'mass communications research'. It is really outside the boundaries of media research in the sense used here. Nevertheless, advertising media researchers may well be able to learn from this work. Reviews are given by Halloran[64], Belson[57], section four, and Tannenbaum and Greenberg[46].

Findings and Application of Television Research with Methodological Implications

Whilst the subject of this chapter is media research and not the use of media, certain findings do have implications for research methodology. Not all are covered by occasional comments in the previous sections and some principal groups are summarized here.

The nature of audiences to single transmissions

The main output of audience size research comprises the ratings for in-dividual transmission times. In the UK the following pattern has been broadly true up to now but may change with the increasing complexity of services available. Ratings for viewers may be broken into two components, sets switched on (from meters) and viewers-per-set (from diaries). The total of sets switched on to all channels is generally consistent for time of day, day of week and season and appears to be based on social habit. The number of sets switched to an individual channel, however, varies with the programming competition. Within the evening, sudden changes in audience level can occur at times of programme change. The quarter hour viewers-per-set factors are much more consistent for time of day and less dependent on programming.

Regularities in the data lead to the question of whether so much need be collected. Ehrenberg[11] has questioned the value of minute by minute and continuous data. Continuing work by JICTAR[12] has investigated whether viewers-per-set factors could be obtained intermittently and applied to continuous set data. In all these cases evaluating the effects of small decreases in accuracy is difficult for the reasons outlined at the beginning of this chapter. The findings in the area, largely unpublished, may become of more importance if other factors, such as rising costs or the need for combination with other research, lead to changes in the research system. Although audience composition data are collected continuously, viewing patterns by sub-groups are now published by JICTAR less frequently. This follows evidence that sub-groups are not particularly selective in their viewing. Some unpublished analyses carried out by the IPA showed a very high correlation between the ordering of the 'best' advertising breaks whether these were defined in terms of cost per thousand for broad audience categories, e.g., men, and small demographic groups (men aged 16 to 24) or purchasing groups, e.g., men who buy aperitifs. Similar conclusions have been published by the Five Agencies Study Group[65] although some possible exceptions were found on AMPS data[66,67]. TAM studies of the viewing patterns of 'heavy', 'medium' and 'light' viewing housewives[68] also showed no difference between the lists of programmes viewed most by each group. The implications are that television is a relatively unselective medium and that advertising schedules can usually be planned on the viewing habits of the main audience. This conclusion can be reached too readily because of the difficulty of isolating small but useful effects in a mass of data full of large effects[66]. Possibly, therefore, there are more exceptions to non-selectivity in British television viewing than have yet been discovered.

The nature of viewing to groups of transmissions

A widespread use of the continuous records obtained from the JICTAR system is in special analyses showing the coverage and frequency of viewing distribution obtained across the target audience group by a schedule of spots. This kind of data reflects the nature of viewing habits over time.

Ehrenberg and Goodhardt[69,70] have extensively analysed the duplication of viewing between pairs of transmissions. Their findings include a duplication law which suggests that all pairs combine in the same way unless the transmissions are adjacent or nearly so. This implies that viewing is not systematic and based on strong personal preferences but more random. Having viewed one programme a viewer is no more likely to view any one other programme more than another unless it is the next or next but one in time. This probably arises because the viewer's own preferences are obscured by components of his viewing arising from the other sources mentioned on p. 614. This non-selectivity does make coverage and frequency data relatively easy to predict in most cases. It is possible to estimate the data from formulae[71] and tables[72] given information such as the number of spots in the schedule and the ratings they achieve. Studies in support of this finding are discussed by Ehrenberg and Twyman[11,12].

Apart from really exceptional and very rare changes in programme schedules, coverage and frequency data could probably be obtained, as adequately as response functions can utilize, from summaries of past analyses or intermittently collected data.

Some findings on media strategy

Results from advertising laboratories[52] show that one strategy may be appropriate for one brand situation and the reverse for another.

Findings on repetition have been reviewed by Broadbent[47] under discussion of the response function and elsewhere. There is also a useful discussion of this work by Bogart[62], chapter 8.

In addition to advertising laboratories and other field studies there are also findings based on physiological measurements taken over a series of advertisement presentations. Some of the work has been reported by Grass[73] and Puther discussed by Krugman.[74,75] It is suggested that the physiological aspects of response to commercials may not be so closely related to their effectiveness as this work implies. They may reflect habituation to the physical stimuli of the advertisement but learning or persuasion may still continue.

Findings on the effectiveness of spot lengths also vary between studies and also according to whether recall or attitude change has been taken as the measure of effectiveness[62].

Reviewing US evidence Bogart[62], chapter 7, finds that the 30 second length generates most recall per second. A study in the UK reported by Treasure and Joyce[53], using pretesting conditions, shows a greater shift in the gift choice measure the shorter the commercial. This may reflect the kinds of shorter commercials available or a distorted relationship between this kind of testing and 'real life'. The present lack of knowledge about response to various possible advertising strategies makes it difficult to use coverage and frequency analyses with any degree of confidence. Probably the most constructive approach to their interpretation is that suggested by Broadbent[47].

Behaviour whilst watching television

Observations of viewers reported by Steiner[34] represent the most detailed attempt to study what happens when people view commercials. Krugman[75] has attempted to extend this further into studying their thinking about commercials whilst viewing.

In the UK, the findings on presence in breaks are most relevant to the existing continuous services. The LPE study[22] showed that more programme viewing housewives were missing from breaks early in the evening than later on. The IPA/ISBA study conflicts with this, showing virtually no time effects for presence in breaks, and some slight evidence for no programme effects. There was little difference between centre and end breaks for adults but more housewives were missing in end breaks. An overall level of absence in breaks of around 20 per cent appears in both US and UK studies. Programme audiences are based on seeing more than half the programme part so that an unknown proportion of viewers will also be missing from programme audiences for any short time periods.

The apparent absence of variability in the proportion of programme audiences present in breaks suggests that these data need be collected less frequently than was originally thought. The hypothesized absence of programme effects does, however, need further checking. If there were even small real programme effects on presence in commercial breaks then this could weaken the meaningfulness of minute by minute data.

Studies including unpublished data from the IPA/ISBA study[20] generally agree that behavioural <u>attention</u> levels rise, moving from early to peak time although relatively little is known about late night viewing. Evidence for the importance of behavioural attention rests solely on its correlation with higher levels of recall. There is evidence of programming effects particularly in relation to programme interest or liking from studies by LPE[22], JWT[63], and TAM[23]. Recently, further work by BMRB has shown that indications of attention level additional to time effects can be deduced from frequency of viewing or loyalty to television programmes[63]. This approach may offer the greatest accessibility to the concept of attention since it can be deduced from regular JICTAR data rather than by the expensive coincidental surveying.

The use of media selection models

Computers are widely used for special analyses such as the assessment of schedules in terms of coverage and frequency of viewing. There are also programmes designed to build, from research data, optimal schedules to certain criteria.

The primary television research input for these is a collection of viewing records of individuals together with their classification information. To select an optimal television schedule involves choosing a response function, or putting a value on each number of advertisement exposures. Other adjustments which might be made include weighting individuals according to their expected market value and perhaps also applying weights to viewing at certain times to take account of hypothesized attentional effects. If a multi-media schedule is to be selected then it is necessary, having chosen advertisement sizes for each medium, to allocate weights to the different types of media exposure. On current knowledge it is virtually impossible to do this satisfactorily.

The use of computer media selection models has been mostly developed by press media owners for the press rather than television. In practice, the problems of time availability and short term buying and adjustments make a computer selected television schedule only relevant in relation to the broad characteristics of the schedule structure. If time availability were also on the computer and schedule selections quickly available these models could be more used in television planning and perhaps even as an aid to buying decisions. Discussion of computer schedule selection models can be found in Broadbent[47,76].

Prediction, feedback and reported value

Arguably, the major advertising function of audience research is to enable predictions to be made about further ratings so that the best time may be bought. Some studies of prediction by advertising agencies are discussed

621

by Ehrenberg and Twyman[11], Twyman[12,77]. Longer term predictions are limited by programming knowledge.

In the short term, predictions are likely to represent a summary of past data combined with estimates of programme popularity. The latter, where successful, have usually been based on subjective experience rather than programming research but there is possibly room for the development of more formalized programme research for use in prediction systems.

Another role for audience research is that it is said to provide feedback to those striving to buy the best television time, so that actions which improve cost per thousand are subsequently reinforced. Whilst this is undoubtedly true to a limited extent, it should be noted that this feedback is entirely in audience research terms and depends on the validity of these terms. It also means that computerization of this function should be possible.

Finally, research is said to provide a record of value for each spot bought. This provides a basis for negotiation between buyers and sellers and an index of success as between agency and advertiser. It is difficult to say what this value amounts to in practice and how much it would be diminished if this activity were based on other than continuous data.

A possible trend in research requirements would be an increasing emphasis on prediction rather than the other research roles, if, through computerization, it becomes easier to assess the pay-off of alternative research systems in terms of time-buying efficiency.

Future Developments with Implications for Television Research

Sources of change

Changes in advertising media research are likely to arise from changes in:

(a) the structure of media;
(b) the marketing of products;
(c) methods of buying and selling media;
(d) research methodology;
(e) the economics of research.

(a) The Structure of Media

The structure of television in the UK after 1976 is still unknown. The development of UHF could mean smaller, more regionally based stations but the economics of running stations seem opposed to that trend. If a second commercial network were established this could lead to a greater fragmentation of audiences and the principle of non-selectivity of ITV audiences might disappear.

Other technical developments include the use of the television set for transmitting material either recorded from transmissions at another time or available separately commercially[78]. Such a development could have implications both for patterns of exposure to media, creating perhaps a new

622

medium, and for the relevance of research techniques. In the longer term, the development of holography[79] is bound to have remarkable effects on all media.

The advent of extensive commercial radio services in addition to any competitive effects, presents an advertising media research problem not yet faced in the UK. One solution may be through combination of radio research with television research. Multi-media diary experiments have sometimes proved quite successful in the US and a number of other precedents exist for combined radio and television research systems such as the BBC and in Holland[1]. Research systems could combine in other ways, however, such as the formation of all-services television research and all-services radio research. Integration with other forms of market research is also a possibility.

(b) *The Marketing of Products*

Manufacturers are increasingly planning products to appeal to segments of markets. This might lead to a greater search for selectivity in media. If this corresponded to increasing selectivity developing in television through more commercial services, then research requirements could well move away from the present emphasis on mass audiences.

The development of new approaches to retailing, clearer thinking about 'below the line' expenditure, and the use of new media such as commercial radio may change the function of television advertising. This could strongly influence ways of measuring its effectiveness and, possibly, the kinds of media measurement required.

(c) *Methods of Buying and Selling Media and Evaluating Research*

The present television research system depends a lot on the sales structure of television and vice versa. If selling methods changed, so would the appropriate research. However, it is still buying methodology that seems to be most influential. Here, an undoubted trend, despite misgivings, is towards computerization. Starting with the use of computers both for accountancy and rather theoretical exercises in media selection, this will ultimately lead to total buying and selling systems being operated on computers. This would involve storing availability, allocation rules and research data. Exercise of media skills would lie in the choice of forms of stating advertising aims and the development of programmes for achieving the consequent requirements.

Such systems would tend to impose the form of data requirements although much of their content would depend on the other factors discussed in this section.

One side-effect of more computerization of media transactions is that alternative forms of research can be systemmatically evaluated to see what effect on decisions they have. At present this is difficult because a human system cannot forget its past experience for the purposes of an evaluation exercise and only rather artificial decision simulating analyses are possible.

(d) and (e) *Research Methodology and the Economics of Research*

These two elements cannot really be considered in isolation. Much depends on how rich a medium television is in the future and how costly research becomes. If there was a decline in the value of the money available for television research, much simpler data collection methods might be adopted despite the potential availability of more sophisticated techniques. There has always been a strong presumption that research and its use does bring a return for the money it costs. There might be greater pressure for evaluating this under any economic stress.

There is room for development in meter techniques but the cost may inhibit this. Meters could get a lot smaller and would then be less obtrusive and suitable for portables or even radios, although it is doubtful whether the latter would ever be economically viable.

The growth of telephone ownership will make available telephone interviewing, which is commonplace in the US and some other European countries.

The development of facilities for transmitting data by line could conceivably mean that on-line meters become a possibility. Something like this was pioneered in the UK by Nielsen and TAM some years ago but were not then viable. Instantaneous measurement systems have also been operated through the monitoring of wire transmitter television services but these relay systems cover a small section of the community. If these services were to grow this approach could become of interest.

The increasing complexity and cost of product and media research has already led to suggestions that more attempt should be made to integrate research systems financed on an industry basis[7,8]. There are additional arguments based on the value of obtaining product and media data from the same source. This is clearly a development which, if progressed, would affect the nature of the television research system as a whole and, possibly, have some influence on the techniques used.

References

1. BBTA *Television in Europe*, Supplement to BBTA Bulletin No. 11, August, 1970.
2. BBTA *Television Audience Measurement*, to be published (see also *Journal of the Society of Film & Television Arts*, No. 38, Winter, 1969–70).
3. GARFINKLE, N. The Brand Rating Index, *ADMAP*, Sept., 1966.
4. All Media & Product Agencies Committee, *AMPS Technical Report*, Research Services Ltd., 1967.
5. CONSTERDINE, G. All Media & Product Survey, *ADMAP*, Sept., 1966.
6. JOYCE, T. What is the Target Group Index?, *ADMAP*, Mar., 1969.
7. Integrated Media & Product Research Working Group, *Review of Media & Product Research Sources*, IPA, 1970.
8. IPA, *The Case for Integrating Media & Product Research*, Occasional Paper No. 19, 1967.
9. TAM, *Comparison Survey of Audience Composition Techniques*, Television Audience Measurement Ltd., 1961.

10. TWYMAN, W. A. *Techniques for Measuring Program vs. Commercial Audiences*, ARF 15th Annual Conference, 1969 (see also IPA Forum No. 25, Jan., 1969).

11. EHRENBERG, A. S. C. and TWYMAN, W. A. On Measuring Television Audiences, *Journal of the Royal Statistical Society*, Series A (General), **130**, 1967.

12. TWYMAN, W. A. *Research into Methods of Measuring Television Audiences & Data Requirements for the British Television Advertising Industry*, ESOMAR, 1969.

13. BUCK, S. F. and WEST, M. J. Consistency of Purchasing and Viewing Behaviour; Optimum period for study, *Journal of the Market Research Society*, **10**, 4, 1968.

14. JICTAR, *Reference Manual*, AGB Ltd., 1970 and revisions thereafter.

15. BEALE, E. M. L., BROADBENT, S., and HUGHES, P. A. B. A Computer Assessment of Media Schedules, *OR Quarterly*, **17**, 4, 1966.

16. AGOSTINI, J. M. The Marriage of Data from Various Surveys: An Expedient or a Unique Way to Make Progress? *ADMAP*, Oct., 1967.

17. BUCK, S. F. and TAYLOR, L. Consistency of Housewives ITV Viewing Intensity over Time, *ADMAP*, July/Aug., 1970.

18. CONSTERDINE, G. Some Recent Evidence on Television Audience Research, *Journal of the Market Research Society*, **10**, 1, 1968.

19. ARF, *Electronic Test of In Home TV Viewing among those Families who Fail to Respond to the Doorbell*, Arrowhead Study No. 8, ARF, 1968.

20. BMRB, *Television Presence Research*, Report to IPA/ISBA Presence Working Party. British Market Research Bureau Ltd., 1968 (see also earlier reports on Pilot Work).

21. CONTAM, *How Good are Television Ratings?* (continued) CONTAM, 1969 (and ARF Conference, 1969).

22. London Press Exchange, *The Audience to Television Advertisements*, Research Services Ltd., 1961.

23. TAM, *Two Studies in Housewife Attention During Commercial Breaks*, Television Audience Measurement Ltd., 1965.

24. BBC, *Audience Research in the United Kingdom: Methods & Services*, BBC 1970.

25. EHRENBERG, A. S. C. A Comparison of TV Audience Measures, *Journal of Advertising Research*, **4**, 4, 1964.

26. SIMMONS, W. R. *Evaluating Television Measurement Systems*, ARF 14th Annual Conference, 1968.

27. WEBB, N. L. The Hardware of Audience Research, *ADMAP*, Sept., 1968.

28. CONSTERDINE, G. AMPS TV Diaries, *ADMAP*, Feb., 1968.

29. RKO General Broadcasting, *1967–8 Television Research Manual*, RKO, 1967.

30. MAYER, M. *How Good are Television Ratings?* CONTAM, 1966.

31. EHRENBERG, A. S. C. Surprise at Poly Channel, *ADMAP*, Dec., 1966.

32. JWT, *Television Viewing Diaries*, British Market Research Bureau Ltd., 1967. (See also *Television Attention Research* Reports 1961–66.)

33. Lintas, *Television in the Family Setting*, Research Bureau Ltd., 1962.

34. STEINER, G. A. The People Look at Commercials, *Journal of Business*, **39**, 2, 1963. (And also The People Look at Television, Knopf, 1963).

35. Television Advertising Representatives Inc., *Observiewing*, 1965.

36. CBS, *Taking the Measure of Two Media*, CBS Television Network, 1962.

37. ALLEN, C. L. Photographing the TV Audience, *Journal of Advertising Research*, **5**, 1, 1965.

38. STUART, A. Reports to JICTAR (unpublished), 1964.

39. CORDELL, W. N. and RAHMEL, H. A. Are Nielsen Ratings Affected by Non-Co-operation, Conditioning or Response Error?, *Journal of Advertising Research*, **2**, 3, 1962.

40. JOYCE, T. Examples of Experimental Work with Media Panels, *ADMAP*, Sept., 1967.

41. HARVEY, B. Non Response in TV Meter Panels, *Journal of Advertising Research*, **8**, 1968.

42. STUART, A. *Sampling in Television Research*, ATV Technical Research Study, Associated Television Ltd., 1960.

43. SILVEY, R. and EMMETT, B. What Makes Television Viewers Choose?, *New Society*, 24, 14 Mar., 1963.

44. GREEN, P. E., CARMONE, F. J., and FOX, L. B. Television Programme Similarities; an Application of Subjective Clustering, *Journal of the Market Research Society*, **11**, 1, 1969.

45. ROTHMAN, J. and RAUTA, I. Towards a Typology of the Television Audience, *Journal of the Market Research Society*, **11**, 1, 1969.

46. TANNENBAUM, P. H. and GREENBERG, B. S. Annual Review of Psychology, *Mass Communication*, **19**, 1968.

47. BROADBENT, S. *Spending Advertising Money*, Business Books, 1970.
48. BROADBENT, S. and SEGNIT, S. *Response Functions in Media Planning*, Thompson Silver Medal Paper, 1967.
49. HASKINS, J. *How to Evaluate Mass Communications*, ARF Monograph, 1968.
50. LAWRENCE, R. J. Report on a Research Programme, *BBTA Bulletin*, 2, Mar., 1968.
51. SEGNIT, S. and BROADBENT, S. *Area Tests & Consumer Surveys to Measure Advertising Effectiveness*, ESOMAR, 1970.
52. ADLER, J. and KUEHN, A. A. *How Advertising Works in Market Experiments*, ARF 15th Annual Conference, 1969.
53. TREASURE, J. and JOYCE, T. *As others see us*, IPA Occasional paper No. 17, 1967.
54. FROST, W. A. K. The Development of a Technique for the Programme Assessment, *The Journal of the Market Research Society*, **11**, 1, 1969.
55. HALDANE, I. R. *Measuring Television Audience Reactions*, MRS Conference, 1970.
56. KIRSCH, A. D. and BANKS, S. Program Types Defined by Factor Analysis, *Journal of Advertising Research*, **2**, 3, 1962.
57. BELSON, W. A. *The Impact of Television*, Crosby Lockwood, 1967.
58. BBC, *The Peoples Activities*, BBC Audience Research Department, 1966.
59. EMMETT, B. P. *A New Role for Broadcasting Research?* WAPOR Conference, 1967.
60. HTI, *Programme Idea Q*, Home Testing Institute Inc., 1966.
61. BROWN, M. M. Attitudes to Programmes and the Effect of Commercials, *ADMAP*, Jan., 1967.
62. BOGART, L. *Strategy in Advertising*, Harcourt Brace and World Inc., 1967.
63. CORLETT, T. and RICHARDSON, D. TV Attention—A Further Step, *ADMAP*, Sept., 1970.
64. HALLORAN, J. D. *The Effects of Mass Communication with Special Reference to Television*, Television Research Committee Paper No. 1, Leicester University Press, 1964.
65. Five-Agencies Study Group, *The Importance of Product Purchase in Relation to ITV Viewing Patterns*, FASG, 1967.
66. TWYMAN, W. A. *Do Housewife Product Purchasing Groups View Differently from All Housewives?* AMPSAC, 1968.
67. TWYMAN, W. A. *How the AMPS Survey was used by its Subscribers*, AMPSAC, 1969.
68. TAM, *Studies of Housewives who are Light ITV Viewers*, Television Audience Measurement Ltd., 1963 and 1966.
69. EHRENBERG, A. S. C. and GOODHARDT, G. T. Practical Applications of the Duplication of Viewing Law, *Journal of the Market Research Society*, **11**, 1, 1969.
70. GOODHARDT, G. T. Constant in Duplicated Television Viewing, *Nature*, **212**, p. 1616, 1966.
71. JOHNSON, D. S. and PEATE, J. L. The Estimation of Television Viewing Frequency, *ADMAP*, July/Aug., 1966.
72. *Housewife Coverage and Frequency Guide*, Television Audience Measurement Ltd., 1966.
73. GRASS, R. C. *Satiation Effects of Advertising*, ARF 14th Annual Conference, 1968.
74. KRUGMAN, H. E. and HARTLEY, E. *Passive Learning from Television*, ESOMAR/WAPOR, 1969.
75. KRUGMAN, H. E. *Processes Underlying Exposure to Advertising*, ARF 14th Annual Conference, 1968.
76. BROADBENT, S. R. *Media Planning and Computers by* 1970, Thomson Award Papers, 1965.
77. TWYMAN, W. A. *The Prediction of Frequency Patterns; An Experiment for JICTAR carried out by the Media Circle*, 1967.
78. COLLIS, J. Media Developments Over the Next Decade and Their Implications for Marketing. *ADMAP*, July/Aug., 1971.
79. LEITH, E. N. and UPATNIEKS, J. *Photography of Laser, Scientific American* (offprint No. 300), **212**, 6, 1965.

See also for general background:
ADAMS, J. R. *Media Planning* Business Books 1971, in addition to BROADBENT[47] and BOGART[6]

25. Radio and cinema research

Frank Teer

The attention of the media researcher is not unnaturally concentrated on the two main advertising media, press and television. Relatively little attention is given to the cinema or radio as subjects for audience research. The reason for this is not hard to find. In advertising expenditure terms, the cinema and radio are minority media. Together, they accounted for less than two per cent of the £535 million spent on advertising in 1969, and less than a tenth of the expenditure on television advertising alone. It is estimated that with the advent of local commercial radio in the UK, which the government plans for 1973, these two media will account for about six per cent of total advertising expenditure.

As advertising media, they are very different from each other in many respects. The quality of exposure to advertising which they offer is at almost opposite ends of the scale. The total absorption of the cinema audience contrasts strongly with exposure to radio advertising where the members of the audience are engaged in activities such as driving, housework, etc., whilst listening. The nature of the advertising is also strongly contrasted. The cinema advertisement gives tremendous creative opportunities to the advertiser through colour and movement on a large screen. Although radio offers creative opportunities of a different type, and can claim high attention among listeners, radio advertising messages tend to be simple and repetitive. Often they are extracted from and used as a reminder of television advertising. Though very different in type, however, they have three characteristics in common. First, they are used by national advertisers mainly as supporting media to press and television campaigns. Second, decisions to use radio or cinema advertising as part of such a campaign are not made principally on considerations of comparative costs per thousand audience reached. Marketing or creative considerations are the principal determinants of the decisions to use these media. Finally, radio in the form of local stations as currently proposed, and cinema, are media which lend themselves to selected area campaigns. Blanket national or regional coverage is not obligatory. Advertisers who have localized interests, e.g., a chain of stores can, therefore, make particularly effective use of these media.

The role given to advertising on radio and in the cinema and the amount of money expended on it affects the type and amount of research conducted. The advertiser requires information before making decisions about media expenditure, but the information he can expect from these two minor media must necessarily be restricted. Decisions about whether to use these media are based on two main information items. The first consists of data which defines the audience of the media in demographic and other terms and, therefore, determines whether the audience reached conforms to the marketing objectives. The other major consideration is the proportion of the target population which is reached by the medium and the number of opportunities to see the advertising which will be achieved by campaigns of varying scope and duration. The advertiser needs not only to know the nature of the audience to the medium but what proportion of that audience is likely to see a given campaign (cover) and how many times, on average, each member of the audience is likely to see the advertisement (repetition). The extent to which these objectives have been met by the audience researcher will be discussed in the context of each medium.

Radio Audience Research

As we are concerned only with advertising media, discussion on radio audience research will be confined to commercial radio. The only commercial station currently broadcasting to the UK is Radio Luxembourg and the only other commercial stations in the British Isles at present are Manx Radio and Radio Eireann.

At the time of writing this chapter the form which commercial radio is likely to take is becoming clear. The chances are that eventually there will be roughly sixty local stations serving areas with populations of 200 000 or more, on the basis of one station per area. The only exception is likely to be Greater London which will have two stations competing for audiences across the whole of the area. Commercial radio is, therefore, going to be local and in general there will be not more than one station per area.

It is also fairly clear that stations will be broadcasting on medium wave during the day and on VHF during the day and at night. This is relevant because ownership of VHF sets is still by no means universal and the plan consequently imposes a restriction on potential evening listening levels. There is little doubt, however, that commercial radio is returning to the UK in force and there is also little doubt that advertisers will call on the radio industry for research information on the nature and size of the radio audience. The 'pirate' stations which burst on the British scene in 1963 were very quick to produce research to show the number and nature of listeners they were reaching, and it seems likely that we shall see history repeating itself by 1973. However, the nature of the research which commercial radio is likely to sponsor will be constrained by the revenue it is likely to yield. It is extremely unlikely that local commercial radio will generate more than £30 million of advertising revenue per annum. This will place obvious limits on the scope and nature of any research carried out. How radio's research resources will be expended is not yet clear, but it is worth reviewing the nature of past research, the problems of researching radio audiences and the special difficulties posed by local radio.

Past radio research

Radio Luxembourg has been transmitting commercial radio to the UK since 1946 and has been carrying out survey research into its audience since 1952. These surveys have been based on personal interviews with 2000 or more individuals for each day's listening surveyed. The questionnaire generally covers claimed listening to programmes on the day before the interview and also broader claims for the previous week. Recently, the questionnaire has been augmented to include an attempt to measure the recall of the previous evening's advertising. The surveys are undertaken on a number of days a year to measure seasonal variations in listening and from the data collected advertisers can estimate the audience figures at different times of the day and at different seasons of the year.

Surveys of this type, which measure listening over the preceding 24 hours (24 hour recall surveys), provide useful data for the advertiser. They measure the characteristics of the audience for any given time period and can be used to estimate the total audience for any given time spot and, thus, the cost per thousand members of the target audience reached by that spot. Because the detailed listening data extends only over a 24 hour period, direct survey evidence of cumulative cover and repetition over a long time period cannot be directly adduced from the survey data. However, the cumulative audience and the amount of repetition delivered by a radio advertising campaign can be estimated and American experience based on work carried out by Westinghouse Broadcasting indicates that these estimates can be refined to a considerable degree of accuracy[2].

Because 24 hour recall surveys do not provide direct measurements of cumulative cover some users have favoured the diary as a method of collecting radio audience data. In November 1968 Radio Luxembourg used a 7 day diary to collect listening data. In this technique, which is also extensively used in the United States, a sample of the general public are asked to keep a record of their radio listening, television viewing and newspaper reading over a 7 day time period. This record then gives the researcher direct evidence on the question of cumulative cover.

During the 'pirate' radio period in the mid-1960's the type of radio research undertaken fell into two distinct types. In the first place, the stations obtained, through using omnibus surveys, weekly audience figures based on questions such as 'Did you listen at all during the last seven days?' and 'When did you last listen?'. Weekly audience figures of this kind were little more than station popularity polls and were used to reinforce the station's claims that they had a wide and interested audience. They were not particularly useful to the media researcher. Consequently, the pirates later undertook 24 hour recall surveys similar to the Luxembourg surveys and on one occasion used a 7 day diary.

Other methods of collecting radio audience data, in particular the telephone interview, which has been used extensively in the US, have not found favour in this country. Because of the low incidence of telephone ownership (only about 35 per cent of homes have a telephone) and the volume of 'out of home' radio listening, there has been considerable doubt about the usefulness of telephone surveys for radio research. The method employed in the US is to use a coincidental check whereby the interviewer telephones a random sample of homes at specified times and asks whether the radio is switched on, and if so, the station to which it is tuned and also who is listening. Without considerable increase in the penetration of telephone ownership, it is unlikely that this method would be used for general radio research in the UK, except possibly for certain minority interest groups, such as high income groups, investors, etc.

Radio research methodology

The deficiencies of the short-term recall surveys conventionally used in radio audience research led the Media Research Group to recommend major experimental work to compare all the techniques available for measuring radio audiences with a view to establishing some form of diary panel[3]. This work was drawn on by the Incorporated Society of British Advertisers (ISBA) who towards the end of the pirate era took steps to establish industry sponsored research. In preparing an initial specification, ISBA stated its basic requirements for audience research. These were:

(a) data should be continuous, or at least up-to-date;
(b) it should be directly comparable across stations;
(c) it should deal with all stations (including BBC);
(d) the data collection methods (including sampling methods) should be validated;
(e) it should tell us
   (i) how many people,
   (ii) in different demographic groups and areas,
   (iii) *ever* listen to each station and
   (iv) listened to each station at each point in time,
   (v) over a 'long' time period (to provide coverage and opportunities-to-see, etc.);

(f) it would also be a good thing if radio could co-operate with other media in due course with a view to
  (i) all media research,
  (ii) solution of other common problems, e.g., the definition of target audiences.

Leaving aside the last of these as being a long term aim, how far do the techniques of 24-hour recall and diary panels meet these requirements? It is clear that of the two techniques, only the diary method will provide audience data over a 'long' time period. 24-hour recall by its very nature can only provide information about opportunities to hear and coverage for a campaign lasting no longer than 24 hours. Because of the frailty of memory, recall surveys for longer time periods are probably ruled out. *Prima facie*, therefore, the diary is probably the best option, but as neither technique has been validated, 24-hour re-call cannot be completely rejected. If this technique was found to be valid and the diary method was not, it might be necessary to use some combination of the two techniques in which recall findings were used to calibrate diary records kept by the same sample of informants.

Before considering how the techniques might be validated, it is worth reviewing the major difficulties which have to be taken into account in the development of the measurement techniques.

Station identification

Because the pirate stations were almost exclusively 'pop' music stations with programmes consisting entirely of almost identical record shows, it has been alleged that listeners might not know to which station they are listening. Some indication of the extent of this problem is shown by a small scale pilot conducted by National Opinion Polls in the latter days of 'pirate' radio in 1966. This pilot consisted of a simple coincidental check in which interviewers called at homes and enquired if the radio was switched on and whether the respondent was listening to it. If the answer to both questions was 'Yes', the interviewer went on to ask to which station the radio was tuned. Having recorded this, the interviewer then checked the set to determine whether it was, in fact, tuned to that station. This is a simple check of simultaneous recall. Out of 322 listeners interviewed, about 10 per cent gave incorrect answers on the question of station. In the case of those who said they were listening to a commercial station, 18 per cent incorrectly identified the station. Of those who said they were listening to a BBC broadcast, about five per cent were incorrect. This experiment was very limited in scope and neither investigated the causes of confusion nor the methods required to minimize it. It goes no further than to demonstrate that station identification is a problem and it was a significantly greater problem for commercial stations of the 'pop pirate' type than it was for BBC stations (as they were then).

The casualness of the event

There is a widespread view that much radio listening especially to 'pop' stations is casual in nature—that the radio does not demand the same degree of undivided attention as press or television. This seems to be borne out by the extent to which radio listening occurs whilst other activities such as housework, driving, work, etc., are in progress. There is, therefore, some doubt whether this type of event can be recalled accurately 24 hours later or whenever the panel member fills in his or her diary. Memory cannot readily be jogged because programme lists consisting almost entirely of names of disc jockeys are unlikely to be adequate recall aids.

It is possible that one of the advantages of the diary may lie in taking some of the casualness from this 'event'. Because panel members know that they have to record their listening, they will pay greater attention to it in terms of taking note of the station they are tuned to and mentally noting the time. At the same time, it should be said that diary-keeping could condition panel members into adopting a listening pattern (especially in the short term) which is not 'normal'. This could be either for prestige reasons or to make their own diary-keeping simpler.

The location of the event

Because of the portability of the transistor radio, listening can take place almost anywhere inside and outside the home. The radio audience is an extremely mobile one. In addition, because the radio is often used as background, it can be played at work or in a car. Although most radio listening does in fact take place in the home, a substantial amount of it occurs outside the home. In a 24-hour recall survey carried out by NOP in 1965, they found that about three-quarters of all listening occurred at home, but during a weekday about one-fifth of all listening took place at work and on Saturday and Sunday 12 per cent to 15 per cent of all listening was either in a car or at some other place outside the home or place of work. Clearly, then, a substantial proportion of listening occurs outside the home, and much of this is to radios not belonging to or tuned in by the listener, making further difficulties of re-call and/or diary keeping. Therefore, before any validation exercise is mounted, the researcher is faced with the problems of:

(a) investigating in detail the extent to which listening claims will be false because of lack of knowledge of the station tuned in to, and determining the direction of any errors;

(b) designing a questionnaire or diary which will adequately prompt out all listening occasions and help the respondent accurately to recall the station—possibly by obtaining a brief account of the day's activities and where they took place.

Validation

Any technique used to measure the audience to any media must have validity, i.e., it must be shown that the measurement technique used reliably reflects the real audience. In using measures which depend on an individual's recall of an event, that measure may not reflect the true audience because of the frailty of memory. Listening occasions may be forgotten and the audience is consequently understated. If a diary method is used, individuals completing the diary might be conditioned to listen more than 'normal'. The act of completing a diary may make them more radio conscious than previously and this might result in an overestimate of the actual audience. As there is no independent audience data against which measurements of the above type can be checked, the only method of validating the information is the coincidental check. This technique requires that the methods being tested are put into operation simultaneously and an independent measure of the audience is taken by a method which is known to be valid. The coincidental check, which is a valid measure, requires that the radio listening of a large sample of individuals be checked at specific moments in time by observation. If a large enough sample of individuals is contacted at, say, precisely 9 p.m., and a note taken of the station to which that individual is listening (if any), a reliable and valid estimate of the listening level at that time can be made. This was the method used by Television Audience Measurement Ltd in the comparison surveys undertaken in the early days of commercial television[4].

A radio audience validation check has been undertaken in the United States. RKO sponsored a comparison study between a multi-media diary, a radio diary, a telephone interview and a coincidental check of 'in home' listening carried out by telephone[5]. This study showed that the results from the multi-media diary corresponded very closely to those from the coincidental check, whereas the radio-only diary considerably overestimated radio audiences. Unfortunately, this study provides no clear guides for 'out of home' listening, but it does show clearly that if a diary is used we might be well advised to collect information on exposure to all media and not just radio.

The need to validate measurement for all listening imposes considerable problems in designing suitable coincidental checking techniques. We have to cover listening in private households, in work places, motor cars, as well as in public places. It is not impossible to devise a coincidental check to cover the audience at home and at work. The former would follow the television pattern and the latter would require sampling work places and determining whether any radios are being played, to which stations they are tuned, and what proportion of employees are listening to them at given moments in time. Listening out of doors is more difficult because the population of any outdoor location is constantly changing. It may, however, be possible to simply sample listeners to determine not the absolute level of listening but to check that the relative listening to each station is correctly recorded in diaries or 24-hour recall. It would be extremely difficult to validate listening in motor cars though a possible answer would be to check motorists as they stop, e.g., for petrol.

The future of radio research

The task of the radio audience researcher is therefore technically a difficult one and, because of the low level of listening to radio, samples have to be large. For the ISBA survey, for example, a coincidental check of 54,000 was suggested. Clearly, therefore, to undertake reliable and valid audience research for commercial radio, the expenditure of considerable time and money would be necessary, and it is doubtful, given the likely form of commercial radio, whether sufficient resources would be forthcoming to undertake all the work which is desirable. The likely structure of commercial radio has already been discussed. It will certainly be of a local nature, though there may be a national element, but what does seem clear is that advertising revenue is unlikely to exceed £30 million and will probably be nearer £10 million. The idea, therefore, of providing information on a continuous basis which fulfils ISBA's requirements in the transmission areas of each of the local stations is clearly out of the question. The research task is completely out of all proportion to the value of the information. Nevertheless, information about the audience will be needed and the only practical solution is for the commercial radio industry to undertake this work on a co-operative basis. Only through industry sponsorship could the necessary finance be found for pilot work and validity studies and this work could be followed by continuing research into the audience on a national scale. A study of this kind using a continuous or semi-continuous diary or a series of 24-hour recall surveys would provide the advertiser with all the information he needs about the national radio audience with appropriate regional breakdowns. This would provide information concerning the audience of any national station but, with the possible exception of Greater London, it would not give audience data specifically relating to any local station without considerable augmentation of sample sizes. Audience figures for local stations could, however, be crudely estimated by allocating national estimates to local areas on a share of population basis. This could only be done, of course, if the populations served by local stations were known. To determine this boundary surveys would be required to establish the extent of the area served by each local transmitter. This information would, in any case, be required. Evidence of the size of the area served by each transmitter would be one of the first requirements of the advertiser.

The great majority of media research is carried out for the benefit of national advertisers who are, generally speaking, interested in national or regional information. Consequently, a national radio survey of the kind outlined above will be sufficient. However, some information of a purely local nature will be required. It is inevitable that the nature and quality of individual stations will vary with a corresponding effect on the size and nature of each station's audience and it is probably that advertisers will call for information which justifies each station's advertising rates in terms of costs per thousand audience reached. Relatively simple surveys in each area

634

in which listeners are asked questions to establish their frequency of listening and, say, the number of hours per day which they listen might provide this type of information.

Audience estimates based on such data would be crude, but would at least demonstrate the relative popularity of each local station surveyed. As a refinement, it might be possible, by including similar questions on the national radio survey, to determine what listening claims of this kind mean in terms of actual listening recorded in diaries. If an approach of this kind proves successful, claimed listening to a specific station could provide a basis for making more accurate estimates of station audiences, spot audiences and even cumulative coverage. However, it seems unlikely that the advertising industry would make demands of this kind on local radio contractors because of the limited use for such data. Local advertisers are unlikely to call for detailed listening figures and national advertisers are not likely to have the inclination or resources to use detailed data for each local market. Provided the local survey data gave crude total audience levels and defined the characteristics of the audience and did both of these things in such a way that comparison can be made with detailed national data, the measures would be adequate for their purpose.

Local radio as an advertising medium does present considerable problems for the survey researcher and a great deal of work will have to be done before reliable, valid, and relevant information can be provided. However, considerable thought has been and is being given to these problems and there is no doubt that the research community is better placed to deal with them than it was ten years ago.

Cinema Audience Research

On the face of it, the cinema should be the simplest of all media for the researcher. The cinema audience is easy to define because qualification for membership depends on the purchase of a ticket and the total opportunities to see delivered by the medium must equal sales of tickets. Although this tells us nothing about the composition of the audience or the number of people represented by the total number of admissions, it is a reliable and accurate measure of 'opportunities' which can be used in conjunction with other research data. Admission figures are published monthly by the Board of Trade, but these figures in themselves are inadequate for campaign planning purposes because the only breakdowns published are by cinema size and the Registrar General's standard region. They do not tell us the total admission for a given period for a given selection of cinemas.

However, reasonable estimates of admissions can be made for individual cinemas because Board of Trade statistics show the percentage of capacity filled (for cinemas in each of four categories of seating capacity) and the average number of performances at these cinemas. Rank Advertising have been able to further improve this by taking into account the actual admissions to individual Rank and ABC cinemas. By deduction they can ascertain average admissions per seat per week to independent cinemas for each of 176 cells (seating capacity by region by quarter of year). By calculating a weekly admission factor for each cell and by applying this to the known seating capacity of an independent cinema, an admission figure can be calculated. Estimates of this kind for independent cinemas can be checked against actual admissions figures from certain independent cinemas who are prepared to supply them. Therefore, although admissions to individual cinemas are not available, reasonable estimates of admissions to cinemas selected for a campaign can be provided by the screen advertising industry through the co-operation of the major cinema chains and a number of independent cinemas.

However, admissions themselves are only part of the story. We need to know the nature of the audience in demographic terms and the number of people attending the cinema at least once in the campaign period, i.e., the cover of the campaign. The calculation of repetition would then be a simple matter of dividing admissions by the cover. Preferably, this information should be available for each demographic sub-group.

The major screen advertisers publish surveys concerning the cinema audience from time to time which have been useful in defining the audience in accurate terms, but the only continuous information available on the cinema audience is derived from the National Readership Survey (NRS). This survey contains three questions concerning cinema-going. These are:

1. *How often these days do you go to the cinema?*

Coded answers: twice a week or more; once a week; once a fortnight; once a month; three or four times a year; less often; never.

2. *How long ago was the last occasion you went to the cinema?*

Coded answers: in last four weeks; over one to three months ago; over three to six months ago; in last six months but can't remember when; longer ago but can't remember at all.

If the answer to question two is 'within last four weeks':

3. *How many times have you been in the last four weeks?*

Coded answers: once; twice; three times; four times; five or six times; seven or eight times; over eight.

On the basis of these questions it is possible to classify individuals into seven cinemagoing frequency categories based on their claimed frequency of visiting the cinema (Q. 1). This frequency distribution has been used to make estimates of the coverage given by campaigns of varying lengths and estimates can be made for any population subgroup classified in the NRS. The obvious method of calculating coverage is to assign probabilities of visiting the cinema in any given period based on an individual's claimed frequency. Thus, those who visit the cinema once or twice a week or more frequently have a probability of one of being covered by a one week campaign. Those who claim to go once in two weeks have a probability of a half, and so on. A probability estimate has to be made about the group who visit the cinema less often than once per month.

In a two week campaign covering all cinemas, the following table illustrates how cover would be calculated, assuming for the sake of simplicity that all cinemagoers go at least once in every four weeks, and that data is available for four groups of people. Having calculated the cover of a

Frequency category	Percentage of Population, say,	Probability of visit in two Weeks	Cover
1 per week	7	1	7%
1 every 2 weeks	4	1	4%
1 every 3 weeks	3	$\frac{2}{3}$	2%
1 every 4 weeks	2	$\frac{1}{2}$	1%
Total			14%

campaign using all cinemas, the assumption then made is that a campaign covering half of all admissions would have half the 'national' cover, i.e., for the above example, seven per cent. Unfortunately, however, calculations of this kind are invalid because individuals tend to overestimate their cinemagoing frequency. This can be evaluated by analysing their replies to the second question on the survey. This shows, for example, that only 96 per cent of the group who claim to go twice a week or more often went to the cinema in the last four weeks preceding the interview.

Stephen Gray, of Computer Projects Ltd, has calculated a cinemagoing probability for each of the seven frequency claim groups and for each of a number of demographic sub-groups. Through this work we can allocate to each individual in the survey a probability that he has visited the cinema in a four week time period. For those who claim to visit the cinema once a month, for example, the probability that they have been in the last four weeks is 0.617. The probabilities derived from this analysis can then be substituted for probabilities based on claimed frequency.

It can be demonstrated that the cinemagoing estimates obtained from this analysis are more accurate than estimates based on claimed frequencies. An analysis of question three produces an estimate of 15.4 million admissions in a four week period compared with the Board of Trade estimate of 16.5 million for a similar period.

The technique developed by Gray can be used for much more sophisticated analysis. Cinema campaigns vary in length but are generally considerably longer than four weeks. It is, therefore, important to be able to estimate cover for various campaign periods. By a simulation process in which cinemagoing probabilities are derived for half-weekly periods it is possible to expand the survey information to give coverage estimates for campaigns of any length. For each individual in the survey the method adopted was to compute his probability of visiting the cinema in a half week and to allocate his visits in an 18-week period on a random basis. Thus, in the case of an individual who goes to the cinema weekly and has a probability of visiting of 0.5 in a half week, he should have made 18 visits in the chosen period. These visits would be randomly allocated to 18 half weeks out of the total of 36. From a file of this kind it is possible to estimate the cover and repetition given by campaigns of any length up to 18 weeks for any sub-group of the population. A complete frequency distribution of opportunities to see the campaign can also be derived.

Estimates of this kind, of course, assume that the campaign is using all cinemas. The method used to relate cover to campaigns using only a proportion of cinemas is a crude one. The assumption made is that if a campaign is using, say, 50 per cent of the total cinema potential (measured in terms of cost) it would achieve 50 per cent of the coverage of a similar campaign using all cinemas. It would, of course, be preferable to use admissions data for the cinemas in question compared with total admissions, but this is not always readily available.

A further problem in making this type of calculation is that it assumes that everyone visits only one cinema. The assumption built into the model is that a person's frequency of visiting a particular cinema is the same as his frequency of visiting any cinema. However, about one-quarter of those who go to the cinema in a four-weekly period visit more than one and as we move from a consideration of national coverage estimates to the coverage given by a selection of cinemas we should take into account an individual's probability of visiting a particular cinema or selection of cinemas rather than any cinema. Coverage estimates made without taking this point into account are probably too low. The extent of that underestimate will depend on which cinemas are actually chosen for the campaign. A cinema in the centre of a large city will attract an audience from a wide area and many of the people visiting it will do so only infrequently. On the other hand, a suburban cinema or a cinema in a small town will tend to attract the same people week after week. It follows, then, that a town centre cinema will give a wider coverage than other establishments. In order to establish the effect of this on coverage estimates, we need to know how many cinemas have been visited by each individual during the campaign period and we need more reliable admissions information.

Apart from coverage and admissions estimates, there are one or two aspects of cinema audience research which are worth a mention. First, the relationship between the total cinema audience and the advertisement audience has always been of interest to advertisers. In the cinema the two must be very close in absolute terms. As any cinemagoer knows, it is almost impossible to avoid seeing the advertisements. Anyone in the auditorium when the advertisements are being shown must be exposed to them. It is, therefore, not unreasonable to assume a one to one relation between the audience of the medium and the audience of the advertisement, though this relationship might be more reliably estimated by determining the proportion of the audience which arrives before and leaves the cinema after the advertisements are screened. The screen advertising industry has also carried out work which demonstrates the high re-call of cinema advertising which makes the medium such a potent one for its relatively small audience. Second, although we have information about the cinema audience in terms of its demographic characteristics, we do not know whether or how this varies according to the location and type of cinema or the type of film screened. Is it possible to grade films or cinemas in terms of the composition of the audience they attract? Perhaps if we knew a little more about why people go to the cinema we could move closer to answering this type of question. Third, what is the catchment area of a cinema? What determines its size and how do these areas overlap? These questions may be important for campaign planning, especially as the number of cinemas declines.

The advertisers' basic requirements are, therefore, reasonably well met so far as the cinema is concerned. The problem of the advertiser lies generally in terms of utilizing the information available. Because of the relatively low level of expenditure on cinema advertising, the amount of effort which goes into campaign planning for this medium is small compared with television and the press. However, the usefulness of analysis based on NRS data will, no doubt, encourage more advertisers to utilize the coverage estimation methods outlined in this chapter, and thus improve cinema campaign planning.

References

Radio

1. Radio Luxembourg Audience Panel, Nov., 1968. Radio Luxembourg Audience Survey, Nov., 1968. Radio Luxembourg Audience Survey, Sept., 1970.
2. Westinghouse Broadcasting Corporation, *Radio's New Math*.
3. Media Research Group Proposals for Commercial Radio, *Admap*, Oct., 1965.
4. Television Audience Measurement Ltd., *Comparison Surveys*, 1963.
5. American Research Bureau/RKO General Broadcasting, *The Individual Diary Method of Radio Audience Measurement*, Feb., 1965.

See also:

Admap, July/Aug., 1970.
Polyphase: *Radio Listening and the Problems of its Measurement*, Radio Advertising Representatives Inc., 1967.
Radio Listening in America, Lazarsfeld and Kendall (Report and an interpretation of a survey conducted by National Opinion Research Centre, 1948).
Modern Radio Advertising, Charles Hull Wolfe of McCann Erickson Inc., Los Angeles, 1953.

Cinema

1. Unpublished Paper on Simulation of Cinema Going Habits, Stephen Gray, Computer Projects Ltd., 1969.

See also:

The Cinema Audience: Duplication of Media Survey, SAA, 1964.
The Cinema Audience: A National Survey, SAA, 1961.

26. Outdoor advertising research

Brian Copland

The limits imposed by the nature and structure of this book do not permit an historical review of the very considerable volume of work accomplished in this field. Those who wish to see the techniques described here in their wider context may care to refer to Copland[1,2]. These works contain extensive bibliographies which can be supplemented for the USA[3].

In the most general terms media research has two distinct but associated functions to perform. First, it must provide audience measurements—that is to say, sound estimates of the number and type of persons who are provided with the chance of seeing and assimilating any advertising messages that may be carried by the medium. At the same time, equally reliable estimates must be provided of the number of such chances or occasions offered to each member of the audience within any given period. Second, some clear indication must be given of the nature, value or effectiveness of these 'opportunities to see'. The decision to employ a given medium, either alone or in conjunction with others, can only be made with confidence if the advertiser and his agency can be assured that the medium in use reaches adequate proportions of the target market with a frequency or level of repetition that will ensure speedy and efficient transmission of his message.

The application of these principles to outdoor advertising—poster and public transport vehicles—presents a number of difficulties which are not present in the study of other media. These difficulties and differences can most readily be explained if comparison be made with the Press. In this medium the unit of measurement is the publication—newspaper or magazine—each with its unique title and a distinct individuality. The extent to which members of the target audience 'read', 'look at', 'glance at', 'leaf through' a given publication and the frequency with which they do this is an immediate measure of the audience provided by the medium. Basic audience measurement for the press, therefore, requires that the extent and regularity of 'reading' of a relatively small number of publications be established together with a clear indication of duplicated and multiplicated 'reading'. In other words, press research rests upon the 'opportunity to see' advertising in known and regularly identifiable media units.

The situation in respect of outdoor advertising, be it static posters or public transport vehicles, is radically different in that the campaign or schedule is made up, not of a relatively small number of identifiable media units (publications) from which a choice is made, but of such a large number of poster sites or vehicles that the individual audience characteristics of each one cannot, in practice, be measured. What is more, the advertiser, whether he selects his sites from an availability list or buys a 'package', does not and cannot know in advance precisely which sites will be used for his campaign; he only knows how many. It is, therefore, necessary in outdoor advertising research to use as the media unit for measurement the 'average' or 'representative' site and to present audience data *not* in terms of specific media units but of campaigns consisting of certain numbers of unspecified sites. Outdoor advertising audience measurement is, therefore, required to estimate in advance the audience, cover and repetition that is likely to be obtained by using a campaign consisting of a given number of average or representative sites distributed widely in a number of named urban areas.

It is, of course, true that individual poster sites (though not individual vehicles) differ very considerably in the audiences they command according to their position in the urban traffic pattern and the size and aspect of the hoarding or panel will condition the extent to which the poster is, in fact, seen and its message assimilated; but these differences, critical, no doubt, in the British process of site selection but not so important when poster packages are bought and sold, can only be appreciated and measured against a datum line which represents the behaviour of average campaigns.

One further, but fundamental, decision is necessary before outdoor media audiences can be measured. Given that a member of the media audience is one who has been presented with some kind of chance or opportunity to receive the message, it is necessary to define this opportunity clearly for each medium. As we have seen, in the press the opportunity is represented by 'reading', 'looking at', 'glancing at' a publication. In outdoor research the qualification for inclusion in the media audience is the passage past a place where the poster is displayed or an 'encounter' between an individual and a public transport vehicle. Whether the individual makes the passage on foot or in a vehicle is, at the initial stages of the measurement, irrelevant. The chance to see and assimilate the message has been provided and, just as the reader of the publication has a chance to see an advertisement in it, so a person passing by a place where a poster is displayed provides for himself an opportunity to see.

It should be emphasized here that the fact that all media use 'opportunities to see' as the basic criterion for inclusion in their audiences does not mean that these opportunities are in any numerical sense comparable. Conceptually they may be identical, but the widely different extent to which these

641

opportunities are translated into actual communication means that inter-media comparisons should not be based upon the number or cost of total 'opportunities to see'. It is the task of media communication research to determine the relative value of the many different types of opportunities to see that are provided by different media.

We may conclude these introductory remarks by drawing attention to the clear distinction that must be made between data collection and model building. It will already be apparent that the generalized nature of outdoor advertising audience measurement allows us to contemplate the construction of a mathematical model illustrating the association between basic data, such as number of campaign sites and town population, and the required levels of cover and repetition. Those concerned with market and media research are sometimes accused of allowing available data collection tech-niques to determine the information required. This is putting the cart before the horse and, particularly in outdoor advertising research, it is necessary first to establish the conceptual framework and only then to consider the various ways in which the essential basic data can conveniently and economically be obtained.

We therefore intend to begin our study of outdoor advertising audience measurement with a description of the mathematical model and its com-ponent parts.

Audience Measurement

Basic characteristic of the audience model

The audience for any poster campaign is generated by the physical interaction between people and places where posters are displayed. Within any given time period—a week, ten days, a month, longer—people pass poster sites and for any given number of sites in an urban area a certain proportion of the total (adult) population is responsible for an equally certain number of passages.

The relationship between these two statistics—audience and total passages, results in a third factor, repetition or frequency, which represents the average number of passages made by each member of the audience. This process of dividing total passages by audience to obtain repetition can be parallelled by dividing total passages by total population to give the average number of passages per head of population.

The relationship between the three factors can now be expressed as follows:

$$\frac{\text{total passages}}{\text{total population}} \div \frac{\text{total passages}}{\text{audience}} = \frac{\text{audience}}{\text{total population}} = \text{cover.}$$

This relationship can be further simplified by dividing by the number of sites

642

in the campaign giving:

$$\frac{\text{Average number of passages per site per head of population}}{\text{Average number of passages per site per member of the audience}} = \text{cover}.$$

Now, if we label the numerator of this fraction A and the denominator R we can illustrate the situation (in any one urban area) thus:

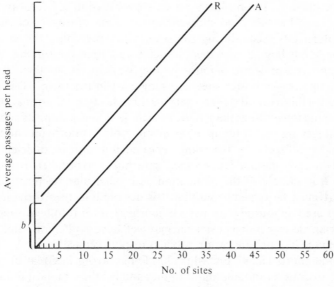

Fig. 26.1

The parameter A represents the average increment in traffic per site and the parameter R the average increment in repetition per site.

It will be apparent from the above that the repetition line can, in this instance, be expressed as A $+$ b, where b is the intercept of the repetition line. This is because, as in the definitive British survey[4] on which the model is based the two lines are parallel. If, as can occur, the two lines are *not* parallel, then R must be expressed as k A $+$ b, where k represents the difference in gradient of the repetition line from the A line.

Thus, the model can be written as C $=$ AS/kAS $+$ b where S represents the number of sites in the campaign. In other words, to calculate cover and repetition for campaigns consisting of any number of sites (in the particular urban area under review) we need to know the value of A (the traffic parameter), the value of b (the repetition intercept) and the value of k (repetition gradient correcting factor).

The establishment of the values of the model parameters, which may well vary from town to town and country to country, calls for survey work, the broad nature of which will be obvious from the foregoing. During the years of development of the model in various European countries the methods of data collection and analysis have been simplified and refined and it is our task in the following paragraphs to describe these methods in sufficient detail.

Data collection and analysis methods

Essentially, the data collection requirements are that the number of passages made by a random sample of the population past a random sample of sites should be known. The problem can be approached in several ways. First, one may record either at an interview or by means of travel diaries exactly where informants went during the seven days preceding the interview[5]. This is a rewarding, if extremely difficult and time consuming, process. Results, in terms of details of journeys, may be mapped and then associated with any number of poster sites that may exist in the town. The obvious advantage of this method is that it permits the collection of information about all sites in the town rather than merely a sample. Chief among its substantial disadvantages are the strain upon the memory of the informant and the very considerable difficulty of recording repeated journeys in sufficient detail. As far as the diary method is concerned, care must also be taken to obtain and retain a true sample of the population with particular reference to travel habits. It must be remembered that it is desirable to record the means of transport used on journeys (or parts of journeys) for it is to be surmised that a pedestrian passage past a poster site may well have a different 'value' from a passage made in a private car or public transport vehicle.

A second approach and one which has found favour in Great Britain and France is to draw a random sample of sites and list these in the questionnaire (describing them as 'key points') and, at the interview, to invite details of journeys made during the past seven days. The number of passages made past each key point is then recorded as the informant describes his or her journeys. In France, an elaboration of this method in order to reduce interview fatigue and memory failure was devised by which each informant was interviewed twice in the course of seven days[6].

Perhaps the most satisfactory method for obtaining the necessary data is that of 'location cards'. By analogy with press readership surveys where the memory stimulus to the informant takes the shape of a reproduction of the publication masthead, a photograph and sketch map of each sampled site location is produced and the resultant pack of location cards is leafed through by the informant at the interview.

The following questions are asked in respect of each location card. 'Now, we just want to check the flow of traffic past various key points in the town. To make the inquiry easier we have prepared these pictures and diagrams of the places we want to ask about'.

NOW TAKE INFORMANT THROUGH THE LOCATION CARDS IN TURN ASKING ABOUT EACH ONE.

'Do you know where this is?'

IF 'YES' ASK, 'Have you ever been to this place?' (Meaning the area marked by dotted lines on the location card map).

IF 'YES' ASK, 'When were you last there, either *at* the exact spot or *passing through* it?' Probe: How long ago was that? 'How were you travelling on that occasion?' 'What was the main purpose of your journey on that occasion?' 'How many times do you go there, or through there, in an average week these days?' IF LESS OFTEN THAN 'ONCE A WEEK' ASK, 'How often do you go there?',[7].

As might be expected, the different methods of data collection—complete journey records, key point recording and location cards—produce slightly different results. It has been found that the location card method, with its more elaborate and efficient stimulus to the informant's memory, results in somewhat higher levels of cover and repetition. This is perhaps due to a 'telescoping' effect in which the informant is inclined to attribute greater recency to intermittent passages past sites. A comparison of the key point and location card methods, together with other observations upon the validity of the model will be found in the IPA Poster Audience Surveys 1964[8].

The analysis of survey data, whether it be obtained by means of maps, key point lists or location cards, was originally a tedious process for it was necessary, in order to establish the graphs of A and R for each town, to determine cover and repetition for average or randomly selected campaigns of various sizes. This originally involved the successive random selection of campaigns of 5, 10, 15, 20, etc., sites. However, along with the improvement in the interviewing techniques brought about by the use of location cards, a shorter and more efficient analysis method has been devised. This method depends upon the assumption that, 'The proportion of the sample of informants passing any given combination of sites is approximately equal to the proportion passing any other different combination of n sites'[9]. The report from which this quotation is taken goes on to say, 'In practice, this is likely to be a reasonable assumption, intrinsic in any concept of "average campaign" '.

The model parameters in detail

(a) A—*The traffic parameter*

The critical position occupied by A—the traffic parameter in the audience model—will already have been appreciated and it has been indicated that values of A may well be different for towns of different populations. An early examination of the results from the definitive British survey showed that this was indeed the case and the differences in A values for the nine towns can be conveniently illustrated in Fig. 26.2. It will be observed that the gradient increases as the population of the town decreases. In other

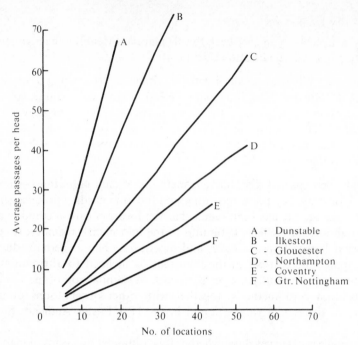

Fig. 26.2. Source: The Size and Nature of the Poster Audience Study Two—
May 1955.

words, A values become greater as population decreases. Naturally, it is to
be expected that the total traffic per site will increase as the population of
the town increases but when this total is divided in every case by the total
population the result is seen to be that the traffic parameter A decreases in
size as town size increases. Put in other terms, the traffic parameter
represents the chance that any one individual in the town would have of
passing any one site. Clearly, this chance is greater in small towns and lesser
in large towns.

Given a situation as depicted in Fig. 26.2 the immediate reaction is to
plot the values of A against population. When this is done it can at once be
seen from Fig. 26.3 that the relationship can be expressed in the form
$\log A = -a \log P + b$. In fact, for British sites the equation reads
$\log A = -0.7250 \log P(000) + 1.4140$.

The extensive work in Europe has enabled us to establish appropriate
equations for the value of A in several different countries. It is pertinent to
observe here that the traffic parameters may be expected to differ quite
markedly for different types of site and in fact in Germany two equations
have been required to cover the different types of site there present. These
equations are:

pillars for multiple posting and normal hoardings—

$$\log A = -0.408 \log P(000) + 1.118;$$

646

pillars for solus posting—

$$\log A = -0.465 \log P(000) + 1.466.$$

In both instances the value of b is 3.74^{10}.

In France, the equation reads:

$$\log A = -0.45 \log P(000) + 0.75,$$

based on five provincial towns. One may note that this equation exhibits a lesser difference between large and small towns than that found in the British equation. Recent pilot survey work in Eire, where a substantial rural population also exists, shows a similar trend.

Different values of A for demographic sub-groups and for different types of site in Great Britain will be commented on in a following section which will be devoted to the application of the model to media planning.

(b)   b—*The repetition intercept*

It is relatively easy to attach a real meaning to A for it represents quite clearly a function of traffic volume which varies according to type of site, town size and demographic sub-group. The situation in respect of *b*—the repetition intercept—is different. As will have been seen in an earlier section, *b* is the intercept of the repetition line and its size therefore conditions the rate of growth of cover as additional sites are added to campaigns and hence the shape of the cover curve. The intercept value of the repetition line is, therefore, of considerable importance. Perhaps the most interesting characteristic of the poster audience model as it has been determined and defined is that the value of *b* remains unchanged within a given country irrespective of the number of sites in the campaign and town size. For static

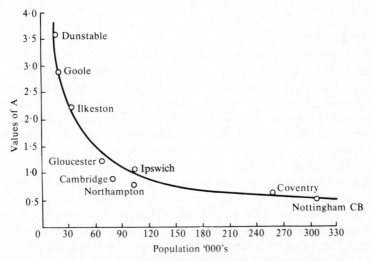

Fig. 26.3. Source: The Size and Nature of the Poster Audience Study Two—May 1955.

posters (in contrast to bus exteriors as we shall see) the values of b range across Europe from 3.5 to 4.75. Recent work in the US (in connection with large urban areas having populations of up to 16 000 000) shows a b value of 2.0.

(c)   k—*The repetition gradient correcting factor*

As we have pointed out earlier, the repetition line need not necessarily be parallel to the A line. In fact, in France, the definitive poster audience survey found that a value of k of 1.11 was necessary in order to correct the repetition line.

It is interesting to speculate on the precise meaning of the constant k. A clue is provided by the fact that in normal circumstances the slope of the A line increases as town size decreases. By analogy from this, we may be entitled to assume that when the slope of the repetition line is greater than that of the A line, i.e., when k has a value in excess of unity as in France, we are seeing a situation where, for one reason or another, the total available population to be covered by the poster campaign is less than the total population of the town. If, for example, the population to be considered was such that a random sample of poster sites could not be expected to reach all of it, i.e., if a substantial proportion never went out of their homes by reason of age or sickness, then we might expect to find a value of k greater than unity. Again, if a geographical distribution of a certain type of site were such that no sample from it could be expected to reach the whole population, then, again, we might expect to find a value of k in excess of unity.

By this argument it is unreasonable to suppose that a value of k of less than unity could be encountered unless, perhaps, the population reached by the campaign was greater than the population from which the sample was drawn.

(d)   t—*The time factor*

Most of the work on poster audience measurement has been based upon the normal time cycle of one week. Journeys made and passages past poster sites have been recorded either for 'the seven days prior to the interview' or, on some occasions, for 'yesterday'. In the latter case, journeys have been categorized as 'regular' or 'casual' and the results multiplied up according to the number of times that 'regular' journeys are made during a normal week. With interviewing correctly distributed between the seven days of the week, 'yesterday's' casual journeys can be multiplied by seven, but, with this method, it is not possible to estimate the growth of audience and, hence, cover and repetition over periods longer than one week. The use of location cards permits the recording of passages at intervals greater than one week and, hence, the extention of the cover growth curve to one month. In fact, it has been found that cover and repetition for periods which are multiples of one week can be predicted simply by a multiplication of the traffic parameter A. The model thus takes the form: $C = t\text{AS}/(t k\text{AS} + b)$ where t is the number of weeks in the campaign. It will be apparent from this that the accumulation of cover over time is the same as that obtained by increasing the number of sites in the campaign, e.g., a campaign of 20 sites for one week produces the same results as a campaign of 10 sites for two weeks.

Applications of the poster audience model

The poster audience model as here described is applicable to all sizes of urban areas and requires only the introduction of the national parameters A, b, and k for its use. In its simplest form,

$$C = \frac{t\text{AS}}{T\text{kAS} + b}$$

it estimates cover and repetition for campaigns of known sizes. More frequently, however, the campaign planner determines in advance the cover and repetition he will require in the various urban areas with which he is concerned and needs to know how many sites in each instance are required to achieve these levels. The model now takes the form (with cover as a percentage):

$$S = \frac{bC}{t\text{A}(100 - C)}.$$

If, for example, a monthly coverage of 80 per cent is required in a town whose A value is 1.0, then with the British values of b at 4.75 and of k at 1.0 the equation reads:

$$S = \frac{4.75 \times 80}{4 \times 1.0 \times 20} = \frac{380}{80} = 4.75 \text{ or 5 to the nearest site.}$$

The monthly repetition level—tAS + 4.75—would be 24.75.

The validity of the model when applied in major conurbations even as large as Greater London has been checked by segmenting the total area and determining the extent to which the resident populations move outside their own sectors[11]. It follows from the structure of the model and the relationship between A and population that, when the town size is, say, doubled or quadrupled, fewer than twice or four times the number of sites is required to achieve the same cover. This is, of course, due to the fact that the inhabitants of the sector can and do pass by sites in sectors other than their own. Provided that account is taken of the distance and use of underground and surface rail transport (which reduces the number of passages past above ground poster sites to a measurable degree) the model can be applied to major conurbations.

The applicability of the model to the largest types of urban area has been tested in the US. In recent years, several poster audience surveys have been carried out covering such markets as New York Metropolitan (population 16 052 047), Los Angeles/Orange Counties (population 8 950 200), Chicago (population 6 125 000), San Francisco (population 2 731 200) and Seattle (population 1 107 200). These surveys, based upon travel diaries, provide figures of cover and repetition for campaigns of various sizes and from these data it is possible to calculate values of A and b. It has been found that the A values for these unusually large urban areas conform to the pattern discovered in Great Britain and Europe and a steady value of b for all campaigns and areas has been found.

In contrast to the larger urban groupings of the population, consideration must also be given to satellite or 'hinterland' populations, i.e., persons living in the catchment area (consisting of very small towns, villages and rural areas) around each urban centre. This problem is relatively minor in Great Britain where more than four fifths of the population live in urban areas, but in Europe and elsewhere it has more importance. The movement of hinterland populations into their appropriate urban centres has been frequently demonstrated[12] and the considerable extent to which these populations are reached by poster sites situated in the town centres has been shown. There is, however, no simple and generally applicable formula for calculating either the relative size of the hinterland or (because of its varying geographical extent) the precise proportion of the hinterland population that will make journeys into their urban centres. This problem can be legitimately evaded in Great Britain where poster advertising is regarded as a purely urban medium but more work remains to be done in countries with substantial rural populations.

Demographic Sub-Groups

Although the outdoor medium claims, with every justification, to reach everyone who moves about out of doors and thus cannot be regarded as a highly selective medium in terms of target markets its coverage of demographic and socio-economic sub-groups of the population is uneven. Both A and b (and possibly k) values may be expected to differ for different sub-groups and recent research has indicated the magnitude of these differences particularly with reference to A. In a section of the Newport Survey an attempt is made to answer the question: 'Who are the heavily exposed people?' On an index basis with all adults as 100, men, the young (aged 16 to 24) and the C social grade score respectively 147, 131, and 121 while the housewife (including workers as well as non-workers) scores only 59. The journey to work, regardless of sex, is naturally a cause of high exposure to posters, for workers as a whole score 147. In sum, the major differences between demographic sub-groups lie not in coverage—the Newport campaign reached 86.1 per cent of housewives and 87.7 per cent of men—but in repetition. Men scored 88.1 and housewives 36.4.

Types of Site

In countries where posters are bought and sold on a package basis, i.e., where site selection is minimal if existent, the known and accepted differences

650

in performance of individual sites are, theoretically at any rate, compensated for within each package: but where schedules and campaigns are built by individual site selection some knowledge of the performance of different types of site, in terms of traffic, is desirable if only to adjust prices. To cope with this requirement, an elaborate system of site classification has been established by the poster industry in Great Britain in which not only traffic but the size and aspect of poster sites has been taken into account[13].

Our concern here is with the application of the poster audience model and in this context its prime purpose is to supply a datum line by which the traffic performance of different types of site can be assessed.

An examination of A values for four different categories of site was carried out in the Newport Survey and this showed that the top category, Road 1 in shopping or mixed areas, has a mean value of A of 1.384 compared with the overall average (as would be calculated by the poster audience model) of 0.878. It is clear from the results shown here that careful selection of sites, even without reference to size or aspect, can produce as much as a 50 per cent improvement in traffic values. It does not necessarily follow, however, that selection solely by traffic values will maximize cover, for this depends (as does the model) on an approximation to a random distribution over the whole of the urban area under review.

The Public Transport Audience Model

The foregoing description of the audience model has been based upon static posters but its use can conveniently be extended to 'moving posters', i.e., advertising on the outside of public transport vehicles. If people pass static poster sites with sufficient regularity to permit the construction of a mathematical model for predictive purposes then we may expect that the regular and repetitive movement of the sites themselves can be easily comprehended in a similar model. In what follows we describe briefly the necessary data collection methods and the modifications to the model structure that are required.

The development of a bus exterior audience model has had to wait upon the discovery of a survey technique which will provide sound estimates not only of the proportion of a sample that has 'seen' or 'encountered' a bus during the period under review but also, and more crucially, of the number of occasions on which a bus has been seen. Various methods have been adopted in the past. The most primitive (and most suspect) of these consists of simple and direct questions: 'Did you see any buses yesterday/during the past seven days?' If yes, 'How many did you see during that period?'[14]. A more sophisticated approach has been adopted in the US in which interviewers retraced the journeys made and recorded by informants in travel diaries. In the course of these simulated journeys a record was made of the number of buses seen. From these basic data cover and repetition figures were derived[15].

What appears to be the most satisfactory data collection method yet devised depends upon the recording, during interviews, of the length of time spent by informants on bus routes and the relation of these potential exposure times to the frequency with which buses traverse the routes. An informant recorded as spending half an hour on bus routes where the frequency is one bus every five minutes, for example, would be credited with six 'bus encounters'. An informant spending less than five minutes on such routes would be excluded from the bus exterior audience. This method seems to have been first applied in Düsseldorf[16] but questioning was confined to 'yesterday'. A more elaborate survey on these lines was conducted on behalf of London Transport in 1968[17]. This covered the whole of the Red London Bus area using a sample of 986 adults and recording time spent on bus routes during the seven days prior to the interview. Corrections were also made to account for variations due to journeys made on foot, in private cars and on buses. This survey provided cover and repetition figures for bus exterior campaigns of different sizes. Similar work has also been carried out in Italy where data was collected from four towns ranging in size from Turin (population 1 131 621) to Arezzo (population 83 716)[18].

Modifications to a.   Structurally, the bus audience model closely resembles the poster audience model in that the value of A—the traffic parameter—is of prime importance. The average number of encounters per bus per head of population decreases in relation to population just as with static posters but the relationship only holds good if the mean bus frequency, i.e., the average number of buses per hour in each town is equalized. In other words, a prediction of total traffic in terms of the number of bus encounters per head of population can be obtained for any town by calculating a value of A based upon any selected common bus frequency and then correcting this to allow for the known variation from the common frequency.

Modification to b.   The shape of the cover curves associated with bus exterior campaigns is seen to be radically different from those encountered in the measurement of static poster audiences. An examination of the results from the London Travel Survey indicates clearly that campaign size has little effect upon cover which is uniformly high. In fact, a campaign of 200 sites (for one week) provides a cover of 82 per cent while one five times the size raises the cover only to 84 per cent. Naturally, repetition levels increase with campaign size; in this instance from 8 to 41. It follows from this that the value of *b* for the bus exterior audience model must be low and in Italy a *b* value of 0.6 was found to be appropriate for all the towns surveyed.

Modifications to k.   Perhaps the most important modification to the audience model relates to the repetition line R. Here, again, the mean bus frequency in each town is of crucial importance in that the lower the bus frequency, i.e., the smaller the chance of seeing a bus, the steeper the slope of the repetition line R and, hence, the higher the value of k. It has been found that in this model the value of k varies inversely with bus frequency and in towns with high frequencies the k values are as near to unity as 1.2 while in low frequency towns they rise to as much as 1.8. One might surmize, therefore, that when the bus frequency rises to a level where k is equal to unity, the bus equation for A will be identified with that for static posters. A situation of this nature has, in fact, been encountered in the US.

We may summarize the situation by saying that the limited amount of work so far carried out indicates that an adequate predictive model for bus exterior advertising can be produced with the following structure: $C = t\text{Af}V/tkA + b$ where C = cover, t = duration of campaign in weeks, A = traffic parameter, i.e., bus encounters, f = mean bus frequency, V = number of vehicles in campaign, k = repetition gradient correcting factor, b = repetition intercept. Full details of the development and validation of this model can be found in the Italian survey referred to above.

Other forms of public transport advertising

It has been logical to extend the audience measurement procedure for poster campaigns to include other forms of advertising to which the whole population can be exposed. The only difference between posters and bus exteriors is that the former are static and the latter mobile. The potential audiences are the same, but the unique feature of public transportation advertising resides in the special 'captive' audience of the public transport users that it can command, and here the problems of audience measurement, i.e., the calculation of cover and repetition, are minimal.

Without exception, audience measurement for advertising on the inside of public transport vehicles—car cards—has been based upon samples of the population which are asked to provide information about the extent of their use of public transport. The results of such surveys[19] can take the form of cover and repetition for campaigns using different numbers of vehicles on the assumption of a random distribution of car cards in campaigns which use fewer than all the vehicles.

It is instructive, however, to consider a unique characteristic possessed by this medium, namely the continuing record of usage in terms of tickets sold. The number of tickets sold by a given public transport system represents in some sense a total of 'opportunities to see' the advertisements carried on that system. If all the tickets related to single and simple journeys with no changes involved then it would be safe to say that each ticket represented one chance to see advertising on the inside of public transport vehicles. This is, in all probability, broadly the case in respect of road transport but the situation in respect of railways, both below and above ground, is different.

Rail travel involves the use of station buildings—forecourts, concourses, platforms and access ways—and in consequence, each journey provides opportunities to see or passages past three distinct types of advertising. The first of these is forecourt and concourse advertising (which can, incidentally, be seen by persons who are not travelling), the second consists

653

of platform advertising and the third vehicle interior advertising or car cards. Thus, a single ticket representing a simple journey without change en route provides two opportunities to see forecourt and concourse advertising, two to see platform advertising and one to see car cards. A simple return ticket provides twice this number and a commuter ticket a greater number still according to its period of currency and extent of use.

Totals of tickets sold, if properly categorized according to type—single, return, commuter, etc.,—can be converted into total opportunities to see each kind of advertising and these totals can, in their turn, be converted into cover and repetition figures. What is required is a continuing panel survey procedure covering a period of at least a year in which rail tickets purchased are recorded together with full details of the journeys made. From such data conversion factors can be calculated such that the raw totals of tickets sold can be converted into the kind of audience data—cover and repetition for different types of transportation advertising—that the media planner and the advertiser require.

As far as ticket analysis for road transport is concerned, it is illuminating to note that the average number of tickets sold per bus per head of population—a car card A value—seems with such limited evidence as exists to bear the same kind of relationship to population as the bus exterior and static poster A values. To the extent that the demand exists one may, therefore, envisage a completely coherent set of movement models based on known data such as population, bus operating statistics and tickets sold which will have the ability of predicting necessary audience data for all forms of 'out of home' advertising.

Communication Effectiveness

Media research is, by definition, concerned with blank spaces; advertising research with the messages that fill them. The dividing line between these two disciplines, however, cannot be clearly drawn, for the techniques of advertising research—the measurement of recall, recognition, attitude change, propensity to buy, etc.—are virtually the only weapons available when it is necessary to make sensible statements about the communication effectiveness of a medium.

The complex and controversial subject of advertising research is treated elsewhere in this book and we must be content here to examine only those practical applications of its techniques which can form a basis, however infirm, for generalizations about the performance of the outdoor medium. Within these limits the task is clear. It is to be in a position to evaluate the different types and sizes of poster site and the medium as a whole in terms of communication effectiveness. To do this it is necessary to examine the performance of large numbers of different posters presented to their audiences in different physical and marketing circumstances. These 'case histories'— for they are no more—may then be subjected to forms of analysis which are intended to distinguish and give numerical value to the many characteristics both of medium and message that are involved.

In pursuance of this aim researchers have, for many years, been in the habit of exposing populations to posters and car cards and then recording the reactions of samples of these populations. In the main, the age-old techniques of spontaneous and aided recall, masked and complete recognition, theme association and general awareness questions have been employed, and the criticisms of these techniques belong as we have indicated, to the study of advertising research. What is of particular importance to the outdoor medium is an appreciation and demonstration of the fact that the weight of advertising exposure—the repetition level—is critical in any evaluation of results. Speaking from the standpoint of the media buyer (a stance which is recommended to the researcher) the outdoor medium, both poster and public transport, has the capacity to deliver uniformly high levels of cover in most target markets and expenditure on this medium is or should be determined primarily by the desired levels of repetition. Hence, the major requirement is that some form of evaluation or weighting should be applicable to the different levels of repetition as predicted by the audience model. Current effectiveness research in this medium is directed to this end.

The direct and visible association of response (however measured) with repetition can be achieved if the survey procedure is such that any sample questioned about response to a given poster campaign can be segmented quite strictly according to its different levels of repetition. This desirable state of affairs can be illustrated by a practical example. In 1968 a new and distinctive test poster was exposed for a period of four weeks in five towns in Great Britain. Efforts were made to reduce 'confusion' by selecting a product (a social service) which was not in the habit of advertising and, in fact, no other advertising in any other medium was employed at this time. Precise details were known of each site in each town where the poster was displayed and location cards were prepared for each. At the expiration of the four week period samples of the population were interviewed and were questioned under two heads:

(a) exposure level questions designed to ascertain whether and how many times each informant had passed each site;
(b) response questions relating to spontaneous and aided re-call and recognition.

Details of the exposure questions have been given earlier in this chapter and the response questions were as follows.

'Can you remember seeing any posters or advertisements on hoardings in . . . . (town) recently?' IF 'YES' SOME POSTERS REMEMBERED, ASK: 'Which poster can you remember seeing in . . . . (town)?' PROBE

TILL NO MORE POSTERS REMEMBERED: 'What others can you remember?' FOR EACH POSTER REMEMBERED, ASK: 'What was the poster about?' 'What did it show?' 'What did it say?' 'These are some well-known advertising slogans. Can you tell me what they are advertising?' SHOW CARD WITH INCOMPLETE SLOGANS. 'Here is a list of some things which have been advertised on posters in . . . . (town) recently. Can you tell me which ones you remember seeing on posters in the town?' FOR EACH ONE REMEMBERED, ASK: 'Did you *definitely* see it or do you just think you *might* have seen it?' SHOW PICTURES OF POSTERS. 'These are pictures of some posters. Let's take this one first'. FOR EACH POSTER, ASK: 'Do you happen to have seen this poster before?' IF 'YES' ASK: 'Have you *definitely* seen it before, or do you just think you *might* have seen it?' 'Whereabouts did you see it?' 'When did you *last* see it?'[7]

Given the answers to these questions it was possible to divide the samples into sub-groups according to the amount of repetition to which they had been subjected and, at the same time, to provide for each of these sub-groups levels of response. The results are summarized in the following charts, Figures 26.4, and 26.5.

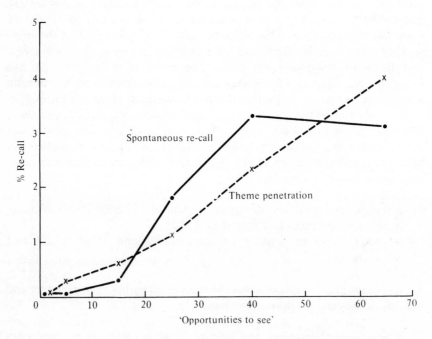

Fig. 26.4. 'Spontaneous Recall' and 'Theme Penetration' generated among housewives by a mixed 16-sheet and 4-sheet campaign (Source: Research Services Ltd. J.5916, November, 1968).

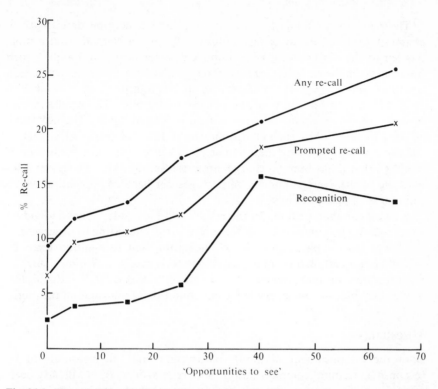

Fig. 26.5. 'Prompted Recall', 'Recognition' and 'Any Recall' generated among housewives by a mixed 6-sheet and 4-sheet campaign (Source: Research Services Ltd. J.5916, November, 1968).

Several conclusions can be drawn from an examination of data of this nature. First, it is clear that the repetition level is a sufficiently important determinant of response to warrant separate attention and analysis. Second, it may be observed that the different types of response measurement generated when plotted against repetition give different shaped curves. Third, the value of this method for pretesting in normal conditions, i.e., in the street, resides in the fact that the campaign size and duration is irrelevant. Provided that comparisons between different test posters are based upon the same levels of repetition, the comparison is valid regardless of campaign size. Finally, it will be appreciated that this technique can be used to evaluate different sizes and types of poster. If the same poster is displayed in different towns using one particular type of site in each then a reasonable comparison can be made on the basis of response. Hitherto, the difficulty of comparing two campaigns using different types or sizes of site has been complicated by the fact that the traffic parameter or A values may not be the same in each case e.g., 48-sheet sites are usually deliberately placed at 'above average' traffic positions and any comparison between the performance of these sites and others of different sizes must take this factor as well as sheer size into account.

The need to accumulate sufficient data, and hence the desirability of examining the behaviour of several (up to 20) poster campaigns at a time, has led to the development of a simplified poster testing technique which has been given the name tAS. This technique makes use of simple recognition questions based upon the presentation to the informant of a number of small colour reproductions of the posters under test. The resultant 'recognition score' expressed as a percentage is plotted against the tAS value of the campaign. For each campaign, the A value or traffic parameter of the town is multiplied by the number of sites used (S) and the number of weeks (t) that it has been 'in charge' up to the survey date. The result is an estimate of the average number of passages per head of population which represents campaign weight.

A curve can then be fitted to the results and the results of any individual campaign design compared with this norm. It is interesting to observe that the curve is of a paraboloid nature indicating that recognition tends to fall off after a certain level of exposure has been reached. We may surmise from this that our measurements here relate to "noticeability" of the poster, a necessary but, of course, not sufficient condition of information transfer.

Miscellaneous

Both the establishment of model parameters and the measurement of response (in terms of communication effectiveness) depend, as will have been seen, upon a fairly precise knowledge of the number of passages past known poster sites. Model parameters for Great Britain and several European countries have now been established and the possibility of a European model can now be envisaged. This will, of course, have considerable advantages particularly for the smaller European countries where resources do not permit the mounting of survey work in several towns. However, it still remains necessary on many occasions to be able to categorize samples of the population according to the levels of their exposure to the outdoor medium. This situation occurs in multi-media and media/product surveys, where exposure to media such as television and press must be measured. It is not possible in such surveys to contemplate the use of location cards and the poster audience model of this provides a single overall average level of exposure in terms of cover and repetition. It has, therefore, been found necessary to attempt to predict at least four levels of exposure to the outdoor medium—'heavy', 'medium', 'light' and 'negligible'—by the use of discriminatory questions. These questions must be short and easily administered and it is to be expected that they will be based upon either the number and type of journeys and/or the length of time spent out of doors.

A significant part of the Newport Survey to which reference has been made above was devoted to a consideration of this subject and the results have been presented in a document produced by the British Joint Industry Committee for Poster Audience Surveys. Apart from social grade and geographical considerations (proximity to town centre) which have an obvious influence upon exposure, the main discriminatory questions relate to the number of times the informant left home during the seven days prior to the interview and details of the journey to work (frequency and means of transport).

An interesting alternative approach to the problem was made some years ago in Germany. The purpose here was to examine response (as described above) in relation to weight of exposure to the medium and for this purpose informants were asked how long they had spent out of doors 'yesterday'. The resultant plot of response against time spent out of doors exhibited characteristics very similar to those which have been found in Great Britain for response against repetition. This encouraging development, which is now in course of elaboration, might well be of assistance in solving the problems of response to bus exterior advertising where, naturally, location cards cannot be used.

This chapter may be concluded by emphasizing once again that the outdoor medium with its regularity of human behaviour is eminently suited to the kind of treatment outlined here. It is possible to predict with sufficient accuracy for commercial purposes the cover and repetition to be expected from campaigns of any size and duration and the demonstrably close association between response and levels of exposure (repetition) provides a basis for the evaluation of the communication effectiveness of the medium.

References

1. COPLAND, B. D. *A Review of Poster Research*, Business Publications Ltd., 1963.
2. COPLAND, B. D. *Transportation Advertising Research*, Institute of Practitioners in Advertising, 1964.
3. *Recommended Research Program for Institute of Outdoor Advertising*, Advertising Research Foundation Inc., 1967.
4. COPLAND, B. D. *The Size and Nature of the Poster Audience, Study II*, Mills and Rockleys Ltd., 1955.
5. NIELSON, A. C. *Survey of Outdoor Advertising Coverage*, Foster and Kleiser, 1960.
6. *Etudes sur l'Audience de l'Affichage* 1963/1964, CESP, 1965.
7. *The Ability to Posters to Communicate*, unpublished, Research Services Ltd.
8. *IPA Poster Audience Surveys*, Institute of Practitioners in Advertising, 1964.
9. *Newport Survey*, Joint Industry Committee for Poster Audience Surveys, 1964.
10. Infratest, *Reichweiten- und Kontaktermittlung des Plakatanschlags in Gemeinden bis zu 300.000 Einwohnern*, 1968.
11. COPLAND, B. D. Towards A Validation of the Poster Audience Model for Greater London, *Journal of the Market Research Society*, Market Research Society, **11**, 4, 1969 (pp. 338–342).
12. Cofremca, *Etude sur les Deplacements des Ruraux Residant dans les Communes de Moins de 1.000 Habitants*, Avenir Publicite, 1968.
13. *Contractor's Handbook for the Use of Contractors Operating in the United Kingdom Only*, British Poster Advertising Association and the Solus Outdoor Advertising Association Ltd., 1968.
14. *Rapport Från en Undersökning I Karlstad om 'King-Size'—Skyltar och 'King-Size'—Bussar*, Svenska Institutet for Opinionsundersökningar, 1961.
15. McKENNA, M. Metromedia Inc., New York.
16. Infratest, *Reichweite der Verkehrsmittelwerbung in Düsseldorf*, 1964,

17. COPLAND, B. D. *The Audience for Advertising on the Outside of the Red London Bus*, London Transport Advertising, 1967.
18. COPLAND, B. D. *La Audience della Pubblicità Esterna sui mezzi di Trasporto Pubblici*, Impresa Generale Pubblicità, 1968.
19. COPLAND, B. D. *London Travel Survey* 1949, London Transport Executive, 1950.
20. *Multi-Media Surveys—The Prediction of Exposure to Posters*, JICPAS, 1970.
21. Institut für Demoskopie Allensbach, *Werbeträger Analyse* 1967, *Zweiter Teil Plakat*, 1967.
22. *The eAS Poster Testing Service*, Outdoor Research Surveys Ltd, London 1971.

Biographies of the contributors

BRIAN ALLT is Deputy Manager, Marketing; Research; and Services Department, of the International Publishing Corporation. After taking a degree in psychology and post-graduate research, he entered market research in 1955. Since 1958 Mr Allt has worked with Odhams' Press (later incorporated into IPC). His department provides full survey facilities, desk research, marketing consultancy and media scheduling services to IPC Divisions. In addition to these activities, he has for many years been a member of several industry committees (JICNARS Technical Sub-Committee, NPA Committees, etc.) concerned with marketing of publications both to the consumer and the advertiser, and he has worked particularly on the development of the JICNARS National Readership Survey. Postal research has been particularly relevant in more recent years as often the only economic means of carrying out research related to minority publications and books, but has also been effectively used for larger publications, reader panels, etc.

GERRY ARNOTT is Managing Director of the Bureau of Commercial Research, in London. Although trained in graphic design, he joined Attwood Statistics in 1955 as a trainee, working first on consumer panels and later in the survey unit. In 1959, he joined Sales Research Services as Audit Controller, engaged on the developments and applications of audit research generally and to a lesser extent on consumer panels. From early 1966 to the end of 1967 he worked at Research Services on consumer panels and audits when he left to join Petfoods where he worked for three years as Market Research Manager. He has had over ten years continuous experience of retail and wholesale audit work, both as a 'seller' and 'buyer'. He has served on Market Research Society Committees, convened weekend courses, and lectured at the Society's summer school.

MICHAEL BROWN is a Partner of Collins Teleki Brown Associates, the marketing, research and communications consultancy he helped to launch in 1971. He obtained a BA degree from the University of Cambridge in natural sciences and economics. In 1954 he entered advertising, initially as an account executive, and then moved to the marketing and market research side. Mr Brown joined Lintas Ltd in 1959 as Head of Media Research. In 1962 he moved to Research Bureau Ltd (the Unilever market research company). In 1963/4 he was attached to the Research Department of Sullivan, Stauffer, Colwell and Bayles, New York. He then returned to RBL as Technical Manager, with responsibility for basic research in the advertising and product areas within an international programme. In 1968 he joined the Newspaper Publishers Association and was later appointed their Head of Marketing.

MICHAEL BURROWS is Director, British Market Research Bureau Ltd, and Head of Industrial and Financial Research. Mr Burrows joined the British Market Research Bureau as a research executive in 1958 and was primarily concerned with continuing studies of the markets for consumer durables and the motor industry. Between 1962 and 1967 he was a director of 'Windett, Burrows and Bonar Law Ltd', a specialist research company in which a merchant bank had an equity interest: as a result, he became particularly involved in portfolio investment research and specialized surveys for City clients. In 1967, Mr Burrows returned to BMRB to develop new business in the industrial and financial field: he was appointed an associate director in 1968 and a director in 1970. His published surveys during this period include the 'GEC bid for AEI' (commissioned by J. Walter Thompson) and the 'Professional Investor' (commissioned by the 'Investor's Chronicle'), and he has become increasingly concerned with corporate communications, particularly in so far as they effect takeover bid situations and the flow of information which should pass from industry to the City, and vice versa. At the same time, the development of the 'City Edition' of the Target Group Index into a basic tool for investment analysts working in the consumer goods field, keeps alive his interests in portfolio investment research and the changing pattern of savings and investment services.

MARTIN COLLINS is a Director of Aske Research Ltd. He is formerly a Director of Research Services Ltd, and a graduate in economics of University College, London.

BRIAN COPLAND is Chairman, Outdoor Research International Ltd. Mr Copland's experience of market research began in 1945 after his return from war service. Three years with Lintas Market Research were followed by a period as Advertising Research Executive with Research Services Ltd and continuing activity in the field of media research with the London Press Exchange Ltd. In 1955 details were first published of his poster audience model which has since been adopted throughout Europe and the American continent. After three years as Director of Research at Lambe and Robinson Ltd (now Benton and Bowles) he joined the Board of Hobson Bates and Partners Ltd where he occupied the position of Research Director for eight years. During the course of his career Brian Copland has been closely associated with the development of media research in general and outdoor advertising research in particular through his continuing membership of the Research Committee of the Institute of Practitioners in Advertising, and the various subcommittees concerned with the establishment of industry research procedures for both press and television. He served as a Member of the Market Research Society Council and is a Fellow of the Institute of Statisticians and the Institute of Practitioners in Advertising. In 1965 he resigned from the Board of Hobson Bates and Partners Ltd to establish with his son, Simon, his own outdoor marketing and research consultancy organization which now serves the industry in all parts of the world. He has contributed extensively to technical journals in Great Britain, Europe and the US and his publications include 'The Study of Attention Value' and 'A Review of Poster Research'. At present, his time is occupied with technical consultations and an extensive programme of lectures and seminars.

JOHN DAVIS is Head of the Operational Research Unit of J. Walter Thompson Co. Ltd. This Unit was set up in 1966 to carry out basic research into problems of advertising and marketing, and to provide consultancy services to clients and others. After graduating in 1948 he worked in statistics and operational research with Gillette, BOAC, and Television Audience Measurement before going to the British Market Research Bureau Ltd in 1956. After three years as a Group Head in the General Research Division, he was appointed Head of the Retail Audit Division in 1959, and was responsible for setting up the first permanent retail audit test panels based on television areas. In 1966 he moved from BMRB to J. Walter Thompson to set up the Operational Research Unit. He is a full member of the Market Research Society and was awarded the Society's Gold Medal in 1966 for his work on test marketing. He is a Fellow and Vice Chairman of the Institute of Statisticians and a Fellow of the Marketing Society.

BERT DE VOS is Media and Marketing Research Director of Masius, Wynne-Williams Ltd, a position he has held since April 1965. Mr De Vos graduated from the London School of Economics in 1952, taking first-class honours in economics. He was a Harold Laski scholar. From 1952 to 1954 he was commissioned in Army Intelligence Service. Since 1954 he has had wide and varied business and academic experience, consisting more recently of six years as a Director of the Gallup Poll, coupled with two years as Director of the Sociological Research Unit at Keele University. He was Chairman of the Market Research Society 1969/70 and is Chairman of the Joint Industry Committee for Television Audience Research technical sub-committee.

JOHN DILLON is Research Director of Market Pulse Ltd, with particular responsibility for its specialist division, Packaging Pulse. He was formerly Managing Director of Packaging and Perceptual Research Ltd, a company specializing in consumer packaging research, which he cofounded in 1967 with William Schlackman Ltd. Dr Dillon was trained primarily as an Experimental Psychologist at University College, London, the University of British Columbia, and McGill University, Montreal, where he obtained his doctorate. His research, both in the academic and business environments, centering upon perceptual behaviour, its emotional correlates, and its relationship to decision-making, led him after a series of developmental studies in 1966 to specialize in packaging research. In the marketing context, Dr Dillon has assisted in the development of several hundred packs for new and existing products.

JOHN DOWNHAM is International Market Research Coordinator of Unilever Ltd, concerned with the development of Unilever's market research facilities and methods internationally. After taking a degree in philosophy, politics and economics at Oxford, Mr Downham joined the British Market Research Bureau in 1948 as a trainee research officer. Subsequently, he reconstructed and developed the BMRB Retail Audit (now a part of Retail Audits Ltd), before assuming responsibility for all consumer research. He became the Managing Director of BMRB in 1960 and towards the end of 1963 joined Unilever. Mr Downham was a council member of the Market Research Society from 1956 to 1962, becoming Chairman in 1959 to 1960. Both then and later he has been a contributor to Market Research Society courses. He is a council member of ESOMAR and has given papers at three of its conferences. He is co-author of 'The Communication of Ideas', and author of a number of papers and articles on market research.

JOHN DRAKEFORD is a Director of Audits of Great Britain Ltd. After graduating in classics at Cambridge University, John Drakeford spent two years in local government accountancy, where his training included the application of computer techniques to financial problems. In 1957, he joined the Research Department of the leading advertising agency, Mather and Crowther Ltd and was Research Manager there from 1960 to 1963, heading a department which serviced the continuous and 'ad hoc' research requirements of agency clients. He then joined Audits of Great Britain Ltd one of the largest independent research companies, specializing in consumer panel research and 'ad hoc' surveys. As a Director of the Company, he now heads AGB Surveys, the division engaged in a wide variety of 'ad hoc' research projects, conducted on behalf of manufacturers, retailers, advertising agencies, media owners, central and local government, and nationalized industries. He is a full member of the Market Research Society and of ESOMAR, and has lectured on research topics both in the UK and in Europe. He also holds the Diploma of the Institute of Practitioners in Advertising.

LEONARD ENGLAND formed England, Grosse and Associates Ltd with Wendy Grosse in 1969. Mr England began his market research career as an interviewer with Mass-Observation Ltd and was trained in many of the techniques described in his chapter; subsequently, he became Managing Director of the Company, a post which he held for over twenty years. He has been Chairman of both the Market Research Society and of the Association of Market Survey Organizations. Among his main research interests are the need to maximize the use of market research techniques in fields such as social welfare, and to improve effective communication of results to management.

COLIN GREENHALGH took a BA with honours in mathematics at Jesus College, Oxford, and started his market research career in 1955 with the British Market Research Bureau. He then moved to Tyne Tees Television, where he was responsible for introducing the market research services supplied to advertisers who were test marketing in that region and, subsequently, to the Research Bureau (Unilever).

In 1963 he joined the Phillips Scot & Turner Company (now Sterling Health Products) where he was largely responsible for setting up and managing a substantial market research department. Later he became Management Services Controller of that company and had new product development responsibilities in Phillips Laboratories, its proprietary medicines division.

He joined Taylor, Nelson & Associates as a Director in 1969, and since 1971, has been Managing Director of Sales Research Services—an associated company of TNA; he has frequently presented papers on product testing and new product development to market research courses and conferences in the UK and Europe. He is a Council Member of the Market Research Society, Chairman of the Society's Professional Standards Committee, and winner of the Society's Gold Medal in 1968.

PAUL HARRIS is the Chief Statistician of NOP Market Research Ltd. He was formerly with the market research department of the Electricity Council and before that with the planning department of the Central Electricity Generating Board. He studied statistics at the Regent Street Polytechnic (now the Polytechnic of Central London) and is an Associate of the Institute of Statisticians. His interests include the application of multi-variate statistical methods to market research data, and the use of computers in statistical analysis, subjects on which he has given lectures for The Market Research Society.

CLIFF HOLMES is the Head of Sampling and Statistics of Research Services Ltd, a position he has held since 1967. After a period of five years in industry Mr Holmes began his market research career with Marplan Ltd, as a statistician. He joined Research Services Ltd in November 1967. He is an Associate of the Institute of Statisticians. In addition to being a part-time lecturer in Market Research at Central London Polytechnic, he gives lectures in Statistics for the Market Research Society and convened the 1970 Advanced Statistics course of multi-variate analysis.

JOHN KENDALL is the Director of Market Research in the International Wool Secretariat, responsible for the control and coordination of market research in the twenty-five or so countries where the IWS operates. He read mathematics and economics at St John's College, Cambridge and joined the British Market Research Bureau in 1959 as a research executive. In 1962 he moved to Masius Wynne-Williams, the leading London advertising agency, where he supervised a wide range of accounts as a research group head. In 1966 he joined the Wool Secretariat to build up and coordinate economic and market research activity throughout Europe. In this position he was involved in great depth in the use of the type of omnibus surveys mentioned in his chapter and was concerned with a number of studies to improve the accuracy and use of this type of research. Finally, in 1967, he took over global responsibility for market research for the Wool Secretariat where he has been responsible for a number of international comparative research programmes, often using omnibus surveys.

MARK LOVELL is Research Director of Leo-Burnett-LPE Ltd. He took a double first in classics and psychology at Cambridge. In 1959 he joined the British Market Research Bureau, where he was made a Group Head, with responsibility for research on a range of consumer accounts. In 1963 he joined Marplan, where he was appointed to the Board. Here he had responsibility for the Communication Research Unit. Communication Research Ltd, then a subsidiary of the London Press Exchange, invited him to join their Board in 1965. He transferred shortly to the LPE Ltd, where he has been in charge of the Research Department since that year. He has delivered many papers at ESOMAR and other international research conferences, and has won several Thomson Awards for Advertising and Media Research: the Silver Medal 1966 and Gold Medals 1967 and 1968.

TONY LUNN is a Senior Manager of Unilever Ltd and a Director of Research Bureau Ltd. His current responsibilities include the administration of the UK section of an international programme of basic market research, designed both to develop new techniques and to advance understanding of consumer decision processes. He took a BA in psychology and philosophy at St John's College, Oxford, and an MA in occupational psychology at Birkbeck College, London. His market research experience includes four years with Attwood Statistics Ltd. He has lectured and published widely on a variety of topics concerning the application of the social sciences to management problems.

ELIZABETH NELSON is Chairman and Joint Managing Director of Taylor Nelson and Associates. After taking a BA degree at Middlebury College and a PhD in psychology at the Institute of Psychiatry, University of London, Dr Nelson entered market research in 1955. She worked as Director and Managing Director of the The Research Unit Ltd, the subsidiary of Benton and Bowles until 1964. In early 1965 she became founder director of Taylor, Nelson. She was Honorary Secretary and Treasurer of the Market Research Society, 1958/1960 and Council Member 1967/1970. She has written several articles on the use of psychological techniques in market research, segmentation analysis and consumer models.

JOHN PARFITT is the Managing Director of Mass-Observation Ltd, a position he has held since 1969. Mr Parfitt graduated in 1951 from the London School of Economics, gaining a BSc (Econ) with first-class honours. He joined Unilever Ltd in 1952 as Management Trainee in the Market Research Division. He spent seven years in consumer research and as Manager of the Television Research Department after the introduction of commercial television in the UK. He joined Attwood Statistics in 1959 as Manager of the Television Consumer Panel, then Manager of the 'Ad Hoc' Surveys Division, Manager of the Consumer Panel and finally Joint Managing Director of Attwood Statistics Ltd. Mr Parfitt has published a number of articles on consumer panels which have appeared in the Journal of Marketing Research, the Journal of Advertising Research, Thomson Gold Medal Papers and ESOMAR.

JAMES ROTHMAN is an independent marketing and research consultant. He is also a Director of Taylor, Nelson and Associates, a marketing research agency within the Taylor Nelson group. Mr Rothman graduated from Cambridge in 1954 with a degree in natural sciences and economics. After National Service in the RAF as an Education Officer, he joined the Solartron Electronics Group as an Organization and Methods Officer and subsequently became assistant to the Research Laboratory Manager. He became interested in market research and left Solartron in 1959 to join BMRB as a research executive. At BMRB he worked both in a consumer research group and as a Group Head in the Special Projects Division. In 1962 he purchased an interest in Sales Research Services and became Chairman of that company. The Taylor, Nelson Group purchased Sales Research Services in 1969 and Mr Rothman became Joint Managing Director of Taylor, Nelson Investment Services and a Director of Taylor, Nelson and Associates. Mr Rothman has spoken both at ESOMAR conferences and at Market Research Society conferences, courses and seminars. He has had papers published in Britain and America on various aspects of marketing, media and research and has received the MRS Gold Medal for his paper on the Formulation of an Index of Propensity to Buy. He has also been a joint winner of the Coglan Award and of the Thomson Gold Medal and Award for Media Research. Besides his business activities, he is a Visiting Research Fellow in Marketing at Lancaster University. He has also served on the Market Research Society Council and as external examiner in marketing to Bradford University.

GEOFFREY ROUGHTON is a Director of Marketing Advisory Services Ltd. Mr Roughton studied english literature and engineering at Trinity College, Cambridge, from which he graduated with a BA in 1952; subsequently he became an MA. His first appointment was with George Newnes Ltd, in a trainee position, following which he was asked to set up the UK subsidiary of a Dutch food materials manufacturing company. In 1956, he joined the Attwood Group of Companies as a client service executive with TAM. He then became a free-lance marketing consultant for a short time early in 1958, before founding Marketing Advisory Services Ltd with John Robertson. For a two year period, 1948/49, he was commissioned in the REME as an electronics instructor. Mr Roughton is a member of the Market Research Society as well as the Royal Statistical Society and has been a council member of the Association of Market Survey Organizations since 1965.

PETER SAMPSON is Director of Gordon Simmons Research Ltd. A full member of the Market Research Society, Mr Sampson graduated from the University of Exeter in 1959 with a degree in social science. He entered market research straight away and worked in the research departments of a number of leading advertising agencies before joining NOP in 1966 to head a group engaged in attitude and motivation research. He has lectured on market research and psychology for the Market Research Society and is currently a part-time tutor in psychology for the University of London Extra-Mural Department. He has published a number of articles on market research topics, and given papers at conferences in Mexico City, Amsterdam, Helsingor, Helsinki and Brighton.

WILLIAM SCHLACKMAN is Chairman and Managing Director of William Schlackman Ltd. Mr Schlackman received his education in psychology at Brooklyn College, the City College and New York University. Prior to his work in market research he was a clinical psychologist working in the area of personnel selection. This was followed by a period of free-lance psychology in the area of motivational research. In 1956 he joined the Dichter organization. Between 1960 and 1962 he was Managing Director of Ernest Dichter Associates in London. He founded William Schlackman Ltd in 1963 and he has been Chairman and Managing Director of that organization from then to the present time.

MARTIN SIMMONS is Joint Managing Director of Gordon Simmons Research Ltd, responsible for its consumer research activities including 'below the line' research. He was previously a Director of the Gallup Poll and before that a Director of Sales Research Services Ltd. He has extensive experience in all forms of consumer and trade research. He has lectured to Market Research Society and ESOMAR meetings. He has served on the Market Research Society's Governing Council and is a Fellow of the Royal Statistical Society. Mr Simmons graduated from the London School of Economics with an honours degree in statistics.

FRANK TEER is Joint Managing Director of NOP Market Research Ltd. He joined NOP as a senior research executive in 1962 from the Board of Inland Revenue. He was made a Director in 1964 and became Joint Managing Director in 1966. Mr Teer studied at the London School of Economics and obtained a BSc(Econ). He has lectured and broadcast on market research and opinion polls. He is a member of the Council of the Market Research Society. He is also a member of the European Society for Opinion and Marketing Research and a member of the World Association for Public Opinion Research.

ANTHONY TWYMAN is currently responsible for programmes of basic research in the areas of advertising and product development at Research

Bureau Ltd. Mr Twyman has degrees in mathematics and law and psychology from Cambridge and London. He was a director of Television Audience Measurement Ltd leaving early in 1965 to combine working as an independent consultant with academic research. He has been a consultant to JICTAR from 1965, becoming Technical Associate in 1966. He has also acted as consultant to the BBTA, IPA and ISBA. Mr Twyman also does some part-time teaching and research in experimental psychology at Birkbeck College, London.

LUCY LAW WEBSTER was educated in the US. Mrs Webster has worked for a number of international organizations and is now an officer of the World Association of World Federalists. Her market research career began in 1958 at the London Press Exchange where she worked for six years, finally as International Division Research Manager, prior to setting up Export Market Research Ltd. Mrs Webster has published a number of articles on international research and multi-country surveys, and has spoken on these topics in Europe and North America.

JEAN MORTON WILLIAMS joined Social and Community Planning Research in 1970, an institute specializing in surveys for government departments, local government and universities, where she is concerned with the application of psychological techniques in this sphere. She is a psychologist with a BA (Hons) from London University and a postgraduate diploma in occupational psychology. She came into survey research via the BBC Audience Research Department where she worked with Dr W. A. Belson on studies of the comprehensibility of programmes and of the effects of programmes on attitudes and knowledge. She joined McCann-Erickson Research Department under Harry Henry in 1957, became a Director of Marplan on its foundation in 1959, and later, Assistant Managing Director. She moved to Market Investigations Ltd in 1966 as Director in charge of psychological research where she was involved in several large scale government attitude studies as well as commercial surveys. She has been a frequent speaker at Market Research Society weekend courses and winter and summer schools on motivation research and attitude measurement and has organized weekend courses on psychological methods and questionnaire design. Her main interest is in the development of attitude research techniques for use in large scale surveys.

ROBERT WORCESTER is Managing Director of Market & Opinion Research International, Ltd, a London-based joint venture of Opinion Research Corporation (US) and NOP Market Research Ltd, (UK). Prior to his London appointment Mr Worcester served in client liaison and research direction posts as well as Controller and Assistant to the Chairman of the Board of ORC, Princeton. He was also Chairman of the Board of Market Insights, a Vice President and Director of E. L. Reilly Co. Inc, and Director of Market Dynamics Inc., ORC subsidiaries. Before joining Opinion Research Corporation in 1965, he was a consultant with McKinsey & Company, Inc. A graduate of the University of Kansas, Mr Worcester has contributed papers to ESOMAR, WAPOR, and Market Research Society Conferences, and articles to a number of journals. He has directed research studies in eighteen countries throughout the world.

Index

Abbey Goodman Display Ltd., 474
ABC (see Audit Bureau of Circulation)
Abelson, R. P., 18, 27, 48, 51
'AB' men, surveys among, 515–516
Abrams, M., 542
Abroad, research (see international research and overseas research)
Accommodation variables, 96
Action studies, 383
Adams, J. R., 626
Additivity, 35
Adler, L., 376, 625
Adler, M. K., 468, 613
Administrative areas, 65
Advertisement audience
   (see audience measurement)
Advertisers' Weekly, 473, 516
Advertising Laboratory, 490
Advertising effectiveness measurement:
   methods, 28, 31, 34, 170
   outdoor advertising, 654–657
   print media, 570–572
   TV commercials, 611–614, 619
Advertising Planning Index, 191
Advertising research, 410–447, 530–531
   (see also cinema, press, outdoor, radio and television)
Advertising Research Foundation, 559, 624, 659
Advertising Theory, 411–413
AEI, 524
AES, 192
Affinity, 325
AGB, 147, 149, 151, 228, 579, 583, 587, 591, 598, 599, 606, 607, 664, 665
Age group classification, 560
Agencies Research Consortium, 560
Agnew, H. E., 468
Agostini, J. M., 351, 358, 376, 564, 575, 624
AGSP, 261
AID, 358, 359
'AIDA', 411
Algebraic visualisation, 317
Allen, C. L., 603, 625
All Media and Product Survey (see AMPS)
Allt, B., 194–219, 661

Alternative hypotheses, 274
Altman, W., 484
American Newspaper Publishers Association Foundation, 575
AMPS, 580, 588, 590, 600, 606, 618, 624
AMPSAC panel, 147, 150, 590
AMSO, 261, 665, 668
Analysis of covariance, 305
Analysis of data, 170–176, 236–238, 249–264
   by hand, 251–253
   by machine, 253–264
Analysis of variance (see variance, analysis of)
Anonymity of respondents in mail surveys, 200–201
API (see Advertising Planning Index)
Appel, V., 446
Area variables, 96
ARF (see Advertising Research Foundation)
Arnott, G., 120–142, 661
Ashton, D., 408
Aske Research Ltd., 662
Association of Market Research Organisations (see AMSO)
Association of Point of Sale Advertising, 475
Association tests, 464–465
Athanasopoulas, D. A., 218
Atkinson, J., 118
Atlas General Survey Program (see AGSP)
'Atomistic' approach, 426
Attention studies, 593
Attitude batteries, 89–94
Attitude change, models of, 48
Attitude measurement, 82–94, 570
Attitude scaling, 89–94, 359
Attitudinal classification, 171, 172, 561–562
Attwood Ltd. (also see AMPSAC), 145, 148, 149, 154, 157, 172, 554, 588, 590, 601, 661, 667, 668
Audience classification, 560–564
Audience concepts 550–560
Audience definition (see audience concepts)
Audience measurement
   cinema media, 635–639
   outdoor media, 642–654
   print media, 549–560
   radio media, 627–635

673

Audience measurement (*cont.*)
 television media, 588–610, 614
Audit Bureau of Circulation, 573
Audits, 120–139, 482
 ad hoc, 139
 briefing interviews for, 112
 case histories, 131–135
 client service, 129
 consumer, 436
 cost, 131
 data from, 123–125
 frequency, 128
 methods, 121–123
 press circulation research in, 573–574
 promotion research in, 479
 sampling for, 126, 137, 141
 test marketing in, 120
 validation of (also see home audits and panels) 129
Audits of Great Britain Ltd. (see AGB)
Automatic interaction detection, 332
Axelrod, J. N., 438
Axes, oblique (see oblique axes)
Axes, orthogonal (see orthogonal axes)

Baby panels, 147, 150
Baby products, 164
Backward segmentation, 351
Baker, J. C., 544
Banded pack (see 'below the line' expenditure)
Banking, 519–532
Banks, S., 615, 625
Bannister, D., 12, 26
Barnes, M. C. J., 480, 483
Barnett, N. L., 367, 376
Bass, F. M., 376
Baur, E. J., 218
Bayesian Statistics, 343, 500
BBC Audience Research (also see British Broadcasting Corporation), 72, 615, 670
BBTA, 141, 624, 670
Beale, E. M. L., 329, 624
Beer, 230, 363
'Before and after test', 31
Behavioral classification, 351
'Behavioural' questions, 79–82, 562–564
Beliefs, 82
'Below the line' expenditure, 471–484, 623
Belson, W., 21, 27, 28, 50, 72, 74, 85, 102, 118, 335, 551, 625, 670
Benchmark, 398
Benn's Hardware Directory, 141
Benton and Bowles, 663
Berelson, B., 22, 27
Berent, P. H., 19, 20, 27, 118
Berlyne, D. E., 468
Bias (in sampling), 56–57, 60
Bias, in T.V. panels, 606
Bingham, J. S., 409
Binomial Theorem, 555

'Bipolar' scales, 87
Bird, M., 575
Birds Eye Foods, 374
'Birthday rule', 67
'Blink rate', 226
Blum, M., 446
BMRB (see British Market Research Bureau)
BOAC, 663
Board of Trade, 141, 635, 637
Bogart, L., 617, 619, 625
Book club—research on, 214–217
Boredom during interview, 72
'Boundary Surveys', 587, 588
Boyd, H. W., 330, 335
Braine, R. L., 12, 15, 16, 26
Brainstorming, 11, 385
Brand image and packaging, 450
Brand image measurement, 87–88, 429
Brand loyalty, 167, 169
Brand name, 395
Brands, companion, 407
Brand saliency, 438–439
Brandsma, P., 118
Briefing (interviewers), 111–113
 for omnibus surveys, 182
British Board of Television Advertisers (see BBTA)
British Broadcasting Corporation (see also BBC), 577, 579, 580, 596, 607, 609, 625
British Market Research Bureau, 191, 192, 213, 525, 526, 557, 564, 575, 590, 594, 595, 601, 604, 606, 624, 662, 663, 665, 666, 668
British Poster Advertising Association, 660
Britt, S. H., 576
Broadbent, S., 162, 177, 376, 447, 562, 568, 576, 612, 619, 621, 624, 626
Brown, J. K., 576
Brown, M., 548–576, 625, 661
Brown, N. A., 233, 446
Brown, R. V., 238
Buchanan, D. I., 446
Buck, S. F., 584, 590, 624
Building Societies Association, 532
Bureau of Commercial Research, 661
Burnett, L., 507, 518
Burrows, M., 519–532, 662
Bus advertising (see public transport advertising)
Bush, C. R., 576
Business analysis, 393
'Business opinions' survey, 526
Business reply licence, 209

Cadbury's, 417
Caffyn, J., 233, 408, 446, 576
Camera, use of in research (also see eye camera), 225, 603
Canadian Facts Co. Ltd., 192
Canonical analysis, 313

Canonical correlation, 330–331
Car cards (see public transport advertising)
Cards, punch (see punch cards)
Cards, show and prompt, 75–76, 188
Carmone, F. J., 328, 335, 376, 625
Carry-over effects, 36
Carson, D., 543
Cars, 362
Cartoon completion, 17
Causal Path Analysis, 373
Cateora, P. R., 544
CBI, 521, 527
CBS, 625
CEIR, (see Scientific Control Systems Ltd.)
Census, 64
Channon, C., 325, 335
Chaplin, J. P., 17, 27
Chemists Directory, 141
Cheskin, L., 468
Chib, R., 473, 483
Children, television viewing by, 604
Chi square table, 283, 285, 332
Chocolate, 417, 418
Christopher, M. A., 319, 335, 484, 493, 504
Christopher, M. G., 376, 493
Cigarettes, 224
Cinema research, 627, 635–639
Circulation research, 572–574
'City block' measure, 45, 49
Clarke, T. J., 408
Clark Thompson, G., 576
Classification data, 94–98, 162, 323–324
Classification (of respondents) (also see demographic classification and television viewing), 94–98, 265–266, 560–564
Classification page, 98–101
Cleaning product, 229
Clemens, N. J. S., 15, 26, 408
'Clumping', 326
Clunies-Ross, C., 408
Cluster analysis, 313, 322, 323–324, 326, 357, 360, 370, 493
'Clustering' (analysis), 326–327
Clustering (sampling), 57, 188
Cochran, W. G., 238, 311
Coding, 239, 247–249
Coding frame, 247–248
Coding instructions, 247
Coefficient of reproducibility, 91
Coffee, instant, 167
Coincidental technique, 593
Collins, B. J. K., 177, 504
Collins, L., 27
Collins, M. A., 52–68, 313, 335, 408, 662
Colour television (in advertising testing), 430
Commercial break, behaviour during, 596
Commercials (see television advertising)
Commercials, radio, 627
Communality, 320–321
Communication with respondents, 70–76

Community Antenna Television, 490
Community leaders, 511–512
Community studies, 511–512
Companies House, 521
Companion brands, 407
Company image (see also corporate image), 520
Competitions (see 'below the line' expenditure)
Competitions—as incentive to respondents, 208, 213
Computer input requirements, 262
Computer media programmes, 556
Computer output, checking, 263–264
Computer Projects, 261, 637
Computers, 237, 258–264
  in editing, 244
  in media research, 565–569, 589, 590, 620–621, 623
Concept association test, 453
Concept development (also see new product development), 9, 347
Concept evaluation, 387
Concept, product (see product concept)
Concept testing, 84, 387–392, 419
Conditioning, 155, 605–606
Confectionery, 355–356, 359
Confederation of British Industries (see CBI)
Confidence limits, 55, 62, 277–278
Congruity principle, 44, 47
Consterdine, G., 624, 625
Construct theory, 12, 15
Construction programs (of media), 565
Consumer confidence, index of, 527
Consumer research applications, 340–344
CONTAM, 594, 605, 624
Content analysis, 22
Content effect, 569
Continuous data, 267
Continuous survey (see also omnibus surveys and panels), 38, 439, 522
Control survey, 32
Cooking, 224
Cooklin, L., 409
Cooley, R. H., 51
Cooley, W. W., 320, 321, 331, 335
Coombs, C. H., 44, 51
Copland, B., 640–660, 662
Coram, Y., 409, 468
Cordell, W. N., 625
Corlett, T., 555, 575, 617, 625
Corporate image research, 505–518, 521, 529
Corporate trademark/symbols, 466–468
Correlation analysis, 314–317, 328
Correlation coefficient, 314–315, 326
Cost-effectiveness, 499–501
Cough mixture, 224
Counter activity (by competitors), 499
Counter/sorter, 244, 256–258
Counts, 221, 228–229

Coupon offers (see 'below the line' expenditure)
Coupon response, 433–434, 572
Coutie, G. A., 238
Covariance, analysis of, 305
Cowling, A. B., 51, 366, 376
Cox, D. R., 35, 50
Cox, W. E. Jnr., 218
Crespi, I., 376
Cybernetics Research Consultants Ltd., 92, 327, 376

DAGMAR, 42, 412, 413
Daily Mirror, 571
Dandruff remover, 453
Data bank, 176, 483
Data matrix, 314
David, H. A., 311
Davis, E. J., 501, 504
Davis, J., 485–504, 663
Day, P. S., 233
De-briefing, 69, 203, 524
De Bono, E., 12, 26
Decision Theory, 343
Degrees of freedom, 284
Dembar, W. N., 446
Demographic classification, readership research and, 95–98, 164, 171, 172, 265–266, 359, 560, 561
Demographic data, 350–351
  abroad, 543
DEMOS, 227, 557, 559
Demoskopea, 192
Dependence (of variables), 314
Depth interview, 9–10, 12–26
Design factor (in sampling), 58–59, 306
Desk research, 4–5
Detectors, television, 603
Detergents, 145, 159, 175, 362
De Vos, A. B., 411, 545–547, 663
Diagrammatic scales, 85–86
Diaries, 75
  multi-media, 622
  panels, 147–149
  radio research, 629, 632
  travel, 644
  television, 590, 599, 600, 601, 603, 618
  (also see panels, and meter diary)
Dichotomization techniques, sequential, 331–332
Dichotomous characters, 325
Dichter, E., 468
Dichter, Ernest, Associates, 669
Difference tests, 36, 280–282
Dillon, J., 448–470, 664
Dimensional system, 46
Dimensionality (of attitude), 83–84
Direct Eye Movement Observation System (see DEMOS)
Discontinuous data, 267
Discrete data, 267

Discriminant analysis, 313, 331
Discrimination (of clusters), 361
Disjunctive reaction time, 459
Display, checks on (see distribution checks)
Display material (see 'below the line' expenditure)
Display stands, 487
Disproportionate sampling, 63–64
Distance coefficient, 326
Distribution, normal, 53, 273
Distribution checks, 137–138
Divergent thinking, 12, 15, 26
Dominance principle, 44
DONOVAN, 261
Downham, J., 340–344
Drakeford, J., 25, 27, 103–119, 664
'Draw a picture' (projective technique), 17
Drives (see motives)
Dun & Bradstreet, 521
Dunn, J., 233
Durand, J., 376
Dustbin audit, 228–229

ECO, 192
Economy, attitudes to, 356
Editing, 115–116, 239–246
Editing instructions, 244, 245
Ehrenburg, A. S. C., 42, 50, 51, 176, 177, 316, 335, 351, 480, 597, 618, 604, 621, 624, 625, 626
Eigenvectors, 317
Electoral register, 66, 198, 205
Electricity Council, 665
Elliot, C. K., 376
Ellis Marketing Research, 192
Emmett, B. P., 326, 335, 616, 625
Employee attitude survey, 516
England, Grosse and Associates Ltd., 665
England, L., 220–234, 665
Enoch, J. M., 469
Ephron, E. H., 575
Equal cell sampling (see sampling, equal cell)
Equal interval, 41, 90
Erdos, P. L., 218
Error, type 1 and type 11 (see type 1 error and type 11 error)
Errors in questionnaire completion, 241
ESOMAR, 543, 665, 667, 668, 669, 671
'Establishment surveys', 586, 587
Euclidean measure, 44, 46
Europe, 538–544
European Common Market, 538
Evaluation programs, 565
Evaluations (see attitudes)
Evening Newspaper Advertising Bureau, 562
Exaggeration (by respondents), 161
Experimental designs, using omnibus surveys, 28–51, 489–490 185
Experimentation in test markets, 485, 504

Exploratory research—use in questionnaire
    design (also see qualitative research), 70
Export Market Research Ltd., 670
Exports, 534
Eyebrow tension, 431
Eye camera, 227, 431
Eyedrops, 451
Eye movement camera, 435, 459

Factor analysis, 89, 92–94, 313, 319–323, 356
Factorial designs, 34–35, 40
Factor rotation, 321–322
Factor score, 322
Fantasy situations, 17
FASG (see Five Agencies Study Group)
Fats, edible, 153
Fayerweather, J., 544
F distribution, tables of, 302–303
Ferber, R., 118, 311, 329, 335
Fessel Institut, Dr., 192
Field control, 103–119
    (also see interviewer(s))
Field-force
    (see interviewer(s))
Field, J. G., 408
Field management, 107–109
    (also see interviewer(s))
Field Readership Index, 557, 559
Fieldwork costs, 178
    (also see interviewing)
Fieldworker
    (see interviewer(s))
Financial research, 519–532
Financial Times, 512, 527
Financial Times Actuaries' Index, 521, 526
Find time procedure, 459, 466
Finite population correction, 56
Fishbein, M., 49, 82, 90, 102, 373
Fishbein model, 49–50
Fish fingers, 366
Five Agencies Study Group, 618, 626
'Five bar gate', 251
Fletcher, R., 233, 469, 559, 576
Flour, 155, 167
Folder test, 432–433
Food products, 370
Ford, A., 469
Ford, N. M., 218
Forecast, 496
'Formula' approach, 567
Fox, L. B., 328, 335, 625
Frame, coding
    (see coding frame)
Frame, sampling
    (see sampling frame)
France, 538
Francel, E. G., 218
Frank, R. E., 330, 335, 351, 376, 504
Frequency counts, 266
Frequency curve, 269

Frequency distribution, 268
Frequency questions, 80–81
Frost, W. A. K., 12, 15, 16, 26, 322, 323, 335,
    408, 615, 625

Gabor, A., 404
Gallup Markedsanalyse AIS, 192
Gallup Poll, 192, 475, 527, 557, 663
Gamma distribution, 42
Gap analysis, 383–385
Garfinkle, N., 624
GEC, 524
Gellerman, S. W., 7, 26
General Foods, 571
Gensch, D. H., 576
Geometric visualization, 317
Getzels, J. W., 12, 26
GfK, 192
Giles, G. B., 409
Gillette, 663
Gilmer, von Haller, 468
Golby, C., 375, 409
'Glue-spot technique', 556
Gold, J. A., 504
Goldman, A. E., 11, 26
Gomme, D., 527
Gomme, Donald, Research Associates Ltd.,
    527
Goodhardt, G. J., 50, 51, 480, 619, 626
Goodyear, J. R., 408
'Goodwill'
    (see corporate image research)
Gordon, W. J. J., 12, 26, 408
Gotham, R., 408
Gould, J. D., 469
Graeco—Latin Squares, 33
Granada Television, 597
Granger, C., 464
Grass, R. C., 619, 626
Gray, M., 468
Gray, S., 637, 639
Graybill, F. A., 311
Green, P. E., 328, 335, 370, 376, 504, 625
Greenberg, H., 576, 612, 617, 625
Greenhalgh, C., 37, 51, 375, 378–409, 665
Gregg, J. V., 238
Grocery purchases, 475
Grocery trade, 139, 472
    (also see audits and trade research)
Grosse, W.
Group discussion, 10–12, 20–25, 385
    analysis, 22–23
    composition, 24–25
    cost, 25
    interpretation, 22–23
    leader, 10, 20
    payment to respondents, 25
    promotional research, use in, 476
    TV programme research, use in, 616
Group interaction, 11

Group Marketing and Research, 192
Guarantee cards, 199
Guss, L. M., 468
Guttman, L., 91, 94, 102
Guttman scales, 91, 94

Haircream, 455
Halbert, M. H., 335, 376
Haldane, I. R., 615, 625
Haley, R. I., 351, 375, 377
Halloran, J. D., 617, 626
Hall tests, 398, 477
Halo effects, 401
Hand analysis, 251–253
'Hardware', 225–227
Harman, H. H., 319, 335
Harris, Louis
        (see Louis Harris Research)
Harris, P., 236–238, 265–311, 665–666
Hartley, E., 626
Harvey, B., 625
Haskins, J. B., 446, 612, 625
Hauck, M., 118
Haug, A. F., 219
Heads, J., 218
Hearne, J. J., 484
'Heavy-half' theory, 351
Heinz, J. and Co. Ltd., 508
Heller, H. E., 362, 376
Hendrickson, A. F., 51, 322, 335, 365, 376, 408
Hepner, H. W., 468
Hess, E., 446
Hess, J. M., 544
'Hidden offers', 434
Hill, P. B., 322, 335, 374, 375
Histogram, 269
Hobson Bates & Partners Ltd., 663
Hochstim, J. R., 218
Hoinville, G., 102, 227
Hoinville, L., 233
Holiday, packaged, 358
'Holistic' approach, 426
Holmes, C., 312–335, 371, 375, 666
Holography, 622
Holsti, O. R., 22, 27
Holzingers B coefficient, 327
Home audits, 75, 147
        (also see 'panels')
Homogeneity of clusters, 361
Hoofnagle, W. S., 50, 484
Hooper, B., 483
Hope, K., 317, 322, 335
Hosiery, 451
Houghton, D., 468
Household sampling, 67
Household variables, 96
Howard, J. A., 373, 376
HTI panels, 153–154, 625
Hudson, L., 12, 26
Hughes, P. A. B., 624

Huxley, J., 234
Hyman, H., 118

IBM, 256, 257, 261
IBM 101 machine, 257
Ice cream, 453
ICL, 256, 261
Ideal brand concept, 372
Identification problem, 461
        (packaging)
Image research, 82, 383–384, 417, 465–466,
        505–518
        (also see brand image
                company image)
                corporate image)
Impulse buying, 481
IMRA
        (see Industrial Market Research Associ-
        ation)
Incentive to respondents, 208
Incorporate Society of British Advertisers
        (see ISBA)
Independent Television Authority, 577, 579,
        615
Index of consumer confidence, 527
Industrial Market Research Association, 218
Industrial research, 106
Inertia effect, 494
Inglis, J., 326, 335
Ink blot test, Rorsach, 17
Institute of Practitioners in Advertising
        (see IPA)
Institute for Research in Communication, 192
Institute of Statisticians, 663
In-store tests, 478–479, 481–482
Instructions (to interviewers), 111, 112–113
        for retail surveys, 140
Insurance, 517, 519–532
Integrated Media and Product Research, 624
Interaction detection, automatic, 332
Interaction effects, 34, 41, 46, 47
Interactive models, 46, 47
Interdependence, of variables, 314
International research, 534–544
        (also see overseas research)
International Publishing Corporation, 661
International Wool Secretariat, 666
Interval scale, 267
Interviewer(s)
        bias, 186
        checks on, 114–116
        control of, 103–106, 114–116, 117, 118
        financial research, for, 522
        full-time, use of, 106–107
        omnibus surveys, for, 182
        piloting and, 78–79
        qualitative research and, 18–20
        questionnaire design and, 77–78
        selection of, 105, 109, 118
        training of, 105, 109–111, 118

Interviewer—effect, 195
Interviewer instructions, 77, 78
Interviewing, 103–119
  financial research, in, 522
  qualitative research, in, 9–20
Interviewing facilities buying of, 116–118
Interviewing manual, 111
INTOMETER, 598
Instructions to interviewer
    (see interviewer instructions)
Investment
    (see financial research)
Investment analysis, 526
Investors Chronicle, 524, 528
Invoice analyses, 136
    (also see audits)
IPA, 68, 595, 601, 604, 606, 618, 620, 624, 645,
  659, 663, 665, 670
Ironmongery—see hardware
Isaacson, H. L., 218
ISBA, 595, 601, 604, 606, 620, 630, 634, 670
Issue audience, 550–553
ITA
    (see independent television authority)

Jackson, P. W., 12, 26
Jahoda, G., 469
Jenkins, J., 193
JICNARS, 214, 531, 661
JICTAR, 151, 579, 583, 584, 586, 587, 589,
  590, 591, 592, 597, 598, 599, 600, 606,
  607, 609, 610, 618, 624, 664, 670
Johnson, D. S., 626
Johns, S., 408, 446
Johnson, D., 326, 335
Joint Industry Committee for Poster Audience
  Surveys, 659
Jones, H., 468, 575
Journal of Marketing, 671
Jowell, R., 102
Joyce, T., 88, 102, 614, 624, 625
J.W.T.
    (see Thompson, J. Walter)

Kaiser, H. F., 321, 335
KMBS, 147, 150, 192, 528
Keane, J. G., 219
Kelly, G. A., 12, 26
Kelly grid
    (see repertory grid)
Kendall, J. P. H., 178–193, 666
Kendall, M. G., 238, 314, 317, 329, 335
Kendall's Coefficient of Concordance, 295
Kendall's tau, 317
Kendall's W., 296
Key depressions, 255
King, S., 446
King, S. J., 408
Kirsch, A. D., 615, 625
Kish, L., 68

Kogan, M., 376
Kollat, D. T., 484
Kolmogorov—Smirnov test, 288–291, 297
Kompass Directory, 521
Kondos, A., 408
Konig, G., 233, 446
Kraushar, P. M., 408
Krugmann, H. E., 446, 619, 620, 626
Kuehn, A. A., 351, 613, 625

Laboratory methods, 221, 225–227, 431, 435,
  459, 571
Lakaschus, C., 461
Languages, foreign
    (see translation)
Lannan, J. M., 415, 446
Lateral thinking, 12
Latin square designs, 32–33, 36, 37, 38, 39, 479
Lawley, D. N., 321, 335
Lawrence, R., 625
Lawson, F., 219
Lazarsfeld, P. F., 102
Least significant difference, 294
'Least squares' methods, 329
Leavitt, C., 446
Leduc, R., 409, 468
Legibility research, 575
Le Grand, Y., 468
Lehner, E., 469
Leighton, D. S. R., 544
Leith, E. N., 626
Le Roux, A. A., 219
Letter, covering, 214
Liander, B., 544
Lichtenstein, M., 469
'Life-cycle' classification, 351, 560
Life-cycle (of product), 379
Likert, R., 102
Likert scales, 90, 92, 94
Linear function, 44
Linear regression, 328
Lintas, 625, 662
Little, Arthur D. Inc., 145
Llewellyn Thomas, E., 469
Loading
    (see weighting)
Location cards, 644
Lodahl, T. M., 376
Lodge, G., 469
Logic of questionnaire, 242
Lohnes, P. R., 320, 321, 331, 335
Loomba, J. K., 22, 27
London Press Exchange, 595, 620, 625, 662,
  666, 670
London Transport, 225, 652
Louis Harris Research, 192
Lovell, M., 233, 408, 410–447, 666
Lowe Watson, D., 506, 509, 518
Loyd, A., 408

LPE (see London Press exchange)
Lucas, D. B., 446, 576
Lunn, J. A., 8, 26, 345–377, 667

McCann Erickson, 670
McDonald, C. D. P., 376, 480, 483, 576
MacFarlane Smith, J., 119
McGloughlin, I., 177, 480, 483
McIver, C., 409
McKenna, M., 660
McKennell, A. K., 102
Macleod, Dr. J. S., 518
McNemar's test, 286
Macworth, J. F., 469
Mackwork, N. H., 469
Maddan, M., 219
Madge, C., 229, 234
Magazine research
    (see print media research)
Mailings, 201–205
Mail surveys, 40, 77, 194–219, 240
    cost, 198
    methods, 200
    questionnaire, 203–205, 217
    readership surveys, 553, 558
    sample, 199–200, 205–206, 210–211
    uses, 195, 196–197, 212, 478, 517
    (also see postal diary)
Mair, J. M. M., 12, 26
Malinowski, R., 234
Mabey, B., 469
Manfield, M. N., 219
Manx Radio, 628
Maps, contextual, 368
Market & Opinion Research International
    Ltd., 670
Market definition, 348
Market Information Services, 192
Marketing, 340–344
    (also see new product development and
    'below the line' expenditure)
Marketing Advisory Services Ltd., 668
Marketing Economics Ltd., 192
Marketing experimentation, 485–504
Marketing Society, 663
Market Investigations Ltd., 670
Market penetration, 167
Market Research Society, 5, 119, 141, 328,
    661–670
Market Search Unit, 192
Market Segmentation, 323–324, 345–377, 384
Market share prediction, 494–496
Market testing, 485–504
Market weights, 565
Marks & Spencer Ltd., 530
Mark sense cards, 240
Marplan Ltd., 136, 192, 597, 666, 670
MAS
    (See Marketing Advisory Services Ltd.)
Masius, Wynne—Williams, 663, 666

Mass Observation, 229, 232, 665, 667
Masson, P., 376
Massy, W. F., 351, 358, 376
Mastheads, 551
Mather & Crowther Ltd., 664
Matrix, data, 314
'Maximum likelihood solution', 321
Maxwell, A. E., 311, 321, 335
Mayer, C. S., 119
Mayer, M., 625
Mean (average), 270
Meaningfulness (of clusters), 361
Measured data, 267
Media effect, 569
Media effectiveness measurement, 569–572
Median, 270
Media profiles, 374
Media programmes, computer, 556
Media research, 545–547, 548–576
    (also see individual media)
Media Research Group, 576, 630, 639
Media schedule—assessment, 42
Media schedule selection, 565–569
Media selection
    (see media research)
Media selection models, 620–621
Media weights, 566
Memory of respondents, 73, 74, 79
Meter-diary system, 592
Meter recording, 597–599, 600, 618, 623
Metheringham, R. A., 556, 576
Metrilog, 599
Midland Market Research, 192
MIL
    (see Market Investigations Ltd.)
Millard, P., 4, 544
Mini-van testing, 477
Minority groups, 184
Mobile testing unit, 430
Mode, 270
Models, 40–50, 342–343
    attitude change, of, 48
    behavioural, 46
    global, 42
    individual, 42
    interactive, 46, 47
    media selection, of, 620–621
    non-interactive, 46, 47
    outdoor advertising, of, 642
    segmentation, 43
    taxonomic, 43
Monadic tests, 398
Monitoring—of mail surveys, 206, 207
'Monopolar' scales, 87
Montgomery, C., 27
Mood, A. M., 311
Mooney, P., 162, 177, 576
Morgan, J. N., 376
Morgan, N., 327, 332, 335, 358, 376, 408
Morgan, Roy, Research Centre, 192

Morgensztern, A., 446
MORI
(see Market and Opinion Research International Ltd.)
Morton Williams, J., 69–102, 670
Moser, C. A., 68
Moss, M., 366, 376
Motivation(al) research, 7–9
Motives, 7–9
Motorists, 230
Motorists panel, 147, 150
MRS
(see Market Research Society)
Multi-country research
(see international research)
Multi-phase sampling, 64
Multiple comparison tests, 305
Multiple discriminant analysis, 331
Multiple regression analysis, 314, 328–330, 515
Multi-state characters, 325
Multi-variate analysis, 9, 12, 238, 312–335, 384, 607
Murphy's Law, 411
Murstein, B. I., 18, 27
'Muters', 490
Myers, J. H., 219

Name testing, 395, 463–466
National Benzole, 420–425
National Industrial Conference Board, 572
National Magazine Company, 562, 576
National Opinion Polls
(see NOP Market Research Ltd.)
National Readership Survey, 58, 67, 98, 551, 552, 554, 555, 557, 576, 588, 590, 636, 639
National Savings Bank, 531
NBD/LSD model, 42, 50
Nederlandse Stichting Voor Statistick, 192
Neidell, L. A., 334, 335
Neisser, U., 469
Nelson, E., 4–6, 51, 366, 376, 408, 667
NEMO, 328, 369
Newnes, George Ltd., 668
New product development, 378–409
(also see market testing)
Newspaper Publishers Association, 661
Newspaper, regional, circulation area of, 63
Newspaper research
(see print media research)
NFO panels, 153, 154
Nicosia, F. M., 373, 376
Nielsen, A. C., 126, 136, 151, 494, 599, 601, 605, 624, 659
Noelle-Neumann, E., 575
Nominal scale, 266
Non-electors (in random sampling), 67
Non-interactive models, 46, 47
Non-metric multi-dimensional scaling, 334
Non-respondents, checks on, 211

Non-response, 59
NOP Market Research Ltd., 18, 192, 528, 631, 665, 668, 669
Normal distribution, 53, 273
Norsk Gallup Institute AIS, 192
North, R. C., 22, 27
'Not answered' category, 241
Nowik, H., 120, 142
NRS
(see national readership survey)
Nuckols, R. C., 219
Null hypothesis, 274
Numerical scales, 85
Nunnaly, J., 376
Nuttall, C. G. F., 575

Oblique axes, 45, 49
Observation techniques, 75, 141, 221, 229–231
O'Dell, W. F., 219
Odhams' Press, 661
Ognibene, P., 219
Omnibus surveys, 38, 178–193
advertising research, 439
companies operating, 192
costs, 183, 187, 192
financial research, use in, 522
overseas, 192
questionnaire, 178, 180, 181
radio research, use in
sampling for, 181, 182, 185, 192
uses, 184, 185, 186, 189
O'Mulloy, J. B., 408
On-air pre-test, 431
One-tailed test, 274
Open-ended questions, 75, 76, 239
coding of, 247
Opinion Research Centre, 18, 192
Opinion Research Corporation, 518
Oppenheim, A. M., 16, 27
Optical reading, 240
Optimisation (of media schedules), 565
Ordinal scale, 267
Orthogonal axes, 45, 49
Orthogonal variables, 317
Osgood, C. E., 86, 102
Outdoor advertising research, 640–660
Outdoor Research International Ltd., 662
Overseas research, 188, 192, 193, 195
(also see international research)

Packaging, 29, 30, 448–470, 488
Packaging and Perceptual Research Ltd., 664
Packaging Pulse, 664
Page audience, 550, 556, 557
Page traffic, 557
Paired comparison, 35, 292–295, 390, 399
Panels, 143–177, 343, 383, 482, 485, 605–607, 612
advertising research, for, 440
companies operating, 147

Panels (*cont.*)
  diary method, 147–149
  product testing, for, 153–154
  promotion research, for, 480
  readership research, for, 553
  shopping, 153
  T.V. media research, for, 580, 590, 597
Pantry check, 82
Parfitt, J. H., 143–177, 480, 504, 667
PARM (see Printed Advertisement Rating
    Methods)
Partial regression coefficient, 329
Participation techniques, 221, 231–232
Patrick, M., 234
Patterson, W., 507, 518
Payment to respondents, 25, 208
Payne, S. L., 72, 102, 219
PCA
    (see principle component analysis)
Pearson's correlation coefficient, 315
Peate, J. L., 410, 626
Penetration research, 175
Penny, J. C., 408
Percentages, 266
Personnel recruitment, 509
Pessemeir, F. A., 376
Petfoods, 661
Petrol, 420–422, 433, 424–425
Phillips, Scott and Turner, 665
Picture interpretation, 17
    (as projective technique)
Pilditch, J., 468, 510, 518
Piloting, 9, 75, 78, 79, 89
  mail surveys, for, 195, 197, 203
  omnibus surveys, using, 186
Pirate radio, 629
Placement tests, 457
Point-of-sale research, 141, 474
Poisson distribution, 42
Poles, emergent and implicit, 14
Polish, furniture/floor, 172, 357
Political research, 38, 327, 392
Polling district, 65
Polygraph, 431
Population correction, finite, 56
Postal checks, 115
    (on interviewers)
Postal diary method, 148
    (also see diaries, mail surveys and panels)
Postal questionnaire return, 185
Postal surveys
    (see mail surveys)
Postal technique, 583
    (also see mail surveys)
Poster audience measurement, 642–654
Poster Audience Surveys (IPA), 645
Poster Audience Surveys,
  Joint Industry Committee for
    (see Joint Industry Committee for Poster
    Audience Surveys)

Poster sites, 641, 650–651
Post-testing advertising, 435–440
Potter, J., 469
Pre-coded questions, 75, 239
Predictions
    (see market share prediction)
Premium bonds, 531
Premium offers
    (see 'below the line' expenditure)
Press research, 432–434, 546, 548–576
  new publication, 574
  product research, 575
Pre-testing advertising, 417–435
Pre-testing promotions, 476, 481–482
Price determination, 402
Principle component analysis, 92, 313, 317–
    319
'Principle factor solution', 321
Print media research, 548–576
Printed Advertisement Rating Methods, 559
Pritchard Brown & Taylor, 261
Probabilities, tables of, 276
Probability proportional to size, 65, 66
Probing, 76, 77
Processing (of data), 239–264
Product compatibility research, 510
Product concept, 366, 380
Product development, 347, 366, 378–409
Product segmentation, 366–371
Product testing, 29, 33, 34, 43
  panels, 153–154, 397
  product development, 393–401
  qualitative, 401
  (also see market testing)
'Profile chart', 322
Projections, 495
Projective techniques, 9, 16–18, 89
Promax, 322
Promotions, 150–151, 175, 176, 471–484, 489
Pronunciation, 464
    (in name testing)
Propensity to purchase, 403
Pseudo-product test, 454
Psychogalvanometer, 221, 226, 431
Psychological classification, 162, 352
Psychologist, 22, 23, 106, 319, 419, 431
Psychometrics, 352
Public Attitude Services, 192
Public transport advertising research, 640,
    651–654
Puddings, canned, 153
Pull-out costs, 491
Punch cards, 245–246, 253, 254
Pupil dilation, 226, 431
Purnell, J. M., 327, 335, 376, 392
Pymont, B. C., 504

Quadratic function, 44
Qualitative research, 6, 7–27
  advertising research, 419

cost, 25
financial research, 523
interpretation, 22–23
new product development, 382–383, 400
segmentation research, 354
techniques, 9–18
uses, 9
Quality control, 114–116
  (of interviewing)
'Quasi-random sampling', 61
Quenoville, M. H., 311
Questionnaire design, 69–102, 314
  advertising post testing, for, 437
  mail survey, for, 203–205, 217–218
  omnibus surveys, for, 180–181, 190
  poster effectiveness surveys, 655–656
  product development surveys, 391, 400
  self completion, 223–225
  (also see piloting)
Questioning techniques, 84–94
Questions, types of, 79–94
QUICKTAB, 261
Quota controls, 60, 61
Quota sampling, 60–61, 95
'Q-technique', 324

Radio audiences, 581, 627–635
Radio, commercial, 622
  (also see radio research)
Radio Eireann, 628
Radio Luxembourg, 628, 629, 630, 639
Radio, Manx
  (see Manx radio)
Radio, pirate
  (see pirate radio)
Radio research, 627–635
Radio Times, 563
Radio, UHF
  (see UHF radio)
Rahmel, H. A., 625
Rampley, B., 408, 446
Random numbers, 66
Random—route sampling, 61, 213
Random sampling, 52–59, 64–68
  for omnibus surveys, 181–182
  (also see quasi-random sampling)
Rank Advertising, 635
Ranked data, 266
'Rapport' with respondent, 71–72
  on telephone, 222
Rating scales, 84–87, 288–292, 297, 322–323, 331, 429
Ratings service, 589
Ratio scale, 267
Rauta, I., 256, 625
RBL
  (see Research Bureau Ltd.)
'Reader', definition of, 550–560
Readership, parallel, 553

Readership, replicated, 553
Readership research, 530, 548–576
Readership scales, 558
'Reading days', 563
Reading frequency, 553–556
Reading locale, 563
Recall questions, 429, 433, 551
  re. t.v. viewing, 595–596
Recognition methods, 552
Recordimeter, 599, 600, 603, 605
Recruitment, personnel, 509
Re-cycling (of products), 341, 379, 405
Refusals, 594
  retail surveys, in, 139–140
Register, electoral
  (see electoral register)
Regression analysis, 313, 329–330, 357, 401
  (see also multiple regression analysis)
'Regret at loss' question, 562
Reminders (for mail surveys), 207
Repeat purchase analysis, 175
Repertory grid, 12–16, 87, 354
  analysis, 313
  cost, 25
  example, 14–15
  t.v. research, use in, 615
Reputation, company's
  (see corporate image research)
Research Bureau Ltd., 147, 150, 153, 192, 477, 602, 662, 665, 667, 670
Research Marketing Services Ltd., 192
Research Services Ltd., 68, 136, 606, 659, 661, 662, 666
Response function, 567
Response rate, 59, 61, 197, 200, 206, 208, 212, 214, 517
Retail audits
  (see audits)
Retail Audits Ltd., 126, 136
Retail outlets, definition of, 141
Retailer research, 139–142
  packaging, 449–450
  (also see 'below the line' expenditure)
Reuss, C. F., 219
Richardson, D., 617, 625
RKO, 625
Roberts, L. D., 518
Robinson, P. J., 335, 376
Roche, M., 469
Rodger, L. W., 409, 468
Role rehearsal, 18
Rolls-Royce, 145
Rorschach Ink Blot Test, 17
Roughton, G. R., 239–264, 668
Rosenberg, M. J., 48, 51
Rotation (of factors), 321–322
Rothman, J., 28–51, 408, 615, 625, 667–668
Round robin, 35
Royal Statistical Society, 527, 669
'R-technique', 324

Running-in period, 605
Ryans, J. K. Jnr., 544

'SABLE', 261
Sainsbury, J. Ltd., 530
Sales Research Services Ltd., 38, 136, 192, 661, 665, 668, 669
Saliency, 83
  brand, 438–439
'SAMPLE', 261
Sample size,
  calculation of, 61–64
  experimental design, in, 30
Sampling, 52–68
  costs, 58–59
  cumulative, 185
  disproportionate, 63–64, 127
  equal cell, 137, 200
  financial research, for, 521, 523
  mail surveys, for, 198–200, 205–206
  methods, examples of, 64–68
  multi-phase, 64
  omnibus survey, for, 181, 182, 185, 189
  panels, for, 154
  quota, 60, 95
  retail audits, for, 126–128
  random, 52–59, 64–68
  random route, 61, 213
  retail audit
  sequential, 63, 185
  serial, 66
Sampling distribution of the test statistic, 274
Sampling error, 29, 52–55
  table, 307
Sampling frame, 59, 64, 66
  for mail surveys, 198, 205–206
Sampling interval, 65
Sampson, P. M. J., 7–27, 87, 354, 385, 408, 483, 668
Samuels, I., 409
Saving,
  examples of research on, 93–94, 531
  (also see financial research)
Scales, 14, 368
    also see diagrammatic, numerical, nominal, oblique, rating, ratio, readership, semantic differential, verbal)
Scalogram, 91
Scatter diagram, 328
Schaffer, A., 469
Scheffe, H., 311
Schlackman, W., 448–470, 516, 518, 669
Schlackman, William Ltd., 664, 669
Schlaeppi, A. C., 575
Schlaiffer, R., 501, 504
Scicon, 261
Scientific Control Systems, 327, 329, 369, 527
Scott, C., 219
Screening (new product ideas), 387
Segmentation criteria, 349–353

Segmentation, market
  (see market segmentation)
Segmentation models, 43
Segment exposure research, 592
Segnit, S., 447, 576, 613, 625
Self-completion questionnaires, 221, 223–225
Self-Service and Supermarkets Directory, 141
Self-service shops, 471
Sellitz, J., 234
Selvin, H. C., 238
Semantic differential, 49
  scales, 86–87, 89, 267
Sentence completion tests, 17
Sequential dichotomization techniques, 331–332, 357
Sequential sampling, 63, 185, 587
SETMETER, 598
Set-switching data, 599
'Seven day aided recall', 597
Shampoo, 440, 442–445, 464
Shelf space allocation, 483
Shepherd Smith, N. H., 576
Sherak, B., 361, 363, 371, 376, 408
Sheth, J. N., 373, 376
Shop-fronts, research on, 38
Shopping List, 452, 475
Shopping panels, 153
Siegal, S., 317, 335
SIFO, 192
Significance level, 277
Significance testing, 265–311
'Significant', 277
Significant differences tables, 307–310
Significant results, 305–306
  interpretation of, 305–306
Sign test, 291–292
Silvey, R., 625
Silvikrin, 440, 442–445
Similarity coefficient, 325
Simmons, Gordon, Research Ltd., 192, 669
Simmons, M., 471–484, 597, 605, 625, 669
Simon, R., 219
Simulation approach, 567
Skelly, F., 408
Skip instructions, 77–78
  (on questionnaire)
Smith, H. A., 575
Smith, W., 375
Smith-Warden Ltd., 408
Smulian, P. A., 408
Sneath, P. H. A., 323, 335, 376
Snedecor, G. W., 311
Soap powder
  (see detergent)
Soap, toilet, 155, 169, 354
Social and Community Planning Research, 96, 670
Social class in group discussions, 24, 25
  (also see classification and demographic classification)

Socio-economic classification, 98, 560
SOFRES, 192
Software package, 258–262
Sokal, R. R., 323, 335, 376
Sonquist, J. A., 332, 335, 358, 376
Soup, 153
Spearman's rank, 317
Speedsearch, 192
'Spherical map', 322
SPL, 261
Split run, 28, 29, 31, 37, 186, 490, 497
Split sample
    (see split run)
SPS, 261
SRS
    (see Sales Research Services)
STAFCO consumer panel, 155
Stafford, J. E., 219
Standard deviation, 271
Standard error, 54, 62, 272
'Stand-out' problem, 458, 460, 461
    (packaging)
Starch, D., 447
Statistical analysis machine, 256, 257
Statistics, 265–311
Statistical significance, 7, 265–311
'Statistician, The', 335
Statisticians, Institute of
    (see Institute of Statisticians)
Stats, M. R., 126, 136
Stefflre, V., 354, 370, 376, 408
Steiner, G. A., 616, 620, 625
Steinkamp, S., 118
'Stepwise' program, 567
St. James model, 49, 365, 370, 373
Stockbrokers, 521
Stock Exchange Council, 532
Stock Exchange Yearbook, 521
STONEWALL, 261
Store-checks, 479
Store tests, 39
Stouffers, A. A., 102
Stratification (in sample design), 58, 319
Stuart, A., 238, 311, 625
Sub-groups
    (see minority groups)
Suchman, E. A., 102
Suci, G. J., 102
Suomen Gallup, 192
Supervisor (of interviewers), 108–109, 110–
    111, 113
Swain, G. R., 219
Symbol research, 448–470
Syndicated research, 129, 138, 190, 191, 528
    (also see omnibus surveys, panels, audits)
Synectics, 11–12, 385

TABLEAU, 261
Tabulations, interpretation of, 48

Tabulator, 256, 257
Tachistoscope, 221, 226, 435, 459, 461, 462
TAM, 151, 579, 583, 594, 595, 597, 599, 601,
    603, 604, 617, 618, 624, 625, 626, 633,
    639, 663, 668, 670
TAMmeters, 598, 603, 605
Tannenbaum, P. H., 102, 612, 617, 625
Tape, paper, 253
    magnetic, 255
Tape recorder, 19, 20–21, 110
Target group definition, 356–366
Target Group Index, 526, 552, 561, 564, 575,
    580, 588, 592, 662
TAT—see thematic apperception test
Taxonomic models, 43
Taxonomy, 313, 323, 327
Tate, B., 408
Taylor, B., 408
Taylor, L., 624
Taylor Nelson & Associates, 526, 665, 667
Teer, F., 627–639, 669
T.C.A., 148, 149, 588, 590, 597
t distribution, 305
Telephone interviewing, 77, 220–223, 523,
    552, 623
    radio research, in, 630
    t.v. viewing research, in, 594, 623
Television areas, 492–493, 577, 582
    definition of, 585
Television Audience Measurement
    (see TAM)
Television audience measurement, 588–610
Television, colour
    (see colour television)
Television commercials, 577–578
    in Europe, 579
Television commercial testing, 427–430, 611–
    614
Television Consumer Audit, 436
Television coverage, 581
Television, future prospects, 622
Television media research, 577–626
Television Opinion Panel, 615
Television programmes
    effects of, 611
    ratings, 322–323, 589, 610
    viewers opinion of, 323, 609, 611, 614–615
Television reception measurement, 583
Television set ownership, 581
Television transmission, 577
Television viewing, 50, 151–152, 546, 589–592,
    603–604, 606, 620
Test areas, 489, 492
Test marketing, 120, 150, 319, 437, 485–504
    of publication, 574
Test towns, 493
Theatre tests, 428
Thematic apperception test, 17
Thomas, J., 544
Thompson, J. Walter, 524, 620, 625, 663

Thomson Medals and Awards for Media Research, 51, 553, 667
Thomson Regional Newspapers, 574
Thornton, C., 15, 26, 376, 408
Thrift, H. J., 218
Thurstone, L. L., 102, 321, 335
Thurstone scales, 90, 92, 94
Tigart, D. J., 376
Time series, 186
Tinker, M., 469
Tobacco, 457
Toothpaste, 167, 172, 173, 174
TOP
    (see Television Opinion Panel)
Trade incentives
    (see below the line expenditure)
Trade marks, 466
Trade research, 120–142
    (also see 'audits')
    invoice analyses
    distribution checks
Trading stamps
    (see 'below the line' expenditure)
Traditionalism scale, 358
Traffic parameter, 645
Transcript of intensive interview, 21
Translation of questionnaires, 543
Treasure, J., 619, 625
Trend analyses,
    panel research in, 163
    omnibus surveys, using, 186
Triadic difference test, 36
't' test, 37, 305, 460
Tube Investments, 507
Tuck, R. T. J., 480, 483
TVQ, 614–615, 617
TV Times, 562
Twedt, D. W., 351, 376
Twigg, J., 119, 376
Two-tailed test, 274
Twyman, W. A., 577–626, 669–670
Tyne Tees Television, 665
Type I error, 277
Type II error, 278

Unilever, 617, 665, 667
Union Carbide, 513
Unit trusts, 519–532
Upatniekj, J., 626
'Users'—definition of, 166–167
Usher, J. N., 409
Van tests, 477

Variance—analysis of, 37, 271, 295, 301, 317
Varimax rotation, 322
Verbal scales, 84–85
Vernon, M. D., 469
VHF radio, 628
Video-tape, 21, 227, 389, 427
Vincent, C. E., 219
Visual factors, in packaging research, 458
Vitamin pills, 451
Voting intention, 38
Votometer machine, 428

Waisanen, F. B., 219
Wales, H. G., 118
Wallace, J. C., 376
Wapor, 671
Warwick, K. M., 377
Washing, clothes, 153
Watsar, J. J., 219
Webb, N. L., 599, 625
Weber, J. H., 484
Webster, L., 534–544, 670
Weighting, 57, 64, 67, 262–263
    attitude scales, 92–94
    mail surveys, 200
Wells, W. D., 376, 446
West, M. J., 584, 624
Westminster Research Bureau, 192
White, C. J., 469
White, P. O., 322, 335
Whittle Data Services, 261
Wicks, A., 576
Wilbett, R. P., 484
Wills, G., 408, 469, 504
Wilson, A., 20, 27, 408
Winick, C., 447, 562, 576
Winkler, A., 354, 376
Wolfe, A., 376
Wolfe, H. D., 576
Worcester, R., 505–517, 670–671
Word association tests, 17
'Word-of-mouth chains', 391
World Association for Public Opinion Research, 669
World Association of World Federalists, 670
Wotruba, T. R., 219
Wright, A. T., 409

Yasin, J., 469
Yate's correction for continuity, 285
Yates, W. A., 120, 142